Bottom Line's HEALTH BREAKTHROUGHS 2014

Bottom Line Books

www.BottomLinePublications.com

ISBN 0-88723-708-8

HealthDay

Articles in this book were written by reporters for HealthDay, an award-winning international
daily consumer health news service, headquartered in Norwalk, Connecticut.

Bottom Line Books® publishes the advice of expert authorities in many fields.
These opinions may at times conflict as there are often different approaches to solving problems.
The use of this material is no substitute for health, legal, accounting or other professional services.
Consult competent professionals for answers to your specific questions.

Telephone numbers, addresses, prices, offers and Web sites listed in this book are accurate
at the time of publication, but they are subject to frequent change.

Bottom Line Books® is a registered trademark of Boardroom® Inc.
281 Tresser Boulevard, Stamford, Connecticut 06901

www.bottomlinepublications.com

Bottom Line Books® is an imprint of Boardroom® Inc., publisher of print periodicals,
e-letters and books. We are dedicated to bringing you the best information from the most
knowledgeable sources in the world. Our goal is to help you gain greater wealth,
better health, more wisdom, extra time and increased happiness.

Printed in the United States of America

Contents

Contents

Contents

11 • EMOTIONAL WELL-BEING

12 • FAMILY MATTERS

13 • HEART & STROKE

Contents

Contents

19 • WOMEN'S HEALTH

Preface

W e are proud to bring you the all-new *Bottom Line's Health Breakthroughs 2014*. This collection represents a year's worth of the latest health news and scientific discoveries in a broad spectrum of fields.

When you choose a Bottom Line book, you are turning to a stellar group of experts in a wide range of specialties—medical doctors, alternative practitioners, renowned nutrition experts, research scientists and consumer-health advocates, to name a few.

We go to great lengths to interview the foremost health experts. Whether it's cancer prevention, breakthrough arthritis treatments or cutting-edge nutritional advice, our editors talk to the true innovators in health care.

How do we find all these top-notch professionals? Over the past 20 years, we have built a network of leading physicians in both alternative and conventional medicine. They are affiliated with the world's premier medical institutions. We follow the medical research, and with the help of our partner HealthDay, an award-winning service that reports on evidence-based health news, we bring the latest information to our readers. We also regularly talk with our advisers in teaching hospitals, private practices and government health agencies.

Bottom Line's Health Breakthroughs 2014 is a result of our ongoing research and contact with these experts, and is a distillation of their latest findings and advice. We hope that you will enjoy the presentation and glean helpful information about the health topics that concern you and your family.

As a reader of a Bottom Line book, please be assured that you are receiving reliable and well-researched information from a trusted source. But, please use prudence in health matters. Always speak to your physician before taking vitamins, supplements or over-the-counter medication…changing your diet…or beginning an exercise program. If you experience side effects from any regimen, contact your doctor immediately.

The Editors, Bottom Line Books, Stamford, Connecticut.

Allergies, Asthma & Respiratory Disorders

Clear Up Nasal Congestion Without Drugs

e all know someone who always seems to have a stuffed nose (or maybe you have one). You can't breathe comfortably, and the stuffiness gets in the way of activities such as eating (you can't taste) and exercising (you're exhausted). It also can lead to pressure around the eyes, headache and difficulty breathing and sleeping.

Nasal congestion may involve a runny nose and mucus production, but the condition actually is due to the inflamed, swollen lining of the nasal passages. If you have nasal congestion, it helps to determine if it's a flare-up (short-term) or a chronic (long-term) problem and treat it accordingly.

Mark Stengler, NMD, a naturopathic medical doctor who is founder and medical director of the Stengler Center for Integrative Medicine in Encinitas, California, pointed out that treating your nasal congestion based on whether it is a short- or long-term problem will help you feel better sooner…

SHORT-TERM NASAL CONGESTION

Seasonal allergies occur in the spring and fall—and other types of allergies to such things as dust mites, pet dander or mold can cause flare-ups when you are exposed.

Test to confirm: A blood test or skin scratch test.

Treatment: Homeopathy for allergy-related nasal congestion.

The idea behind these remedies: A substance similar to the allergen but not the allergen itself is given in minute doses. It causes a healthy person to have symptoms similar to those caused by the allergen. This exposure desensitizes the

---

Mark A. Stengler, NMD, naturopathic medical doctor in private practice, Encinitas, California…adjunct associate clinical professor at the National College of Natural Medicine, Portland, Oregon…author of *The Natural Physicians Healing Therapies* and coauthor of *Prescription for Natural Cures* (both from Bottom Line Books). *http:// markstengler.com*

immune system to the allergen. Allium cepa, for example, can help pollen-related congestion.

Another form of homeopathy is isopathy, in which small amounts of the actual allergen are given in very diluted form. If you know what you are allergic to, you can purchase the associated remedy—or seek the help of a holistic doctor. Homeopathic remedies for common allergens are available from Newton Homeopathics (800-448-7256, *www.newtonlabs.net*).

Also recommended: Using a HEPA filter air purifier and taking the supplement quercetin, a plant derivative with natural antihistamine effects that reduces allergic response. Follow label instructions. Quercetin has mild blood-thinning properties, so speak to a physician if you take blood-thinning medication.

LONG-TERM NASAL CONGESTION

When a patient has nasal congestion that has gone on for months (or even years), there could be several causes, such as…

•**Food sensitivity.** Food sensitivities often are caused by gluten (a protein found in wheat, rye and barley) or by cow's milk. You can perform a simple food-elimination diet on your own to see if you have a sensitivity to one of these foods. Eliminate gluten, for example, for two weeks to see if your nasal congestion clears up during that time. If it does, then you know you have a sensitivity to gluten and need to stay away from it on an ongoing basis.

•**Fungal infection.** Fungal growth in the sinuses stimulates an inflammatory immune system response—and is a common cause of year-round nasal congestion. People who frequently use antibiotics and/or nasal decongestant sprays or who consume a high-sugar diet are especially prone to these infections.

Treatment: The way to determine a fungal infection is to follow an antifungal regimen for two to four weeks. If nasal congestion clears up, then we know that the patient has a fungal infection. After following the antifungal regimen below, the infection usually clears up and the patient can go back to eating a healthful diet.

Following an antifungal diet involves avoiding all refined sugars, all grains (including bread, pasta, rice and corn), potatoes, legumes (including peas, beans, soy and peanuts) and

---

New Treatment for Nasal Allergy Symptoms

Qnasl, a powdered form of the corticosteroid *beclomethasone dipropionate,* recently won FDA approval for treating allergic rhinitis, which causes runny nose, sneezing and watery eyes. Liquid forms of this and similar medicines have been available for years, but many patients dislike them because of the drip down the back of the nose. Qnasl is approved for seasonal and yearlong allergies in patients ages 12 and above.

Consumers Digest. *www.consumersdigest.com*

---

cheese…and eating lots of vegetables, fruits, berries (naturally occurring sugar is OK to consume), fresh fish and lean poultry. In particular, eat a lot of broccoli, cabbage and garlic, all of which have antifungal properties.

Also recommended: Oregano oil supplements, which have antifungal effects.

Brand to try: Oreganol, from North American Herb & Spice (800-243-5242, *www.northamericanherbandspice.com*). Follow label directions. A too-high dose of oregano oil can cause digestive upset. You also can take quercetin (mentioned above) and a daily probiotic containing Lactobacillus acidophilus and Bifidobacterium.

OTHER TREATMENTS FOR NASAL CONGESTION

Anyone with nasal congestion, regardless of the cause, should avoid mucus-producing foods, such as dairy products, refined flour, chocolate, eggs, and fried and processed food. This includes people who have repeated bouts of nasal congestion following a respiratory infection. *The following natural approaches also can help…*

•**N-acetylcysteine (NAC).** This amino acid works to thin mucus and reduce excessive inflammatory responses of the immune system.

Dose: 500 mg, three times daily.

•**Bromelain.** This enzyme reduces inflammation in the nasal passages.

Dose: 500 mg, twice daily between meals. Since bromelain has blood-thinning properties, speak to a doctor before taking it if you take blood-thinning medication.

•**Vitamin C,** for its antiallergy and immune-boosting effects.

Dose: 1,000 mg, four times daily.

•**A nasal spray or rinse to relieve nasal passage irritation.** *Follow label instructions. Choose the one that works best for you...*

•Grapefruit-seed extract nasal spray has antifungal and antimicrobial properties.

Brand to try: NutriBiotic Nasal Spray (800-225-4345, *www.nutribiotic.com*).

•Saline nasal spray containing xylitol. Xylitol is a natural substance that relieves irritation caused by allergies or infection.

Brand to try: Xlear Nasal Spray (877-599-5327, *www.xlear.com*). Also available at *www. amazon.com.*

•**Neti pot.** Another form of nasal rinse is provided by this small pot, which is designed to flush out nasal passages with a saline solution.

Growing an Allergy-Free Garden

Mary L. Jelks, MD, clinical assistant professor of medicine in the department of allergy and immunology at the University of South Florida in Tampa, a fellow of the American Academy of Allergy, Asthma and Immunology, and author of *Allergy Plants that Cause Sneezing and Wheezing* (World-Wide).

I f you are like many of the 40 million Americans who suffer from seasonal allergies, you love puttering in the yard but hate the way plant pollens and molds make your eyes water and nose run. Antihistamines and symptom-easing supplements only help to a certain degree, but there's more help on the horizon—low-allergy landscaping.

Key: Various factors—including a plant's appearance, provenance, pollination method, even its sex—affect how allergenic it is. So the idea is to fill your yard with the types of plants least likely to trigger symptoms, according to Mary L. Jelks, MD, author of *Allergy Plants that*

Cause Sneezing and Wheezing and a clinical assistant professor of medicine in the department of allergy and immunology at the University of South Florida in Tampa. *Smart landscaping choices for the allergy-prone include...*

•**Trees with showy leaves or year-round greenery rather than profuse blossoms.** Trees that bloom plentifully and for long periods tend to disperse more pollen...in contrast, eye-catching leaves and evergreens look lovely without sending your yard's pollen count sky-high.

Good tree choices: Apple, cherry, larch, plum and red maple (which are deciduous)...and hemlock, pine and spruce (which are evergreens).

Avoid: Aspen, birch, elm, hickory, mulberry, oak, olive, pecan, sycamore, walnut.

•**Female cultivars.** Some plant species are separate-sexed (dioecious). In the nursery, you may have seen plants labeled fruitless or seedless, terms that often indicate male plants. Some people like male plants because they don't produce any messy seeds, fruits or flowers—but because they do produce pollen, they are not good choices for allergy patients, Dr. Jelks cautioned.

Better: Opt for the pollen-free female cultivars if you want your yard to include ash, box elder, cottonwood, date palm, poplar or willow.

•**Brightly hued flowers and blooming bushes.** Colorful blooms generally are the type that attract butterflies and bees for pollination—and these plants also tend to have large, heavy pollen deeply embedded in the flowers rather than lightweight pollen that's easily dispersed into the air (and into your airways).

Consider: Azalea, begonia, bougainvillea, columbine, crape myrtle, daffodil, dahlia, daisy, geranium, iris, pansy, peony, periwinkle, petunia, phlox, ranunculus, salvia, snapdragon, sunflower, tulip, verbena, zinnia.

•**Native plants.** Indigenous species are more disease-resistant—and, as Dr. Jelks explained, healthy plants are less vulnerable to allergy-promoting infestations of mildew, rust and black spot.

Resource: To find plants native to your region, check the Web site of the Lady Bird Johnson Wildflower Center at the University of Texas at

New Device for Allergy Emergencies Is Easier to Use Than the EpiPen

The Auvi-Q is shaped like a slim smartphone and offers voice instructions that guide a user through the injection process. Just place the device against the outer thigh, push firmly and the needle injects and retracts automatically. Both the Auvi-Q and the EpiPen are equally effective.

Stephen J. Apaliski, MD, allergist and immunologist at Allergy & Asthma Centres of the Metroplex, Arlington, Texas, and author of *Beating Asthma* (Smashwords.com).

Austin (go to *www.wildflower.org* and click on native plant information).

•**Grass that has a short pollen season.** Some grasses produce pollen for four or more months of the year—for instance, bahia, Bermuda, bluegrass, fescue, redtop and saltgrass. But pollen season is limited to just two or three months for other grasses, such as grama, orchard, timothy and velvet. Pollen season length varies from region to region, so consult a local landscaper to see what would work best for you.

Also: If you are highly sensitive to grasses, Dr. Jelks suggested minimizing grassy areas in favor of stone paths or water features. At the very least, let someone else cut your lawn—although a well-mown lawn produces less pollen than unmown grass, the mowing itself releases pollen and mold spores into the air.

•**Mulch that won't mold.** Wood chips and shredded wood mulch decompose rapidly, especially in areas where mulch tends to remain damp—and thus are likely to harbor mold spores.

Better: Nonorganic options, such as gravel, crushed granite or rubber chips.

More helpful strategies for allergy-prone gardeners…

•**Choose low-risk times for yard work.** It's best to garden in the late afternoon, when pollen counts generally are lowest…and when the wind is calm, so pollens are not being blown about. To check local pollen counts, visit the Web site of the American Academy of Allergy, Asthma & Immunology's National Allergy Bureau at *www.aaaai.org*—and stay indoors when counts soar.

•**Wear the right gardening garb.** Wear gloves, long sleeves, pants and, if necessary, a mask when you garden to reduce contact with allergens. Designate a pair of shoes just for yard work, and keep them in the garage or mudroom so you don't track allergens into the house. Also, be sure to shower, shampoo and put on clean clothes as soon as possible after coming indoors—otherwise, pollens and molds on your body, hair and clothes may trigger symptoms long after you leave the yard.

What You Never Knew About Sneezing— Including How to Stop It

Neeta Ogden, MD, adult and pediatric allergist, asthma specialist and immunologist with private practices in New York City and Closter, New Jersey. She is spokesperson for and Fellow of the American College of Allergy, Asthma & Immunology (*www.acaai.org/allergist*). *www.neetaogdenmd.com*

It's probably not something you think about too often, but there are some fascinating facts about the old ah-choo. Also called *sternutation*, sneezing is the body's way of clearing the nose of bacteria, viruses and irritants such as dust or perfume.

When nerve endings in the lining of the nasal passages are stimulated, the "sneeze center" in the lower brain stem sends out signals that cause you to take a deep breath and hold it. Air pressure in the lungs increases…chest muscles tighten…and your throat and eyes close. Then your chest muscles contract vigorously and your throat muscles relax, abruptly forcing air from your nose and mouth at about 100 miles per hour and sending out a wet spray that can radiate five feet.

Curious triggers: Sneezing doesn't occur only when you have a cold or allergies. The sneezing reflex can be provoked by all kinds of odd things, from sunlight to exercise to sex, according to allergist Neeta Ogden, MD, a spokesperson for the American College of Allergy, Asthma and Immunology. Here are some surprising sneeze triggers…and what you can do to halt inopportune sneezes before they erupt.

•**Eyebrow plucking.** This stimulates the trigeminal nerve that supplies sensation to the face, firing impulses that reach the nerve endings inside the nose and sparking the sneezing reflex.

Preempt the sneeze: "Press a fingertip on your eyebrow while tweezing to interrupt this nerve messaging and dampen the impulse to sneeze," Dr. Ogden suggested.

•**Exercising.** Working out causes you to hyperventilate, which can dry out your nasal passages. In response, your nose increases its mucous secretion—and that can stimulate the nerve endings that provoke sneezing. Heavy breathing also stimulates the diaphragm, contributing to the sneezing reflex.

Preempt the sneeze: Hydrate your nose with a few spritzes of saline mist just before a vigorous workout, Dr. Ogden advised. If sneezing is truly disruptive, try a lower-intensity exercise such as walking, yoga or Pilates.

•**Bright light.** Do you sneeze after walking out of a dark theater and into the bright afternoon sunlight? Called the *photic* sneeze reflex, this inherited trait affects an estimated one-third of people.

Possible explanation: When the optic nerve is stimulated by a sudden flood of bright light, it fires a signal to the brain to constrict the pupils—but some of that electrical signal is picked up by the nearby trigeminal nerve and mistaken as a nasal irritant.

Preempt the sneeze: Put on a pair of sunglasses before going out into bright light…or try breathing through your mouth while pinching the end of your nose for a few moments to disrupt the errant nerve signal.

•**Sex.** Physical intimacy activates the parasympathetic nervous system that controls involuntary reflexes—reflexes that include sexual arousal and sneezing. This link may be behind the "nuisance sneezing" that occurs during sex, Dr. Ogden said. Also, the nose (like the genitals) contains erectile tissue that may become engorged during arousal, provoking a sneeze.

Preempt the sneeze: Try using the length of your index finger to press gently but firmly on the area between your nose and your upper lip until the sneezing urge passes—then you can carry on with what you were doing, free of distractions.

Last word: The brain's sneeze center and related nervous system circuitry relax during sleep, Dr. Ogden noted, which is why we generally don't sneeze while asleep…so as you drift off, rest assured that sneezes won't disturb your post-afterglow slumber.

Spice Allergy Affects 2% to 3% Of the Population

It is more common in women than men and often is triggered by cinnamon, garlic, vanilla, black pepper or spice blends. Reactions, which can range from mild sneezing to life-threatening anaphylaxis, can be caused by breathing, eating or touching spices. Spices also are found not just in food but in a variety of cosmetics and dental products.

Sami Bahna, MD, past president, American College of Allergy, Asthma & Immunology, Arlington Heights, Illinois. *www.acaai.org*

Acupuncture May Help Ease Hay Fever

Benno Brinkhaus, MD, professor, Charite-University Medical Center, Berlin, Germany.

Harold Nelson, MD, professor, medicine, National Jewish Health, Denver.

Remy Coeytaux, MD, PhD, associate professor, community and family medicine, Duke University School of Medicine, Durham, North Carolina.

Annals of Internal Medicine

Hay fever sufferers may find some relief with acupuncture, a recent study suggests, though the therapy's appeal in the "real world" is yet to be seen.

The study included 422 people with grass and pollen allergies. Researchers found that those randomly assigned to a dozen acupuncture sessions fared better than patients who did not receive the procedure.

On average, they reported greater symptom improvements and were able to use less antihistamine medication over eight weeks. The advantage, however, was gone after another eight weeks, according to findings reported in the *Annals of Internal Medicine*.

Still, that doesn't necessarily mean that acupuncture's benefits fade, said lead researcher Benno Brinkhaus, MD, of Charite-University Medical Center in Berlin.

Many studies have suggested that acupuncture helps ease various types of pain, such as migraines and backaches, as well as treat nausea and vomiting related to surgery or chemotherapy. According to traditional Chinese medicine, acupuncture works by stimulating certain points on the skin believed to affect the flow of energy, or "qi" (pronounced "chee"), through the body.

But some recent research suggests that the needle stimulation also triggers the release of pain- and inflammation-fighting chemicals in the body. No one is sure why acupuncture would help with hay fever, but there is evidence that it curbs inflammatory immune-system substances involved in allergic reactions.

STUDY DETAILS

For the recent study, Dr. Brinkhaus and colleagues recruited 422 adults with hay fever.

They randomly assigned the patients to one of three groups—one that received 12 acupuncture sessions over eight weeks; one that received

a "sham" version of acupuncture; and one that received no acupuncture.

In the sham version, acupuncturists used real needles, but inserted them only superficially and into areas of the skin that are not traditional acupuncture points. Patients in all three groups were allowed to take antihistamine medication when their symptoms flared up.

After eight weeks, the study found, patients given real acupuncture reported more symptom improvement than those in either of the comparison groups. On average, their quality-of-life "scores" were 0.5 to 0.7 points better—which, in real life, should translate to a noticeable difference in hay fever symptoms, according to Harold Nelson, MD, an allergist at National Jewish Health, a Denver hospital that specializes in respiratory diseases.

Hay fever symptoms were much better in all three study groups by week 16. Dr. Brinkhaus said that's probably because pollen season was dying down at that point.

Dr. Brinkhaus, who is a medical doctor and acupuncturist, said he would recommend acupuncture to patients who are not satisfied with allergy medication—either because it's not working or because of the side effects.

Remy Coeytaux, MD, who cowrote an editorial published with the study, agreed that acupuncture is worth a shot.

"Absolutely, give it a try if you are interested," said Dr. Coeytaux, an associate professor of community and family medicine at Duke University School of Medicine, who studies acupuncture.

According to Dr. Coeytaux, one of the strengths of this study is that it compared acupuncture against both antihistamines alone and sham acupuncture. The fake procedure was used to help control for the "placebo effect"—where people feel better after receiving a treatment just because they believe it will work.

But Dr. Coeytaux said it's also time for studies to move beyond testing real acupuncture against sham versions. One reason is that those fake procedures may actually have physiological effects of their own—making them poor placebos.

It's in Her Kiss

If you give your partner a kiss and your lips tingle, swell or itch, you could be having an allergic reaction, especialy if he or she has eaten a certain food or taken a particular medication. Saliva can excrete the allergen up to 24 hours after being consumed. You also might be reacting to lipstick or lip balm. See an allergist who can develop a treatment plan for you.

Leonard Bielory, MD, professor of environmental sciences, Rutgers University, New Brunswick, New Jersey.

Instead, Dr. Coeytaux said, it would be good to compare acupuncture head-to-head with other therapies, to see how it stacks up.

For now, hay fever sufferers who want to try acupuncture may face some obstacles. Depending on where patients live, there may not be many licensed acupuncturists nearby. In the United States, most states require practitioners to be licensed.

Then there is the cost. Acupuncture prices vary, but they typically run around $100 for a session, and health plans often do not cover it.

MORE OBSTACLES AND OPTIONS FOR HAY FEVER HEALING

The study was well done and "positive," because acupuncture seemed helpful, said Dr. Nelson.

But Dr. Nelson doubted whether the time, inconvenience and expense of acupuncture sessions would seem worthwhile to many hay fever sufferers—especially because there are simpler ways to manage the condition.

"I don't know how many people will want to wait in an acupuncturist's office, then sit with 16 needles in them for 20 minutes, and do that 12 times, when they could use a nasal spray," Dr. Nelson said.

Specifically, Dr. Nelson pointed to prescription nasal sprays that contain anti-inflammatory corticosteroids. The sprays—which include brand names like Flonase and Nasonex—are taken daily to help prevent hay fever symptoms.

Patients in this study were not using nasal steroids. They were taking antihistamines as needed—which, Dr. Nelson said, is not the most effective way to manage hay fever.

Still, he added, there are people who want to avoid medication, and they may be interested in acupuncture as an option.

Dr. Nelson also suggested that people who want a "natural" remedy for their hay fever woes might also consider allergy shots. That means getting a series of injections that expose you to tiny amounts of the substance causing your allergies, to train your immune system to tolerate it.

info For more information about hay fever, visit the American Academy of Allergy, Asthma & Immunology Web site, *www.aaaai. org/conditions-and-treatments/allergies/rhinitis. aspx.*

The Superfood Spirulina And What It Can Do For Your Allergies

Jennifer Adler, MS, CN, a certified nutritionist, natural foods chef and adjunct faculty member at Bastyr University, Seattle. *www.passionatenutrition.com*

When you think of a superfood, you probably think of salmon or blueberries—not the algae that floats on the surfaces of lakes, ponds and reservoirs.

But there's a type of blue-green algae that has been used for food and medicine in developing countries for centuries...that NASA has recommended as an ideal food for long-term space missions...that is loaded with health-giving nutrients...and that might be a key component in a diet aimed at staying healthy, reversing chronic disease and slowing the aging process.

That algae is spirulina.

Spirulina grows mainly in subtropical and tropical countries, where there is year-round heat and sunlight. It is high in protein (up to 70%), rich in antioxidants and loaded with vitamins and minerals, particularly iron and vitamin B-12. And it has no cellulose—the cell wall of green plants—so its nutrients are easy for the body to digest and absorb.

GREEN MEDICINE

Dried into a powder, spirulina can be added to food or taken as a tablet or capsule. And ingested regularly, spirulina can do you a lot of good.

Spirulina has anti-inflammatory properties and can prevent the release of histamine and other inflammatory factors that trigger and worsen allergic symptoms. Studies also show that spirulina can boost levels of IgA, an antibody that defends against allergic reactions. In one study, people with allergies who took spirulina had less nasal discharge, sneezing, nasal congestion and itching.

IDEAL DOSE

A preventive daily dose of spirulina is one teaspoon. A therapeutic dose, to control or reverse disease, is 10 grams, or one tablespoon.

Spirulina has been on the market for more than a decade, and it's among the substances listed by the FDA as "Generally Recognized as Safe" (GRAS).

Caution: If you have an autoimmune disease, such as multiple sclerosis, rheumatoid arthritis or lupus, talk to your doctor. Spirulina could stimulate the immune system, making the condition worse.

BEST PRODUCTS

Like many products, the quality of spirulina varies. *What to look for...*

Pets Reduce Childhood Allergies

Recent findings show that children younger than age one who lived with a cat were 50% less likely to become sensitive to cats later in life. (Exposure to pets after the age of one is not associated with allergy risk.)

Theory: Being exposed to pet allergens and bacteria at a young age may allow infants' immune systems to develop in such a way as to avoid being sensitive to pets.

Study of 566 children by researchers at Henry Ford Hospital, Detroit, published in *Clinical & Experimental Allergy.*

•**Clean taste.** Top-quality spirulina tastes fresh. If spirulina tastes fishy or "swampy" or has a lingering aftertaste, it's probably not a good product.

•**Bright color.** Spirulina should have a vibrant, bright blue-green appearance (more green than blue). If spirulina is olive-green, it's probably inferior.

•**Cost.** You get what you pay for—and good spirulina can be somewhat pricey.

Example: Spirulina Pacifica, from Nutrex Hawaii—grown on the Kona coast of Hawaii since 1984 and regarded by many health experts as one of the most nutritious and purest spirulina products on the market—costs $50 for a 16-ounce, 454-gram jar of powder. Store it in the refrigerator.

•**Growing location.** The best spirulina is grown in clean water in a nonindustrialized setting, as far away as possible from an urban, polluted environment. If you can, find out the growing location of the product you're considering buying.

HOW TO ADD IT TO FOOD

There are many ways to include spirulina in your daily diet...

•**Put it in smoothies.** Add between one teaspoon and one tablespoon to any smoothie or shake.

•**Add to juice.** Add one teaspoon or tablespoon to an eight-ounce glass of juice or water, shake it up and drink it.

•**Sprinkle it on food.** Try spirulina popcorn, for instance—a great conversation starter at a potluck. To a bowl of popcorn, add one to two tablespoons of spirulina powder, three to four tablespoons of grated Parmesan cheese, two or three tablespoons of olive oil, one-half teaspoon of salt and one-eighth teaspoon of cayenne pepper.

•**Add it to condiments.** Put one-quarter teaspoon in a small jar of ketchup, barbecue sauce, mustard or salad dressing. This way you'll get a little each time you use these products.

Does Eating Fish During Infancy Cut Asthma Risk?

Jessica Kiefte-de Jong, PhD, pediatrics, epidemiology, Erasmus Medical Center, Rotterdam, Netherlands.

Antonio Rodriguez, MD, director, pediatric pulmonology, Miami Children's Hospital.

Pediatrics

Adding fish to babies' diets during the first year of life might reduce their risk of asthma later on, a study by Dutch researchers suggests.

This window of protection appears to occur between six months and 12 months of age. Adding fish to the diet before that or not at all in the first year seems to carry an increased risk of wheezing and shortness of breath, the researchers said.

"This study provides insight into what the optimal timing of introduction can be for fish," said lead study author Jessica Kiefte-de Jong, PhD, from the pediatrics and epidemiology departments at Erasmus Medical Center in Rotterdam.

"The results may assist health care workers about the recommendations regarding the introduction of complementary feeding in infants," she added.

Pediatricians may not agree with the findings, however. One expert objects to feeding children fish at such a young age because of potential harms.

"I have never heard that fish is a preventive against asthma," said Antonio Rodriguez, MD, director of pediatric pulmonology at Miami Children's Hospital.

"There is a danger of an allergic reaction feeding fish to children under one year of age," he said. "In addition, there is always concern about the toxicity of mercury in fish."

This is why fish is not fed to infants, he said.

Dr. Kiefte-de Jong agreed that before parents start introducing fish to their infants these findings need confirmation in a real clinical trial. She also said the researchers aren't quite sure why eating fish at this age might benefit children's lung health.

RESEARCH DETAILS

For the study, published online in the journal *Pediatrics*, the research team collected data from a population-based study of more than 7,200 children born between April 2002 and January 2006 in Rotterdam.

Reviewing questionnaires on overall diet, the researchers looked at when parents introduced fish to their infants' diets. They also looked at symptoms of asthma that developed at ages three and four years.

Children who started eating fish at six to 12 months had a significantly lower risk of wheezing when they were four years old compared with children who began eating fish later, Dr. Kiefte-de Jong's group found.

For children who started eating fish earlier—or not at all—within the first year, the risk for wheezing increased at four years, they noted. The risk of shortness of breath increased slightly as well.

The researchers acknowledged that other factors besides when the children started eating fish might have influenced the children's breathing ability at preschool age. And the study did not prove that the introduction of fish during the first year of life prevented asthma later on.

C-Section May Raise Child's Risk of Allergies, Asthma

Henry Ford Health System, news release.

Babies born by cesarean section are more likely than others to develop allergies, a recent study says.

Researchers evaluated more than 1,200 newborns when they were one month, six months, one year and two years old.

By age two, babies born by cesarean section were five times more likely to have allergies than those born naturally when exposed to high levels of common household allergens such as pet dander and dust mites.

The findings "further advance the hygiene hypothesis that early childhood exposure to microorganisms affects the immune system's development and onset of allergies," study lead author Christine Cole Johnson, chairwoman of the health sciences department at Henry Ford Hospital in Detroit, said in a hospital news release. "We believe a baby's exposure to bacteria in the birth canal is a major influencer on their immune system."

Babies born by C-section have a pattern of "at-risk" microorganisms in their gastrointestinal tract that may make them more susceptible to developing the antibody immunoglobulin E (IgE) when exposed to allergens, Johnson said.

IgE is linked to the development of allergies and asthma.

The study was presented at the annual meeting of the American Academy of Allergy, Asthma and Immunology in San Antonio, Texas.

The study found an association between cesarean birth and allergy risk, but it did not prove cause-and-effect.

info The American Academy of Pediatrics has more about allergies and asthma in children at its Web site, *www.healthychildren.org.*

Chronic Heartburn Could Spur Asthma in Some Patients

Blair Jobe, MD, director of the Institute for the Treatment of Esophageal and Thoracic Disease at the West Penn Allegheny Health System.
David Bernstein, MD, gastroenterologist and chief, division of hepatology, North Shore University Hospital, Manhasset, New York.
West Penn Allegheny Health System, news release.

Chronic heartburn is a major cause of asthma in adults, a recent study suggests.

The finding could help add asthma to the known health risks—including esophageal cancer—already associated with chronic heartburn, which is formally known as gastroesophageal reflux disease (GERD) and is one of the most common digestive disorders in Western nations.

What Exercises Are Best for You?*

If you have asthma...

Asthma, one of the most common lung diseases in the US, generally does not interfere with exercise unless you are performing an activity that's especially strenuous such as running, which can trigger an attack ("exercise-induced asthma").

With exercise-induced asthma, the triggers vary from person to person. For example, very vigorous exercise, such as squash or mountain biking, can cause difficulties for some people with asthma, who may do better alternating brief periods of intense and slower-paced activity (as used in interval training). Swimming is also a good choice—the high humidity helps prevent drying of the airways, which can trigger an asthma attack.

If you use an inhaler such as albuterol to treat an asthma attack: Ask your doctor about taking a dose immediately before you exercise to help prevent an attack, and always.

If you have chronic obstructive pulmonary disease (COPD): Exercise doesn't improve lung function, but it does build muscle endurance and improve one's tolerance for the shortness of breath that often accompanies COPD (a condition that typically includes chronic bronchitis and/or emphysema).

Aerobic exercises that work the lower body (like walking or stationary cycling) are good, but the Schwinn Airdyne or NuStep provides a lower- and upper-body workout with the option of stopping the upper-body workout if breathing becomes more difficult.

*Always talk to your doctor before starting a new exercise program. If you have a chronic illness, it may be useful to consult a physical therapist for advice on exercise dos and don'ts for your particular situation.

John P. Porcari, PhD, program director of the Clinical Excercise Physiology (CEP) program at the University of Wisconsin-La Crosse.

GERD occurs when a muscle at the end of the esophagus fails to close properly. This allows stomach contents to leak back (reflux) into the esophagus and irritate it. GERD symptoms include frequent heartburn, chest discomfort,

Asthma Drug Helps Relieve Chronic Hives

According to a recent study, three injections of the asthma drug *omalizumab* (Xolair) reduced the amount of itching in patients resistant to antihistamines by up to 71%.

Marcus Maurer, MD, research director and professor of dermatology and allergy at Charité-Universitätsmedizin, Berlin, Germany, lead author of study, published in *The New England Journal of Medicine*.

dry cough, difficulty swallowing, hoarseness or sore throat, and regurgitation of food.

IDENTIFYING GERD-INDUCED ASTHMA

In this study, researchers used a new, specially designed catheter that measures levels of acid reflux exposure within the patient's airway. They believe that this new method (known by the acronym HMII) was much more effective than conventional techniques in identifying patients with GERD-induced asthma.

The researchers also found that for the majority of patients, asthma symptoms eased after they underwent surgery for GERD, according to the study published in the journal *JAMA Surgery*.

"We have observed for some time a strong association between GERD and certain pulmonary [lung] diseases, including adult-onset asthma," study author Blair Jobe, MD, director of the Institute for the Treatment of Esophageal and Thoracic Disease at the West Penn Allegheny Health System, said in a health system news release.

"The real challenge, however, has been our limited ability to effectively diagnose these patients and determine who precisely may benefit from surgical intervention," he added. According to Dr. Jobe, the newly devised test "is much more sensitive as means of detecting GERD in asthmatic patients than what we have traditionally relied upon."

The findings are strong enough to warrant consideration of HMII testing in adults with asthma that is not responding to asthma medications or in those who also have GERD symptoms, he said.

One expert wasn't surprised by the findings.

EXPERT COMMENTARY

"GERD is a common condition affecting millions of Americans," noted David Bernstein, MD, gastroenterologist and chief of the division of hepatology at North Shore University Hospital in Manhasset, New York. "And reflux of gastric acid through the esophagus and into the lungs is a common cause of chronic cough and asthma."

But it may be too early to advocate for widespread diagnostic testing using the new method, he added.

"This new technique is interesting and needs to be further evaluated before it can replace currently accepted diagnostic techniques," Dr. Bernstein said.

However, he believes that surgery is not always warranted for patients with reflux-linked asthma symptoms.

"Surgery for GERD-induced asthma is seldom necessary due to the ability of high-dose anti-acid medications in controlling the vast majority of reflux cases," Dr. Bernstein contends. "It is premature to recommend anti-reflux surgery without an adequate trial of anti-acid medications."

info The US National Institute of Diabetes and Digestive and Kidney Diseases has more about GERD at its Web site, *www.digestive.niddk.gov/ddiseases/pubs/gerd/*.

Experimental Drug Calms Severe Asthma

Ian Pavord, MB, consultant physician, University Hospitals of Leicester NHS Trust, England.
Rubin Cohen, MD, director, Asthma Center, North Shore-LIJ Health System, New Hyde Park, New York.
The Lancet, online.

An experimental drug known as *mepolizumab* may reduce outbreaks by almost 50% in people with a type of hard-to-treat asthma, an early study finds.

About a third of people with severe asthma have what is called *eosinophilic* asthma, in which inflammatory cells called *eosinophils* cause swelling of lung airways. Standard asthma treatment with inhaled steroids isn't effective, so these patients take oral steroids, which have many side effects, the researchers explained.

Mepolizumab blocks the production of eosinophils and reduces the frequency of severe asthma outbreaks, which may reduce the need for steroids, the researchers said.

The new drug is a monoclonal antibody, a class of drugs involving naturally occurring human antibodies that are genetically altered in a laboratory, cloned in large numbers and introduced into the patient to target disease sites.

"This is a promising new drug treatment," said lead researcher Ian Pavord, MB, a consultant physician at the University Hospitals of Leicester NHS Trust, in England. "I think it's going to become a viable treatment and it offers hope to a group of people that are having really big problems with their asthma."

The purpose of this trial was to find out the best dose of the drug and to identify the type of patients most likely to benefit from it, Dr. Pavord said.

"It's been a successful study, because we have established the drug is effective even in low doses and patients can be identified through a blood test," he added.

Some patients taking mepolizumab may be able to reduce the amount of steroids they take, according to Dr. Pavord.

"If that were the case it would be very attractive to the patient," he said.

GlaxoSmithKline, the maker of mepolizumab, funded the trial. The findings were published in the online edition of the journal *The Lancet*.

STUDY DETAILS

For the study, Dr. Pavord's team randomly assigned more than 600 patients with severe asthma to receive one of three doses of mepolizumab or a placebo. The drug is given intravenously once a month. Participants included asthma patients from 81 medical centers in 13 countries, and their ages ranged from 12 to 74 years old.

After a year, the researchers found that patients taking mepolizumab had about half the number of severe outbreaks requiring ER visits

---

New Help for Sleep Apnea

When 23 adults with sleep apnea were given 60 mg of *pseudoephedrine* and 10 mg of *domperidone* before bed, all but one reported fewer symptoms, such as loud snoring and daytime fatigue.

Theory: Pseudoephedrine is used to treat nasal congestion, and domperidone is used for acid reflux, so the combination of these drugs may help reduce airway blockages and swollen tissue in the throat that may contribute to sleep apnea.

If you have sleep apnea: Ask your doctor if this drug combination would be effective for you.

Murray Grossan, MD, a Los Angeles–based otolaryngologist in private practice.

---

or hospitalizations as patients taking a placebo. Patients taking mepolizumab also had half as many outbreaks that required oral steroids.

Although mepolizumab effectively reduced outbreaks, it didn't produce consistent improvements in symptoms or lung function, the study found. "It's not a cure," Dr. Pavord said. "It's likely to be a long-term treatment."

Headaches and swelling of the nasal passages were seen among patients taking the drug and those on placebo, the researchers noted. Side effects from oral steroids include mood changes, increased appetite, weight gain and acne.

The potential cost of the drug, if approved, isn't known. Approval of mepolizumab for asthma isn't expected for at least three to four years, Dr. Pavord said.

EXPERT COMMENTARY

"The results of this study are very impressive," said Rubin Cohen, MD, director of the Asthma Center at North Shore-LIJ Health System in New Hyde Park, New York.

"If this pans out, patients with severe asthma would have a different treatment option and be able to control their asthma without the side effects of steroids," he said. "They may actually be able to get off steroids completely or reduce the amount of steroids they take substantially."

info To learn more about asthma, visit the US National Library of Medicine at *www.nlm. nih.gov/medlineplus/asthma.html.*

Treat Sleep Apnea and Ease High Blood Pressure

American Academy of Sleep Medicine, news release.

Continuous positive airway pressure (CPAP), a type of therapy for the sleep disorder known as obstructive sleep apnea, significantly lowered blood pressure in men with hypertension, researchers have found.

"All types of patients may benefit from this treatment, even those with other chronic medical conditions," principal investigator Bharati Prasad, MD, said in a news release from the American Academy of Sleep Medicine. "It's important to now do a prospective study enrolling different types of patients with sleep apnea."

STUDY DETAILS

The study included 221 men who were newly diagnosed with obstructive sleep apnea and also had either high blood pressure (hypertension) or type 2 diabetes. Obstructive sleep apnea causes disrupted sleep and pauses in breathing during the night.

The men were prescribed CPAP therapy to treat their sleep apnea. CPAP uses mild air pressure to keep airways open while a patient sleeps.

Significant decreases in both systolic and diastolic blood pressure readings (the top and bottom numbers in the reading) were seen in the men at three to six months after starting CPAP therapy, and also when tested again at nine to 12 months after starting the treatment.

IMPLICATIONS

The results indicate that, for men with obstructive sleep apnea and high blood pressure, CPAP may not only be an effective way to treat their sleep disorder, but also their hypertension, the authors of the study reported in the *Journal of Clinical Sleep Medicine.*

The study found an association between CPAP therapy and reductions in high blood pressure levels, but it didn't prove a cause-and-effect relationship.

info For more information on sleep apnea, visit the Web site of the US National Heart, Lung, and Blood Institute at *www.nhlbi. nih.gov/health/health-topics/topics/sleepapnea/.*

Lifestyle Changes That Stop Sleep Apnea

Chris Meletis, ND, executive director, Institue for Healthy Aging and author of *The Hyaluronic Acid Miracle* (Freedom Press). *www.drmeletis.com*

Self-care strategies…

•**Sleep on your side.** This helps keep airways open.

•**Lose weight,** because extra pounds mean extra tissue in the throat. Just a 10% weight loss can decrease apnea events by 26%. However, thin people and children can have apnea, too.

•**Don't drink alcohol within three hours of going to bed.** It relaxes the airway.

•**Sing some vowels.** In a study by UK researchers, three months of singing lessons helped decrease snoring, which could in turn decrease apnea.

What to do: Sing the long vowel sounds a-a-a-e-e-e, taking two or three seconds to sing each vowel. Do this once or twice every day for five minutes a session.

Human Airways' "Brush" Mechanism Gives Clues To Lung Diseases

Michael Rubinstein, PhD, John P. Barker Distinguished Professor, University of North Carolina, Chapel Hill.

American Association for the Advancement of Science, news release.

A recent study that helps explain how human airways rid the lungs of mucus could give insights into asthma, cystic fibrosis and chronic obstructive pulmonary disease (COPD), researchers say.

Human airways rely on mucus to expel foreign matter—including toxic and infectious particles—from the body, the study authors said in a news release from the American Association for the Advancement of Science.

"The air we breathe isn't exactly clean, and we take in many dangerous elements with every breath," said study coauthor Michael Rubinstein, PhD. "We need a mechanism to remove all the junk we breathe in, and the way it's done is with a very sticky gel called mucus that catches these particles and removes them with the help of tiny [hair-like] cilia," he explained.

"The cilia are constantly beating, even while we sleep," Dr. Rubinstein said. "In a coordinated fashion, they push mucus containing foreign objects out of the lungs, and we either swallow it or spit it out. These cilia even beat for a few hours after we die. If they stopped, we'd be flooded with mucus that provides a fertile breeding ground for bacteria."

HOW MUCUS MOVES

It's long been believed that mucus clearance occurs through a "gel-on-liquid" method, in which a watery layer acts as a lubricant and separates mucus from cells that line the airways. However, this does not explain how mucus remains in its own distinct layer.

In this study, published in the journal *Science*, Dr. Rubinstein and colleagues at the University of North Carolina at Chapel Hill suggest a "gel-on-brush" form of mucus clearance, in which mucus moves atop a brushlike layer rather than a watery layer.

"This layer—this brush—seems to be very important for the healthy functioning of human airways," Dr. Rubinstein said. "It protects cells from sticky mucus, and it creates a second barrier of defense in case viruses or bacteria penetrate through the mucus. They would not penetrate through the brush layer because the brush is denser," he added.

"We found that there is a specific condition, below which the brush is healthy and cells are happy," Dr. Rubinstein said. "But above this ideal condition, in diseases like [cystic fibrosis]

or COPD, the brush becomes compressed and actually prevents the normal cilia beating and healthy flow of mucus."

If the mucus layer becomes too dense, it can crash through the brush layer, collapse the cilia and stick to the cells lining the airways, the study authors noted.

"The collapse of this brush is what can lead to immobile mucus and result in infection, inflammation and eventually the destruction of lung tissue and the loss of lung function," Dr. Rubinstein explained. Insights like those might someday help researchers develop new treatments for lung diseases, he added, and also provide a way to assess the effectiveness of those treatments.

info The American Academy of Family Physicians has more information about chronic obstructive pulmonary disease at its Web site, *http://familydoctor.org/familydoctor/en/diseases-conditions/chronic-obstructive-pulmonary-disease.printerview.all.html.*

Most Coughs Don't Respond to Antibiotics

Philipp Schuetz, MD, MPH, Kantonsspital Aarau, Tellstrasse, Aarau, Switzerland.
Len Horovitz, MD, pulmonologist, Lenox Hill Hospital, New York City.
The Lancet Infectious Diseases, online.

Commonly prescribed antibiotics don't help cure most coughs in adults, recent research confirms.

Patients with a cough or bronchitis are often prescribed antibiotics, and previous studies have had conflicting results about their effectiveness.

STUDY DETAILS

For this study, researchers randomly assigned more than 2,000 adults complaining of a cough to take either the antibiotic *amoxicillin* for a week or an inactive placebo.

Overall, the antibiotic was no more effective at relieving symptoms or their duration than the placebo, the study found. The findings also held among people who were older than 60.

Study participants were 18 and older and had sought treatment for an acute cough—meaning they'd had the cough for less than a month—which is one of the most common illnesses seen by primary care doctors. There was no reason to suspect that any of them had the lung infection pneumonia, which is treated with antibiotics.

Participants took the antibiotic three times daily for seven days. While they had no better recovery than those taking the dummy pills, they were more likely to report side effects such as nausea, rash and diarrhea, according to the study.

That said, more people in the placebo group did experience new or worsening symptoms, but this did not occur frequently enough to justify treating everyone with antibiotics. Thirty people would need to be treated with antibiotics to prevent one person from developing new or worsening symptoms, the study found.

The study was published in a recent online edition of *The Lancet Infectious Diseases.*

MAIN MESSAGE CONCERNING COUGHS AND ANTIBIOTICS

"The main message here is that antibiotics are usually not necessary for respiratory infections, if pneumonia is not suspected," said Philipp Schuetz, MD, of the Kantonsspital Aarau in Switzerland.

"Only a few patients benefit from antibiotics and these may be identified with new blood tests for bacterial infections," said Dr. Schuetz, who wrote an editorial accompanying the study. "Physicians and patients should generally refrain from antibiotic use, yet, if they feel unsure, the blood test helps them to further minimize risks."

The study is the largest to date that shows antibiotics do not help treat lower-respiratory infections, the researchers say.

PROBLEMS WITH INDISCRIMINATE USE

Indiscriminate use of antibiotics may also pose risks, Dr. Schuetz said. "The main risk from antibiotics is related to direct side effects such as severe diarrhea," he said. "The other risk relates to emergence of multi-resistant bacteria, which on a population level are a threat to society as antibiotics may not work properly."

Len Horovitz, MD, a pulmonologist at Lenox Hill Hospital in New York City, said that many patients beg for antibiotics to nip a cold in the bud. "This is not how it works," he said. "Viruses such as the common cold do not respond to antibiotics."

TAKING CARE OF COLDS AND COUGHS

So what does work? "Comfort care, such as more sleep, drinking lots of fluids, and using a humidifier at night," Dr. Horovitz said. "If you have a cough or lower respiratory tract infection, go to the doctor and let him examine you." The doctor can take a culture of any mucus that comes up with the cough to see if there is a bacteria present, he explained.

"Getting antibiotics for a dry cough without taking a culture is doing a disservice," he said. "There is no benefit and there may be a slight risk."

info Learn more about the common cold by visiting the US Centers for Disease Control and Prevention Web site at *http://www.cdc.gov/getsmart/antibiotic-use/uri/colds.html.*

Calm That Nagging Cough Fast

Jamison Starbuck, ND, naturopathic physician in family practice and a guest lecturer at the University of Montana, both in Missoula. She is past president of the American Association of Naturopathic Physicians and a contributing editor to *The Alternative Advisor: The Complete Guide to Natural Therapies and Alternative Treatments* (Time Life).

You may think that you've just about kicked a cold or bout of the flu, but what about the nasty-sounding cough that won't go away? It could be bronchitis, the term for inflammation of the bronchi—the air "tubes" that connect the trachea and the lungs.

While a viral illness, such as a cold or the flu, is a common cause of bronchitis, it's not the only one. People who have a cough but no other symptoms, such as body aches or a runny nose, may have developed bronchitis after prolonged or significant exposure to lung irritants, such as dust, smoke or chemical fumes. If you're a smoker or have allergies or asthma, you're more vulnerable to bronchitis because your lungs are already inflamed. Bronchitis due to a bacterial infection is relatively rare.

You might think of bronchitis as "just a cough," but it can be dangerous for some people. Pneumonia can be a complication of bronchitis—especially in children under age two and in older adults who are frail and/or debilitated. In people with a history of cardiac arrhythmia, the exertion of prolonged, hard coughing can trigger a rapid or irregular heartbeat. If you have bronchitis, it's important to see your doctor if you notice an unusual heart rate, have shortness of breath, a fever or bloody sputum, or you are frail and elderly. Even if you're otherwise healthy, see a doctor if your cough lasts for more than two weeks.

Antibiotics are of no use for viral or inflammatory bronchitis. Instead, conventional doctors usually tell their patients to simply rest and drink plenty of fluids. This is solid advice, but there are several natural medicines to speed the healing process, often cutting the course of the illness in half. *Top remedies for bronchitis…*

•**Try a botanical expectorant.** It not only helps you cough up phlegm but also acts as an antiviral and soothes irritated tissues in the throat.

My favorite: Elecampane in tincture (an alcohol extract) form.

Typical dose: 30 drops in one ounce of water. Take this at least 15 minutes before or after eating or drinking, six times per day for up to seven days.

Caution: Elecampane may cause an allergic reaction in people with ragweed allergies.

•**Eat the right foods.** Avoid dairy products, meat and sugar during bronchitis—these foods promote inflammation and slow your healing. Instead, have vegetable soup, broth, whole grains and steamed vegetables.

•**Drink peppermint tea.** Nausea due to frequent coughing and swallowing phlegm commonly occurs with bronchitis. Peppermint tea relieves nausea and helps break up the swallowed mucus.

•**Take a hot bath or steamy shower.** Either one will soothe your respiratory tract and help eliminate mucus.

Also helpful: Apply a thin layer of Vicks VapoRub or Mentholatum Ointment to the center of your chest after the bath or shower and again just before bed to make breathing easier and reduce coughing while you sleep.

Important: With viral bronchitis, people are usually contagious (via air droplets from a cough or direct contact) for up to a week.

Blood Pressure & Cholesterol

Are You Taking the Right Blood Pressure Medication?

If you're one of the roughly 75 million Americans with high blood pressure (hypertension), you might like to believe that lifestyle changes, such as losing weight, exercising and cutting back on salt, can control it. In some cases, it can. But like it or not, most people who have hypertension end up on medication.

The problem is that more than one-third of patients on medication still have elevated blood pressure readings. In many instances, they are not on medication or a dosage that is right for them. Millions also are suffering from avoidable side effects.

There are more than 60 drugs for hypertension—too many for most physicians (even specialists) to know about in detail. What's more, your drug treatment needs to be targeted to match the cause of your hypertension.

WHAT'S YOUR HYPERTENSION?

Of the millions of Americans with inadequately controlled hypertension, nearly all could have blood pressure in the normal range simply by adjusting their medication. What most patients don't realize is that hypertension is driven by different mechanisms that respond to different treatments.

The three mechanisms underlying hypertension in most cases—and the best treatments for each…

#1: Hypertension driven by sodium/ volume. This is the most common form of high blood pressure, affecting at least half of hypertensive patients.

The kidneys do not excrete sodium efficiently and, as a result, the body starts to accumulate sodium and fluid. This increase in fluid volume raises blood pressure. In addition,

Samuel J. Mann, MD, professor of clinical medicine at Weill Medical College of Cornell University and a hypertension specialist at New York-Presbyterian Hospital, both in New York City. He is also author of *Hypertension and You: Old Drugs, New Drugs and the Right Drugs for Your High Blood Pressure* (Rowman & Littlefield).

elevated sodium can trigger arterial constriction in some patients, which further raises blood pressure.

Telltale signs: Fluid retention in the legs (edema) and low levels of the hormone renin (as measured with a widely available blood test). African-Americans, people over age 65 and those who are "salt-sensitive" are more likely to have sodium/volume hypertension.

Main treatment: A diuretic (water pill) that increases sodium excretion or a calcium-channel blocker, such as *amlodipine* (Norvasc), that dilates arteries.

#2: Hypertension driven by the renin-angiotensin system (RAS).

The kidneys have sensors that monitor blood pressure and blood volume. When either is low, the kidneys secrete the hormone *renin*, which triggers the formation of angiotensin II, constricting arteries and raising blood pressure.

Telltale signs: High renin levels in the blood, the absence of edema and lack of response to diuretics prescribed to reduce blood pressure. It's more common in Caucasians under age 50.

Four classes of drugs that block RAS activation…

•**Angiotensin-converting enzyme (ACE) inhibitors,** such as *enalapril* (Vasotec) and *captopril* (Capoten).

•**Angiotensin-receptor blockers (ARBs),** such as *losartan* (Cozaar) and *valsartan* (Diovan).

•**Direct renin inhibitor (DRI).** *Aliskiren* (Tekturna)—the only drug within this new class.

•**Beta-blockers,** an older drug class, which includes *metoprolol* (Toprol). In most patients with RAS-mediated hypertension, ACE inhibitors and ARBs are preferred over beta-blockers—outcomes are better, and they cause fewer side effects, such as fatigue.

Approximately 80% of hypertension patients will respond to drugs that target sodium/volume or the RAS, or to a combination of drugs that targets both.

#3: Hypertension driven by the sympathetic nervous system (SNS).
The SNS is responsible for hypertension in about 15% of cases and frequently is overlooked by physicians. Stimulation of the SNS, which is the primary link between our brain and our blood pressure, results in adrenaline-induced increases in heart rate and cardiac output (the amount of blood pumped by the heart) and arterial constriction. Emotions stimulate the SNS and may be the source of SNS hypertension.

Effective drugs include beta-blockers, which slow down the heart, often in combination with an alpha-blocker, such as *doxazosin* (Cardura), which dilates arteries. Drugs like *clonidine* (Catapres), a central alpha-receptor stimulator, reduce SNS outflow from the brain but cause fatigue in most patients.

Telltale signs: Conditions such as alcohol abuse and sleep apnea can trigger SNS-driven hypertension. Other indicators are episodic hypertension and hypertension that is not controlled by drugs that target sodium/volume and the RAS.

PRESCRIPTION PITFALLS

There are many effective drugs on the market, but unless they are correctly prescribed, hypertension won't be controlled and avoidable side effects may occur. *Common errors you should watch out for…*

•**Widespread overtreatment.** Millions of Americans are on more medication than they need, including many people who might not need any at all.

The most common reasons doctors overprescribe: Anxiety that raises blood pressure when visiting the doctor, incorrect measurement of blood pressure at the doctor's office and/or at home, and the addition of medication in patients with well-controlled hypertension who have an occasional elevated reading.

•**Not enough diuretics.** In many people, a low dose of a diuretic, such as 25 mg of *hydrochlorothiazide*, is sufficient—a higher dose is not needed and even can be harmful. But in some, a higher dose or a combination of two diuretics is essential. Studies show that in half of people with uncontrolled hypertension, blood pressure can be brought under control by strengthening the diuretic regimen.

•**Underuse of some highly effective older drugs.** New drugs are promoted, while some older drugs are nearly forgotten. Older diuretics such as *amiloride* (Midamor) and *torsemide* (Demadex), and beta-blockers such as *betaxolol*

(Kerlone) and *bisoprolol* (Zebeta) are examples of excellent older drugs that are not commonly prescribed but should be.

•**Overuse of beta-blockers.** Beta-blockers can cause fatigue and, in older patients, can affect cognitive function. Modifying or eliminating use of the beta-blocker can improve cognitive function in some patients and should not be overlooked as a consideration in the evaluation of cognitive decline. Many patients taking a beta-blocker for hypertension don't need to be on one!

•**Lack of appreciation for emotional factors.** Decades of studies have failed to prove that such factors as stress, anger and anxiety lead to hypertension. However, some studies suggest that repressed emotions, the emotions we are unaware of, might contribute. If your hypertension is driven by emotional factors, you will respond better to drugs that target the SNS.

Summing up, nearly all patients with hypertension can be treated successfully with available drugs. The goal is a normal blood pressure without drug side effects. You should not settle for less.

Should you see a hypertension specialist? If your hypertension is under control with one or two drugs, and you have no side effects, you don't need to see a specialist.

Otherwise, consider seeking the opinion of a physician specializing in hypertension. To find one, go to *www.ash-us.org*, the Web site of the American Society of Hypertension (under "Patients," click on "HTN Specialists Directory").

Foods That Help Control Blood Pressure

Janet Bond Brill, PhD, RD, a registered dietitian and a nationally recognized expert in nutrition and cardiovascular disease prevention. She is author of *Blood Pressure Down: The 10-Step Plan to Lower Your Blood Pressure in 4 Weeks Without Prescription Drugs* (Three Rivers). *www.drjanet.com*

Considering all the dangers of high blood pressure (including increased risk for heart attack, stroke and dementia), we definitely want to do everything we can to keep our blood pressure levels under control. But are we? Unfortunately, one surprisingly simple step—eating the right foods—consistently gets ignored as an effective technique for controlling blood pressure.*

Of course everyone knows that a low-sodium diet helps some people maintain healthy blood pressure levels. But there's a lot more to blood pressure control than avoiding that bag of potato chips, extra dash of soy sauce or a crunchy dill pickle (just one dill pickle contains about 875 mg of sodium, or nearly 40% of recommended daily sodium intake).

What most people are missing out on: With the right combination of blood pressure–controlling nutrients, you often can avoid high blood pressure altogether...or if you already have the condition and are being treated with medication, you may be able to reduce your dosage and curb your risk for troubling side effects, such as fatigue, depression and erectile dysfunction.

The best foods for blood pressure control...

EAT MORE BANANAS

Bananas are among the best sources of potassium, a mineral that's crucial for blood pressure control. A typical banana contains about 450 mg of potassium, or about 10% of the amount of potassium most people should aim for each day.

Potassium works like a "water pill." It's a natural diuretic that enables the kidneys to excrete more sodium while also relaxing blood vessels—both functions help control blood pressure.

Scientific evidence: In a large study of nearly 250,000 adults published in the *Journal of the American College of Cardiology,* people who increased their intake of potassium by 1,600 mg daily were 21% less likely to suffer a stroke than those who ate less.

Kiwifruit also is a concentrated source of potassium with more than 200 mg in each small fruit.

Recommended daily amount of potassium: 4,700 mg. A good potassium-rich breakfast

*In addition to smart eating habits, a blood pressure–controlling action plan includes regular exercise (ideally, 30 minutes of aerobic activity, such as brisk walking or swimming, at least five times a week) and a stress-reducing regimen.

is oatmeal made with soy milk (300 mg), one cup of cantaloupe (430 mg), one cup of fresh-squeezed orange juice (496 mg) and one cup of coffee (116 mg).

Other good potassium sources: Potatoes (purple potatoes have the most), avocados, pistachios and Swiss chard.

Good rule of thumb: To control blood pressure, try to consume three times more potassium than sodium.

PILE ON THE SPINACH

Even if you eat plenty of bananas, all of that potassium won't lower your blood pressure unless you also get enough magnesium. It is estimated that about two-thirds of Americans are deficient in magnesium—and while magnesium supplements might help in some ways, they do not reduce blood pressure. Only magnesium from food—such as spinach, nuts, legumes and oatmeal—offers this benefit due to the nutrients' synergistic effect.

Recommended daily amount of magnesium: 500 mg. One cup of cooked spinach provides 157 mg of magnesium.

Also good: Two ounces of dry-roasted almonds (160 mg).

DIP INTO YOGURT

Calcium helps the body maintain mineral balance that regulates blood pressure. Calcium also contains a protein that works like a natural ACE inhibitor (one of the most common types of blood pressure medications) and prevents the constriction of blood vessels that raises blood pressure.

Important: Stick to low-fat or no-fat yogurt, milk and cheese—the saturated fat in whole-fat dairy products appears to cancel the blood pressure–lowering effects. In addition, opt for "plain" yogurt to avoid the added sugar that's found in many brands of yogurt. If you don't like the taste

---

Slow Breathing Lowers Blood Pressure

You've probably heard that yoga, meditation and other forms of relaxation can reduce blood pressure.

An even simpler solution: Merely breathing more slowly, for just a few minutes a day, can do the same thing—and research shows that for some people, combining slow breathing with relaxation techniques can be as effective as drug therapy.

What to do: Once a day, take a little time to slow your breathing. Breathe in deeply for 10 seconds, then breathe out at the same rate. Repeat the cycle for 15 minutes.

Or try Resperate, an electronic breathing device that helps you synchronize your breathing ($300, *www.resperate.com*).

---

of plain yogurt, add a little granola, honey, nuts, seeds, fresh berries or banana.

For a tasty "pumpkin pie" snack: Add plain canned pumpkin, walnuts, pumpkin pie spice and Splenda to plain yogurt and top it with fat-free whipped cream.

Other high-calcium foods: Leafy greens and sardines (with the bones). Calcium supplements also can help keep blood pressure down, but recent research has linked them to increased cardiovascular risk. Talk to your doctor about these supplements.

Recommended daily dose of calcium: 1,000 mg for men age 51 to 70…1,200 mg for men age 71 and older, and women age 51 and older. Eating two fat-free yogurts (830 mg), one cup of cooked spinach (245 mg) and three kiwifruits (150 mg) will easily get you to your daily calcium goal.

ENJOY SOY

Soy foods, including tofu, soy nuts and soy milk, may be the most underrated blood pressure–lowering foods. Research shows that people who regularly eat soy can reduce their blood pressure as much as they would by taking some medications. Soy increases nitric oxide, a naturally occurring gas that lowers blood pressure.

Helpful: If you can't get used to the taste (or texture) of tofu, drink chocolate soy milk. An eight-ounce glass has 8 g of soy protein. Unsalted, dry-roasted soy nuts are an even richer source with about 10 g in a quarter cup.

Recommended daily amount of soy: 20 g to 25 g of soy protein. This translates to two to four servings of soy nuts or soy milk. Women at high risk or who are being treated for breast, ovarian or uterine cancer should discuss their soy intake with their doctors—it can affect hormone levels that can fuel these cancers.

SIP RED WINE

Too much alcohol increases risk for high blood pressure—as well as heart disease and stroke. In moderation, however, red wine relaxes arteries and reduces risk for diabetes, a condition that often increases blood pressure. White wine and other forms of alcohol also reduce blood pressure, but red wine is a better choice because it contains more heart-protecting antioxidants known as flavonoids.

You'll get significant flavonoids from wines with a deep red color, such as cabernets. Specifically, grapevines that face harsher sun exposure and nutrient deprivation produce more flavonoids—cabernet sauvignon tops the list. Red wine also is high in resveratrol, another antioxidant. One glass of red wine contains enough resveratrol to stimulate the body's production of nitric oxide. Pinot noir wine has more resveratrol than other types.

Recommended daily limit for red wine: No more than two glasses for men or one glass for women.

For people who can't drink alcohol, purple grape juice has some flavonoids and resveratrol but doesn't contain the full benefit provided by red wine.

What's Slowly Killing Your Brain

Owen Carmichael, PhD, associate professor of neurology and computer science, Center for Neuroscience, University of California, Davis. His study was published in The Lancet Neurology.

There are lots of "young-ish" people—say, people in their 30s or 40s—who have been told by their doctors that they have borderline high blood pressure and whose reaction is basically, "Eh, whatever."

If this describes you—or a sibling or child of yours—you need to know that this youngish person with highish blood pressure is committing suicide of the brain.

That's because, as a recent study shows, even slightly high blood pressure starts eating up the brain even when a person is quite young.

There generally aren't any symptoms, and the person looks and feels fine (for now).

But here's where the mental trouble starts...

HOW HIGH BLOOD PRESSURE HURTS THE BRAIN

Most blood pressure research focuses on older people, so researchers were interested in exploring its effects on younger individuals. In an analysis of data from the famous Framingham Heart Study, they examined the neurological effects of systolic blood pressure—the top number in blood pressure readings—on adults with an average age of 39.

What they found should be considered a wake-up call for some younger folks. Using high-tech scans (a traditional MRI and a special type of MRI called diffusion tensor imaging), Owen Carmichael, PhD, a coauthor of the study, and his colleagues discovered that the higher a person's blood pressure, the lower the volume of gray matter in the brain and the lesser the structural "integrity" of the white matter. So those with hypertension (a reading of 140/90 or higher) had more cognitive damage than those with prehypertension (a reading between 120/80 and 139/89)...those with prehypertension had more than those with "normal" blood pressure (a reading under 120/80)...and even those with "high-normal" blood pressure had more than those with "low-normal" blood pressure.

Gray matter is like a set of computers that perform the calculations that enable you to remember things, concentrate, follow a sequence of events, speak, see and hear, for example. When you have less gray matter, it's like having fewer computers to do those calculations, so it's harder to do those brain-related tasks mentioned above. White matter, on the other hand, is like the Internet wiring that allows the gray matter "computers" to communicate with each other and do those mental tasks efficiently. When the integrity of the white matter is compromised, it's as if your brain wiring has been frayed. So that also makes performing those brain-related tasks mentioned above more difficult.

Now, these aren't effects that you would necessarily notice in your 30s or 40s—you won't suddenly start forgetting your children's names or getting lost in your own house, said Dr.

Blood Pressure Drugs May Fight Dementia

Recent finding: People treated for hypertension with beta-blockers had less brain atrophy...fewer signs of small strokes...and a lower level of plaques associated with Alzheimer's disease than people who were not taking the medications.

Study by researchers at Pacific Health Research and Education Institute, Honolulu, presented at the annual meeting of the American Academy of Neurology in San Diego.

Carmichael. But if blood pressure isn't controlled, the negative effects begin—today—and then worsen with age. This can make you more susceptible to serious cognitive conditions, such as Alzheimer's disease.

GET YOUR NUMBERS DOWN

The great news, though, is that prehypertension (and even high-normal blood pressure) is very treatable. Making certain lifestyle changes (such as, of course, eating healthier foods and exercising more) and, as a last resort, even taking a medication (such as a thiazide diuretic, beta-blocker, angiotensin-converting enzyme inhibitor or calcium channel blocker) can lower your blood pressure and prevent any further brain damage. Is it possible to reverse damage that's already been done? Dr. Carmichael said that the answer isn't known, but hopefully future research will address it.

Once again, if your blood pressure is 140/90 or more, it's high. If it's under 120/80, it's normal. If it's between 120/80 and 139/89, you have prehypertension—which means that you don't have high blood pressure but are likely to develop it in the future. Even people with prehypertension in the study had more signs of brain damage than those with normal blood pressure—so you should take even a borderline reading such as that seriously.

Don't let your age give you a false sense of security.

The Sweet Snack That Does Wonders For Blood Pressure

Harold Bays, MD, medical director and president of the Louisville Metabolic and Atherosclerosis Research Center in Louisville, Kentucky, and principal investigator of a study on the effects of raisins on blood pressure, presented at the American College of Cardiology's 61st Annual Scientific Session.

Isn't it a rare joy when a new study produces scientific evidence in support of something sweet and yummy? In this case, the tasty news is that raisins can reduce blood pressure.

Why is this important? Blood pressure that is even slightly elevated—a condition called prehypertension—increases the risk for heart attack, stroke and kidney disease. Prehypertension is defined as a systolic pressure (the top number in a blood pressure reading, as measured in "millimeters of mercury" or mmHg) of 120 to 139...or a diastolic pressure (the bottom number) of 80 to 89.

For the recent study, researchers randomly assigned 46 prehypertension patients, average age 61, to eat a snack three times a day for 12 weeks. For one group, each snack consisted of a one-ounce package of raisins. The other group ate prepackaged processed commercial snack foods, such as crackers or cookies, that did not contain raisins, other fruit or vegetables. The raisins and the other snacks each contained about 90 to 100 calories per serving. Participants' blood pressure was measured at the start of the study and after four, eight and 12 weeks.

Results: Blood pressure did not change significantly among participants in the commercial snacks group. In comparison, in the raisin group, systolic pressure decreased significantly, with reductions ranging from 5 mmHg to 7 mmHg—an amount that has cardiovascular benefits, clinical trial evidence suggests. Raisin eaters' diastolic pressure also dropped, though not as much.

Explanation: Raisins are high in potassium, a mineral that reduces blood pressure by promoting the proper balance of electrolytes and fluids in the body...helping offset the adverse effects of dietary sodium...and increasing the amount of sodium excreted via the urine. Raisins also have antioxidants and other components that may make blood vessels less stiff.

Best: If your blood pressure is elevated—or if your blood pressure is fine and you want to keep it that way—consider forgoing processed snack foods in favor of a handful of natural raisins. Not fond of raisins or crave more variety? Other potassium-rich snack options include bananas, cantaloupe, carrots, honeydew melon, papayas and yogurt.

Reduce High Blood Pressure By Tapping Your Toes

Ann Marie Chiasson, MD, family practitioner and clinical assistant professor of medicine, Arizona Center for Integrative Medicine, University of Tucson. She is author of *Energy Healing: The Essentials of Self-Care* (Sounds True).

High blood pressure increases your risk not only for heart attack, heart failure and stroke, but also for grave maladies that you may never have considered, such as kidney failure, dementia, aneurysm, blindness and osteoporosis.

Medications help reduce blood pressure...but their nasty side effects can include joint pain, headache, weakness, dizziness, heart palpitations, coughing, asthma, constipation, diarrhea, insomnia, depression and erectile dysfunction!

Vitamin C Can Reduce Blood Pressure

In a recent study, about 500 milligrams (mg) of vitamin C taken daily for eight weeks reduced systolic pressure—the more important top number—by 3.84 Hg...and by 4.85 Hg in patients with hypertension. The dose is well below the daily limit of 2,000 mg.

Edgar Miller III, MD, PhD, associate professor of medicine and epidemiology at Johns Hopkins University School of Medicine, Baltimore, and senior author of an analysis of 29 studies, published in *American Journal of Clinical Nutrition*.

Now there's a promising alternative therapy that's completely risk-free—and costs nothing. This easy-to-use therapy is "tapping," which is based on the principles of Chinese medicine. *Here's how it works...*

SOMETHING OLD, SOMETHING NEW

The tapping method is used by Ann Marie Chiasson, MD, of the Arizona Center for Integrative Medicine. For her own patients with high blood pressure, Dr. Chiasson has adapted a tapping technique that is part of the ancient Chinese practice called qigong.

Qigong involves simple movements, including tapping on the body's meridians, or "highways" of energy movement. These meridians are the same as those used during acupuncture and acupressure treatments. According to a review of nine studies published in *The Journal of Alternative and Complementary Medicine*, qigong reduced systolic blood pressure (the top number) by an average of 17 points and diastolic blood pressure (the bottom number) by an average of 10 points. Those are big reductions! In fact, they are comparable to the reductions achieved with drugs—but the qigong had no unwanted side effects.

Though Dr. Chiasson has not conducted a clinical trial on her tapping protocol, she has observed reductions in blood pressure among her patients who practice tapping. The technique she recommends also could conceivably benefit people who do not have high blood pressure if it reduces stress and thus helps lower the risk of developing high blood pressure.

TAP AWAY

Some tapping routines are complicated, involving tapping the top of the head, around the eyes, side of the hand and under the nose, chin and/or arms. But Dr. Chiasson's technique is a simpler toe-and-torso method that is quite easy to learn. It is safe and can be done in the privacy of your own home—so if it might help you, why not give it a try?

First, you may want to get a blood pressure reading so you can do a comparison later on. If the tapping technique is helpful, you eventually may be able to reduce or even discontinue your high blood pressure drugs (of course, for safety's sake, you should not stop taking any drugs without first talking to your doctor about it).

Dr. Chiasson's plan: Each day, do five minutes of toe tapping (instructions below)…five minutes of belly tapping…and five minutes of chest tapping. You may experience tingling or a sensation of warmth in the part of the body being tapped and/or in your hands, which is normal. You can listen to rhythmic music during your tapping if you like. As you tap, try to think as little as possible, Dr. Chiasson said—just focus on your body, tapping and breath.

Rate: For each tapping location, aim for a rate of about one to two taps per second.

•**Toe tapping.** Lie flat on your back on the bed or floor. Keeping your whole body relaxed, quickly rotate your legs inward and outward from the hips (like windshield wipers), tapping the sides of your big toes together with each inward rotation. Tap as softly or as vigorously as you like.

•**Belly tapping.** Stand with your feet a little wider than shoulder-width apart. Staying relaxed, gently bounce up and down by slightly bending your knees. At the same time, tap softly with gently closed fists on the area below your belly button and above your pubic bone. Try to synchronize your movements to give one tap per knee bend.

•**Chest tapping.** Sit or stand comfortably. Using your fingertips, open hands or gently closed fists, tap all over your chest area, including the armpits. Tap as softly or as vigorously as you like without pushing past your comfort level.

Cautions: If you are recovering from hip or knee surgery, skip the toe tapping (which might strain your joint) and do only the belly tapping and chest tapping. If you are pregnant, stick with just the chest tapping—lying on your back during toe tapping could reduce blood flow to the fetus…and tapping on your belly may not feel comfortable and could stimulate the acupressure points used to induce labor, Dr. Chiasson said.

Follow-up: Continue your tapping routine for eight weeks, then get another blood pressure reading to see whether your numbers have improved. If they have—or if you simply enjoy the relaxing effects of the tapping—you might want to continue indefinitely.

Hidden Salt in Six Favorite Foods

Linda Van Horn, PhD, RD, professor of preventive medicine, Northwestern University Feinberg School of Medicine, Chicago, spokesperson, American Heart Association, and coauthor of a recent AHA advisory published in *Circulation*.

C an you remember the last time you filled the saltshaker on your kitchen table? After all, you're probably well aware that excess salt contributes to high blood pressure, cardiovascular disease and stroke risk (not to mention bloating and under-eye bags). And it's linked to

Top Doctor's Natural Cure…

L-arginine for High Blood Pressure

L-arginine is an amino acid found in meats, grains, fish and other foods. When you take higher, supplemental doses, it increases blood levels of nitric oxide, which dilates arteries and reduces blood pressure. Studies have shown that patients who take L-arginine can reduce their blood pressure by 20 points or more. Also, L-arginine appears to reduce atherosclerosis, buildups in the arteries that lead to most heart attacks.

How to use it: Take 1,000 milligrams (mg) twice a day. Use a time-release form—it will stay active in the body throughout the day.

Caution: L-arginine can interact with some medications, including high blood pressure medications and nitroglycerin.

C. Norman Shealy, MD, PhD, founding president of the American Holistic Medical Association, a leading advocate for the use of holistic and integrative medicine by healthcare providers. A neurosurgeon, he is director of the Shealy Institute in Springfield, Missouri, and author of *The Healing Remedies Sourcebook* (Da Capo). *www.normshealy.com*

kidney stones, asthma, osteoporosis and gastric cancer, too.

But simply ignoring the saltshaker won't keep you safe, because only 11% of the sodium consumed by the average American comes from adding salt while cooking or eating a meal. And just 12% comes from naturally salty foods. This means that more than three-fourths of the sodium in the typical US diet comes from packaged foods and restaurant fare.

Yet some of the worst sodium-stuffed offenders are foods that people generally do not think of as salty. That's why the American Heart Association (AHA) recently released its "Salty Six" list of common foods that are surprisingly high in sodium.

Which of the six are sneaking salt into your system?

THE DIRTY HALF-DOZEN

The AHA recommends that all Americans keep their salt intake to less than 1,500 mg per day—less than half of the current average intake of about 3,400 mg per day. To achieve that, watch out for…

•**Breads.** Even though bread doesn't usually taste salty, a single slice has as much as 230 mg of sodium. If you have two slices of toast at breakfast, a sandwich at lunch and a roll or two with dinner, you're darn close to your whole day's allotment of sodium before you've factored in any other foods. And if you spread that bread with regular butter (butter not labeled "unsalted"), which has about 100 mg of sodium per tablespoon, you're over the limit.

•**Poultry.** The amount of sodium varies depending on how poultry is prepared—but did you know that even raw chicken or turkey may contain salt? Often salt is added during packaging to help keep poultry fresh…poultry may be brined to make it kosher…or a salty broth may be added to raw poultry to ensure that it will be moist after cooking. This process can add 100 mg of sodium or more to each serving of poultry—including the ground poultry that's so popular these days. Of course, poultry that's breaded and fried is typically far worse. For instance, a 3.5-ounce serving of chicken nuggets usually contains about 600 mg of sodium.

•**Cold cuts.** You know that bologna, salami, ham and other such meats are high in sodium, but you may not realize just how salty they really are.

Reality check: A modest four-ounce serving of deli meat can use up your entire day's allotment of sodium in one fell swoop. Deli turkey isn't necessarily much better—four ounces of smoked turkey breast typically has nearly 1,100 mg of sodium.

•**Soup.** What seems like a healthy choice— a nice bowl of vegetable or chicken noodle soup—can sabotage you because prepared soups, broths and bullions are loaded with salt. Just one cup of canned soup contains as much as 940 mg of sodium…so if you consume the whole can (as many of us do), you're way above the limit for the day.

•**Pizza.** This fast food has salt in the cheese, in the crust and in the sauce. Just one four-ounce slice of cheese pizza contains up to 760 mg of sodium—and that's assuming you don't add pepperoni or another salty topping.

•**Sandwiches.** Since bread and cold cuts are loaded with salt, putting them together in a sandwich is a sure way to exceed your salt quota, particularly if you include other sodium-packed extras such as cheese (176 mg per ounce for cheddar) and/or mustard (171 mg per tablespoon).

PASS THE SALT…RIGHT ON BY

Fortunately, there's a lot you can do to cut back on salt…

•**Instead of having a whole sandwich at lunch, have half** a sandwich plus a small side salad.

•**When you order a pizza, ask for a thin crust** and half the usual amount of cheese.

•**Make your own soup** so you control how much salt is added.

•**Opt for low-sodium versions of your favorite foods,** particularly breads, meats and soups. And be sure to compare the serving size listed on the label with how much you actually eat—for instance, do the math to see how much sodium that full bowl of soup actually contains.

•**When buying raw fresh or frozen poultry, choose packages** labeled "no added salt" or "no added broth."

•**On food labels and restaurant menus,** look for foods with the AHA Heart-Check mark—these meet AHA nutritional standards, including for sodium content.

High Blood Pressure May Protect Some Frail Seniors

Michelle Odden, PhD, public health epidemiologist, Oregon State University, Corvallis, Oregon.

Bradley Flansbaum, MD, DO, director, Hospital Medicine, Lenox Hill Hospital, New York City.

Howard S. Weintraub, MD, clinical director, Center for the Prevention of Cardiovascular Disease, NYU Langone Medical Center, New York City.

Archives of Internal Medicine, online.

Frail, elderly people with high blood pressure may live longer than their peers with lower blood pressure, recent research suggests.

In the study of 2,340 seniors, low blood pressure protected those who were healthier and more robust, but the same could not be said for their frail counterparts. In general, high blood pressure, or hypertension, is a major risk factor for heart attack and stroke.

Researchers used data from two yearly US National Health and Nutrition Examination Surveys. The recent findings were published in the *Archives of Internal Medicine.*

STUDY DETAILS

Frailty and fragility were assessed via walking-speed tests. Study participants were asked to walk for about 20 feet at their normal pace. Those who walked less than 2.6 feet per second were "slower walkers." Their faster-walking counterparts had lower rates of diabetes, heart disease and other health problems. A third group included participants who were unable to complete the walking test.

In this third group, those frail seniors with higher blood pressure levels were 62% less likely to die during the study period when compared with their counterparts with lower blood pressure levels.

"Older frail adults might benefit from slightly higher blood pressure," said study author Michelle Odden, PhD, a public health epidemiologist at Oregon State University, in Corvallis, Oregon. "As the blood vessels get more stiff with age, it may be necessary to have more pressure to keep blood pumping to the central organs, like the brain and heart."

It's too early to make any treatment recommendations, Dr. Odden said. "Our study does support lower blood pressure in healthy elderly people," she said.

Each patient is different, she noted. "If you have seen one older adult, you have seen one older adult," she said. "This really sums up the wide variety of health status we see in older adults."

The study linked data from the nationwide health surveys in 1999–2000 and 2001–2002 to US National Death Index data through December 2006. During the study, 589 people died. Faster walkers with high blood pressure were 35% more likely to die, compared with those fast walkers with normal blood pressure levels, the study showed. There was no link seen between high blood pressure and death among slow walkers.

Meat May Be Linked to Hypertension in Older Adults

Researchers examined data on 2,241 people (average age 65) to explore links between intake of various types of protein and high blood pressure.

Result: Among people over age 70, only one-half ounce more than the average daily intake of two ounces of animal protein, such as red meat and poultry, was associated with a 37% increased risk for hypertension. Protein from other sources (plant, dairy, fish, etc.) did not affect hypertension risk.

Wieke Altorf-van der Kuil, researcher, Wageningen University, Wageningen, The Netherlands.

According to the American Heart Association, normal blood pressure is a systolic pressure of less than 120 and a diastolic pressure of less than 80. Systolic pressure (the upper number in a blood pressure reading) refers to pressure in the arteries when the heart beats. Diastolic pressure (the lower number) measures pressure in the arteries between heart beats.

EXPERT RESPONSE

One expert said the new results would have a direct impact on clinical practice.

Among older people with chronic conditions "hypertension is among the most common, and choosing one, two or three drugs to reduce blood pressure is an all-too-common dilemma," said Bradley Flansbaum, MD, director of Hospital Medicine at Lenox Hill Hospital in New York City. "These pills all have costs and side effects," he said. "Now, by walking our patients and determining those folks that can exceed 2 mph or greater—30 minutes per mile—doctors can select who will benefit from these classes of drugs."

He added that blood pressure treatments that could help a relatively healthy 80-year-old might not benefit a frailer patient. "Those who cannot achieve a similar [walking] speed signal a burden of illness and debilitation that does not warrant therapy, which if used, might even be harmful."

Another expert agreed.

When it comes to blood pressure, "one size fits all' doesn't really hold," said Howard Weintraub, MD, clinical director of the Center for the Prevention of Cardiovascular Disease at NYU Langone Medical Center in New York City. "For elderly, frail individuals, our primary focus should not necessarily be getting their blood pressure down."

Some of the medications used to treat high blood pressure, including diuretics and beta blockers, may confer more risk than benefit in this group, he said.

"We need to focus on hypertension, but give a little slack," he said, adding that not every patient will benefit from efforts to lower their blood pressure. However, he said, "If the systolic pressure is 180, I am not leaving it alone. I

would also treat someone who also has diabetes and has high cholesterol or other risk factors."

A systolic blood pressure of higher than 180 is considered a hypertensive crisis, according to the American Heart Association.

info Learn more about high blood pressure (hypertension) at the American Heart Association Web site, *www.heart.org.*

Treating Kidneys With Radio Waves May Ease Tough-to-Control Hypertension

Varinder Singh, MD, chairman of cardiology, Lenox Hill Hospital, New York City.
Gregg Fonarow, MD, spokesman, American Heart Association, and professor of cardiology, University of California, Los Angeles.
American Heart Association, news release.

For patients whose high blood pressure cannot be controlled despite taking several medications, a short burst of radio waves at the nerves around the kidneys may do the trick, a small recent study says.

According to the American Heart Association, more than 78 million adults in the United States have hypertension, which is blood pressure readings at 140/90 mmHg or higher.

Among these adults, about 9% have resistant hypertension, which means that even while taking three or more medications to control their blood pressure, it remains at 140/90 mmHg or higher.

The findings from this recent study could be a significant step in treating people with resistant hypertension, which is a major risk factor for heart attack and stroke, the researchers said.

The technique studied—called catheter-based renal denervation—is minimally invasive. In it, doctors use a catheter inserted through the artery in the groin, which sends radio waves that burn away nerve tissue around the arteries to the kidneys.

The procedure destroys nerves that help control and filter salt in the body, which may be overactive in patients with high blood pressure. The US Food and Drug Administration has not yet approved its use.

STUDY DETAILS

For the study, an international team lead by Dr. Murray Esler, professor and senior director of the Baker IDI Heart and Diabetes Institute in Melbourne, Australia, assigned 35 patients to renal denervation and compared them with 47 patients who had already had the procedure.

All the patients suffered from drug-resistant hypertension. Their systolic blood pressure— the top number in a blood-pressure reading— remained dangerously high at 160 millimeters of mercury (mmHg) or above despite having taking three or more drugs to control blood pressure, the researchers noted.

Dr. Esler's team found that more than 83% of those who had denervation treatment before had a drop in systolic blood pressure of at least 10 mmHg after six months and almost 79% maintained the reduction at 12 months.

The 35 patients in this phase of the study had similar results to the initial group. Almost 63% of these patients saw a reduction in systolic blood pressure of 10 mmHg or more six months after treatment.

The study was funded by medical device maker Medtronic. The findings were published in the journal *Circulation*.

SAFE AND EFFECTIVE

The procedure is safe as well as effective, the study authors said.

"Participants' kidneys were not damaged or functionally impaired," Dr. Esler said. "We also found no ill effects on long-term health from the procedure."

Whether this technique might be useful in treating less severe high blood pressure hasn't yet been tested. If it is applicable, patients could possibly discontinue using blood-pressure drugs, Dr. Esler suggested.

EXPERTS VARY ON RESULTS

"This is a very promising approach for managing medication-resistant hypertension," said Dr. Gregg Fonarow, MD, a spokesman for the American Heart Association and professor of cardiology at the University of California, Los Angeles.

"High blood pressure is a major contributor to heart attack, stroke, heart failure and [kidney] failure," said Dr. Fonarow, who was not involved in the study. "Despite the availability of a number of effective medications, many patients with hypertension have not achieved adequate control of their blood pressure. There is thus an important, but currently unmet, need for additional therapies to effectively control hypertension."

Dr. Fonarow noted: "In all, reductions in systolic blood-pressure levels on the order of 25 to 30 mmHg were achieved and maintained without any loss in efficacy."

Another expert, however, said that scenario is likely overoptimistic.

"Hypertension is a hard disease to treat because there are so many things that go into getting blood pressure under control," said Varinder Singh, MD, an interventional cardiologist at Lenox Hill Hospital in New York City. "There's lifestyle and diet, there is getting to the right doses of medications, there are adherence issues. So anything that will help patients get their goals is exciting."

Even with this technique, people will most likely still have to take blood-pressure medications, Dr. Singh said. "You may have to take less medication or you may have to take lower doses, but we all expect that patients will still have to take some medication," he said.

Dr. Singh also noted that although this procedure is used in other countries it is not yet approved in the United States.

Dr. Fonarow added: "While this study demonstrates that renal denervation provides sustained reduction of blood pressure up to one year and appears safe, additional studies with longer-term follow-up are needed."

info To learn more about hypertension, visit the US National Library of Medicine Web site at *http://www.nlm.nih.gov/medlineplus/highbloodpressure.html*.

In Search of Oil— For Heart Health

Devarajan Sankar, PhD, MD, a research scientist in the department of cardiovascular disease at Fukuoka University Chikushi Hospital in Chikushino, Japan, and lead author of the study, which was presented at a recent American Heart Association meeting.

Are you concerned about your heart health? If so, you may want to add a few uncommon cooking oils to your collection.

Recent research shows that using a certain combination of two particular Asian cooking oils may reduce blood pressure...reduce levels of "bad" LDL cholesterol...and raise levels of HDL "good" cholesterol.

Just from using certain oils!

THE QUEST FOR HEALTHIER COOKING OIL

Earlier research from lead study author Devarajan Sankar, PhD, MD, had shown that cooking with unrefined sesame oil could reduce blood pressure and improve cholesterol levels in people with high blood pressure. "This is probably because sesame oil contains many antioxidants, as well as mono- and polyunsaturated fats—the healthiest kinds of fats," noted Dr. Sankar.

The drawback? Sesame oil has a low smoke point, which makes it difficult to use while cooking. So Dr. Sankar's team set out to find an oil that could withstand higher cooking temperatures and be blended with sesame oil without detracting from its health benefits.

After much analysis, researchers settled on refined rice bran oil, which is also rich in antioxidants and healthful fats but has a much higher smoke point. They created a blend using 80% rice bran oil and 20% sesame oil, and then used it in their latest study.

Now, researchers used types of refined rice bran oil and unrefined sesame oil that are not commercially available. (The unrefined sesame oil was filtered and expelled in a manner that helped it maintain a high amount of nutrients called lignans, and the rice bran oil was enzymatically degummed and refined—without chemicals—so it would maintain a high amount

of nutrients such as oryzanol, tocotrienols, tocopherols and phytosterols.) In other words, think of them as oils on steroids.

But don't let that discourage you from reading on. Refined rice bran oil and unrefined sesame oil are available in stores, and though they may not pack quite as dramatic a punch as what was used in the study, they still are likely to have a beneficial effect, said Dr. Sankar.

You might be thinking, Aren't unrefined oils generally healthier than refined oils? Why would the researchers use refined rice bran oil? Rice bran oil that humans consume is always refined to some extent. Dr. Sankar explained that refin-

---

ing the rice bran oil removes some of its undesirable properties—such as its dark color and its overly powerful flavor—but the oil retains almost all of its nutrients.

And you don't have to worry that heating unrefined sesame oil might cancel out its health benefits. The sesame lignans are not destroyed when using normal cooking temperatures, said Dr. Sankar.

A COMBINATION OIL: BETTER OR WORSE?

For the study, the researchers analyzed adults who had varying degrees of high blood pressure and were using palm oil, sunflower oil and/or peanut oil in their cooking. Their blood pressure was measured. Then they split them into three groups. One group took a common calcium channel blocker medication (*nifedipine*) that's used to treat high blood pressure and did not cook with the study's special oil blend (they used whatever fats they normally use). A second group that did not take any blood pressure drugs replaced their usual cooking and salad dressing oils with approximately 2 ⅔ tablespoons per day of the special combination oil. The third group did both—they took the drug and used the special oil blend in place of the fats that they normally use.

Results after two months…

Blood pressure: Participants who simply used the special oil blend saw an average drop in systolic blood pressure (the top number) of 14 points and an average drop in diastolic blood pressure (the bottom number) of 11 points. Incredibly, their blood pressure improved almost as much as the drug-only group, which saw a drop of 16 points (systolic) and 12 points (diastolic). Results in the group that used both the oil blend and the drug were even more dramatic—a systolic drop of 36 points and a diastolic drop of 24 points.

Cholesterol: The blood pressure drug did next to nothing for cholesterol levels. But participants who used the oil blend saw, on average, a 26% drop in LDL "bad" cholesterol and a 10% increase in HDL "good" cholesterol. How great is that?!

"These two oils appear to have a synergistic, beneficial effect on health that is rather incredible," said Dr. Sankar. "The blend could play a significant role in the treatment and prevention of heart disease."

Another plus: "They have no unpleasant side effects," he added.

USE "HEARTY" OILS IN YOUR KITCHEN

Future studies may explore how the oil blend stacks up against other types of blood pressure medications, such as ACE inhibitors and beta-blockers…and how the oil blend compares with other oils (such as olive oil, long-touted for its cardiovascular benefits) and other blends.

In the meantime, Dr. Sankar encouraged people who are concerned about their heart health to substitute sesame oil and rice bran oil into their diets in place of other fats as much as possible. While this precise oil blend was made specially for the study and isn't yet commercially available, you can find sesame and rice bran oils in many supermarkets, as well as at health-food stores and Asian grocery stores, and you can replicate the mix that was used in the study at home (80% rice bran, 20% sesame).

If you're currently taking blood pressure medication or cholesterol medication, don't stop—the oil blend should be used to supplement, not replace medications (for now, at least).

The Cholesterol Myth— Why Lowering Your Cholesterol Won't Prevent Heart Disease

Jonny Bowden, PhD, CNS, a nutritionist and nationally known expert on weight loss, nutrition and health. Based in Los Angeles, he is board-certified by the American College of Nutrition and a member of the American Society of Nutrition. He is author, with Stephen Sinatra, MD, of The Great Cholesterol Myth: Why Lowering Your Cholesterol Won't Prevent Heart Disease—and the Statin-Free Plan That Will (Fair Winds). www.jonnybowden.com

Many people believe that managing cholesterol is key to preventing heart disease. That is not necessarily so. *Here are six common misconceptions…*

Not true: **Most heart attack patients have high cholesterol.**

About half of heart attack patients turn out to have perfectly normal cholesterol. When Harvard researchers analyzed data from the Nurses' Health Study, they found that about 82% of heart attacks and other "coronary events" were linked to smoking, excessive alcohol consumption, obesity, a lack of exercise and poor diet—not high cholesterol.

Not true: **All LDL "bad" cholesterol is dangerous.**

Some forms of LDL are harmful, but others are not. The standard cholesterol test doesn't make this distinction. You can have sky-high LDL with a low risk for heart disease. Conversely, even if your LDL is low, your risk for heart disease could be high.

Scientists have identified several subtypes of LDL that act in totally different ways. For example, subtype A is a large, pillowy molecule that does not cause atherosclerosis, the underlying cause of most heart attacks. Subtype B, a small, dense molecule, is dangerous because it is prone to oxidation and can penetrate artery walls, one of the first steps in heart disease.

What to do: Ask your doctor for an expanded cholesterol test. It will measure the different types of LDL particles and the number of particles as well as triglycerides, HDL and other substances. The test probably won't be covered by insurance, but it's reasonably priced—usually around $100.

Not true: **Cholesterol should be as low as possible.**

It doesn't matter if your total cholesterol is above or below 200 mg/dL. What matters is your size pattern, the ratio of small-to-large LDL molecules.

Suppose your LDL is high, with a large concentration of fluffy, subtype-A particles. This is known as Pattern A. Your cholesterol-associated risk for heart disease is negligible.

You do have to worry if you have Pattern B. It means that you have a lot of the artery-damaging subtype-B particles and that your risk for heart disease is elevated. The expanded cholesterol test can help determine this.

Not true: **You need a statin if you have high LDL.**

The statin medications, such as *simvastatin* (Zocor) and *atorvastatin* (Lipitor), can help some patients with high LDL. If your LDL is Pattern B, a statin could save your life. You probably don't need a statin, or any other cholesterol-lowering drug, if you have Pattern A.

There's good evidence that statins are effective for secondary prevention—they help prevent subsequent heart attacks in patients (especially middle-aged men) who already have had a heart attack. This is not because of a cholesterol-lowering effect but because statins stabilize plaque, thin the blood and are anti-inflammatory.

Overall, however, statins don't do much for primary prevention (preventing a heart attack in patients who don't have existing heart disease).

If you're generally healthy and your only "symptom" is high cholesterol, you probably don't need a statin or any other cholesterol-lowering drug.

Not true: **Saturated fat is dangerous.**

Forget what you've heard—the saturated fat in red meat, butter and eggs does not increase your risk for heart disease.

Researchers from Harvard and other institutions analyzed 21 previous studies that looked at the relationship between saturated fat and heart disease. Their meta-analysis included nearly 350,000 subjects who were followed for between five and 23 years.

Conclusion: Saturated fat did not cause an increase in heart disease or stroke.

Not true: **Carbohydrates are healthier than fats.**

The conventional advice to substitute carbohydrates for dietary fat is misguided—and dangerous.

A Harvard study compared the progression of heart disease in postmenopausal women who changed their intakes of certain foods, including carbohydrates and saturated fat. The researchers found that women who ate more saturated fat had less disease progression. Those who ate more carbohydrates got worse.

Another study found that the risk for a heart attack was higher in patients who replaced saturated fat with refined carbohydrates.

Not all carbohydrates are bad. People who eat healthy carbs—such as whole grains, legumes and vegetables—will probably do better, regardless of their fat intake. What people tend to eat, however, is refined carbohydrates—white bread, white rice and desserts.

Sugar is particularly bad because it increases arterial inflammation, insulin levels and blood pressure. It also elevates triglycerides, one of the main heart disease risk factors.

What helps: The best ways to reduce your risk for heart disease include maintaining a healthy weight, exercising regularly and not smoking.

No Need to Fast Before Cholesterol Blood Test

Christopher Naugler, MD, assistant professor of clinical pathology, University of Calgary, Alberta, Canada.

Samia Mora, MD, assistant professor of medicine, Brigham and Women's Hospital, Boston.

Gregg Fonarow, MD, associate chief, division of cardiology, University of California, Los Angeles and director, Ahmanson-UCLA Cardiomyopathy Center.

Archives of Internal Medicine, online.

Current practice calls for patients to fast at least eight hours before having their cholesterol levels checked, but Canadian researchers report that may be unnecessary.

"For routine screening, fasting for cholesterol is largely unnecessary," because it has only a slight effect on test results, said lead researcher Christopher Naugler, MD, assistant professor of clinical pathology at the University of Calgary, in Canada. "Eliminating fasting as a general requirement for cholesterol testing could greatly increase convenience for patients without significantly altering test results."

There are some patients, however, such as those with abnormally high triglycerides, where a repeat fasting cholesterol measurement may be necessary, Dr. Naugler said.

The report was published in the journal *Archives of Internal Medicine.*

STUDY DETAILS

For the study, Dr. Naugler looked at laboratory data on cholesterol tests from more than 200,000 patients.

The researchers compared fasting time with resulting cholesterol levels. Overall, they found fasting time made little difference in the accuracy of the blood test. Levels of total and HDL (good) cholesterol varied less than 2% with different fasting times.

In addition, levels of LDL (bad) cholesterol varied less than 10% and levels of triglycerides, a marker linked with inflammation, varied less than 20%, the researchers noted.

EXPERT COMMENTARY

"In our opinion, physicians and health care providers may consider doing non-fasting lipid tests based on the current evidence," said Samia Mora, MD, assistant professor of medicine at Brigham and Women's Hospital in Boston and coauthor of an accompanying journal commentary.

Either non-fasting or fasting blood tests may be used for cholesterol testing, Dr. Mora said.

"This is based on a growing body of evidence—including the present study, but also several other recent studies—that non-fasting lipids are generally not substantially affected by the fasting," she said.

Summer Cholesterol Alert

If your LDL "bad" cholesterol level is borderline high in the summer, you may want to be tested again in winter.

Here is why: In a two-year review of more than 227,000 adults, researchers found that LDL levels increased an average of 7 mg/dL during the winter months compared with summer. This led to an overall increase of 8% in the prevalence of high cholesterol levels.

Theory: The shorter days of winter result in less exposure to sunlight and lower concentrations of vitamin D—low levels of this vitamin may increase LDL levels.

Filipe Moura, MD, researcher, State University of Campinas, Brazil.

Another expert noted that non-fasting test results may also be a more reliable predictor of heart trouble.

"While most guidelines recommend obtaining a cardiovascular lipid panel after at least eight hours of fasting, many studies suggest for most individuals a non-fasting lipid panel provides similar lipid values," said Gregg Fonarow, MD, associate chief of the cardiology division at the University of California, Los Angeles. "Some analyses have even suggested that non-fasting lipid levels are more accurate for predicting the risk of cardiovascular events compared with those obtained in the fasting state."

info For more information on cholesterol, visit the American Heart Association's Web site, *www.heart.org*, and search "cholesterol."

Gene-Tweaked Probiotics And Tomatoes Can Lower Your Cholesterol

Mitchell Jones, PhD, MD, chief scientific officer and co-founder, Micropharma, Montreal.
Suzanne Steinbaum, MD, preventive cardiologist, Lenox Hill Hospital, New York City.
Presentation, American Heart Association annual meeting, Los Angeles.

People who took a probiotic supplement containing a beneficial bacteria saw their cholesterol levels improve, and a freeze-dried concoction made from a genetically engineered tomato had a similar effect on mice, two recent studies show.

The research, presented at the American Heart Association annual meeting in Los Angeles, is the latest to use nonpharmaceuticals or specially designed foods to rein in high cholesterol—a major risk factor for heart disease, heart attack and stroke.

STUDY DETAILS ON PROBIOTICS AND CHOLESTEROL

In one study involving 127 people with high cholesterol, those who took a twice-daily supplement of a special strain of the *Lactobacillus reuteri* bacterium for nine weeks experienced an average 11.6% drop in LDL "bad" cholesterol and a 9.1% drop in total cholesterol, compared with those taking a placebo.

Other strains of L. reuteri are found naturally in breads and yogurts, but researchers at the Canadian probiotics company Micropharma, which funded the study, say they've formulated a strain that seems to help block the absorption of cholesterol.

The strain, called L. reuteri NCIMB 30242 and marketed as Cardioviva, is thought to help break up bile salts, which helps lower absorption of cholesterol.

Mitchell Jones, PhD, MD, chief scientific officer at Micropharma, helped develop the product, which he said can also be added to food products such as yogurts. "Cardioviva is a novel, natural approach to one of the most prevalent heart problems of our time, high cholesterol," Dr. Jones said. As to safety, he added that, "like other probiotics, if there are gastrointestinal side effects, they are rare and usually minor."

According to Dr. Jones, Micropharma has launched Cardioviva in supplement form in Canada and the United States. It has been available since late May, 2013.

TOMATO STUDY AND HEART HEALTH

A second study looked at a genetically engineered tomato that produces a peptide (a type of protein) that mimics the effect of HDL "good" cholesterol when eaten.

The study involved mice that were specially bred to have uncontrolled LDL "bad" cholesterol. The mice were fed a high-calorie, fatty "Western"-style diet plus a freeze-dried, ground version of the genetically tweaked tomato for two weeks. The tomato powder made up 2.2% of the rodents' total diet.

The researchers, led by Alan Fogelman, MD, chair of the department of medicine at UCLA's David Geffen School of Medicine in Los Angeles, said that mice given the powder displayed lower blood levels of inflammation, higher levels of good cholesterol and less signs of atherosclerotic plaques ("hardening of the arteries"), among other signs of improving cardiovascular health.

"We have found a new and practical way to make a peptide that acts like the main protein in good cholesterol, but is many times more effective and can be delivered by eating the plant," said Dr. Fogelman, who is also director of the Atherosclerosis Research Unit at UCLA.

The study was funded by the US National Heart, Lung and Blood Institute.

EXPERT RESPONSE

One heart expert said that products such as Cardioviva might help reduce cholesterol, but they should be seen as just one added weapon in the battle against heart disease.

"As a well-tolerated substance, and easily taken at a lower dose than other supplements, Lactobacillus may be a beneficial supplement in reducing cholesterol," said Suzanne Steinbaum, MD, a preventive cardiologist at Lenox Hill Hospital in New York City.

However, she said that any effective attempt to lower cholesterol should always involve healthy diet and exercise.

Reviewing the data from the tomato study, Dr. Steinbaum said, "Although interesting, a

---

Statins Can Cause Memory Problems

The FDA has reported that long-term use of cholesterol-lowering statin medications can lead to cognitive issues in some people.

Self-defense: Patients and families should stay alert for any cognitive changes that seem to go beyond age-related declines.

Examples: Difficulty balancing a checkbook, trouble recognizing people, problems remembering what was just said.

Beatrice A. Golomb, MD, PhD, associate professor of medicine, University of California, San Diego, School of Medicine, La Jolla. She has collected and studied more than 3,000 reports of side effects of statin use.

Statins Cause Fatigue

In a recent finding, users of the cholesterol-lowering drugs *pravastatin* (Pravachol) and *simvastatin* (Zocor) were significantly more likely to report lower energy or fatigue after exertion than people taking a placebo. Other statins also may cause fatigue. The higher the dose, the greater the effect. Some patients, but not all, seem to have less fatigue if they take coenzyme Q10 or vitamin D along with statins.

Beatrice A. Golomb, MD, PhD, associate professor of medicine, University of California, San Diego, School of Medicine, La Jolla, and leader of a study published in *Archives of Internal Medicine.*

---

mice trial like this cannot necessarily be extrapolated to the choices that human beings make, in terms of the foods that they eat."

And she warned against hoping for too much from research into "medicinal foods."

"Based on this trial alone in mice, the concept of 'medicinal' genetically engineered foods are not the do-it-yourself pharmacies of the future," Dr. Steinbaum said.

Again, she stressed that a smarter, old-fashioned choice would be simply to eat more healthily.

"We know that a diet rich in fruits and vegetables and multigrains, and low in fats, can also decrease the incidence of heart disease in humans," Dr. Steinbaum said. "Yet the Western diet filled with fat and simple sugars still is more preferred."

info Find out more about cholesterol at the American Heart Association Web site, *www.heart.org.*

Brain Health & Memory

How Healthy Is Your Brain?

For most people over age 40, glitches in memory are high on their lists of health concerns. Whether it's lost keys, forgotten names or other "senior moments," we fear each is a sign of a deteriorating brain.

What science now tells us: Memory is not necessarily the most important measure of brain health. And no matter what your age, there are ways to improve the mind. However, many of the popular beliefs about improving mental performance are outdated and incorrect.

Most common myths...

MYTH #1. Brain health steadily declines with age. Scientists used to believe that people were born with all of the neurons (brain cells) that they'd ever have and that the ability to form new brain connections ended in adolescence.

It's now known that the brain is the most modifiable part of the body. It's constantly being changed by how we use it, and the changes can be measured within just hours. That's why you can be confounded by, say, a new cell phone in the morning and then be using it proficiently by the end of the day.

While you are focused on new learning—such as writing an original report or preparing new recipes—neural activity increases and promotes the development of new neurons. But if these neurons are not put to proper use, they die.

As you age, your ability to think more broadly and deeply can continue to grow if your brain is exercised properly—thanks to the functions of your frontal lobes, the part of your brain that sits just behind and above your eyes in your skull. Even though brain health is tied to all parts of the brain, the majority of the heavy lifting is

Sandra Bond Chapman, PhD, a cognitive neuroscientist who is the founder and chief director of the Center for BrainHealth and the Dee Wyly Distinguished University Chair, both at The University of Texas at Dallas. She is coauthor, with Shelly Kirkland, of *Make Your Brain Smarter: Increase Your Brain's Creativity, Energy, and Focus* (Free Press). *www.brainhealth.utdallas.edu*

How Fit Are Your Frontal Lobes?

Are you challenging your brain in your everyday life? *Ask yourself...*

•Do you have the same dinner guests repeatedly?	or	•Do you invite unexpected guests to vary the conversation?
•Do you express the same ideas repeatedly to convey your position on timely issues?	or	•Do you continually try to see things from new perspectives when discussing a timely topic?
•Do you resist new technology such as a new cell phone?	or	•Do you stay open to moving from old to new technology?
•Do your e-mails sound the same? Do you send cards following predictable traditions?	or	•Do you think of creative ideas and unique timing to convey personal messages?

If the left column describes you more accurately, you may need to more actively engage your frontal lobes.

directed through the frontal lobe networks. The frontal lobes are responsible for decision making, judgment, planning and other "executive" functions. (To get an idea of how effectively you're engaging your frontal lobes in everyday life, see box above.)

My advice: Engage your frontal lobes by being curious and creative and by solving problems whenever you can. Challenge your brain by thinking deeply and extracting meaning from information you are given.

Example: Think back to a favorite book that you read several years ago, and come up with five to eight different take-home messages that are applicable to different contexts.

Better yet: Read it again, and then come up with the list.

MYTH #2. A good memory indicates mental robustness. Surprisingly, memory skills do not correspond to everyday-life performance as much as frontal lobe functioning. This means that you can have an excellent memory but not be very innovative, insightful, creative or mentally productive.

My advice: Don't worry when you can't remember everything. Although we tend to note what we forget, we rarely take stock of all the things we do remember.

A brain that gets too occupied with remembering everything works less efficiently and becomes stressed, overwhelmed and bogged down in the details. If something is important

in your life—it could be your work, a hobby or even a weekly card game—you'll remember the details that really matter.

Do not worry about, say, occasional forgotten names or unimportant tasks. But when forgetting regularly interferes with your performance, it may be a sign that something more than benign memory glitches is taking over. Many things can impair memory—not enough sleep, some medications, such as antidepressants and blood pressure drugs, and stress. Memory issues do not always mean Alzheimer's disease. See your doctor if you're concerned about your memory.

MYTH #3. Multitasking gives your brain a good workout. Again, not true. When you multitask, the brain has to call on different regions to handle the load. It works inefficiently because the communication isn't synchronized. When you "overuse" your brain in this way, the frontal lobes become fatigued. This slows efficiency and decreases performance.

My advice: Whatever you're doing, focus on that and nothing else for at least 15 minutes. Put a "do not disturb" sign on the door. Turn off your phones, and don't check your e-mail. You'll think more clearly in those 15 minutes than someone who multitasks for an hour.

MYTH #4. People with a high IQ have the most brainpower. Today's IQ tests are based on measurements that were developed more than a century ago. They mainly emphasize such skills as knowledge, memory and speed in ability to perform mathematical equations—all of which were much more important in the days before computers and the Internet.

What's more important is knowing how to use knowledge in novel ways and bringing together facts from disparate areas to create original ideas. As Einstein said, "Imagination is more important than knowledge. Knowledge is limited. Imagination encircles the world."

My advice: Whenever you're confronted with a problem, stop and think deeply about the knowledge you already have. Connecting it and generating original ideas is crucial to brain health.

MYTH #5. Unrelenting mental work boosts brain capacity. It's true that high achievers can put in long hours and consider lots of information when they try to solve vexing problems. But they also know when to stop looking at more information—and they reach that point earlier than most people do.

Productivity and achievement are not linked to how many hours are worked and how much information is accessed. In fact, decreasing exposure allows your frontal lobes to be deployed to focus on key data, and, even more importantly, to know what information to ignore.

My advice: Keep your key frontal lobe operations finely tuned by blocking, discarding and ignoring less relevant tasks and information. Consolidating facts and options into big ideas and perspectives is necessary to cultivate creative thinking and problem solving.

Best Way to Fight Memory Loss

The combination of computer use and exercise is better than mental or physical activity alone. The exact reason is not yet known, but it may be that physical activity improves blood flow to the brain and therefore delivers more nutrients...while mental activity works at the molecular level to boost synaptic activities.

Yonas E. Geda, MD, MSc, a neuropsychiatrist at Mayo Clinic, Scottsdale, Arizona, and leader of a study of 926 people, ages 70 to 93, published in *Mayo Clinic Proceedings.*

Women and Men Need Different Foods for Ultimate Brain Power

Daniel G. Amen, MD, a brain-imaging specialist who is founder, CEO and medical director of Amen Clinics. Based in Newport Beach, California, he is author of more than 30 books, including *Unleash the Power of the Female Brain* (Harmony). *www.amenclinics.com*

Women and men need different foods to accommodate very different brains. Daniel Amen, MD, and his staff at Amen Clinics did a study of 46,000 brain scans involving about 26,000 patients. Using a brain-imaging test called SPECT (single photon emission computed tomography), they found clear differences between male and female brains.

In general: Women's brains are more active than men's brains. Much of this activity is in the region known as the prefrontal cortex, which controls judgment, impulse control and organization. Women also produce less serotonin than men. Serotonin is the neurotransmitter that makes you less worried and more relaxed, so women are more prone to anxiety and depression.

Men, on the other hand, produce less dopamine. Dopamine is involved with focus and impulse control, so men are more likely to be impulsive and have trouble concentrating.

BEST FOODS FOR WOMEN

Foods that increase serotonin are critical for women. *When their serotonin levels rise, women naturally experience less anxiety and are less likely to get upset...*

•**Chickpeas.** Also known as garbanzo beans, chickpeas increase the brain's production of serotonin. Other carbohydrates do the same thing, but chickpeas are better because they're high in nutrients and fiber, with about 12 grams of fiber per one-cup serving. Fiber slows the body's absorption of sugars...prevents sharp spikes in insulin...and helps the brain work at optimal levels.

•**Sweet potatoes.** They're a favorite starch of Dr. Amen because they taste good, are high in vitamin C and fiber and don't raise blood sugar/insulin as quickly as white potatoes. They're a "smart" carbohydrate that causes a gradual increase in serotonin.

•**Blueberries.** They're called "brain berries" for a reason. Blueberries are a concentrated source of flavonoids and other antioxidants that reduce brain inflammation. This is important for good mood and memory. Studies have shown that people who eat blueberries may have less risk for dementia-related cognitive declines.

You will get some of the same benefits with other berries, including strawberries, but blueberries are a better choice for brain function.

•**Dark chocolate.** It is one of the healthiest foods that you can eat. Chocolate increases levels of nitric oxide, a molecule that dilates arteries throughout the body, including those in the brain. One study found that women who ate the most chocolate had greater improvements in verbal fluency and other mental functions than those who ate the least. Chocolate also can improve your mood and energy levels. Because it's high in antioxidants, it reduces the "oxidative stress" that can impair memory and other brain functions.

Dr. Amen recommends dark chocolate with natural sweeteners. His company, Amen Clinics, makes a Brain on Joy Bar with dark chocolate and coconut.

BEST FOODS FOR MEN

Men naturally gravitate to high-protein foods. The protein increases dopamine and provides fuel for a man's greater muscle mass. *The trick for men is choosing healthier protein sources…*

•**Salmon.** Between 15% and 20% of the brain's cerebral cortex consists of docosahexaenoic acid (DHA), one of the omega-3 fatty acids found in salmon and other fatty fish such as tuna, trout, sardines, herring and mackerel. Men who don't eat fish are more likely to have brain inflammation that can impair the transmission of nerve signals.

A study published in *Alzheimer's & Dementia: The Journal of the Alzheimer's Association* found that elderly adults who got more DHA had improvements in memory and learning. The study focused on supplements, but you can

get plenty of DHA and other omega-3s by eating fatty fish more often.

•**Eggs.** They are not the dietary danger that people once thought. Recent research has shown that people who eat a few eggs a week—or even as many as one a day—are no more likely to develop heart disease or have a stroke than those who don't eat eggs.

Eggs are an excellent source of protein, inexpensive and easy to prepare. They also are high in vitamin B-12, which can reduce age-related brain shrinkage and improve cognitive function.

•**Sesame seeds and Brazil nuts.** In addition to increasing dopamine, they contain antioxidants that protect brain cells. Like other nuts and seeds, they're high in protein and monounsaturated fats that reduce LDL "bad" cholesterol.

Nuts and seeds are good for the heart as well as the brain. The landmark Adventist Health Study, conducted by researchers at Loma Linda University, found that people who ate nuts five or more times a week were only about half as likely to have a heart attack as those who rarely ate them.

Boost Your Memory in Minutes—(And Have Fun Doing It)

Cynthia R. Green, PhD, founder and president of Memory Arts, LLC, and author of *30 Days to Total Brain Health: A Whole Month's Worth of Daily Tips to Boost Your Memory and Build Better Brain Power* (Memory Arts, LLC). *www.totalbrainhealth.com*

We all have heard that the brain, like a muscle, requires regular mental exercise to stay fit. Most people assume that this means hard work—learning a new language, attending university classes, etc.

There are fun and easier ways. The following "brain workouts" immediately exercise the brain and help you stay mentally sharp and agile, improving both memory and thinking skills.

Bonus: Similar types of brain workouts can help prevent later-life cognitive declines. A *New England Journal of Medicine* study found that people who spent the most time engaged in mentally stimulating activities, such as playing board games and writing for pleasure, were 63% less likely to develop dementia than those who did the least.

Activities to try…

•**Tap a tune.** While imagining your favorite song, drum your fingers on a table or desktop to re-create the notes you are hearing in your head. This encourages the brain to coordinate memory, movement and auditory skills.

Expressing yourself this way cross-challenges the brain and causes it to activate different neural networks than the ones it normally uses.

•**Rework a word.** Write down a multisyllable word, such as "resolution," "sufficient" or "beneficence." Then see how many other words you can come up with, using the letters of the original word. This exercise forces you to see familiar things (the original word) in new ways. You can make it harder by giving yourself only two minutes to do the "word search." Timed activities encourage the use of different mental skills, such as speed, attention and flexibility.

•**Juggle.** Some of the best mental activities also have a physical component. German researchers found that complex motor integration activities, such as juggling, increased the brain's white matter, tissue that is composed of nerve fibers that transmit information to different areas of the brain.

You can learn basic juggling techniques by watching Internet videos.

Helpful: Start with juggling lightweight scarves. They're easier for beginners to juggle than, say, tennis balls.

•**Wear your watch upside down.** Can you tell what time it is when the numbers on your watch are reversed? It's harder than you think. This type of subtle change forces your brain to practice neurobics, activities that engage your attention and involve using one or more of your senses in a new way.

Another example: Using your nondominant hand to brush your teeth. It takes practice!

•**Doodle.** Doodling does more than keep your hands busy. Using a pen or colored pencils to doodle or draw can change the ways in which you see your environment. It also requires mental focus to look closely at what's around you.

Worried About Your Memory? How to Tell What's Normal and What's Not

Aaron P. Nelson, PhD, chief of neuropsychology in the division of cognitive and behavioral neurology at Brigham and Women's Hospital and an assistant professor of psychology at Harvard Medical School, both in Boston. He is coauthor, with Susan Gilbert, of *The Harvard Medical School Guide to Achieving Optimal Memory* (McGraw-Hill).

With all the media coverage of Alzheimer's disease and other forms of dementia, it's easy to imagine the worst every time you can't summon the name of a good friend or struggle to remember the details of a novel that you put down just a few days ago.

Reassuring news: The minor memory hiccups that bedevil adults in middle age and beyond usually are due to normal changes in the brain and nervous system that affect concentration or the processing and storing of information. In fact, common memory "problems" typically are nothing more than memory errors. Forgetting is just one kind of error.

Important: Memory problems that are frequent or severe (such as forgetting how to drive home from work or how to operate a simple appliance in your home) could be a sign of Alzheimer's disease or some other form of dementia. Such memory lapses also can be due to treatable, but potentially serious, conditions, including depression, a nutritional deficiency or even sleep apnea. See your doctor if you have memory problems that interfere with daily life—or the frequency and/or severity seems to

Retinal Damage Linked to Memory Problems

Scientists tested the eye and brain health of 511 women (average age 69) over a 10-year period.

Result: Women with retinopathy (which affects blood vessels in the eye and often is associated with hypertension and diabetes) had lower average cognitive scores and larger memory-disrupting vascular brain lesions than those without it.

Theory: Retinopathy may be an early marker for vascular brain disease, which can lead to cognitive and memory problems.

If you have retinopathy: Talk to your physician about getting screened for vascular brain disease and memory problems.

Mary Haan, DrPH, MPH, professor of epidemiology, University of California, San Francisco.

be increasing. *Five types of harmless memory errors that tend to get more common with age…*

Memory error #1. Absentmindedness. How many times have you had to search for the car keys because you put them in an entirely unexpected place? Or gone to the grocery store to buy three items but come home with only two? This type of forgetfulness describes what happens when a new piece of information (where you put the keys or what to buy at the store) never even enters your memory because you weren't paying attention.

My advice: Since distraction is the main cause of absentmindedness, try to do just one thing at a time. Otherwise, here's what can happen: You start to do something, and then something else grabs your attention—and you completely forget about the first thing.

We live in a world in which information routinely comes at us from all directions, so you'll want to develop your own systems for getting things done. There's no good reason to use brain space for superfluous or transitory information. Use lists, sticky notes, e-mail reminders, etc., for tasks, names of books you want to read, grocery lists, etc. There's truth to the Chinese proverb that says, "The palest ink is better than the best memory."

Helpful: Don't write a to-do list and put it aside. While just the act of writing down tasks can help you remember them, you should consult your list several times a day for it to be effective.

Memory error #2. Blocking. When a word or the answer to a question is "on the tip of your tongue," you're blocking the information that you need. A similar situation happens when you accidentally call one of your children by the name of another. Some patients are convinced that temporarily "forgetting" an acquaintance's name means that they're developing Alzheimer's disease, but that's usually not true.

Blocking occurs when the information that you need is properly stored in memory, but another piece of information is getting in the way. Often, this second piece of information has similar qualities (names of children, closely related words, etc.) to the first. The similarity may cause the wrong brain area to activate and make it harder to access the information that you want.

My advice: Don't get frustrated when a word or name is on the tip of your tongue. Relax and think about something else. In about 50% of cases, the right answer will come to you within one minute.

Memory error #3. Misattribution. This is what happens when you make a mistake in the source of a memory.

More than a few writers have been embarrassed when they wrote something that they thought was original but later learned that it was identical to something they had heard or read. You might tell a story to friends that you know is true because you read about it in the newspaper—except that you may have only heard people talking about it and misattributed the source.

Misattribution happens more frequently with age because older people have older memories. These memories are more likely to contain mistakes because they happened long ago and don't get recalled often.

My advice: Concentrate on details when you want to remember the source of information.

Focus on the five Ws: *Who* told you…*what* the content was…*when* it happened…*where* you were when you learned it…and *why* it's important. Asking these questions will help to strengthen the context of the information.

Memory error #4. Suggestibility. Most individuals think of memory as a mental video-tape—a recording of what took place. But what feels like memories to you could be things that never really happened. Memories can be affected or even created by the power of suggestion.

In a landmark study, researchers privately asked the relatives of participants to describe three childhood events that actually happened. They were also asked to provide plausible details about a fourth scenario (getting lost in a shopping mall) that could have happened, but didn't.

A few weeks later, the participants were given a written description of the four stories and asked to recall them in as much detail as possible. They weren't told that one of the stories was fictional.

What happened: About 20% of the participants believed that they really had been lost in a shopping mall. They "remembered" the event and provided details about what happened. This and other studies show that memories can be influenced—and even created—from thin air.

My advice: Keep an open mind if your memory of an event isn't the same as someone else's. It's unlikely that either of you will have perfect recall. Memories get modified over time by new information as well as by individual perspectives, personality traits, etc.

Memory error #5. Transience. You watched a great movie but can't remember the lead actor's name two hours later. You earned an advanced degree in engineering, but now you can hardly remember the basic equations.

These are all examples of transience, the tendency of memories to fade over time. Short-term memory is highly susceptible to transience because information that you've just acquired hasn't been embedded in long-term storage, where memories can be more stable and enduring.

This is why you're more likely to forget the name of someone you just met than the details of a meaningful book that you read in college—although even long-term memories will fade if you do not recall them now and then.

My advice: You need to rehearse and revisit information in order to retain it. Repeating a name several times after you've met someone is a form of rehearsal. So is talking about a movie you just watched or jotting notes about an event in a diary.

Revisiting information simply means recalling and using it. Suppose that you wrote down your thoughts about an important conversation in your journal. You can review the notes a few weeks later to strengthen the memory and anchor it in your mind. The same technique will help you remember names, telephone numbers, etc.

Olive Oil Helps Your Memory

Saturated fat, such as that found in meat and cheese, contributes to declines in memory and cognition—but monounsaturated fat, like that in olive oil, seems to protect the brain.

Recent study: Women over age 65 who ate the most saturated fat were up to 65% more likely to experience cognitive decline over time than those who ate the least. Women who ate the most monounsaturated fat were 44% less likely to decline in verbal-memory scores and 48% less likely to decline in overall cognition.

Olivia I. Okereke, MD, associate psychiatrist, Brigham and Women's Hospital, Boston, and leader of a study of 6,183 women, published in *Annals of Neurology*.

Supplements to Power Up Your Brain

Daniel G. Amen, MD, a brain-imaging specialist who is founder, CEO and medical director of Amen Clinics. Based in Newport Beach, California, he is author of more than 30 books, including *Unleash the Power of the Female Brain* (Harmony). *www.amenclinics.com*

Can supplements help you find your car keys? Some just might. Research shows that taking the right supplements, in combination with a healthy lifestyle, can preserve and improve brain function.

Renowned brain specialist Daniel G. Amen, MD, knows this firsthand. During his studies of single-photon emission computerized tomography (SPECT) imaging, he decided to have some scans done of his own brain. What he found was that years of unhealthy habits—drinking diet soda, eating fast food, not exercising—had caught up with him. He started a healthy brain program, which included brain-building supplements. Now his brain is healthier than it was 20 years earlier.

Here, Dr. Amen shares the best supplements for your brain.

Caution: Most people can safely take all of them daily, but always check with your health-care provider first, particularly if you have any health problems such as high blood pressure or if you are on any medications, including blood thinners.

MEMORY VITAMIN

Americans don't get enough sun, and because of this, about two-thirds of adults don't meet their vitamin D needs through sunshine exposure.

You probably know that vitamin D is essential for bone strength as well as for preventing some cancers, including breast cancer.

What's new: Vitamin D appears to help the immune system remove beta-amyloid, an abnormal protein, from the brain. This is important because beta-amyloid causes the "tangles" that are associated with Alzheimer's disease.

Brain cells use vitamin D for learning, memory and other cognitive functions. It also is an antioxidant that protects neurons from cell-damaging inflammation. A Tufts University study found that elderly adults with optimal levels of vitamin D performed better on cognitive tests and had better brain-processing speeds than those with lower levels.

Recommended: 2,000 international units (IU) of vitamin D daily is a typical dose, but I advise patients to get their blood levels of vitamin D tested before taking supplements. Everyone synthesizes and absorbs vitamin D differently.

FISH OIL

There's compelling evidence that the omega-3 fatty acids in fish-oil supplements can improve your mood as well as your memory and other cognitive functions. I take fish oil every day, and I advise everyone to do so.

A large portion of the brain consists of *docosahexaenoic acid* (DHA), one of the main omega-3s in fish oil. The brain uses DHA to form cell membranes. People who consume fish oil, either by taking supplements or eating fish, have better brain functions, including a faster transmission of nerve signals and improved cerebral blood flow.

When Danish researchers compared the diets of more than 5,000 older adults, they found that those who ate the most fish were less likely to get dementia and more likely to maintain robust memories.

Important: The American diet is high in omega-6 fatty acids—found in processed foods, red meats, cooking oils, etc. Even if you eat a lot of fish, you still will need supplements to achieve the recommended ratio of one part omega-3s to every three parts omega-6s.

Recommended: 1 to 2 grams daily. Look for a supplement that provides roughly equal amounts of DHA and eicosapentaenoic acid (EPA).

MULTIVITAMIN

Most Americans don't eat the recommended five daily servings of fruits and vegetables. A multivitamin, particularly one that includes B vitamins, is good insurance and can help your brain. In a 2010 study, researchers tested the mental performance of 215 participants. The participants then were given either a daily multivitamin or a placebo. When they were retested a month later, those in the vitamin group showed better mental performance than they had in the beginning. There wasn't a change in the control group.

B vitamins nourish the myelin layer that covers brain cells. Studies have shown that adults who don't get enough of these nutrients, particularly vitamins B-6, B-12 and folic acid, tend to have the greatest declines in memory and other cognitive functions.

Recommended: Look for a product with all seven of the major B vitamins.

VINPOCETINE

This vasodilator comes from the periwinkle plant. Unlike many supplements, it's able to cross the blood-brain barrier and improve brain circulation. Studies show that it significantly increases the oxygenation of brain tissue and improves memory, particularly when used in combination with other brain-boosting supplements.

Recommended: 5 milligrams (mg) to 10 mg daily.

GINKGO

When I examine blood flow and activity patterns with SPECT, the "prettiest" brains often are found in people who take ginkgo. This popular herb is among the best-studied supplements. It dilates blood vessels and reduces the "stickiness" of platelets, cell-like structures in blood that increase the risk for clots. Ginkgo contains flavonoids as well as terpenoids, potent antioxidants that prevent damage to brain cells.

There's strong evidence that ginkgo improves memory. It is also thought to help reduce the risk for vascular dementias and, possibly, Alzheimer's disease.

Recommended: 60 mg to 120 mg, twice daily.

ST. JOHN'S WORT

Anxiety, stress and depression cause serious impairments in mental functions. Chronic stress, for example, increases levels of hormones that can damage the hippocampus (the part of the brain involved in memory). People who are depressed tend to sleep poorly and don't take care of themselves. These and other factors can interfere with clear thinking.

The herb St. John's wort is one of the best treatments for depression. It also is used for treating anxiety and stress. It improves mental focus and helps stop your mind from "spinning."

A review of 29 studies involving 5,489 patients, published by The Cochrane Collaboration (an organization that analyzes medical research), concluded that St. John's wort was just as effective as prescription antidepressants, while causing fewer side effects.

Recommended: If you feel depressed or anxious, take 900 mg of St. John's wort daily, divided into two doses.

Caution: St. John's wort rarely causes side effects, but it can interact with other medications. Talk to your doctor.

The New Nutrient That Boosts Brain Function

Erin McGlade, PhD, a clinical psychologist at the University of Utah Brain Institute and University of Utah Department of Psychiatry in Salt Lake City. Her research includes the effects of citicoline supplementation on healthy adults and adolescents.

The older we get, the longer our to-do lists get (so it seems) and the tougher it seems to focus and get things done.

If that frustration sounds familiar, you'll want to pay attention to news from a recent study about a nutrient called citicoline. Researchers say that it helps sharpen mental focus.

Citicoline is a naturally occurring chemical found in cells, including brain cells. Earlier studies showed that citicoline (also called CDP-choline) improved memory and attention in seniors with mild-to-moderate memory loss. It also helped individuals with dementia caused by small strokes to recover some cognitive functions. The recent study, though, is thought to be the first to examine the compound's effects on healthy middle-aged people.

Published in *Food and Nutrition Sciences*, the recent study included 60 healthy women ages 40 to 60. For 28 days, participants took either 250 mg of citicoline daily…500 mg of citicoline daily…or a placebo. Neither the women nor the investigators were told which participants had been assigned to which regimen until the study was over. On day 28, each participant completed a 14-minute computerized version of a standard test often used to gauge sustained attention and focus. Specifically, they were asked to pay close attention as individual letters flashed on a computer screen for one-quarter of a second each and to press the keyboard's space bar whenever any letter other than X appeared. Mistakes were either by commission (hitting the bar when an X flashed by) or omission (not hitting the bar when another letter appeared).

Impressive results: Women who had taken citicoline at either dosage made fewer errors of both commission and omission than women who had taken a placebo. Interestingly, the lower-dose citicoline group performed best of all.

The study's lead author, Erin McGlade, PhD, a clinical psychologist at the University of Utah Brain Institute in Salt Lake City, explains, "This study suggests that citicoline helps with what I call the 'spacing out' that can accompany aging. For example, if I'm at work trying to read article after article, instead of my mind wandering to, 'Where am I going tonight?' the citicoline helps me focus on what I need to do at that moment."

Why it works: Researchers theorize that citicoline increases brain levels of *dopamine*, a neurotransmitter that is closely linked to our ability to focus. As we get older, it becomes harder to rein in our focus, a phenomenon that has been linked to having fewer available dopamine receptors, Dr. McGlade said. Citicoline may boost dopamine to help us pay attention to the task at hand. The nutrient also helps keep brain cell membranes healthy.

If you want to give citicoline a try: Unless you're fond of organ meats such as liver and brains, you're unlikely to get a substantial amount of citicoline in your diet. Because the

---

DID YOU KNOW?

A Diabetes Drug May Be Good For the Brain

Metformin encourages neuron growth in laboratory tests and enhances memory in mice. If further research confirms the findings, the drug may be used to help repair the brains of patients with neurological disorders.

Study by researchers at University of Toronto, published in *The Journal of the American Medical Association*.

---

nutrient appears in only small quantities in other foods, taking supplements of citicoline may be the easiest way to be sure of getting a therapeutic dosage. Remember, the current study found that a dose as low as 250 mg resulted in increased attention (the brand used in the study was Cognizin). Certain energy drinks also have citicoline—but these typically do not contain the efficacious amount, Dr. McGlade noted, so be sure to check product labels.

Though long-term studies of the potential side effects of citicoline have yet to be done, side effects appear to occur only occasionally and mostly involve mild gastrointestinal upset. As a general precaution, citicoline should not be used by women who are pregnant or breast-feeding.

Five Surprising Ways to Prevent Alzheimer's

Marwan Sabbagh, MD, director of Banner Sun Health Research Institute, Sun City, Arizona. He is research professor of neurology at University of Arizona College of Medicine, Phoenix. He is author of *The Alzheimer's Prevention Cookbook: 100 Recipes to Boost Brain Health* (Ten Speed). *www.marwansabbaghmd.com*

Every 68 seconds, another American develops Alzheimer's disease, the fatal brain disease that steals memory and personality. It's the fifth-leading cause of death among people age 65 and older.

You can lower your likelihood of getting Alzheimer's disease by reducing controllable and well-known risk factors (see box below). *Here Marwan Sabbagh, MD, shares new scientific research that reveals additional little-known "secret" risk factors that you can address...*

CHECK YOUR TAP WATER

A scientific paper published in *Journal of Trace Elements in Medicine and Biology* theorizes that inorganic copper found in nutritional supplements and in drinking water is an important factor in today's Alzheimer's epidemic.

Science has established that amyloid-beta plaques—inflammation-causing cellular debris found in the brains of people with Alzheimer's—contain high levels of copper. Animal research shows that small amounts of inorganic copper in drinking water worsen Alzheimer's. Studies on people have linked the combination of copper and a high-fat diet to memory loss and mental decline. It may be that copper sparks amyloid-beta plaques to generate more oxidation and inflammation, further injuring brain cells.

What to do: There is plenty of copper in our diets—no one needs additional copper from a multivitamin/mineral supplement. Look for a supplement with no copper or a minimal amount (500 micrograms).

I also recommend filtering water. Water-filter pitchers, such as ones by Brita, can reduce the presence of copper. I installed a reverse-osmosis water filter in my home a few years ago when the evidence for the role of copper in Alzheimer's became compelling.

INCREASE VITAMIN D INTAKE

Mounting evidence shows that a low blood level of vitamin D may increase Alzheimer's risk.

A 2013 study in *Journal of Alzheimer's Disease* analyzed 10 studies exploring the link between vitamin D and Alzheimer's. Researchers found that low blood levels of vitamin D were linked to a 40% increased risk for Alzheimer's.

The researchers from UCLA, also writing in *Journal of Alzheimer's Disease*, theorize that vitamin D may protect the brain by reducing amyloid-beta and inflammation.

What to do: The best way to make sure that your blood level of vitamin D is protective is to ask your doctor to test it—and then, if needed, to help you correct your level to greater than 60 nanograms per milliliter (ng/mL). That correction may require 1,000 IU to 2,000 IU of vitamin D daily...or another individualized supplementation strategy.

Important: When your level is tested, make sure that it is the 25-hydroxyvitamin D, or 25(OH)D, test and not the 1.25-dihydroxyvitamin D test. The latter test does not accurately measure blood levels of vitamin D but is sometimes incorrectly ordered. Also, ask for your exact numerical results. Levels above 30 ng/mL are considered "normal," but in my view, the 60 ng/mL level is the minimum that is protective.

RECONSIDER HRT

Research shows that starting hormone-replacement therapy (HRT) within five years of entering menopause and using hormones for 10 or more years reduces the risk for Alzheimer's by 30%. But a recent 11-year study of 1,768 women, published in *Neurology*, shows that those who started a combination of estrogen-progestin therapy five years or more *after* the onset of menopause had a 93% higher risk for Alzheimer's.

What to do: If you are thinking about initiating hormone replacement therapy five years or more after the onset of menopause, talk to your doctor about the possible benefits and risks.

FALL-PROOF YOUR HOME (AND LIFE!)

A study published in *Neurology* in 2012 showed that NFL football players had nearly four times higher risk for Alzheimer's than the general population—no doubt from repeated brain injuries incurred while playing football.

Crucial Steps to Fight Alzheimer's

- Lose weight if you're overweight.
- Control high blood pressure.
- Exercise regularly.
- Engage in activities that challenge your mind.
- Eat a diet rich in colorful fruits and vegetables and low in saturated fat, such as the Mediterranean diet.
- Take a daily supplement containing 2,000 milligrams of omega-3 fatty acids.

What most people don't realize: Your risk of developing Alzheimer's is doubled if you've ever had a serious concussion that resulted in loss of consciousness—this newer evidence shows that it is crucially important to prevent head injuries of any kind throughout your life.

What to do: Fall-proof your home, with commonsense measures such as adequate lighting, eliminating or securing throw rugs and keeping stairways clear. Wear shoes with firm soles and low heels, which also helps prevent falls.

If you've ever had a concussion, it's important to implement the full range of Alzheimer's-prevention strategies in this article.

HAVE A PURPOSE IN LIFE

In a seven-year study published in *Archives of General Psychiatry*, researchers at the Rush Alzheimer's Disease Center in Chicago found that people who had a "purpose in life" were 2.4 times less likely to develop Alzheimer's.

What to do: The researchers found that the people who agreed with the following statements were less likely to develop Alzheimer's and mild cognitive impairment—"I feel good when I think of what I have done in the past

---

Help for Alzheimer's Patients and Their Families

Best Web sites include Alzheimer's Association (*www.alz.org)*, which lists warning signs, disease stages, treatments, care options and financial-planning advice. It has message boards for patients and caregivers. Alzheimer's Disease Education and Referral Center (*www.nihseniorhealth.gov*), from the National Institute on Aging, has information on the latest studies about the disease's causes and possible cures. PBS offers a 90-minute documentary on Alzheimer's patients and their families (*www.pbs.org/ theforgetting*). This Caring Home (*www.this caringhome.org*), from Weill Cornell Medical College, gives room-by-room safety recommendations and solutions to problems.

Kiplinger's Retirement Report. www.kiplingers.com

---

and what I hope to do in the future" and "I have a sense of direction and purpose in life."

If you cannot genuinely agree with the above statements, there are things you can do to change that—in fact, you even can change the way you feel about your past. It takes a bit of resolve…some action…and perhaps help from a qualified mental health counselor.

One way to start: Think about and make a list of some activities that would make your life more meaningful. Ask yourself, *Am I doing these?*…and then write down small, realistic goals that will involve you more in those activities, such as volunteering one hour every week at a local hospital or signing up for a class at your community college next semester.

Measuring Brain Plaques May Yield Clues to Alzheimer's Risk

American Academy of Neurology, news release.

A large amount of beta amyloid, or "plaques," in the brain may trigger more significant memory loss in healthy older people than the genetic risk factor associated with Alzheimer's disease, known as the ApoE-ε4 allele, according to recent research from Australia.

"Our finding that brain-plaque-related memory decline can occur while people still have normal memory and thinking shows that these plaque-related brain changes can be detected and measured while older people are still healthy," said study author Yen Ying Lim, of the University of Melbourne. "This provides an enormous opportunity for understanding the development of early Alzheimer's disease and even a sound basis for the assessment of plaque-targeting therapies."

STUDY DETAILS

The researchers had nearly 150 older adults with no thinking or memory problems undergo a PET brain scan. The participants, who were an average age of 76, also were tested for the APOE gene.

The group's brain function was monitored for 18 months using computer-based tests, card games and memorized word lists.

Over the course of the study, the people who began with more brain plaques had up to 20% greater decline on the computer-based assessments of memory than the people who had fewer brain plaques.

The researchers also found the participants who carried the APOE gene had greater memory loss than those who did not have this genetic risk factor. They noted, however, that carrying the gene did not affect memory decline associated with the plaques.

The study results were published in the journal *Neurology*.

IMPLICATIONS

"Our results show that plaques may be a more important factor in determining which people are at greater risk for cognitive impairment or other memory diseases such as Alzheimer's disease," Lim said in a journal news release. "Unfortunately, testing for the APOE genotype is easier and much less costly than conducting amyloid imaging."

Although the researchers discovered an association between plaques and increased memory loss, they did not prove a cause-and-effect relationship.

 For more information on Alzheimer's disease, visit the Web site of the US National Institute on Aging at *www.nia.nih.gov/alzheimers*.

Alzheimer's May Progress Differently in Women, Men

Maria Vittoria Spampinato, MD, associate professor, radiology, Medical University of South Carolina, Charleston.
Clinton Wright, MD, MS, scientific director, Evelyn F. McKnight Brain Institute, University of Miami Miller School of Medicine.

Alzheimer's disease may look and act differently in men and women, recent research suggests.

When Doctors Get It Wrong...

Alzheimer's Disease

It's impossible to diagnose this condition with 100% certainty because the only definitive "test" is an autopsy of the patient's brain after death. Even though there are fairly accurate ways to determine that a patient might have Alzheimer's (see below), mistakes are common.

Examples: Depression is one of the most common causes of Alzheimer's-like symptoms, but doctors often fail to recognize it. Other problems, including nutritional deficiencies and medication side effects—for example, from anticholinergic drugs, such as antihistamines, incontinence medications and tricyclic antidepressants—also can cause symptoms that mimic Alzheimer's.

Surprising fact: It's estimated that 10% to 25% of patients with symptoms of dementia (such as memory problems and/or peculiar behavior) may have a non-Alzheimer's condition that could be reversed with proper treatment.

What to do: Don't accept a diagnosis of Alzheimer's disease after a single office visit or after taking a simple questionnaire. Specialists (such as neurologists) take a very detailed personal and family history...conduct neurological and mental-status tests...and order a variety of blood and imaging tests to determine whether other conditions might be involved.

Joe Graedon, MS, and Teresa Graedon, PhD, consumer advocates. *www.peoplespharmacy.com*

An emerging field known as gender-specific medicine has shown pronounced differences among the sexes in terms of heart disease and other conditions. These latest findings—if confirmed by further research—may have significant implications for diagnosing and treating Alzheimer's among the sexes.

When people develop Alzheimer's disease, their brains atrophy or shrink. In the study of 109 people with newly diagnosed Alzheimer's, brain scans showed that this atrophy happened earlier in women than men. Women also lost more gray matter in their brains in the year before their diagnosis. However, men seemed to have more problems with their thinking ability when diagnosed with Alzheimer's than their female counterparts did. What's more, men and women lost gray matter in different areas of their brain.

"It is commonly known that loss of volume in hippocampus coincides with cognitive decline, but this is more true in males than females," said study author Maria Vittoria Spampinato, MD, an associate professor of radiology at the Medical University of South Carolina.

The hippocampus is the part of the brain tasked with memory formation, organization and storage.

"The next step is to integrate this information on brain volume loss with other markers of Alzheimer's disease to understand if gender differences exist with other modalities or just brain volume alone," Dr. Spampinato said.

The study was presented at the annual meeting of the Radiological Society of North America.

EXPERT COMMENTARY

Clinton Wright, MD, scientific director of Evelyn F. McKnight Brain Institute at the University of Miami Miller School of Medicine, said it's too soon to draw any conclusions about gender differences in Alzheimer's disease.

"Additional information would need to be provided to know if the findings are attributable to sex differences or other factors," Dr. Wright said. "In particular, it is not clear if the authors adjusted for age. If women were older they might have had greater volume losses over the study period."

Poor Sleep Linked to Alzheimer's

People who wake up frequently (more than five times in an hour) or who are awake for more than 15% of the time that they are in bed are significantly more likely than better sleepers to show physiological changes associated with early Alzheimer's disease, according to a recent study.

Not yet known: Whether it is poor sleep that causes the brain changes—or vice versa.

Yo-El Ju, MD, assistant professor of neurology and a sleep medicine specialist at Washington University School of Medicine, St. Louis.

The finding that women had greater brain volume losses while men had worse mental function at the time of Alzheimer's diagnosis is also hard to explain, Dr. Wright said: "One would expect greater atrophy in those with worse cognition unless additional factors such as vascular damage explained these differences."

info For more information about Alzheimer's disease risk factors, visit the Alzheimer's Association Web site, *www.alz.org* (search "risk factors").

Damage to Tiny Blood Vessels in Brain May Raise Alzheimer's Risk

Adam Brickman, PhD, assistant professor, neuropsychology, Taub Institute for Research on Alzheimer's Disease and the Aging Brain, Columbia University, New York City.
Sam Gandy, MD, associate director, Mount Sinai Alzheimer's Disease Research Center, New York City.
JAMA Neurology

D amage to tiny blood vessels in the brain might be a secondary contributor to Alzheimer's disease, a recent, small study suggests.

Areas of this blood vessel damage, called white matter hyperintensities, are found in the brains of patients with Alzheimer's disease and appear to raise the risk for the condition, the researchers report.

It is believed that the accumulation of beta amyloid plaques in the brain are a primary factor in the development of the memory-robbing condition.

"If you have both these white matter hyperintensities and amyloid in the brain, then you are more likely to get Alzheimer's disease down the road than if you just have one of these," said study senior author Adam Brickman, PhD, an assistant professor of neuropsychology at Columbia University's Taub Institute for Research on Alzheimer's Disease and the Aging Brain.

The exact connection between this vessel damage and Alzheimer's disease isn't exactly clear, he added. While the study showed an association between the two, it did not prove a cause-and-effect relationship.

"There are a number of things that happen through aging that can influence the vessels of the brain, but there also might be an interaction with Alzheimer's disease itself, where the disease is damaging the vessels or the vessel damage is causing the Alzheimer's disease," Dr. Brickman explained.

These tiny vessels might also become damaged through a variety of conditions, including high blood pressure, low blood pressure, oxidative stress, diabetes or inflammation, he explained.

The goal of the research is to one day target these damaged vessels as a way to slow or prevent Alzheimer's disease, Dr. Brickman said.

"Maybe not a primary target, but certainly a potential target," he said. "If we know what the risk factors for white matter disease are, they are perfectly reasonable targets for either prevention or possible treatment."

Limiting the damage to the brain's blood vessels is also important, Dr. Brickman said. Keeping body weight and blood pressure levels in the normal range and not smoking can go a long way in preventing Alzheimer's disease, he said.

STUDY DETAILS

For the study, Dr. Brickman's team looked for blood vessel damage in the brains of 20 patients diagnosed with Alzheimer's disease and in 21 people without the condition.

The researchers found that people with Alzheimer's disease had larger areas of damage than those who were not diagnosed with Alzheimer's.

In addition, blood vessel damage in 59 people with mild memory problems who were included in the study were signs that they were at risk for Alzheimer's disease, the researchers added.

Dr. Brickman noted that these areas of blood vessel damage are seen in most patients with Alzheimer's disease. "I think the reason we don't see it in every patient is because the MRI technology we use might not be sensitive enough to pick up all the changes in white matter disease," he said.

The report was published in the online edition of *JAMA Neurology*.

EXPERT RESPONSE

One expert said the damage to the tiny blood vessels is yet another aspect to the development of Alzheimer's disease, but it complicates understanding the condition.

"This study provides clear evidence that dementia patients in the real world are more complex than those with the pristine pure Alzheimer's disease that we select in research centers," said Sam Gandy, MD, associate director of the Mount Sinai Alzheimer's Disease Research Center in New York City.

The causes of this blood vessel damage in the brain aren't well understood, but it appears that these white matter hyperintensities do signal brain damage linked to dementia, he said.

Dr. Gandy also noted these areas of blood vessel damage make it harder to evaluate the effectiveness of drugs being tested to reduce plaque in Alzheimer's patients.

info For more information on Alzheimer's disease, visit the Alzheimer's Association Web site at *www.alz.org*.

Brain Scans May Explain Memory Problems in Some MS Patients

Fred Lublin, MD, director, Corinne Goldsmith Dickinson Center for Multiple Sclerosis, Mount Sinai Medical Center, New York City.

Steven Mandel, MD, neurologist, Lenox Hill Hospital, New York City.

Hanneke Hulst, MSc, VU University Medical Center, Amsterdam.

Neurology, online.

Besides problems with gait and vision, people who have multiple sclerosis often complain they have trouble remembering things, and now recent research may explain why.

MS is an autoimmune disease that occurs when the body attacks myelin, a fatty substance that insulates the nerve fibers of the central nervous system. Symptoms range in severity and may include problems with gait, balance, vision, memory and thinking abilities.

According to a small study from the Netherlands, people with MS who report memory and thinking problems have more extensive damage to the white matter in their brains than their counterparts with MS who don't report such problems.

Up to 70% of all people with MS will experience a mental decline at some point, said study author Hanneke Hulst, MSc, at the VU University Medical Center, in Amsterdam. And the recent research "confirmed that cognitive symptoms in MS have a biological basis," Hulst said.

STUDY DETAILS

To get a better picture of what was going on in the brains of people with MS, Hulst and colleagues used a new type of brain scan called diffusion tensor imaging along with traditional MRI scans on 20 people with MS-related thinking problems, 35 people with MS whose thinking ability was not affected by the disease and 30 people without MS.

More damage appeared in the brain's white matter of people with MS who reported memory and thinking impairments than in those who had MS but no such complaints about mental decline: 76% vs. 49%, respectively. This was especially apparent in areas of the brain linked to memory, attention and concentration, the researchers said.

"Imaging can now be used to capture a wider spectrum of changes in the brains of people with MS, and will therefore help determine more accurately whether new treatments are helping with all aspects of the disease, including cognitive [mental] impairment," Hulst said. "Unfortunately, at the moment there are no treatments available to prevent or cure cognitive problems in MS."

The findings were published online in *Neurology*.

Coconut Oil May Fight Alzheimer's

Coconut oil may fight Alzheimer's disease and other cognitive disorders, says Andrew L. Rubman, ND.

Theory: A brain compromised by Alzheimer's does not use glucose efficiently. Coconut oil helps the brain compensate for its reduced ability to use glucose as fuel. Several studies have shown promising results, but more research is needed. In the meantime, substituting several tablespoons of coconut oil for other vegetable oils in cooking and salads cannot hurt.

Preferred brand: Source Naturals, *www.sourcenaturals.com*.

Andrew L. Rubman, ND, founder and director of Southbury Clinic for Traditional Medicines, Southbury, Connecticut. *www.naturopath.org*

EXPERTS COMMENT

Steven Mandel, MD, a neurologist at Lenox Hill Hospital in New York City, said the recent study validates some of the complaints he hears from people with MS. "The test is not ready for prime time, but in the future, it can help us sort out how impaired these individuals are in regard to everyday life and daily living."

It may also serve as a marker to assess whether a treatment is making a difference, he said.

Fred Lublin, MD, director of the Corinne Goldsmith Dickinson Center for Multiple Sclerosis at Mount Sinai Medical Center in New York City, said that memory and thinking problems are common in people with MS, but they are usually subtle.

"People with MS are more aware of [these problems] than are the people around them," Dr. Lublin said. Still, he added, "this is an important finding that helps us better understand how cognitive impairment occurs and therefore can be a marker for treatments in the future."

info Learn more about how MS affects memory and concentration at the Web site of the National Multiple Sclerosis Society, *www.nationalmssociety.org* (search "Cognitive Dysfunction").

Botox May Ease Tremors in Multiple Sclerosis Patients

Anneke van der Walt, MBChB, neurologist and research fellow, Royal Melbourne Hospital, Australia.

Thomas Guttuso Jr., MD, assistant professor, neurology, University at Buffalo SUNY, New York.

Neurology

The drug Botox, best known for paralyzing muscles in the forehead to reduce wrinkles, can also relieve shaking in the limbs of patients with multiple sclerosis, a small recent study suggests.

The treatment, which requires several times the amount of Botox (botulinum toxin type A) used for wrinkles, could be expensive and is not yet approved by the US Food and Drug Administration for this use. However, multiple sclerosis (MS) patients can still legally get the treatment in the United States.

"Most patients tolerate the injections very well and are keen to continue the treatment once they see the benefits they get from it," said Anneke van der Walt, MBChB, lead study author and a neurologist and research fellow at the Royal Melbourne Hospital in Australia.

The shaking, known as a tremor, can affect one or both arms, or less commonly the legs, in MS patients. "The shaking affects them when they're just trying to hold the arms up or do common daily tasks such as eating and drinking, shaving and, particularly, writing," van der Walt said. "As with many MS symptoms, the tremor can be worse on very hot days and worse when the person is tired."

Physicians may turn to medications to treat the tremors, but the drugs often have little effect, van der Walt said. Brain surgery to implant electrodes is another option to relieve the tremors, but the benefits may not last long.

STUDY DETAILS

In the recent study, researchers randomly gave Botox or an inactive placebo by injection to 23 MS patients with tremors in their arms. Twelve weeks later, patients who had received Botox the first time got the placebo, and vice versa.

The investigators assessed tremor severity and a variety of motor skills before and after treatment.

According to the study, published in the journal *Neurology*, after Botox injection, the patients had "significant" improvement in tremors as well as in drawing and writing ability, as rated on a 10-point scale.

One side effect, weakness in the limb, was very common in the patients who received Botox—42% reported it, compared with 6% among those who received the placebo. However, the weakness was mild to moderate in the patients and went away within two weeks.

It's not clear how the drug relieves tremors, but it may have something to do with changing the way muscles, nerves and the brain interact, van der Walt said.

The patients received an average of 83 international units of Botox, about three to four times the amount used for wrinkles, although less than the typical amount that migraine patients get. The injections are needed from two to four times a year and cost the equivalent of about $500 to $1,000 in Australia, van der Walt said.

She recommended that "patients who are interested in exploring Botox treatment for their tremor [should] make sure that they are referred to a movement disorder specialist with both an interest in tremor and expertise in complex Botox injections."

EXPERT COMMENT

Commenting on the study, Thomas Guttuso Jr., MD, an assistant professor of neurology at the University at Buffalo in New York, said Botox currently is usually reserved for patients with severe, continuing tremor "that is markedly interfering with certain activities of daily living."

Dr. Guttuso added, "My own experience with these patients is that Botox can be effective when the tremor occurs more at the shoulders and elbows but not as effective when the tremor occurs more at the wrists and fingers."

He added that it's not clear if Botox leads to "meaningful" differences in the lives of patients, and future research will need to examine that issue.

info For more about multiple sclerosis, visit the US National Library of Medicine at its Web site, *www.nlm.nih.gov/medlineplus/multiplesclerosis.html*.

The Mineral Deficiency That Can Cause Restless Leg Syndrome

James R. Connor, PhD, professor of neurosurgery and vice-chair for neurosurgical research at Penn State College of Medicine and director of the Center for Aging and Neurodegenerative Diseases at the Neuroscience Institute of the Penn State Milton S. Hershey Medical Center, both in Hershey.

You climb into bed longing for sleep, but just as you start to relax, your legs begin to twitch, tingle and ache. You feel an overwhelming urge to move your legs around to dispel the creepy-crawling sensation, but those kicks keep you awake into the wee hours. Night after night, the pattern repeats until you're ready to jump out of your skin.

If this sounds depressingly familiar, you probably have restless legs syndrome (RLS), an aptly named neurological disorder that affects 10% of the US population, with women outnumbering men two-to-one. RLS has been linked to a wide variety of conditions, including pregnancy, diabetes, nerve damage, high blood pressure and varicose veins. But now a growing body of research suggests that a key component—or perhaps even the key component—of the disorder is insufficient iron in the brain.

This is not your garden-variety type of iron deficiency typically associated with anemia, in which the whole body is low in iron. Instead, said James R. Connor, PhD, director of the Center for Aging and Neurodegenerative Diseases at the Penn State Milton S. Hershey Medical Center, the RLS-related iron insufficiency affects the brain specifically. *Here's the deal...*

Iron is carried in the bloodstream. Regular blood vessels throughout the body have porous spots that allow nutrients (including iron) to get out and do what they're supposed to do to sustain the body's tissues. However, blood vessels in the brain do not have such porous spots—that is part of a mechanism called the blood-brain barrier, which helps keep harmful substances from invading the body's central command system. Instead, brain blood vessels are specially modified to serve as a nutrient reservoir for the brain to draw upon as needed.

People with RLS can't seem to keep enough iron in that reservoir, Dr. Connor explained. The resulting iron deficiency in the brain interrupts production of dopamine, a neurotransmitter needed to produce smooth, purposeful muscle movement. "RLS symptoms get worse at night because that's when iron levels drop naturally. It's a physiological rhythm that we normally can handle when reservoir levels are OK. But when the iron reservoir is too low, RLS symptoms emerge," he said.

If you have signs of RLS: Do not try to treat yourself with over-the-counter iron supplements, Dr. Connor cautioned. "Iron supplements aren't absorbed very well. In order to get enough iron to affect your RLS, you may have to take high doses of iron tablets, which sometimes may make you very sick with constipation and stomach cramps," he said.

Instead, see your physician for a blood test to check your iron levels and perhaps a brain MRI to look at the amount of iron in your brain. If your iron levels are indeed low, you may be treated with iron supplements or given iron intravenously—for some people, this appears to effectively "refill" the reservoir, Dr. Connor said.

Certain RLS patients also may benefit from medications that target dopamine activity, such as *gabapentin* (Horizant), *ropinirole* (Requip) or *pramipexole* (Mirapex). Your doctor also should review any other medications you are taking to determine whether they could be contributing to your problems. For instance, certain antidepressants, antihistamines and antinausea drugs can aggravate RLS symptoms. Switching or discontinuing such medications may help you get some restful RLS-free slumber at last.

What If It's a Brain Tumor?

Alessandro Olivi, MD, a professor of neurosurgery and oncology and director of neurological oncology at Johns Hopkins University School of Medicine and chairman of neurosurgery at Johns Hopkins Bayview Medical Center, both in Baltimore.

No one wants to hear a doctor say, "It's a brain tumor." But what most of us don't realize is that for the majority of people who hear these words, the diagnosis is not a death sentence.

Meningioma is the most common kind of brain tumor—and the majority of these, 85%, are benign. This does not mean that these tumors are not harmful or do not cause serious problems. But understanding of these tumors has advanced, and research is ongoing to determine why these tumors occur and in whom—and this has produced new detection and treatment options.

Findings you should know about…

WHAT ARE MENINGIOMAS?

Meningiomas are tumors that do not grow within the brain tissue itself, but on the meninges, the membrane that covers the brain and lines the spinal cord. Commonly, meningiomas develop between the upper surface of the brain and the skull.

Meningiomas also can occur on the skull base—including forming in the bones at the bottom of the skull and the bony ridge in the back of the eyes.

Symptoms can occur as the meningioma grows large enough to exert pressure on the brain or if it irritates the surrounding areas. Depending on its location and which brain areas and nerves are disrupted, symptoms may include blurred vision, impaired hearing or sense of smell, loss of balance or facial pain or numbness. Symptoms such as headaches, seizures, muscle weakness and/or memory loss may also occur.

WHO IS AFFECTED?

Meningiomas are two to three times as common in women as in men and are found more frequently in blacks than in any other ethnic group. The higher rate among women has led scientists to wonder whether hormones might play a role—and whether hormone treatment may increase risk.

So far, the data from large population studies in both the US and Finland have found no connection between oral contraceptives and meningiomas and no more than a weak association between postmenopausal hormone-replacement therapy (HRT) and the occurrence of brain tumors.

A large 2011 study that looked at lifestyle factors suggested that the risk for meningioma after menopause rose for women who were overweight but dropped slightly for active women.

THE CAUSE IS UNKNOWN

Researchers are still working on what causes meningiomas. One area of interest is radiation. Several studies have shown that very large amounts of radiation appear to increase the risk for these tumors. Most susceptible are children and young adults who had high doses of radiation to treat a previous cancer. A connection between cell-phone use and meningioma has not yet been determined.

Now researchers at Brigham and Women's Hospital and Yale University are using genetic analysis to help understand why some individuals develop meningiomas after radiation exposure while other people do not.

A study that was published in the journal *Cancer* in 2012 suggested that there may be a connection between bitewing dental X-rays and meningioma, but the evidence is not definitive. For now, the best advice is simply to have dental X-rays no more often than is necessary.

DIAGNOSIS OF MENINGIOMAS

Sometimes, meningiomas are diagnosed by accident, even before they cause symptoms—for example, in the course of examination for an unrelated problem such as head trauma.

For other patients, meningiomas are not diagnosed until they have been growing for years and reached a substantial size. Slow-growing tumors are almost always benign and rarely become cancerous.

When symptoms (such as those mentioned earlier) make physicians suspect a meningioma, they turn to computed tomography (CT) and magnetic resonance imaging (MRI), with contrast dye to better see the tumor, for diagnosis.

Recent progress: The development of powerful magnets has made MRI scans far more precise than they were in the past—and they are able to detect brain tumors that might have been missed a few years ago.

TREATMENT STRATEGIES

Once found, not all meningiomas need to be treated. Physicians may opt for the "watchful waiting" approach for small, benign tumors that do not create symptoms.

Researchers are studying these benign tumors. At Johns Hopkins, they are looking at the genetic differences between benign meningiomas that stay benign and those that become malignant. This will help doctors determine which tumors need treatment and when it is safe to wait and watch a tumor.

Surgery may become necessary if symptoms develop or if periodic brain scans show that the tumor is starting to grow rapidly. The usual surgical treatment is removal of the entire tumor.

Major advances: With image-guided surgery, the surgeon uses CT or MRI as a kind of 3-D internal GPS to tell him/her just where the tumor ends and to navigate around blood vessels and neural structures.

This type of advance makes it possible to remove tumors that would previously have been considered too risky to remove, and to remove them more completely, making recurrence less likely. The use of intraoperative CT and MRI in the operating room enables surgeons to verify that the entire tumor has been removed.

Sometimes the location of the tumor makes surgery impossible. For instance, a meningioma in the middle of the skull base is likely to be surrounded by crucial nerves and blood vessels that make surgery too risky.

In cases like these, radiation therapy (also called radiotherapy) is used. Radiation therapy has also advanced. Today, stereotactic radiosurgery uses imaging and computerized programming to precisely target high-intensity radiation to the tumor while limiting damage to nearby brain tissue. Gamma Knife, CyberKnife and similar methods deliver this type of concentrated radiation. Stereotactic radiosurgery usually keeps tumors from growing but only occasionally shrinks them.

One possible side effect is brain swelling, which can cause symptoms such as headaches or neurological problems such as seizures or loss of balance.

Antinausea Drug Stops Brain Tumor Growth

Emend, a medication that reduces nausea from chemotherapy, blocks the action of substance P, an inflammatory substance in brain tumors. This discovery may result in a new treatment.

The University of Adelaide.

Chemotherapy plays a small role in meningioma—it is reserved for aggressively malignant or recurrent tumors that cannot be treated effectively with surgery or radiotherapy alone.

Research is ongoing to develop new drugs. At Johns Hopkins, scientists have identified a molecular pathway within meningioma cells that spurs their growth—and this could lead to the development of drugs to block their growth.

Researchers at Harvard Medical School, Memorial Sloan-Kettering Cancer Center and elsewhere also are testing medications approved for pancreatic and gastrointestinal cancers with hopes of identifying more effective chemotherapy for those meningiomas that do become aggressive or recurrent.

Air Pollution Harms the Brain

People over age 50 who live in areas with high levels of air pollution do not score as well on tests of memory and thinking skills as people who live in areas with cleaner air. For every 10-point increase in air pollution, participants' scores dropped by an average of one-third point—the equivalent of aging three years.

Self-defense: Don't exercise outdoors on high-pollution days. (For local air-quality conditions, go to *www.airnow.gov.*)

Study of nearly 15,000 people by researchers at Andrus Gerontology Center of the University of Southern California, Los Angeles, presented at the 65th annual meeting of the Gerontological Society of America in San Diego.

Increase Your Brain Power in Less Than Two Minutes

Jason Selk, EdD, former director of mental training, St. Louis Cardinals. He is best-selling author of *10-Minute Toughness* and *Executive Toughness: The Mental-Training Program to Increase Your Leadership Performance* (both McGraw-Hill), and is featured regularly on ABC, CBS, NBC and ESPN. *www.enhancedperformanceinc.com*

A top major league baseball mental-toughness trainer has devised a mental workout that helped his team clinch the World Series (twice!)—and it can help you build the brain power and mind-set you need to achieve your own ambitions, too. Yet it's so simple that it takes only 100 seconds per day.

The technique works on all sorts of goals, whether your dream is to lose weight or win a marathon…strengthen your muscles or strengthen your friendships…or achieve a life-altering personal or professional aspiration.

This 100-second brain workout was formulated by Jason Selk, EdD, former director of mental training for the St. Louis Cardinals and the best-selling author of *Executive Toughness: The Mental-Training Program to Increase Your Leadership Performance.*

He explained that a tired, overwrought brain is vulnerable to the formation of bad habits, such as watching TV instead of exercising… or mindlessly bingeing on junk food instead of preparing a nutritious meal. A quick, daily mental workout revitalizes your mind, releasing stress and boosting mental energy and clarity, the same way that physical exercise increases your body's strength and endurance. Basically a combination of the physiological effects of controlled deep breathing plus the psychological benefits of a very specific type of visualization, the 100-second brain workout can benefit just about anyone.

FIVE STEPS TO YOUR SUCCESS

Once a day with your eyes closed, do Dr. Selk's 100-second daily brain workout…

Step 1: **Centering breath** (15 seconds). Inhale for six seconds…hold the breath for two seconds…then slowly exhale for seven seconds. This calming, controlled breathing technique helps slow your heart rate and prepares your mind for a natural and effective work pattern, Dr. Selk said.

Step 2: **Identity statement** (5 seconds). Think of a goal—personal, physical, professional, financial or whatever—then turn it into a statement about yourself, phrasing it as if you had already achieved that goal. Recite this statement silently to yourself. For instance, you might inwardly say, *I am slim and health-conscious,* and *I follow a nutritious diet with ease and enjoyment*…or *I am a dedicated runner with the skill and determination to win a marathon*…or *I am a caring, compassionate person with many deep and emotionally fulfilling friendships.*

Should you use the same statement every day or change it up sometimes? Dr. Selk said, "The identity statement is essentially a personal mantra that reflects who you are becoming and what you hope to achieve. Over time, as you reach or revise your goals, you may revise your identity statement as well. But the real power of the identity statement is in the repetition and imprinting of this singular vision you've created for yourself."

Step 3: Personal highlights reel (60 seconds). You can see how the name of this step comes from someone who works with athletes, since watching sports highlights is not only fun for fans, but also a valuable training tool for players. "This step boosts confidence, setting your brain on a positive path so you don't get bogged down with stress," Dr. Selk said.

Here's how to visualize your own "highlights" in this step—first, spend 30 seconds remembering three things that you did well in the previous 24 hours…then spend 30 seconds envisioning three things you are going to do well in the next 24 hours. (You don't need to set a timer—it doesn't matter whether you spend precisely 30 seconds on each portion of the exercise.) For maximum effect, visualize these accomplishments in as much detail as you can. For example, you might recall how you ordered a nutritious chopped salad for lunch, took a pass on dessert, then walked the two miles home from the restaurant. Or you might imagine yourself tomorrow morning, scheduling your overdue dental cleaning, then lifting weights at the gym, then ordering that supplement your doctor recommended.

An alternative type of personal highlights reel projects farther into the future. For the first 30 seconds, visualize yourself in five years' time, having already succeeded at your current goal…

then for the next 30 seconds, visualize yourself in the day that lies before you, accomplishing tasks that will contribute to the achievement of your five-year plan.

Step 4: Repeat your identity statement (5 seconds). This confirmation of the mantra from Step 2 reinforces your successful self-image.

Step 5: Repeat the centering breath (15 seconds), using the technique from Step 1, to further encourage calmness to take root in your brain.

Ready reminder: Visit *www.bottomlinepublications.com/downloads/BrainBoost.pdf* for a short version of these steps that you can save or print.

SCHEDULING YOUR MENTAL PUSH-UPS

Exactly when during each day should you do your 100-second brain workout? Don't worry too much about that—just experiment to see what suits you best. Dr. Selk said, "Some people like to do the exercise within a few minutes of waking up, when the mind is clear and uncluttered. Others prefer the start of the workday, just before things really get rolling, so that they are focused and fully ready for what lies ahead. Bedtime is a great option, since research suggests that visualizing right before sleep may influence the subject of your dreams. You may find that your dreams answer questions, solve problems and provide guidance related to your before-bed visualization." Whatever time and place you choose, reserve that spot in your electronic or paper calendar so that the mental workout becomes a daily habit.

If you miss a day here or there, there's no need to stress about it. "Just like one missed appointment with your trainer won't sink your overall physical fitness, the occasional missed mental workout won't kill your progression to clarity and reduced stress," said Dr. Selk. Simply make the commitment to get back on track the following day.

Once you begin your mental workout, within a matter of days you should start to see improvement in your ability to achieve your goals—whatever they may be.

Even Mild Dehydration Hurts Your Brain

Lawrence Armstrong, PhD, professor of kinesiology, Neag School of Education, University of Connecticut, Storrs, Connecticut. His study on men was published in *British Journal of Nutrition* and his study on women was published in *Journal of Nutrition*.

It's easy to know when you're really dehydrated—your mouth is parched, you're likely overheated and all you can think about is chugging a giant glass of ice-cold water.

But knowing when you're mildly dehydrated is much harder, because the signs aren't always as apparent.

And, it's far more common for people to be mildly dehydrated than to be in dire straits.

The problem is, even running just a little bit low on fluids can mess with our brains, according to two recent studies—one on men and one on women.

Both studies included healthy college-aged men and women who took part in cognitive evaluations over the course of a few weeks in order to compare scores from their well-hydrated and dehydrated states.

Results: In women, compared with when they were hydrated, mild dehydration caused them to have trouble concentrating and to perceive mental tasks as more difficult, though they didn't score any worse on the mental tasks. The mild dehydration also caused the women fatigue and headaches. In men, compared with when they were hydrated, mild dehydration caused them to not score as well on mental tasks, especially tasks involving vigilance and working memory. Mild dehydration did not cause the men fatigue or headaches. Researchers reported that differences in hormones may be the reason that men and women experienced different effects.

DRINK UP THESE TIPS

Why would mild dehydration produce such pronounced effects? Lawrence Armstrong, PhD, a professor of kinesiology at the University of Connecticut in Storrs, who led both studies, offered an intriguing theory. It's possible that the billions of neurons in our brains detect mild dehydration early and negatively impact those bodily functions listed above as a warning to us: We need to get water before more dire consequences occur!

It's really important to pay attention not just to thirst, but also to some of those other more subtle signs mentioned above, said Dr. Armstrong, such as fatigue, headache, and difficulty concentrating, remembering or learning. "If you feel any of those things, think about how much you've had to drink over the last 24 to 48 hours," he said.

As a rule of thumb, Dr. Armstrong advises drinking eight cups of water each day to stay properly hydrated. If you exercise for under an hour, drink an extra 1.5 to 2.5 cups of water, advises the Mayo Clinic—and if you exercise for over an hour or if you sweat intensely, drink even more water than that. For every glass of alcohol that you drink, have an extra cup of water. Of course, keep an eye on your urine color—dark yellow or tan means that you need more to drink. Pale yellow is ideal.

Remember, it certainly doesn't require running a marathon to run low on fluids. Mild dehydration can occur even when we're doing mundane tasks—such as eating or watching TV—because we constantly lose water through our skin and during the simple act of breathing, Dr. Armstrong said. What about soft drinks, juice drinks and the many other beverages available? Water is the simplest and most natural fluid—so always keep some nearby, and sip away!

Breast Cancer

How Red Wine Affects Breast Cancer Risk

If you're a woman, then you already know that one daily drink of alcohol may raise your risk for breast cancer by about 12%, according to some research. But a recent study suggests that not all alcohol is created equal...when it comes to wine, in particular, white wine may be more risky than red.

Now picture a restaurant full of people ordering wine—what are most of the women having? White, of course. What's their risk?

WHAT'S IN THAT GLASS?

Glenn D. Braunstein, MD, chairman of the department of medicine at Cedars-Sinai Medical Center in Los Angeles, got the idea to study red wine versus white wine because of substances called aromatase-inhibitors (AIs). AIs are naturally present in red grape skins, red grape seeds and red wine—but not in white grapes or white wine—and, in prior studies they have been

shown, in drug-form, to decrease the body's production of estrogen (which many breast cancers require to grow). So Dr. Braunstein wanted to see whether the natural AIs found in red wine might help healthy women blunt the added risk of drinking red wine, making it less risky than white wine.

RED WINE TRUMPS WHITE

In the study, Dr. Braunstein and his team randomly assigned 36 healthy women (average age 36) to drink eight ounces of either red or white wine with food each evening during the first 21 days of their menstrual cycle. They drank either Cabernet Sauvignon or Chardonnay made by the same company in the same year. After the 21st day, they were told to drink no wine (and consume no grape-related products) until their next menstrual cycle began, at which point they were asked to switch to drinking the other color of wine for 21 days. Twice during the same phases of each menstrual cycle, physicians drew

---

Glenn D. Braunstein, MD, chairman, department of medicine, vice president for clinical innovation, Cedars-Sinai Medical Center, Los Angeles.

blood from the women to measure their levels of estrogen and other hormones.

The results: Researchers found that when the women drank red wine, they had lower levels of estrogen compared with when they drank white wine. When the women drank red wine, they also had higher levels of several other hormones, which are additional indicators that the red wine was acting as an AI. The researchers concluded that given its effect on estrogen and other hormones, drinking red wine may be less risky than drinking white, in terms of breast cancer risk.

In fact, it is possible that a certain amount of red wine reduces breast cancer risk, said Dr. Braunstein, but additional research will be needed to see whether that's true. The study was published in the *Journal of Women's Health*.

BELLY UP

Dr. Braunstein said that although the only red wine tested was Cabernet Sauvignon, it's likely that red wines made from other red grapes would have similar effects. So, he said, if you're a healthy woman with no history of breast cancer and you like to indulge in alcohol on occasion, then you might want to stick with red wine. But he emphasized that if you don't already drink alcohol, this research does not suggest that you pick up the habit, since you can still get the AI benefit from a glass of purple grape juice or a bowl of red grapes. And if you currently have breast cancer or have already had breast cancer, he added, it may also be wise to stay away from alcohol altogether. Talk to your doctor about your particular risk factors.

Foods That Lower Risk for Breast Cancer

Eating dark green or deep orange vegetables and fruits that are rich in carotenoids reduces the risk for estrogen-receptor-negative cancers by 13%. Eat spinach, broccoli, cantaloupe, carrots, apricots and other dark green or orange fruits and vegetables.

Review of data from 18 studies involving more than one million women by researchers at Harvard School of Public Health, Boston, published in *Nutrition Action Healthletter*.

Tender Breasts May Mean Trouble for Women Who Take Hormones

Carolyn Crandall, MD, professor in the department of medicine at the David Geffen School of Medicine and associate research director of the National Center of Excellence in Women's Health, University of California, Los Angeles, and lead author of a study on hormone therapy published in *Breast Cancer Research and Treatment*.

I f you are considering or currently using hormone therapy (HT) to ease menopausal symptoms such as hot flashes and night sweats, you're probably keenly aware of the concerns about a link between HT and breast cancer. Recent study results help identify which HT users are and are not at increased risk for this dreaded disease.

The surprising clue: Sore breasts.

Background: There are two basic types of menopausal HT—estrogen alone…and a combination of estrogen plus progestin (a synthetic progesterone-like hormone). A woman who has had a hysterectomy can take estrogen alone. For a woman with an intact uterus, the combination form of HT is given because the progestin protects against uterine cancer. A common side effect of both types of HT is breast tenderness.

Researchers examined the medical records of more than 27,000 postmenopausal participants in a study called the Women's Health Initiative. The women took either estrogen-only HT, combination HT or a placebo for about five to seven years, on average, then were followed up for several more years. They received annual mammograms and breast exams and periodically answered questions about their health and symptoms, including breast tenderness.

Findings: Women whose breasts became tender within a year after starting combination HT were 33% more likely to get invasive breast cancer during the study period than combination HT users who did not develop new breast tenderness. Among women who were already prone to breast tenderness before the start of the study, use of combination HT doubled the risk for breast cancer. However, for women taking estrogen-only HT, no link was found between breast soreness and cancer risk—in fact, women in the estrogen-only group were less likely to develop breast cancer than women in the placebo group.

Explanation: Combination HT use appears to increase breast density (the proportion of glandular or connective tissue to fatty tissue)—and dense breasts are a known risk factor for breast cancer.

Self-defense for women who are using or thinking about starting HT: Alert your doctor to any breast tenderness you may experience and include this factor in your discussion about the risks and benefits of HT...and be extra-sure to get regular mammograms and breast exams.

Breast Cancer Gene Tests Won't Help Most Women

US Preventive Services Task Force, news release.

The benefits of genetic testing to assess the risk of breast and ovarian cancers linked to the BRCA gene are limited to a small number of women, a recent report indicates.

Mutations in the BRCA1 and BRCA2 genes greatly increase a woman's risk of developing these cancers. Women with these mutations have a 70% chance of developing breast cancer—which is five times greater than in the general population—and increase their lifetime risk of ovarian cancer from less than 2% to as high as 46%.

An important step in preventing these cancers is helping women understand their risk, according to the US Preventive Services Task Force.

RESEARCH AND CONCLUSIONS

In preparing a draft report and recommendations, the task force examined available evidence to determine if genetic counseling and testing could benefit women most likely to have BRCA mutations.

The task force concluded that more than 90% of American women—those whose family history does not indicate an increased risk for BRCA1 or BRCA2 mutations—will not benefit from genetic testing or counseling.

This is because current tests often provide inconclusive results and these women could be burdened with the uncertainty of whether they are at increased risk for cancer. Many of these women might choose to take powerful medications or have major surgery to reduce their risk of cancer, which would be unnecessary if they were not at increased risk.

Therefore, the task force said it continues to recommend against genetic counseling and BRCA testing in these women.

"At this point, scientific evidence only shows that BRCA1 and BRCA2 testing is beneficial for women who have reviewed their family history of breast or ovarian cancer with a primary-care professional and discussed the pros and cons of the screening test with a trained genetic counselor," task force chairwoman Virginia Moyer, MD, MPH, said in a task force news release.

"We hope that further research into ways to use genomic science, such as identifying women who have harmful BRCA genes but do not have a family history of cancer, could improve screening practices and even prevent some cancers," she added.

RECOMMENDATIONS FOR HEALTH-CARE PROVIDERS

The task force said it also found evidence to recommend that primary-care health providers screen women who have family members with breast or ovarian cancer to determine if their family history is associated with an increased possibility of having BRCA1 or BRCA2 mutations.

In situations where this is the case, women should receive in-depth genetic counseling to thoroughly review family history and—if indicated and after weighing the pros and cons of BRCA testing—undergo the test, the report said.

The recommendations apply to women who have not been diagnosed with breast or ovarian cancer but who have family members with breast or ovarian cancer and whose BRCA status is unknown.

"Every year, too many American women and families are faced with the challenge of dealing with breast and ovarian cancer diagnosis and treatment," Dr. Moyer said. "We need better treatments, better screening methods and, most importantly, better ways to prevent cancer."

info The US National Cancer Institute has more about BRCA mutations and cancer risk at its Web site *www.cancer.gov/cancertopics/factsheet/risk/brca.*

The Breast Cancer Risk That's as Bad as the Gene

Chaya Moskowitz, PhD, associate attending biostatistician at Memorial Sloan Kettering Cancer Center in New York City.

A s they reach adulthood, some childhood cancer survivors need to be extra-wary about yet another cancer threat, a recent study reveals.

Researchers looked at long-term data (the median follow-up period was 26 years) on 1,268 female childhood cancer survivors who had been treated with radiation to the chest. It's not news that radiation raises a person's risk for future cancers—but what was surprising was the degree to which risk increased.

How the numbers stacked up: Among childhood cancer survivors who had received chest radiation, 24% developed breast cancer by age 50...the median age at diagnosis was just 38. Risk was especially elevated among women who as children got high doses of chest radiation to treat Hodgkin lymphoma (cancer of the immune system)—their rate of 30% was comparable to the 31% rate that the researchers estimated for women who carry the BRCA1 gene mutation.

It is worrisome to note that only about half of women treated with chest radiation as youngsters follow the current breast cancer screening guidelines from the Children's Oncology Group, a consortium supported by the National Cancer Institute. Those guidelines recommend that childhood cancer survivors who received 20 Gy (the unit of measure for radiation) or more to the chest area undergo twice-yearly clinical breast exams, annual mammograms and annual breast MRIs starting at age 25 or eight years after radiation, whichever comes later. And the recent study findings suggest that these same

guidelines also may be appropriate for women who were treated with lower chest radiation dosages, researchers said.

Childhood cancer survivors: Talk to your doctor about breast cancer screening—and make sure that he or she is aware of your chest radiation treatment history.

Depo-Provera Birth Control Might Raise Breast Cancer Risk

Christopher Li, MD, PhD, breast cancer epidemiologist, Fred Hutchinson Cancer Research Center, Seattle.
Elizabeth Poynor, MD, PhD, gynecologic oncologist and pelvic surgeon, Lenox Hill Hospital, New York City.
Freya Schnabel, MD, director of breast surgery, NYU Clinical Cancer Center, New York City.

T here appears to be a link between an injectable form of progestin-only birth control, best known as Depo-Provera, and an increased risk of breast cancer in young women, recent research suggests.

For the study, researchers compared more than 1,000 Seattle-area women, aged 20 to 44, who were diagnosed with breast cancer, and more than 900 women without breast cancer.

Recent use of the injectable contraceptive (formally called depo-medroxyprogesterone acetate or DMPA) for a year or longer was associated with a 2.2-fold increased risk of invasive breast cancer, the study found.

This increased risk appeared to fade within months after women stopped using the contraceptive, and women who used the contraceptive for less than a year or who had stopped using it more than a year earlier did not have any increased risk of breast cancer, according to the findings published online and in the journal *Cancer Research.*

"Although breast cancer is rare among young women and the elevated risk of breast cancer associated with DMPA appears to dissipate after discontinuation of use, our findings emphasize the importance of identifying the potential risks associated with specific forms of contraceptives given the number of available alternatives," study leader Christopher Li, MD, PhD, a breast cancer epidemiologist at the Fred Hutchinson Cancer Research Center in Seattle, and colleagues wrote.

"In the United States, many women have numerous options for contraception, and so it is important to balance their risks and benefits when making choices," Dr. Li noted.

While the study uncovered an association between Depo-Provera and raised breast cancer risk, it could not prove a cause-and-effect relationship.

EXPERT COMMENTARY

Commenting on the study, Elizabeth Poynor, MD, PhD, a gynecologic oncologist and pelvic surgeon at Lenox Hill Hospital in New York City, said, "This study further confirms that some types of progestins are not healthy for the breast. For women who are at elevated risk to develop breast cancer based on family history, or even age, this type of contraception may not be a good choice for them."

But another expert cautioned that the study did have its limits.

Freya Schnabel, MD, director of breast surgery at NYU Clinical Cancer Center in New York City, noted that the women in the study who seemed at highest risk of developing breast cancer while on Depo-Provera were those with a family history of the disease or women who had never had children (another risk factor).

Furthermore, she said, "the study did not include information about all breast cancer risk factors in the participants, and this is a real limitation of the analysis which could impact on the results. Also, the mechanism by which the progesterone would increase risk only in current users is not clear."

"More detailed studies are needed to clarify the relationship between this contraceptive method and risk of breast cancer," she said.

The research was funded by the US National Cancer Institute and the Department of Defense Breast Cancer Research Program.

info Planned Parenthood has more about Depo-Provera at its Web site, *www.plannedparenthood.org* (search "birth control shot").

Breast Implants Linked to a Rare Cancer

About 60 women with silicone or saline breast implants have developed *anaplastic large cell lymphoma* (ALCL). As many as 10 million women have received implants, so any disease risk is very low, but removing the implants will eliminate the risk.

Self-defense: See your doctor if you develop persistent swelling or pain around the implant. Symptoms usually appear many years after implantation—eight years, on average, and as long as 23 years.

William Maisel, MD, MPH, chief scientist, Center for Devices and Radiological Health, Food and Drug Administration, Silver Spring, Maryland.

3D Mammography Finds More Breast Cancers

Diane LoRusso, MD, clinical assistant professor, Weill Cornell Medical College, New York City, and cofounder, Rye Radiology Associates, Rye Brook, New York. *www.ryeradiology.com*

Breast tomosynthesis, commonly called 3D mammography, is a relatively new imaging technique that catches more breast cancers than regular 2D mammograms—while more accurately identifying harmless spots as benign.

Recent research reveals how well it works…

•**A study from Norway included 12,631 women who were screened with both 2D and 3D mammography.** When radiologists had access to both the 2D and 3D exams, they detected 40% more cases of invasive breast cancer (the type that has spread outside the milk duct or lobule and into the breast tissue itself) than when they saw only the 2D exams.

•**In a separate study from Massachusetts General Hospital, the combination of 2D and 3D mammography reduced false-positive results** (when a suspicious-looking abnormality is found but turns out to be benign) by 39%.

Diane LoRusso, MD, a clinical assistant professor at Weill Cornell Medical College who has practiced radiology for nearly four decades, calls 3D mammography a "remarkable breakthrough and a major improvement in our ability to detect breast cancer."

But: There are some downsides to the 3D test. *Should you be asking your doctor for a 3D mammogram? Here's the info you need to decide…*

THE BENEFITS OF 3D

A regular mammogram is a two-dimensional picture of a three-dimensional object that's been flattened out by those uncomfortable breast-squishing plates. Because the compressed breast tissue ends up overlapping itself, one feature can hide in the shadow of another, making it difficult to find tiny cancers hidden in the breast. (Imagine a bunch of letters of the alphabet being layered one on top of the other. They'd be hard to read, right? That's similar to what happens with a 2D mammogram image.)

For the 3D mammogram, the breast is still compressed between the plates—but the arm of the X-ray machine rotates in an arc above the breast, taking 15 separate images. Those are then processed on a computer to create a 3D image that the radiologist can manipulate to view 50 to 60 individual millimeter-thin "slices" of breast tissue. By eliminating overlapping structures, abnormalities are more easily seen. (Imagine that pile of alphabet letters being separated layer by layer. You could view each letter individually, so they would be easy to read.)

The 3D images help radiologists pin down the size, shape and precise location of abnormalities—details that tend to be obscured on 2D images. The improved visibility explains why 3D mammograms detect tumors that 2D mammograms miss…and why the new technology is less likely to yield those anxiety-producing false-positive results that lead to unnecessary (and expensive) extra testing.

THE DOWNSIDES

Currently, 3D mammography is used in addition to regular mammography, not instead of it—so even if you opt for the 3D test, you'll still need regular 2D mammograms as well. One reason is that an important aspect of mammogram reading is to compare a patient's new images with her previous images to see whether anything has changed. Since those previous images were all 2D, for comparison's sake, you need a 2D version of your current images, too. Fortunately, both scans can be performed on the same mammography equipment in rapid succession. (In May 2013, the FDA approved the use of a low-dose 3D mammography alone [the software is manufactured by Hologic, Inc.]—but separate 2D tests are still the norm.)

Radiation is another concern. Though the 3D scan uses about the same amount of radiation as the 2D scan, combining the two doubles your radiation exposure. Still, the total radiation dose for the combined test is well below three milligray, which is the FDA limit for a single mammogram—and it's less than the radiation dose from the film (rather than digital) 2D mammograms of the past. As Dr. LoRusso pointed out, because 3D mammograms produce fewer false-positive results, your overall radiation dose may be lower in the long run since you're less likely to be called back for additional mammograms.

The amount of breast compression involved in 3D mammography is no different from that required for a 2D scan. However, to do both the 2D and 3D tests, you have to endure that breast squishing a bit longer—for about six to 12 seconds per breast, compared with the two to four seconds needed for just the 2D test alone.

The good news: The design of the compression device on the 3D unit is more comfortable for most patients, Dr. LoRusso said.

Another downside is the expense. Insurance companies generally do not cover 3D mammography because they still consider it experimental. Hopefully, this will change in the not-to-distant future (and it certainly couldn't hurt to ask your insurance company to cover your 3D test). For now, though, you'll probably have to pay the extra cost yourself. Typically this ranges from about $50 to $100, depending on your location and your doctor—a small price to pay for improved cancer detection.

MAKING YOUR CHOICE

Dr. LoRusso recommends the 3D test for all her mammography patients because research shows that it benefits women with all breast types.

However, it is particularly important for the 30% of women whose breasts are dense (meaning that they contain more glandular or connective tissue than fatty tissue). Mammogram X-rays do not see through dense tissue as easily as they see through fat tissue—cancerous tissue and dense areas both appear white on the mammogram, so identifying cancer is like trying to pick out a particular cloud in a cloud-filled sky.

Ask your local radiology center or hospital whether it provides 3D mammography…or use the manufacturer's locator service. Currently about 300 radiology centers in the US offer this test. To learn more about 3D mammography and see the machine in action, check out this video from Dr. LoRusso's Web site at *www.rye radiology.com/3d-digital-mammography*.

Finally, Dr. LoRusso said, it is very important to realize that 3D mammography should not replace other breast tests that your doctor may recommend. For instance, if you have dense breasts or palpable masses, you also may need breast ultrasound screening…if you are at very high risk for breast cancer due to genetic factors, you also may need a breast MRI. In short, 3D mammography is an important new tool in the fight to detect breast cancer, but it is not the only tool.

How False-Positive Mammograms Hurt You

John Brodersen, PhD, researcher, University of Copenhagen Department of Public Health, Denmark.

Matthew Loscalzo, LCSW, Liliane Elkins Professor in Supportive Care Programs, City of Hope Comprehensive Cancer Center, Duarte, California.

Annals of Family Medicine

Women who have a false-positive mammogram result—when breast cancer is first suspected but then dispelled with further testing—can have lingering anxiety and distress up to three years after the misdiagnosis, a recent study finds.

The emotional fallout is probably so long-lasting, "because the abnormal screening result is seen as a threat to your own mortality," said study author John Brodersen, PhD, a researcher at the University of Copenhagen in Denmark.

The report is published in the *Annals of Family Medicine*.

BACKGROUND

Public health experts often cite false-positive mammograms as a downside to mammography screening. They believe these false-positive findings need to be considered when making recommendations about who should be screened, at what age and how frequently.

They aren't uncommon: The risk of a false positive for every 10 rounds of screening ranges from 20% to 60% in the United States, Dr. Brodersen said.

After an abnormal mammogram, doctors typically order additional mammograms and, depending on those results, more tests such as an ultrasound or MRI, and finally a biopsy.

Studies about the short-term and long-term consequences of false-positive mammogram results have produced mixed findings, which Dr. Brodersen said spurred him to conduct his study.

THE STUDY

Dr. Broderson and his team evaluated more than 1,300 women, including 454 who had abnormal findings on a screening mammogram and others who received normal results.

Of those 454 who first had abnormal results, 174 later found they had breast cancer. Another 272 learned the result was a false positive. (Eight others were excluded from the study due to unknown conclusions or a diagnosis of cancer other than breast cancer.)

The women answered a questionnaire about their psychological state, such as their sense of calmness, being anxious or not about breast cancer and feeling optimistic or not about the future. They repeated the questionnaire at one, six, 18 and 36 months after the final diagnosis.

Six months after the final diagnosis, those with false positives had negative changes in inner calmness and in other measures as great as the women with breast cancer. Even at the three-year mark, women with false-positives had more negative psychological consequences compared with women with normal findings.

The differences among those with normal, false-positive and breast cancer findings only began to fade at the three-year mark, the study found.

Dr. Brodersen can't say if women who were more anxious about health or life in general to begin with were more likely to have long-term distress. "I have not investigated this aspect," he said.

EXPERT REACTION

Even without this information, the study is a good one, said Matthew Loscalzo, LCSW, the Liliane Elkins Professor in Supportive Care Programs at the City of Hope Comprehensive Cancer Center in Duarte, California.

"They looked at large enough numbers, so the data they are sharing is valid and should be taken very seriously," he said.

The finding that some women are still stressed three years later does not surprise Loscalzo. From his experience working with patients, Loscalzo said, women who receive a false-positive result do often feel at risk, even after getting the news they are cancer-free.

Many, he said, will definitely worry—"Will the next one be a breast cancer?"

According to the American College of Radiology, "Anxiety regarding inconclusive test results is real and is only natural." However, the organization of radiologists also cited what it said are study flaws. For instance, the researchers did not take into account whether women with false-positive results had a family history of breast cancer, or whether some women were ordered to have more frequent mammograms, both of which would likely raise anxiety levels.

WHAT TO DO

Women who get an abnormal mammogram result need support, Loscalzo said. Women who undergo additional testing after an abnormal mammogram should ask to get their results as soon as possible, he added. If they are feeling anxious, he suggests they also tell their doctor they want to talk with a counselor, he said.

info To learn more about mammography results, visit the American Cancer Society Web site, *www.cancer.org*, and search "Breast Imaging Reporting and Data System."

Good News for Women with Breast Cancer

Jill Dietz, MD, director of the Hillcrest Breast Center, Cleveland Clinic Foundation. She is a fellow of the American College of Surgeons and member of several professional organizations, including the American Society of Breast Surgeons and Society of Surgical Oncology. A researcher and teacher, Dr. Dietz is also program director for the surgical breast fellowship at Cleveland Clinic.

Women who have breast cancer are now living longer than they did only five years ago—and not simply due to improved mammography techniques.

Reason: Recent scientific evidence is changing the way physicians can treat the disease—making these treatments much more selective and effective. *Key findings breast cancer patients need to know about...*

•**New thinking on double mastectomy.** Many women with breast cancer opt to surgically remove the breast with the malignancy and the healthy breast. Their decision to remove both breasts is driven by the fear that a new breast cancer will develop in the healthy breast. But recent research suggests that double mastectomy for these women may be overused.

Recent scientific evidence: Researchers who followed up with 1,525 early-stage breast cancer patients four years after they had received mastectomy, double mastectomy or lumpectomy (a breast-conserving procedure that removes only the malignancy and surrounding tissue) found that women who had both breasts removed would have had a very low risk of developing cancer in the healthy breast.

Who should consider having a double mastectomy? According to the Society of Surgical Oncology, it may be warranted for a woman who is at increased risk for breast cancer because she has two or more immediate family members (a mother, sister or daughter) with breast or ovarian cancer...or has tested positive for mutations in the BRCA1 or BRCA2 gene. These criteria apply to women who have early-stage breast cancer as well as those who haven't developed the disease.

Self-defense: If you don't have a family history or genetic predisposition to develop breast cancer, carefully review your reasons for considering a double mastectomy.

•**Better results with *tamoxifen*.** Doctors have long advised certain breast cancer patients to use an estrogen-blocking drug (tamoxifen) for about five years to stave off future breast malignancies.

Recent scientific evidence: For 15 years, researchers followed 6,846 breast cancer patients who took tamoxifen for an additional five years after five years of initial use while another group stopped the drug at five years.

Result: Those who used the drug for 10 years had a significantly reduced risk for breast cancer recurrence and death.

The benefits of longer-term tamoxifen use apply primarily to premenopausal women. That's because postmenopausal women have the option of taking another class of drugs called aromatase inhibitors, including *letrozole* (Femara), which are slightly more effective than tamoxifen at preventing future breast cancers but do not, for unknown reasons, offer the same benefit to premenopausal women. Research has not yet determined whether postmenopausal women would benefit from taking letrozole for 10 years rather than the standard five-year recommendation.

Self-defense: If you're a premenopausal woman with breast cancer (especially if the tumor was large and/or you had lymph nodes that tested positive for cancer), ask your doctor about the risks and benefits of taking tamoxifen for more than the standard five years. Using the drug increases risk for endometrial cancer and pulmonary embolism.

•**Less invasive treatment may improve survival for early-stage breast cancer.** Women with early-stage breast cancer perceive mastectomy to be more effective at eliminating their future risk for breast cancer, but research shows that this is probably not true.

Recent scientific evidence: In an analysis of more than 112,000 women with stage I or stage II breast cancer who were tracked for an average of 9.2 years, those who received lumpectomy plus radiation had odds of survival that were as good as or better than those who underwent mastectomy.

Self-defense: If you are diagnosed with stage I or stage II breast cancer, ask your doctor about lumpectomy plus radiation.

•**More women could benefit from reconstruction.** With breast reconstruction, a woman who has received a mastectomy (or, in some cases, a lumpectomy) can have her breast shape rebuilt with an implant and/or tissue from another part of her body (typically the abdomen, back or buttocks). When a patient opts for reconstruction, it is ideally performed with the initial breast cancer surgery for the best cosmetic result.

Breast reconstruction does not restore the breast's natural sensation or replace the nipple. However, a new "nipple-sparing" mastectomy, a technically difficult procedure in which the surgeon preserves the nipple and areola (the brownish or pink-colored tissue surrounding the nipple), is gaining popularity with women whose malignancy does not interfere with this type of surgery.

Recent scientific evidence: Even though breast reconstruction can offer cosmetic and psychological advantages, not very many women choose to have it. In a study of more than 120,000 women who underwent mastectomy, fewer than one in four of the women with invasive breast cancer opted for reconstruction, while only about one in three of those with early-stage disease got it. Almost all women are candidates for reconstruction, which does not impact survival rates. In some cases, women require one or more subsequent surgeries to fine-tune the reconstruction.

Self-defense: Ask about reconstruction before your treatment begins. If you're a candidate, the breast surgeon can coordinate with a plastic surgeon. Breast reconstruction is often covered by insurance, but some insurers may require a co-pay. (See the following article on breast reconstruction for more information.)

•**Targeted therapies save lives.** Until 40 years ago, breast cancer was treated almost uniformly with radical mastectomy, radiation and some form of hormone therapy.

Recent scientific evidence: Using new genomic DNA–based tests, doctors are now able to customize treatment based on tumor biology, helping them better predict a patient's risk for recurrence and response to particular treatments. This may help thousands of women avoid chemotherapy, including anthracyclines, which are linked to heart damage and leukemia.

Self-defense: Ask your doctor whether you could benefit from genomic testing to help determine which breast cancer therapies would be most effective for you.

Love Your Post-Cancer Breasts

Frank J. DellaCroce, MD, cofounder of the Center for Restorative Breast Surgery and the St. Charles Surgical Hospital (a hospital dedicated to breast reconstruction), both in New Orleans. *www.breastcenter.com*

Two recent surgical breakthroughs provide good news and new options for breast reconstruction after mastectomy.

If a loved one is facing breast cancer surgery, please pass along this information. Don't assume she already knows—sadly, only 30% of patients are fully informed about their options for reconstruction prior to their breast cancer surgery, according to a study from the University of Michigan.

For details on these surgical advances, we contacted Frank J. DellaCroce, MD, cofounder of the Center for Restorative Breast Surgery in New Orleans, who pioneered the new techniques. *Here's what women should know about…*

•**Nipple-sparing mastectomy.** Traditionally, mastectomy has meant surgical removal of the entire breast…and reconstruction has included the need to rebuild a nipple by grafting skin from elsewhere and tattooing the area to simulate the areola (the colored ring around the nipple). However, with the new nipple-sparing mastectomy (NSM), the surgeon preserves the breast skin and nipple area while removing the underlying breast tissue, including the cancer, through a small incision below the nipple. This is immediately followed with breast reconstruction using either an implant, a "flap" procedure (described below) or another technique to fill the pocket of breast skin—so the woman leaves the operating room with the cancer gone and the reconstructed breast already in place.

While no reconstruction technique can guarantee a breast that looks exactly as it did before surgery, NSM minimizes scarring…provides optimal cosmetic results…and helps women feel more "whole" after surgery, Dr. DellaCroce said. (For before-and-after photos, visit *www.breast center.com/nipple-sparing-mastectomy.php* and click on "View Result Photos.")

After NSM, sensation in the nipple may be reduced or eliminated, but results vary and many women report a substantial return of touch sensation in the months after surgery. What about the risk for cancer recurrence? "All studies to date, from multiple institutions, have shown equal cure rates with preservation of the nipple as compared with techniques that sacrifice it," said Dr. DellaCroce.

Who can benefit? While candidates for NSM must be evaluated case by case, the procedure generally is most appropriate for women who have relatively small areas of cancer that are a safe distance away from the nipple, Dr. DellaCroce said. NSM also may be considered when a woman opts to undergo prophylactic mastectomy because she is at very high risk for breast cancer due to a BRCA gene mutation.

•**Stacked flap.** To understand the new "stacked" procedure, you first need to know about the standard deep inferior epigastric perforator flap breast reconstruction technique. With the standard procedure, a flap of complete tissue—blood vessels, skin and fat—is taken from the abdominal area beneath the breast and used as a "donor" to reconstruct a breast of soft, warm, living tissue. But this may not work well for thin women who are full-breasted, as they may not have adequate abdominal tissue to reconstitute their breast volume, Dr. DellaCroce said. In such women, breast implants may be used to supplement the abdominal donor tissue—but implants can lead to complications, such as painful capsular contracture (hardening of tissue), which may require removal of the implant.

This is where the new stacked flap technique comes in—because it enables even thin women to have implant-free reconstruction using only their own natural tissue (without sacrificing abdominal muscle, as some other reconstruction techniques require). The procedure stacks two layers of abdominal fat under the preserved skin envelope by carefully connecting the blood vessels between them using microsurgery, Dr. DellaCroce explained. This allows for full restoration of volume in the new breast.

Who can benefit? Thin women undergoing mastectomy who prefer not to use implants… and women who have had radiation treatment to the breast, for whom implants generally are not appropriate because of the likelihood of severe capsular contracture. "The stacked flap may be performed at the same time that mastectomy is performed. Or if mastectomy has already been done, the stacked flap can serve as a wonderful way to recreate a breast out of soft, living tissue at any point at which the patient is ready to proceed with restoration," Dr. DellaCroce said.

Finding a surgeon: Because NSM and stacked flap procedures are so new, you will need to hunt to locate a surgeon experienced with the technique you are interested in. To start, get referrals from the American Society of Plastic Surgeons (*www.plasticsurgery.org*), then interview several candidates. Dr. DellaCroce recommended choosing a surgeon who confirms that he or she has done at least one per week for a full year of the procedure you're considering and whose success rate exceeds 95%. Also, ask to see photos of the surgeon's work…and get contact information for several patients who have undergone the same procedure so you can ask them about their experiences.

Having the option of reconstruction can be an important facet in a patient's full recovery. Dr. DellaCroce said, "When you lose some component of your physical self, you also lose some of your emotional self. To have the breast rebuilt erases some of the injury of a very difficult event." And that makes the victory of surviving breast cancer all the sweeter.

Common Treatment Creates More Complications

Common breast cancer treatment brachytherapy may cause more complications than traditional external-beam radiation therapy (EBRT). Brachytherapy involves placing radioactive material inside the breast. The treatment usually lasts a week. EBRT projects radiation from a machine outside the body and usually is done over four to six weeks. Researchers estimated the complication rate to be 16.8% higher with brachytherapy than with EBRT.

Cary P. Gross, MD, associate professor of medicine, Yale School of Medicine, New Haven, and leader of a study, published in Journal of Clinical Oncology.

The Noncancer Breast Cancer

Irene Wapnir, MD, chief of breast surgery at the Stanford Cancer Institute and an associate professor of surgery at the Stanford University School of Medicine, both in California. For information on clinical trials currently recruiting participants, visit *http://med.stanford.edu/profiles/cancer/faculty/Irene_Wapnir/*.

Patients are confused, and no wonder—because doctors don't even agree on the name, much less on how aggressively to treat the breast condition officially known as *ductal carcinoma in situ* (DCIS). Some women with DCIS wind up doing nothing, while others opt for extensive surgery and/or years of pharmacological treatment. *Here's why this confounding condition presents such a dilemma…*

DCIS, which develops when genetic mutations occur in the DNA of cells within a milk duct, is generally considered the earliest form of breast cancer. Also called stage 0 breast cancer, it is noninvasive, meaning that the abnormal cells have not spread beyond the milk duct to invade surrounding breast tissue. Because it seldom produces symptoms, it usually is discovered during a routine mammogram. In itself, DCIS is not life-threatening—in fact, some doctors refer to it as precancer rather than cancer.

The concern, of course, is that if these cancer cells do develop the ability to break down the wall of the milk duct and grow, then they will have become invasive cancer—with the potential to spread and be fatal. The local treatments offered to DCIS patients are similar to those for patients with invasive breast cancer. For some women, this may be overtreatment, as their DCIS cells may never develop the capacity to invade or spread. Problem is, as yet there's no way to foretell whose disease will become invasive and whose won't.

We spoke with Irene Wapnir, MD, chief of breast surgery at the Stanford Cancer Institute and a leading breast cancer researcher. Her recent analysis of two long-term studies on the efficacy of various treatments helped bring increased clarity to the question of how to handle DCIS.

An estimated 60,000 US women are diagnosed with DCIS each year. If you are ever among them, remember that DCIS is not an emergency, so you can safely take several weeks or more to investigate your options. *Here are the treatments—from the least to the most aggressive—to discuss with your oncologist...*

•**Lumpectomy** (surgical removal of the abnormal tissue and a surrounding margin of healthy tissue). This preserves the breast, allows a quick recovery and has a minimal effect on appearance. In Dr. Wapnir's study, which followed patients for an average of about 15 years, 19% of DCIS patients who received lumpectomy alone developed subsequent invasive breast cancer. Dr. Wapnir said that a DCIS patient over age 70 who also has another medical problem that is potentially life-threatening might consider lumpectomy alone rather than lumpectomy plus radiation and *tamoxifen* (described below).

•**Lumpectomy plus radiation.** The goal of radiation is to kill any lingering cancer cells. Compared with lumpectomy alone, the addition of radiation reduced breast cancer recurrence risk by more than half, Dr. Wapnir found. Also, radiation potentially allows for narrower margins—for instance, the surgeon might remove a 1-mm margin of healthy tissue rather than the 2-mm to 5-mm margin recommended with lumpectomy alone—thus allowing superior cosmetic results.

Downside: Radiation can have long-term side effects at the treatment site, such as skin darkening or thickening and mild shrinkage of breast tissue.

•**Lumpectomy, radiation and tamoxifen.** A "triple therapy" that includes several years of use of the oral drug tamoxifen is appropriate for patients whose DCIS is determined to be hormone receptor positive. The drug blocks the action of estrogen, a hormone that promotes cancer cell growth. Dr. Wapnir found that, compared with lumpectomy plus radiation, triple therapy reduced tumor recurrence by another 32%.

Bonus: Tamoxifen protects both breasts, not just the DCIS-affected breast...and it reduces the number of new cancers by half, Dr. Wapnir said.

•**Single mastectomy.** Surgically removing the breast with DCIS eliminates nearly all the risk of developing invasive cancer in that breast and also eliminates the need for radiation. However, women may consider mastectomy more disfiguring than lumpectomy...and there is no known survival advantage to mastectomy. Dr. Wapnir said that mastectomy makes most sense for women whose DCIS is large (more than 5 cm) or in multiple sites in the breast. Alternatively, she added, some women may choose mastectomy due to personal preference or because they wish to avoid radiation or tamoxifen therapy.

•**Double mastectomy.** According to a study from the University of Minnesota, the number of patients opting to remove the healthy breast as well as the DCIS-affected breast has soared since 1998. For women at extremely high risk for invasive breast cancer—for instance, because they carry a BRCA breast cancer gene mutation—it may be reasonable to consider this approach to prevention. But otherwise, Dr. Wapnir said, physicians should take care not to foster patients' fears by overemphasizing the dangers of DCIS and thus subjecting women to double mastectomy for a condition that may never become life-threatening.

Bottom line: For most DCIS patients, breast-conserving lumpectomy plus radiation (and tamoxifen, when appropriate) would be Dr. Wapnir's treatment of choice. In her study, fewer than 1% of the 2,612 participants who underwent lumpectomy, with or without radiation and/or tamoxifen, ended up dying as a result of breast cancer recurrence—a very reassuring statistic.

For help making treatment decisions: A second opinion is always a good idea. To find a National Cancer Institute-designated comprehensive cancer center, check *http://cancercenters. cancer.gov.*

Novel Drug Approach Shows Promise Against Breast Cancer

Sunil Verma, MD, medical oncologist, Sunnybrook Odette Cancer Centre, and assistant professor, University of Toronto.

Daniel Hayes, MD, clinical director, breast oncology program, and professor, department of internal medicine, University of Michigan Comprehensive Cancer Center, Ann Arbor, Michigan.

New England Journal of Medicine

Presentation, European Society for Medical Oncology meeting, Vienna, Austria.

Cancer treatment could one day be more effective and less difficult to endure if a new breast cancer therapy that offers high-precision targeting of tumors proves successful.

The new approach uses a unique three-pronged combination of agents that simultaneously attack cancer cells but prevent the release of chemotherapy until the drug reaches its specific target, said the authors of a recent study on the technique.

As a result, the treatment attacks cancer with greater power and effectiveness, yet less toxicity, so patients experience fewer side effects, such as nausea and vomiting, hair loss and infections, the study authors said.

The drug therapy, called T-DM1, appears to be effective in prolonging life and reducing tumor growth with less impact on the body's healthy cells in a significant proportion of women in the late stages of a specific kind of breast cancer known as HER2-positive. It was approved by the US Food and Drug Administration in early 2013.

T-DM1 is what's known as an "antibody-drug conjugate," designed to deliver potent anti-cancer drugs to tumors while limiting toxicity to healthy cells in the body.

"This is a new model for attacking cancer," explained study author Sunil Verma, MD, a medical oncologist at Sunnybrook Odette Cancer Centre and an assistant professor at the University of Toronto. "It opens up the doors for antibody-drug conjugates to be used potentially with early-stage breast cancers, lung, colon and colorectal cancers," he said.

Breast cancer is the most common female cancer in the United States. Up to 20% of women with breast cancer have tumors that have high levels of HER2, which is a protein that is involved in cell growth, differentiation and blood vessel formation, Dr. Verma said.

The experimental drug is made up of *trastuzumab* (Herceptin, an existing breast cancer drug) and the cancer-cell-destroying agent *emtansine* (DM1), plus a substance that prevents the drug from becoming active until it reaches the targeted cancer cells.

Trastuzumab delivers DM1 to the tumor where it kills cells overproducing HER2, Dr. Verma explained. By combining these components, T-DM1 targets cancer cells while minimizing harmful side effects, he said.

In the case of HER2-positive cancer, the antibody-drug conjugate includes Herceptin. But with other forms of cancer, the antibody could be different, depending on the genetic composition of the cancer, Dr. Verma explained.

STUDY DETAILS

In the study, a phase 3 trial, 991 patients with HER2-positive breast cancer were randomly assigned to receive either T-DM1 or standard therapy—the anti-cancer drugs *lapatinib* (Tykerb) and *cepecitabine* (Xeloda). All the participants had locally advanced or metastasized breast cancer previously treated with Herceptin and a taxane, a type of drug that blocks cell proliferation by stopping cell division, the study authors said.

Of the participants, 43.6% of those on T-DM1 had tumor shrinkage, while 30.8% of those on the other medications did. Mean progression-free survival was 9.6 months in the T-DM1 group compared with 6.4 months among those getting standard therapy.

"That's significant," said Dr. Verma. "And this improvement comes with less toxicity and fewer side effects."

The research was published online in the *New England Journal of Medicine* and presented at the European Society for Medical Oncology, in Vienna.

EXPERT COMMENTARY

Daniel Hayes, MD, clinical director of the breast oncology program at the University of Michigan Comprehensive Cancer Center, said the question is whether this three-pronged approach will be effective with other cancers.

"We don't know yet, but it's likely," he said. "But people will definitely benefit from this drug."

Dr. Hayes said that while science has made remarkable progress against breast cancer during the last 30 years, "we still have 30,000 to 40,000 women die of breast cancer every year. We need to do better."

info To learn more about breast cancer, visit the US National Cancer Institute Web site at *www.cancer.gov/cancertopics/types/breast*.

For Early Cancer, Lumpectomy Beats Mastectomy for Survival

E. Shelley Hwang, MD, MPH, chief, breast surgery, Duke Cancer Institute, Durham, North Carolina.

Wendy Woodward, MD, PhD, section chief for breast radiation oncology, and associate professor, University of Texas MD Anderson Cancer Center, Houston.

Laura Kruper, MD, MPH, director, Cooper Finkel Women's Health Center and co-director, breast oncology program, City of Hope Comprehensive Cancer Center, Duarte, California.

Cancer

Breast-conserving surgery for early stage breast cancers may result in better survival than mastectomy, according to a recent study.

For those with early stage breast cancer, "lumpectomy is just as effective if not more effective than mastectomy," said researcher E. Shelley

Hwang, MD, MPH, chief of breast surgery at Duke Cancer Institute in Durham, North Carolina.

In this procedure, just the tumor and some healthy tissue are removed, sparing the rest of the breast

"There are lots of women who think the more [treatment] they do, the better they will do," she said. "This refutes that."

The findings, published online in the journal *Cancer,* are especially strong for women over 50 with hormone-sensitive cancers, the researchers found.

Earlier research had also concluded that the two procedures are similarly effective, but Dr. Hwang's is a more "real-world" study.

STUDY DETAILS

Dr. Hwang's team looked at 14 years of data from the California Cancer Registry, following more than 112,000 women with early stage breast cancer (stages 1 or 2) between 1990 and 2004. Ages ranged from 39 to 80.

More than half (55%) had lumpectomy and radiation, while 45% had mastectomy (complete breast removal) alone.

Dr. Hwang compared lumpectomy and radiation with mastectomy alone, not mastectomy plus radiation. "We wanted to look at early stage disease, and those patients typically don't get radiation after mastectomy," she said.

The researchers tracked the women's progress for a median of more than nine years (half followed longer, half less). During that time, more than 31,000 women died, nearly 40% of them from breast cancer. The others died of other causes.

For the first three years after treatment, those who had a mastectomy had a higher risk of dying from heart disease and other ailments than those who had lumpectomy. This may indicate that the women who underwent lumpectomy were generally healthier, Dr. Hwang said.

Over the entire follow-up, those who underwent lumpectomy were more likely to survive the breast cancer.

"The group that benefited the most—who had the biggest difference in breast cancer survival—were those women over 50 with estrogen-receptor positive disease," Dr. Hwang said.

This means their cancer depends on estrogen to grow.

Among those women, the lumpectomy group had a 13% lower risk of death from breast cancer and a 19% lower risk of death from any cause than those who had a mastectomy.

Not all women with early stage breast cancers can have a lumpectomy, Dr. Hwang said. Among the exceptions are those whose cancers are too large, or those who have other cancers in the same breast.

RECENT TREND TOWARD MASTECTOMY

The percent of women with early breast cancers choosing a mastectomy has risen recently, after a dip in previous years. Dr. Hwang and others suspect that women who were told they could safely opt for lumpectomy were still afraid to try it.

The recent research, which was funded by the US National Cancer Institute, suggests that if a lumpectomy is possible, it may actually increase survival, Dr. Hwang said.

EXPERT REACTION

The findings may reverse the mastectomy trend, said Laura Kruper, MD, MPH, co-director of the breast oncology program at the City of Hope Comprehensive Cancer Center in Duarte, California, who was not involved in the study.

The study is scientifically sound in many ways, Dr. Kruper said. "They broke it down by year of diagnosis and by age category," she said.

"They looked at socioeconomic status, and they kept it early stage."

Wendy Woodward, MD, PhD, section chief for breast radiation oncology at the University of Texas MD Anderson Cancer Center in Houston, said that for women with early cancers, the study "clearly reiterates there is no detriment to cancer control in having a lumpectomy and radiation for breast-conserving surgery candidates."

But, Dr. Woodward added, "I am not sure the study convinces us that lumpectomy and radiation is better for breast cancer survival, but it may be."

CONCLUSION

The study was observational, Dr. Hwang stressed. It found a link or association but could not provide cause-and-effect proof that the breast-conserving treatment is more effective than mastectomy in early stage breast cancer.

Dr. Hwang believes the study does arm women with valuable information. However, "I don't want women who chose mastectomy to think they did the wrong thing," Dr. Hwang said. "At the end of the day, personal preference trumps everything else. I fully support the patient's options to choose the best treatment for themselves."

info To learn more about lumpectomy and other breast cancer surgery options, visit the Web site of the American Cancer Society, *www.cancer.org,* and search "breast cancer surgery."

No Long-Term Heart Risks From Breast Radiation

American Society for Radiation Oncology, news release.

A recent study allays concerns that early-stage breast cancer patients who receive radiation treatment might have a long-term increased risk for heart problems.

STUDY FINDINGS

The study included 50 stage 1 and stage 2 breast cancer patients who underwent either breast-conservation therapy using radiation (26 patients) or modified radical mastectomy alone (24 patients). Mastectomy is a type of surgery that involves removing the breast. Doctors consider both to be effective treatments, but they have different side effects.

More than 25 years after treatment, both groups had similar levels of heart function and rates of heart problems. For example, the rate of heart attack within 10 years of breast cancer diagnosis and treatment was 5.1% for breast-conservation patients and 5.7% for mastectomy patients.

The study was presented at the annual meeting of the American Society for Radiation Oncology in Boston.

IMPLICATIONS

"Over the past two decades, radiation therapy has become more precise and safer with modern techniques," said lead author Charles Simone II,

MD, a radiation oncologist at the Hospital of the University of Pennsylvania in Philadelphia.

"We are pleased to find that early-stage breast cancer patients treated with modern radiation therapy treatment planning techniques do not have an increased risk of long-term cardiac toxicity and that breast-conservation therapy with radiation should remain a standard treatment option," he added.

info For more information on treating breast cancer, visit the Web site of the US National Cancer Institute, *www.cancer.gov* and search "breast cancer treatment."

Multivitamins and Breast Cancer Recurrence

Heather Greenlee, ND, PhD, assistant professor of epidemiology at the Mailman School of Public Health and an assistant professor of medical oncology at the College of Physicians and Surgeons, both at Columbia University in New York City, and coauthor of a study on multivitamin/mineral use among breast cancer patients.

Any woman who has faced breast cancer wants to do all within her power to prevent a recurrence, of course, and now a recent study suggests a simple step that may be beneficial—taking multivitamin/mineral supplements.

Here's the scoop: 2,239 women who had been diagnosed with early-stage breast cancer between 1997 and 2000 completed questionnaires about their use of multivitamins before and after their diagnoses. By 2010, 363 of the women had had a breast cancer recurrence... 202 had died from the disease.

Results: Women who benefited most from taking multivitamin/mineral supplements were those who had radiation to treat their breast cancer. *Details...*

•**Among women who received radiation and chemotherapy,** long-term multivitamin/mineral users (those who took supplements three or more times weekly for at least 12 months in the five years prior to their initial diagnoses and continued after their diagnoses) were about 50% less likely to experience a breast cancer recurrence than women who never took multivitamins.

•**Among women who received radiation treatment only,** long-term users were about 50% less likely to experience a breast cancer recurrence...75% less likely to die from breast cancer...and 46% less likely to die from any cause than women who never took multivitamins.

Using a vitamin product without minerals did not make a difference in cancer recurrence or death rates, though the significance of this result was limited because few participants used that type of multivitamin.

The study does not prove that multivitamins prevent breast cancer recurrence or death—the apparent benefit could be due to the fact that women in the study who took vitamins typically followed a more healthful lifestyle overall. However, researchers noted that, despite the controversial viewpoint that antioxidant supplements may counteract cancer treatment, multivitamin/mineral use did not appear to have any negative effects for these breast cancer patients.

Acupuncture Might Ease Breast Cancer Fatigue

Alex Molassiotis, RN, PhD, professor, cancer and supportive care, School of Nursing, Midwifery and Social Work, University of Manchester, England.
Laura Kruper, MD, MSCE, director, Cooper-Finkel Women's Health Center, and chief, Breast Surgery Service, and assistant professor, division of surgical oncology, City of Hope Cancer Center, Duarte, California.
Journal of Clinical Oncology, online

Offering breast cancer patients a relatively short regimen of acupuncture alongside standard treatment can help alleviate some of the crippling fatigue that often accompanies the disease, according to a recent study.

The magnitude of help that patients undergoing acupuncture experienced was deemed by the study team to be "both statistically and clinically important."

"I am quite excited with these results," said study lead author Alex Molassiotis, RN, PhD, a professor of cancer and supportive care with the school of nursing, midwifery and social work at the University of Manchester in England. "They provide some good evidence of an effect of acupuncture for the management of a very debilitating and burdensome symptom for patients."

"The addition of a new treatment approach gives patients and health professionals more options," Dr. Molassiotis added, noting that the range of options specifically designed to address fatigue issues among cancer patients has been limited.

The study appeared in the *Journal of Clinical Oncology.*

FATIGUE AND BREAST CANCER

More than 40% of breast cancer patients experience significant cancer-related fatigue, according to background information included in the study. For some patients the problem may persist at a moderate or even severe level for years following the cessation of treatment.

RECENT STUDY

To explore the potential of acupuncture treatment, the authors focused on more than 300 women with breast cancer who were being cared for as outpatients at one of nine health care facilities across the United Kingdom.

At the time of the study, participants had been diagnosed with either stage 1, 2 or 3 breast cancer, and all had been experiencing at least moderate levels of fatigue for an average of 18 months. Most were white, and their average age was 53.

For a six-week period, all patients continued to receive the same care they had been receiving before the study, and all were additionally given an information booklet that tackled the issue of fatigue management.

However, more than 200 of the patients also were randomly chosen to undergo weekly 20-minute acupuncture sessions that involved needle placement at three different entry points.

By the end of the six-week period, those who had received acupuncture appeared to fare better on every measure of fatigue that the team assessed.

Specifically, those in the acupuncture group reported feeling notably better than the "usual-care" group in terms of overall fatigue, physical and mental fatigue, anxiety and depression levels, functional well-being, emotional well-being, social functioning, and overall quality of life.

POSSIBLE EXPLANATION

"Acupuncture is a complementary therapy that not only can have direct effects on the symptom experience of patients, but also...provide the opportunity [for] patients to be more involved with their symptom management and empower them more," Dr. Molassiotis said. "Patients also like 'natural' and 'traditional' approaches to health management."

"[However], we still do not understand how acupuncture may work to manage fatigue," he acknowledged. "Within the results may also be a so-called placebo effect, which is common in many complementary therapies. So in future work we need to look into objective and physiological outcome measures, too, although the patient-reported outcomes used in the current trial are equally very important."

EXPERT COMMENTARY

Laura Kruper, MD, MSCE, director of the Cooper-Finkel Women's Health Center and chief of the breast surgery service at the City of Hope Cancer Center in Duarte, California, described the British effort as both "well done" and "strong."

"Acupuncture has been used in a variety of settings within medicine, such as to control chemotherapy-related nausea, post-operative nausea, migraines and chronic pain," she said. "It is still not exactly known how acupuncture works, but that does not mean it does not have therapeutic benefit."

But, while noting that "many patients turn to complementary therapies to bridge the gaps that Western medicine does not fill," Dr. Kruper stressed the need "to ensure that these therapies are safe, effective and reliable."

"In the world of medicine, we rely on investigational studies to guide our treatment decisions so that we provide evidence-based medicine," she said. "Complementary therapies need to undergo the same rigorous tests that Western medicine does. This study was exemplary in that it was conducted with adherence to the principles of scientific method, and hopefully a study like this will be the first of many."

info For more information on acupuncture, visit the Web site of the US National Center for Complementary and Alternative Medicine, *http://nccam.nih.gov/health/acupuncture.*

High-Fat Dairy Foods Linked to Worse Survival After Breast Cancer

Candyce Kroenke, ScD, MPH, staff scientist, Kaiser Permanente Division of Research, Oakland, California.
Leslie Bernstein, PhD, professor, and director, division of cancer etiology, Beckman Research Institute, City of Hope Comprehensive Cancer Center, Duarte, California.
Journal of the National Cancer Institute

Eating high-fat dairy products may raise the risk of death years later for breast cancer survivors, according to a recent study that followed almost 1,900 women for up to nearly 15 years.

High-fat dairy includes foods such as whole milk, cream for coffee and butter. Low-fat dairy includes skim milk, nonfat milk, low-fat yogurt or nonfat yogurt.

Women "who ate one or more servings of high-fat dairy a day had a 49% higher risk of breast cancer death compared with those who ate up to half a serving a day," said study author Candyce Kroenke, ScD, MPH, a staff scientist with the Kaiser Permanente Division of Research in Oakland, California.

The women in the higher-intake group—eating one serving or more of high-fat dairy per day—had a 64% higher risk of dying from any cause compared with those who consumed little or none, she added.

The link was much weaker for high-fat dairy and a recurrence of the breast cancer, she said, and was not strong enough to be significant statistically.

BACKGROUND

Previous research by others, Dr. Kroenke said, has not found that a low-fat diet protects against dying from breast cancer.

She decided to explore high-fat dairy foods since they contain more estrogens—which tend to reside in fat—than do low-fat dairy foods. Breast cancers known as estrogen receptor-positive (ER-positive) are more common than ER-negative and require estrogen to grow.

RECENT STUDY

The women in the recent study were diagnosed with early breast cancer between 1997 and 2000. They were patients at Kaiser Permanente in California or were registered with the Utah Cancer Registry.

Women supplied information about their diet at the study start. Most also gave information on diet six years later.

In all, 349 women had a cancer recurrence over the follow-up period. Of the 372 women who died during that time, 189 deaths (about half) were due to breast cancer.

The researchers divided the women into three groups, from low to high intake of high-fat dairy foods. The lowest group ate less than a daily half-serving (or none) of high-fat dairy. The highest group had a serving a day or more.

One limitation, Dr. Kroenke said, is the reliance on self-reported food records, subject to mistakes as no one remembers perfectly. So the link between high-fat dairy and death risk may be underestimated, she said.

Dr. Kroenke accounted for other factors that might play a role in cancer recurrence and death risk, such as stage of cancer at diagnosis, education level and other diet habits.

There were not enough women in the study to evaluate if the links between high-fat dairy and risk of death held for women with both ER-positive and ER-negative cancers, she said.

"I would expect to find a stronger link for ER-positive," she said.

The study, supported by the US National Cancer Institute, was published in the *Journal of the National Cancer Institute*.

EXPERT COMMENTARY

"This is really one of the early studies of this topic," said Leslie Bernstein, PhD, director of the division of cancer etiology in the Beckman Research Institute at the City of Hope Comprehensive Cancer Center, in Duarte, California. She was not involved with the recent study.

"It's an interesting finding," she said. But the researchers found an association, she said, not a cause-and-effect link. "The women were not [randomly assigned] to getting different diets."

Other factors could have played a part. For instance, eating patterns may be different right after diagnosis or treatment compared with earlier or later, she said.

The strongest result is for high-fat dairy and risk of death from other causes, she said.

High-fat diets can cause weight gain, a risk factor for heart disease.

ADVICE

Meanwhile, it wouldn't hurt to eat low-fat dairy, Dr. Bernstein said.

"If women have breast cancer and are trying to reduce their estrogen exposure, shifting away from high-fat dairy to lower-fat dairy would make sense," Dr. Kroenke said.

info To learn more about diet and cancer risk, visit the American Cancer Society Web site, *www.cancer.org,* and search "diet and activity factors for certain cancers."

More Women Consider Gene Test After Angelina Jolie Revelation

Debbie Saslow, PhD, director, breast and gynecologic cancer, American Cancer Society, Atlanta.
Harris Interactive/HealthDay poll, July 16-18, 2013

After hearing about film star Angelina Jolie's double mastectomy, a growing number of US women now say they may ask their doctors whether the same preventive measure is right for them, according to a Harris Interactive/HealthDay poll.

The survey of nearly 1,100 US women found that almost all women (86%) had heard of Jolie's double mastectomy. And 5% of those women said they would seek medical advice on having a preventive mastectomy or ovary removal because of Jolie's decision.

That may seem like a small percentage, but it translates to about 6 million women nationwide, noted Harris Poll chairman Humphrey Taylor.

Back in May 2013, Jolie announced that she had undergone a double mastectomy and also planned to have her ovaries removed, after learning that she carried a gene mutation linked to breast and ovarian cancers.

Jolie, 38, carries a mutation in a gene called BRCA1. According to the American Cancer Society, defects in that gene and another, called BRCA2, substantially raise a woman's lifetime risks of breast and ovarian cancers—to a roughly 60% chance of developing breast cancer, and a 15 to 40% risk of ovarian cancer.

By comparison, the average US woman has a 12% chance of being diagnosed with breast cancer over her lifetime, and only a 1.4% risk of ovarian cancer.

Experts stress that most breast cancers are not inherited, and gene mutations—mainly in the BRCA genes—account for only about 5 to 10% of all breast cancers.

And while many women in the new survey might have been interested in BRCA gene testing, most do not need it, experts said (see page 60 for more information).

"Genetic testing is only recommended for women at high risk," said Debbie Saslow, PhD, director of breast and gynecologic cancer for the American Cancer Society in Atlanta.

"High risk" involves a number of factors, Dr. Saslow said, including the age at which relatives were diagnosed.

For example, "if your grandmother was diagnosed with breast cancer at the age of 70, that's not a reason to have genetic testing," she said.

Certain other family history patterns, though, are linked to a higher risk of carrying a cancer-linked BRCA mutation. Some of those include having two first-degree relatives with breast cancer, one of whom was diagnosed at age 50 or younger; a first-degree relative with cancer in both breasts; or two or more relatives with ovarian cancer at any age.

Your doctor, Dr. Saslow said, should take a thorough family history—which means you need to know about any breast or ovarian cancers on both sides of your family. If that raises a red flag, your doctor should refer you to a genetic counselor to see if BRCA testing is a good idea, Dr. Saslow said.

Cancer Breakthroughs

Little-Known Risk Factors for Cancer

Believe it or not, your bedside alarm clock —and even your morning glass of orange juice—could possibly increase your risk for cancer.

Scientists in many parts of the world are now making intriguing new discoveries about such surprising and little-known factors that may increase your likelihood of developing, or dying from, cancer.

For example...

FRUIT JUICE

Fruit is loaded with cancer-preventing antioxidants and fiber. But when you remove the fiber and drink the juice, which is high in sugar, you trigger greater spikes in blood sugar (glucose) and the glucose-regulating hormone insulin. High levels of glucose and insulin, acting as a growth stimulant, can promote more rapid cellular growth and division, which may increase one's risk of developing cancer or promote existing disease.

Scientific evidence: In a study of nearly 1,800 people, those who drank the most fruit juice (more than three glasses a day) were 74% more likely to develop colorectal cancer than those who drank the least, reported researchers in the October 2011 issue of the *Journal of the American Dietetic Association.*

Cancer self-defense: This study, which was based on responses to food-frequency questionnaires, is not definitive, but according to Keith Block, MD, the evidence is strong enough to advise people to avoid fruit juice and eat the whole fruit instead. If you don't want to give up fruit juice, mix three ounces of pure fruit juice

---

Keith I. Block, MD, medical director of the Block Center for Integrative Cancer Treatment in Skokie, Illinois, which combines advanced conventional medicine with research-based complementary therapies. He is founding editor-in-chief of *Integrative Cancer Therapies,* a peer-reviewed journal. He is author of *Life Over Cancer* (Bantam). *www.blockmd.com*

with three ounces of water. Drink no more than two to three servings of the diluted fruit juice mixture a day.

Also avoid other fast-digesting, glucose-spiking carbohydrates (such as sugar and white flour). Emphasize foods that stabilize blood sugar and insulin, such as whole grains, legumes and vegetables. If you regularly eat pasta, cook it al dente (to minimize blood sugar increases). Choose whole-wheat pasta or brown rice pasta.

LIGHT AT NIGHT

Fascinating research is now being conducted on possible cancer risks associated with a phenomenon known as "light at night" (LAN)—that is, any type of light exposure at night…even from a bedside alarm clock.

Research on the health effects of light exposure began more than two decades ago when scientists first identified an increased risk for breast, prostate, colorectal and other cancers in night-shift workers. Researchers theorize that night-shift work disrupts the body's natural circadian rhythm of daytime activity and nighttime rest, leading to imbalances in the hormones melatonin, estrogen and cortisol, which may play a role in triggering cancer. Now the research extends far beyond night-shift work.

Scientific evidence: Researchers at the University of Haifa in Israel measured light levels in the "sleeping habitats" of 1,679 women. They found that those with the highest "bedroom-light intensity" had a 22% higher risk for breast cancer. A 2009 study discovered that risk for prostate cancer increased as the exposure to LAN increased.

To help protect yourself…

•**Use an alarm clock with a red light.** An alarm clock that's too close to your head and illuminated with any color other than red generates light in the blue spectrum, which may be associated with disruption in sleep and cut the production of melatonin, the circadian-regulating hormone.

In addition, if you need a light to help you find your way to the bathroom, use a dim nightlight. Avoid direct exposure to light.

Helpful: Use a sleep "mask" to cover your eyes when you're sleeping.

HEAVY TRAFFIC

It's logical that breathing air pollution from traffic might increase the risk for lung cancer.

Recent unexpected finding: Research published in various peer-reviewed journals in the last year links air pollution from traffic to a higher risk for ovarian, cervical, brain and stomach cancers. Researchers are still studying the association, but it may be due to volatile organic compounds (VOCs), polycyclic aromatic hydrocarbons and other toxic substances in car exhaust that cause cellular damage not just in the lungs but throughout the body. *To avoid exposure to pollution from automobiles…*

•**When driving, maintain a reasonable distance from the car in front of you.** Use the rule of thumb from safety experts—at least one car length for every 10 miles per hour (mph) of speed. So if you're driving 60 mph, there should be at least six car lengths between your car and the one in front of you. And in stop-and-go traffic or at a stoplight, leave one car length of space between your car and the one in front of you.

•**Turn on the air-recirculation system in your car**—and leave it on when you are in heavier traffic. This helps ensure that no outdoor air is circulating in your car.

•**If you live near a busy road, close your home's windows during peak traffic hours** and place one or two air filters in appropriate locations in your home.

•**Avoid driving, bicycling or walking in or near rush-hour traffic whenever possible.**

•**Wear a breathing mask,** often used by motorists, joggers and cyclists to filter out noxious odors and fumes, if you can't avoid areas with high levels of pollution from traffic.

Examples: Filt-R Reusable Neoprene Commuter Pollution Mask (about $30) and Respro Techno Face Mask (about $40)—both are available online. Or, if you can't wear a mask, breathe through your nose instead of your mouth. Breathing through the nose helps filter out particles that get trapped in the mucous membranes. When breathing through your mouth, pollutants may directly enter the lungs.

•**Eat an antioxidant-rich diet** with leafy greens, melons and dark-colored fruits such as plums and berries (for example, blueberries and blackberries)—these protect your body's cells from harmful pollutants.

•**Check the Web site *www.airnow.gov* for air quality in your area,** and avoid going outside when the air-quality index is higher than the "moderate" range.

VITAMIN E

Research investigating vitamin E's effect on prostate cancer has been mixed. At one time, it was reported that vitamin E could reduce men's risk for prostate cancer.

However, a recent study published in *The Journal of the American Medical Association,* which analyzed existing data, found that men who took vitamin E alone had a 17% increase in prostate cancer compared with men who took a placebo. Men who took vitamin E and selenium (a supplement with cancer-suppressing properties) had no increased risk for prostate cancer.

What's now been discovered: In the research linking vitamin E use to increased prostate cancer risk, men took a form of vitamin E called alpha-tocopherol, which has several drawbacks.

For example, it is synthetic (not natural), and it does not include the vitamin's seven other compounds—three tocopherols (gamma, beta and delta) and four tocotrienols.

Many experts now think that gamma-tocopherol—not alpha-tocopherol, which was shown in research to increase prostate cancer risk—is the type of vitamin E with the greatest cancer-fighting activity.

Cancer self-defense: If you take vitamin E, look for a supplement that contains mixed tocopherols (including gamma-tocopherol) and tocotrienols.

All people, especially those with a history of cancer, should consult a doctor who is experienced in nutrition and the use of dietary supplements before starting a supplement regimen. Also, be sure to make a varied antioxidant-rich diet part of your cancer-fighting defense.

Medical Conditions That Can Cause Cancer— How to Lower Your Risk

Lynne Eldridge, MD, medical manager of the Lung Cancer site for About.com and a former clinical preceptor at the University of Minnesota Medical School in Minneapolis. Dr. Eldridge practiced family medicine for 15 years and now devotes herself full time to researching and speaking on cancer prevention. She is author of *Avoiding Cancer One Day at a Time* (Beaver's Pond).

If you don't have any of the well-known risk factors for cancer, including smoking, a family history of cancer or long-term exposure to a carcinogen such as asbestos, you may think that your risk for the disease is average or even less than average.

What you may not realize: Although most of the cancer predispositions (genetic, lifestyle and environmental factors that increase risk for the disease) are commonly known, there are several medical conditions that also can increase your risk.

Unfortunately, many primary-care physicians do not link these conditions to cancer. As a result, they fail to prescribe the tests and treatments that could keep cancer at bay or reduce the condition's cancer-causing potential. *Medical conditions that increase your risk for cancer...*

1. Diabetes. The high blood sugar levels that occur with type 2 diabetes predispose you to heart attack, stroke, nerve pain, blindness, kidney failure, a need for amputation—and cancer.

Recent research: For every 1% increase in HbA1c—a measurement of blood sugar levels over the previous three months—there is an 18% increase in the risk for cancer, according to a study published in *Current Diabetes Reports.*

Other current studies have linked type 2 diabetes to a 94% increased risk for pancreatic cancer...a 38% increased risk for colon cancer...a 15% to 20% higher risk for postmenopausal breast cancer...and a 20% higher risk for blood cancers such as non-Hodgkin's lymphoma and leukemia.

What to do: If you have type 2 diabetes, make sure your primary-care physician orders regular screening tests for cancer, such as colonoscopy and mammogram.

Screening for pancreatic cancer is not widely available, but some of the larger cancer centers (such as the H. Lee Moffitt Cancer Center & Research Institute in Tampa, Florida, and the Mayo Clinic in Rochester, Minnesota) offer it to high-risk individuals. This typically includes people with long-standing diabetes (more than 20 years) and/or a family history of pancreatic cancer. The test involves an ultrasound of both the stomach and small intestine, where telltale signs of pancreatic cancer can be detected.

Also work with your doctor to minimize the cancer-promoting effects of diabetes. For example, control blood sugar levels through a diet that emphasizes slow-digesting foods that don't create spikes in blood sugar levels, such as vegetables and beans...get regular exercise—for example, 30 minutes of walking five or six days a week...and consider medical interventions, such as use of the diabetes drug *metformin* (Glucophage).

2. Helicobacter pylori infection. This bacterial infection of the lining of the stomach can cause stomach inflammation (gastritis) and ulcers in the stomach or upper small intestine. It also causes most stomach cancers.

Startling statistic: An infection with H. pylori triggers a 10-fold increase in your predisposition to stomach cancer. Getting treatment for an H. pylori infection lowers your risk for stomach cancer by 35% but does not eliminate the risk—perhaps due to lingering inflammation. What's most important is to avoid other inflammation-causing habits such as smoking.

What to do: If you are diagnosed with gastritis or a stomach or intestinal ulcer, ask your doctor to check for an H. pylori infection—and to treat it with antibiotics if it is detected. Research shows that a fecal analysis is the most accurate way to detect H. pylori.

3. "Iron overload" disease. This hereditary condition (known technically as hemochromatosis) affects one out of every 200 people, causing them to absorb and store too much dietary iron—in the liver, heart, joints and pancreas. Hemochromatosis also increases a person's risk for cancer (particularly liver cancer).

Stress Fuels Cancer Spread

In laboratory studies, stress was shown to increase the spread (metastasis) of breast cancer cells to the bone. Stress-reducing therapies appear to decrease levels of a molecule that promotes cell migration (for more on cancer and stress management, see page 85).

PLOS Biology

Recent research: In a study of more than 8,000 people reported in the *Journal of Internal Medicine,* iron overload increased the risk for any cancer nearly fourfold.

Iron overload should be suspected if you have or had a relative (including a second-degree relative such as a grandparent) with the condition...you have a family history of early heart disease (beginning at age 50 or earlier)... you have a family history of cirrhosis without obvious reasons such as alcoholism or hepatitis...or you have the symptoms of hemochromatosis (joint pain, fatigue, abdominal pain and a bronze appearance to the skin).

What to do: Ask your doctor for a serum ferritin test. If the test confirms iron overload, your doctor can simply and quickly correct the problem with regular bloodletting—a pint of blood once or twice per week until iron levels return to normal, and then three to four times per year.

4. Inflammatory bowel disease (IBD). This autoimmune disease attacks the lining of the intestine, causing symptoms such as abdominal cramping and bloating, bloody diarrhea and urgent bowel movements. The disease takes two main forms—ulcerative colitis (affecting the colon) and Crohn's disease (usually affecting the small intestine). Both forms predispose you to colon cancer.

Recent research: People age 67 and older with ulcerative colitis have a 93% higher risk for colorectal cancer...people of the same age group with Crohn's disease have a 45% higher risk, according to a 2011 study reported in *Digestive Diseases and Sciences.*

Problem: IBD can come and go in flare-ups that occur only once every five or 10 years. This can lead your primary-care physician to underestimate the severity of the problem and your risk for colon cancer.

What to do: IBD usually is diagnosed between the ages of 15 and 30. If you have ulcerative colitis that involves the entire colon, you should have your first colonoscopy eight years after diagnosis or at the standard age of 50 (whichever comes first) and then have another every one to two years thereafter.

If you have ulcerative colitis that involves only the left colon (which represents a somewhat smaller cancer risk than when the entire colon is affected) or Crohn's disease, you should receive your first colonoscopy 12 to 15 years after your diagnosis or at age 50 and then another every one to two years thereafter.

5. Polyps detected in a relative. Most people think that a hereditary predisposition to colon cancer means that you have a first-degree relative (parent, sibling or child) who was diagnosed with the disease.

Surprising fact: If you have a first-degree relative who had a colonoscopy that detected an adenomatous polyp (adenoma)—a type of growth that can turn into cancer within two to five years—you also have a predisposition to colon cancer.

Recent research: Having a first-degree relative with an adenoma appears to make you four times more likely to develop colorectal cancer, according to a report in *Annals of Internal Medicine.*

What to do: Have a first colonoscopy 10 years earlier than the age at which your relative's adenoma was detected and repeat it every five to 10 years (depending on results). That should give plenty of time to detect (and remove) an adenoma so it can never turn into cancer.

Interesting: Some cancer centers also advise earlier screening if a second-degree relative, such as a grandparent, had colon cancer.

Good Buzz: Coffee Helps Protect Against Endometrial Cancer

Youjin Je, ScD, nutrition researcher in the department of nutrition at Harvard School of Public Health in Boston and leader of a meta-analysis on coffee and endometrial cancer risk published in *International Journal of Cancer.*

Java lovers, rejoice—recent research reveals yet another potential health perk from drinking coffee. We already have evidence that coffee can reduce the risk for diabetes, stroke and Parkinson's disease, and perhaps for Alzheimer's, depression and basal cell skin cancer, too. And now it appears that coffee also reduces a woman's odds of getting cancer of the endometrium (uterine lining), the most common gynecologic cancer in the US.

What we all want to know: How much joe would we need to drink to help guard against endometrial cancer? To get the answer, Harvard researchers analyzed data from 16 studies involving a total of 369,004 women (including 6,628 endometrial cancer patients) who were followed for up to 26 years.

Findings: Women who drank the most coffee—an average of three to four cups daily—were 29% less likely to get endometrial cancer than women who drank little or no coffee. Overall, each eight-ounce cup of coffee consumed per day reduced a woman's endometrial cancer risk by 8%. (These stats were for women who drank regular coffee or regular as well as decaf…there was not enough data on decaf alone to draw firm conclusions about its effects on endometrial cancer risk.)

Drink think: Coffee is an excellent source of chlorogenic acid, an antioxidant that helps prevent the damage to cells' DNA that triggers the cancer process. Also, caffeine and/or other bioactive compounds in coffee may have favorable effects on hormones, including estrogen and insulin, thus inhibiting cancer cell growth.

New Test Will Reduce Cancer Biopsies

A new saliva test to diagnose oral cancer is in clinical trials. If effective, dentists will be able to administer—important because most patients with warning signs (white growths and/or lesions in the mouth) do *not* have cancer. An accurate saliva test could reduce unnecessary biopsies. Oral cancer is the world's sixth most common cancer.

Michigan State University.

Downside: For some people, excess caffeine can cause irritability, anxiety, restlessness, headaches, sleep problems and/or abnormal heart rhythms.

Is black best? This study did not specifically assess the effects of drinking coffee black versus adding cream and/or sugar. But reseachers cautioned that consuming lots of cream or sugar could contribute to insulin resistance and excess weight gain—both of which can increase endometrial cancer risk.

Bottom line: Go ahead and enjoy your java (provided the caffeine doesn't bother you), but don't go too light or too sweet.

Lifesaving Screening for Ex-Smokers

Christine D. Berg, MD, chief of the Early Detection Research Group in the Division of Cancer Prevention at the National Cancer Institute in Bethesda, Maryland, and project officer for the National Lung Screening Trial.

Maybe you started as a teen, lighting up to be cool—then got hooked. Hopefully, you put cigarettes aside years ago or are working hard to kick the habit now. But if you have a history of smoking (or if someone you love does), you'll want to know about a painless screening test that significantly reduces the odds of dying from lung cancer. It's a type of computed tomography (CT) scan called a low-dose helical CT (aka spiral CT) of the chest.

Background: The deadliest malignancy, lung cancer claims more lives than breast, ovarian, colon and prostate cancers combined. Lung cancer causes no symptoms in its earliest and most curable stages, and by the time people develop telltale signs (chest pain, wheezing, coughing up blood), it's usually too late. The five-year survival rate for all lung cancer patients is less than 16%...and previous attempts to develop an early-detection test failed to reduce the death rate.

Encouraging: The recent National Lung Screening Trial (NLST) involved 53,454 symptom-free former or current heavy smokers ages 55 to 74. Participants underwent three annual screenings using either standard chest X-ray (which produces a single image in which anatomic structures of the chest overlie each other)...or helical CT (in which a CT scanner rotates around the person for seven to 15 seconds, producing multiple detailed images). Participants were followed for an average of 6.5 years from the first screening, during which time 442 people in the X-ray group and 354 in the CT group died of lung cancer.

Translation: Low-dose helical CT screening reduced lung cancer death risk by 20%.

Explanation: A screening test does not reduce a person's odds of getting lung cancer, of course. What a helical CT can do is find lung abnormalities when they are still so small that they can be completely removed surgically, said Christine D. Berg, MD, chief of the Early Detection Research Group in the Division of Cancer Prevention at the National Cancer Institute and NLST project officer.

Risks: Though the radiation exposure from a low-dose helical CT is significantly less than from a regular diagnostic chest CT, it is about 30 times higher than from a single-view chest X-ray. Another concern is the high rate of false-positive results (37% with helical CT versus 14% with X-ray), which can lead to unnecessary testing and anxiety.

Who should consider testing? Dr. Berg stated that screening with low-dose helical CT is reasonable for anyone between ages 55 and 74 who meets the NLST entry criterion of at least 30 "pack-years." (To calculate your pack-years, multiply the average number of packs smoked per day by the number of years you smoked.) Research is being done to determine whether the test's benefits outweigh its potential harms for younger individuals and/or those with less of a smoking history, such as 20 pack-years. The test is not appropriate for people with a history of light smoking or no smoking, even if they have a family history of lung cancer.

Low-dose helical CT scans of the chest are available at most imaging facilities that provide CTs. Cost ranges from about $350 to $2,000, depending on location. At present, insurance generally does not cover helical CT lung cancer screening—though Dr. Berg stated that this may change within the next few years as the US Preventive Services Task Force weighs in based on the new evidence of the test's benefits.

Easier Colonoscopy Preparation

A new colon-prep solution consists of only two five-ounce servings—much less than the two to four liters of salty-tasting fluid that patients usually drink before a colonoscopy. Patients take the first five-ounce dose of the new prep, Prepopik, the evening before the procedure, and the other five ounces five hours before the colonoscopy. Each dose is followed by several eight-ounce servings of a clear liquid such as water or clear broth to prevent electrolyte imbalances. Ask your doctor whether the new preparation is appropriate for you.

Mayo Clinic Health Letter. www.healthletter.mayo clinic.com

How Often Do You Need a Colonoscopy?

Durado Brooks, MD, director, colorectal cancer, American Cancer Society, Atlanta.
Journal of Clinical Oncology, online

People who have had a colonoscopy during which a high-risk potentially cancerous polyp was removed may not need another colonoscopy for five years, German researchers report.

If this suggestion were to be adopted, it would be a change from the current recommendation in the United States, which calls for another colonoscopy three years after a high-risk polyp —one that is likely to become cancerous—is removed.

"This is a case control study, so they didn't follow a group of individuals over time to assess the impact of polyp removal," said Durado Brooks, MD, director of prostate and colorectal cancers at the American Cancer Society.

That kind of patient follow-up, however, did take place in the study that established the current US recommendations for colonoscopy, he noted.

In addition, while the German study looks at the odds of cancer developing over time, the older study that set the US guidelines looked at the odds of a new polyp developing, Dr. Brooks said.

"The time frames they are recommending are something that might be considered, but you cannot make changes in current guidelines based on this study," he said.

The report was published online in the *Journal of Clinical Oncology*.

STUDY DETAILS

For the recent study, a team lead by Dr. Hermann Brenner, at the German Cancer Research Center, in Heidelberg, looked at medical records of more than 2,500 people who had a cancerous polyp removed and compared them with nearly 1,800 people without such polyps.

They compared surveillance intervals of less than three years, three to five years, and six to 10 years before receiving another colonoscopy.

Looking at the risk of finding colorectal cancer, even for those with high-risk polyps, "strong, statistically significant risk reduction by 60% was seen for the less-than-three-years time window and by 50% for the three-to-five-years time window," the researchers wrote.

This was true for men, women, young and old, they added.

IMPLICATIONS

Their results suggest that surveillance colonoscopy could take place five to 10 years after the low-risk polyp was found and removed, and possibly also be prolonged to five years for high-risk polyps, the researchers concluded.

If new polyps aren't found, then another colonoscopy isn't needed for 10 years, he said.

The 10-year span between colonoscopies is the recommendation for anyone who has a normal colonoscopy, Dr. Brooks added.

The advantage of extending the time between colonoscopies from three to five years in patients with high-risk polyps is the use of resources, he said.

The problem is that doctors don't follow the current guidelines.

"If we could get clinicians just to follow the current recommendations we could expand our resources considerably," Dr. Brooks said. "Right now far too many people are getting colonoscopies done at intervals that are not recommended by anyone's guidelines."

Some people who have had high-risk polyps get a colonoscopy every year. Many people who have normal colonoscopies get another after five years, Dr. Brooks said.

All the evidence shows that colonoscopies every five years is much too frequent, he said.

"We are doing far too many colonoscopies on people who are in the system, but there are at least 40% of adults at risk who have never been screened," Dr. Brooks said. "If you're 50 and older and never been screened—get screened."

info For more information about colon cancer, visit the American Cancer Society at its Web site, *http://www.cancer.org/cancer/colon andrectumcancer/index.*

New DNA-Based Blood Test Spots Cancer

Science Translational Medicine

A recent study raises the possibility of a DNA-based blood test that doctors could routinely use to determine whether a patient has cancer.

There are many caveats. The research is preliminary, and the test is not cheap. Even if it does detect cancer, the test—like the one currently used to detect prostate cancer—could raise big questions about how to deal with the results.

Even so, a genetic test for cancer would be a major advance, experts say.

"This would be a way of detecting cancers earlier, and to tell you the level of cancer as you're going through the therapy," said Victor Velculescu, MD, codirector of the Cancer Biology Program at Johns Hopkins Kimmel Cancer Center in Baltimore.

Several blood tests detect the body's reaction to cancer, and others are being developed, including one that may spot stray cancer cells in the blood. This test is unique because it examines the blood for signs of DNA that's spilled out of cancerous cells into the bloodstream when they die, Dr. Velculescu explained.

In the study, researchers found that the test picked up differences in 10 patients with breast or colorectal cancer when compared with 10 healthy patients. The test didn't falsely suggest any of the healthy patients had cancer, he added.

"We're looking at the entire genome and can apply the test to any cancer type or individual cancer," Dr. Velculescu said.

The test costs hundreds of thousands of dollars, but Dr. Velculescu expects the price would eventually drop.

In the future, he said, the test could be performed at regular intervals and detect cancer without requiring a biopsy. For now, however, the test needs to undergo more research.

EXPERT COMMENT

If the test detects signs of cancer, then what? A blood screening test for prostate cancer, known as the PSA test, is a topic of hot debate because some patients may undergo unnecessary treatment.

Still, Otis Brawley, MD, chief medical officer and executive vice president of the American Cancer Society, said he can foresee a cancer screening blood test becoming a routine part of medicine, although it may take 20 years or more to get there.

In some cases, Dr. Brawley said, doctors could potentially choose to use the screening test to evaluate the extent of cancer in a patient instead of performing a biopsy. For example, in certain types of lung cancer, a biopsy can be dangerous because a needle is inserted into the lung, he noted.

For now, Dr. Brawley said, the test is "extremely expensive and extremely preliminary, and it's probably several years before anybody's going to be able to buy this."

The study appears in the journal *Science Translational Medicine.*

Best Ways to Beat Cancer Now

Isaac Eliaz, MD, integrative physician and medical director of the Amitabha Medical Clinic & Healing Center in Santa Rosa, California, an integrative health center specializing in cancer and chronic conditions. Dr. Eliaz is a licensed acupuncturist and homeopath and an expert in mind/body medicine. *www.dreliaz.org*

Radiation, chemotherapy and surgery are widely known to be the main treatments for cancer. But to fight the disease more effectively and to maximize the odds of recovery, doctors and patients are increasingly turning to integrative oncology.

This approach combines the conventional treatments mentioned above with natural or alternative treatments that can minimize the complications and side effects from cancer treatments, help relieve pain and improve overall health, increasing chance of survival.

Isaac Eliaz, an integrative physician, shared integrative treatments that scientific studies and his clinical experience show are likely to be effective for a wide range of cancer patients...

EXERCISE

Research shows that cancer patients who walked three to five hours a week improved their outcomes, compared with cancer patients who didn't exercise.

My advice: Try to exercise every day. Walking is usually best—it's easy to do on a regular basis and is proven to work. Other helpful exercises include yoga, tai chi and qi gong, all of which stretch and strengthen muscles, relax the body and even improve immunity.

Caution: Too much strenuous exercise can produce inflammation, thought to be a factor in cancer development, and cause wear and tear on the body. Do not exercise to the point of exhaustion.

STRESS MANAGEMENT

Stress management is essential for cancer patients—stress, anxiety and even pessimism weaken immunity and may spark inflammation, possibly spurring the progression and aggressiveness of cancer. In my clinical experience, cancer patients who practice stress management often have better outcomes than those who don't.

Recent finding: Women with breast cancer who practiced mindfulness-based stress reduction, including meditation, indicated that they were better able to cope with stress, anxiety and panic, were more confident and had improved personal relationships, reported researchers in *Complementary Therapies in Clinical Practice.*

My advice: Regular meditation—even 10 minutes a day—is a proven stress-reduction technique with results comparable to or better than antidepressants and antianxiety medications. Strong social support and social networking also can reduce stress and improve outcomes in cancer patients. Creative outlets—such as drawing or painting, writing, playing an instrument and dancing—also help ease stress and improve emotional well-being.

DIET

Dietary needs vary from patient to patient. For example, some cancer patients may require a high-protein diet (those who are weak), while others may need a diet emphasizing plant foods (those who are overweight). *But all cancer patients should follow these essential basics...*

A low-glycemic diet that minimizes or eliminates refined carbohydrates such as sugar and white flour, both of which fuel inflammation and may promote the growth and aggressiveness of tumors...and avoidance of processed trans fats and fried foods, which spur inflammation and damage DNA. Also, eat as much organically grown food as possible—it's free of synthetic pesticides, many of which are linked to cancer in humans...and drink eight eight-ounce glasses of filtered water every day to stay hydrated and eliminate toxins.

SUPPLEMENTS

Here are four supplements that research and my own clinical experience confirm are uniquely effective for cancer—all are available at health-food stores, well-tolerated and safe for adults, the elderly and children...*

•**Honokiol.** This extract from the bark of the magnolia tree interferes with the growth and spread of cancer and can increase the effectiveness of chemotherapy and radiation. Studies have shown that honokiol may be useful for many types of cancer, including leukemia and cancer of the brain, breast, bone, colon, pancreas, skin and stomach.

•**Artemisinin.** The herb *Artemisia annua* (commonly called *sweet wormwood*) is as powerful as quinine in treating malaria. Recent research shows that artemisinin, a compound derived from the herb, has strong anticancer effects, reducing tumor size and blocking metastases.

•**Modified citrus pectin (MCP).** This substance, derived from citrus fruit peels and apples, controls *galectin-3,* a protein linked to cancer formation and metastases. MCP also boosts the immune system and safely removes heavy metals and other toxins from the body.

Recent research: Combining MCP with chemotherapy was more effective in killing prostate cancer cells than chemotherapy alone, reported researchers in *Cell Biology International.*

•**Mushroom extracts.** Extracts from medicinal mushrooms such as coriolus, reishi, cordyceps, maitake and shiitake can boost immunity...improve digestion...increase energy ...and help prevent side effects from chemotherapy and radiation as well as improve their effectiveness.

Standout scientific evidence: In a study of patients who had undergone surgery for liver cancer, those who took active hexose correlated compound (AHCC), an extract of shiitake, had a longer time to recurrence and a higher survival rate.

*Consult an integrative physician before taking any of these supplements. He/she can advise you on the best supplements for your cancer, dosage and possible side effects. Inform your doctor of all drugs/supplements you are taking to avoid possible interactions.

ACUPUNCTURE

Acupuncture can help cancer patients in many ways, including providing relief from pain and nausea. It also has been shown to reduce inflammation and boost immune function.

Recent research: In an analysis of 15 studies on acupuncture published in *Supportive Care in Cancer,* researchers found that combining acupuncture with drug therapy was 36% more effective in relieving pain in cancer patients than drug therapy alone.

To find an integrative physician: Online, go to Cancer Decisions (*www.cancerdecisions. com*), and click on "Professional Associates"...or go to the Society for Integrative Oncology (*www. integrativeonc.org*).

Less-Invasive Surgery Better for Esophageal Cancer

Jonathan E. Aviv, MD, FACS, clinical director, Voice and Swallowing Center of ENT and Allergy Associates and clinical professor, otolaryngology, Mount Sinai Medical Center, New York City.
The Lancet, news release

Besides being easier on the body, minimally invasive surgery to remove the esophagus of patients with esophageal cancer can also greatly reduce the risk of lung infection compared with traditional open surgery, a recent study finds.

Dutch researchers also found that patients who undergo this less-invasive procedure have much shorter hospital stays and a better short-term quality of life than those who have open surgery, which requires cutting through a patient's chest.

Removal of part of or the entire esophagus (a procedure called esophagectomy) is the mainstay of esophageal cancer treatment. This study compared open esophagectomy and minimally invasive esophagectomy, which uses a tiny scope and two small incisions rather than large cuts typical of traditional surgery.

What to Ask Your Doctor Before a Colonoscopy

Before scheduling a colonoscopy, ask the doctor for his/her adenoma detection rate (ADR).

Choose a doctor with an ADR of at least 20%—that is, the doctor should be able to detect adenomas (precancerous polyps) in one of five patients getting a colonoscopy (the current recommended national benchmark). Even higher ADRs may become standard with the use of high-definition scopes and training to detect very subtle and flat polyps.

Michael Wallace, MD, MPH, professor of medicine, division of gastroenterology and hepatology, Mayo Clinic, Jacksonville, Florida.

The minimally invasive procedure was first used two decades ago. According to the American Cancer Society, it requires a highly skilled surgeon and at this point in time is only used with small cancers. This is the first study to compare minimally invasive with open esophagectomy, according to Miguel Cuesta, researcher at the VU University Medical Centre in Amsterdam, and colleagues.

STUDY DETAILS

The researchers looked at the outcomes of 56 patients who had open surgery and 59 patients who had the minimally invasive procedure. In the two weeks after surgery, lung (or pulmonary) infections occurred in 29% of those who had open surgery but only 9% of those who had minimally invasive surgery.

Overall, 34% of the patients who had open surgery developed a lung infection, compared with 12% of those who underwent minimally invasive surgery, the study found.

The researchers also noted that patients who had minimally invasive surgery had less blood loss, far shorter hospital stays and better quality of life (much less pain and vocal-cord paralysis).

Importantly, minimally invasive surgery was as effective as open surgery, the study authors concluded in the report published online in *The Lancet*.

EXPERT COMMENT

One US expert was impressed with the findings. The study "goes a long way to encouraging esophageal surgeons to seriously consider minimally invasive surgery for their patients with surgically resectable [removable] esophageal cancers," said Jonathan Aviv, MD, clinical professor of otolaryngology at Mount Sinai Medical Center in New York City.

"If these results can be confirmed in other settings, minimally invasive esophagectomy could truly become the standard of care," Simon Law, of the University of Hong Kong, China, wrote in an accompanying editorial.

For his part, Dr. Aviv also believes that the study "underscores the need for continued early screening of patients with symptoms suggestive of esophageal cancer—cough and hoarseness, likely even more important than 'typical' gastrointestinal symptoms such as heartburn and regurgitation."

Dr. Aviv, who is also clinical director of the Voice and Swallowing Center of ENT and Allergy Associates, New York City, added that "esophageal cancer both in western Europe and here in the USA is the only cancer that is markedly increasing in incidence the past 30 years."

info *More information:* The US National Cancer Institute has more about esophageal cancer at its Web site, *www.cancer.gov/cancertopics/wyntk/esophagus*.

Chemo + Radiation Best for Bladder Cancer

Nicholas James, PhD, professor, clinical oncology, and codirector, Research and Development (Cancer) University Hospitals, University of Birmingham, England.
Manish A. Vira, MD, director, fellowship program in urologic oncology, the Arthur Smith Institute for Urology, Lake Success, New York.
New England Journal of Medicine

The addition of two well-tolerated chemotherapy drugs to radiation therapy led to significantly longer survival rates among patients with muscle-invasive bladder cancer.

About 385,000 cases of bladder cancer are diagnosed annually worldwide, according to study authors, with the average age at diagnosis over 70. For those whose cancer has invaded the bladder muscle, five-year survival rates are about 45% regardless of treatment.

For younger, healthier patients, bladder removal—known as radical cystectomy—is considered the gold standard of care for invasive bladder cancer. But older patients with co-existing medical conditions may not be as well-equipped to tolerate complications of the procedure, experts said.

STUDY DETAILS

The recent study, the largest late-stage trial of its kind, was conducted at 45 medical facilities in the United Kingdom. Researchers divided 360 patients into groups receiving radiation alone or radiation plus chemotherapy: Patients were randomly assigned to undergo daily radiation alone or radiation along with two chemotherapy drugs, *fluorouracil* and *mitomycin C.*

Those undergoing the combined therapies had a 67% rate of local disease-free survival after two years, compared with 54% in the radiation group. Five-year overall survival rates were 48% in the chemo-radiation group, compared with 35% in the radiation-only group.

In addition to improved survival rates, the number of patients needing bladder removal as a "salvage therapy"—because other treatments failed—was lower among those receiving radiation plus chemotherapy.

"Overall, the results establish that the addition of chemotherapy to radiotherapy should become standard practice for organ-preserving treatments of bladder cancer," said Manish Vira, MD, director of the fellowship program in urologic oncology at the Arthur Smith Institute for Urology in Lake Success, New York. "The tried-and-true treatment method is still [bladder removal] and certainly we are moving toward a more multi-disciplinary approach."

The study is published in the *New England Journal of Medicine.*

Adverse effects from the chemotherapy—including diarrhea, sore mouth or suppression of blood cell production—were low among participants and were managed by lowering drug dosages, said study author Nicholas James, PhD,

professor of clinical oncology at the University of Birmingham in England.

Cost of the chemotherapy drugs is relatively inexpensive, he said—about $1,600, plus pharmacy and intravenous administration costs.

"We were pleasantly surprised by the overall results, particularly the low reported toxicity in the chemo-radiotherapy arm compared to the radiotherapy-only group," Dr. James said. "We feel the results are sufficient to change practice...the drugs are cheap and safety was good in an elderly population."

Melanoma Is On the Rise

Albert Lefkovits, MD, an associate clinical professor of dermatology at Mount Sinai School of Medicine and codirector of the Mount Sinai Dermatological Cosmetic Surgery Program, both in New York City.

Melanoma is the most dangerous form of skin cancer. It's particularly frightening because it's more likely than other cancers to spread (metastasize) to other parts of the body. More than 76,000 Americans are diagnosed with melanoma each year, and between 8,000 and 9,000 will die from it.

Good news: New technology increases the chances that a melanoma will be detected early—and when it is, you have a 95% to 97% chance of surviving. The prognosis is worse after the disease has spread, but two new drugs can significantly increase survival times—and medications that may be even more effective already are in the pipeline.

WHO'S AT RISK?

A study published in *Journal of Investigative Dermatology* found that melanoma rates increased by 3.1% annually between 1992 and 2004—and the incidence continues to rise.

The increase is due to several reasons. The US population is aging, and older adults are more likely to get melanoma (though it is a leading cause of cancer death in young adults). Public-awareness campaigns have increased the rate of cancer screenings (though officials would like the screening rates to be even higher), and more screenings mean an increase in melanoma diagnoses.

If you are a fair-skinned Caucasian, your lifetime risk of getting melanoma is about one in 50. The risk is lower among African Americans, Hispanics and Asians, but they're more likely to die from it because they often develop cancers on "hidden" areas (such as the soles of the feet), where skin changes aren't readily apparent.

Important: Don't be complacent just because you avoid the sun or use sunscreen. Many cancers appear in areas that aren't exposed to the sun, such as between the toes or around the anus.

STATE-OF-THE-ART SCREENING

Melanomas grow slowly. Patients who get an annual skin checkup are more likely to get an early diagnosis than those who see a doctor only when a mole or skin change is clearly abnormal.

Doctors used to depend on their eyes (and sometimes a magnifying glass) to examine suspicious areas. But eyes-only examinations can identify melanomas only about 60% of the time.

Better: An exam called epiluminescence microscopy. The doctor takes photographs of large areas of skin. Then he/she uses a device that magnifies suspicious areas in the photos. The accuracy of detecting melanomas with this technique is about 90%.

The technology also allows doctors to look for particular changes, such as certain colors or a streaked or globular appearance, that indicate whether a skin change is malignant or benign. This can reduce unnecessary biopsies.

Few private-practice physicians can afford the equipment that's used for these exams. You might want to get your checkups at a medical center or dermatology practice that specializes in early melanoma detection. If this isn't possible, ask your doctor if he/she uses a handheld dermatoscope. It's a less expensive device that's still superior to the unaided eye.

NEW TREATMENTS

In the last few years, the FDA has approved two medications for patients with late-stage melanoma. These drugs don't cure the disease but can help patients live longer.

Ipilimumab (Yervoy) is a biologic medication, a type of synthetic antibody that blocks a cellular "switch" that turns off the body's ability to fight cancer. A study of 676 patients with late-stage melanoma found that those who took the drug survived, on average, for 10 months after starting treatment, compared with 6.4 months for those in a control group.

Vemurafenib (Zelboraf) may double the survival time of patients with advanced melanoma. It works by targeting a mutation in the BRAF V600E gene, which is present in about 50% of melanoma patients. Researchers who conducted a study published in *The New England Journal of Medicine* found that more than half of patients who took the medication had at least a 30% reduction in tumor size. In about one-third of patients, the medication slowed or stopped the progression of the cancer.

Combination treatment: Each of these medications attacks tumors in different ways. They can be used in tandem for better results. For example, a patient might start by taking the first drug, then, when it stops working, he/she can switch to the second drug. This approach can potentially extend survival by up to a year.

Both drugs can have serious side effects. For now, they're recommended only for a select group of patients.

SELF-PROTECTION

Take steps to protect yourself…

•**Check your skin monthly.** It's been estimated that deaths from melanoma could be reduced by 60% if everyone would do a monthly skin exam to look for suspicious changes. Look for asymmetric moles in which one part is distinctly different from the other part…moles with an irregular border…color variations…a diameter greater than 6 millimeters (mm), about one-quarter inch…or changes in appearance over time.

•**Get a yearly checkup with a dermatologist.** It's nearly impossible to self-inspect all of the areas on your body where melanoma can appear. Albert Lefkovits, MD, advises patients to see a dermatologist every year for full-body mapping. The doctor will make a note (or photograph) of every suspicious area and track the areas over time.

Important: New moles rarely appear in people over the age of 40. A mole that appears in patients 40 years and older is assumed to be cancer until tests show otherwise.

- **Use a lot of sunscreen.** Even though melanoma isn't caused only by sun exposure, don't get careless. Apply a sunscreen with an SPF of at least 30 whenever you go outdoors. Use a lot of sunscreen—it takes about two ounces of sunscreen (about the amount in a shot glass) to protect against skin cancer. Reapply it about every two hours or immediately after getting out of the water.

- **Don't use tanning salons.** Researchers who published a study in *Journal of the National Cancer Institute* found that people who got their tans at tanning salons—that use tanning lamps and tanning beds that emit UV radiation—at least once a month were 55% more likely to develop a malignant melanoma than those who didn't artificially tan.

Hidden Melanoma—It Can Strike Where You Least Expect It

Marianne Berwick, PhD, MPH, division chief and head of cancer epidemiology and prevention at the University of New Mexico School of Medicine and associate director of the Cancer Population Sciences Program at the University of New Mexico Cancer Center, both in Albuquerque.

If you spotted a mole on your leg that had changed colors or grown larger or asymmetrical, chances are that you would do the right thing and make an appointment to see your doctor. But melanoma, the deadliest of all skin cancers, often doesn't follow the rules and can develop in an unexpected place, such as the sole of your foot, under a fingernail or even in your eye.

The hidden threat: Even though we don't hear much about it, up to 30% of melanomas have an almost normal appearance or develop in areas where most people—including many doctors—don't think to look.

The Ultimate Skin Exam

All adults should see a dermatologist at least once a year for a skin exam…or promptly if you notice a change in your skin, including any of those described in the adjacent article. A thorough skin exam from a dermatologist—of every inch of your skin including areas of the body that do not receive sun exposure—is one of the best defenses against melanoma. You might also be checked with a device called MelaFind, which takes digital pictures of abnormal areas and analyzes them for signs of cancer. It can help your doctor decide if a biopsy is needed.

The first step of a skin exam is to take off all your clothes (and jewelry) and slip into a gown that's open at the front. *See graphic for important areas that are sometimes missed…*

To protect yourself further: Examine every inch of your skin once a month. Don't forget to use a hand mirror to check your buttocks, between the buttocks and the backs of both legs. While sitting, use the mirror to also check the area around (and under) the genitals.

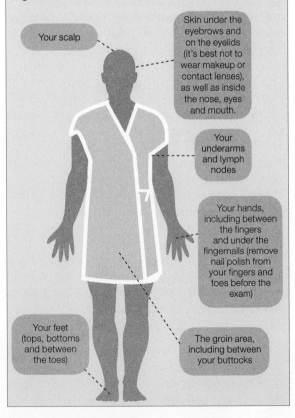

Your scalp

Skin under the eyebrows and on the eyelids (it's best not to wear makeup or contact lenses), as well as inside the nose, eyes and mouth.

Your underarms and lymph nodes

Your hands, including between the fingers and under the fingernails (remove nail polish from your fingers and toes before the exam)

Your feet (tops, bottoms and between the toes)

The groin area, including between your buttocks

Good news: The overwhelming majority of patients will survive if the melanoma is detected early. *Where to look—and what to look for…*

A LUMP OR UNUSUAL PATCH

About 15% of all melanomas diagnosed in the US are due to so-called nodular melanomas. They can occur anywhere on the body, and they don't necessarily arise from preexisting moles. These melanomas are particularly dangerous because they grow into the skin more rapidly than they expand in width. That's why most people don't notice them until they've already spread.

What to look for: Nodular melanomas can appear as a lump (usually black, red or skin-colored) that may be firm and dome-shaped or as a dark- or light-colored patch of skin that does not quite resemble the surrounding area.

Self-defense: When you examine your skin, make note of any unusual lump…or area that doesn't resemble the surrounding skin, and see a dermatologist promptly.

UNDER THE NAILS

About 5% of all melanomas—and the most common form in Asians and people with dark skin—appear under a fingernail or toenail or on the palms of the hands or the soles of the feet. They also can occur in mucous membranes in the nose, mouth or other areas. This cancer, acral lentiginous melanoma, is dangerous because most people don't recognize it.

What to look for: A melanoma under a nail often appears as a brown or black streak that grows larger over time. If a melanoma affects the mucous membranes in the nasal passages, it can cause persistent congestion or nosebleeds.

Self-defense: See your dermatologist right away if you notice a nail streak that's getting bigger and is not due to an injury. Go to your doctor if you have nosebleeds for no obvious reason or develop unexplained chronic congestion. Ask your dentist to check your mouth at routine dental exams.

"AGE" SPOTS

These flat areas of sun-damaged skin vary in size, are gray-brown or black and usually appear on the face, arms, shoulders and/or hands. If a spot changes over time, it could be lentigo maligna melanoma.

What to look for: A flat "spot" that gradually spreads and develops an irregular shape. It will be a brownish color and usually appears on the face, neck or other sun-exposed areas.

Self-defense: Have a dermatologist check age spots when they first appear. If an area changes quickly (over a period of about two weeks) or has irregular borders, see a dermatologist promptly.

SCALP CHANGES

Unless you have thinning hair or you are bald, your scalp isn't an area that's easy to see. That's why melanomas on the scalp are so dangerous—most people don't notice them until they're already advanced.

What to look for: Scalp melanomas usually follow the normal rules of ABCDE—Asymmetry…Border irregularities…Color changes…Diameter (larger than about one-quarter inch)…and Evolving (changes in appearance over time). Areas that itch or bleed persistently also should be checked promptly.

Self-defense: Once a month, take a few minutes to examine every part of your scalp. You can use a comb and/or hair dryer to move your hair out of the way. Use a mirror to help you see the top and back of your scalp and/or ask a family member or your hairdresser to check those places for you.

THE GROIN AND MORE

Melanomas can occur in areas that have never been exposed to sun.

What to look for: Any sensation (such as itching or bleeding) around the testicles or penis or in the vulvar area or vagina…or anus that doesn't seem normal. You might notice a mole or a discolored area that's changing.

Self-defense: See your doctor right away if you experience unexpected vaginal bleeding or discharge or blood in the urine. Blood that appears during bowel movements is sometimes caused by hemorrhoids but may also indicate cancer, so see your doctor promptly.

VISION CHANGES

You aren't likely to see an ocular melanoma (a rare type of eye cancer), because it's usually not apparent when you look in a mirror.

What to look for: See an eye doctor if you notice a scratchy sensation under the eyelid or possibly changes in vision, such as blurring or a loss of peripheral vision.

Self-defense: There is little evidence that wearing sunglasses will prevent eye melanomas. The best way to protect yourself is with an annual eye exam from an ophthalmologist or optometrist.

Daily Aspirin Linked to Lower Risk for Deadly Skin Cancer in Women

Jean Tang, MD, PhD, assistant professor of dermatology, Stanford University School of Medicine, Palo Alto, California.

Michele Green, MD, dermatologist, Lenox Hill Hospital, New York City.

Cancer, online

Older women who take an aspirin regularly may be lowering their risk of developing the deadly skin cancer melanoma, a recent study suggests.

And the longer postmenopausal women take aspirin, the more melanoma risk appears to diminish.

The effect is only seen with aspirin, not with other pain relievers such as *acetaminophen* (Tylenol), the researchers noted.

Each year in the United States there are nearly 77,000 new cases of melanoma and more than 9,000 deaths from it, according to the US National Cancer Institute.

THE STUDY

For the study, the research team collected data on nearly 60,000 white women who were part of the Women's Health Initiative, a long-term national study. The women, aged between 50 and 79, were asked about what medications they took and other lifestyle preferences.

Over 12 years of follow-up, the investigators found that women who took aspirin had a 21% lower risk of developing melanoma compared with women who didn't take aspirin.

The study found that women who took aspirin for at least five years had their melanoma risk drop by 30%, compared with women who didn't take aspirin.

To try to isolate the effect of aspirin on melanoma, the researchers accounted for other factors such as skin tone, tanning and use of sunscreen.

The new report was published in *Cancer*.

MORE STUDY NEEDED

But it's too soon to make firm conclusions, a researcher cautioned.

"Aspirin could be potentially used to prevent melanoma, but a clinical trial is needed," said lead author Jean Tang, MD, PhD, an assistant professor of dermatology at Stanford University School of Medicine in Palo Alto, California.

This type of population-based study can only show an association between aspirin and the reduced risk for melanoma, not that aspirin actually helps prevent it.

Dr. Tang doesn't believe women should start taking aspirin solely to try to prevent melanoma. "It's too early to say this," she said.

POSSIBLE EXPLANATIONS

It is possible that aspirin's anti-inflammatory properties might be responsible for lowering the risk of melanoma, Dr. Tang suggested.

"Aspirin may also promote cell death of melanoma cells," she added.

Whether a protective effect also occurs in men is not known, said Dr. Tang, who plans to look at that in her next study.

EXPERT RECOMMENDATIONS

One expert doesn't see any problem taking aspirin to prevent melanoma, especially for people with a family history of the disease.

Prolonged use of aspirin is not without risks, including stomach bleeding, but the benefits of preventing melanoma outweigh the risk for vulnerable people, said Michele Green, MD, a dermatologist at Lenox Hill Hospital in New York City. She praised the recent research.

"I think it's fantastic. It's really a remarkable study," Dr. Green said.

"If you have a family history of melanoma, I don't see any downside of taking aspirin for this," she said. "I would urge my patients who have a family history of melanoma to take aspirin based on this study."

info To learn more about melanoma, visit the US National Cancer Institute's Web site, *www.cancer.gov*, and search "melanoma."

Face-Saving Skin Cancer Surgery

Margaret W. Mann, MD, assistant professor of dermatology at Case Western Reserve University School of Medicine in Cleveland and director of the Skin Cancer & Mohs Surgery program at University Hospitals/Westlake in Westlake, Ohio. She is fellowship-trained in Mohs skin surgery, cosmetic and vein procedures.

After her dermatologist diagnosed the spot on her nose as the skin cancer basal cell carcinoma (BCC), Lana went online to check out photos of other patients. She was shocked by some of the images and terrified of ending up with a huge scar.

Fortunately, Lana's doctor was skilled in a treatment called Mohs micrographic surgery. After weighing her options, Lana went ahead with the surgery—and now she describes the technique as "literally face-saving."

BCC, the most common skin cancer in the US, is rarely fatal but can be disfiguring, explained Mohs expert Margaret W. Mann, MD, an assistant professor of dermatology at Case Western Reserve University School of Medicine in Cleveland. It develops in the bottom of the epidermis (outermost layer of skin). What is visible on the surface is the "tip of the iceberg," with more tumor cells growing downward and outward into surrounding skin—like the roots of a tree. The cancer most often occurs on the face, scalp or neck but can develop anywhere. Lana's nose lesion emerged as a red, raised spot that itched, flaked, bled, healed and then returned repeatedly. In other cases, BCC appears as a waxy bump...flat, scaly, brown or flesh-colored patch...crusty or oozy lesion...or sore with a sunken center.

If you notice any such spot: See a dermatologist immediately. "The longer you leave it, the larger it grows, so the larger the scar will be when it's removed," Dr. Mann cautioned.

Treatment options for BCC include excision (cutting out the tumor)...curettage and electrodesiccation (scraping off the tumor, then cauterizing the base to destroy any remaining abnormal cells)...cryosurgery (freezing)...radiation...and laser. With these methods, the surgeon must estimate how much tissue to treat, which can lead to unnecessary removal of healthy tissue and/or tumor recurrence if any cancer is inadvertently left behind.

What makes Mohs different is that it allows the surgeon to precisely identify and remove the entire tumor—virtually eliminating the chance that it will grow back and thus providing the highest success rate among treatments—while it leaves surrounding healthy tissue intact to minimize scarring.

How it works: Mohs is usually performed as an outpatient procedure under local anesthesia. The tumor is shaved off in ultra-fine layers, one layer at a time, and each bit of tissue is immediately examined under a microscope. A special dye allows the surgeon to distinguish normal cells from cancer cells. The surgeon can then map the exact location of each projecting "root" of the tumor, so that—layer by layer—every last microscopic portion of cancer can be removed without undue harm to healthy tissue. Although time-intensive, the technique's cure rate is near 99%, Dr. Mann said. For an infographic on the method, visit *http://bit.ly/iKNVMJ* and click on the Step-by-Step Process icon.

Another unique aspect of Mohs is that wound reconstruction usually is done immediately because there is no need to wait for a pathologist's report to confirm that the cancer is gone. Depending on the wound's size, it may be stitched...or a graft of skin may be taken from elsewhere...or a flap of living tissue from an adjacent area may be used to fill in the wound. If the treated area is very extensive, plastic surgery may be performed later.

Mohs typically costs more than other types of BCC treatment—and those other methods often

Dental Plaque and Cancer

In a recent study, scientists tracked almost 1,400 healthy adults (average age 40) for 24 years.

Findings: Of the 58 people who died prematurely, cancer was the most common cause of death. Additionally, those who died of cancer had more dental plaque on their teeth and gums than those who did not die prematurely. In fact, dental plaque was found to increase risk for premature death due to cancer by 79%—perhaps due to a systemic inflammatory response.

Birgitta Söder, PhD, professor of odontological prophylaxis, department of dental medicine, Karolinska Institutet, Stockholm, Sweden.

work fine, depending on the tumor's extent and location. But Mohs generally is considered the treatment of choice for BCC that is large, deep, fast-growing, irregularly shaped, recurrent or located near scar tissue or on the face. Discuss your options with your doctor and your insurance company.

Many doctors perform Mohs, but for the best outcome, Dr. Mann recommended using a board-certified dermatologist who is a member of the American College of Mohs Surgery (ACMS). Membership in ACMS requires completion of a one- to two-year fellowship training program and at least 500 supervised Mohs surgery cases—so these physicians are specially trained as cancer surgeons, pathologists and reconstructive surgeons. Visit *www.mohscollege.org* and click on "Find an ACMS Mohs surgeon."

Important news: A recent study from Brown University revealed that patients who have had one BCC are likely to have multiple carcinomas over time—suggesting that this type of cancer should be considered a chronic disease. So even after your BCC is successfully treated, it is best to remain on guard for signs of new skin tumors elsewhere on your body.

New Drug Effective for Rare Genetic Skin Cancer

Jean Tang, MD, assistant professor, department of dermatology, Stanford University School of Medicine.

John Lear, MD, consultant dermatologist, Manchester Royal Infirmary, Manchester, England.

New England Journal of Medicine

When a clinical trial is stopped abruptly just eight months after its start, it's either very good or very bad news.

In the case of a study on a skin cancer drug, the results were so impressive that the trial's independent data and safety monitoring board decided to offer the drug immediately to the study participants who were taking placebos.

The drug, *vismodegib* (Erivedge), was approved in January 2012 by the US Food and Drug Administration for people with aggressive, large basal cell carcinoma that had spread to the lymph nodes or other body systems. The researchers wanted to test the oral medication against a disfiguring form of skin cancer called basal cell nevus syndrome, a rare genetic condition.

Basal cell nevus syndrome typically starts at puberty. The condition can involve hundreds of basal cell lesions, often requiring many surgical and nonsurgical procedures to treat.

Basal cell carcinoma of the skin is the most common cancer worldwide, and its prevalence is increasing. There are about 2.1 million new cases of non-melanoma skin cancer treated in the United States every year, according to journal background information. Some 750,000 of these are cases of basal cell carcinoma. Basal cell nevus syndrome—also known as Gorlin syndrome—occurs in fewer than 1% of them.

The study tracked more than 2,000 existing basal cell skin cancers and documented 694 new lesions in the study group.

STUDY DETAILS

Researchers followed 41 patients with basal cell nevus syndrome and found that those taking vismodegib got an average of slightly more than two new cancers, while those not taking the drug developed 29.

"This is one of the first clinical trials that show the drug can be used in prevention," said Jean Tang, MD, a coauthor of the study and assistant professor in the department of dermatology at Stanford University School of Medicine.

Dr. Tang said the positive effects of the drug are visible within a month after starting to take it. "This is a life-changing drug for these patients," she said.

The research also provides new evidence about a key genetic pathway in the development of basal cell and other cancers. Vismodegib targets what is called the "hedgehog-signaling pathway." (It was named after mutant mouse embryos in early studies that looked like hedgehogs.)

The pathway directs cell growth in embryos and also regulates adult stem cells involved in maintaining and regenerating tissue. If the pathway malfunctions, it can result in basal cell carcinoma and other cancers.

"The research trial demonstrates proof of the impact of the hedgehog-signaling pathway in basal cell cancers," Dr. Tang explained. The findings may have broader relevance to treating other types of basal cell skin cancer, she said.

The study was reported in the *New England Journal of Medicine*.

SIDE EFFECTS AND COST

The drug's side effects, including muscle cramps, changes in taste perception, weight loss, hair loss and fatigue, can be debilitating. In order to reduce their impact, the researchers are testing whether dosing the drug intermittently—two months on, two months off—will reduce the symptoms while still being at least 90% effective. They're also testing reduced dosages to better understand how to strike the right balance, Dr. Tang said.

At this point, vismodegib costs $250 a day, Dr. Tang said. The drug's maker, Genentech, contributed nearly $1 million to support the research, including the costs of patient travel, office visits and biopsies, she said.

A second, related study in the same journal issue found that some patients responded to vismodegib for locally advanced and metastatic basal cell carcinomas. This study also received funding from Genentech.

An Antibody That Shrinks Cancer Tumors

A single antibody caused tumors from seven different human cancers (including breast, colon and prostate) transplanted into mice to shrink or disappear, according to a recent study led by Stanford University School of Medicine. The antibody blocks a protein that cancer cells use to signal immune system cells not to kill them. It will be tested on humans within two years.

Study by researchers at Stanford University School of Medicine, published in *Proceedings of the National Academy of Sciences*.

EXPERT COMMENT

John Lear, MD, a consultant dermatologist at the Manchester Royal Infirmary in England, wrote an editorial on the studies. "It is a landmark day for patients with basal cell carcinoma," he said in an interview. "The next step is to develop topical applications and injections that could minimize side effects while effectively preventing and treating lesions."

info To learn more about basal cell nevus syndrome, visit the Web site of the US National Library of Medicine at *http://ghr.nlm.nih.gov/condition/gorlin-syndrome*.

Drug Attacks Advanced Thyroid Cancer

Martin Schlumberger, MD, Institut Gustave Roussy, Villejeuf, France.
Dennis Kraus, MD, director, Center for Head & Neck Oncology, New York Head & Neck Institute, Lenox Hill Hospital, New York City.
The Lancet Oncology, online

A recent study shows that the chemotherapy drug *vandetanib* (Caprelsa) may extend life for some thyroid cancer patients.

The results of phase 2 trials showed that patients taking the drug lived for 11 months without the cancer progressing, compared with six months for those receiving a placebo.

"This study is confirmation that vandetanib is effective in advanced thyroid cancer patients, not only in terms of overall response, but also in terms of progression-free survival," said lead researcher Martin Schlumberger, MD, of the Institute Gustave Roussy in Villejuif, France. "Vandetanib should be used as first-line treatment in patients with progressive, untreatable thyroid cancer."

STUDY DETAILS

For the study, Dr. Schlumberger's team randomly assigned 145 patients with late-stage thyroid cancer either to vandetanib or a placebo.

In addition to a longer period when the cancer didn't progress, patients taking vandetanib had their disease better controlled, with more patients having a complete or partial response to the drug, the researchers found.

Among patients taking the drug, 72% had disease progression, compared with 84% taking placebo.

Neither those taking vandetanib or placebo, however, showed better overall survival, the researchers noted. Among those taking vandetanib, 26% died; 29% of those taking a placebo died.

Patients with papillary thyroid cancer—the most common type of thyroid cancer—who took vandetanib had progression-free disease for an average of 16 months, compared with patients with rarer forms of cancer, where progression-free disease lasted an average of almost eight months.

Patients taking vandetanib had greater side effects, including abnormal heart rhythms (which can be deadly), diarrhea, weakness and fatigue. Two patients taking vandetanib died from the treatment, the researchers noted.

Vandetanib works by targeting three proteins known to play a role in the growth and spread of thyroid cancer.

A month's supply of vandetanib can cost more than $10,000, according to the American Society of Clinical Oncology.

IMPROVED SURVIVAL FOR ADVANCED CANCER

If caught early, thyroid cancer is often curable. "Typically, we talk about thyroid cancer being the great cancer," said Dennis Kraus, MD, director of the Center for Head & Neck Oncology at Lenox Hill Hospital in New York City. "If you've got to have a cancer, this is the one."

In most cases of thyroid cancer, the risk of dying of the disease is 1%, Dr. Kraus noted. Treating the disease usually involves surgically removing the thyroid and the lymph nodes if they are involved. In addition, patients can receive radioactive iodine.

"It's only the minority of patients who…develop recurrent disease or metastatic or locally advanced cancer, who go on to die of their disease," Dr. Kraus said.

With vandetanib, these types of patients may have improved survival, Dr. Kraus said.

"It's not a panacea," he said. "But in a group in which we thought we had no viable treatment, we now have something we can try to treat people with and either control their disease or prolong their survival."

info For more on thyroid cancer, visit the Web site of the US National Library of Medicine at *www.nlm.nih.gov/medlineplus/thyroid cancer.html*

Nausea Meets Its Match

Nausea and vomiting were reduced in more than half of 80 cancer patients who took the antipsychotic drug *olanzapine* (Zyprexa) after not being helped by standard antinausea medication.

Theory: Olanzapine is thought to help prevent chemotherapy drugs from activating the brain's "vomiting center," which triggers chemo-related nausea. Side effects of olanzapine include depression, difficulty walking, and difficulty falling or staying asleep. Elderly patients with dementia should not take this drug because it may increase their stroke risk.

Sandra M. Swain, MD, medical director at the Washington Cancer Institute, Washington Hospital Center, Washington, DC.

After Cancer: You Really Can Get Back to Normal

Julie K. Silver, MD, who cofounded Oncology Rehab Partners, a Northborough, Massachusetts–based firm that trains and certifies hospitals and cancer centers in cancer rehabilitation. She is author of *After Cancer Treatment: Heal Faster, Better, Stronger* (Johns Hopkins). *www.oncologyrehabpartners.com*

Until relatively recently, there was no such thing as "cancer rehab" to help cancer patients cope with the grueling and sometimes lasting physical and psychological effects of chemotherapy, radiation, surgery or other treatment. Patients, many of whom considered themselves lucky just to be alive, dealt with the problems largely on their own.

Now: Just as patients who have suffered a heart attack or stroke are likely to receive guidance on how to cope with the aftereffects of treatment, more and more cancer patients are beginning to get the help they need to regain the quality of life they had before getting sick.

Who can benefit: Of the 12.6 million cancer survivors in the US, an estimated 3.3 million continue to suffer physical consequences of their treatment, such as fatigue and/or chronic pain…and another 1.4 million live with mental health problems, such as depression and/or a form of mild cognitive impairment known as "chemo brain."

Latest development: As cancer rehab becomes more prevalent throughout the US—hundreds of facilities nationwide offer such programs—there is mounting evidence showing how this type of care can help accelerate recovery, improve a patient's quality of life and perhaps even reduce risk for cancer recurrence.* In fact, the American College of Surgeons' Commission on Cancer now requires cancer centers in the US to offer rehab services in order to receive accreditation.

WHEN CANCER REHAB HELPS

Even though it was first conceived as a resource for patients immediately after their acute phase of treatment, cancer rehab can help long after treatment has taken place. For example, people who were treated years ago and are now cancer-free—but not free of side effects from treatment—can benefit from cancer rehab. Just because you went for, say, physical therapy two years ago after you finished cancer treatment, it doesn't mean that you can't get more help now for the same problem or a different one.

Insurance picks up the tab: Because the benefits of cancer rehab are now so widely accepted, insurance generally covers the cost—regardless of when you were treated for cancer—including consultations with physiatrists (medical doctors who specialize in rehabilitation medicine), physical therapists, occupational therapists, speech language pathologists and others.

Even though cancer rehab therapies tend to be short term (typically requiring two to three sessions weekly in the provider's office for a period of a few weeks), insurance plans often limit the number of visits for such therapies. Be sure to check with your insurer for details on your coverage.

Each cancer patient's situation is different, but here are some common problems and how they are treated with cancer rehab…

MILD COGNITIVE IMPAIRMENT ("CHEMO BRAIN")

Cancer patients who have received chemotherapy often complain that they don't think

*To find a medical center near you that offers cancer rehab services, consult Oncology Rehab Partners, *www.oncologyrehabpartners.com*.

Cancer "Prehab" Can Help, Too

Cancer "prehab" is useful during the window after a patient is diagnosed with cancer but before treatment begins to help boost his/her physical and emotional readiness for cancer treatment. For example, a specific exercise program, such as interval training, may be advised to increase strength before surgery. A nutrition program may be used to improve a patient's nutritional status before treatments that may sap appetite or lead to nutrition problems such as anemia. Working with a psychologist can help identify and deal with anxiety and stress before treatment starts. Cancer prehab usually is offered at centers that provide cancer rehab services.

as well and that they have less energy and decreased attention spans. If anxiety or hot flashes due to chemo interfere with sleep, that can decrease cognitive functioning, too.

How cancer rehab helps: A physical therapist might work with a cancer patient by using a specific therapeutic exercise plan. Exercise has been shown to improve cognitive functioning—perhaps by improving blood flow to the brain.

An occupational therapist or speech therapist may recommend strategies to help concentration, attention and memory. This may involve computer-based programs that improve short-term memory.

ANEMIA AND FATIGUE

Anemia is common with many hematological (blood) cancers, such as leukemia and lymphomas.

How cancer rehab helps: In a young person who has just undergone a bone marrow transplant, for example, if there is a low red blood cell count (an indicator of anemia) or a risk for infection, a tailored exercise program can build strength and endurance to help fight fatigue.

For an older adult, exercise is also a key part of a fatigue-fighting regimen that improves endurance and overall fitness. If fatigue results in problems with balance and gait, an occupational therapist can help the patient remain independent at home by suggesting a smartphone-based monitoring device such as a motion sensor that notifies a family member or friend if the patient falls.

BREATHING PROBLEMS

Difficulty breathing and feeling short of breath are common problems in lung cancer survivors. These patients also may experience pain after surgery and have trouble exercising and performing their usual daily activities due to shortness of breath.

How cancer rehab helps: In addition to improving strength and physical performance through targeted exercises, a cancer patient who is having breathing problems would need to improve his/her ability to get more air into the lungs. This may involve "belly breathing" exercises that will allow him to complete his daily activities without getting out of breath so quickly.

What Exercises Are Best for You?*

If you have cancer...

Exercise may help fight the nausea and muscle wasting that sometimes occur with cancer and its treatment. In fact, a recent meta-analysis of 56 studies found that aerobic exercise, including walking and cycling—both during and after treatment—reduced fatigue in cancer patients.

Interestingly, strength training was not found to reduce fatigue. But strength training helps maintain muscle mass, so some use of weights or resistance machines should be included for 15 to 20 minutes twice a week, if possible.

Because cancer patients sometimes have trouble maintaining their body weight, it's especially important for those who are exercising to increase their calorie intake.

*Always talk to your doctor before starting a new exercise program. If you have a chronic illness, it may be useful to consult a physical therapist for advice on exercise dos and don'ts for your particular situation.

John P. Porcari, PhD, program director of the Clinical Excercise Physiology (CEP) program at the University of Wisconsin-La Crosse.

Common Heart Drug Might Improve Lung Cancer Survival

Daniel Gomez, MD, assistant professor, department of radiation oncology, University of Texas M.D. Anderson Cancer Center, Houston.
Len Horovitz, MD, pulmonologist, Lenox Hill Hospital, New York City.
Annals of Oncology

Recent research suggests that beta blockers, medications that are used to control blood pressure and heart rhythms, may also help lung cancer patients live longer.

The researchers found that patients with non-small-cell lung cancer being treated with radiation lived 22% longer if they were also taking these drugs.

"These findings were the first, to our knowledge, demonstrating a survival benefit associated with the use of beta blockers and radiation therapy for lung cancer," said lead researcher Daniel Gomez, MD, an assistant professor in the department of radiation oncology at the University of Texas M.D. Anderson Cancer Center in Houston.

"The results imply that there may be another mechanism, largely unexplored, that could potentially reduce the rates of tumor spread in patients with this very aggressive disease," he added.

STUDY DETAILS

For the study, Dr. Gomez's team compared the outcomes of more than 700 patients undergoing radiation therapy for lung cancer.

The investigators found that the 155 patients taking beta blockers for heart problems lived an average of nearly two years, compared with an average of 18.6 months for patients not taking these drugs.

The findings held even after adjusting for other factors such as age, stage of the disease, whether or not chemotherapy was given at the same time, presence of chronic obstructive pulmonary disease and aspirin use, the researchers noted.

Beta blockers were also associated with improved survival without the disease spreading to other parts of the body and survival without the disease recurring, they added. Beta blockers, however, appeared to make no difference in the length of survival without the disease progressing in the part of the lungs where it started, the study authors pointed out.

The study was published in the *Annals of Oncology*.

THEORY

How beta blockers might slow cancer's spread isn't known. However, the researchers speculate that these drugs may work by suppressing a hormone called norepinephrine, which is known to promote the spread of cancer cells.

EXPERT COMMENTARY

According to one expert, the study raises questions. "It is unclear whether beta blockers need to be started before the cancer is found, or if they still have a utility once the diagnosis is

Ginseng Relieves Cancer-Related Fatigue

According to a recent study, cancer patients who took a 2,000-milligram supplement of American ginseng twice a day for eight weeks experienced a 20-point improvement on a 100-point fatigue scale. Those taking a placebo showed only a 10-point improvement.

Study of 340 patients with cancer-related fatigue from 40 community medical centers by researchers at Mayo Clinic, Rochester, Minnesota, presented at the American Society of Clinical Oncology's annual meeting.

made," said Len Horovitz, MD, a pulmonologist at Lenox Hill Hospital in New York City.

In addition, Dr. Horovitz wonders whether other drugs that block hormones might serve the same purpose.

ADVICE

"Right now, we would not advocate that patients take beta blockers for this purpose, until these findings can be validated by prospective trials," Dr. Gomez said. "In addition, future studies will help us to understand if the mechanism that we propose is correct, and thus if beta blockers are indeed directly affecting the aggressiveness of this cancer or if these findings are due to the activation or inhibition of another pathway."

One thing is clear, added Dr. Horovitz, people should not start taking beta blockers in hopes of preventing or controlling lung cancer.

Dr. Horovitz did say he thinks trials testing whether or not beta blockers or other hormone-blocking drugs prevent the spread of lung cancer should be done.

info For more on lung cancer, visit the National Cancer Institute's Web site, *http://www.cancer.gov/cancertopics/types/lung*.

Consumer Health Alerts

Hidden Toxins in Your Home

I f you don't think that toxins are lurking, undetected and invisible in your home, this fact will make you sit up and take notice. The air inside our homes may be anywhere from two to 100 times more polluted than the air just beyond our front doors, according to the Environmental Protection Agency. How could this be? It turns out that the air we breathe in our homes may contain contaminants, fungi or chemical by-products that can harm our health.

It is easy to feel overwhelmed when reading about all of these dangers, but the good news is that by taking simple steps you can stay ahead of the game in terms of protecting yourself and your family...

THE THREAT: MOLD

Especially in the wake of Superstorm Sandy on the East Coast, information about mold contamination has been making headlines.

This may come as no surprise to you: It is estimated that about half of all US homes are contaminated with mold. Mold (and its cousin, mildew) are fungi, and their spores are everywhere, both indoors and out. But mold needs moisture to grow, which is why it thrives wherever there is moisture in your home—in large areas, such as damp basements, or even in small piles of damp clothing.

If you're exposed long enough—mainly through inhaling mold spores—you may become allergic, experiencing a chronic runny nose, red eyes, itchy skin rashes, sneezing and asthma. Some types of mold produce secondary compounds called *mycotoxins* that can even cause pneumonia or trigger autoimmune illness such as arthritis.

What you may not know: Moisture control must begin promptly—you have about 24 to 48

Mitchell Gaynor, MD, assistant clinical professor of medicine at Weill Medical College of Cornell University in New York City. He is founder and president of Gaynor Integrative Oncology and is board-certified in oncology, hematology and internal medicine. He has written several books, including one about environmental dangers.

hours to completely dry out wet areas or dampness before mold starts to grow. This time frame can help you cope with small areas of moisture and reduce your exposure to mold.

Examples: It's important to quickly dry wet clothes left in a gym bag or in a washer or dryer…damp windowsills…and spills in the refrigerator. You can reduce or eliminate mildew in your bathroom by running the exhaust fan for a half-hour after showering—and leaving a window open if possible. When cleaning pillows and duvets, make sure to wash and dry them according to manufacturers' instructions—otherwise the filler may retain moisture, encouraging mold growth.

To remove small areas of mold (it can be black, brown, green, yellow or white and may have an acrid smell), scrub them with a mixture of one-eighth cup of laundry detergent, a cup of bleach and a gallon of water.

Mold on a wall often is a sign that mold is also within the wall, so you'll need to consult a professional about removal, especially if the area is larger than 10 square feet.

THE THREAT: WATER

Up to 700 chemicals have been found in tap water, many of which have been linked to cancer, hypothyroidism and immune system damage. Chemicals such as cadmium (a highly toxic metal used in batteries)…perfluorochemicals (used in making Teflon-coated pans)…and polychlorinated biphenyls or PCBs (the coating on electrical transformers used in fluorescent lighting), among others, make their way into our tap water when they are dumped into soil, contaminating groundwater.

You can find out details about the water in your area by going to *www.ewg.org/tap-water* and entering your Zip code. At this site, you will find out about some of the contaminants in your tap water, such as lead and barium. You also will find out which ones might exceed health guidelines. In high amounts, these contaminants may cause brain damage, cancer and liver and kidney damage.

What you may not know: Contaminants in tap water, when heated, can become inhalable gasses in the shower. When inhaled while showering, chloramines and chlorine, which

Dishwashers Can Be Breeding Grounds for Dangerous Fungi

In a recent finding, of 189 dishwashers tested, 62% tested positive for fungi…and 56% had a fungal species known as Exophiala, which looks like black slime and can cause fatal infections. The fungi is highly resistant to heat and detergents. You can wipe away the slime, but researchers are working on methods for permanently removing the fungi from dishwashers.

Nina Gunde-Cimerman, PhD, chair of molecular genetics and microbiology, University of Ljubljana, Slovenia, and leader of a study of 189 dishwashers from 18 countries, published in *Fungal Biology.*

often are used to treat drinking water, vaporize and can raise risk for bladder cancer, hypertension, allergies and lung damage.

To prevent exposure to inhalable gasses and chlorine, buy a showerhead filter. It should remove chloramines, chlorine, lead, mercury and barium.

Good brand: Santé (*www.santeforhealth.com*, various models are available for under $200).

THE THREAT: RADON

Radon is an invisible, odorless toxin created naturally during the breakdown of uranium in soil, rock and water. This radioactive gas can sneak into your home via cracks in the foundation. It is the number-one cause of lung cancer among nonsmokers—and smokers are even more susceptible.

Most people know about testing for radon when they sell or buy a home. The EPA recommends in-home testing for anyone who lives in a basement or on the ground, first or second floors. You can purchase an affordable short-term test kit. (One brand to try is Kidde Radon Detection Kit, about $15.)

Long-term radon testing kits take into account weather variations and humidity levels that can throw off short-term results. If a short-term kit reveals elevated levels, then you need to do long-term testing.

What you may not know: The EPA sets an acceptable level of radon at anything below 4 picocuries per liter (pCi/L). However, in 2009 the World Health Organization determined that a dangerous level of radon was 2.7 pCi/L or higher.

My advice: Do periodic testing and keep 2.7 in mind for acceptable radon levels.

THE THREAT: PCBS

These toxic chemicals could be wafting through your home and you wouldn't know it. PCBs were used to line and insulate electrical wiring and were in paint, caulk and fluorescent light ballasts in homes until it was found that they off-gas, which means that the chemicals in them begin to evaporate, causing health problems for residents. Besides increasing risk for cancer, PCBs can adversely affect the immune, reproductive, nervous and endocrine systems.

What you may not know: PCBs were banned in the late 1970s but remain in many older homes built before 1977. Once released into the environment, PCBs don't easily break down. You won't know if PCBs are being released.

Most electricians are now trained to check your home's wiring to ensure that it isn't rotting or producing PCBs. A PCB remediation company can test for the toxin and remove it. Air-quality testing costs approximately $550.

Don't Cook Danger into Your Food

Sandra Woodruff, RD, registered dietitian and nutrition consultant based in Tallahassee, Florida, and Helen Vlassara, MD, an endocrinologist and professor at Mount Sinai School of Medicine in New York City, where she directs the Experimental Diabetes and Aging Division. They are also coauthors of *The AGE-Less Way: Escape America's Overeating Epidemic* (*www.theage-lessway.com*).

Some of the most serious chronic health problems in the US, including Alzheimer's disease, cancer, diabetes and kidney and heart disease, have been linked to what we eat—processed foods, fast food, red meat, etc. What may surprise you is that the increased health risks from these foods may be due in large part to how they are cooked.

Dry-heat cooking, such as grilling, broiling, frying and even baking and roasting, greatly increases levels of *advanced glycation end-products* (AGEs), also known as glycotoxins. Small amounts of these chemical compounds are naturally present in all foods, but their levels rise dramatically when foods are subjected to dry heat, which frequently occurs both in home cooking and in commercial food preparation.

The danger: AGEs are oxidants that produce free radicals, damage DNA, trigger inflammation throughout the body and accelerate the aging process. They also make cholesterol more likely to cling to artery walls, the underlying cause of most heart attacks. Some researchers now believe that AGEs can be linked to most chronic diseases.

A NEW THREAT

A century ago, people mainly ate fresh, homemade foods, such as grains, vegetables, legumes and fruits, with relatively small amounts of meat. The processed food industry was still in its infancy.

However, in the following decades, meat portions grew larger, and Americans acquired a strong desire for the intense flavors, aromas and colors in commercially prepared "browned" foods, such as crackers, chips, cookies, grilled and broiled meats, french fries, pizza, etc. During this time, the rates of heart disease, diabetes and other chronic diseases started to rise. This wasn't a coincidence—the rich taste, smell and appearance of these foods primarily come from AGEs.

Use Copper Cookware to Fight Salmonella

The oxidation of copper in copper-alloy pots and pans produces a residue that kills salmonella and some other bacteria that cause food poisoning. Stainless steel cookware has no effect on salmonella at all.

Study by researchers at University of Arizona, Tucson, reported in USA Today Magazine.

Our bodies can neutralize the small amounts of AGEs that are naturally found in foods (and that we produce as a by-product of metabolism). But our defense mechanisms are overwhelmed with the high amounts that are now very common in the typical American diet.

HOW MUCH IS TOO MUCH?

AGEs are measured in kilounits (kU). We recommend consuming no more than 5,000 kU to 8,000 kU per day (see box on next page for examples of kU levels in some common foods). Recent studies have shown that the average American typically consumes more than 15,000 kU daily, and many people eat well over 20,000 kU daily.

Reducing dietary AGEs may be especially important for people with diabetes because high blood sugar levels cause more AGEs to form. It's also crucial for people with kidney disease because they are less able to remove AGEs from the body. AGEs also are elevated in patients with heart disease, obesity and dementia.

Researchers can measure the amounts of AGEs in the blood, but doctors don't commonly use this test because it's not currently available for commercial use. What your doctor can do is measure levels of C-reactive protein (CRP), a marker for inflammation. If your level is high (above 3 mg/dL), you may have excessive AGEs in your blood. If you eat a lot of grilled, broiled and roasted meats, for example, and/or heat-treated processed foods, this also means your AGE levels are likely too high.

AN "AGE-LESS" DIET

Our studies have shown that people who make simple dietary changes can reduce their levels of AGEs by more than 50% in four months. The reduction is accompanied by a similar decrease in CRP levels. *Helpful strategies…*

•**Eat less animal protein.** Animal protein, especially red meat, is among the main sources of AGEs—and the levels can multiply tenfold when the meat is grilled, broiled, baked or roasted.

Helpful: Eat beef no more than three times a week.

Because animal fat also contributes to AGE intake, eat lean meats. They have fewer AGEs than higher-fat meats. Animal fats such as butter also are higher in AGEs than plant fats such as olive oil.

Best approach: Fill three-quarters of your plate with plant foods, such as vegetables, whole grains, legumes and fruits, and leave no more than one-quarter of the plate for animal foods, such as meats and cheeses.

Soups and stews are tasty ways to serve small portions of meat. Also enjoy more meatless meals, such as vegetarian chili or veggie burgers. Nonfat milk and yogurt are low in AGEs and are a good way to add protein to meals and snacks.

•**Avoid dry-heat cooking,** such as grilling, broiling, baking, roasting and frying. High, dry heat greatly increases AGEs.

Example: A piece of raw meat might have 500 kU to 700 kU of AGEs. But after the meat is broiled, the level can rise to 5,000 kU to 8,000 kU.

Better approach: Cook with moist heat—stew, poach, steam, boil or microwave. A piece of chicken that's poached or boiled, for example, will have about 1,000 kU. The same piece of chicken will have about 5,000 kU when it's broiled.

If you have a desire for grilled or roasted foods, vegetables and fruits are better choices than meats. These foods have far fewer AGEs than meats and fats when cooked with dry heat.

If you do cook with dry heat, marinate first. The eventual formation of AGEs is reduced by about 50% when raw meats are marinated in acidic ingredients, such as vinegar or lemon juice. For each pound of meat, use the juice from two lemons or an equivalent amount of vinegar or lime juice plus enough water to cover the meat (about one cup). Add some garlic and/or herbs for extra flavor. Avoid commercial marinades since they're usually high in sugar and/or oil, which will increase AGEs.

•**Reheat gently.** Microwaving is a good method for reheating meats and other foods. Be sure to include plenty of liquid and reheat to a safe temperature to prevent the possibility of food-borne illness due, for example, to E. coli or salmonella.

Reduce AGEs in Your Meals

You can easily reduce AGEs in your food with simple modifications in meal preparation. AGE amounts listed are based on standard serving sizes.

High-AGE Menu	AGE ku	Low-AGE Menu	AGE ku
BREAKFAST			
Fried egg sandwich	1,300	Scrambled egg sandwich	120
Coffee with cream	330	Coffee with whole milk	10
LUNCH			
Salad topped with grilled chicken, cheddar cheese and Italian dressing	6,330	Salad topped with poached chicken, light cheddar cheese and light Italian dressing	1,890
Toasted wheat crackers	275	Whole-grain pita wedges	15
DINNER			
Grilled steak	6,600	Braised beef	2,200
Baked oven fries	490	Mashed potatoes, no butter	20
Steamed green beans with butter	650	Steamed green beans with sliced almonds	320

Source: http://theage-lessway.com/estimating-your-age-intake

Warning: Any food that has been browned or crisped, such as cookies, crackers, chips, etc., will be high in AGEs.

Tricky Food Labels

Deanna Minich, PhD, CN, nutritionist and author, has written four books on nutrition and health, including An *A-Z Guide to Food Additives* (Conari), in which she gives an "A to F" safety rating for widely used food additives. *www.foodandspirit.com*

A bottle of Gatorade sounded like the perfect thirst quencher to 15-year-old Sarah Kavanagh on a hot, humid day in her Mississippi hometown. But this teenager, a committed label-reader, was surprised to learn from an Internet search that the popular sports drink contained brominated vegetable oil, an ingredient that comes with a long list of possible side effects, including changes in thyroid hormones and function and neurological disorders.

The additive, used in some citrus-flavored drinks to keep the fruit flavoring evenly distributed, does not sound ominous—how bad could it be with "vegetable" in the name? But Kavanagh, whose story was told in *The New York Times*, had done her research and started a petition to convince Gatorade-maker PepsiCo to change the drink's formulation.

Here are other food additives (some even healthy-sounding) that are bad for us—along with some scary-sounding additives that are good for us...*

ADDITIVES TO AVOID

•**Cottonseed oil.** Made from the seeds of the cotton plant, cottonseed oil is used to thicken food or add texture. Cottonseed oil is found in many fried snack foods, especially potato chips, as well as in salad oil, sauces, marinades and baked goods.

Some individuals are allergic to cottonseed oil. Cotton crops also tend to be genetically modified and grown with high levels of pesticides.

•**Diacetyl.** This additive, which provides a buttery aroma and flavor, is most often found

Soups, sauces and gravies should be brought to a boil. Leftovers such as meats and casseroles should be reheated to 165°F.

•**Don't eat certain foods together.** Consuming meats with foods that are high in sugar—for example, having a slice of cake after eating a hamburger—allows existing AGEs in the meat to interact with the sugars in the cake, creating higher levels of AGEs. Similarly, eating meats with very high-fat foods, such as a hamburger topped with bacon and cheese, will produce far more AGEs than consuming these foods by themselves.

•**Focus on fresh foods.** Because processed foods have high levels of AGEs, fresh foods and foods that have been minimally processed are a much better choice.

A serving of rice, for example, will have almost no AGEs, but the same amount of crispy rice cereal will have 600 kU. Avoid takeout and convenience foods, such as fast-food burgers, fries and pizza.

*To research potential health risks of food additives, consult the Web site of the Center for Science in the Public Interest, *www.cspinet.org*.

in microwave popcorn. And its pairing with hydrogenated fats, also typically found in microwave popcorn, equals an extremely unhealthy combination that increases LDL "bad" cholesterol and lowers HDL "good" cholesterol.

In addition, a preliminary 2012 lab study suggests that consuming diacetyl may worsen the effects of beta-amyloid accumulation, a hallmark of Alzheimer's disease.

•**Hydrolyzed vegetable protein.** This meaty-tasting flavor enhancer, classified as a "natural flavoring" on some labels and used in soups, meats, sauces and stews, often masks the presence of monosodium glutamate (MSG). Found in many canned, packaged and prepared foods, MSG is known to trigger headaches and may lead to weight gain.

MSG is sometimes also a hidden source of wheat, which should be avoided by people who are sensitive to gluten, a protein found in wheat, barley and rye.

•**Potassium bromate.** Potassium alone is an essential mineral for health, but potassium bromate (found in bromated flour) has been linked to cancer in lab animals. The threat is strong enough to have prompted all European countries as well as Canada and China to ban bromated flour, an additive that helps dough rise. In the US, the FDA has stopped short of such a measure, instead only encouraging commercial bakers to voluntarily stop using it.

Many national manufacturers of baked goods, such as Arnold and Pepperidge Farm, switched to nonbromated flours years ago, but others have not. Check the label.

ADDITIVES THAT ARE SAFE

•**Alginate.** It may sound like it comes from algae, but seaweed is the source of this additive, which serves as a thickener in jellies, salad dressings, custards, ice cream and soups. Its ability to trap cholesterol in its gel-like structure may lower cholesterol, and some studies suggest it also can help us feel full.

•**Canthaxanthin.** Healthful food colorings are difficult to find, but this orange-red pigment —found in crustaceans, fish and mushrooms— is an antioxidant. Canthaxanthin is sometimes added to fruit spreads, syrups and drinks and may have benefits similar to those found in other antioxidants such as beta-carotene.

•**Dioctyl sodium sulfosuccinate.** This food stabilizer and thickener is known for its stool-softening and laxative properties. The white, waxy solid, which is added to dairy-based cheeses, beverages and sauces, has been researched extensively in animal studies and is considered essentially nontoxic.

•**Fructo-oligosaccharides (FOS).** Just trying to pronounce this additive scares some people away, but don't let it deter you if you spot it on a food label. FOS are plant sugars derived from such healthful foods as asparagus and Jerusalem artichokes.

FOS, typically added to certain dairy products such as some yogurts and ice cream, act as healthful "prebiotics," which promote the production of "good" bacteria in your gut.

Toxic Toilet Paper?

Kurunthachalam Kannan, PhD, research scientist with the New York State Department of Health in Albany, a professor in the department of environmental health sciences in the School of Public Health at the State University of New York at Albany, and coauthor of two recent studies on BPA and BPS in paper products published in *Environmental Science & Technology*.

The FDA recently refused to ban bisphenol A (BPA), the toxic chemical that leaches out of plastic containers and cans and into our foods. Now there is more disturbing news about BPA and its chemical "cousin" bisphenol S (BPS)—according to two recent studies, both these toxins are present in an array of paper products, including toilet tissue!

Background: BPA has estrogen-like effects on the body, acting as an endocrine disruptor and interrupting our hormonal signals. It has been linked to heart disease, diabetes, cancer, liver disease, thyroid dysfunction, obesity and birth defects. In addition to its use in food containers, BPA also serves as a color developer in thermal paper, such as cash register receipts—and when we touch that paper, the chemical can be absorbed through our skin or enter our bodies via hand-to-mouth contact.

What you may not know: As the evidence against BPA grows, some paper manufacturers have been replacing the compound with the structurally similar BPS—which also has estrogen-like effects.

Recent studies: Researchers looked at hundreds of samples of common paper products— paper towels, napkins, newspapers, magazines, flyers, tickets, luggage tags, business cards, envelopes, currency, facial tissues and, yes, TP— and found that the vast majority contained BPA and/or BPS. How did these chemicals get into such a wide array of products? Thermal paper often is recycled, so contamination of other types of paper products can occur during the recycling process…ink may be another source, though this requires further study.

Self-defense: Avoid touching thermal paper by turning down receipts you don't need…if you must touch such paper frequently (for instance, because you're a cashier), wear gloves. Wash your hands immediately after handling newspapers, magazines, flyers or paper money. Use cloth dishtowels, napkins and handkerchiefs rather than paper ones. As for that toxic toilet paper, researchers suggested skipping recycled TP and instead using virgin pulp toilet paper. And how about continuing to lobby the FDA to take action on BPA and BPS, too?

High BPA Levels Seen in Narrowed Arteries

Peninsula College of Medicine and Dentistry, news release.

For the first time, researchers have uncovered evidence that a chemical found in a wide range of everyday plastic products may be tied to the risk for arterial narrowing, and thereby heart disease, among those found to have elevated levels of the chemical in their urine.

The finding builds on prior concerns regarding bisphenol A (BPA), which is used in the manufacture of food and drink containers, and other common household items. The recent study results are based on an analysis of data from nearly 600 men and women participating in a coronary artery disease study in the United Kingdom.

"Our latest study strengthens a growing body of work that suggests that BPA may be adding to known risk factors for heart disease," study author David Melzer, PhD, professor of epidemiology and public health at the Peninsula College of Medicine and Dentistry at the University of Exeter in the United Kingdom, said in a college news release.

Dr. Melzer and colleagues published their findings in the journal *PLoS ONE*.

To explore the chemical's potential impact on heart disease, the research team divided the study participants into three groups based on their arterial narrowing status: those with severe coronary artery disease (385 patients); those with moderate disease (86 patients); and those with no signs of coronary artery disease (120 patients).

The investigators then measured the levels of BPA found in each participant's urine.

Cross-referencing of arterial narrowing with urinary levels of BPA revealed that those with severe coronary artery disease had "significantly" higher levels of urinary BPA.

"These results are important because they give us a better understanding of the mechanisms underlying the association between BPA and heart disease," Tamara Galloway, PhD, the study's lead toxicologist, said in the news release.

However, while the recent study uncovered an association between arterial narrowing and BPA levels in urine, it did not prove a cause-and-effect relationship.

The study authors noted in the news release that research published by the Peninsula College of Medicine and Dentistry in 2008 prompted many countries to ban BPA from the manufacture of baby bottles and other feeding equipment, based on the suggestion that the chemical may pose a specific health risk to infants.

In addition, other research by the same team has suggested that BPA exposure may affect testosterone levels in men.

info For more information on BPA, visit the US National Institute of Environmental Health Sciences Web site at *www.niehs.nih.gov* (search "BPA").

Surprising Dangers in the Hospital

Marty Makary, MD, MPH, associate professor of surgery and health policy at Johns Hopkins School of Public Health, Baltimore. He is author of *The New York Times* best seller *Unaccountable: What Hospitals Won't Tell You and How Transparency Can Revolutionize Health Care* (Bloomsbury). *www.unaccountablebook.com*

When you're admitted to a hospital, you probably don't stop and wonder what your chances are of getting out alive. But the odds are worse than you might imagine—and you can literally save your own life (or that of a loved one) by knowing how to investigate a hospital's record before you're checked in.

Frightening statistics: An estimated 98,000 hospital patients die from medical errors in the US annually. That's more than twice the number of Americans killed in car crashes each year. Many other hospital patients will suffer from serious—and preventable—complications. *Examples:* About one of every 20 hospital patients will develop an infection…and surgeons operate on the wrong body part up to 40 times a week.

Getting the information you need: Because few hospitals publish statistics about their performance, it's difficult for patients to know which ones are worse—in some cases, much worse—than average.

For advice on avoiding the most common threats to hospital patients, we spoke to Marty Makary, MD, MPH, one of the country's leading experts on hospital safety.

WHAT YOU CAN FIND OUT

When I've asked patients why they chose a particular

hospital, they typically say something like, "Because it's close to home." Others might say, "That is where my doctor has privileges." But those are bad answers. Before you get any medical care in a hospital, you should find out everything you can about the track record of the hospital. *Five clues to consider…*

Clue #1: **Bounceback rate.** This is the term that doctors use for patients who need to be rehospitalized within 30 days. A high bounceback rate means that you have a higher-than-average risk for postsurgery complications, such as infection or impaired wound healing. Patients also can look up bounceback rates for conditions such as heart attacks and pneumonia. The rate for a particular procedure should never be higher than the national average.

Why this matters: A high bounceback rate could indicate substandard care or even a lack of teamwork in the operating room. It could also mean that the hospital is discharging patients too soon or that patients aren't getting clear discharge instructions that tell them what to do when they get home.

What to do: Check your hospital's rating on the US Department of Health and Human Services' Web site Hospital Compare (*www. hospitalcompare.hhs.gov*), where the majority of US hospitals are listed. You can see if the bounceback rate is better than, worse than or the same as the national average for the procedure you need.

Hospitals that are serious about reducing readmissions go the extra mile. For example, they will provide patients with detailed instructions on such issues as medication use and proper wound-cleaning procedures. Some even give patients a 24-hour hotline number to call if they have symptoms that could indicate a problem.

Clue #2: **Culture of safety.** My colleagues and I at Johns Hopkins recently surveyed doctors, nurses and other hospital employees at 60 reputable US hospitals and asked such questions as, "Is

---

Extra Help When Picking a Hospital

When you meet hospital workers in your community, ask which hospital they would choose if they needed care. A recent survey conducted at 60 reputable US hospitals found that in one-third of them, half or more of health-care workers would not feel comfortable receiving medical care in the unit in which they work.

the teamwork good?" "Is communication strong?" "Do you feel comfortable speaking up about safety concerns?"

We found a wide variation in the "safety culture" at different hospitals—and even within different departments at the same hospital. At one-third of the hospitals, the majority of employees reported that the level of teamwork was poor. Conversely, up to 99% of the staff at some hospitals said the teamwork was good.

Why it matters: Hospitals with a poor safety culture tended to have higher infection rates and worse patient outcomes.

What to do: Few hospitals that have conducted this type of survey make the findings public. Patients have to find other ways to get similar information. To do this, I suggest that before you choose a hospital you ask employees—including nurses and lab technicians—if they'd feel comfortable getting medical care where they work. Even if some hospital employees put a positive spin on their answers, you can generally tell a lot from their demeanor and comfort level when they respond.

Clue #3: **Use of minimally invasive procedures.** Compared with "open" surgeries, minimally invasive procedures—such as knee arthroscopy and "keyhole" gallbladder surgery—require shorter hospitalizations. They're also less painful, less likely to result in an infection and less likely to lead to the need for subsequent surgery.

In spite of this, some surgeons still prefer open procedures. During my training, for example, I worked with a surgeon who was not skilled at minimally invasive surgery. His procedures were always open and involved large incisions—his wound-infection rate was about 20%. But his colleagues, who had trained in the newer minimally invasive techniques, had infection rates that were close to zero.

Why it matters: For the reasons above, you should usually choose a minimally invasive procedure if it's appropriate for your condition.

What to do: When discussing surgery, ask your doctor if there's more than one approach...the percentage of similar procedures that are done in a minimally invasive way...and

What Your Hospital Knows That You Don't

Here are six things your hospital might not tell you that could hurt you...

• **Your surgeon has experience—just not with the operation you require.**

What to do: Ask your doctor how many times each year he/she performs the operation you need. Be cautious about the surgeon who performs it far less than the average specialist in the field would.

• **You can't trust marketing claims.**

What to do: The hospital's advertised "number-one ranking" might be restricted to a very specific measure or malady that has little to do with your needs. Go to *www.hospitalcompare.hhs.gov* for unbiased info.

• **You might be better off going to your local community hospital than a prestigious research hospital.**

What to do: Lean toward prestigious research hospitals if you have a high-risk or complex condition such as cancer or a high-risk pregnancy...but toward well-regarded community hospitals for routine conditions.

• **You're probably better off with a doctor who doesn't seem omniscient.**

What to do: Raise the topic of seeking a second opinion with your doctor. It's a good sign if he encourages this...a bad sign if he becomes defensive.

• **Doctors recommend the procedures that they know best, not the ones that are best for you.**

What to do: Do a Web search for the name of the operation you require, along with the words "minimally invasive." If there is a minimally invasive alternative that your doctor didn't mention, ask him/her about it. Seek a second opinion (see CLUE #3 on this page).

• **The hospital's plastic surgeons may have little or no training in plastic surgery.**

What to do: Confirm that a plastic surgeon is certified by the American Board of Plastic Surgery (*www.abplsurg.org*).

the percentage that he/she does that way versus the percentage done each way nationwide.

Important: Get a second opinion before undergoing any ongoing or extensive treatment, including surgery. About 30% of second opinions are different from the first one.

***Clue #4*: Volume of procedures.** "See one, do one, teach one" is a common expression in medical schools. The idea is that new doctors have to start somewhere to learn how to perform medical procedures. Don't let them start on you.

Why it matters: Surgical death rates are directly related to a surgeon's experience with that procedure. The death rate after pancreas surgery, for example, is 14.7% for surgeons who average fewer than two procedures a year. It is 4.6% for those who do four or more. A survey conducted by the New York State Department of Health found that hospitals with surgeons who did relatively few procedures had patient-mortality rates that were four times higher than the state average.

What to do: Ask your doctor how often he does a particular procedure. For nonsurgical care, ask how many patients with your condition he treats.

Helpful: If 50% or more of a doctor's practice is dedicated to patients with exactly your condition, he will probably be a good choice.

***Clue #5*: The availability of "open notes."** Doctors make detailed notes after every office visit, but many patients have never seen these notes. Hospitals may not make them easily available, or the office/hospital can make it difficult (or expensive) to get copies.

Why it matters: Transparency builds trust. Patients who know what's in their medical records will not have to wonder what the doctor is writing about them.

Patients who read the notes will remember details about treatment advice…ask questions if they are confused…and often correct errors that can make a difference in their diagnosis and/or treatment. Also, these records are needed for a second opinion.

I purposely dictate notes while my patients are still in my office sitting next to me. Once, I was corrected when I said that a prior surgery was on the left side—it was actually on the right side. Another patient corrected me when I noted a wrong medication dose. Another reminded me to mention a history of high blood pressure.

What to do: Get copies of all of your medical records, including test results. If your doctor or hospital refuses to share them, ask to speak to an administrator. The records are yours—you have a right, under federal law, to see them and get copies. Fees range from a few dollars for a few pages to hundreds of dollars for extensive records.

When to Follow Your Doctor to a New Practice

Charles B. Inlander, consumer advocate and health-care consultant based in Fogelsville, Pennsylvania. He was the founding president of the nonprofit People's Medical Society, a consumer advocacy organization, and is author or coauthor of more than 20 consumer-health books.

Recently, one of my wife's trusted doctors sold his practice to a local hospital. Now, instead of owning his own surgical practice, he is an employee of a large and growing hospital system. This is a trend that is revolutionizing how our health care is being delivered. By the end of 2012, 55% of all doctors in the US were employed by hospitals, and the number keeps growing—largely because of the rising costs of maintaining private practices and hospitals' desire to keep their beds full by having their own sources of referrals. By 2020, only about 20% of US doctors are expected to be in their own private practices.

If your doctor has notified you that he/she is joining a hospital system or if you're looking for a new doctor, be sure to ask these questions…

•Will your doctor refer his patients outside the hospital's system? Referrals among hospital doctors, including specialists, are easy and usually don't require long waits for appointments. And because they work for the same entity, these doctors more frequently consult with one another than independent physicians do. That type of coordinated care often results in better outcomes. But what happens if the best referral is outside that hospital's system? Believe it or not, some hospitals require doctors to refer only in-house even when they believe an outside colleague may be better.

To protect yourself: Ask your doctor whether he can refer outside the hospital system. If not, do not use that doctor.

•**What happens if your doctor leaves the hospital?** Some hospitals require doctors to sign a noncompete clause that prohibits them from practicing in the local area if they quit or are let go by the hospital.

To protect yourself: Ask your doctor whether he would still be available to treat you if he leaves the hospital for any reason. If not, consider choosing another doctor so that you can be ensured continuity of care.

•**Will you be shuffled around?** Some people who have followed their doctors to hospital practices have been disappointed because they are sometimes forced to see other doctors in the practice when they show up for their appointments.

To protect yourself: Ask your doctor whether you will be notified in advance (and given a chance to reschedule) if he is not available to see you at your appointment time.

•**Are your medical records transferable?** Every hospital now uses electronic medical records, which help ensure that your care is coordinated because all your tests, treatments and medical history are in one electronic file. The problem is, most hospitals have their own unique electronic medical record system that

is available only to their personnel. If you use doctors outside the hospital system, the hospital practice is not likely to handle the transfer of a paper copy of your records.

To protect yourself: Ask for paper copies of your medical history, the results of all your tests and doctors' notes on major treatments you have had. This way, you can take these records with you when you see practitioners outside the system rather than relying on the hospital practice to take care of it.

The Epidemic of Overdiagnosis

H. Gilbert Welch, MD, MPH, professor of medicine at The Dartmouth Institute for Health Policy and Clinical Practice and general internist at the White River Junction VA in Vermont. He is author of *Overdiagnosed: Making People Sick in the Pursuit of Health* (Beacon) and *Should I Be Tested for Cancer? Maybe Not and Here's Why* (University of California).

There's a dangerous epidemic out there. It's called overdiagnosis—when you are diagnosed with a condition that will never hurt your health.

Overdiagnosis can lead to potentially harmful medical care, as you undergo invasive tests, take medications or have surgery—all for a condition that is harmless. Medical care also can be expensive, time-consuming and anxiety-producing. *Here, according to H. Gilbert Welch, MD, MPH, the conditions that are frequently overdiagnosed...*

HIGH BLOOD PRESSURE

There is tremendous value in treating moderate-to-severe hypertension—a reading of 160/100 or higher—because it can prevent heart attack, heart failure, stroke and kidney failure. But below that range (very-mild-to-mild hypertension), overdiagnosis is likely. In statistical terms, almost everyone treated for severe hypertension will benefit, but 18 people with mild hypertension have to be treated for one person to benefit.

And all that unnecessary treatment can involve added expense, hassle (doctor appointments, lab tests, refills, insurance forms, etc.) and drug side effects such as fatigue, persistent cough and erectile dysfunction.

My viewpoint: Don't automatically take medication to lower mild high blood pressure. Losing weight and getting more exercise generally are the way to go.

TYPE 2 DIABETES

More than 20 million Americans have type 2 diabetes, which can cause complications such as heart disease, kidney failure, blindness, nerve pain and leg infections that lead to amputation.

However: Like high blood pressure, type 2 diabetes has a range of abnormality, from the asymptomatic to the severe. Some people with diabetes will never develop complications.

That's even more likely nowadays because the medical definition of type 2 diabetes—and therefore, the criteria for who should and should not be treated—has changed. The definition of type 2 diabetes used to be a fasting blood sugar level higher than 140 mg/dL. Today, it is a fasting blood sugar level higher than 126 mg/dL—turning millions of people into diabetics. A newer test—hemoglobin A1C, a measurement of long-term blood sugar levels that detects the percentage of red blood cells coated with glucose (blood sugar)—defines diabetes as a level of 6.5% or higher.

My viewpoint: Physicians should use medication to reduce blood sugar in patients with an A1C of 9% or higher…discuss treatment with patients between 8% and 9%…and typically not treat patients under 8%.

In a randomized trial designed to test the effect of aggressive blood sugar reduction, more than 10,000 people with type 2 diabetes and A1C levels above 8% were divided into two groups. One group received intensive glucose-lowering therapy aimed at reducing A1C to less than 6%. The other group received standard therapy, targeting a level of 7% to 7.9%. After three years, the intensive-therapy group had about 25% increased risk for death, and because of that, the trial was stopped.

PROSTATE CANCER

In 2012, the US Preventive Services Task Force recommended against screening for prostate cancer with the prostate-specific antigen (PSA) test, concluding that "many men are harmed as a result of prostate cancer screening and few, if any, benefit."

Recent research shows that 1,000 men need to have a PSA test annually for a decade to prevent one death from prostate cancer. However, between 150 and 200 of those men will have a worrisome PSA test (a level higher than 4) that will lead to a biopsy of the prostate—an invasive procedure that can cause blood in the urine, infections and a high rate of hospitalization in the month after the procedure. Of those biopsied, 30 to 100 will be treated for a cancer that was never going to bother them. As a result, between one-third and one-half of those men will become impotent and 20% to 30% will become incontinent.

My viewpoint: I am a 57-year-old man—I have not had a PSA test, nor do I intend to. I understand that I may develop symptoms of prostate cancer (such as trouble urinating and bone pain), that I may die from prostate cancer (as about 3% of men do) and that lifelong screening might reduce my risk (maybe down to as low as 2.5%). But I also recognize that most men (about 97%) will die from something else, and I don't want to spend my life looking for things to be wrong. Most prostate cancers found by the PSA test are slow-growing and not life-threatening, but because there is no way to determine which prostate cancers are dangerous and which are nonthreatening, most of them are treated. Given the limited benefits in saving lives and the terrible risks of overtreatment, I don't recommend PSA testing. (For other views and studies on PSA testing, see page 310.)

BREAST CANCER

Diagnostic mammography—testing a woman when a new breast lump is found to see if she has cancer—is an absolute must. Screening mammography—for early detection of breast cancer—is not.

Recent scientific research: A study I coauthored, published in *The New England Journal of Medicine,* links three decades of mammographic screening for breast cancer to a doubling in the number of cases of early-stage breast cancer, from 112 to 234 cases per 100,000 women. Our study estimated that over those 30 years, 1.3 million American women have been overdiagnosed—tumors that were detected on screening would never have led to clinical symptoms.

The result is more tests…more anxiety from "suspicious" findings…and more harsh anticancer treatments, including more mastectomies.

My viewpoint: It is probably true that some women will die of breast cancer if they don't get screened for it. But it is much more common to be hurt by screening than helped by it. Mammography is a choice, not an imperative.

How to Communicate With Your Doctor to Get the Care You Need

Leana Wen, MD, emergency physician at Brigham and Women's Hospital and Massachusetts General Hospital, both in Boston. She is coauthor, with Joshua Kosowsky, MD, of *When Doctors Don't Listen: How to Avoid Misdiagnoses and Unnecessary Tests* (St. Martin's). *www.drleanawen.com*

When you have a doctor's appointment (or go to an emergency department), the diagnosis process starts the moment the physician steps into the examination room. That's why what you say and how you say it are so critical to getting an accurate diagnosis and the best possible medical care.

You have probably heard that the average patient has less than 20 seconds (some studies say just 12 seconds) to describe the ailment before being interrupted by the doctor.

What's even more interesting is that the average doctor will have already made a diagnosis during those crucial first seconds. But if he/she hasn't gotten your full medical history, your odds of getting a correct diagnosis dramatically decline.

TALK SO YOUR DOCTOR WILL LISTEN

To prevent this scenario, when you see any doctor—whether it's your primary care physician, an emergency department physician or a specialist—what's most important is to tell your story in a way that will help him truly understand what's happening. My advice…

•**Plan what you're going to say beforehand.** If you have a doctor's appointment, write down your complete story and practice beforehand how you'll deliver it with a family member or a friend. While practicing, work out the details that most accurately describe what you are feeling.

•**Don't use medical jargon or diagnose yourself.** Because you probably haven't been trained in medical terms, you may use them incorrectly. In your own words, give a clear, chronological and vivid description of what's going on without a self-diagnosis. For example, instead of saying, "My stomach ulcer pain is an eight out of 10," you might state, "I woke up with a terrible stomachache. I felt like my belly was on fire."

•**Describe how symptoms have impacted your life.** You could say, "I have had such a bad headache that I could not get out of my bed for three days." If a symptom is chronic, describe how it's changed over time. For example, "My joint pain improved for a month, but it has now come back and is worse than ever."

•**Answer your doctor's yes/no questions with details.** Doctors use yes/no questions because it is a quick (though incomplete) way to gather information. What works best for you, the patient, however, is to answer your doctor's questions your way, giving pertinent details.

Example: If your doctor asks, "Do you have pain in your chest?" you might say, "Not pain, exactly…but I felt a kind of dull discomfort right here, around the time I got up. It lasted about an hour, and now I have a throbbing sensation in the same place from time to time."

•**Don't let go of your real concerns.** If you think the doctor is ignoring your concerns, you might say, "I've tried to answer your questions about my chest pain, but I also want to know why I've been feeling so queasy after most meals for the last two weeks."

GET THE INFORMATION YOU NEED

If you want to be fully involved in your medical care, you'll also need to understand the reasoning behind a diagnosis. When making a diagnosis, doctors develop a list of possibilities (known as the "differential diagnosis"). From this list, doctors select one (or more) that seems most likely (called the "working diagnosis"). After you've told your story, ask your doctor what could possibly be wrong and what he thinks your problem is.

Important: If the diagnosis—or anything the doctor says—doesn't make sense to you, ask more questions. For example, you might say, "Does this explain why I've been feeling so tired for weeks?" As the doctor performs a physical exam, participate actively by asking questions such as, "Just what is it we're looking for?"

If the doctor orders tests: Find out why.

Specific questions might include: Just what will the test show? Will it change treatment? Are there risks? Are there risks in not doing the test? Are there alternatives? Is waiting an option?

Important: If your regular doctor is not open to this type of dialogue, it might be time to find a new one—or if you're in an emergency room, offer to wait until the doctor can spend a little more time with you.

Nine Things Nursing Homes Won't Tell You

Robert Kane, MD, director of the Center on Aging at University of Minnesota, Minneapolis. Dr. Kane holds an endowed chair in the department of long-term care and aging at University of Minnesota School of Public Health, where he previously served as dean. He is author of *The Good Caregiver: A One-of-a-Kind Compassionate Resource for Anyone Caring for an Aging Loved One* (Avery).

You trust your parent's nursing home to take care of him or her. Unfortunately, some homes do not deserve this trust. Nine secrets you need to know about nursing homes—public and private...

1. You would lose your taste for this facility if you visited during mealtime. Mealtimes are when nursing home employees are under the greatest stress. Some residents have meals served in their rooms, but most eat in a dining room. Try to look in on a meal—if employees are interacting with residents in a friendly and respectful manner, they probably treat residents well all the time.

2. Our nurses aren't really our nurses. When nursing homes can't find enough permanent nurses, they arrange for "agency nurses" to fill the manpower gaps. These agency nurses work for staffing agencies, not the nursing home, and they rarely stay long enough at a home to form a bond with the residents or get to know their needs.

Most facilities use agency nurses from time to time, but it's a bad sign if more than 15% to 20% of a home's manpower is provided by agency nurses. The facility should provide this statistic upon request.

3. Our physical therapy facilities and staff fall well short of our claims. Insist on touring the physical therapy department especially if your parent requires rehab. Does the equipment look modern and extensive? Ask your parent's doctors if any special rehab equipment would be helpful, and confirm that this is present. Also ask whether the nursing home's physical therapists are on staff or on contract—facilities with physical therapists on staff likely have made a greater commitment to rehab services.

4. We have less than four stars in the overall rating. The Medicare system's Web site includes the Nursing Home Compare database (*medicare.gov/nursinghomecompare*), which rates every Medicare- or Medicaid-certified nursing home on a star system, with five stars indicating the best. Avoid facilities with an overall rating lower than four stars if you can afford to do so.

5. Our activities schedule is just for show—the main activity here is sitting and staring. Every nursing home has an "activities schedule" that inevitably lists an impressive array of things for residents to do each day. Look in on one or two of these activities next time you visit your parent. Is the activity really taking place? How many residents are participating? Does it look like they're having fun? Be concerned if the main activity of most residents appears to be clustering around the nurses' station in wheelchairs staring into space or at a TV.

(Residents sitting around is perfectly fine—if they are chatting together, playing cards or interacting in some other way.)

6. Trust your nose. Some subpar nursing homes manage to make their facilities look presentable for visitors, but making them smell pleasant is a tougher challenge. Walk down a few corridors where doors to patient rooms are open and take a whiff. A bad facility might reek of urine, feces or large amounts of Lysol.

7. We can't provide what our residents really want—privacy. The contentment of nursing home residents is closely correlated with their ability to obtain privacy, according to our research. Unfortunately, many homes offer mostly shared rooms. It doesn't really cost that much more to build nursing homes with private rooms—it's just a matter of adding a few extra walls—but many nursing homes were constructed before the importance of single rooms was widely recognized.

Helpful: If single rooms are not available in your parent's price range, consider how much privacy the facility's shared rooms offer. Some feature sturdy partitions...others just thin curtains or nothing at all between beds.

8. The more you visit, the better the care your parent will receive. Residents whose families visit often typically receive significantly more attentive care from nursing home employees than those who rarely receive guests. If you live far away, perhaps a friend or relative can visit regularly.

Helpful: Each time you visit, ask a question or two of a staff member. This sends the message that you are paying close attention to your parent's care. But always be polite, and don't let these questions become excessive or frivolous—you want the staff to consider you involved, not annoying.

9. We can kick your parent out at any time. Nursing homes cannot legally expel residents because they've run out of savings and must resort to Medicaid to pay. But nursing homes are allowed to send away residents who have come to require more care than the home can provide. Some disreputable facilities expel

What Hospitals Aren't Telling You About Nursing Homes

If your parent requires nursing home care following a hospital stay, there's a good chance that the hospital discharge planner will give you just a few days to choose a nursing home. The longer your parent stays in the hospital, the less profit the hospital makes. (Medicare and health insurance plans typically pay a predetermined fixed amount for the treatment of a particular health problem, with no additional payments for longer-than-average stays.)

What most families don't realize is that they can push back when discharge planners try to push their parents out the door. If you haven't selected a nursing home yet, tell the discharge planner that you require more time and that you will file an appeal with Medicare if he/she doesn't relax the deadline. The threat alone often is enough to make discharge planners back down—they don't like the paperwork hassles associated with appeals. If not, file the appeal. Even if your appeal is rejected, the appeals process will buy you some additional time.

Helpful: The hospital's patient advocate should be able to provide details about how to file this appeal. Or hire a long-term-care case manager who can help with filing the appeal and selecting a nursing home. You will have to pay this case manager a few hundred dollars, but it's money well-spent. Your local Area Agency on Aging might be able to help you find a local case manager.

residents who run out of money by claiming that their care needs have increased.

If this happens to your parent, you could contact your state's long-term-care ombudsman to file a complaint. (Find your state's ombudsman through the Web site *ltcombudsman.org*.) But even if the ombudsman agrees that the facility cannot kick out your parent, you probably don't want your parent staying in a nursing home that would act this way, assuming that you can afford other options.

When a Specialist Is NOT a Good Choice for Specific Care

Dennis Gottfried, MD, an associate professor of medicine at the University of Connecticut School of Medicine, Farmington, and an internist with a private practice in Torrington, Connecticut. He is author of *Too Much Medicine: A Doctor's Prescription for Better and More Affordable Health Care* (Paragon House).

You might assume that you will get better care when you spend extra time and extra money to see a medical specialist. But is that really true?

Not always. Generalists—such as internists, general practitioners and family physicians—have a broader, more holistic view of the patient's condition and provide integrated care, but they lack the in-depth knowledge that specialists have in their area of medicine. Specialists may provide more fragmented care and order unnecessary tests and more procedures that are risky, studies show.

So when does the benefit of a specialist's added expertise outweigh the problem of sometimes disjointed medical care and excessive testing?

Rule of thumb: Specialists are generally preferable when a single medical condition that requires expert knowledge dominates all other medical concerns, such as a cardiologist treating an acute heart attack or an oncologist prescribing chemotherapy. Generalists, however, are usually more suitable when multiple chronic conditions, such as hypertension, diabetes and high cholesterol, are present.

How to get the best care for specific medical problems…

ARTHRITIS

Where to start: If you have osteoarthritis, you'll probably do better in the care of a general physician.

Osteoarthritis, a condition in which the cartilage in joints gradually wears down, often occurs with aging.

DID YOU KNOW?

4,000 Surgical Mistakes Occur in the US Every Year

These include leaving a foreign object such as a sponge or a towel in a patient…performing the wrong procedure…or operating on the wrong side of the body.

Analysis of national malpractice claims by researchers from Johns Hopkins University School of Medicine, Baltimore, published in *Surgery.*

Most patients do well with basic approaches: Regular exercise, physical therapy, glucosamine supplements and/or the use of *naproxen* (Aleve) or *ibuprofen* (Motrin).

See a specialist when: The pain is constant or severe and is not relieved by any of the above treatments. Orthopedists (specialists who often treat arthritis patients) frequently advise joint replacement for arthritic hips, knees and shoulders.

For rheumatoid arthritis: A specialist (rheumatologist) is needed. Rheumatoid arthritis is an autoimmune disease that causes widespread swelling and pain in the joints.

Patients frequently are treated with powerful anti-inflammatory and immune-modulating medications, such as *etanercept* (Enbrel), *adalimumab* (Humira) or *cyclophosphamide*. These and other related drugs have serious side effects, including depressed immunity and an increased risk for infection and cancer. They are best administered by a rheumatologist who has experience in their use.

DIABETES

Where to start: A primary care physician. Type 2 diabetes is largely a lifestyle disease caused by obesity and inactivity. It is initially managed with diet, exercise and oral medications, although insulin may be required as the disease progresses. Cardiovascular risk factors, such as high blood pressure, as well as lifestyle factors and blood sugar levels need to be monitored. Because of the comprehensive care that they require, people with type 2 diabetes should optimally be cared for by a generalist.

Diabetes specialists, or diabetologists, endocrinologists who specialize in diabetes, often take a narrow view. For example, they emphasize the importance of lowering blood sugar, frequently with insulin or oral medications.

Overall blood glucose control is monitored by the A1C blood test, which measures average blood sugar levels over the past two to three months. The major health risks for type 2 diabetics are heart disease and stroke, but lowering blood sugar too much (more than a full point in those at high risk) can actually increase risk for heart attack.

See a specialist when: Your A1C level is consistently above 8. (A normal level is below 6.3.) Elevated A1C increases the risk for some diabetes complications, including kidney disease. A specialist might be better able to lower consistently elevated A1C to healthier levels.

For type 1 diabetes: These patients should almost always see a diabetologist. Type 1 diabetes occurs more commonly in young adults and requires insulin shots from the onset. Also, the use of insulin and insulin pumps, which is recommended for type 1 diabetes patients, requires specialized knowledge.

HEART ATTACK

Where to start: People who have had heart attacks always need to see a cardiologist. The first hours (even minutes) after a heart attack are critical, and an emergency room physician will work with a cardiologist. A cardiologist will know what medication should be rapidly administered to minimize long-term damage to the heart and what tests (such as an angiogram) or procedures (such as stenting) need to be ordered. This specialist also will have significant experience prescribing the best drugs for common problems such as dissolving clots and restoring normal heart rhythms.

Most patients who have had a heart attack should see a specialist once or twice a year for the rest of their lives. The patient will be monitored to determine whether treatment such as surgery or stenting is necessary.

See a generalist when: Your condition is stable—that is, you are not having symptoms, such as shortness of breath or heart irregularities. Patients who have fully recovered from a heart attack may want to seek care from an internist or family doctor who has good communication with the cardiologist.

Example: Cardiologists often prescribe multiple medications to aggressively treat heart patients with high LDL "bad" cholesterol by lowering levels from, say, 100 mg/dL to 70 mg/dL. Yet there's little evidence that reducing LDL that much improves life expectancy. The medication needed to achieve such a low level may increase the risk for muscle pain and memory loss.

Primary care doctors often give a lower dose of the same medication to slightly improve cholesterol and minimize the risk for memory loss and muscle pain.

For heart failure: People with this condition, in which the heart is too weak to efficiently pump blood throughout the body, are best managed jointly by a cardiologist and a generalist. However, people with cardiac risk factors, such as hypertension or elevated cholesterol, but no history of heart attack, are best cared for by a generalist.

MENTAL HEALTH

Where to start: Almost 20% of patient visits to primary care doctors are for psychiatric problems. Primary care doctors can prescribe antidepressants and antianxiety medications and, if necessary, provide referrals to therapists and

---

Texting Works for Medication Reminder

After analyzing multiple studies, researchers found that text messaging is an effective way to remind patients with chronic conditions, such as high blood pressure, asthma and glaucoma, to take their daily medications.

Journal of the American Medical Informatics Association

support groups. This is appropriate and sufficient for most psychiatric disorders.

See a psychiatrist when: The treatment isn't working. A psychiatrist will have the knowledge to recommend other medications or medication combinations. Patients with more severe psychiatric problems, such as bipolar disorder or schizophrenia, should always be treated by a psychiatrist.

STROKE

Where to start: A neurologist should treat anyone who has suffered an acute stroke. If carotid artery disease is the suspected cause of the stroke, a vascular surgeon should be seen to monitor and treat the patient's risk for blood clots.

An analysis of 10 randomized clinical trials found that patients who were treated in hospital stroke units (with a neurologist on call 24 hours a day) had better survival rates than those who were treated in general hospital wards. Similarly, patients who were treated by neurologists were more likely to maintain brain function than those who were treated by nonspecialists.

See a generalist when: A neurologist has identified and treated all of the possible causes of stroke, such as hypertension and atrial fibrillation. Once a patient has recovered from the stroke itself, a general physician can manage the anticlotting and blood pressure medications.

Why We Need Compounding Pharmacies

Jamison Starbuck, ND, a naturopathic physician in family practice and a guest lecturer at the University of Montana, both in Missoula. She is past president of the American Association of Naturopathic Physicians and a contributing editor to *The Alternative Advisor: The Complete Guide to Natural Therapies and Alternative Treatments* (Time Life).

Compounding pharmacies have recently received a lot of bad publicity in the wake of a multistate fungal meningitis outbreak (see page 291). That's because the source of the contaminated steroids responsi-

ble for the illnesses and deaths was a so-called compounding pharmacy. But unlike traditional compounding pharmacies that create customized medications—one at a time, according to a physician's prescription—this pharmacy was mass-producing them.

Even though the meningitis outbreak has been tragic, legitimate compounding pharmacies that create customized medication do play an important role in the practice of medicine. With about 3,000 compounding pharmacies now operating in the US, when is it appropriate to use one? *In my practice, for example, I often recommend compounding when a patient needs a...*

•**Low-dose medication.** If a patient requires hormone replacement with testosterone or estrogen, for instance, I often send him/her to a local compounding pharmacy with a customized prescription for that individual. This approach allows me the flexibility to prescribe very small or unusual doses that are not available commercially in conventional pharmacies.

•**Nonpill preparation.** Liquid or sublingual (under-the-tongue) preparations often are required for patients with swallowing or absorption problems. For example, the sleep hormone melatonin is commercially available as a pill. However, I often find that a sublingual melatonin preparation, available from compounding pharmacies, is better for patients who have swallowing difficulties.

•**Preparation with a short shelf life.** Some natural medicines, such as glutathione (a powerful antioxidant), have a short shelf life (depending on the preparation, it can be as short as 10 days). Compounding pharmacies can produce such preparations with fresh medicinal ingredients.

Of course, you don't need to go to a compounding pharmacy for every medication, and compounded drugs are not always better than ones that are commercially manufactured. In some cases, compounded drugs are more expensive than their commercially made counterparts. The decision to use a compounded medication is usually made by your physician. However, if you have unique needs that you think could be better addressed with

Surgery Preparation Myth

Is there any truth to the "nothing by mouth after midnight" rule when preparing for surgery?

Decades of research have shown that having a light breakfast, such as black coffee and dry toast, six or more hours before surgery is safe for most healthy patients. So is drinking clear liquids two or more hours before surgery. In fact, surgical patients who drink clear liquids are less thirsty and hungry, less worried about surgery and less likely to get a headache from forgoing their morning coffee. Surgical patients should just be sure to first check with their doctors.

Those facing surgery should also ask their doctors about carbohydrate loading. Several European health organizations now recommend drinking a carbohydrate-rich, clear liquid, such as Clearfast, the evening before and the morning of surgery. It can ease recovery by reducing some of the negative side effects of surgery, such as nausea, vomiting and impaired insulin response.

Jeannette T. Crenshaw, DNP, RN, assistant professor of nursing, Texas Tech University Health Sciences Center, Lubbock, Texas.

a compounded medication, be sure to discuss them with your doctor and ask if a compounded medication would be best for you.

Compounding pharmacies operate in a variety of ways—as small, individual stores limited to compounding…within a conventional locally owned pharmacy…or as sections of large commercial pharmacy chains. Like regular pharmacies, compounding pharmacies are regulated by individual states, though the oversight may be expanded in the wake of the recent meningitis outbreak. Pharmacists who work in compounding pharmacies are licensed just as those who work in traditional pharmacies are licensed. Your doctor should be able to recommend a reputable compounding pharmacy in your area.

Ugly Truths About Plastic Surgery

Anthony Youn, MD, a plastic surgeon in private practice in Troy, Michigan, and an assistant professor of surgery at Oakland University William Beaumont School of Medicine in Rochester, Michigan. He is author of *In Stitches: A Memoir* (Gallery).

Americans set a new record in 2012 for the number of cosmetic procedures performed. All told, there were 13.8 million face-lifts, nose jobs, liposuctions, Botox injections and other elective procedures done for beauty's sake.

But some of these quick fixes aren't what they're cracked up to be, and not every potential patient is well-suited for a nip, tuck, implant or injection. What's more, some of these procedures carry little-known—and often serious—risks.

What you need to know…

Secret #1: **You can't stop the clock.** Some patients assume that a face-lift is a long-term fix. But that's a myth.

What most people don't realize: It's true that a good face-lift (with a typical cost of $8,000 to $15,000)* can take several years off your appearance and last for 10 or more years. But the moment surgery is over, the clock starts ticking again, and droopy jowls, wrinkles, etc., eventually will return.

There are, however, alternatives to going under the knife. For example, a laser procedure ($2,000 or more) can, to a somewhat lesser extent than a face-lift, tighten skin for the short term (about one to three years).

Secret #2: **Fillers can make you go blind.** Among the fastest-growing cosmetic treatments are soft-tissue fillers that can plump up lips, soften facial wrinkles and minimize folds around the nose and mouth. The most popular of these—used 1.3 million times last year in the US—is hyaluronic acid, better known as Juvéderm or Restylane. This substance is extracted

*Elective cosmetic procedures that do not correct a functional defect are usually not covered by insurance.

from rooster combs or derived from bacteria in a laboratory setting.

What most people don't realize: Injecting hyaluronic acid between the eyebrows to diminish furrows that make an individual look angry (at about $600 a pop) can, in rare cases, cause instant, incurable blindness.

The ophthalmic artery—part of the internal carotid artery that supplies the eyes with blood—can accidentally be injected with filler, irreversibly clotting the artery. Even an experienced plastic surgeon can make this mistake. That's why I advise patients to avoid any between-the-brow fillers.

Hyaluronic acid can, however, be safely injected into the lips and nasolabial folds (laugh lines).

The best treatment to correct eyebrow furrows is Botox ($325 per treatment), which does not carry the same risk for blindness. Headache commonly occurs after the procedure but is only temporary. Receiving Botox injections every three to four months will eliminate "angry" furrows without potentially robbing you of your eyesight.

Secret #3: **A brow wax is often as effective as a surgical "brow lift."** More than 28,000 Americans received brow lifts (also called forehead lifts) last year at an average cost of about $5,000.

With this procedure, the surgeon makes an incision along the front of the scalp so that he/she can peel back and "lift" the forehead in order to give the patient a more youthful, well-rested appearance. However, a far less invasive and less expensive procedure offers similar—or even better—results.

What most people don't realize: A simple brow wax ($15 to $30) reshapes the arc of the eyebrow, which gives the appearance of "lifting" the eyebrow several millimeters, just as surgery does. The trick?

A good brow wax removes hair from the lower area of the eyebrow, not from the top. The beneficial effect is especially noticeable if the person starts out with bushy eyebrows and goes to a professional aesthetician for the service.

To find a qualified aesthetician, consult Associated Skin Care Professionals at *www.ascp skincare.com* (click on "Find an ASCP Skin Care Professional"). The aestheticians referred by ASCP have completed appropriate training and have met state requirements.

Secret #4: **Fat sucked out during liposuction may come back.** Some plastic surgeons tell their patients that body fat removed during liposuction—a surgical procedure that can "sculpt" problem areas such as the thighs and buttocks by removing up to 12 pounds—is gone for good.

What most people don't realize: The jury is still out on the long-term results of liposuction, the third most popular plastic surgery in the US, with a cost of up to $10,000.

A 2011 study, published in *Obesity*, concluded that with liposuction the body merely redistributes fat to untreated areas—especially the abdomen, shoulders and arms, which leads to a top-heavy "Popeye effect."

Meanwhile, a 2012 study, published in *Plastic and Reconstructive Surgery*, found that fat sucked away during liposuction had not returned one year later—perhaps living up to the promise of permanence (barring any significant weight gain).

Ask for Less Blood to Be Drawn

Drawing blood too many times may cause hospital-acquired anemia in patients with acute myocardial infarction.

Recent finding: For every 50 milliliters of blood drawn, the risk for anemia rises by 18%. Drawing just under one-half pint of blood can lead to moderate-to-severe anemia.

Self-defense: Ask your doctor if the amount of blood drawn can be reduced or if pediatric-sized blood tubes can be used.

Mikhail Kosiborod, MD, associate professor of medicine, University of Missouri-Kansas City School of Medicine, and coauthor of a study of 17,676 people, published in *Archives of Internal Medicine*.

New Vitamin D Blood Tests Can Be Inaccurate

A review of 163 randomly selected blood samples found that results from 40% of patients screened by doctors with Abbott's Architect test and 48% with Siemens' Centaur-2 test were either more than 25% too high or more than 25% too low when compared with a widely used definitive testing method called liquid chromatography/mass spectrometry (LCMS). The Abbott and Siemens tests, which were introduced in 2011, most often overestimated vitamin D deficiency.

If you need a vitamin D test: Ask your doctor to make sure the lab uses the LCMS test or the radioimmunoassay blood test, which is also considered to be highly accurate.

Earle W. Holmes, PhD, professor of pathology and pharmacology, Loyola University Chicago Stritch School of Medicine.

Of course, diet and exercise are ultimately the best ways to lose weight and shape your body.

Secret #5: **Some people should see a therapist instead of a surgeon.** Cosmetic surgery is simply not advisable for some individuals who have it.

What most people don't realize: Up to 15% of people seeking cosmetic enhancements have a condition known as *body dysmorphic disorder* (BDD), sometimes called "imagined ugliness" because sufferers obsessively fixate on perceived physical defects that do not seem prominent to others. To a person who has BDD, a small, hardly noticeable bump on the nose, for example, could, in his mind, be a real deformity.

Some opportunistic plastic surgeons view BDD patients as "cash cows." That is because there is seemingly no end to the flaws these patients notice on their faces and bodies, and they are usually willing to pay big bucks to "fix" these supposed defects.

In my practice, I'd estimate that one of every six or seven people I see has BDD. I won't

treat these patients but, rather, gently suggest that they'd be better off seeing a psychiatrist or other mental-health professional. This is often a difficult message for these patients to receive because they have a skewed perception of reality. But it's the right thing to do!

Thumbs Up or Down for Mini-Bunion Surgery?

Ed Davis, DPM, a podiatrist and board-certified foot surgeon in private practice in San Antonio and Live Oak, Texas. *www.southtexaspodiatrist.com*

A bunion—which is an enlargement of the bone or swelling of tissue around the joint at the base of the big toe—often is caused by faulty foot mechanics, meaning that the foot rolls in too much when you walk. Bunion surgery generally is appropriate only if the bunion is painful...or there is limitation in the range of motion...or the big toe is drifting toward the second toe. The so-called mini-bunionectomy—surgical correction of a mild and painless bunion using a small incision—is rarely necessary or advisable given that surgery carries some risk for infection, nerve damage or other complications. What's more, because such surgery does not address the underlying cause of the problem, the bunion would probably just come back anyway.

The best way to keep a mild bunion from progressing to the point where surgery is needed is to correct the faulty foot mechanics that caused the bunion to form in the first place. Your podiatrist can help you learn how to walk properly so your foot does not roll inward. He or she also can prescribe custom-made orthotic inserts for your shoes to help keep your foot in the correct position. High-heeled, pointy-toed shoes can definitely make a bunion worse, so it is a good idea to stick with shoes that have a low heel (no higher than 1½ inches), wide toe box and adequate arch support.

Referral to a podiatrist: American Podiatric Medical Association, *www.apma.org*.

Health Web Sites: The Best-Kept Secret To Better Care

Trisha Torrey, a patient advocate in Baldwinsville, New York. She is the patient empowerment expert for About.com and also runs the Web site EveryPatientsAdvocate.com. She is one of the original members of the Society for Participatory Medicine.

If you have been diagnosed with a condition—any condition—you might be tempted to hop online and join other patients in a discussion group. But you can do much more online. Today, social networking is changing the look and feel of patient support Web sites—and providing much more help for groups of people with the same conditions.

The "old style" patient support groups, forums and discussion boards enable patients to exchange a great deal of information online—interacting...asking questions...providing opinions...and sharing emotions.

But several newer Web sites enable patients to do even more—such as interact with health professionals...build communities for lesser-known conditions...and share medical tests with doctors and researchers. These patient-to-patient/patient-to-doctor exchanges are known as "participatory medicine," because they give patients a chance to interact and work with various knowledgeable health professionals.

TODAY'S ONLINE SUPPORT GROUPS

Sites such as HealthBoards.com, DailyStrength.org and Inspire.com enable patients to choose from hundreds of groups, including ones for medical conditions, mental health problems and life situations, such as loneliness or parenting.

Here are some highlights...

•HealthBoards.com

•Easy-to-navigate site with about 899,000 registered members and six million monthly visits.

•Offers hundreds of message boards on health issues, from abuse support and acid reflux to West Nile virus and women's health.

•There is a section where you can ask doctors questions.

•DailyStrength.org

•Offers more than 500 support groups on topics ranging from fibromyalgia and Crohn's disease to smoking cessation and the emotional pain of divorce.

•Members can send one another "virtual hugs" for support.

•Inspire.com

•Covers hundreds of conditions, both common and rare.

•Has a high level of user "engagement." There are about 1,600 members in the encephalitis community. This is a large group considering that the condition, characterized by swelling of the brain, is rare.

Many of these sites enable patients to start their own groups. This happened, for example, to a group of young women with a rare heart condition called spontaneous coronary artery dissection (SCAD) who found one another on Inspire.com. Since most doctors don't see many cases of SCAD (which occurs when the layers of the coronary artery separate, causing blockage and sometimes a heart attack), there wasn't much research in the area. That changed when the "SCAD Ladies," as they are known, inspired Mayo Clinic researchers to conduct the largest-ever SCAD study.

DATA FOR RESEARCH

Doctors are taking note of how the Internet can be used to gather patients for research.

PatientsLikeMe.com is a for-profit Web site that brings together people with the same diagnosis who share data, including their medical test results, blood values, bone density or whatever information is appropriate to their disease.

The idea behind it: Sharing health information greatly benefits patients.

The site, which began in 2004 as a resource for people with amyotrophic lateral sclerosis (ALS), is now available to patients with 1,200 health conditions. PatientsLikeMe.com has its own team of researchers and collaborates with researchers from other institutions, such as Oxford University and Johns Hopkins University, among others. Patients who participate on this site realize that they are sharing their medical information (photos and hometowns also are used), but they believe that the potential medical benefit outweighs any loss of privacy.

GETTING BETTER HELP ONLINE

Since there are so many online patient support groups, how do you know which is best for you? And what can you offer by visiting the site?

•**Test out a few Web sites.** Search through several different online support groups to get a good idea of the comments and replies that are exchanged. Ask yourself if you are comfortable with the tone of the conversation and whether the topics match your needs. Note too that there might be more people and a livelier discussion about your condition on one site than on another.

•**Offer support to others.** Web site users say that it feels good to be able to share their medical information and to help others.

Important: Always verify information that could affect your health. If you find out about a new treatment online, be sure to consult your physician before trying it.

Don't Let Supplements Sabotage Your Lab Tests

Joseph Lamb, MD, a faculty member of The Institute for Functional Medicine in Federal Way, Washington, and director of intramural clinical research at Metagenics, Inc., in Gig Harbor, Washington. He has authored numerous articles on nutritional supplements in scientific publications such as *Nutrition Research.*

If you take vitamin and/or herbal supplements, you probably already know that these products can interact—sometimes harmfully—with other supplements and medications.

What few people realize: Taking such supplements may also interfere with a wide variety of laboratory tests, including blood work and urine tests.

Bed Rails Can Be Deadly

During the last nine years, 150 patients (mostly older, frail and in nursing homes) were reported to have died after their heads or chests became trapped in hospital bed rails—about 36,000 more required emergency room treatment for their injuries. The FDA issued public safety warnings about adult bed rails in 1995, but manufacturers weren't required to put safety labels on their products.

Alternative: A mattress with raised edges.

Steven Miles, MD, professor of medicine and bioethics, University of Minnesota Medical School, Minneapolis.

WHAT CAN HAPPEN

More than half of the adults in the US take one or more dietary supplements every day. And nearly seven billion lab tests are given each year. In most instances, supplements do not affect the results of lab tests.

However, case reports in the medical literature indicate that certain supplements can...

•**Produce a "false-positive" or "false-negative" test result** that may lead to additional tests and unnecessary treatments.

•**Change your body chemistry in a way that the test accurately reflects**—but leads to incorrect treatment if your doctor doesn't know that the supplement is causing the change.

SUPPLEMENTS TO WATCH

Commonly used supplements that may affect certain lab tests...

•**Vitamin C.** This vitamin can produce a false-negative reading for a fecal occult blood test, which detects digestive tract bleeding, a possible sign of colon cancer. Vitamin C can interfere with the test's chemical reaction, which signals the presence of hidden blood in the stool. (A fecal occult blood test may be done yearly if you have a family history of colon cancer.)

What to do: Three days before testing, stop taking vitamin C, including multivitamins.

Also important: An iron supplement can produce a false-positive reading on a fecal occult

Best Place to Buy Vitamins

The best place to buy vitamins is in a natural-foods store or other place that focuses on dietary supplements. Their products, unlike those at chain pharmacies, are most likely to contain the most potent forms—and no artificial colors or preservatives. *What to look for…*

•**Vitamin E.** The gamma tocopherol form is natural and more potent than dl-alpha tocopherol, the synthetic form.

•**Vitamin C.** The best forms come from rose hips, tapioca or other natural sources. In addition to ascorbic acid, they contain powerful bioflavonoids.

•**Vitamin B.** Supplements should contain equal amounts of B-1 (thiamine), B-2 (riboflavin) and B-6 (pyridoxine). The best ones are made from rice, yeast or other natural products.

Also important…

•**If possible, buy vitamins in dark-colored or opaque containers.** They will last longer.

•**Don't purchase more than a two-month supply at a time.** And make sure that products are not past their expiration dates.

•**Keep vitamins away from moisture.** When you open the container, remove any cotton balls, which absorb moisture and can cause vitamins to disintegrate. Don't store vitamins in the bathroom or refrigerator unless the label tells you to.

Earl Mindell, RPh, PhD, nutritionist in Beverly Hills, California, and author of *New Vitamin Bible* (Hachette) and *Prescription Alternatives* (McGraw-Hill).

blood test. Excess iron in red blood cells can be mistaken for blood in the stool. Iron supplements also can skew the results of iron tests.

If you are scheduled for a fecal occult (or iron) blood test, be sure to tell your doctor if you're taking iron. (See the next page for advice on the best ways to discuss your supplement use with your doctor.)

•**Riboflavin.** High doses of this B vitamin (usually above the recommended daily intake of 1.3 mg for men, 1.1 mg for women) can turn your urine bright yellow, potentially interfering with any urine test that uses a dipstick indicating a color change.

These tests include a urine protein test (to monitor kidney function)…a urine glucose test (to monitor blood sugar levels)…a urine ketone test (for diabetes)…a urine pH test (to monitor the body's acid/alkaline balance)…and a urinalysis itself (which doesn't use a dipstick, but may evaluate the color of the urine).

What to do: Riboflavin is quickly cleared from the body. Don't take a supplement or multivitamin with riboflavin the night before or the morning of a urine test—riboflavin can be safely resumed afterward.

•**Folic acid.** The B vitamin folic acid works in conjunction with another B vitamin (B-12) in many body functions, including cell division. However, a high intake of folic acid can mask one of the telltale laboratory signs of vitamin B-12 deficiency—abnormally large red blood cells—by making the cells appear normal.

A deficiency of vitamin B-12 can cause anemia…neuropathy…and memory loss and other mental difficulties.

What to do: If you are being tested for a B-12 deficiency and take a large dose of folic acid (above 800 mcg) in a supplement or multivitamin, tell your doctor.

Also important: Inform your doctor if you are taking the drug *L-methylfolate* (Deplin). This is a high-dose folate supplement that's sometimes prescribed with an antidepressant to help produce neurotransmitters that regulate mood (including serotonin, norepinephrine and dopamine).

•**Calcium supplements.** Undigested or unabsorbed calcium in the intestines may cause an artificially high reading on a bone-density scan.

What to do: Avoid calcium supplements and multivitamins that contain calcium for 48 hours before a bone-density scan.

•**Vitamin E, fish oil, ginkgo biloba, hops extract, red clover, ginger and garlic.** These supplements have blood-thinning properties that can cause problems for people taking the anticoagulant drug *warfarin* (Coumadin). This medication is prescribed to thin the blood in individuals at risk for blood clots, such as those with heart disease.

To make sure that the medication is working, patients should regularly have their Prothrombin Time and International Normalized Ratio checked. These tests measure the amount of time it takes for blood to clot. Because the supplements listed above can thin the blood, they can change the results of the tests.

What to do: If you take (or are about to be prescribed warfarin), be sure to tell your doctor if you use one of these blood-thinning supplements. Your doctor will need to closely monitor your prothrombin time and adjust your medication dose accordingly.

•**Dan Shen and Chan Su.** These are Chinese herbs. Dan Shen is used for heart and circulatory problems and Chan Su for sore throats and chest congestion. Both herbs can interfere with the test to determine if a patient's blood level of *digoxin*, a drug prescribed for heart failure or arrhythmias, is within the normal range. This interference can be very dangerous, because too little digoxin is not therapeutic, while too much can be toxic.

What to do: If you're taking digoxin, don't use either of these herbs.

WORK WITH YOUR DOCTOR

The best strategies to help avoid a false or misinterpreted lab test result caused by a supplement…

•**Tell your practitioner about all the supplements you take.** When you visit your doctor, bring along a written list of your supplements that can be photocopied. If a supplement contains a unique, multi-ingredient formula, photocopy the package insert or bottle label and attach it to your list.

Mistake to avoid: Do not bring a bag filled with your supplements. If your doctor is writing down a list of your supplements, he'll have less time to attend to other, equally important aspects of your care.

•**Take quality supplements.** They are less likely to interfere with lab tests. A poorly manufactured supplement may include ingredients not listed on the product label or the amounts could be less (or more) than what is on the label.

To ensure that you're taking a high-quality product…

•**Look for a "GMP Certified" product.** A GMP certification on the label means that "good manufacturing practices" have been verified by an independent third party that checks such important features as the product's strength, composition and purity.

•**Do not purchase anything without a complete listing of ingredients.** Avoid all products with only vague ingredient listings such as "proprietary blend"—neither you nor your practitioner should be in the dark about the contents or dosages of any supplement you're taking.

Organic Foods Are Not More Nutritious

Crystal Smith-Spangler, MD, instructor, Stanford University School of Medicine, and physician-investigator, VA Palo Alto Health Care System, Palo Alto, California.

Charles Benbrook, PhD, chief science consultant, Organic Center, Enterprise, Oregon.
Annals of Internal Medicine

Organic foods are almost invariably more expensive than their conventionally produced counterparts but they aren't necessarily healthier or more nutritious, recent research suggests.

Scientists found no consistent differences in vitamin content between organic and conventional foods and few significant differences in health benefits. They did note, however, that organic produce is 30% less likely to be contaminated with pesticides than conventional fruits and vegetables—though the pesticide levels of all foods fell within allowable limits—and that organic chicken and pork appeared to lessen exposure to antibiotic-resistant bacteria.

"I think different people will make different decisions based on our findings," said study author Crystal Smith-Spangler, MD, an instructor at Stanford University School of Medicine and a physician-investigator at the VA Palo Alto Health Care System, in California. "We thought we'd find more significant differences, but there are many reasons why someone might consume organic foods. Health is one, but they may be concerned about the environment, animal welfare practices or taste, and we weren't evaluating that."

The study was published in the *Annals of Internal Medicine*.

BACKGROUND

Organic foods, often twice as costly as their conventional counterparts, have become big business in the United States in recent years, with estimated sales skyrocketing from $3.6 billion to $26.7 billion between 1997 and 2010.

Organic products are generally grown without synthetic pesticides, fertilizers, irradiation or chemical food additives and without routine use of antibiotics or growth hormones. Organic livestock are offered freedom of movement and access to the outdoors and are fed pesticide- and animal by-product-free organic feed.

STUDY DETAILS

Dr. Smith-Spangler and her colleagues analyzed 237 previous studies, including 17 involving human consumption of organic versus conventional diets and 223 comparing either the nutrient levels or the bacterial, fungal or pesticide contamination of products such as fruits, vegetables, grains, meats, milk, poultry and eggs produced organically and conventionally.

Only one nutrient, phosphorous, was found to be significantly more abundant in organic produce, but researchers felt this had little clinical significance since few people are deficient in phosphorous. Also, no difference in protein or fat content was observed between organic and conventional milk, though limited previous studies did suggest organic milk contains markedly higher levels of omega-3 fatty acids, which may lower the risk of conditions such as heart disease, cancer and arthritis.

Certain Herbal Remedies Can Interact with Drugs

Certain herbal remedies are more likely to interact with prescription drugs. When scientists analyzed 85 articles and studies, they found numerous interactions between herbal remedies, supplements and prescription drugs—with 26% resulting in a major interaction. Flaxseed, echinacea and yohimbe had the largest number of contraindications.

Conclusion: Some ingredients in herbal remedies alter the way prescription drugs are absorbed, distributed, metabolized and eliminated.

When you get a new prescription: Make sure your doctor and pharmacist are aware of any supplements or herbal remedies you may be taking.

Hsiang-Wen Lin, RPh, PhD, assistant professor, College of Pharmacy, China Medical University, Taichung, Taiwan.

CONCLUSIONS

Dr. Smith-Spangler said she and her team were inspired to undertake the research to find answers for themselves, their families and their patients about the potential merits of organic foods. But, "we didn't find strong evidence that organic food was significantly more nutritious or healthier," she said, "and similar levels of both types are contaminated with bacteria" such as E. coli, which can be deadly.

"We can't exclude the idea that some organic practices may increase nutrient levels…or increase or decrease bacteria," she said. "But at the market you don't often get to look at the organic practices used. Many studies mention that other factors can influence nutrient content, such as ripeness, season and storage practices."

EXPERT REACTION

Charles Benbrook, PhD, is chief science consultant at the Organic Center in Enterprise, Oregon, which says it conducts "credible evidence-based science on the health and environmental benefits of organic food and farming." He praised the study authors' "ambitious undertaking" but said the study underestimated the impact of organic livestock farming on reducing antibiotic resistance and missed analyzing research attributing important health benefits from organic produce on prenatal development.

"We need to recognize that finding strong evidence of clinically significant health benefits for eating organic food is a tall order," Dr. Benbrook said. "But I don't think their study rules out some of the more subtle benefits of consuming organic foods that are more in the nature of promoting healthy pregnancies and preventing disease."

info For more information on organic foods, visit the Web site of the US Department of Agriculture, *http://fnic.nal.usda.gov/food-labeling/organic-foods*.

Frozen Orange Juice Is Better for You Than Premium Not-from-Concentrate Juice

Frozen juice is made with the whole fruit, including the peel, so it has more *hesperidin*—a potent antioxidant found in the orange rind. And frozen juice costs much less.

Example: A 12-ounce can of frozen (48 ounces prepared) is about $2.50. A 64-ounce jug of premium is about $6.75.

Yearly savings if you have an eight-ounce glass a day: $154.76 (excluding the cost of water).

Prevention. www.prevention.com

Diabetes

Can Your Cosmetics Give You Diabetes?

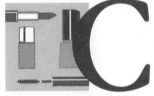

Consumer watchdogs have warned for years that chemicals called *phthalates*—types of plasticizers contained in many products, including furniture, toys, plastic bags and detergents, as well as in some cosmetics, including lotions, hair sprays and perfumes—can knock our endocrine systems out of whack, potentially raising our risk for obesity and hardening of the arteries.

What's worse—a recent study suggests that we can now add type 2 diabetes to the list of phthalate dangers.

The cosmetics part is especially creepy, since we do more than simply touch that stuff—we often massage lotions or makeup into our skin and spray perfume onto our necks, where we breathe it right in. And if you should kiss some-

one wearing phthalate-containing cosmetics or perfume—what's getting into your mouth?

WHAT LURKS IN OUR COSMETICS

The phthalates are put into many types of cosmetics because they do have some benefits. In perfume, for example, they help the scent linger longer…in nail polish, the chemicals reduce cracking by making polishes less brittle… and in hair spray, phthalates allow the spray to form a flexible film on hair, avoiding stiffness. But phthalates in these products can be either absorbed through the skin or inhaled, which causes them to enter the bloodstream…and then, watch out!

In the study, the researchers from Uppsala University in Sweden drew fasting blood samples from more than 1,000 adults, looking for several toxins, including four substances specifically formed when the body breaks down phthalates. Even after adjusting for typical type 2 diabetes risk factors such as obesity, cholesterol

Monica Lind, PhD, associate professor of occupational and environmental medicine, Uppsala University, Uppsala, Sweden. Her research was published in *Diabetes Care*.

127

levels, smoking and exercise habits, researchers found that participants whose phthalate levels were among the highest 20% of the group were twice as likely to have type 2 diabetes when compared with those whose phthalate levels fell into the lowest 20% of the group.

Study author Monica Lind, PhD, an associate professor of occupational and environmental medicine at the university, explained that since she and her colleagues are among the first scientists to measure phthalate levels in blood, "high" and "low" are relative to this study—in other words, it's difficult to discern whether the levels of phthalates in this study were "high" on any kind of absolute scale. And researchers didn't track the amount of phthalate-containing products that participants used. But the study does suggest that the higher the levels of phthalates in the blood, the higher the risk of getting type 2 diabetes, and that might reflect a greater use of products that contain them.

CHECK THE LABELS

Phthalates may increase the risk for type 2 diabetes by disrupting insulin production and/or inducing insulin resistance, Dr. Lind said. But those ideas are disputed by the FDA, which states that "it's not clear what effect, if any, phthalates have on health."

In the US, the FDA does not require cosmetics or perfumes to be phthalate-free. It does require nonfragrance ingredients to be listed on

Curcumin Stops Diabetes from Progressing

According to recent research, when given a curcumin extract (1.5 grams daily) for nine months, study participants at risk for diabetes did not develop the disease. Among a similar group given a placebo, 16.4% developed the disease. Curcumin is the main compound in turmeric, a spice in curry powders and mustards.

Study of 240 people by researchers at Srinakharinwirot University, Bangkok, Thailand, published in Tufts University Health & Nutrition Letter.

cosmetic products, but the loophole is that any ingredients that are parts of a fragrance don't have to be listed—a manufacturer can simply put "fragrance" on the label. As a result, according to the nonprofit Campaign for Safe Cosmetics, most cosmetics and perfumes that contain phthalates don't list them on the label. In other words, if the word "fragrance" is listed, then you won't know for sure what's in the product, unfortunately.

WHAT YOU CAN DO TO PROTECT YOURSELF

You can search online for cosmetics that are "fragrance-free" using the nonprofit Environmental Working Group's Skin Deep cosmetics database at *www.ewg.org/skindeep* and then choose among the products that are also phthalate-free. For perfumes, specifically, search the phrase "phthalate-free perfumes," which leads to many brands, such as Zorica of Malibu, Kai, Pacifica, Agape & Zoe Naturals, Rich Hippie, Honoré des Prés, Blissoma Blends, Red Flower Organic Perfumes, Tsi-La Organic Perfume and Ayala Moriel Parfums.

Skipped Diabetes Screening Puts Moms and Babies at Risk

Jon M. Nakamoto, MD, PhD, is laboratory medical director for Quest Diagnostics and an associate professor of pediatrics and endocrinology at the University of California, San Diego. He is coauthor, with other Quest Diagnostics medical experts, of a study on gestational and postpartum diabetes screening published in *Obstetrics & Gynecology*.

There's a vitally important screening test that expectant and new moms need to protect their babies' health and their own. So it's shocking to learn from a recent study just how often this test is omitted. We're talking about screening for diabetes during and after pregnancy. *What women must know...*

Gestational diabetes develops when a pregnant woman's blood sugar is too high and her body cannot make and use all the insulin it needs. Based on updated diagnostic criteria, the

Walking Just a Half-Mile a Day Helps Fight Diabetes

Researchers studied the health outcomes of 592 adults without diabetes who wore pedometers to measure their steps on two typical days five years apart.

Result: Every half-mile increase in daily steps (about 1,000 steps) was associated with a lower body mass index (BMI), a ratio of weight to height, and higher insulin sensitivity, which keeps blood sugar levels in check. Even a moderate amount of exercise helps prevent diabetes.

Terry Dwyer, MD, director, Murdoch Childrens Research Institute, Melbourne, Australia.

American Diabetes Association now estimates that this condition affects 18% of pregnancies—a far higher percentage than previously believed.

Risks: Unless diagnosed and controlled, gestational diabetes increases the mother's risk for high blood pressure and triples the likelihood that a cesarean delivery will be needed...it also doubles the baby's risk for serious injury at birth, quadruples the odds of being admitted to the neonatal intensive care unit, and increases the child's risk for obesity and diabetes in adulthood. For most women with gestational diabetes, the condition goes away after childbirth, but about 10% develop type 2 diabetes—a chronic and potentially deadly condition—during the postpartum period. That's why the American College of Obstetricians and Gynecologists recommends that all pregnant women get tested for gestational diabetes between the 24th and 28th week of pregnancy...and that all those diagnosed with gestational diabetes get retested six to 12 weeks after delivery.

Alarming recent findings: Analyzing data on 924,873 women from pregnancy through six months after delivery, researchers found that 32% were never tested for gestational diabetes...and, worse, that 81% of women who had been diagnosed with gestational diabetes, and therefore should have been screened for postpartum diabetes, did not receive the test.

Based on recent studies, the International Association of Diabetes and Pregnancy Study Groups now recommends that doctors use the 75-g oral glucose tolerance test to screen for diabetes. If you are pregnant or postpartum, discuss this with your obstetrician.

Does Black Tea Reduce Diabetes Risk?

BMJ Open, news release

Rates of type 2 diabetes are lower in countries where many people drink black tea, a finding that supports previous research suggesting that regular consumption of black tea is associated with a reduced risk of diabetes, according to a recent study.

The number of people with type 2 diabetes is projected to rise to 438 million by 2020, the International Diabetes Federation estimates.

Researcher Ariel Beresniak of Data Mining International, in Geneva, Switzerland, and colleagues looked at black tea consumption in 50 countries on every continent and compared that with rates of diabetes and cancer, as well as respiratory, infectious and cardiovascular diseases in those nations.

Ireland had the highest level of black tea consumption (more than 4.4 pounds a year per person), closely followed by the United Kingdom and Turkey. Nations with the lowest levels of black tea consumption were South Korea, Brazil, China, Morocco and Mexico.

Statistical analyses showed that diabetes rates were low in countries with high levels of black tea consumption. There was no association between black tea consumption and any of the other health conditions included in the study, according to a *BMJ* news release.

"These original study results are consistent with previous biological, physiological and ecological studies conducted on the potential of [black tea] on diabetes and obesity," and provide "valuable additional scientific information at the global level," the researchers wrote.

HOW BREWED BLACK TEA HEALS

Black tea contains a number of complex flavonoids that have been linked with several potential health benefits, the researchers noted. The brewing process releases these flavonoids.

While the study found a mathematical association between black tea consumption and type 2 diabetes rates, it did not prove a cause-and-effect relationship.

info The US National Institute of Diabetes and Digestive and Kidney Diseases has more about type 2 diabetes at its Web site *http://dia betes.niddk.nih.gov/dm/pubs/type2_es/.*

What Women on Statins Need to Know About Diabetes

Yunsheng Ma, MD, PhD, MPH, an associate professor in the division of preventive and behavioral medicine at the University of Massachusetts Medical School in Worcester and coauthor of a meta-analysis published in *Archives of Internal Medicine.*

No doubt you're aware that cholesterol-lowering statin medications can have side effects, such as muscle pain, digestive problems and liver damage. What you may not realize is that statins also significantly increase the risk for diabetes, as a recent large-scale study showed.

Participants included 153,840 postmenopausal women ages 50 to 79, none of whom had diabetes at the start of the study. The women were tracked for an average of 7.6 years, during which time 10,242 or nearly 7% of them developed diabetes.

Finding: Even after researchers adjusted for other diabetes risk factors (such as age, race, diet, physical activity level, smoking, high blood pressure and a family history of diabetes), women who took statins were 48% more likely to develop diabetes during the course of the study than those who did not take statins. All types of statins had this effect, regardless of the dosage, potency or how long the medication was used.

What this means for you: Remember that lifestyle changes—adopting a healthy diet, get-

Blood Sugar Danger

Does high blood sugar mean a higher risk for colorectal cancer?

Yes, there is a small increased risk, according to recent research. What's most important is to talk to your doctor about ways to maintain a healthy weight by eating a balanced diet, exercising regularly and, if necessary, taking medication.

Elevated blood sugar levels are associated with obesity, which is a known risk factor for colorectal cancer. High blood sugar may also be linked to higher levels of inflammatory factors that spur the growth of polyps that can develop into cancer.

Geoffrey Kabat, PhD, senior epidemiologist, Albert Einstein College of Medicine of Yeshiva University, New York City.

ting regular exercise, losing excess weight—are safe, effective, drug-free ways to reduce cholesterol and help guard against both heart disease and diabetes. If your doctor suggests that you start taking a statin, ask about the risks and benefits as well as possible cholesterol-lowering alternatives. If you already use a statin, do not simply stop taking it on your own, researchers cautioned. Instead, talk to your doctor about ways to reduce your need for the drug…discuss an appropriate schedule for screening for diabetes…and immediately alert your doctor if you develop any possible warning signs of diabetes, such as increased thirst, increased urination and/or blurred vision.

If You Love to Bake…

Suzanne Havala Hobbs, DrPH, licensed, registered dietitian and author of *Living Vegetarian for Dummies and Living Dairy-Free for Dummies* (both from Wiley).

Here's the problem—you need to watch your blood sugar, but you love to bake (and sample your wares!). What are the best nonsugar alternatives for baking?

Sugar adds sweetness and flavor to quick breads, cookies, cakes, muffins and other baked goods, but it also affects texture, moistness and color. In some recipes, you can reduce the amount of sugar by 25% with good results. In other recipes, you can't replace or reduce the sugar at all.

You sometimes can compensate for the loss of sweetness by adding extra vanilla, almond flavoring, cinnamon, nutmeg or even bits of fruit such as raisins, diced apples, dried cherries or mashed, ripe banana, which come with fiber and nutrients in exchange for the small number of added calories.

Sugar substitutes such as *aspartame* (Equal) and *sucralose* (Splenda) aren't ideal for baking because their sweetening power is degraded by heat and they don't contribute to the texture or color of baked goods. Sugar substitutes that incorporate sugar, such as Equal Sugar Lite and Splenda Sugar Blend, make for better baking.

A Red Flag for Diabetes

Joel M. Gelfand, MD, associate professor of dermatology and epidemiology at Perelman School of Medicine, University of Pennsylvania, Philadelphia. He was senior author of a study published in Archives of Dermatology.

If you have psoriasis—as millions of Americans do—the scaly, itchy patches of skin on your scalp and/or other body parts aren't the only health problems to be concerned about.

You probably know about the increased risks for heart attack, stroke, arthritis and certain cancers. Yet there's another disease to add to the already long list.

A recent study found that people with psoriasis are at increased risk for also developing type 2 diabetes—even if they don't have any of the risk factors that are common to both diseases, such as obesity. And the more severe the psoriasis, the greater the risk of type 2 diabetes.

How much extra risk do you have? In the study, people with mild psoriasis had an 11% greater risk of developing type 2 diabetes, compared with those who did not have psoriasis… and people with moderate-to-severe psoriasis had a 46% higher risk.

THE COMMON THREAD: INFLAMMATION

"Both diseases are caused by chronic inflammation," senior study author Joel M. Gelfand, MD, noted, "and we think that the same inflammation that causes psoriasis also prevents the body from responding to insulin as well as it should, which is what leads to type 2 diabetes."

WHAT PSORIASIS SUFFERERS NEED TO DO

So if you have psoriasis, what should you do?

Dr. Gelfand said that it's important to get regular blood sugar screenings to test for type 2 diabetes, since the earlier you find out that you have diabetes, the easier it is to keep it in check. For many people, blood sugar is checked as part of their annual physical. And, do everything you can to help prevent (or at least delay) type 2 diabetes from developing. That means—you guessed it—following a healthy diet, exercising regularly and losing excess weight, Dr. Gelfand said.

"Think of your psoriasis as a window into what's happening in your body," he continued. "Those rashes on your skin aren't necessarily just exterior problems—they may be a sign of other metabolic issues that are happening in the interior of your bloodstream."

He also stressed that these recommendations are especially important for people with psoriasis who are 40 or older because the risk of developing diabetes increases with age.

Can reducing psoriasis symptoms lower your risk of type 2 diabetes? "There is some evidence that it might help, so it's worth a shot, but scientists don't yet know," Dr. Gelfand said.

Tea with Crackers

Animals given a green tea–based antioxidant (EGCG) had about a 50% lower blood sugar spike after eating starch than those that didn't have it. In humans, about a cup and a half of tea with meals could produce a similar effect.

Penn State University

Study Examines Link Between Breast Cancer and Diabetes

Diabetologia, news release

Postmenopausal breast cancer survivors are at increased risk for developing diabetes and should be screened for the disease more closely, a recent study suggests.

THE STUDY

Researchers analyzed data from 1996 to 2008 from the province of Ontario, Canada, to determine the incidence of diabetes among nearly 25,000 breast cancer survivors ages 55 or older and nearly 125,000 age-matched women without breast cancer.

During a median follow-up of more than five years, nearly 10% of all the women in the study developed diabetes. Compared with those who had not had breast cancer, the risk of diabetes among breast cancer survivors was 7% higher two years after cancer diagnosis and 21% higher 10 years after cancer diagnosis, the investigators found.

The risk of diabetes, however, decreased over time among breast cancer survivors who had undergone chemotherapy. Their risk compared with women without breast cancer was 24% higher in the first two years after cancer diagnosis and 8% higher 10 years after cancer diagnosis, according to the study, which was published in the journal *Diabetologia*.

POSSIBLE EXPLANATIONS

"It is possible that chemotherapy treatment may bring out diabetes earlier in susceptible women," said study author Lorraine Lipscombe, MD, director, Centre of Integrated Diabetes Care of Women's College Hospital and Women's College Research Institute in Toronto. "Increased weight gain has been noted [after receiving] chemotherapy for breast cancer, which may be a factor in the increased risk of diabetes in women receiving treatment."

"Estrogen suppression as a result of chemotherapy may also promote diabetes," Dr. Lip-

Keep an Eye on Your A1C

A1C tests measure the average levels of blood glucose (also called blood sugar) over the past three months. A normal A1C level is below 5.7%. Diabetes is diagnosed at 6.5% or above, and 5.7% to 6.4% is considered to be prediabetes. If you are borderline—prediabetic or close to it—you have a higher risk of developing diabetes, especially if you have a family history of the disease.

If you are prediabetic, you can do a lot to lower your blood sugar levels. For example, if you are overweight, follow a healthful diet and make regular exercise a part of your routine. Even a 10- to 15-pound weight loss can bring the A1C level back into the normal range. You also may want to talk with your doctor about medication, such as *metformin* (Glucophage), to help keep blood sugar levels under control.

Anne Peters, MD, director, University of Southern California Clinical Diabetes Program, Beverly Hills, California.

scombe added. "However, this may have been less of a factor in this study where most women were already postmenopausal."

The study authors suggested that there may be other factors involved for women who received chemotherapy, including glucocorticoid drugs, which are used to treat nausea in patients receiving chemo and are known to cause spikes in blood sugar. In addition, breast cancer patients undergoing chemotherapy are monitored more closely and thus are more likely to have diabetes detected, they noted.

The researchers said it is unclear why diabetes risk increased over time among breast cancer survivors who did not receive chemotherapy.

"There is, however, evidence of an association between diabetes and cancer, which may be due to risk factors common to both conditions," Dr. Lipscombe said. "One such risk factor is insulin resistance, which predisposes to both diabetes and many types of cancer—initially insulin resistance is associated with high insulin levels and there is evidence that high circulating insulin may increase the risk of cancer."

"However, diabetes only occurs many years later when insulin levels start to decline," she said. "Therefore, it is possible that cancer risk occurs much earlier than diabetes in insulin-resistant individuals, when insulin levels are high."

ADVICE

Overall, the "findings support a need for closer monitoring of diabetes among breast cancer survivors," Dr. Lipscombe concluded.

info The American Cancer Society outlines what happens after breast cancer treatment. Visit *www.cancer.org* and search "after breast cancer treatment."

No Two Diabetes Patients Are the Same

Ildiko Lingvay, MD, MPH, an assistant professor in the departments of internal medicine and clinical science and a practicing endocrinologist at The University of Texas Southwestern Medical Center in Dallas.

Chances are you know one or more people who have type 2 diabetes, or perhaps you have been diagnosed with the condition yourself.

The number of Americans with diabetes is truly staggering—a new case is diagnosed every 17 seconds. And, of course, the consequences of uncontrolled diabetes are dire, including increased risk for heart attack and other cardiovascular problems…blindness…leg amputation…kidney failure…and, ultimately, premature death.

To help meet this enormous challenge, medical research has been stepped up.

Now: American researchers have joined forces with their European counterparts to devise new strategies to diagnose and manage diabetes more effectively than ever before.

What you need to know…

EASIER DIAGNOSIS

In the US, about 26 million people have diabetes. This includes roughly 19 million who have been diagnosed and an estimated seven million who are undiagnosed. Experts hope that a change in the diagnostic process will lead to more widespread testing and fewer undiagnosed cases.

Until recently, diabetes was typically diagnosed using one of two standard tests—a blood test that requires an overnight fast to measure blood glucose levels…and an oral glucose tolerance test, which involves drinking a high-sugar mixture and then having blood drawn 30 minutes, one hour and two hours later to show how long it takes blood glucose levels to return to normal.

The problem: Both of these tests are inconvenient for the patient, and they measure blood glucose levels only at the time of the test. Many people never get tested because they don't like the idea of having to fast overnight or wait hours to complete a test.

New approach: More widespread use of the A1C test. For decades, the A1C test, which provides a person's average blood glucose levels over a period of two to three months, has been used to monitor how well people with diabetes were controlling their disease. However, it wasn't deemed a reliable tool for diagnosis.

Now, after major improvements that have standardized the measurements from laboratory to laboratory, the A1C test is considered a practical and convenient diagnostic option.

The A1C requires no fasting or special preparation, so it's the perfect "no excuses" test. A1C

Diabetes Drugs Linked to Vision Loss

Macular edema—swelling in the central retina that can lead to blindness—is more common among patients taking Actos or Avandia. But the medicines, known as *thiazolidinediones*, generally have more benefits than risks, and the risk for macular edema is small. Patients taking the medications should have more frequent eye examinations to detect early signs of the condition.

Joel Zonszein, MD, FACE, FACP, a certified diabetes educator, professor of clinical medicine and director of the Clinical Diabetes Center, University Hospital of the Albert Einstein College of Medicine, Montefiore Medical Center, Bronx, New York.

New Diabetes Treatment On the Way

An FDA advisory panel has recommended approval of *canagliflozin*, which causes blood glucose to be excreted in urine. The drug, used in combination with a standard treatment, *metformin*, leads to weight loss and reductions in blood pressure, so it may be particularly helpful for diabetics with cardiac problems.

Joel Zonszein, MD, director of the Clinical Diabetes Center, University Hospital of the Albert Einstein College of Medicine, Montefiore Medical Center, Bronx, New York.

tests analyzed by accredited labs (such as Lab-Corp and Quest Diagnostics) meet the latest standardization criteria.

NEW TREATMENT GUIDELINES

Recently, the American Diabetes Association and the European Association for the Study of Diabetes collaborated on recommendations for best treatment practices for type 2 diabetes. The most significant change in the new guidelines is the concept of individualized treatment.

The problem: In the past, diabetes care was based on a one-size-fits-all strategy—with few exceptions, everyone with the condition got basically the same treatment.

New approach: The recently released guidelines acknowledge that there are multiple treatment options for each patient and that the best treatment for one patient may be different from what another patient requires.

This is important because diabetes affects an enormously wide range of people. For example, diabetes can strike a thin 77-year-old woman or a 300-pound teenage boy, and their treatment needs and goals will be as different as their characteristics.

After reviewing a patient's medical history and individual lifestyle, the doctor and patient consider treatment options together and decide on the best fit. *Factors that are more explicitly spelled out in the new guidelines include...*

•**Other medical conditions and medications.** If diabetes treatments interact badly with a patient's current medications, it may cause one of the medications to become ineffective...amplify the effects of the drugs...or cause allergic reactions or serious, even life-threatening side effects. This is especially true for people being treated for kidney disease or heart problems, as many diabetes medications may exacerbate those health issues.

•**Lifestyle and daily schedule.** Diabetes management is easier for people who have predictable schedules. For example, a full-time worker who regularly wakes up at 7 am, eats breakfast, takes a lunch hour and is home for dinner will have simpler treatment needs than a college student who sleeps past noon, eats cold pizza for breakfast, then pulls an all-nighter.

If a physician gives standard insulin recommendations to someone who has an unusual eating and sleeping schedule, it is easy to have blood sugar drop too low—a dangerous condition called hypoglycemia. That's why it is important that patients share as many details of their lives as possible, even if the information seems irrelevant.

BETTER TREATMENT STRATEGIES

Until recently, diabetes has been treated with a stepwise approach—starting with conservative treatment, adding medication later only when needed. This sounds good, except that new treatments are incorporated only after previous treatments fail and blood glucose rises.

The problem: Depending on scheduled doctor visits, blood sugar may remain elevated for months or even years before anyone catches the change.

New approach: Research suggests that if physicians intervene more intensively at the beginning, they have the potential to stop the progression of diabetes. With this in mind, treatment aims to decrease the rate at which the body loses insulin-producing ability...and prevent diabetes complications by not allowing blood sugar to exceed safe levels.

Under this new scenario, doctors hit diabetes full force with the patient's individualized treatment plan (including lifestyle changes and

How to Dispose of "Sharps"

Every year, Americans throw away more than three billion used needles and other so-called sharps—things such as EpiPens (which treat life-threatening allergies) and the finger-stick devices diabetics use to monitor blood sugar levels. *To dispose of them properly…*

Purchase a sharps disposal container, which is leakproof and has a puncture-resistant lid. (You can find one on Amazon.com for less than $7.) Never place sharps in trash cans or recycling bins or flush them down the toilet.

When the container is full, close it and contact your local trash-removal service to find out how you can dispose of it. (Disposal guidelines vary—for example, you might be able to drop your container off at a local hospital or fire department…or you might need to mail the container to a collection site.) Get more information at www.*safeneedledisposal.org*.

Morgan Liscinsky, spokesperson, US Food and Drug Administration's Office of Public Affairs, Silver Spring, Maryland. *www.fda.gov/safesharpsdisposal*

medication), instead of with graduated, step-up treatments.

What the new guidelines mean for anyone diagnosed with diabetes: If your current diabetes treatment plan does not address the points described in this article, see your doctor. Your treatment may need to be more customized.

The Diabetes Complication That Kills

James M. Horton, MD, chair of the Standards and Practice Guidelines Committee of the Infectious Diseases Society of America. *www.idsociety.org*

A foot or leg amputation is one of the most dreaded complications of diabetes. In the US, more than 65,000 such amputations occur each year.

But the tragedy does not stop there. According to recent research, about half of all people who have a foot amputation die within five years of the surgery—a worse mortality rate than most cancers. That's partly because diabetic patients who have amputations often have poorer glycemic control and more complications such as kidney disease. Amputation also can lead to increased pressure on the remaining limb and the possibility of new ulcers and infections.

Latest development: To combat the increasingly widespread problem of foot infections and amputations, new guidelines for the diagnosis and treatment of diabetic foot infections have been created by the Infectious Diseases Society of America (IDSA).

What you need to know…

HOW FOOT INFECTIONS START

Diabetes can lead to foot infections in two main ways—peripheral neuropathy (nerve damage that can cause loss of sensation in the feet)…and ischemia (inadequate blood flow).

To understand why these conditions can be so dangerous, think back to the last time you had a pebble inside your shoe. How long did it take before the irritation became unbearable? Individuals with peripheral neuropathy and ischemia usually don't feel any pain in their feet. Without pain, the pebble will stay in the shoe and eventually cause a sore on the sole of the foot.

Similarly, people with diabetes will not feel the rub of an ill-fitting shoe or the pressure of standing on one foot too long, so they are at risk of developing pressure sores or blisters.

These small wounds can lead to big trouble. About 25% of people with diabetes will develop a foot ulcer—ranging from mild to severe—at some point in their lives. Any ulcer, blister, cut or irritation has the potential to become infected. If the infection becomes too severe to treat effectively with antibiotics, amputation of a foot or leg may be the only way to prevent the infection from spreading throughout the body and save the person's life.

A FAST-MOVING DANGER

Sores on the foot can progress rapidly. While some foot sores remain unchanged for months, it is possible for an irritation to lead to an open wound (ulcer), infection and amputation in as little as a few days. That is why experts recommend that people with diabetes seek medical care promptly for any open sore on the feet or any new area of redness or irritation that could possibly lead to an open wound.

Important: Fully half of diabetic foot ulcers are infected and require immediate medical treatment and sometimes hospitalization.

Don't try to diagnose yourself—diagnosis requires a trained medical expert. An ulcer that appears very small on the surface could have actually spread underneath the skin, so you very well could be seeing just a small portion of the infection.

WHAT YOUR DOCTOR WILL DO

The first step is to identify the bacteria causing the infection. To do this, physicians collect specimens from deep inside the wound. Once the bacteria have been identified, the proper antibiotics can be prescribed.

Physicians also need to know the magnitude of the infection—for example, whether there is bone infection, abscesses or other internal problems. Therefore, all diabetes patients who have new foot infections should have X-rays. If more detailed imaging is needed, an MRI or a bone scan may be ordered.

The doctor will then classify the wound and infection as mild, moderate or severe and create a treatment plan.

HOW TO GET THE BEST TREATMENT

Each person's wound is unique, so there are no cookie-cutter treatment plans. *However, most treatment plans should include…*

•**A diabetic foot-care team.** For moderate or severe infections, a team of experts should coordinate treatment. This will be done for you—by the hospital or your primary care physician. The number of specialists on the team depends on the patient's specific needs but may include experts in podiatry and vascular surgery. In rural or smaller communities, this may be done via online communication with experts from larger hospitals (telemedicine).

•**Antibiotic treatment.** Milder infections usually involve a single bacterium. Antibiotics will typically be needed for about one week. With more severe infections, multiple bacteria

---

Foot Care Is Critical if You Have Diabetes

To protect yourself from foot injuries…

•**Never walk barefoot,** even around the house.

•**Don't wear sandals**—the straps can irritate the side of the foot.

•**Wear thick socks with soft leather shoes.** Leather is a good choice because it "breathes," molds to the feet and does not retain moisture. Laced-up shoes with cushioned soles provide the most support.

In addition, pharmacies carry special "diabetic socks" that protect and cushion your feet without cutting off circulation at the ankle. These socks usually have no seams that could chafe. They also wick moisture away from feet, which reduces risk for infection and foot ulcers.

•**See a podiatrist.** This physician can help you find appropriate footwear—even if you have foot deformities. Ask your primary care physician or endocrinologist for a recommendation, or consult the American Podiatric Medical Association, *www.apma.org.*

Also: Inspect your feet every day. If you see any sign of a sore, seek prompt medical care. You should also see a doctor if you experience an infected or ingrown toenail, callus formation, bunions or other deformity, fissured (cracked) skin on your feet or you notice any change in sensation.

---

are likely involved, so you will require multiple antibiotics, and treatment will need to continue for a longer period—sometimes four weeks or more if bone is affected.

If the infection is severe…or even moderate but complicated by, say, poor blood circulation, hospitalization may be required for a few days to a few weeks, depending on the course of the recovery.

•**Wound care.** Many patients who have foot infections receive antibiotic therapy only, which is often insufficient. Proper wound care is also necessary. In addition to frequent wound cleansing and dressing changes, this may include surgical removal of dead tissue (debridement)... and the use of specially designed shoes or shoe inserts—provided by a podiatrist—to redistribute pressure off the wound (off-loading).

•**Surgery.** Surgery doesn't always mean amputation. It is sometimes used not only to remove dead or damaged tissue or bone but also to improve blood flow to the foot.

If an infection fails to improve: The first question physicians know to ask is: "Is the patient complying with wound care instructions?"

Which Exercises Are Best for You?

If you have diabetes...

Exercise can lower blood sugar almost as well as medication. Recent guidelines for people with diabetes recommend 150 minutes of moderate to strenuous aerobic exercise weekly, in addition to three strength-training sessions that work all the major muscle groups—increasing muscle mass is believed to be a particularly effective way of controlling blood sugar.

All aerobic exercises are beneficial, but those that use both your upper- and lower-body muscles are best because they help deliver blood glucose to muscle cells throughout your body—try an elliptical machine, the Schwinn Airdyne (a stationary bike that adds arm movements) or NuStep (a recumbent stepper that incorporates arm movements). If you walk, use poles to involve your arms. Try to do some type of exercise every day—this helps ensure its blood sugar–lowering benefits.

If you use insulin on a regular schedule:
Exercise at the same time each day, if possible, to help maintain even, predictable blood sugar levels. Insulin should typically be used 60 to 90 minutes after your workout—check with your doctor or diabetes educator.

To prevent excessive drops in blood sugar:
Eat something before or just after exercise and adjust your insulin dose on the days you work out. Talk to your doctor for specific advice.

John P. Porcari, PhD, program director of the Clinical Exercise Physiology (CEP) program at the University of Wisconsin-La Crosse.

Too many patients lose a leg because they don't take their antibiotics as prescribed or care for the injury as prescribed.

Never forget: Following your doctors' specific orders could literally mean the difference between having one leg or two.

Popular Diabetes Meds Put to the Test

Christianne Roumie, MD, MPH, Nashville Veterans Affairs Medical Center, Geriatric Research Education Clinical Center, Nashville, Tennesee.
Steven Nissen, MD, chairman, division of cardiovascular medicine, Cleveland Clinic, Cleveland, Ohio.
Annals of Internal Medicine

P atients with diabetes who were treated with the popular oral medication *metformin* face a lower risk of heart attack, stroke or death than those taking *sulfonylureas*, another common option, according to a large, multiyear study.

About 8% of people in the United States have diabetes. Most have type 2 diabetes, which means they don't metabolize blood sugar (glucose) properly. Some people can reverse all signs of type 2 diabetes via weight loss, while others require medication to manage the condition.

Researchers who tracked hundreds of thousands of veterans with type 2 diabetes found that users of metformin (brand names include Glucophage and Fortamet) faced a "modest but clinically important" 21% lower risk of hospitalization because of cardiovascular complications than users of sulfonylureas (*glyburide* and *glipizide*).

Study lead author Christianne Roumie, MD, MPH, of the Geriatric Research Education Clinical Center at the Nashville Veterans Affairs Medical Center in Tennessee, cautioned, however, that they couldn't pinpoint whether metformin protects against heart issues or whether, by contrast, sufonylureas pose a specific threat to heart health. It's possible that both are true.

Although the researchers said the findings suggest metformin should be the preferred oral treatment for diabetes, they also stressed that it's not yet clear whether their findings would apply to women or other racial and ethnic groups, given that 97% of their study participants were men and 75% were white.

According to the American Diabetes Association, sulfonylurea drugs are insulin-production stimulants that have been in use since the 1950s. Metformin, also dating to the 1950s, works by lowering blood glucose levels.

EXPERT COMMENT

At least two-thirds of people with diabetes will die of heart disease, added Steven Nissen, MD, chairman of the department of cardiovascular medicine at the Cleveland Clinic in Ohio.

"The kind of information provided by a study like this on a diabetes drug's impact on heart disease is pretty important to have, when you think of it in that context," he said.

info For more information on diabetes medication, visit the American Diabetes Association Web site at *www.diabetes.org/living-with-diabetes/treatment-and-care/medication/.*

Guerrilla Tactics to Control Your Diabetes

Richard K. Bernstein, MD, a diabetes specialist in private practice in Mamaroneck, New York. He is a fellow of the American College of Endocrinology, the American College of Nutrition and the American College of Certified Wound Specialists. Dr. Bernstein is also author of nine books on diabetes, most recently *Dr. Bernstein's Diabetes Solution: A Complete Guide to Achieving Normal Blood Sugars* (Little, Brown). *www.diabetes-book.com*

I f you have diabetes, you may think that you are taking all the right steps with your diet, medication and exercise habits.

But the truth is, virtually all people with this common disease make mistakes in managing their condition—and unknowingly increase their risk for diabetes complications, such as heart attack, stroke, kidney failure and blindness.

Guerrilla tactics that really work: Richard K. Bernstein, MD, who was diagnosed himself with type 1 diabetes at age 12, is vigorous and healthy at almost 80. He swears by the sometimes unconventional but highly effective approach that he has developed and adopted for

Top Doctor's Natural Remedy

Alpha-lipoic Acid for Diabetics

According to Richard Horowitz, MD, of the Hudson Valley Healing Arts Center in Hyde Park, New York, *alpha-lipoic acid,* which is found in foods such as red meat and liver, works as an antioxidant, and improves insulin sensitivity, so it reduces your risk for cardiovascular disease and diabetes, and it may help reduce blood sugar levels. Dr. Horowitz typically prescribes 300 mg to 600 mg per day in pill form...while those patients with diabetes and/or cardiovascular risk factors will often be prescribed up to 1,200 mg per day.

Richard Horowitz, MD, Hudson Valley Healing Arts Center, Hyde Park, New York.

himself and the thousands of patients with type 1 and type 2 diabetes he has treated.

Here's where Dr. Bernstein thinks people with diabetes—and many mainstream medical authorities—have got it all wrong...

Mistake #1: **Settling for blood sugar levels that are too high.** Everyone agrees that elevated blood sugar is at the root of all long-term diabetic complications. But the blood sugar goals established by the American Diabetes Association (ADA) are *much too high.* The ADA has set a hemoglobin A1c (HbA1c) of 6.5% or above as the level that indicates diabetes. Most doctors accept these levels.

To virtually eliminate risk for complications: I advise that nearly all people with diabetes strive for an HbA1c of 4.5%—an average blood sugar level of 83 mg/dL. In fact, I often advise people with diabetes to ask their own doctors why their blood sugar shouldn't be as low as that of someone *without* diabetes.

Also important: Your blood sugar shouldn't vary by more than 10 mg/dL before and after meals. Many doctors are unconcerned if blood sugar spikes as high as 200 mg/dL after a meal, as long as it returns to an acceptable average level. But people with such blood sugar spikes tend to develop the same cardiovascular complications as those whose blood sugar levels are always high.

Mistake #2: **Not recognizing hidden causes of elevated blood sugar.** *Acute stress*—such as a fight with your boss or anxiety about a key presentation—can raise it. If your glucose reading is higher than expected when you're stressed, an injection of rapid-acting insulin will bring it down if you have type 1 diabetes. If you have type 2, your own insulin secretions will likely lower blood sugar within 24 hours.

Infection raises blood sugar levels—and high blood sugar increases infection risk. Suspect infection if your glucose level is up and insulin isn't working as well as usual. Get prompt treatment so that your blood sugar will go down and the infection will heal. Beware of dental infections and gum disease.

What I do: I brush twice daily, floss after meals and get tartar and plaque scrapings from a periodontist every three months.

Mistake #3: **Using the wrong glucose meter.** Whether you inject insulin for type 1 diabetes or take oral drugs for type 2, or control your disease with diet and exercise alone, you must accurately track your blood sugar with home testing.

My advice: Test a meter you are considering buying in the store—take 10 readings in succession using the manufacturer's "normal" control solution. A pharmacy with glucose meters on display will usually let you test them—ask the pharmacist. Readings should be within 6 mg/dL of the midpoint of that normal range.

Important: Make sure that you can return the device if you find it to be inaccurate later. If your insurance company won't cover a meter you like, file an appeal.

My favorite glucose meter: Of the many glucose meters for home use that I have tried, the FreeStyle Freedom Lite by Abbott, available at most drugstores or on Amazon.com for about $13, has been the most accurate.

Mistake #4: **Pricking your finger the wrong way.** If you use a glucose meter, your doctor will probably tell you to wipe the site with alcohol before pricking it. I disagree.

First, it isn't necessary to wipe your finger with alcohol—this dries out the skin and can lead to calluses, which makes it difficult to get a blood sample. Neither my patients nor I have ever developed an infection from not using alcohol.

However, you should wash your hands before drawing blood. This is especially true if you've been handling food or glucose tablets or applied hand cream—all of which can cause false high readings.

Helpful: Rinse your finger with warm water to get the blood flowing, and prick the back of your finger between the joints—this area may produce more blood and cause less pain.

Mistake #5: **Overdoing vitamin C.** In excess, vitamin C raises blood sugar and inactivates the glucose-processing enzyme in the test strip, resulting in deceptively low glucose readings. You'll probably get all the vitamin C you need from vegetables (you shouldn't rely on fruit—it has too much natural sugar). If you must take supplements, 250 mg daily in a sustained-release form is tops. These formulations are less likely to cause blood sugar spikes.

Diet, Fitness & Nutrition

To Lose Weight... Eat More

There is a science to weight loss, but the facts often are obscured by the myths. For example, the calories-in, calories-out theory says that for every 3,500 calories you lose, you drop a pound of fat. If you follow this logic, a 150-pound woman who reduced her daily caloric intake by 100 calories (the amount in less than one cup of reduced-fat milk) for 10 years would give up 365,000 calories—and would weigh only 46 pounds!

Despite what you've heard, calories are not all that matter...they're not all the same...and the government's dietary guidelines are not effective for weight control.

What really works...

•**Eat more to lose weight.** It's true. People who consume more food gain less weight than those who cut calories—but only as long as the calories come from the right foods.

Example: When researchers at the University of Pennsylvania compared the effects of higher- and lower-calorie diets, they found that people who ate more lost 200% more weight.

A diet high in high-quality foods (such as protein-rich seafood, nuts and seeds and nonstarchy vegetables, such as celery, asparagus and salad greens) increases satiety, the ability of calories to fill you up and keep you full. The same foods are less likely to be stored as body fat than, say, processed foods, and they're more likely to be burned off with your normal metabolism.

People who eat less to lose weight usually fail because the body interprets calorie restriction as starvation. For self-protection, it hangs on to body fat and instead utilizes muscle tissue for energy. Up to 70% of the weight that people

Jonathan Bailor, a health-and-fitness researcher based in the Seattle area, who analyzed more than 10,000 pages of academic research related to diet, exercise and weight loss for his book *The Smarter Science of Slim: Scientific Proof, Fat Loss Facts* (Aavia). *www.thesmarterscienceof slim.com*

lose on a low-cal diet actually is muscle tissue, not fat.

When we eat more—but smarter—we are satisfied…eat only the number of calories that we really need…and provide our body with an abundance of nutrition. This enables us to sustainably burn body fat.

•**Focus on protein.** Protein is a high-satiety nutrient that triggers the release of hormones that send *I've had enough* signals to the brain. In a University of Washington study, participants were allowed an unlimited amount of calories as long as 30% of those calories came from protein.

Result: They consumed 441 fewer calories a day—without feeling hungry.

Protein is less likely to be converted to fat. When you eat an egg omelet or a chicken breast, about one-third of the protein calories are burned during digestion…another one-third are burned when the liver converts protein to glucose (a process called gluconeogenesis).

Compare this to what happens when you eat bread or other starchy foods. About 70% of those calories can be stored as fat.

Recommended: Get one-third of your calories from protein—in the form of seafood, poultry, meat or nonfat dairy, such as plain Greek yogurt or cottage cheese.

•**Don't neglect fiber.** This isn't new advice, but most people still don't get enough fiber—or understand why it helps.

The fiber in plant foods isn't digested or absorbed. Instead, it takes up space in the digestive tract…and makes you fill up faster and stay full longer. This is why you will feel more satisfied when you eat, say, 200 calories worth of celery instead of 200 calories worth of candy. The celery takes up about 30 times more space.

•**You don't have to "count" fiber grams.** As long as you get about one-third of total calories from nonstarchy vegetables (discussed previously), you'll get enough.

•**Don't believe the claims about grains.** Whole-wheat bread, oatmeal, brown rice and other grains will not help you lose weight.

Reason: The calories in grains are aggressive, which means that they're more likely to be stored as fat than the calories that you get

from protein or nonstarchy carbohydrates. Grains—even whole grains—are rapidly converted to glucose (blood sugar) in the body. The rapid rise in glucose is followed by an equally rapid drop-off. This stimulates the appetite and causes you to crave more calories.

Also, fast-rising glucose is hard for the body to handle. It responds by attempting to rid itself of glucose—by storing it in fat cells.

•**Eat fat.** It's true that fat has about twice as many calories as protein or carbohydrates, but that would matter only if the calories-in, calories-out equation had anything to do with weight loss—which it doesn't.

Decades ago, doctors encouraged Americans to consume fewer calories from fat.

Result: The average person got heavier, not leaner. Experts now agree that people who consume more fat are no more likely to be overweight or obese than those who eat less—if anything, the people who eat less fat are more likely to gain weight.

Recommended: Get about one-third of your calories from fats, including olive and canola oils (monunsaturated fats that lower your risk for heart disease) and the fats in meats, poultry and fish.

•**Drink a lot of green tea.** You will naturally burn more fat when you drink more water. If you get much of this water in the form of green tea, you will do even better. The polyphenols in green tea are among the healthiest antioxidants ever discovered. These compounds, along with

---

Food Diaries Make Diets More Effective

Recent finding: Women who consistently kept food diaries lost about six more pounds (or about 4% more) in a year than women who didn't.

Reason: Writing down what and how much you eat makes it seem more real—if you do not write food down, it is easier to tell yourself that you did not eat so much.

Study of 123 overweight or obese postmenopausal women by researchers at Fred Hutchinson Cancer Research Center's Prevention Center, Seattle, published online in *Journal of the Academy of Nutrition and Dietetics.*

the caffeine in tea (about one-fifth the amount in coffee), increase fat metabolism. If you drink decaffeinated tea, you still will burn more fat than you would just by drinking water.

Recommended: Between five and 15 cups of green tea daily. For maximum efficiency, put all the tea bags you need for the day in hot water. Let the tea brew for a few minutes, and then drink the tea throughout the day like iced tea…or put it in the microwave if you prefer hot tea.

"Small" Secret to Outwitting a Big Appetite

Devina Wadhera, a PhD candidate in the department of psychology at Arizona State University in Tempe and lead author of a study on food piece size and satiety presented at the recent Annual Meeting of the Society for the Study of Ingestive Behavior in Zurich.

A recent study outlines a simple cut-food-up-and-eat-less strategy that may work as a painless weight-loss technique for dieters. The 301 study volunteers fasted overnight and skipped breakfast before the experiment began. Then they each were given a bagel and cream cheese. One group of participants got bagels that were whole…the other group got identical bagels, except that theirs had been cut into four pieces. After eating as much of their bagels as they wanted, they spent 20 minutes filling out questionnaires about food preferences—a delaying tactic, because it takes

about 20 minutes after eating for the brain to get the message that the stomach is full. Next, each participant was invited to eat as much as desired of a complimentary lunch that included a turkey sandwich, veggies with dressing, crackers with meat and cheese, mozzarella sticks, pasta, potato salad and a cupcake.

Fascinating findings: Compared with participants who had received whole bagels, those whose bagels had been cut up ate 8% less of their bagels—but the real revelation was that they also ate 40% less of the big lunch! Apparently, the cut-up bagels had done a much better job of satisfying participants' appetites, so when offered additional food later, they were less tempted by it.

Especially in this era of out-of-control portion sizes, it's smart for us to make regular use of this simple tactic—cut up food to make it seem more plentiful and thus more satisfying. We have nothing to lose but weight.

How to Walk Away from Cravings

Adrian H. Taylor, PhD, professor of exercise and health psychology and director of research, sport and health sciences at the College of Life and Environmental Sciences at the University of Exeter in England. He is coauthor, with Hwajung Oh (who recently completed her PhD at the University of Exeter), of a study on walking and chocolate consumption published in *Appetite*.

Do you often have cravings for a food treat, especially when under pressure, say, while working? It happens to pretty much anyone who enjoys eating. *But sometimes the treat is not a good fix for our psyche or our waistline....*

Here's a simple step for cutting back on treats and giving into cravings—just take a short walk. Sounds wacky, but it works. The tip comes from chocolate researcher Adrian Taylor, PhD, professor of exercise and health psychology at the University of Exeter in England. *The skinny on Dr. Taylor's recent study...*

Participants included 45 women and 33 men who habitually ate at least 3.5 ounces of chocolate daily and reported frequent chocolate cravings. They did not know that the study was about chocolate—instead, they were told that the focus was on how exercise affects thinking. The participants were randomly divided into four groups. Those in groups one and two walked briskly on a treadmill for 15 minutes. Then, for 15 minutes, they worked at a computer (in a setup similar to what you'd find in an office), with group one performing an easy task...and group two performing a difficult task. Groups three and four rested for 15 minutes instead of exercising, then worked on either the easy task or the challenging task.

Key element: Each participant had a bowl of small chocolate candies next to his or her computer and was "casually" invited to have some. Afterward, researchers weighed the bowls to see how much chocolate each person had eaten.

Results: Among participants who rested before their task, the average amount of chocolate consumed during the 15-minute work period was 28 grams (about one ounce)...whereas participants who walked before working ate only 15 grams, on average, or nearly 50% less. Surprisingly, the ease or difficulty of their task did not significantly alter how much chocolate the participants ate.

Dr. Taylor's earlier research showed that exercise dampens chocolate cravings. But this is the first study to show that simply walking reduces the amount of the treat people actually eat— perhaps because exercise releases endorphins that leave you feeling more content and less in need of comfort food.

Bottom line: Up to 97% of women (and 68% of men) get food cravings, most commonly for chocolate. So unless you're part of the 3% who are immune, try taking a quick walk before settling down to work—it could help keep chocolate cravings and consumption under control. How briskly should you move? Dr. Taylor suggested walking at a pace you might use if you were late for an appointment but not so fast as to leave you breathless.

Diners Eat Less In Soft Ambience

Cornell University, news release.

It may not help the restaurant's bottom line, but a recent study suggests that diners are happier and eat less in fast-food restaurants when the lighting and music go soft.

STUDY DETAILS

"When we did a makeover of a fast-food restaurant, we found that softer music and lighting led diners to eat 175 fewer calories and enjoy it more," said study lead author, Brian Wansink, PhD, professor of marketing and director of the Food and Brand Lab, at Cornell University.

Simple Secret to Improving Health Habits

After tracking 204 adults who didn't eat well or exercise regularly, researchers found that the most effective way to improve the study participants' habits was to reduce their TV and computer time and have them eat more fruits and vegetables. Participants maintained healthier habits even after the three-week study ended.

Explanation: Focusing on just two simple changes is not overwhelming, and the behaviors reinforce each other.

Bonnie Spring, PhD, professor of preventive medicine, Northwestern University Feinberg School of Medicine, Chicago.

The researchers found that people ate less—775 calories instead of 949, or a decrease of 18%—thanks to the changes in the atmosphere. People also said they enjoyed their food more.

"These results suggest that a more relaxed environment increases satisfaction and decreases consumption," Dr. Wansink said. "This is important information for fast-food restaurants, which are often accused of contributing to obesity: Making simple changes away from brighter lights and sound-reflecting surfaces can go a long way toward reducing overeating—and increase their customers' satisfaction at the same time."

The findings were published in the journal *Psychological Reports*.

info For more information about managing weight, visit the US National Library of Medicine Web site, *www.nlm.nih.gov,* and search "weight control."

Can't Get Yourself To Exercise?

Michael W. Otto, PhD, a professor of psychology at Boston University. He is coauthor, with Jasper A.J. Smits, PhD, of *Exercise for Mood and Anxiety: Proven Strategies for Overcoming Depression and Enhancing Well-Being* (Oxford University).

It's proven to lower your risk for heart disease, diabetes, stroke and certain cancers—and may protect against Parkinson's and Alzheimer's disease. It boosts mood and curbs anxiety. It also helps you lose weight. On top of all that, it costs virtually nothing.

Exercise is hands-down one of the best things you can do for your health. So why is it so difficult to stick with it?

Latest development: Even though the many physical and mental benefits of exercise are undeniable, researchers are now making surprising discoveries about common psychological barriers that can sideline even the most health-conscious individuals…

Lift Lighter Weights

Lifting lighter weights more times is just as effective at building muscle as lifting heavy weights.

Recent finding: After 10 weeks of training three times a week, participants who lifted light weights for more repetitions gained as much muscle as people who lifted heavy weights but with fewer repetitions.

Study by researchers at McMaster University, Hamilton, Ontario, Canada, published in *Journal of Applied Physiology*.

THE EXERCISE HABIT

Surely, you've heard all the popular ways to make exercise more appealing—for example, listening to music while you do it or finding an exercise buddy. For some people, these steps are all that's needed to become consistent exercisers. But for others, more subtle forces may be at work.

For example, people who must negotiate the "will I…won't I" dialog before every exercise session are making it too hard on themselves. That's because people who consistently exercise do not have to stop and think about it each time—they simply have made it a habit.

One of the most powerful ways to establish an exercise habit is to always do it at the same time of day—this way, your whole schedule becomes arranged in a way that lets you exercise without "juggling." This could mean getting up a little earlier each day and going for a brisk walk or going directly to the gym after work.

Other ways to make exercise a habit for you…

•**Dress the part.** Changing into a special exercise outfit makes you feel like a different person—the same way dressing for work or for a party puts you in the proper mood. Even when motivation is very low, putting on your exercise clothes can help you feel more like your "exercising self" and get you moving. Paying a little more for stylish fitness gear also may help.

What to do: Begin by taking one step at a time—first change clothes, then walk out the door, then focus on walking, for example, then start jogging.

Avoid "inertia zones." Once you park yourself in front of the TV or pick up the newspaper, it will be much harder to get moving. So, when you get home after a long day, remember that exercise is far more likely to help you feel better than watching television.

Helpful: Put the TV remote in a drawer and tell yourself you can't get it out until you've exercised.

LOOK FOR THE RIGHT REWARD

You would think that exercise's promised health benefits would be enough to motivate anyone to get moving. Not so.

The reason: It usually takes weeks—sometimes months—before you'll see results on the scale or your waistline…and perhaps even years before the health benefits pay off in a big way.

These delayed rewards hold little appeal for humans, who are hardwired to respond more readily to immediate gratification, such as sleeping an extra half-hour or stretching out on the couch after work.

What most people fail to realize: Exercise does offer its own immediate reward—it improves mood. Within five minutes of finishing physical activity, most people feel happier and less stressed.

However, until you experience this mood shift for yourself, you may not believe it. So make a conscious effort to tune in to your emotional state—you may be surprised by the dramatic mood boost that exercise can provide.

Need proof? For two weeks, keep a written record of your mood before and after you exercise. This should give you hard evidence to show how much better you can feel after exercising.

BE A GOOD COACH

It's common for people who want to get more exercise to tell themselves that they "must" do it. Soon, this inner voice sounds more like a drill sergeant than a sympathetic, helpful coach. This doesn't help because shame and guilt don't motivate us much—except, perhaps, to avoid the whole issue.

What works better: Rather than nagging yourself to exercise, try to be rational. *How to respond to common exercise-avoiding messages…*

In the morning: "It won't matter if I stay in bed now. I'll work out tomorrow"…"I'll exercise later in the day"…"I'm still tired—I'll feel better if I sleep in."

What to tell yourself: "I chose to work out in the morning for a reason…it fits my schedule and makes me feel good later"…"Of course I feel tired—I'm still in bed. Once I get moving, I'll be energized."

If you plan to exercise after work: "I just need to relax for a little while, then I'll go to the gym."

What to tell yourself: "Exercise is a real break from what I've been doing…a good workout will leave me feeling mentally refreshed"… "If I work out now, I'll sleep better and be ready for tomorrow."

If you're feeling tired or depressed: "I'm just not up to exercising…I need to indulge myself and lie down or just watch TV."

What to tell yourself: This is like saying, "I have a headache, so I can't take an aspirin." Instead, tell yourself, "Since I'm feeling down, exercise is exactly what I need. Remember how much better I feel after a workout?"

SET THE RIGHT PACE

A lot of people think that a "real" workout must be strenuous. But a good coach will have you walking, running, biking or swimming fast enough to be beneficial—but not so fast that you'll avoid the workout.

Two-Minute Yoga Practice

Two-minute yoga practice is an effective overall stretch. Doing the Downward Dog pose every day uses the strength of your arms and legs to stretch your spine, hips, hamstrings and calves. It also strengthens your quadriceps and ankles…and tones your arms and abdominals.

Annie Carpenter, yoga instructor, Exhale Center for Sacred Movement, Los Angeles, quoted in *Yoga Journal.* www.yogajournal.com

Important secret: Just 2.5 hours weekly of moderate aerobic exercise—for example, walking at a pace that raises your heart rate but leaves you able to carry on a conversation (that is, you can talk but not sing)—confers all the major health benefits described earlier.

Also helpful: Structure your workout so that the ending is pleasurable. If you're getting tired, coast for a bit, then finish with a victory sprint. Studies show that we tend to remember the end of an experience more vividly than the beginning or middle. Ending a workout on a positive note allows you to recall those good feelings later on.

Get More from Your Workouts!

Tom Holland, CPT, a certified personal trainer and exercise physiologist based in Darien, Connecticut. *Women's Health* magazine named him one of the top 10 fitness professionals in the country. He is author of *Beat the Gym* (William Morrow) and *The Marathon Method* (Fair Winds).

Anyone who sticks to an exercise program knows that the commitment involves a lot of time and, in some cases, money if you belong to a gym or fitness center.

Trap: All too often, people follow ineffective routines that cause them to waste their time and money. *Here are my secrets for getting the most from your workout…**

SECRET #1: Do the right amount of cardio. If you don't do enough cardiovascular exercise, you won't get the maximum benefits. But, if you do too much, you'll increase your risk for injury. So how much cardio should you do?

My advice: Follow this simple formula—for every pound you weigh, do one minute of cardio each week. For example, if you weigh 150 pounds, you should do 150 minutes of cardio (incorporating a variety of exercises) per week.

Because women in general will end up doing less cardio than men with this formula, it's wise

*Consult your doctor before beginning or significantly changing an exercise regimen.

for them to spend more time doing strength training (see next page). Genetically, women have less muscle than men, and as a woman ages, the preservation of lean muscle becomes vital.

SECRET #2: Understand what the programs on cardio machines really mean. Let's say that you opt for a "fat-burning" program on a treadmill because you want to lose (or maintain) body weight. Based on the "calories burned from fat" percentages given with these programs, it appears that you will burn more fat if you work out at a lower intensity. But that's not true. Because these fat-burning calculations are based on percentages—not total calories burned—they are easily misunderstood. *For example…*

Workout #1: A 30-minute cardiovascular workout at an easy intensity burns 250 calories and 20 g of fat. With this workout, 72% of calories burned are from fat.

Workout #2: A 25-minute intense cardio workout burns 330 calories and 25 g of fat. That's the equivalent of 68% of calories burned from fat.

The easier workout burns a larger percentage of fat, but the more intense workout burns more fat and calories in total—and in less time. The more calories and fat burned, the more weight you will lose.

SECRET #3: Skip the heart-rate zone charts. The most widely used maximum heart-rate zones are calculated by subtracting the exerciser's age from 220. For example, if you are age 50, your maximum heart rate would be 170 (220 − 50 = 170). This is supposed to be the highest heart rate you should reach during a workout. However, research has found that in most cases the number is too low.

My advice: Whether you choose to use a treadmill, StairMaster, stationary bike, elliptical trainer, etc., simply focus on varying the intensity of your workout. Use a scale of one to 10, with 10 being the most intense. On some days do a lower intensity workout (around a five or six), and on other days bring it up to a seven or eight. Mix in short intervals (10 to 60 seconds) of high-intensity (nine to 10) exercise.

Better Way to Measure Belly Fat

Researchers reviewed nine years of health-survey data for 12,785 people (average age 41).

Result: People with excess belly fat but still within the "normal" body mass index (BMI) range were almost three times more likely to die of cardiovascular disease as those with normal BMIs and waist-to-hip ratios (a marker of belly fat).

Theory: BMI alone is not an accurate gauge of deadly visceral fat, which surrounds the heart, liver and other organs.

To determine your waist-to-hip ratio: Divide your waist measurement by your hip measurement. The ratio should be 0.85 or lower for women and 0.90 or lower for men.

Francisco Lopez-Jimenez, MD, professor of medicine, Mayo Medical School and Mayo Clinic, Rochester, Minnesota.

Important: Always get your doctor's approval before following any maximum heart-rate formulas.

SECRET #4: Don't slight your strength-training regimen. Many people complain that, as they age, they eat and exercise the same amount but still gain weight. One of the main causes of this is loss of muscle mass. The more muscle mass you have, the more calories you burn. Strength training preserves and even increases muscle mass, keeping metabolism at a high level.

Strength training also increases bone density and functional strength and preserves joint health.

My advice: As with cardio workouts, vary your strength-training routines. Some days use machines, others use dumbbells or stretch bands. You also could do squats, push-ups and lunges. If you have trouble incorporating separate strength-training sessions into your workout, an efficient method is to do circuit training. This approach involves strength exercises with short bursts of cardio in between.

Important: Don't spend too much time on ab crunches. The appearance of abs is largely due to diet. The best way to reduce abdominal fat is with healthful eating and cardio exercise. Spend only 10% of your strength-training sessions on ab exercises. This will define the abdomen once you have decreased abdominal fat.

SECRET #5: Start with an exercise you hate. Because you're less likely to perform exercises you hate, doing them will have a big impact on your body.

My advice: Do just one exercise you don't like at the beginning of a workout—if you put it off until the end of your exercise session, chances are you won't do it. Incorporate one exercise you hate for a few weeks, then switch to another you dislike. This prevents your body from getting used to the hated exercise.

The Secret to a Slim Belly After Liposuction

Study on the effects of exercise after liposuction by researchers at the University of Sao Paulo in Brazil, published in *The Journal of Clinical Endocrinology and Metabolism.*

Having the fat instantly sucked out of a too-big belly does hold a certain appeal when a healthy diet and regular exercise cannot overcome a family trait toward a wide waist. So it's no wonder that liposuction—which targets pesky pockets of subcutaneous fat lurking just below the skin—is one of the world's most popular cosmetic surgeries.

Problem: That sudden loss of body fat may trigger a feedback mechanism that promotes fat regain. Even worse, a recent study from Brazil shows that the type of fat regained is far more harmful to health than the type of fat that was sucked out! Fortunately, the study also suggests a simple way to prevent that dangerous fat from forming. *Ladies contemplating lipo, take note…*

The study included 36 non-obese women who were not in the habit of exercising regularly. Each had liposuction to remove a modest amount (about 2.2 pounds) of abdominal subcutaneous fat. After two months, one group of participants was assigned to do a combination of strength training plus aerobic exercise for about 60 to 75 minutes three times weekly for four months…the other group did not exercise. Both groups had similar dietary habits.

What the researchers found: Six months after surgery, CT scans showed that both groups still had less subcutaneous belly fat than they had had prior to their liposuction. However, the nonexercisers had a 10% increase in visceral fat, a dangerous type of fat that lies deep within the abdomen, surrounding internal organs. Visceral fat produces hormones and other substances that can raise blood pressure, negatively alter blood cholesterol levels and interfere with the body's ability to properly use insulin—thus increasing the risk for heart disease, diabetes and death. In contrast, the exercisers showed no such increase in visceral fat, indicating that exercise can counteract a liposuction-induced increase of this harmful fat.

Bottom line: If you are considering liposuction, ask your doctor about the possibility of increased visceral fat and discuss an appropriate postsurgery exercise plan.

Aerobic Exercise Seems Best for Weight, Fat Loss

Leslie Willis, MS, exercise physiologist, Duke University Medical Center, Durham, North Carolina.

Timothy Church, MD, PhD, MPH, director, preventive medicine research, Pennington Biomedical Research Center, Baton Rouge, Louisiana.

Journal of Applied Physiology

I f you want to burn fat and lose weight, aerobic exercise beats resistance training, a recent study says.

"We are not trying to discourage people from resistance training," said study author Leslie Willis, MS, an exercise physiologist at Duke University Medical Center in Durham, North Carolina.

BACKGROUND

Previous studies have shown that resistance training has many benefits, including improving blood sugar control, she said, but the effects of it on fat reduction have not been conclusive.

STUDY DETAILS

The recent study, published in the *Journal of Applied Physiology,* compared resistance training to aerobic exercise to determine which is best for weight and fat loss.

Willis's team assigned 234 middle-aged men and women, all overweight or obese, to one of three groups for the eight-month study. The resistance-training group worked out three times a week, with instructions to exercise about three hours total. They used eight different weight machines.

The aerobic group put in about 12 miles a week on elliptical machines or treadmills, putting in about 133 minutes a week, or about 2 ¼ hours.

The combination group worked out three days a week, putting in the combined effort of the resistance training and the aerobic groups.

STUDY RESULTS

Those who did aerobic exercise only or a combination of aerobic and resistance training reduced total body mass and fat mass more than those in the resistance only group. However, the aerobic only group and the combination group were not substantially different from each other, Willis said.

For instance, the aerobic only group lost 3.8 pounds and the combination group lost 3.6 pounds.

Exercise Levels Should Be Considered a "Vital Sign"

Recent report: Physicians should put more emphasis on a patient's overall physical activity level—much as they do with blood pressure readings and body weight.

Prediction: The number of people who exercise regularly would likely increase, as did the number of people who quit smoking when doctors began recommending smoking-cessation programs.

Self-defense: At your next doctor visit, be sure to discuss your physical activity levels.

Karim Khan, MD, PhD, professor of kinesiology, The University of British Columbia, Canada.

Drink Cold Water During Intense Exercise

Cold water regulates internal body temperature and prevents dehydration more efficiently than room-temperature water.

Study of 45 physically active men, average age around 30, by researchers at Stanford University, Stanford, California, and several athletic training facilities, published in *Journal of the International Society of Sports Nutrition.*

The combination group did experience the largest reduction in waist circumference. A large waist (over 35 inches in women, over 40 in men) is a risk factor for heart disease and other problems.

IMPLICATIONS

The recent study results suggest for people short on time, focusing on aerobic exercise is the best way to lose weight and fat, Willis said.

The combination group "did double the time commitment without significantly improving the result over the aerobic group alone for fat mass," Willis noted.

"If fat mass is something a person wants to target, I would say your most time-efficient method would be to focus on the cardiovascular exercise," she said.

"Resistance training did increase lean mass, but it doesn't change fat mass, so the pounds didn't change," she said.

RESISTANCE TRAINING STILL IMPORTANT

Timothy Church, MD, PhD, MPH, director of preventive medicine research at Pennington Biomedical Research Center in Baton Rouge, Louisiana, said experts have known that "aerobic exercise really helps with weight loss."

However, he said, the study results are no reason to dismiss resistance training. People lose muscle mass as they age, he said, and resistance training, which helps maintain muscle strength, can help with quality-of-life issues.

It can help people perform such small but important everyday tasks as lifting their grand-

children and getting luggage into overhead bins on airplanes, he said.

info To learn more about aerobic exercise, visit the Web site of Georgia State University at *www2.gsu.edu/~wwwfit/aerobice.html*

Can You Be Fit and Fat?

C. Noel Bairey-Merz, MD, professor of medicine, Women's Guild Chair in Women's Health and director of the Barbra Streisand Women's Heart Center and the Preventive and Rehabilitative Cardiac Center at Cedars-Sinai Medical Center, Los Angeles. She is chair of the National Institutes of Health–sponsored Women's Ischemic Syndrome Evaluation.

Good news if you're overweight—you still can be fit, as long as you're physically active.

THE RESEARCH

Researchers at Dallas's Cooper Institute recruited 22,000 men in a study designed to look at the relationship between body fat and fitness. First, they measured the participants' body compositions and gave them treadmill tests. Then they tracked the men for eight years.

Result: Men who were overweight but fit were two times less likely to have died than those who were lean but unfit. Those who were lean and exercised were healthier than fat people who exercised, but the difference was small.

Exercise Safely in Hot Weather

Dilute sports drinks—mix two parts water with one part sports drink. Sports drinks are high in sugar, which can cause an energy spike that can lead to early fatigue, especially on hot days.
Do not overstretch—muscles move more easily in hot weather, but overstretching can lead to injury.
Be on the lookout for signs of heat exhaustion—headaches, dizziness, blurred vision and nausea. If you experience any of these, stop your workout, rest and hydrate.

Lisa Corsello, certified personal trainer and nutrition consultant, and creator and owner of the Burn workout, San Francisco.

Walking Inhibits Weight-Promoting Genes

A brisk hour-long walk each day cuts the effect of weight-promoting genes in half. The opposite is also true—the effect of the genes rises 25% for every two hours of daily TV-watching or other sedentary behavior.

Study of 12,000 people by researchers at Harvard School of Public Health, Boston, reported at the American Heart Association's annual meeting in San Diego.

Being fit does not require high-level athletic training—it simply means that you should aim for a cumulative 30 minutes of moderate-intensity daily activity such as walking.

THE GOAL THAT COUNTS

If you have to pick a single health goal, it's generally better to get fit than to lose weight. *To begin...*

•**Check your fitness.** If you're fit, you should be able to walk 30 minutes without stopping... and climb a flight of stairs without gasping for breath. If you can't, you'll want to see a doctor and ease into an exercise plan. Heart attacks often occur when sedentary people suddenly face a cardiovascular stressor, such as overly vigorous exercise.

•**Exercise consistently.** The duration of exercise—and doing it regularly—is important.

•**Make exercise easy.** You can achieve fitness as you go about your day. *Examples...*

•**Walk.** Every hour of walking can increase your life expectancy by two hours. At work, take the stairs instead of the elevator...go for a walking break instead of a coffee break...make walking tours part of your vacations.

•**Squeeze in exercise.** Bring a resistance band to work, and do short workouts at your desk. At home, stand up rather than sit when watching TV or talking on the phone. When reaching for something on a high shelf, stretch up on your toes to get it. Squat down to pick up something low.

How Much Vitamin D Do Bones Need? Probably More Than You Think

Bess Dawson-Hughes, MD, director of the Bone Metabolism Laboratory at the Jean Mayer USDA Human Nutrition Research Center on Aging at Tufts University in Boston and coauthor of an article on vitamin D supplementation and fracture risk in *The New England Journal of Medicine.*

It was just a few years ago that the Institute of Medicine (finally) increased its recommendations on vitamin D intake. The previous guidelines called for a scant 200 international units (IU) to 600 IU daily, depending on age... the current recommendations are 600 IU daily for most Americans and 800 IU for those over age 70. Now a huge recent study suggests that those levels are still too low to keep our bones from breaking as we age.

Researchers pooled data from 11 clinical trials involving a total of 31,022 seniors ages 65 and up, 91% of whom were women. The trials focused on the effects of vitamin D supplements taken with or without calcium. Rather than looking at how much vitamin D participants were given as part of a study, as is typically done, the researchers zeroed in on how much vitamin D people actually did take. Based on that, participants were divided into four groups, or quartiles, ranging from the highest to the lowest levels of actual vitamin D intake.

Findings: In the highest quartile, vitamin D supplementation averaged 800 IU (and ranged from 792 IU to 2,000 IU) per day. People in this quartile were 30% less likely to break a hip and 14% less likely to suffer a nonverterbral fracture, such as in a wrist or forearm, than people in all of the other quartiles. In fact, the results showed no benefit in terms of fracture prevention from taking less than 800 IU daily.

Take-home message: Talk to your doctor about supplementing with at least 800 IU of vitamin D daily. (Note that many multivitamins provide only 400 IU of vitamin D.) But don't fall into a "lots more is lots better" mind-set—excessive vitamin D can lead to high blood levels of calcium, which can cause kidney damage and blood vessel calcification.

How to Get More Nutrients From Your Veggies

It's always best to chew your vegetables and other foods thoroughly to grind them into a soft form for optimal digestion. This is especially important for anyone who has *gastroparesis* (a condition that reduces the ability of the stomach to grind food and empty its contents) or any other gastrointestinal movement disorder. You need to break down the tough cell walls in vegetables so your body can absorb the flavonoids, polyphenols and other nutrients in the cells.

Studies show that up to 70% of the nutrients in raw vegetables are not absorbed by the body. If you have gastroparesis or just want to boost your nutrient intake, lightly steam or briefly microwave vegetables. Mixing them in a blender or juicer will also help the body absorb more of their nutrients.

Try to eat a variety of brightly colored vegetables, including red, orange and dark green.

Gerard E. Mullin, MD, associate professor of medicine, The Johns Hopkins University School of Medicine, Baltimore, and coauthor of *The Inside Tract: Your Good Gut Guide to Great Digestive Health* (Rodale).

Stop Flushing Your Calcium Down the Drain

Elson M. Haas, MD, founder and director of the Preventive Medical Center of Marin in San Rafael, California. He also is author of numerous books on health and nutrition, including *Staying Healthy with Nutrition: The Complete Guide to Diet and Nutritional Medicine* (Celestial Arts). *www.pmcmarin.com*

Are you conscientiously eating calcium-rich foods and following your doctor's orders about calcium supplement use? That's good—but not good enough to ensure that your bones benefit.

Reason: Some foods contain substances that interfere with calcium absorption, so whatever else you eat along with your calcium influences how much of the mineral goes to your bones…

and how much literally gets flushed away when you go to the bathroom.

To tip this balance in your favor, it helps to allow a few hours to elapse between eating the foods that you rely on for calcium and eating the types of foods that reduce calcium absorption, according to Elson M. Haas, MD, an integrative physician in San Rafael, California, and author of *Staying Healthy with Nutrition: The Complete Guide to Diet and Nutritional Medicine*. So just what kinds of foods are we talking about?

Calcium-rich foods: These include beans (great northern, navy, white)…Chinese cabbage…dairy products…fortified cereals…leafy greens (beet greens, collards, dandelion greens, kale, turnip greens)…nuts…okra…rice…seafood (crab, salmon, ocean perch, sardines, shrimp)…seeds…and soy products.

HERE'S WHAT INTERFERES WITH CALCIUM…

•**Sodium.** When you eat too much sodium, the excess is excreted in your urine—but when that sodium leaves your body, it drags calcium with it.

Best: Limit daily consumption of sodium to no more than 2,300 mg or about the amount in one teaspoon of salt. What if you do go overboard on salt? Potassium helps limit sodium-induced calcium excretion, so have a high-potassium

Do You Need a Multivitamin?

Individuals over 50 generally do not need a multivitamin. It is best to get your nutrients from a healthful diet that includes plenty of brightly colored fruits and vegetables, whole grains and legumes.

If you eat dairy, make it nonfat or use non-dairy alternatives, such as almond or soy milk.

However, those over age 50 may have trouble absorbing vitamin B-12 from food, so a supplement may be needed. Ask a doctor to test your level and recommend a supplement, if needed.

Suzanne Havala Hobbs, DrPH, clinical associate professor, Gillings School of Global Public Health, University of North Carolina at Chapel Hill.

Foods for Better Sleep

Try salmon and spinach salad for dinner at 7 pm—omega-3s in the fish help you relax, and magnesium in spinach can calm your nerves. For dessert at 7:30, eat tart cherries—they contain the sleep hormone melatonin—or drink tart cherry juice. For a bedtime snack at 9 pm, make warm milk part of a soothing ritual—it is the routine, not the tryptophan in the milk, that is calming.

Health. www.health.com

---

food (banana, cantaloupe) with your calcium, Dr. Haas suggested.

• **Caffeine.** Do you often have calcium-rich yogurt for breakfast or take your calcium pill with your morning meal—then wash it down with a big mug of coffee or tea? Caffeine from any source works against strong bones by interfering with calcium absorption and causing more of the mineral to be lost through the urine.

Better: Have your morning yogurt with a glass of orange juice instead, since its vitamin C and magnesium improve calcium absorption… or take your supplement in the afternoon or evening, after you've finished drinking coffee for the day.

• **Phytates.** Found in high-fiber foods such as berries, corn, nuts, oatmeal, rye and especially wheat bran, phytates are substances that bind calcium, reducing its absorption. Fiber-rich foods have many health benefits, so of course you don't want to shun them…but if you're increasing your fiber intake (for instance, to help regulate digestion), be sure to increase your calcium intake, too.

• **Phosphorus.** This mineral, which is plentiful in meat and poultry, has many important functions in the body. But for proper bone density, a delicate balance must be maintained between phosphorus and calcium—which means that as phosphorus intake increases, the need for calcium increases, too.

Problem: Ideally, people should eat more calcium than phosphorus, but the typical meat-focused Western diet contains roughly two to four times more phosphorus than calcium. Also,

because both phosphorus and calcium require vitamin D for absorption, phosphorus-rich foods compete with calcium-rich foods for the available vitamin D.

Bone smart: Ask your doctor about supplementing with vitamin D. Also, cut back on meat and focus more on plant foods…and be aware that carbonated beverages such as colas have as much as 500 mg of phosphorus in one serving—so say "so long" to soda.

Nighttime note: Has your doctor recommended calcium supplements? Choose a brand that also includes magnesium for maximum absorption…and take half of your daily dose at bedtime, Dr. Haas suggested—it may even help you relax and sleep better.

Raw? Cooked? How to Eat Your Veggies

Joel Fuhrman, MD, nutrition researcher and board-certified family physician in Flemington, New Jersey, who specializes in preventing and reversing disease through nutritional and natural methods. He is author of *Super Immunity: The Essential Nutrition Guide for Boosting Your Body's Defenses to Live Longer, Stronger and Disease Free* (HarperOne). *www.drfuhrman.com*

There's a pervasive belief that heating foods—especially vegetables—destroys disease-fighting nutrients and digestion-enhancing enzymes. But recent research contradicts the "raw is always best" contention.

Joel Fuhrman, MD, a nutrition researcher, family physician and author of *Super Immunity: The Essential Nutrition Guide for Boosting Your Body's Defenses to Live Longer, Stronger and Disease Free,* confirmed this. He explained: "With some vegetables, the micronutrients are heat-sensitive and can be destroyed by cooking. But with others, cooking allows the body to absorb more of the beneficial compounds because heat releases the nutrients from the cell matrix to which they are bound."

Which veggies should you cook and which are best raw? *Dr. Fuhrman had some specific recommendations…*

Best cooked: By cooking a tomato, you break down its cell walls and release more of its lycopene, a cancer-fighting antioxidant. Dr. Fuhrman also suggested cooking carotenoid vegetables (think red, orange and yellow) such as bell peppers, carrots and corn, because the heat increases the bioavailability of their nutrients. He particularly recommended that mushrooms be cooked. "Cooking mushrooms for even a few minutes dissipates most of the mild toxins they contain," he explained. Why eat mushrooms at all if they have toxins? Because they also provide powerful polysaccharides thought to inhibit tumor growth. For instance, one recent study found that eating mushrooms daily was associated with a 64% reduction in breast cancer risk.

Best raw: A vegetable Dr. Fuhrman singled out to eat raw is perhaps the one you'd least want to eat that way—the onion. When you chop an onion, a chemical reaction releases compounds called organosulfides. These compounds cause your eyes to tear...but more importantly, they help halt cancer cell growth and may have anti-inflammatory effects that protect against osteoarthritis. Unless you chop or purée the onion while it is still raw, the organosulfides will not form because heat can deactivate the enzymes that create them. You don't have to eat a raw onion the way you would an apple—just put some slices on your salads and sandwiches. And when you do cook with onions, be sure that they are thinly sliced or chopped and blended into the recipe while still raw so the organosulfides have a chance to form.

Best when raw and cooked are combined: Green cruciferous vegetables such as broccoli, cabbage, collards and kale contain more vitamins and minerals per calorie than any other foods, Dr. Fuhrman said. But some are released when raw and others need to be heated to be bioavailable. In particular, myrosinase, an enzyme that is released only when the cell walls are damaged (for instance, by chewing, chopping or juicing) triggers a chemical reaction that activates the body's own antioxidant system, providing potent protection against cancer. Cooking deactivates myrosinase. So why not always go raw with these vegetables? Because some of their nutrients are more bioavailable when cooked. Dr. Fuhrman recommended eating both raw and cooked green cruciferous vegetables at the same meal—for instance, by having a raw kale salad along with your stir-fried broccoli-and-chicken entrée—because synergistic effects will produce maximum benefits.

• **Cooking methods matter.** Of course, how you cook has a big effect on veggies' healthfulness. Dr. Fuhrman advised against roasting, grilling or deep frying because high-heat cooking methods that brown, darken or dry out foods lead to the formation of carcinogenic acrylamides. If you love grilled vegetables, choose juicy ones such as tomatoes and peppers, which don't dry

Better Broccoli

Beneforté brand broccoli is grown to contain two to three times the normal amount of glucoraphanin, a nutrient that may help to break down fat and lower cholesterol. It tastes sweeter than regular broccoli and contains slightly more cancer-fighting sulphur. Beneforté is available at grocery stores in Alabama, California, Georgia, Minnesota, North Carolina, South Carolina, Tennessee and Texas— and is expected in other states by 2014.

Richard Mithen, PhD, programme leader, Institute of Food Research, Colney, Norwich, UK.

Peanuts Have More Protein

Peanuts (a legume) have more protein than tree nuts, and just as much as fish, poultry and red meat, ounce for ounce.

Also: Peanuts contain healthy B vitamins, such as folate...cholesterol-lowering phytosterols...phytochemicals, such as arginine, that help relax blood vessels...and hearthealthy resveratrol.

Other key nutrients in peanuts: Vitamin E, magnesium, iron, copper and potassium.

University of California, Berkeley Wellness Letter. www.wellnessletter.com

Healthful Fish at a Good Price

Catfish is an excellent source of vitamin D. It has more than 400 international units (IUs) of the vitamin per three-ounce serving, more than many other fish including salmon. It also is an excellent source of protein, contains omega-3 fatty acids and is low in mercury. And it is cheaper than many other fish.

Best: Bake or broil the fish...don't bread or fry it.

Consumer Reports on Health. www.consumerreports .org/health

out with cooking—their moisture helps keep acrylamides from forming.

Generally, a quick steaming is best because it makes beneficial nutrients more absorbable while causing minimal damage to heat-sensitive ones. Microwaving and sautéing are OK, but take care not to overcook the veggies (which is all too easy to do). Boiling isn't recommended because many nutrients are discarded with the cooking water. Soups and stews are fine, however, Dr. Fuhrman said—water-soluble nutrients are not lost because we eat the tasty liquid portion, too.

Digestive Disorders

"Silent" Heartburn Can Kill—Here's How to Get Relief...

If you have heartburn, you feel a burning sensation in your chest, usually after eating a meal of spicy or acidic foods. Right?

What you may not realize: Heartburn can occur without causing typical symptoms. With a "silent" form of heartburn known as laryngopharyngeal reflux (LPR), a chronic cough, hoarseness, frequent throat-clearing, difficulty swallowing and/or asthma-like symptoms, such as noisy breathing, are among the red flags to watch for.

Unfortunately, many patients with LPR suffer for years because their doctors mistakenly blame these symptoms on allergies, postnasal drip or other common health problems. Don't let this happen to you or a loved one. Untreated LPR increases risk for asthma, pneumonia—and even potentially deadly esophageal and throat cancers.

WHAT HAPPENS

It's normal for acids and enzymes in the stomach to surge upward (reflux) into the esophagus (the muscular tube that connects the throat to the stomach). This happens up to 50 times a day in the average adult, often without causing any symptoms or long-term damage. The esophagus is designed to withstand these assaults. But tissues in the throat are more sensitive.

Each episode of reflux causes material from the stomach to surge upward at incredibly fast speeds. At this high velocity, liquid droplets can spray past a valve called the upper esophageal sphincter and into the throat.

Doctors often refer to LPR as acid reflux, but this is somewhat misleading. Some acid does

---

Jamie Koufman, MD, professor of clinical otolaryngology at New York Medical College in Valhalla, New York, and founder and director of the Voice Institute of New York in New York City. She is coauthor, with Jordan Stern, MD, and Marc Bauer, of *Dropping Acid: The Reflux Diet, Cookbook and Cure* (The Reflux Cookbooks). *www. refluxcookbook.com*

surge upward—but so does pepsin, an enzyme that breaks down proteins during digestion. The actual damage to the throat is caused by pepsin.

When you have an episode of reflux, pepsin molecules cling to tissues in the throat. The pepsin is harmless until it's activated by acid.

It takes only trace amounts of acid to activate pepsin. As long as you continue to consume acid-containing foods and beverages, the pepsin will stay in an active state.

HOW TO AVOID MISDIAGNOSIS

The prevalence of reflux disease, including LPR, has increased by about 4% every year in the last few decades. This increase is thought to be due to obesity, a risk factor for reflux, and higher levels of acidic foods and beverages in the American diet.

Despite the increasing prevalence of LPR, it still can be tough to get a correct diagnosis. You should suspect that you have it if you experience frequent or intermittent difficulty swallowing, hoarseness, persistent postnasal drip and/or the sensation of a lump in the throat. A cough that often occurs after eating or when lying down is another sign of LPR.

Important: Your family doctor might not be familiar with the symptoms of LPR or its treatments, so it is wise to go to an otolaryngologist (ear, nose and throat doctor) if you think that you may have the condition. He/she will probably be able to diagnose LPR from your medical history and a description of your symptoms.

Most patients with LPR are advised to take standard heartburn medications, such as *cimetidine* (Tagamet) or *omeprazole* (Prilosec). However, these medications only partially relieve symptoms for most LPR patients.

A Low-Acid Diet

People who have LPR will need to follow a strict, low-acid diet to give damaged tissues time to heal and to deactivate any remaining pepsin molecules.

What to do: For two weeks, avoid carbonated beverages, fruit juice and alcohol. During this time, eat only low-acid foods (with a pH higher than 5).

Examples: Fish…tofu…poultry…egg whites…bananas…melon…potatoes (plain or salted, no butter)…vegetables (raw or cooked, no onions, tomatoes or peppers)…milk (low fat, soy or Lactaid Fat Free)…chamomile tea…and water. You can find the pH levels of foods at a number of Web sites, such as *www.pickyourown.org/ph_of_foods.htm.*

After this period, you can gradually reintroduce other foods, as long as your diet consists primarily of low-acid foods.

BEST TREATMENT OPTION

A reduced-acid diet is the most effective treatment for LPR. Pepsin is activated at a pH of 5 or lower. (A lower pH indicates a higher acid concentration.)

The majority of patients who follow a low-acid diet (see box) for two weeks, then continue to restrict acidity by mainly eating low-acid foods, can greatly reduce or even eliminate their symptoms. *To begin…*

•**Give up certain beverages.** Soft drinks are one of the main causes of LPR because they're highly acidic.

Examples: Coca-Cola has a pH of 2.5…and Tab and Diet Pepsi are each 2.9. Even less acidic beverages, such as sparkling water, can lead to reflux due to the carbonation.

I advise patients to avoid all carbonated drinks, fruit juice and alcohol. You can continue to drink coffee—but have no more than one cup each day. If you prefer tea, try chamomile.

•**Avoid canned and bottled foods and beverages.** The FDA requires that these foods and beverages (except water) be acidified to pH 4.6 or lower to prevent bacterial growth and prolong shelf life. However, this particular practice is believed to be one of the main reasons for the rise in LPR.

•**Drink Evamor water.** It's an alkaline bottled water with a pH of 8.8. It contains bicarbonate, which neutralizes acids. Research shows that the pepsin in throat tissues can't survive at pH levels above 7.7. Patients who drink this water regularly may recover more quickly than those who drink tap water. You can purchase Evamor Natural Artesian Water online at *www.evamor.com* or at most health-food stores and many major grocery stores.

•**Reduce fats.** Even when they're not high in acid, high-fat foods weaken the "holding" power of the esophageal muscle that prevents reflux. All high-fat foods will increase risk for LPR—and fried foods are particularly bad.

My advice: Don't give up fats entirely—just use them in smaller amounts, as though they're seasonings rather than main ingredients.

Example: All the fat in an egg is in the yolk, but a plain egg-white omelet is too bland for most people. For more richness while reducing reflux, add one egg yolk to three egg whites. You also should cut back significantly on cheese, meats, butter, etc.

•**Balance acids.** After following the low-acid diet for two weeks, most LPR patients can have acidic foods as long as they eat small amounts and combine them with nonacidic foods to keep the overall pH at safe levels.

Examples: Combine strawberries (which are too acidic to eat alone) with low-fat milk. The milk will buffer the acid and keep the total pH where it should be. Similarly, you could combine apple slices (which are acidic) with low-fat cheese.

My favorite combo: A smoothie with bananas, a cup of skim milk and a little plain yogurt (all nonacidic) with some strawberries (acidic).

•**Learn your particular trigger foods.** Most patients with LPR have more episodes/symptoms when they eat tomatoes, onions, garlic or peppers.

Also a problem: Fatty nuts (such as macadamia nuts and walnuts) and chocolate.

Zap Away Heartburn

According to recent research, heartburn symptoms were reduced or eliminated in 77% of patients who were implanted with an experimental device that delivered shocks to the sphincter that's responsible for heartburn, researchers reported at a recent scientific meeting. This approach may allow heartburn patients to take less medication for their condition.

American College of Gastroenterology.

Other foods are idiosyncratic: They cause symptoms in some patients, but not in others. You will have to experiment with foods to discover what causes symptoms and what does not.

The Simple Cure for Fatigue, Pain and Digestive Distress

Alessio Fasano, MD, a professor of pediatrics, medicine and physiology at the University of Maryland School of Medicine in Baltimore, where he is the director of the Center for Celiac Research. He cochaired the international committee that published the new classifications for gluten-related disorders.

If you've always assumed that gluten-free foods are for someone else, it may be time to reconsider. Scientists are now finding that many more people than once believed are suffering ill effects from bread, cereal, pasta and other foods that contain gluten.

Until recently, most doctors thought that you could safely consume gluten unless you had celiac disease, an autoimmune disorder that damages the intestine and causes symptoms such as abdominal pain, bloating, chronic diarrhea and/or foggy thinking.

Now: An international panel of experts recently concluded that millions of Americans who do not have celiac disease also could benefit from giving up gluten. A new classification system, published in the peer-reviewed online journal *BMC* (BioMed Central) *Medicine*, now identifies gluten sensitivity as a distinct disease, one that's related to, but not the same as, celiac disease.

It's an important distinction because people who tested negative for celiac disease in the past often were told that they didn't need to give up gluten, even when their symptoms were virtually identical to those of celiac patients. Some doctors even insisted that the symptoms were imaginary—and that these patients should get psychiatric help.

Gluten sensitivity also can lead to other conditions, such as irritable bowel syndrome (IBS), fibromyalgia and chronic fatigue syndrome.

We now know that gluten sensitivity is not only real but common, possibly affecting about 5% to 7% of Americans. Celiac disease affects about 1%. Could gluten be affecting you—and you don't even know it?

WHAT'S THE DIFFERENCE?

If you have celiac disease or gluten sensitivity, your immune system reacts to gluten—but in different ways...

With celiac disease, gluten triggers the activation of the immune system, which mistakenly attacks the small intestine. A similar process is involved in other autoimmune diseases, such as rheumatoid arthritis and lupus.

If you have celiac disease and eat gluten, the immune system attacks villi, hairlike projections in the small intestine that absorb nutrients. Abdominal discomfort and digestive problems, including the malabsorption of essential vitamins and minerals, can result.

The symptoms can differ among celiac patients—some may have sharp abdominal pains that come and go...others could experience a chronic squeezing ache. They also can have a higher risk of developing intestinal cancer or neurological disorders, such as migraines and peripheral neuropathy.

With gluten sensitivity, a part of the immune system known as the innate immune system is affected. Unlike people with celiac disease, those with gluten sensitivity don't produce antibodies to gluten, nor do they suffer damage to the small intestine or have a higher-than-average risk for cancer. They do have an immediate reaction to gluten—the body releases inflammatory substances that can cause abdominal pain and other symptoms similar to those seen in celiac disease.

Similarly, a person who has a wheat allergy can have many of the same symptoms of celiac disease or gluten sensitivity. With a wheat allergy, however, the patient may have an itchy skin rash, asthma or even, in extreme cases,

What Is Gluten?

Gluten is a protein that occurs naturally in wheat, barley and rye—as well as in bulgar and spelt (forms of wheat). Breads, cereals, pastas and cakes are among the foods that typically contain gluten. It also can be found in thousands of processed foods, including salad dressings, ice cream, yogurt and soup (in the form of ingredients such as "filler flour," "vegetable starch" and "hydrolyzed wheat gluten").

anaphylaxis, a severe, whole-body allergic reaction that can be life-threatening.

A GROWING THREAT

The incidence of celiac disease has quadrupled in about the last half-century. Researchers suspect that gluten sensitivity has increased at a similar rate. The reasons for these increases aren't yet known.

One possible explanation is that our bodies haven't had time to adapt to the processed foods and the increased gluten content found in several grains during the last 50 years. As a result, the immune systems in people genetically predisposed to gluten-related disorders may not recognize these foods as "friendly."

WHEN TO SUSPECT GLUTEN

Many people with celiac disease or gluten sensitivity eventually see a diet-related pattern to their symptoms—they feel worse when they eat such foods as bread and pasta.

Good news: The symptoms of both celiac disease and gluten sensitivity typically disappear following the adoption of a gluten-free diet. With celiac disease, symptoms may improve within a few weeks, although the intestinal damage may take several months or even years to completely heal. If you're sensitive to gluten, the relief can be much faster, often within a few days.

WHAT TESTS DO YOU NEED?

If you suspect that you have celiac disease, get tested before giving up gluten-containing foods. People with celiac disease who quit consuming gluten will have a false-negative blood test—it will show that they don't have the disease even if they really do. *Here's how celiac disease is detected...*

•**Blood test.** This is a simple and an accurate way to identify two antibodies, anti-endomysium and anti-tissue transglutaminase, that are produced when patients are exposed to gluten.

When Doctors Get It Wrong

Celiac Disease

More than three million Americans have this intestinal disease in which the immune system reacts to a protein (gluten) found in wheat, barley and rye.

Because this used to be considered a rare disease, physicians—particularly older doctors who went to medical school decades ago—don't always look for it. In addition, some of the most common symptoms, such as fatigue, abdominal pain, anemia and headaches, can be caused by dozens of other conditions.

What to do: Get tested. A blood test that looks for abnormal immune activity and other factors, perhaps followed by an intestinal biopsy, can detect celiac disease. If you test positive, you'll need to follow a gluten-free diet. Web sites such as *www.celiac.org* list foods/products that are gluten-free. Patients who eliminate all gluten will usually make a full recovery.

Don't eliminate gluten before testing—the partial recovery of the intestinal lining will make it harder to get an accurate diagnosis.

Joe Graedon, MS, and Teresa Graedon, PhD, consumer advocates. *www.peoplespharmacy.com*

•**Biopsy.** A diagnosis of celiac disease (but not gluten sensitivity or a wheat allergy) can be verified with a biopsy. It's done by endoscopy, which involves the insertion of a thin tube through the mouth, esophagus and stomach and into the small intestine. A small piece of tissue is removed and examined in a laboratory to look for damage to the villi. Those with gluten sensitivity or wheat allergies will not have damaged villi.

There are no reliable tests for gluten sensitivity. The condition is a diagnosis of exclusion—your doctor will say that you have gluten sensitivity if you test negative for celiac disease and a wheat allergy (diagnosed by a skin prick or blood test), but your symptoms and personal history indicate gluten is the problem.

GO GLUTEN-FREE

If you have celiac disease, you must avoid all obvious and hidden sources of gluten for life. Widely recognized sources of gluten are wheat, barley and rye, and lesser-known sources include bulgar and spelt (both forms of wheat).

Ask your doctor for a referral to a licensed dietitian to help you adhere to the gluten-free diet. Read food labels to learn which packaged foods contain gluten, and join a support group in your area to learn about gluten-free resources. For a list of gluten-free foods, go to *www.celiac.org*…or to get recipes, go to *www.gluten.net*. For more information on gluten-related disorders, go to *www.celiaccenter.org*.

If you have gluten sensitivity, you also may need to follow a gluten-free diet. However, some people with gluten sensitivity can tolerate small amounts of gluten, such as a few bites of pizza or a taste of bread. In some cases, tolerance can change over time.

Caution: If you have celiac disease, even trace amounts of gluten can trigger a reaction. For example, foods without gluten, such as oats, can cause a problem for celiac sufferers if gluten-containing foods are processed on the same machinery.

The Real Causes of Stomach Trouble

Steven Lamm, MD, internist and faculty member at New York University School of Medicine in New York City. He appears regularly as the "house doctor" on ABC's *The View*. He is author, with Sidney Stevens, of *No Guts, No Glory* (Basic Health). *www.drstevenlamm.com*

The average adult has two to four pounds of bacteria in the digestive tract. The vast majority of these organisms, about 85%, are beneficial. The remaining 15% are potentially harmful, but they won't make you sick as long as they're outnumbered by the good guys.

Any change in this microbial balance, known as *dysbiosis*, can lead to a host of digestive problems, such as diarrhea, bloating and constipation. If the harmful organisms continue to multiply, they can contribute to more serious diseases, including inflammatory bowel disease and even cancer.

It doesn't take much to disturb the balance. *Here are the main risks and how to combat them...*

ANTIBIOTICS

The ability of antibiotics to kill bacteria also is their downside. They can save you from infection, but they can wipe out beneficial organisms at the same time.

Researchers have found that a single course of antibiotic therapy can disrupt the balance of some intestinal bacteria for years. Many antibiotic patients get yeast infections—Candida, the organism that causes them, flourishes when beneficial organisms are killed by antibiotics. The use of powerful, broad-spectrum antibiotics (such as Cleocin) has resulted in an increase in infections with C. difficile, a dangerous organism that thrives when the body's natural balance is disturbed.

What to do: Tell your doctor that you would rather not take an antibiotic unless you really need it. It's estimated that up to half of antibiotic prescriptions are unnecessary. For example, millions of Americans every year are given antibiotics for colds, sinus infections and sore throats—illnesses that usually are viral, not bacterial.

If you do need an antibiotic, ask your doctor if you can take a narrow-spectrum agent, such as penicillin. Narrow-spectrum antibiotics kill fewer beneficial organisms than broad-spectrum antibiotics such as Cipro.

Also helpful: Take a probiotic supplement (see box) while using antibiotics—and keep taking it for about a week afterward. Take the supplement about four or five hours after taking

Supplements for Gut Health

If you experience any type of digestive discomfort—heartburn, constipation, diarrhea, bloating —more than once or twice a month, you could benefit from daily supplements.

Probiotics can help counteract the effects of modern life (antibiotics, chemicals in food and water, etc.). They also can help ease discomfort from diarrhea and inflammatory diseases such as IBS.

Look for a product that contains a combination of live organisms—it will replenish a range of beneficial organisms in the intestine. I recommend brands such as Pharmax, Metagenics and Enzymatic Therapy, which produce high-quality supplements. Follow the dosing instructions on the label.

Also, broad-spectrum digestive enzymes are particularly helpful for adults age 50 and older, who tend to produce low levels of digestive enzymes and often have difficulty with digestion.

The same companies that produce probiotics manufacture high-quality digestive enzymes. Follow the label instructions.

the antibiotic. Otherwise, the antibiotic will kill the beneficial organisms in the probiotic supplement. You may want to continue to take a probiotic daily. (See page 169 for more information on antibiotics and digestive disorders.)

POOR DIET

The foods that most Americans eat every day are chemically processed, low in fiber and high in fat and sugar. They're among the main causes of bacterial overgrowth, the proliferation of harmful intestinal bacteria.

Many chronic digestive problems—gas, diarrhea, constipation—are thought to be caused by bacterial overgrowth.

What to do: Probiotics can help, but you also will need to cut down on the processed foods in your diet. Better yet, try to eliminate them completely. Be particularly wary of refined carbohydrates such as white bread, pasta, candy, pastries, cookies and chips, which are rapidly digested by your gut, causing a spike in blood sugar.

EMOTIONAL STRESS

We all get "butterflies" when we're anxious. For reasons that still aren't clear, stress-related signals from the brain travel to the intestine, causing an upset stomach and other symptoms. The worse the stress, the more intense the symptoms.

Example: Patients with irritable bowel syndrome (IBS) tend to have higher stress levels than those without it. Also, when animals in laboratory studies are stressed, they have a 20% to 25% reduction in a particular "good" organism in the intestines and a corresponding increase in one that's harmful.

What to do: Schedule time every day for something that helps you unwind. Some people enjoy a half-hour of yoga, doing a hobby or working in the garden.

Exercise is ideal because it decreases levels of stress hormones while increasing endorphins, brain chemicals that impart a feeling of well-being.

TRAVEL

Sooner or later, just about everyone who travels will suffer from sudden diarrhea that usually is attributed to bad water or unsanitary conditions.

Fact: It can be caused by the mere act of traveling. Travel disrupts your circadian rhythm—physical, mental and behavioral changes driven by the 24-hour biological clock that regulates sleep and wakefulness. You probably don't sleep well before a trip…you're rushing around getting ready…and you may suffer from jet lag after you arrive at your destination.

The nerves, hormones and blood vessels that regulate the intestines are very sensitive to circadian changes. It's common for travelers to experience dysbiosis, along with the digestive problems that accompany it, even with no foreign organism present.

What to do: Take care of your digestive health before you leave for your trip. Try to get enough sleep. Go for long walks. Keep your stress level to a minimum. Avoid drinking alcohol (it causes dehydration and disrupts your circadian rhythm)—and avoid alcohol on the plane as well.

Also important: Fortify your system with a healthy breakfast, such as oatmeal, on the day you leave. Pack healthy snacks, such as high-protein bran bars, so you don't have to eat the food served in airports or on the plane. Nutritious meals will help maintain the optimal bacterial balance.

The Pills That Cause Lifelong Gut Problems

Matthew P. Kronman, MD, an assistant professor of pediatric infectious diseases at Seattle Children's Hospital and the University of Washington School of Medicine in Seattle and lead author of a study on antianaerobic antibiotic exposure and IBD published in Pediatrics.

By now, we all know better than to press our doctors for antibiotics when we have nonbacterial infections, such as colds. After all, we don't want to contribute to the growing problem of antibiotic resistance in a vain attempt to squelch viruses and other germs with drugs that only work against bacteria.

But public-health concerns aside, there's another important reason to curtail antibiotic use. Recent research links antibiotics to an increased risk for an especially nasty ailment called inflammatory bowel disease (IBD).

An umbrella term for a group of disorders that includes Crohn's disease and ulcerative colitis, IBD causes diarrhea, constipation, abdominal pain and cramping, gas, bloating and/or rectal bleeding—and the symptoms can be lifelong. Though IBD can develop at any age, it is particularly worrisome to note that its incidence has doubled among kids over the last decade.

Study scoop: Researchers analyzed data on more than a million children under age 18 who were followed for at least two years. They found that kids who took common oral antianaerobic antibiotics (which target bacteria that don't need oxygen to thrive)—such as *penicillin, amoxicillin* and *amoxicillin/clavulanate* (Augmentin)—were 84% more likely to develop bowel problems than kids who did not take such antibiotics. The more antibiotics the children took and the younger they were when they took them, the higher their IBD risk. Babies were especially vulnerable—IBD risk was more than five times greater for infants given the antibiotics before their first birthdays, compared with babies who didn't get the drugs.

Widespread risk: It's estimated that about 49 million antibiotic prescriptions are written for kids in the US every year. The study researchers suggest that those prescriptions will result in an additional 1,700 cases of pediatric IBD per year. What's the connection? The antibiotics may alter bacteria in the gut, triggering chronic inflammation.

Gut advice: IBD tends to run in families. If you have a legacy of Crohn's disease or ulcerative colitis in yours, don't automatically press your child's pediatrician for an antibiotic. If the doctor offers up a prescription? Before you accept, ask whether there are any other treatment options or whether it's appropriate to use a narrow-spectrum antibiotic that targets a narrower range of bacteria.

As for whether taking antibiotics in adulthood might also increase IBD risk, the jury is still out—but the possibility does exist. So the prudent course for all of us, regardless of age, is to renew our commitment to avoiding unnecessary antibiotics, reserving their use for times when such treatment truly is needed.

Hypnosis Help For a Bad Gut

Perjohan Lindfors, MD, PhD, is on the faculty of health sciences at the Sahlgrenska Academy of the University of Gothenburg in Sweden and is lead author of two studies on IBS, one published in *American Journal of Gastroenterology* and one in *Scandinavian Journal of Gastroenterology*.

P lace your hand on your belly and imagine creating soothing sensations of warmth and comfort. This is a hypnosis technique—and yes, it may sound funky. But if you suffer from the chronic, incurable and tough-to-treat condition called irritable bowel syndrome (IBS), this kind of mind-over-matter method may bring amazing relief.

Recent research from Sweden shows remarkable effects from a form of hypnosis known

---

Better Treatment for Irritable Bowel Syndrome (IBS)

Treatment for IBS has traditionally focused on relieving symptoms, such as diarrhea.

Recent study: Researchers have uncovered a primary cause of IBS—bacteria.

Finding: When cultures were collected from the guts of 320 volunteers, more than one-third of those with small intestinal bacterial overgrowth (SIBO) also had IBS, compared with only 10% without the disorder. Of those whose IBS also caused diarrhea, 60% had this type of bacterial overgrowth.

If you have IBS: Talk to your physician about being tested for SIBO and, if present, treatment with the antibiotic *rifaximin* (Xifaxan).

Mark Pimentel, MD, director, GI Motility Program, Cedars-Sinai Medical Center, Los Angeles.

---

as gut-directed hypnotherapy. During treatment, a patient receives hypnotic "suggestions" such as visualizing her gastrointestinal tract as a smoothly floating river. The idea is to bring forward a deeper feeling of being able to control symptoms, for instance, by relaxing the gut muscles so the bowel doesn't go into spasm.

Why is this such good news? Because IBS is common, affecting an estimated 10% to 15% of Americans, with women outnumbering men by about two to one…and because the nasty symptoms—abdominal pain, cramps, bloating, gassiness, diarrhea and/or constipation—can seriously diminish quality of life. While medication and lifestyle changes may help when symptoms are mild, patients with severe IBS often don't respond to such treatments.

The new evidence: Patients with severe IBS had 12 weekly hour-long hypnotherapy sessions, either at psychologists' private offices or at a small county hospital…control groups did not get hypnotized but instead were given info on IBS physiology, diet and/or relaxation techniques.

Results: Patients who underwent hypnosis reported significantly reduced symptoms, decreased anxiety and improved quality of life… whereas there was no significant improvement in the control groups. What makes this especially encouraging is that, unlike earlier studies conducted at highly specialized research centers, the recent research was done in the type of ordinary health-care settings readily available to the average patient.

Best of all, the benefits seem to be long-lasting. In a related study, the majority of IBS patients who had been helped by hypnotherapy reported that their symptoms had improved further in the two to seven years following treatment…and most continued to use the techniques they had learned on a regular basis.

Interested? To find licensed health professionals who practice hypnosis, visit the Web sites of the American Society of Clinical Hypnosis (*www.asch.net*) and the Societies of Hypnosis (*www.societiesofhypnosis.com*).

Protect Your Pancreas!

Jerry R. Balentine, DO, chief medical officer and executive vice president of St. Barnabas Hospital in New York City. He also is a professor of emergency medicine at the New York College of Osteopathic Medicine in Old Westbury, New York, and is the medical editor of *The New York Medical Journal*, a quarterly online publication. *www.newyorkmedicaljournal.org*

Pancreatitis is a condition that most people associate with heavy drinking. But the causes are more widespread. Nearly two-thirds of the pancreatitis cases in the US may be caused by using certain prescription medications, including antibiotics, blood pressure drugs and antidepressants…or by having other conditions, especially gallstones…high triglycerides (a type of blood fat)…infection (such as mumps, herpes or food poisoning)…or autoimmune disease (such as lupus or Sjögren's syndrome). Trauma that damages the pancreas also can lead to pancreatitis.

Why this is important: Pancreatitis is not only painful but also associated with an increased risk for pancreatic cancer. Even if you don't have pancreatitis now, you still want to do everything you can to avoid the condition. *Fortunately, if you do develop pancreatitis, the simple steps described in this article will help prevent attacks…*

THE DANGER OF INFLAMMATION

When the pancreas gets inflamed, digestive enzymes that normally travel from the pancreas to the small intestine get trapped. These enzymes, which are potent enough to digest food in the stomach, start "digesting" the pancreas itself.

Result: Tissue damage and intense pain. With treatment, attacks due to acute pancreatitis usually subside within about one week. However, about 20% of patients who suffer acute pancreatitis go on to develop chronic pancreatitis, in which lingering inflammation may cause extensive damage and scarring.

RED FLAGS

Most patients with acute pancreatitis experience sharp pains in the upper-left part of the abdomen, and the pain may extend all the way to the back. The pain, which usually is accompanied by nausea and/or vomiting, may be mild initially but almost always gets more severe over a period of hours.

With chronic pancreatitis, flare-ups can be mild. But you'll probably lose weight, get occasional indigestion and have pale or clay-colored stools—all due to impaired digestion from a reduced supply of pancreatic enzymes.

GETTING THE RIGHT CARE

The pain of acute pancreatitis is very intense, so you will probably need to be hospitalized during an attack. Your doctor will give you medications for pain and probably administer IV fluids to keep you hydrated. Because the pain worsens after eating, people often stop eating and drinking during a pancreatitis attack.

Your doctor will then focus on what's causing the pancreatitis. For example, you may need surgery to remove gallstones or the gallbladder. Gallstones can cause reflux of

---

What Is Pancreatitis?

Pancreatitis is inflammation of the pancreas, a gland that plays a crucial role in the digestive process. Located behind the stomach, the pancreas secretes enzymes that combine with bile, produced in the liver, to digest food. The pancreas also releases hormones that help regulate glucose derived from food.

bile into the pancreas, producing inflammation. Other treatments might include antibiotics that don't damage the pancreas to treat infection… or treating an alcohol addiction.

The conditions that cause pancreatitis are easily diagnosed with blood tests, stool tests to check for proper digestion/absorption of nutrients and/or imaging tests, such as ultrasound or a CT or MRI scan, to detect pancreatic inflammation, gallstones and blockages.

THE NEXT STEP

Doctors routinely review medications in people who have been diagnosed with acute pancreatitis. In some cases, discontinuing a "problem" medication (see box) will eliminate the risk for future flare-ups. Lifestyle changes and other self-care measures can help you reduce discomfort and prevent future attacks. *Steps to follow…*

•**Use the right painkiller.** *Ibuprofen* (Motrin) and aspirin are among the best choices. Do not take *acetaminophen* (Tylenol). People with pancreatitis are at greater risk for liver damage, which can occur in anyone who takes acetaminophen.

•**Don't drink.** You'll want to avoid alcohol if you've been diagnosed with pancreatitis. It can trigger flare-ups even if the initial inflammation wasn't caused by alcohol.

•**Limit dietary fat.** It's harder for the body to digest fat than the carbohydrates and protein in foods such as legumes, fresh vegetables and whole grains. In addition to fast food and most desserts, foods that are relatively high in fat include meats, eggs and whole-fat dairy products.

•**Eat frequent, small meals.** Large meals stress the pancreas. I advise patients with pancreatitis to eat six or eight times a day instead of the traditional three daily meals.

•**Try supplemental enzymes.** They seem to ease symptoms in some patients with acute or chronic pancreatitis. Products such as Nature's Life Pancreatin or Pancreatic Enzyme Formula haven't been proven to help, but they're worth a try if you're having trouble with digestion and/or abdominal pain.

•**Get a lipid test.** For reasons that aren't clear, some pancreatitis cases are caused by very high triglycerides (above 1,000 mg/dL in a blood test).

Drugs That Can Harm Your Pancreas

The following are among the frequently prescribed drugs that may trigger pancreatitis…*

•**Antibiotics** such as *ciprofloxacin* (Cipro), *azithromycin* (Zmax) and *demeclocycline* (Declomycin).

•**Antidepressants** such as *escitalopram* (Lexapro) and *bupropion* (Wellbutrin).

•**Blood pressure drugs** such as *enalapril* (Vasotec), *amlodipine* (Norvasc) and *metolazone* (Zaroxolyn).

•**Cholesterol drugs** such as *atorvastatin* (Lipitor) and *gemfibrozil* (Lopid).

•**Heartburn drugs** such as *omeprazole* (Prilosec) and *cimetidine* (Tagamet).

To check other drugs, go to the FDA Web site, *www.fda.gov/drugs.*

*Do not discontinue any drug without consulting your doctor.

If you test high, you can lower triglycerides with exercise, weight loss, fish-oil supplements and a diet that's low in saturated fat. Medications, including *niacin* or a fibrate drug, such as *gemfibrozil* (Lopid), also may be needed if your triglycerides are this high.

Surprising Foods That Can Upset Your Stomach

Christine L. Frissora, MD, assistant attending physician at New York-Presbyterian Hospital and an associate professor of medicine at Weill Medical College of Cornell University, both in New York City.

I f you have a sensitive stomach, you probably experience frequent bouts of digestive distress. While in some cases it's obvious what has caused the discomfort—for example, eating spicy foods or taking seconds, or even thirds—other times it seems to be a mystery.

What you may not know is that it could have been something seemingly harmless, or even healthful—like green tea or yogurt—that caused you to feel nauseated or bloated.

FOODS TO AVOID

Surprising triggers of digestive discomfort…

• **Energy bars.** Because these bars, such as Zone Perfect bars and PowerBars, contain added nutrients and vitamins, they typically are eaten as a healthful snack, a meal replacement or for a pre-workout energy boost. Some bars, especially low-sugar or low-carb varieties, contain sugar alcohols, such as glycerin and maltitol syrup, which can cause bloating, gas and diarrhea. Other bars are simply too high in complex carbohydrates and calories for someone with a sensitive stomach to digest easily.

What to do: If you want to have an energy bar, be sure to eat only a small portion of it at a time.

• **Green tea.** Although green tea is widely recognized for its disease-fighting properties—it's full of antioxidants and other compounds that help fight cancer and heart disease and stave off diabetes, stroke and dementia—it contains irritants that can make you feel nauseated.

For example, green tea contains caffeine—anywhere from 24 mg to 40 mg per eight-ounce cup—which can irritate the gastrointestinal (GI) tract. Even decaffeinated green tea has some caffeine. But it's not the caffeine by itself that makes green tea a cause of digestive distress in some people. Green tea is also very high in tannins (polyphenols responsible for its astringent taste), which are associated with nausea and stomach upset in some individuals.

What to do: If green tea makes you nauseated, avoid it altogether or have a very weak cup. Chamomile tea is soothing to the GI tract and is a good alternative.

• **Vegetable skins.** Eggplant, bell pepper and potato skins can be difficult to digest, especially if you have diverticulitis (inflamed or infected pouches in the intestinal wall) or colitis (inflammation of the large intestine)…or have

---

What Causes a Sensitive Stomach?

Your stomach mixes food with digestive juices, then empties its contents into the small intestine. If you have a sensitive stomach, the muscles of the stomach may function more slowly, which can lead to indigestion. Or the nerves of the stomach may be overly sensitive to distension (enlargement of the stomach after eating), resulting in uncomfortable bloating. Eating certain foods can make these symptoms worse.

---

had complicated abdominal surgery (involving infection or perforation).

What to do: Peel thick-skinned vegetables, then purée, mash or stew the insides before eating to aid digestion.

• **Grapes.** Red and black grapes contain the phytochemical resveratrol, a powerful antioxidant thought to help protect against coronary disease, some cancers and viral infections. But eating too many grapes—or even just a few if you are sensitive to them—can cause nausea and diarrhea.

Reason: Grapes are high in fructose, a natural sugar that often causes gas. Green grapes contain a lot of tannins, like green tea, which can lead to stomach upset.

What to do: Eat only a small amount of grapes, or avoid them altogether if you are sensitive to them. Instead, try eating other fruits rich in resveratrol, such as cranberries, blueberries and bilberries.

• **Nuts.** The high fiber and fat content of nuts slow their movement through the digestive tract, which increases the risk for gas and bloating. Nuts also contain stomach-irritating tannins.

What to do: Avoid eating nuts if you experience digestive discomfort when consuming them…have had a complicated abdominal surgery…have peritonitis (inflammation of the inner abdominal wall)…or have diverticulosis (small pouches that bulge through the large intestine) or diverticulitis. Some alternatives to whole nuts include nut butters or oatmeal with berries.

• **Probiotics.** The balance of healthful and potentially unhealthful bacteria in your digestive system can be thrown off due to illness, medications and diet, causing diarrhea and constipation. Probiotic supplements and foods contain live, healthful bacteria that can help restore balance to the digestive system. Examples of the bacteria contained in probiotics include Lactobacillus and Bifidobacterium.

Certain probiotic supplements and foods are helpful for specific situations. For example, Activia yogurt can help alleviate constipation…the supplement Align can ease bloating...and Florastor (Saccharomyces boulardii lyo) helps diarrhea caused by antibiotics.

What to do: Many probiotic supplements and foods can produce bloating (due to the ingestion of billions of bacteria). Avoid probiotics if this is a problem for you.

Caution: If you are severely ill or your immune system is compromised, avoid probiotics (and check with your doctor before having yogurt). Probiotics can enter the bloodstream and cause sepsis, a potentially life-threatening condition caused by the body's inflammatory response to bacteria or other germs.

Important: A sensitive stomach, marked by gas and bloating, may be caused by celiac disease, an immune reaction to gluten in wheat, barley and rye. If you have these symptoms, get tested for celiac disease.

BETTER-KNOWN TROUBLEMAKERS

You may already know that the following foods can cause stomach upset, but they're worth a reminder...

•**Artificial sweeteners.** Some artificial sweeteners, such as Splenda (sucralose), Equal (aspartame) and Sweet'N Low (saccharin), are difficult for the body to break down, which can lead to bloating, nausea, headache and other symptoms.

What to do: Be on the lookout for artificial sweeteners, which are found not only in diet sodas and sugarless gum, but also in many other processed foods, including some yogurts, cereals, snacks and juices.

•**Carbonated beverages.** These drinks contain carbon dioxide gas, which distends the stomach.

What to do: Avoid beer, soda, seltzer and other "fizzy" drinks if you have bloating. Plain water is best.

•**Monosodium glutamate (MSG).** This flavor enhancer often is added to Chinese food, canned vegetables, soups and processed meats. It can cause nausea, headache, cramping, fatigue and other symptoms.

What to do: Avoid Chinese food, unless it is free of MSG, and avoid canned or processed foods with MSG on the label.

WHAT HELPS

How you eat and drink also can help prevent discomfort. For example, it's widely known that having six small meals per day, rather than three larger meals, makes it easier for the stomach to empty properly. *Other helpful approaches...*

•**Drink liquids between meals.** While the digestive system needs to be well-hydrated to function optimally, too much water or other liquids during meals can overdistend the stomach, especially in patients with gastroesophageal reflux disease (GERD), in which stomach contents backwash into the esophagus...hiatal hernia, in which part of the stomach sticks upward into the chest through an opening in the diaphragm...and gastroparesis, delayed emptying of the stomach.

Small sips of liquid during a meal are fine.

Helpful: Avoid having a lot of liquids about 15 minutes before you eat and at least an hour after you eat.

•**Don't talk while eating.** This can lead to aerophagia, a condition caused by swallowing too much air, which can result in abdominal bloating, frequent belching and gas.

•**Eat slowly and chew well.** Make sure to thoroughly chew foods before swallowing.

•**Stew meats.** They are digested more easily than those that are broiled, grilled or fried.

•**Take chewable supplements.** Many supplements can cause bloating or nausea. If possible, use chewable forms, which are less likely to cause discomfort.

The "Other" Incontinence

Arnold Wald, MD, gastroenterologist and professor of medicine in the section of gastroenterology and hepatology at the University of Wisconsin School of Medicine and Public Health in Madison. Dr. Wald has written dozens of articles on bowel incontinence and has treated about 1,000 patients for this condition.

The media frequently cover urinary incontinence. What doesn't get reported on is the other type of incontinence—even though it affects nearly 18 million American adults.

The inability to control bowel movements, known as bowel incontinence, is more common in older adults (over age 65), but it can affect adults of all ages. It is both uncomfortable and embarrassing—so much so that many people never discuss it with their doctors. Too often, those who do ask for help are told that it's "just a natural part of getting older." The fact is, there is nothing natural about bowel incontinence. Fortunately, it's always caused by an underlying, and usually treatable, problem.

WHAT GOES WRONG

You should see your primary care physician or a gastroenterologist if you're having difficulty controlling your bowel movements. No one should have trouble "holding" his/her bowel movements except in unusual situations, such as when you have diarrhea. *Main causes...*

•**Constipation.** Paradoxically, this is a common cause of bowel incontinence.

Here's why: Patients who are frequently constipated may develop an impaction, the accumulation of stool inside the rectum. Impacted stool can stretch the rectum, leading to seepage of liquid stool and creating overflow incontinence.

•**Weak pelvic floor.** The pelvic floor muscles control bowel movements and urination. These muscles tend to get weaker with age, particularly in those who typically strain to have a bowel movement. Pregnancy and childbirth also can weaken or harm these muscles.

•**Damage to the rectum.** This is generally a side effect of medical treatments.

Example: Men who have had radiation for prostate cancer may develop rectal scarring, which reduces the amount of stool that the rectum can hold and diminishes its ability to stretch. Decreased capacity to store stool leads to urgency. Inflammatory bowel diseases such as Crohn's disease can have similar effects.

•**Damage to the anal sphincters (rings of muscle that control bowel movements) also can be involved.** In men, this damage sometimes occurs during prostate surgery...in women, it may be caused by childbirth, particularly when the birth requires an episiotomy (creating a surgical incision to enlarge the vaginal opening) or the use of forceps. Hemorrhoids can prevent the anal sphincters from completely closing.

•**Nerve damage.** Nerve damage can reduce your ability to tighten the sphincters—or even to sense when stool is about to come out. Nerve damage can result from diabetes, diseases such as multiple sclerosis or a lifetime of straining during bowel movements.

FOR BETTER CONTROL

It is difficult for someone with bowel incontinence to determine the cause, so it is crucial to seek medical treatment.

When you see a doctor for bowel incontinence, it's important to receive a digital rectal exam. It is among the most effective ways to identify possible causes. For example, your doctor may feel a stool impaction or weakness in the sphincter muscles.

Doctors who don't perform a digital exam are more likely to depend on tests that may not be necessary, such as rectal sonograms or anal manometry, in which a narrow tube with a small balloon at the tip is inserted into the rectum to measure the sensitivity and function of the rectum and anus.

Some patients with bowel incontinence require surgery, such as repair of the anal sphincter muscles, but the majority do not.

Best treatments...

•**Removal of excess stool.** This is sometimes the only treatment needed if impacted stool is causing the problem. The doctor will use his gloved fingers to break apart and remove the excess stool. This is followed by an enema and then a laxative to fully empty the colon, which can be done at home or in the doctor's office. Some bowel incontinence patients recover completely after the treatment, but only if they have regular bowel movements every day or every other day—or, when necessary, with additional enemas or laxatives.

•**Laxatives.** Doctors used to discourage patients from using stimulant laxatives, such as *bisacodyl* (Dulcolax) or senna extracts. However, recent research shows that these products are not as harmful to the colon as previously believed. They can prevent stool impaction as well as constipation. You can use them daily or every other day, depending on your doctor's advice. If you prefer, you can try a bulk laxative, such as *psyllium* (Metamucil).

• **Moderate fiber intake.** In my experience, patients with rectal damage—for example, from radiation or inflammatory bowel disease—often do better when they consume less dietary fiber. That's because fiber increases the amount of stool that's produced. This is helpful for healthy adults, but it may not be so for people with bowel incontinence.

Because people vary in how they react to dietary fiber, it's wise to ask your doctor whether you should be on a low- or high-fiber diet.

• **Habit training.** This is a behavioral approach for patients with poor sphincter control or for those who can't feel when a bowel movement is imminent. Patients are instructed to go to the toilet at specific times—for example, 15 to 30 minutes after breakfast or right after drinking a cup of coffee.

The goal is to establish a regular routine so that you work with your body's natural rhythms and bowel movements become more predictable.

• **Medication.** *Loperamide* (Imodium) is an antidiarrheal medication that can help if your stools tend to be loose or watery. It slows the passage of stools and makes them firmer and less likely to leak out.

Loperamide works best when it's taken before you have problems. Someone who tends to have accidents in the morning, for example, should take the medication an hour before breakfast. You can also take it to prevent problems when you won't have easy access to a bathroom. Ask your doctor about the best times to take it. Side effects are rare but can include constipation.

Helpful: Patients with minor leakage due to anal sphincter weakness can insert a cotton ball, twisted into a "tampon" shape, into the anal opening. It's less expensive than pads or adult diapers—and, if your accidents involve only a little leakage, just as effective.

Also helpful: If sphincter muscles are weak, you can strengthen them by performing anal Kegel exercises—tighten and release muscles several times a day.

BREAKTHROUGH APPROACH

Approved by the FDA in 2011, InterStim Therapy is effective for patients with severe bowel incontinence (or urinary incontinence) caused by muscle damage that can't be corrected surgically.

How it works: Surgically implanted electrodes stimulate the sacral nerves where they exit the spinal cord. These nerves activate the pelvic floor and sphincter muscles. Delivering electricity to these nerves helps them function properly.

Patients who are candidates for InterStim are first given a temporary device. If it's effective, a permanent, stopwatch-sized power pack is implanted under the skin in the lower back.

Recent finding: A study published in *Diseases of the Colon & Rectum* found that 86% of patients who used InterStim had at least 50% fewer bowel incontinence episodes. Forty percent had total remission of bowel incontinence.

New Drug Appears Effective, Safe for Ulcerative Colitis

William Sandborn, MD, chief, gastroenterology, and head, Inflammatory Bowel Disease Center, University of California, San Diego.

Michael Poles, MD, gastroenterologist and associate professor of medicine, New York University School of Medicine, New York City.

New England Journal of Medicine

An experimental drug called *tofacitinib* reduces the symptoms of ulcerative colitis, at least in the short term. The drug appears relatively safe, with few serious side effects, a recent study found.

More than three-quarters of those taking the highest dose of the drug—which is given as a pill—had a response to the medication, and 41% of these patients achieved a remission, according to the study.

"Tofacitinib…affects a group of proteins expressed in the white blood cells. It has a suppressive effect on the immune system," explained the study's lead author, William Sandborn, MD, chief of gastroenterology and head of the Inflammatory Bowel Disease Center at the University of California, San Diego.

Better Ulcer Treatment

Standard therapy for *Helicobacter pylori* (H. pylori) infection, a common cause of ulcers, includes the antibiotic *ampicillin*, a second antibiotic and an acid-reducing proton-pump inhibitor (PPI), such as *omeprazole* (Prilosec).

Recent study: When stomach pH levels in H. pylori patients were too acidic, ampicillin did not work effectively.

If you have an H. pylori infection: Talk to your doctor about a higher prescription PPI dose to keep acid levels down and improve treatment.

Elizabeth Marcus, MD, clinical instructor of pediatrics, David Geffen School of Medicine, University of California, Los Angeles.

Probiotics Can Harm As Well as Heal

These dietary supplements contain bacteria that can help remove disease-causing microorganisms from the digestive tract, relieving such problems as bloating, irregularity and gastroesophageal reflux disease (GERD). But probiotics can increase the risk for colitis, diverticulitis, irritable bowel syndrome (IBS) and other disorders—and they can cause allergic reactions. Probiotics vary in the types of bacteria…how they affect the body…and how they interact with medications. Talk to your doctor.

Andrew L. Rubman, ND, a naturopathic physician, is founder and director of Southbury Clinic for Traditional Medicines, Southbury, Connecticut.

Ulcerative colitis is a chronic inflammatory disease of the colon that affects about 700,000 Americans, according to the Crohn's and Colitis Foundation of America. The treatment options for the disease are somewhat limited, and the treatments that are available, such as corticosteroids, have many unwanted side effects. Drugs may be used to bring a flare-up of ulcerative colitis into remission or to maintain a remission. Corticosteroids are generally used to induce a remission, but not maintain it, because of their numerous side effects.

"Ulcerative colitis leads to rectal bleeding, diarrhea and other symptoms that affect a patient's quality of life. The immune system is attacking the colon in ulcerative colitis, and the theory behind this drug is that you would block the function of the immune system cells that are causing the problems and lead to an improvement in the disease," Dr. Sandborn said.

Another drug, called *infliximab* (Remicade), is used to induce and maintain remission in ulcerative colitis. The current study only looked at short-term use of tofacitinib. It's unclear yet whether the drug could be used for maintenance therapy.

STUDY DETAILS

The current study included 194 adults with moderately to severely active ulcerative colitis who were randomly assigned to receive one of four doses of the drug or an inactive placebo twice daily for eight weeks. The drug dosages used were 0.5 milligrams (mg), 3 mg, 10 mg or 15 mg.

Clinical responses occurred in 32%, 48%, 61% and 78% of those receiving the medication, respectively, correlating directly with the dose they were taking. The lowest response rate was seen for the 0.5-mg dose, while the highest response was seen in those taking the 15-mg dose. In those taking a placebo, 42% had a clinical response.

Remission was achieved by eight weeks in 13%, 33%, 48% and 41% of those taking the lowest to highest doses. Ten percent of those on placebo achieved remission, the report noted.

The researchers noted a rise in both good and bad cholesterol that increased as the dose of medication went higher. Three patients had low white blood cell counts, which increases the possibility of infection, according to the study.

Results of the study were published in the *New England Journal of Medicine*. The drug's manufacturer, Pfizer, provided funding for the study, and Pfizer researchers were involved in the design and implementation of the study, according to Dr. Sandborn.

info For more information about ulcerative colitis, visit the Web site of the Crohn's and Colitis Foundation at *www.ccfa.org*.

Drugs

Are You Overdosing on OTC Drugs?—Here Are The Worst Offenders

We hear a lot about overuse of prescription drugs. That's because every year, more than 20,000 Americans die from a prescription drug overdose. About 75% of those fatalities are from painkillers such as *oxycodone* (OxyContin) and *hydrocodone* (Vicodin). But there's another unexpected threat—and that's overdosing on over-the-counter (OTC) painkillers.

Believe it or not, the main culprit is *acetaminophen*—the common pain reliever in Tylenol and other brands. It hospitalizes 30,000 people annually, many of whom develop acute liver failure.

Studies show that one-half to two-thirds of acetaminophen overdoses are the result of victims' poor understanding of the product's dosing instructions. One 2012 study published in the *Journal of General Internal Medicine* tested 500 people to determine their knowledge about and use of acetaminophen.

By their answers, many of the study participants showed that they would overdose—24% by using one product and unknowingly taking more than the safe limit of 4,000 mg (4 g) every 24 hours…and about 46% by using two acetaminophen-containing products at the same time without realizing the combined dosage would be an overdose.

The same misuse of medications and misunderstanding of labels occurs with other types of OTC medications described throughout this article—with potentially disastrous long-term consequences for health. *Here's how to make sure that you don't overdose on or overuse OTC drugs…*

Suzy Cohen, RPh, a licensed pharmacist in Boulder, Colorado, and author of the *"Dear Pharmacist"* syndicated column, which reaches 20 million readers nationwide, *The 24-Hour Pharmacist* (William Morrow) and *Diabetes Without Drugs and Drug Muggers* (both from Rodale). *www.suzycohen.com*

ACETAMINOPHEN

Acetaminophen is the most commonly used OTC drug in the US—every week, one out of every five adults takes it. And for good reason—the drug works fast to reduce pain and fever. In fact, acetaminophen works so well, it's the main pain-relieving, fever-lowering ingredient in many OTC products for headache, arthritis, back pain, colds, coughs, sinus problems and more. But the effectiveness and availability of the ingredient is a setup for overdosing.

Fortunately, a few simple precautions can help prevent an acetaminophen overdose…

•**Read the labels and do the math.** Read the ingredient list on every OTC drug you take and know which contain acetaminophen and how much. Keep careful track of your daily intake—and don't ever take more than 1,000 mg at any one time or exceed 4,000 mg in a day. The more acetaminophen-containing products you take, the more likely it is you'll overdose.

Example: In the *Journal of General Internal Medicine* overdose study, three drug combinations were most likely to cause an overdose—a pain reliever and a PM pain reliever…a pain reliever and a cough and cold medicine…a sinus medication and a PM pain reliever.

•**Know if you are at high risk**—and be extra-cautious if you are. In the overdose study, people who were "heavy users" of acetaminophen (taking it a couple of days a week or more) were more likely to underestimate their intake—and to overdose.

Important: If you suffer from chronic pain, see your primary care physician or a pain specialist, and ask for a stronger medication that is taken once or twice a day. That way, you won't have to take as many OTC painkillers.

•**Know the signs of an overdose.** An overdose of acetaminophen typically causes nausea and vomiting, sweating, yellowing of the skin and eyes and a general feeling of flulike illness. Within one to three days, it causes pain in the upper right quadrant of the abdomen (the location of the liver). If you develop those symptoms after regular use of acetaminophen (or after a single dose that is excessive)—seek immediate medical care.

Self-defense: Call 911 or go to a hospital emergency department if you have severe symptoms, such as gasping for air. The standard treatment for acetaminophen overdose is *n-acetyl-cysteine* (NAC), an antioxidant that reverses liver toxicity, often given intravenously. Although NAC capsules are available at health-food stores, it's best to be treated by medical personnel since an overdose is a serious medical condition. If you suspect that you may be experiencing symptoms of an overdose, you can call a 24-hour poison control center such as the National Capital Poison Center at 800-222-1222.

PROTON PUMP INHIBITORS (PPIs)

These popular drugs work by slowing down your body's production of stomach acid, preventing and relieving the symptoms of heartburn. They also are used to treat indigestion (dyspepsia), ulcers and other upper gastrointestinal (GI) problems. Two kinds are available OTC—*lansoprazole* (Prevacid 24HR) and *omeprazole* (Prilosec OTC, Zegerid OTC).

The danger: These drugs, if taken daily, should not be used for more than two weeks without a doctor's approval, according to label instructions. Studies show that overuse can increase risk for hip, wrist or spine fractures in adults over age 50…and cardiac arrhythmias, intense diarrhea, colds, flu and pneumonia, and vitamin and mineral deficiencies in users of all ages. In addition, when you stop taking one of these drugs abruptly, it can trigger rebound acid hypersecretion—a surge of stomach acid that worsens symptoms, forcing you back on the drug for relief.

Self-defense: Slowly wean yourself off long-term use of a PPI. Speak to your doctor about the best way to do this. Afterward, treat heartburn with OTC antacids, a much safer choice (follow label instructions).

NASAL DECONGESTANTS

Many people suffer from *rhinitis medicamentosa* (RM)—a chronically stuffy nose caused by overuse of nasal decongestant spray. For example, you might use a spray, such as Afrin or Neo-Synephrine containing the ingredient oxymetazoline or phenylephrine, during a cold or allergy season. It provides relief, but there is "rebound congestion" when the spray wears off. You use it again...there is rebound congestion... and you use it again. Soon, you have RM—and are addicted to the nasal spray for "relief."

Self-defense: If you are addicted to a nasal spray, wean yourself off slowly. (*Examples:* Alternate nostrils with each use, rather than spraying both nostrils. Or use the spray only at bedtime to get you through the night.) As you decrease use, try a nonmedicated saline spray or a menthol nasal spray and a humidifier or steam vaporizer. You might also ask your doctor for a short-term prescription for nasal corticosteroids, which will relieve congestion while you withdraw from the spray. Plus, address underlying health problems that may cause nasal congestion, such as food allergies or structural problems in the sinuses.

LAXATIVES

Constipation is a common problem, and daily use of OTC laxatives, such as Miralax and Milk of Magnesia, is frequently the "solution."

The danger: Laxative overuse can lead to abdominal cramping, nausea and vomiting, blood in the stool, mineral deficiencies, electrolyte imbalances that cause heart and kidney damage—and, in rare cases, death.

Self-defense: Wean yourself slowly off laxatives. For example, switch from daily use to every-other-day use for one week.

Use Over-the-Counter Sleep Aids Only Occasionally

Over-the-counter sleep aids—such as *diphenhydramine* (found in Tylenol PM) and melatonin—should not be taken for more than five consecutive days. Taking them longer can cause side effects, such as dry mouth and dizziness.

Best approach: Lifestyle changes—cutting back on caffeine and alcohol...exercising...and going for therapy if stress and anxiety are disturbing your rest.

Health. www.health.com

As you're reducing use, add more fiber to your diet, with fruits, vegetables, whole grains and beans—and, if necessary, take a daily fiber supplement—to help ensure regular bowel movements. Take a probiotic, a supplement of "friendly" bacteria that aids digestive health. Other digestive aids that can help cure constipation include aloe vera, essential fatty acids and digestive enzymes. Talk to your doctor about which of these digestive aids might work best for you. Drink water throughout the day and exercise regularly, which stimulates bowels.

STAY SAFE

Keep all your prescriptions at the same pharmacy. That way, your pharmacist has your complete medication profile and can accurately advise you about your OTC medications.

When buying an OTC product, ask your pharmacist to check for interactions between your prescription drugs and your OTC choices. You are not being a "pest"—the pharmacist wants to help keep you safe.

Meds That Make You Sick: Side Effects You Need to Know

Armon B. Neel, Jr., PharmD, certified geriatric pharmacist and author of *Are Your Prescriptions Killing You? How to Prevent Dangerous Interactions, Avoid Deadly Side Effects, and Be Healthier with Fewer Drugs* (Atria). *www.medicationxpert.com*

Robert Steven Gold, RPh, hospital pharmacist and author of *Are Your Meds Making You Sick? A Pharmacist's Guide to Avoiding Dangerous Drug Interactions, Reactions and Side Effects* (Hunter House). *www.areyourmeds makingyousick.com*

Nearly 60% of the prescription medications taken by patients aren't needed. That's what researchers discovered in a study published in *Archives of Internal Medicine*. The study also revealed that 88% of patients said they felt healthier when taking fewer drugs.

The fact is that adverse effects from medications are the fourth-leading cause of death in the US (after heart disease, cancer and stroke).

This means that, every year, approximately 100,000 deaths in the US are caused, in part, by dangerous drug reactions—more deaths annually than homicides, car accidents and airplane crashes combined.

About 6% of patients who take two medications daily will experience a drug interaction. If you're taking five medications a day, the risk rises to 50%.

According to Armon B. Neel, Jr., PharmD, a certified geriatric pharmacist, the following are medications that often are overprescribed and can produce serious side affects…

STATINS

The cholesterol-lowering statins, such as *atorvastatin* (Lipitor) and *simvastatin* (Zocor), are among the highest-selling prescription drugs in the US. They are not as effective as you might think…and the potential side effects, including muscle pain and memory loss, can be serious.

A recent study, published in *Pharmacotherapy,* found that 75% of patients who took statins reported memory loss or other cognitive problems. The same study found that 90% of patients who stopped their medication had rapid mental improvements.

Statins can be life-saving drugs for patients with high cholesterol and existing heart disease or other cardiovascular risk factors. But generally, they are not effective for primary prevention (preventing a heart attack in healthy patients with few risk factors).

Before starting a statin, ask your doctor about the drug's Number Needed to Treat (NNT). The NNT for Lipitor is 168. This means that 168 patients would have to take it (for 4.1 years) to prevent one cardiovascular event. Those are impressively bad odds, particularly when the risk for muscle pain/memory loss can be as high as one in 10.

Advice: Try to lower your cholesterol with nondrug approaches. These include taking fish-oil supplements…and eating less saturated fat and more fiber. Take a statin only if you have high cholesterol and other cardiovascular risk factors, such as a family history, high blood pressure and/or diabetes.

BLOOD PRESSURE DRUGS

About 40% of the patients Dr. Neel sees are taking at least four different drugs to control hypertension. Some patients need this many drugs to lower blood pressure, but they are the exceptions. If you are taking more than two drugs for blood pressure, you probably are taking the wrong drugs.

Example: Beta-blockers for hypertension. Millions of older Americans take these drugs, even though the drugs often cause fatigue, dizziness and other side effects. In addition, doctors often prescribe both an ACE inhibitor (such as *captopril*) and an angiotensin receptor blocker (such as *losartan*), even though they work in similar ways. Patients using this combination are 2.4 times more likely to have kidney failure—or die—within six months as those taking just one of them.

Advice: If you are like most patients with hypertension, you probably need to take only a diuretic (such as *chlorthalidone*) and perhaps a calcium channel blocker (such as *diltiazem*). Don't assume that you need additional drugs if your blood pressure still is high—you might just need a higher dose—though some patients do need other medications.

Important: Some patients who reduce their salt intake, exercise and lose weight can take lower doses of medication. A study published in *The New England Journal of Medicine* found that salt restriction for some people has about the same effect on blood pressure as medication does.

PAINKILLERS

Ibuprofen and related analgesics, known as *nonsteroidal anti-inflammatory drugs* (NSAIDs), are among the most commonly used medications in the US. People assume they're safe. They're not.

One study found that 71% of patients who used NSAIDs experienced damage to the small intestine, compared with just 5% who didn't take them. These medications also increase the risk for stomach bleeding, ulcers and hypertension.

Advice: Take an NSAID only if you need both the painkilling and anti-inflammatory effects—for a flare-up of knee pain, for example.

Take the lowest possible dose, and take it only for a few days at a time.

If you're 60 years old or older, you may need to avoid these drugs altogether. The risk for stomach or intestinal damage is much higher than in younger adults. A safer medication is *tramadol* (Ultram), a prescription analgesic that doesn't cause gastrointestinal irritation.

Millions of Americans take narcotic painkillers, such as *codeine, oxycodone* (OxyContin) or other *narcotic analgesics.* They are used for post-surgical pain, dental pain, etc. They can cause constipation even at doses that are four times lower than the doses needed for pain relief. Constipation that continues for more than one or two weeks can result in an intestinal blockage from hardened stools.

All narcotic analgesics slow the intestinal contractions (peristalsis) that move nutrients and wastes through the digestive tract. A study of cancer patients found that 95% of people who used these medications experienced constipation.

Advice: If you need these drugs, ask your doctor to prescribe the lowest possible dose… and ask whether you can use a stool-softening medication such as *docusate* (Colace) and take a stimulant laxative such as *bisacodyl* (Ex-Lax, for example) if you're not having regular bowel movements. The combination of stool softener and stimulant laxative is more effective than either one used alone.

Also important: Drink a glass of water every few hours, and get regular exercise. Fluids and exercise moisten stools and increase the frequency of bowel movements.

SEDATIVES

Valium and related drugs, known as *benzodiazepines*, are among the most dangerous medications for older adults.

Reason: They aren't efficiently broken down (metabolized) in the liver. This means that high levels can accumulate in the body.

Patients who take these drugs daily for conditions such as insomnia or anxiety are 70% more likely to fall—and 50% more likely to have a hip fracture—than those who don't take them. Also, patients who use them regularly have a 50% chance of experiencing memory loss.

Sedatives such as *diazepam* (Valium), *triazolam* (Halcion) and *zolpidem* (Ambien) should never be taken for extended periods.

Advice: If you are going through a stressful time, ask your doctor to write a one- or two-week prescription for a short-acting medication such as *lorazepam* (Ativan). It is eliminated from the body more quickly than other drugs.

For long-term insomnia/anxiety, ask your doctor about *venlafaxine* (Effexor). It's good for depression as well as anxiety, and it's safer than sedatives for long-term use.

ANTIDEPRESSANTS

Doctors routinely prescribe *SSRI antidepressants,* such as *fluoxetine* (Prozac) and *paroxetine* (Paxil), to patients who don't really need them.

One study, based on data submitted to the FDA, concluded that these and other antidepressants are no more effective than a placebo for most patients. Yet the risks, including falls, bone fractures and even seizures, are high, particularly in older patients.

Important: Depression often is episodic. Patients who have suffered from a traumatic event—the loss of a job, divorce, the death of a spouse—will often have a period of depression that eventually clears up without treatment.

My advice: Start with nondrug approaches. If you're going through a rough patch, see a psychologist or meet with a pastor or another type of counselor. For many patients, talk therapy is as effective as medication.

According to Robert Stevens Gold, RPh, a hospital pharmacist and author of *Are Your Meds Making You Sick?,* the following medications can also produce serious, often surprising, side effects…

BLOOD THINNERS

Warfarin (Coumadin), a "blood thinner" that inhibits blood clotting and often is prescribed to patients with heart disease or who have had a heart attack. Warfarin, as well as other anti-clotting drugs, can make the blood so thin that bleeding occurs from the stomach, intestine or gums. And since bleeding can take longer to stop, blood can leak from a capillary and cause a bruise without an injury.

An article by Canadian researchers published in *Annals of Internal Medicine* analyzing the results of 33 previous studies, found that patients taking warfarin had about a one in 39 chance of serious bleeding. About one in eight patients with major bleeding episodes died.

Solution: Warfarin can be a life-saving drug if you need it, but you should work closely with your doctor to find the dosage that is best for you. Also, it's crucial to be aware that other medications, supplements and even foods can thin your blood. These medications include nonsteroidal anti-inflammatory drugs (NSAIDs), such as aspirin and *ibuprofen* (Motrin), and *clopidogrel* (Plavix), an antiplatelet drug—all of which have bleeding as a side effect. Before taking any other drug, let your doctor know that you're also taking warfarin.

Caution: Many herbs and supplements, such as fish oil, licorice, ginseng and coenzyme Q10, can increase/worsen the effects of warfarin.

Also important: Foods that are high in vitamin K, such as spinach and kale, affect the rate at which your blood clots and could require a change in your dose of warfarin. If you take a blood thinner, speak to your doctor about the effects of other medications, supplements and foods on your blood.

ANTIBIOTICS

The *sulfonamide* class of antibiotics (Bactrim is one of the main ones) can trigger an immune reaction called Stevens-Johnson syndrome. This side effect is rare—it affects only between one and three patients per 100,000—but requires immediate medical attention. The immune system causes a burning rash that spreads and often gets infected. Sores and blisters in the mouth can spread to the stomach, lungs and colon. Some patients die from it.

Because it's so serious, everyone should know the warning signs—a cough, headache, fatigue, blisters and joint pain followed by a rash.

Advice: Get to the emergency room immediately. You may be hospitalized and switched to a different medication.

Levofloxacin (Levaquin) is a broad-spectrum antibiotic given for infections. The fluoroquinolone class of antibiotics, which includes le-

vofloxacin and *ciprofloxacin* (Cipro), has been linked to torsades de pointes, a rare but dangerous heart irregularity (arrhythmia) that can cause instant death in some cases.

Warning: Patients who take one of these antibiotics along with a *thiazide diuretic,* such as *hydrochlorothiazide* (Microzide), may have a higher risk for heart irregularities.

Recent development: A study published in *The New England Journal of Medicine* has found that *azithromycin* (Zithromax and others), an antibiotic used to treat bacterial infections, may increase risk for irregular heartbeat and sudden death in patients with, or at risk for, heart disease.

Solution: If you take any of these antibiotics and experience a change in your heart's rhythm (a feeling of fluttering in the heart or a heart rate greater than 100 beats per minute), go to the emergency room. Episodes that last for more than about 10 seconds can cause a loss of consciousness and sometimes seizures.

HEARTBURN DRUGS

Patients with gastroesophageal reflux disease (GERD) or heartburn sometimes take *metoclopramide* to reduce discomfort and accelerate the healing of ulcers in the esophagus. The medication works by blocking the effects of dopamine. Doing this reduces nausea and helps food pass more easily from the stomach through the digestive tract.

Metoclopramide causes Tardive dyskinesia (uncontrolled muscle movements, especially in the face) in about 20% of patients who take it for three months or longer. It blocks the effects of dopamine, a brain chemical that plays a role in cognition and movement, the loss of which also occurs in Parkinson's patients.

Caution: Patients who combine metoclopramide with *prochlorperazine* (Compzine), used for some mental disorders as well as nausea, are more likely to have movement disorders because it also blocks the effects of dopamine.

Solution: Switch to a different heartburn drug—for example, an antacid or a medication such as *cimetidine* (Tagamet), an H2 blocker, that does not typically block dopamine.

Important: Uncontrolled movements caused by medication may not appear for up to six months. If you are experiencing tremors or other movement disorders, ask your doctor to review all of your medications, not just the ones that you've recently started.

DIABETES DRUGS

Patients with diabetes often take *metformin*, an oral medication that decreases the production of glucose in the liver and increases the ability of cells to use insulin. Metformin has a black-box warning (the most serious warning on medication labels) about lactic acidosis, a rare but dangerous complication that's fatal in about 50% of cases. It occurs when a metabolic by-product (lactate) accumulates in the bloodstream. Diabetic patients with kidney disease have the highest risk of getting it.

Early warning: Fatigue and severe muscle pain even when you're sedentary.

Advice: Call your doctor immediately if you're taking metformin and develop muscle pain. You might need to discontinue the medication. Patients who take metformin should have blood tests to check serum creatinine every three months—the tests will show if lactate is being removed from your body.

Also important: Don't take the heartburn medication *cimetidine* (Tagamet) if you're using metformin. The combination increases blood levels of metformin by up to 40%. You can switch to a different heartburn drug, such as *famotidine* (Pepsid).

Insulin is another diabetes medication that can produce serious side effects, such as hunger, nervousness and heavy sweating.

Patients who use insulin to lower their blood sugar often forget that it's an extremely potent drug. Unless you use it exactly as prescribed, it can lower blood glucose to dangerous levels, causing hypoglycemia. This triggers the hunger, nervousness and heavy sweating.

Hypoglycemia occurs occasionally in every diabetic who uses insulin—it takes time to learn how to use insulin appropriately. Doctors routinely advise patients to take diabetes-education classes, in which they learn how to recognize the signs of high and low blood sugar...how

---

Chewing Gum to the Rescue!

Dimenhydrinate, a drug commonly used in medication to prevent nausea, vomiting and motion sickness, can now be delivered in the form of chewing gum rather than pills.

Advantage: Chewing gum is more convenient and allows for faster absorption than pills.

American Association of Pharmaceutical Scientists

---

and when to test blood sugar...and the best times to take medication.

Advice: If you're using a fast-acting form of insulin, always have something to eat within 30 minutes. Otherwise, the medication will lower your blood sugar too much.

Also important: Keep a "quick fix" snack, such as a box of fruit juice or a package of crackers, in your pocket, purse or briefcase. A snack quickly will elevate your blood sugar if you develop symptoms of hypoglycemia.

DRUGS FOR BONE HEALTH

Alendronate (Fosamax), taken to prevent/treat osteoporosis, is known to cause stomach ulcers in about 1% of patients and ulcers in the esophagus in up to 2%. These are small percentages, but the risk rises when patients also take an NSAID, such as ibuprofen or *naproxen* (Aleve).

Solution: If you need a drug such as alendronate to preserve bone strength, changing how you take the medication can reduce the side effects.

Examples: Take alendronate first thing in the morning when your stomach is empty, washing it down with six to eight ounces of plain water. Taking it with some beverages or foods, particularly orange juice or acidic foods, increases the risk for ulcers. Don't lie down for 30 minutes after taking it—this can cause stomach acids to reach, and damage, the esophagus.

Also important: Avoid NSAIDs. Take *acetaminophen* (Tylenol), a non-NSAID painkiller.

Drugs That Harm Your Eyes

Robert Abel, Jr., MD, an ophthalmologist at Delaware Ophthalmology Consultants in Wilmington. He is author of *The Eye Care Revolution: Prevent and Reverse Common Vision Problems* (Kensington). *www.eyeadvisory.com*

When it comes to drug side effects, among the most widely recognized are nausea, fatigue, headache and dizziness.

What often gets overlooked: The eyes, like other parts of the body, are vulnerable to side effects from prescription drugs. Some of these side effects are merely annoying, but others, including an increased risk for cataracts and glaucoma, can threaten your ability to see—and, in some cases, the damage can persist even after you stop taking the medication.

Drugs that can harm your vision—and how to protect yourself…

•**Alpha-blockers.** These medications, commonly used to lower blood pressure and improve urine flow in men with enlarged prostate glands, relax blood vessels and muscles in many parts of the body.

The risk: Tamsulosin (Flomax), *terazosin* (Hytrin) and other alpha-blockers can change the refraction of the eyes, resulting in blurred vision that usually subsides when the drug is discontinued but can continue to worsen if you don't stop taking the medication. Alpha-blockers also have been linked to an increased risk for glaucoma. In people who already have glaucoma, these drugs may trigger an acute attack due to the sudden buildup of pressure in the eye.

Solution: If you take an alpha-blocker and develop blurred vision and/or have glaucoma, ask your doctor about using a lower dose. If you still have eye symptoms, your doctor can prescribe a different drug, such as a beta-blocker (for blood pressure) or saw palmetto (for an enlarged prostate).

Very important: If you're going to have cataract surgery, tell your doctor if you have ever taken an alpha-blocker (even years ago). These drugs can prevent the pupil from staying dilated during surgery, a major cause of complications. If your doctor knows that you've taken an alpha-blocker, he/she will use an intraocular pupillary expander to keep the pupil open during the procedure.

•**Antidepressants.** The popular SSRI (selective serotonin reuptake inhibitor) antidepressants, such as *fluoxetine* (Prozac), *sertraline* (Zoloft), *escitalopram* (Lexapro) and *paroxetine* (Paxil), can reduce the body's natural secretions.

The risk: Chronic eye dryness. Patients who take these medications often suffer from dry, itchy eyes. Persistent dryness can lead to blurred vision and an increased risk for infection.

Solution: Be sure to use artificial tears whenever your eyes are dry or irritated. *Best:* Choose preservative-free products, such as TheraTears and Refresh Plus…get adequate hydration by drinking plenty of water…and increase your intake of omega-3 fatty acids (for example, eat salmon, sardines, mackerel or other cold-water fish at least two to three times a week).

•**Corticosteroids.** These drugs—cortisone, prednisone and similar medications—are taken by millions of Americans to reduce inflammation from many chronic conditions, including asthma.

The risk: About 16% of patients who use corticosteroids regularly will develop an increase in intraocular pressure that can lead to glaucoma. Corticosteroids also increase risk for cataracts and accelerate their growth in patients who already have them.

Solution: Consider Chinese herbal remedies rather than a corticosteroid. Studies have shown that they work nearly as well as corticosteroids for some inflammatory conditions, such as asthma and osteoarthritis—but without the side effects that can occur with steroids.

I advise patients who take corticosteroids to consult a Traditional Chinese Medicine (TCM) practitioner. Patients should let their doctors know that they're exploring the use of herbal remedies and not stop taking their steroids abruptly. To find a TCM practitioner near you, consult the National Certification Commission for Acupuncture and Oriental Medicine, *www.nccaom.org.*

177

•**Digoxin (Lanoxin).** This medication, often used to treat congestive heart failure, increases the force of the heartbeat.

The risk: Digoxin and other cardiac glycosides, such as digitoxin, can accumulate in the retina and/or optic nerve, causing a green/yellow tint in vision and sometimes blurred vision—both of which usually go away when the drug is discontinued.

Solution: Lower the drug dose—but first consult your doctor. Also, consider trying coenzyme Q10 (CoQ10)—it has been linked to a 30% increase in the efficiency of the heartbeat. As a result, patients who take CoQ10 (30 mg to 60 mg, one to two times daily) can often take a lower dose of digoxin or another cardiac glycoside. (Talk to your doctor if you take diabetes, blood pressure or blood-thinning drugs—CoQ10 may interact with these medications.)

•**Erectile dysfunction (ED) drugs.** *Sildenafil* (Viagra), *tadalafil* (Cialis), *vardenafil* (Levitra) and other such ED drugs can affect photoreceptor cells in the eyes that are responsible for color vision.

The risk: Men who take these drugs may notice a bluish tint in their field of vision. Fortunately, the tint will quickly fade as the drug wears off. Some doctors speculate that the daily use of these ED drugs also could cause long-term damage to the eyes' photoreceptors in rare cases. For this reason, patients with macular degeneration or other eye diseases are sometimes advised not to take these medications.

Solution: If your doctor says that ED drugs are safe for you, take the lowest dose that you need to achieve an erection. Also consider nondrug approaches that do not cause vision problems.

Examples: FDA-approved vacuum pumps and drugs that are injected into the penis—this is less painful than you might imagine.

•**Tamoxifen (Nolvadex, others).** This drug is used for some breast cancers and often is prescribed to women at high risk for the disease.

The risk: The eyes absorb chemical compounds from tamoxifen and other cancer-fighting medications, triggering a breakdown of cells in the eyes that decreases color perception and increases risk for cataracts and diseases of the retina.

Solution: Women who take tamoxifen should schedule a test called optical coherence tomography. It detects minute changes in tissues of the eyes. With annual tests, it's possible to predict future eye changes before symptoms occur—and to stop the medication, if necessary, before damage results.

When a Patch Is Better Than a Pill

Jack E. Fincham, PhD, RPh, a registered pharmacist and professor in the division of pharmacy practice and administration at the University of Missouri, Kansas City.

If you take medication, chances are it's a pill. But topical versions of many widely used drugs (in the form of patches or a topical gel or cream) are often more effective—and safer—than pills.

What's new: Even though some patch-based medications, such as *nicotine* and *scopolamine* (for motion sickness), have been on the market for many years, a variety of popular drugs have recently been formulated as topical drugs. Topical medications now are available to treat a wide range of conditions, including high blood pressure, chest pain (angina), depression, Alzheimer's disease and hormonal deficiencies.

Why use a patch? Let's say you have arthritis and often take a nonsteroidal anti-inflammatory drug (NSAID), such as *ibuprofen* (Motrin) or *diclofenac* (Voltaren), to control pain. If you experience gastric bleeding—a side effect of NSAIDs and a common reason for hospitalization—the topical version of the drug may be a much better choice for you.

Medicated patches also are a good choice for patients with swallowing difficulties…those who forget to take their pills…or those who can benefit from steady dosing.

WHY THE SKIN?

Pills seem like an obvious way to take medication, but that's only because we are used to them. In Europe, about one-quarter of the medication taken for pain relief comes from patches and gels or creams.

What's the benefit of patches and other skin-applied medications? First, they are generally easier to use for some patients and work just as quickly or even faster than pills.

Here's why: The skin is one of the best organs for administering drugs into the bloodstream, where the drug's active ingredients are then distributed throughout the body. With oral medications, the active ingredient is metabolized (broken down) in the digestive tract, liver and kidneys, which often leads to side effects. While topicals also pass through the liver and kidneys, they don't go through the digestive tract. *Advantages of topical medications...*

•**Lower doses.** When you take an oral medication, some of the active ingredient may be destroyed by acids in the digestive tract or reduced when broken down in the liver and kidneys. In fact, with some oral drugs, only about 10% of the active ingredient reaches its intended target—the bloodstream, then a specific organ or system. As a result, you must take a high dose to offset losses. Higher doses mean more complications and side effects.

•**Fewer side effects.** Topical medications are not risk-free. But side effects are typically limited to minor skin irritation. Oral medication side effects are a major cause of hospitalization and sometimes even death.

Example: Topical medications can be helpful for patients who need narcotic painkillers. Oral narcotics often cause constipation and stomach upset. Patches are much less likely to cause these types of side effects.

•**Steadier dosing.** When you take an oral drug, you achieve a high initial blood concentration of the active ingredient. Then, the levels slowly decline until you take the next dose. With a patch, drug levels are more evenly sustained throughout the day—or even for days at a time.

Time-released oral medications can mimic this effect, but they're unpredictable. Many factors—the acid in your stomach, what you've eaten, etc.—can affect how quickly the medication is released. There's less variability with patches.

•**More convenient.** It's estimated that 55% of older adults don't take their medications the way they're supposed to—because of forgetfulness or limited mobility, for example. Some patches can be applied once a week. It's easier to remember once-a-week dosing than multiple daily pills.

Downside: The main drawback of topicals is the cost. They are more expensive than pills because they're more complicated to manufacture.

PATCHES NOW AVAILABLE

Medicated patches you should know about...*

•*Clonidine* (Catapres-TTS) patch for high blood pressure. Because it is applied just once a week, it is much easier to use—and easier to remember—than daily oral drugs.

•**Deponit** for angina. Patients who have angina due to coronary artery disease can take a nitroglycerin tablet for quick relief. Deponit, the same medication used in patch form, delivers a steady dose of the medication and can prevent these attacks from happening. It is applied for 12 to 14 hours at a time, with 10 to 12 hours off.

•**Exelon patch** for mild-to-moderate Alzheimer's disease. This patch, applied once every 24 hours, provides the same benefits as the equivalent oral drug *rivastigmine* (Exelon), with less nausea and/or vomiting.

Check first with your doctor if you have heart or lung disease, bladder problems or seizures—the Exelon patch may worsen these conditions. Caregivers often prefer the patch because they can see that they have given the medication.

•**Ortho Evra birth-control patch,** applied once a week, produces blood-hormone levels that are higher than what can be achieved with a typical pill.

It's a good choice for women who do not want to take—or who sometimes forget to take—a daily pill. Each of these factors can make the Ortho Evra patch a more reliable form of birth control than the pill.

---

*Talk to your doctor if you take any medications (patches could interact with them). Some patches, such as Catapres-TTS, contain aluminum and have been reported to cause skin burns during MRI. Remove patches before MRIs.

•*Oxybutynin* (Oxytrol) for overactive bladder. Applied twice weekly, this medicated patch helps patients achieve better control by inhibiting involuntary contractions of the bladder. It is less likely than the oral medication to cause other side effects such as constipation or dry mouth.

•**Testosterone patch, applied once every 24 hours—generally between 8 pm and midnight to match a man's daily hormonal cycles.** Men who suffer from fatigue, low libido or other symptoms of testosterone deficiency can use a patch (Androderm or Testoderm) that delivers a steady supply of the hormone—with less risk for liver damage than oral drugs.

Leading Drugs That Stop Working (or Worse)… And Natural Alternatives

Michael T. Murray, ND, a licensed naturopathic physician based in Paradise Valley, Arizona, and author of more than 30 books, including *What the Drug Companies Won't Tell You and Your Doctor Doesn't Know: The Alternative Treatments That May Change Your Life—and the Prescriptions That Could Harm You* (Atria). *www.doctormurray.com*

Many people try a pill, find that it helps, and then keep on taking it for weeks, months or years—never realizing that certain medications tend to lose their effectiveness for some people over time. What's even more worrisome is that, in some cases, such drugs eventually can lead to a worsening of the very conditions they were supposed to treat.

According to Michael T. Murray, ND, author of more than 30 health-related books, including *What the Drug Companies Won't Tell You and Your Doctor Doesn't Know: The Alternative Treatments That May Change Your Life—and the Prescriptions That Could Harm You,* certain nutritional supplements provide effective, safer alternatives that allow some patients to reduce or discontinue conventional drugs. And because the supplements help address the underlying causes of disease—rather than simply acting as what Dr. Murray called "biochemical

Band-Aids" to reduce symptoms in the short term—they keep on working in the long term, he said.

Here are common prescription and nonprescription medications that can lose effectiveness over time, plus possible natural alternatives…

Important: If you are using any of these drugs, do not simply discontinue them on your own. Instead, consult a qualified holistic doctor to find out whether switching to supplements or adding supplements to your medication regimen is appropriate for you and to determine optimal dosages. Also note that, while the supplements mentioned below generally are safe, some may not be appropriate for pregnant women or people with certain medical conditions—another reason why you should discuss their use with a knowledgeable practitioner. *Talk to your doctor about…*

•**Nonsteroidal anti-inflammatory drugs (NSAIDs) for osteoarthritis.** These include aspirin, *ibuprofen* (Advil), *naproxen* (Aleve) and *celecoxib* (Celebrex). NSAIDs often produce short-term benefits by initially reducing osteoarthritis pain and inflammation…but over time, Dr. Murray said, they can accelerate the progression of joint destruction by inhibiting cartilage formation, leading to greater pain and disability.

Natural alternative: Glucosamine sulfate. With age, some people appear to lose the ability to produce sufficient levels of glucosamine, a substance the body uses to manufacture the cartilage that acts as a shock absorber in the joints. Though glucosamine sulfate supplements are not anti-inflammatory or pain-relieving drugs per se, over time they reduce inflammation and ease pain by helping the body repair damaged joints…and in numerous studies, the supplements produced much better results than NSAIDs in relieving osteoarthritis.

Typical dosage: 1,500 mg of glucosamine sulfate daily. Results may be seen after two to four weeks of use…the longer glucosamine is used, the greater the therapeutic benefit.

•**Blood sugar–lowering drugs for type 2 diabetes.** One common side effect of oral diabetes medications such as *glyburide* (Micronase) and *pioglitazone* (Actos) is weight gain—yet excess weight makes blood sugar levels

Coated-Aspirin Alert

Aspirin helps prevent heart attack and stroke, and coated aspirin has been promoted as being gentler on the stomach.

Recent study: Researchers gave 400 healthy people a single dose of 325-mg immediate-release (uncoated) or enteric-coated aspirin and measured absorption. Nearly half of the participants did not fully absorb the coated aspirin within eight hours, but all absorbed the uncoated aspirin.

If you take coated aspirin: Ask your doctor whether you can safely switch to regular aspirin—many patients can. Coated aspirin has never been shown to reduce bleeding in the stomach.

Tilo Grosser, MD, research assistant professor, Perelman School of Medicine, University of Pennsylvania, Philadelphia.

even harder to control. As a result, Dr. Murray said, blood sugar–lowering medications may be prescribed at even higher dosages or in combination with other medications, creating an even greater risk for side effects.

Natural alternative: Mulberry leaf. Research has shown that mulberry therapy reduced fasting blood glucose concentrations in diabetic patients more significantly than glyburide…as a bonus, mulberry also decreased LDL "bad" cholesterol and triglyceride levels. Dr. Murray noted that mulberry supplementation may improve blood sugar levels to the point that some patients, under their doctors' supervision, may be able to reduce or discontinue oral diabetes medications.

Typical dosage: 1,000 mg of mulberry leaf powder three times daily, taken before meals.

Caution: Mulberry may not be appropriate for patients with impaired liver function.

•**Bisphosphonates for osteoporosis.** Medications such as *alendronate* (Fosamax), *risedronate* (Actonel) and *ibandronate* (Boniva) help protect against fractures by increasing bone density—but when used for more than five years, they actually increase the risk for fractures of the thighbone as well as for osteonecrosis

(bone death caused by poor blood supply) of the jaw.

Natural alternatives: BioSil and vitamin D. BioSil contains a highly bioavailable form of the trace mineral silica, which improves bone mineral density and increases the collagen content of bone. Vitamin D supplementation also helps by ensuring that the body absorbs and retains calcium, a mineral critical for building strong bones.

Typical dosages: 6 mg to 10 mg of BioSil daily…plus 2,000 international units (IU) of vitamin D daily.

Caution: BioSil may not be appropriate for people with kidney problems…vitamin D may not be appropriate for patients with high blood calcium levels.

•**Sedatives for insomnia.** When sleep medicines are taken every night for a long time, they tend to lose their effectiveness. Some such drugs can impair the ability to reach the deeper stage-three and stage-four levels of sleep, thus worsening sleep quality—which is one reason why they can produce a morning "hangover" feeling, Dr. Murray noted. What's more, sedatives have a variety of possible side effects (dizziness, drowsiness, impaired coordination) and are potentially addictive—all of which make them poor candidates for long-term use.

Natural alternatives: Melatonin and 5-hydroxytryptophan (5-HTP). Melatonin is a hormone that normally rises at bedtime, promoting sleepiness. According to Dr. Murray, melatonin supplementation is particularly effective in treating insomnia in seniors, in whom low melatonin levels are quite common. 5-HTP is an amino acid that converts to serotonin, a brain chemical that helps initiate sleep. Supplementing with 5-HTP increases deep sleep without lengthening total sleep time, Dr. Murray said.

Typical dosages: 3 mg of melatonin per day, taken at bedtime…plus 50 mg of 5-HTP per day, taken at bedtime.

Caution: Melatonin may not be appropriate for patients with bleeding disorders…5-HTP may not be appropriate for patients taking SSRI antidepressants.

Referrals to holistic physicians: American Holistic Health Association (*www.ahha.org*)… American College for Advancement in Medicine (*www.acam.org*)...American Association of Naturopathic Physicians (*www.naturopathic.org*).

Too Many Meds Cause Frequent Fainting Spells

David A. Friedman, MD, chief, Heart Failure Services, North Shore-LIJ's Plainview Hospital, New York. American Heart Association, news release.

Taking too many medications at the same time could lead to repeated fainting episodes, a recent study reveals.

"Simply stated, the more antihypertensive pills a patient takes, the greater the likelihood of a possible fainting spell under certain circumstances," explained one cardiologist, David Friedman, MD, chief of Heart Failure Services at North Shore-LIJ's Plainview Hospital in New York. He was not involved in the recent research.

STUDY DETAILS

In the study, Danish researchers led by Martin Ruwald, MD, of Copenhagen University Hospital Gentofte, looked at more than 127,000 patients, median age 64, who were hospitalized for fainting between 1997 and 2009.

Of those patients, more than one-fifth had experienced at least two fainting episodes.

The researchers found that the risk of repeat fainting rose with the number of medications that patients were taking at the same time. For example, compared with people who took no medications, recurrent fainting was 16% more likely for those taking one drug; 20% more likely for those taking two drugs and 32% more likely for those taking three or more drugs, the team reported.

Dr. Ruwald's team focused on drugs known to cause a sudden drop in blood pressure when a person stands up after lying down. These drugs included widely used types of heart medications such as alpha blockers, beta blockers, diuretics, calcium channel blockers and ACE inhibitors.

The study was presented at the annual meeting of the American Heart Association.

Better Drug Storage

When 2,131 parents and grandparents of kids ages one to five were surveyed, nearly one-quarter of grandparents (5% of parents) reported keeping prescription drugs, including daily dose pill storage boxes that children can easily open, in readily accessible places. Unintentional poisonings from medications are a leading cause of emergency room visits for children ages six and under.

Vital: Store all medications out of reach of young children—on upper shelves of cabinets or the top of the refrigerator.

And remember: Childproof lids work only when closed correctly.

Matthew M. Davis, MD, associate professor of pediatrics, internal medicine and public policy, University of Michigan Medical School, Ann Arbor.

WHAT YOU AND YOUR DOCTOR SHOULD DO

Dr. Friedman said fainting, which doctors call "syncope," isn't uncommon among heart patients.

"In my practice, patients who have demonstrated recurrent syncope or near syncope while on several blood pressure pills for various multiple health-related reasons, benefit from medication dose adjustments on a variable schedule or staggering pills at different hours along the day as needed," he said. Often, detailed discussions with patients or their caregivers allow them to adjust dosing schedules on their own based on blood pressure readings or other medical factors, Dr. Friedman added.

"I find these measures help patients adhere to potentially difficult medication regimens, maximize drug optimization, and minimize the chances of dizziness, lightheadedness or overt passing out spells," he said.

info The US National Institute of Neurological Disorders and Stroke has more about fainting at its Web site, *www.ninds.nih.gov/disorders/syncope/syncope.htm.*

Cancer Drug May Flush Out 'Hidden' HIV

David Margolis, MD, professor, medicine, University of North Carolina at Chapel Hill.

Joseph Kulkosky, PhD, associate professor, biology, Chestnut Hill College, Philadelphia.

Alberto Bosque, PhD, research assistant professor, University of Utah School of Medicine, Salt Lake City.

Nature

Medications can eliminate any sign of HIV from the bloodstream, but the virus that causes AIDS never vanishes for good. Instead, it hides in the body, waiting to strike again.

Now, researchers report that they may have discovered a way to use a cancer drug to make the infected cells more visible, potentially allowing them to be killed.

It's too early to know if the approach will actually help patients get rid of the virus forever. The optimistic hopes of scientists, who are forever seeking an AIDS cure, could be snarled by side effects or some other medical hitch.

But the findings are a promising start, said study author David Margolis, MD, a professor of medicine at University of North Carolina at Chapel Hill.

"We just wanted to show that we could get the virus to come out and show itself," he said. "This doesn't tell you that we have a cure for AIDS that everyone can take tomorrow. It begins us on a road to accomplish that goal."

At issue is HIV's ability to hide in the body. Scientists suspect that the virus "hijacks" certain kinds of immune cells—the ones that remember how to deal with certain kinds of germs—and lurk inside them. Thanks to this hijacking ability, medications and the immune system itself can't find and kill the virus or prevent it from multiplying.

The virus can move out of the immune cells if AIDS medications fail or if patients stop taking them. That means HIV can't currently be cured.

In the recent study, researchers gave single doses of a skin cancer chemotherapy drug called *vorinostat* (Zolinza) to eight HIV-infected patients. The drug seemed to flush out the hidden virus so it was more easily visible.

Bone-Loss Drugs Make Artificial Joints Last Longer

Patients who were on a bisphosphonate, such as *alendronate* (Fosamax) or *risedronate* (Actonel), for at least six months before hip- or knee-replacement surgery were half as likely to need a new implant within the next five years as patients who did not take a bisphosphonate.

Caution: Bisphosphonates have been associated with increased risk for atypical femur fractures and bone-related jaw disease.

Nigel K. Arden, MD, professor in rheumatic diseases, University of Southampton, England. He is coauthor of a study of 41,995 patients, published in *BMJ*.

None of the patients reported side effects, but they only took one dose.

Manufacturer information for cancer patients who take the drug lists serious side effects including dehydration, clots (rare), low red blood cell levels and high blood sugar.

As far as AIDS treatment, the next steps will be to figure out the best dose of the cancer drug and discover if medications or the immune system will kill the virus once it's loose.

"We don't know how to use this drug yet, and we don't know if we have to use it all the time every day for weeks or months and months," study author Dr. Margolis said. "We may just need to use it a few days here, then rest, on and off, until we get to the goal we need to get to."

One big question is whether it's possible to fully eliminate the "reservoir" of hidden virus in the body, said AIDS researcher Joseph Kulkosky, PhD, an associate professor of biology at Chestnut Hill College, in Philadelphia. Still, he said, it may be possible to at least get at some of it.

Another AIDS researcher, Alberto Bosque, PhD, a research assistant professor at the University of Utah School of Medicine, praised the study but cautioned that "we are at the beginning of the race towards HIV eradication, where the unknowns and uncertainties exceed our knowledge."

The study appears in the journal *Nature*.

info For more about AIDS, visit the US National Library of Medicine at its Web site, *www.nlm.nih.gov/medlineplus/hivaids.html.*

Emotional Well-Being

What to Do If You Think a Loved One Is Depressed...

It's difficult for healthy people to fully understand what depression feels like. It's more than feeling "down." People with depression don't experience normal emotions. They blame themselves for things that aren't their fault...or get angry for trivial reasons...or misinterpret disagreement as rejection and increasingly withdraw from normal interactions.

Important: Don't expect someone with depression to "snap out of it." It is a disease. You can't solve depressed people's problems, but you can help them get the help they need. *What to do...*

•**Don't take it personally.** It's easy for your feelings to be hurt when you're dealing with someone who is depressed. His/her communication skills may be impaired, and he will find it difficult to give the expressions of support that are normal in healthy relationships.

•**Remind yourself that it's not about you.** When you are helping someone who is depressed, try to be objective and keep your emotions out of it.

•**Point out recent changes.** Denial is one of the main defense mechanisms of depressed people. They often don't recognize—or choose not to recognize—that they're depressed.

•**Without being judgmental, explain what you've noticed.** Stick to the facts. Maybe he sleeps all the time or is less active than he used to be. He might have given up activities that he used to enjoy. He probably spends more time alone—watching TV, using the Internet, etc. He might be overly sensitive or get angry easily.

Richard O'Connor, PhD, a psychotherapist in private practice with offices in Canaan, Connecticut, and New York City. He is former executive director of the Northwest Center for Family Service and Mental Health and author of *Undoing Depression: What Therapy Doesn't Teach You and Medication Can't Give You* (Berkley Trade). *www.undoingdepression.com*

You can suggest (but not insist) that the changes might be due to depression. Encourage him to get professional help.

Important: Don't expect that one conversation will change things. You might have to bring it up repeatedly. Also, men and women tend to react differently when people bring up their depression. Men are more likely to get angry and defensive…while women tend to feel hurt.

•**Explain why he needs help.** A depressed person is highly vulnerable to criticism. Try not to give the impression that you're blaming or judging. Do help him understand that his behavior is affecting his loved ones.

Example: You might point out that some behaviors, such as a hair-trigger temper, are frightening. Simply saying, "You're different than you used to be," might encourage him to get help.

•**Encourage exercise.** Studies have shown that people with mild-to-moderate depression who exercise three or more times a week for about 30 minutes each time improve about as much as those taking antidepressants. Those who continue to exercise are less likely to have future episodes of depression than those who rely on medications alone.

Any form of exercise is likely to be helpful, but aerobic exercise—swimming, biking, fast walking—is probably superior to other types of workouts. It increases brain levels of endorphins, the so-called "happy hormones." It also boosts confidence.

•**Join him in social activities.** Social isolation is one of the hallmarks of depression. But people with depression want human contact even when they're too insecure or withdrawn to seek it out.

You can help him overcome his reluctance by introducing him to safe social settings without a lot of pressure. You could, for example, accept a dinner invitation from close friends, those with whom your loved one won't feel as though he has to perform. Or you could go to an art opening or other social event where you will be around other people but your loved one won't have to engage unless he wants to.

•**Keep at it.** Start conversations. Ask about his day. Make plans to meet for lunch or dinner.

You'll probably get a lot of rejection, but keep trying.

Important: Being around someone with depression is draining. Allow yourself to back away when you feel that you can't cope with it anymore. Take a break, and take care of yourself. Then, when you're feeling strong, reach out again.

•**Ask about suicide.** It's an uncomfortable topic, but it is essential to talk about. Up to 15% of those with serious depression will end their lives by suicide.

If you've talked to your loved one about depression and he admits that it's a problem, follow up by asking something such as, "Are you having thoughts of hurting yourself? Have you thought about suicide?"

Few people will admit to having these thoughts unless they're asked—the majority of suicides come as a complete surprise to loved ones. People who are depressed are ashamed of having these thoughts, and they don't want to put a burden on their loved ones.

Bringing up the subject gives him permission to talk about it. If he is having suicidal thoughts, you will know that the depression is serious and that it is urgent that he get immediate help.

Sweet Drinks Are Linked to Depression

People who drank more than four cups per day of regular soda were 30% more likely to develop depression within a decade…and those who drank diet soda were at greater risk than those who drank regular soda. People who drank fruit punch had a 38% higher risk for depression…and drinkers of diet fruit punch were at higher risk. But people who drank four cups of coffee a day had a 10% lower depression risk.

Self-defense: Consider switching from sweetened drinks to unsweetened coffee.

Study of nearly 264,000 people, ages 50 to 71, by researchers at National Institute of Environmental Health Sciences, Research Triangle Park, North Carolina, presented at the annual meeting of the American Academy of Neurology in San Diego.

Seven Daily Servings of Fruits, Veggies Best for Happiness

University of Warwick, news release.

People who eat seven servings of fruit and vegetables a day have the highest levels of happiness and mental health, according to a recent study.

STUDY DETAILS

In a joint effort with Dartmouth University in Hanover, New Hampshire, researchers at the University of Warwick in Coventry, England, examined the eating habits of 80,000 people in England and found that mental well-being rose with the number of daily servings of fruits and vegetables, peaking at seven servings a day.

The study, which appears in the journal *Social Indicators Research,* defined a serving as about 80 grams (2.8 ounces).

"The statistical power of fruit and vegetables was a surprise. Diet has traditionally been ignored by well-being researchers," said study coauthor Sarah Stewart-Brown, BM, BCh, PhD, a professor of public health.

Further research is needed to learn more about the reasons behind the findings, she added.

"This study has shown surprising results, and I have decided it is prudent to eat more fruit and vegetables. I am keen to stay cheery," said study coauthor Andrew Oswald, DPhil, a professor in the economics department.

CURRENT GUIDELINES

Currently, many Western governments recommend that people eat five servings of fruit and vegetables a day to protect against heart disease and cancer. The USDA recommends seven to nine daily servings, which varies depending on the age and sex of an individual. (Visit *choosemyplate.gov* for tips on how to follow guidelines.)

While the study found an association between fruit and vegetable servings and well-being, it did not prove a cause-and-effect relationship.

info The US Centers for Disease Control and Prevention has more about fruits and vegetables at *www.cdc.gov/nutrition/everyone/fruits vegetables/index.html.* Or to find out more about dietary guidelines, visit the US Department of Health & Human Services Web site at *http://www. health.gov/dietaryguidelines/2010.asp.*

The Burger That Prevents Depression

Felice Jacka, PhD, research fellow and associate professor, Barwon Psychiatric Research Unit, Deakin University, School of Medicine, Geelong, Australia.

Depending on your age, you may have grown up thinking that red meat was either great for your health or horrible for your health.

More recently, when health-savvy individuals inquire about a "bottom line" on red meat based on the latest studies, they're usually told that it's probably best to limit their intake to very small amounts.

Now, a recent Australian study shows that eating a moderate amount—not a small amount—of red meat may be good for our mental health. *But it needs to be a certain type of red meat…*

EAT TO BEAT DEPRESSION & ANXIETY

Interestingly, researchers found that women who consumed the equivalent of one to two ounces of red meat—beef or lamb—per day were about half as likely to be diagnosed with anxiety or depression as women who ate more or less red meat. The association was found only when they ate unprocessed red meat—which knocks out cold cuts, hot dogs and many fast-food burgers. (The researchers aren't sure whether the same would hold true for men, but they will be testing that next.)

Did you notice the eyebrow-raiser in there? Eating little meat, which is what many people do to stay healthy, was associated with increased anxiety and depression, compared with eating some (but not a lot of) red meat. To put the amount of meat in everyday terms, a burger patty is typically about four ounces, so eating one to two ounces a day, the "sweet spot" in the study, is the equivalent of eating about two or three modestly sized burgers a week.

But as was mentioned above, this meat wasn't just any old meat. It was a specific kind…

ALL BEEF IS NOT CREATED EQUAL

To learn more about which red meat is best, we spoke with Felice Jacka, PhD, associate professor at the Deakin University School of Medicine in Australia, who led the research.

In Australia, they feed their cows and sheep grass—and that is the first thing that Dr. Jacka pointed out. Here in the US, the vast majority of cattle and sheep are fed mostly grains, mainly because a grain-fed cow or sheep can reach "slaughter weight" faster than one that is grass-fed. But what animals eat affects what we eat when we eat them.

Here are the nutritional benefits of grass-fed meat…

•**Compared with grain-fed meat, grass-fed meat is leaner, containing less saturated fat and fewer calories.** This is beneficial because a diet high in saturated fat may activate the body's stress response system, and that has been shown to trigger anxiety and depression.

•**Grass-fed meat also contains a smaller amount of omega-6 fatty acids and a greater amount of omega-3 fatty acids.** Eating a lot of omega-6s stops omega-3s from performing their anti-inflammatory responsibilities. And inflammation may be a cause of anxiety and depression, said Dr. Jacka, just like it contributes to so many other disorders. This may be one reason why the Australian women who ate little red meat had higher rates of anxiety and depression than those who ate a moderate amount.

•**Grass-fed meat contains more conjugated linoleic acid** (which is good for you because it may reduce body fat and improve immunity), more of vitamins A and E, more antioxidants and more beta-carotene than grain-fed beef. Dr. Jacka isn't sure if those factors also helped decrease the risk for depression and anxiety, but it's possible.

GO FOR GRASS-FED

It's critical to point out that Dr. Jacka's study does not prove that red meat prevents or cures depression or anxiety—what it shows is an association, but not necessarily causation.

Still, if depression or anxiety runs in your family, or if you suffer from one of the disorders, eating a moderate amount of unprocessed red meat (seven to 14 ounces a week) might be a good idea, said Dr. Jacka. Of course, it's important not to go overboard, because other studies have linked large amounts of red meat to increased risk for health problems such as cardiovascular disease, type 2 diabetes and cancer. One recent study from the Harvard School of Public Health in Boston linked eating one serving a day (or 21 ounces a week) of

---

Online Counseling Can Help With Depression

•**Telemedicine works.** Therapists using Skype and other computer-based connection methods can talk with patients anywhere. The practice, called telemedicine, is becoming more accepted among doctors and can be as effective as in-person therapy. Private insurers generally will not pay for it, although Medicare will in some circumstances.

To find an online therapist: Go to *www.breakthrough.com* or *www.etherapyweb.com.*

Lynn F. Bufka, PhD, American Psychological Association, Washington, DC.

•**Free Online CBT.** A review of 22 trials involving computerized cognitive behavioral therapy (CBT), conducted via the Internet or in a clinic, found that this method may be an effective treatment option for depression and anxiety. In five studies that compared computerized and face-to-face CBT, both seemed to be equally beneficial. CBT helps by reversing destructive and distorted thought patterns.

If you have difficulty traveling to a therapist's office or finding time for treatment: Check with your doctor, then consult the free self-help CBT program at *https://thiswayup.org.au.*

Gavin Andrews, MD, professor of psychiatry, The University of New South Wales at St. Vincent's Hospital, Darlinghurst, Australia.

Better Way to Detect Depression

A recent study indicates that people who are depressed or anxious may decide not to seek treatment if they perceive their suffering to be less severe than that of family, friends or others. Conversely, people surrounded by those who rarely feel depressed may believe their symptoms are abnormal because they appear more severe by comparison.

Problem: Making comparisons can lead to missed or false diagnoses.

If you feel depressed or anxious: Try not to compare your feelings with those of others. See a doctor for an evaluation.

Karen Melrose, researcher, department of psychology, The University of Warwick, Coventry, UK.

Natural Boost for Depression Sufferers

Recent study: Severe depression symptoms eased twice as fast in women who took 5 g of the muscle-building amino acid creatine along with the antidepressant *escitalopram* (Lexapro), compared with those who took only the antidepressant.

Theory: Creatine may boost energy levels in the brain, helping selective serotonin reuptake inhibitors (SSRIs), such as escitalopram, work faster.

If you are taking an SSRI and your depression hasn't improved: Ask your physician about adding creatine to your regimen.

Perry Renshaw, MD, professor of psychiatry, The University of Utah, Salt Lake City.

unprocessed red meat with a 13% increased risk for premature death.

If you're basing your diet decision on the evidence, then you'll have to eat only grass-fed meat. Look for the word "grass-fed" or, ideally, "grass-finished" (meaning grass all the way to slaughter) on the package—you can find this type of meat at many markets now. Be prepared to pay more than you would for grain-fed meat…but if it's better for your health, it may be worthwhile to "pay the price" now as opposed to later!

Forget Self-Esteem!

Kristin Neff, PhD, associate professor of human development and culture at The University of Texas at Austin. She is author of *Self-Compassion: Stop Beating Yourself Up and Leave Insecurity Behind* (William Morrow). *www.self-compassion.org*

For years, self-esteem has been touted as the key to happiness and fulfillment. But there's increasing evidence that another quality is even more important to a successful life—self-compassion.

Recent research: A 2012 analysis of 14 studies found that people high in self-compassion were less vulnerable to depression, anxiety and stress. Other research has shown that with self-compassion comes higher motivation to exercise, greater likelihood to have regular doctor checkups, less susceptibility to eating disorders and better ability to cope with chronic pain.

THE PROBLEM WITH SELF-ESTEEM

Our highly competitive culture tells us we need to be special or at least above average to feel good about ourselves. But this can lead to constant, debilitating self-criticism. And in people who do have high self-esteem, it can contribute to a sense of superiority or entitlement, which can feed into prejudice and bullying.

What's more, self-esteem can be very fragile. It lasts only as long as you see yourself as successful, smart or attractive…and evaporates when you stumble or don't like what you see in the mirror.

Conversely, self-compassion is stable and constructive. When you see yourself clearly—both positive and negative traits—you can more easily cope with the setbacks and mistakes that are inevitable in life and make the changes needed to reach your full potential.

TREASURE YOURSELF

Self-compassion means treating yourself in the same way you would treat a treasured friend.

The biggest reason most people don't do this is that they think they need self-criticism to motivate themselves. They're afraid that if they permit self-compassion, they will keep making the same mistakes and never improve themselves.

But growing research confirms that self-criticism is a poor success strategy. Rather than motivating, it makes people feel anxious, incompetent and depressed.

BUILDING SELF-COMPASSION

Gestures of caring—a kind word or warm embrace—trigger the release of oxytocin, a brain chemical that promotes feelings of trust, calm and safety. *To do this for yourself...*

• **Say soothing words to yourself when you're upset.** Use the same kind of language you would use to comfort a friend in need. You might say to yourself, "I know you're feeling bad right now, and I want you to be happy. I'm here to support you in any way I can."

• **Listen in on your self-talk.** If you hear harsh tones of self-judgment, quiet your inner critic. You could tell yourself, "I know you're trying to make me a better person, but your angry words aren't helping. Please don't be so critical." But if there's a character flaw you would like to address, you might say, "This behavior is causing problems, and I don't want you to suffer. Can you try harder to change? I believe in you." These words can help put you in the calm and safe state required to do your best and make needed changes.

• **Find an inconspicuous self-caress that soothes you.** Physical gestures of kindness and warmth are the most direct way to calm anyone, including yourself. For some people, gently placing a hand on the heart or belly turns self-blame into self-compassion. You also can try cradling your face in your hand or wrapping your arms around your body for a brief embrace.

MORE SELF-COMFORT

To have self-compassion, you must accept certain painful feelings without denying or fighting against them. Notice where in your body you experience emotions like sadness and anger—maybe it's a feeling of constriction in your throat or tight muscles in your chest.

When Doctors Get It Wrong...

Is It Depression or Hypothyroidism?

Patients who produce too little thyroid hormone (hypothyroidism) may have the condition for years before it is diagnosed because symptoms are usually vague and seemingly minor.

Common scenario: A doctor might assume that a patient who complains of fatigue, recent weight gain or apathy is suffering from stress or depression and write a prescription for an antidepressant.

What to do: Insist on a blood test to check your thyroid hormone levels if you have any of the above symptoms. Fatigue that's accompanied by an increased sensitivity to cold often is a sign of hypothyroidism. So is hair loss (but not that due to male-pattern baldness). For unknown reasons, thinning of the outer one-third of the eyebrows is also a red flag for hypothyroidism.

Experts disagree on the optimal range for thyroid stimulating hormone (TSH). Current guidelines suggest that it should fall somewhere between 0.45 mIU/L and 4.49 mIU/L. (The specific values will depend on the laboratory that your doctor uses.) If your TSH is normal but your symptoms persist, ask your doctor about other blood tests, such as free T3/T4 or anti-thyroglobulin. In some patients, these tests are useful in detecting hypothyroidism.

Most people do well with a thyroid replacement regimen. Some benefit from levothyroxine (Levoxyl, Levothroid, Synthroid, etc.), while others find that natural desiccated thyroid hormone, such as Armour Thyroid, Nature-Throid or Westhroid, provides a better balance of T3 and T4 hormones.

Joe Graedon, MS, and Teresa Graedon, PhD, consumer advocates. www.peoplespharmacy.com

---

Helpful: Lie down in a quiet place and do a body scan. Start with the soles of your feet and slowly move upward. Consciously offer comfort to areas where unpleasant feelings arise—by putting a warm hand on the spot...relaxing tightness in the area by tensing then releasing the muscle...or by saying some comforting words.

WRITE YOURSELF A LETTER

In one study, people who wrote themselves one-paragraph self-compassionate letters (daily for one week) reported feeling happier and less depressed three months later.

You can do this for yourself. In your daily letter, focus on whatever troubles you. Write your letter from the perspective of a truly compassionate friend or wise grandmother who unconditionally loves you. Express the kind of understanding and gentle encouragement you would offer someone you care deeply about.

Take the quiz: To find out how self-compassionate you are, go to *www.self-compassion.org*.

Fear No More: A Simple Fix for Phobias

Matthew D. Lieberman, PhD, is a professor of social psychology and director of the social cognitive neuroscience laboratory at the University of California, Los Angeles, and coauthor of a study on phobias published in *Psychological Science.*

W hat scares you? Speaking in public...driving over bridges...finding a creepy-crawly bug in your bedroom? Whatever the object of your phobia may be, you'd no doubt feel relieved if you could free yourself from that fear.

Well, you can do that by using a simple "talk to yourself" technique. But the words you use are key—and they're the opposite of the type of self-talk you've probably tried in the past, recent research revealed.

The study recruits included 88 spider-phobic people, mostly women. First, for the "pretest," participants were asked to walk as close as they dared to an open container housing a live tarantula (a big, hairy one with a six-inch leg span!). Researchers recorded how near each person got to the spider...and also measured how much each person's hands sweated, a physical indication of fear level.

Next, participants were randomly divided into four groups and went through repeated "exposure trials" during which they had to sit two feet away from a screen covering another (equally big and hairy) live tarantula. One group, which served as a control, did not receive any instructions about what to say to themselves as they sat by the spider. *Each of the other three groups were taught one of the following techniques for verbally describing the experience...*

•**Affect labeling**—using negative words to describe the spider and their own emotional response to it (for instance, "I feel anxious that the disgusting tarantula will jump on me").

•**Reappraisal**—using neutral words in an attempt to feel less negatively about the spider. ("Looking at the little spider is not dangerous for me".)

•**Distraction**—talking about something unrelated to the feared object ("There is a television in front of my couch in the den").

Immediately after the exposure trials and again a week later, participants were once more asked to walk as close as they could to a tarantula's container, while researchers again noted how close they approached and how much their hands sweated.

Surprising phobia-fighting finding: It is common for people to either downplay their fears or distract themselves in an attempt to relieve phobias. Yet in this study, it was the "affect labelers"—those who openly admitted to feeling freaked out—who sweated the least and

---

Surprising: Depression May Weaken Shingles Vaccination

Researchers gave a shingles vaccination or a placebo to 92 patients, roughly half of whom had major depression.

Result: The shingles vaccine was less effective in patients with untreated depression than in those who were not depressed or undergoing treatment for depression.

Conclusion: Untreated depression weakens the body's immune response to the vaccine. The shingles vaccine is recommended for adults age 60 and older.

Michael Irwin, MD, Cousins Professor of Psychiatry, University of California, Los Angeles.

were able to move closest to the spider. Some of them even touched the beast!

Why it works: The researchers speculate that giving voice to fear helps discharge the emotion by first stimulating but ultimately calming the amygdala, the area of the brain linked to anxiety. The process may be similar to mindfulness, a relaxation technique in which you become more aware and accepting of ongoing experiences.

Though this study focused strictly on fear of spiders, it's possible that the anxiety-easing affect-labeling technique would work equally well with other fears, from acrophobia (fear of heights) to zoophobia (fear of animals) and everything in between. So try talking honestly about how you're feeling the next time you encounter whatever it is that gives you the willies. You have nothing to lose but fear itself.

Natural Cures For Phobias

Jamison Starbuck, ND, naturopathic physician in family practice and a guest lecturer at the University of Montana, both in Missoula. She is past president of the American Association of Naturopathic Physicians and a contributing editor to *The Alternative Advisor: The Complete Guide to Natural Therapies and Alternative Treatments* (Time Life).

P hobia is from the Greek word *phobos*, meaning mortal fear. It is the most common anxiety disorder, affecting up to 14% of Americans during their lifetimes. Whether it's a fear of flying (aviophobia), fear of heights (acrophobia) or any of the dozens of other phobias, the condition causes a persistent and unreasonable fear that severely limits the sufferer's ability to freely work, play or socially interact. A rapid heart rate, shortness of breath, trembling and a strong desire to flee are among the common symptoms of phobias. People with phobias often make irrational choices in order to avoid the feared object.

Sadly, many people with phobias go untreated. Others become dependent on sedatives, such as *alprazolam* (Xanax) or *clonazepam* (Klonopin). But there are other options that not only relieve symptoms, but also address the root cause of the problem. *Recommended...*

•**Therapy.** One way to cure or reduce the severity of a phobia is to understand it. Talk therapy, hypnotherapy, exposure therapy and eye movement desensitization and reprocessing (EMDR), a type of mental "reprocessing" of the phobia reinforced by eye movements, can help. Ask your doctor to recommend a mental-health professional specializing in one of these areas.

•**Gamma amino-butyric acid (GABA).** This amino acid, available as an over-the-counter supplement, is excellent for treating phobias. Preliminary studies confirm what I have seen in my practice—taking a GABA supplement helps calm the brain and create a sense of well-being while maintaining one's mental alertness.

Typical dose: 200 mg up to three times a day or 15 minutes before exposure to the object of your phobia. I prefer a sublingual or chewable form since it's quickly absorbed.

•**Rescue Remedy.** This is a Bach flower remedy, a type of natural medicine made from the distilled essences of five flowers. Available in stores that sell homeopathic and natural medicines, it calms the nervous system and helps ease stress.

Typical dose: Starting 15 minutes before the fear-inducing event, take four drops on the tongue. Repeat every 15 minutes for an hour, then take four drops every three hours, if needed. Use Rescue Remedy alone or with GABA. Rescue Remedy contains alcohol, so speak to your doctor if you take medication that interacts with alcohol.

•**Strength training and aerobic exercise.** Though not discussed in the medical literature on treating phobias, a combination of strength training and aerobic exercise has enhanced the results for my patients who have tried the approaches described above. Becoming physically strong often leads to mental strength and a sense of control—both of which can lessen or completely cure phobias. Consider starting with an exercise class, such as cycling or Zumba, or work with a personal trainer.

Good Riddance to Bad Nightmares

Simon Kung, MD, an assistant professor of psychiatry at the Mayo Clinic in Rochester, Minnesota, and coauthor of a review of studies on *prazosin* and PTSD-related nightmares, published in *Mayo Clinic Proceedings*.

For most of us, thank goodness, bad dreams disturb our slumber only occasionally. But for people who suffer from recurrent nightmares, falling asleep can be a truly scary experience…and getting enough rest can be next to impossible.

So it is welcome news that a medication called *prazosin* (Minipress) can help, according to a recent study. And even though this research focused on a particular type of patient, it's quite possible that the drug could help a much wider range of nightmare-prone people. *Here's the story…*

For many patients with post-traumatic stress disorder (PTSD), nightmares are so frequent and so frightening that they seriously affect sleep and quality of life—and can even contribute to substance abuse and suicide. While psychotherapy and other treatments may help PTSD, there is not much available from a medication standpoint for banishing nightmares. Because the blood pressure drug prazosin is sometimes prescribed off-label to ease PTSD-induced nightmares, researchers set out to see how well it worked by reviewing 12 studies involving a total of 259 PTSD patients.

Findings: While the methods and results varied from study to study, overall, prazosin was indeed found to be helpful in reducing the severity and frequency of PTSD-related nightmares—within a few days to a few weeks.

The drug was well-tolerated by patients of all ages, even at higher dosages. Though brief and temporary dizziness was a fairly common side effect, the drug did not cause significant unwanted changes in blood pressure.

How it seems to work: Nightmares involve an excess of the brain chemical norepinephrine. Prazosin blocks norepinephrine receptors, calming the body's overstimulated fight-or-flight response.

For sweeter dreams: Though this study review found evidence of prazosin use only in PTSD patients, the researchers said that "it seems logical to extend the use of prazosin to non-PTSD nightmares" to explore whether the drug also might help in those cases, too. *Bottom line:* If you suffer from frequent nightmares, ask your doctor whether prazosin is appropriate for you.

The Right Amount of Exercise Can Boost Mental Health

Teachers College, Columbia University, news release

People who exercise 2.5 to 7.5 hours a week have better mental health, but more than that is associated with poorer mental health, a recent study suggests.

THE STUDY

Researchers compared mental health with exercise by analyzing self-reported data from

Loneliness Reduces Productivity

Employees who are lonely are less productive both as individuals and in teams. Loneliness tends to increase hostility, negative thinking and anxiety, as well as reduces cooperation—all changes that can have a negative impact in the workplace.

Self-defense: Help yourself or a lonely colleague by connecting in small ways, such as taking time for a chat…asking for input on a project…or going out for coffee or lunch together. Talk to a manager or company counselor if your loneliness or that of another employee seems to be persistent and is having an effect on productivity.

Study of more than 650 workers by researchers at California State University, Sacramento, and The Wharton School, University of Pennsylvania, Philadelphia, reported in The New York Times.

more than 7,600 adults who took part in a US national survey.

"The largest mental health differences occurred with two to four hours of exercise per week. Beyond four hours, the trend begins to reverse—about 65% of those with poorer mental health exercised more than four hours per week, compared to 55% of adults in better mental health," according to Yeon Soo Kim, MD, a visiting scholar in the departments of biobehavioral sciences and health and behavior studies, and colleagues at Teachers College, Columbia University.

MORE EXERCISE IS NOT BETTER

They were surprised to find that after 7.5 hours of exercise per week, symptoms of depression and anxiety increased sharply. This was true in both men and women, and in people of all ages and different levels of health.

The study, published in the journal *Preventive Medicine,* is the first to show an association between too much exercise and poor mental health, according to the researchers.

However, further research is needed to determine whether people who tend to be depressed and anxious are more likely to be more physically active as a way to keep their mental symptoms under control, or whether greater amounts of exercise actually cause symptoms of depression and anxiety.

IMPLICATIONS

The researchers also emphasize that their findings support "the notion that regular activity may lead to prevention of mental health disorders."

"If physical activity can prevent mental health disorders or improve overall mental health, the public health impact of promoting physical activity could be enormous," according to the study authors.

While the study found an association between high amounts of exercise and worse mental health, it did not prove a cause-and-effect relationship.

info For recommendations on the right amount of exercise for you, visit the Web site of the Centers for Disease Control and Prevention, *www.cdc.gov,* and search "physical activity guidelines."

Why "TM" Is Making a Comeback

Norman E. Rosenthal, MD, a clinical professor of psychiatry at Georgetown University School of Medicine in Washington, DC. He is author of *Transcendence: Healing and Transformation Through Transcendental Meditation* (Tarcher-Penguin). *www.normanrosenthal.com*

Few of us get through life without experiencing trauma of some sort, be it a frightening accident, worrisome illness or heart-breaking loss. Distressing thoughts and internal stress can reverberate long after a traumatic incident. Transcendental meditation (TM) can help.

What is TM? Given its profound effects, you may be surprised to hear that TM is easy to learn and do. There's nothing mystical, religious or cultlike about the practice (despite what the media put forth in the 1960s when the Beatles embraced the practice). TM is a straightforward technique involving silent repetition of a mantra, a particular sound with no meaning that serves as a vehicle to settle the mind into a profound state of restful alertness. Once mastered, TM ideally is practiced with eyes closed for 20 minutes twice per day.

How it works: Psychiatrist Norman Rosenthal, MD, author of *Transcendence: Healing and Transformation through Transcendental Meditation,* explained that TM is among the most powerful "stress busters" he has encountered in his many years of psychiatric practice and confirmed that it is a useful tool for getting through painful times or recovering from posttraumatic stress disorder (PTSD).

Reason: People who have experienced intense stress often have difficulty calming down because the body's alarm-signaling mechanism goes awry and the "fight or flight" response becomes their normal state of being. "Stress can be like an alarm bell that just keeps ringing. Transcendental meditation helps to settle down both the mind and body, so people become more resilient and less vulnerable to stress," Dr. Rosenthal said.

Research has demonstrated that TM helps people to achieve equanimity because it literally changes their brain waves. TM promotes alpha brain waves, slow-frequency signals that

Meditation Staves Off Loneliness and Disease

Forty healthy adults were divided into two groups—one group attended an eight-week course in mindfulness meditation, an ancient practice that focuses on creating awareness of the present moment, while the other group did not.

Result: The meditation group reported lower levels of loneliness (a risk factor for death) and had lower levels of C-reactive protein and pro-inflammatory gene expression (which contribute to cardiovascular and neurodegenerative diseases and cancer). Mindfulness meditation is taught throughout the US. For locations, consult the Center for Mindfulness at the University of Massachusetts Medical School, *http://umassmed.edu/cfm/stress.*

J. David Creswell, PhD, assistant professor of psychology, Carnegie Mellon University, Pittsburgh.

So That's Why Some People Clam Up

Researchers recently found that *alexithymia,* a condition marked by an inability to identify and express emotions, occurs in about 6.5% of women and 7.5% of men. Alexithymics tend to avoid intimate relationships, but many do get married—often to the detriment of their spouses' emotional health.

University of Missouri.

are associated with calmness. There also is an increase in coherence, meaning that brain waves from different parts of the brain are more closely in step with one another. In other words, "TM spreads a great wave of calmness across the brain," Dr. Rosenthal said. Brain scans have shown that this can happen the first time a person meditates...with regular practice, those changes become lasting and can be seen even at times when the person isn't meditating. Dr. Rosenthal added, "TM also may help by a process of systematic desensitization—allowing worrisome thoughts and feelings to emerge in the context of profound relaxation and transcendent joy, thereby weakening the neural links that were forged by the trauma."

To learn TM: For maximum effectiveness, TM is taught through personalized instruction tailored to each individual, as it has been for thousands of years. Just as you can't master playing piano or swinging a golf club by reading about it, you can't really learn TM from a book. You can find a certified TM teacher through the Maharishi Foundation USA (*www.tm.org*), a nonprofit educational organization. (Dr. Rosenthal receives no financial compensation from this or any other TM organization.)

You may think a private TM tutor is more expense than you wanted to pay for meditation. Consider this—a study in *American Journal of Health Promotion* recently reported that people with consistently high health-care costs experienced a 28% cumulative reduction in physician fees after practicing TM for five years.

New Help for BPD

Joan Farrell, PhD, director of the Schema Therapy Institute Midwest–Indianapolis Center, and coauthor, with Ida Shaw, of *Group Schema Therapy for Borderline Personality Disorder* (Wiley-Blackwell).

Borderline personality disorder (BPD), a mental illness marked by difficulty managing emotions, extreme fears of abandonment and self-destructive behaviors, has been notoriously difficult to treat—until now. BPD patients finally can get the help they need, thanks to a novel form of psychotherapy called schema therapy. (Unhealthy or early maladaptive "schemas" are self-defeating, core themes or patterns that we keep repeating throughout our lives.)

The research is encouraging. In one study, for instance, one group of BPD patients received the typical treatment consisting of weekly individual psychotherapy sessions—but after eight months, 84% of these patients still met the diagnostic criteria for the disorder. However, a second group received the typical treatment plus weekly sessions of schema therapy—and after eight months, only 6% still had BPD!

Who develops BPD? Though not as well-known as bipolar disorder or schizophrenia, BPD is actually more common, affecting from 2% to 6% of US adults. People who develop BDP tend to have sensitive, reactive temperaments. Study coauthor Joan Farrell, PhD, director of the Schema Therapy Institute Midwest–Indianapolis Center and coauthor of the book *Group Schema Therapy for Borderline Personality Disorder*, explained that often their core emotional needs were not met during childhood. Perhaps they had an unstable home environment…did not form a secure attachment with a caregiver…and/or were physically, sexually or emotionally abused. Genetics also may play a role, as the disorder appears to run in families.

Although more US women than men are treated for BPD, Dr. Farrell noted that this could be due to a gender bias in diagnosis. For instance, men with certain BPD symptoms, such as intense anger and aggressiveness, often are diagnosed instead with antisocial personality disorder (a long-term pattern of manipulating and exploiting others). In many cases, for both women and men, BPD goes unrecognized.

The treatment that can help: Schema therapy combines cognitive behavioral and emotion-focused techniques. It centers on helping patients change longstanding, negative self-images and self-defeating behaviors, incorporating methods such as role-playing, letter writing, assertiveness training, anger management, guided imagery, relaxation, gradual exposure to anxiety-producing situations and challenges to negative thoughts and beliefs.

A unique key element of schema therapy is limited reparenting in which, within the bounds of a professional relationship, the patient establishes a secure attachment to the therapist. "Many patients with BPD missed some critical emotional learning as children. They were not adequately validated and encouraged to express their emotions and needs. In schema therapy, the therapist meets some of those core childhood needs—for example, by setting limits, expressing compassion and providing nurturance," Dr. Farrell said. The goal is for patients to become emotionally healthy and autonomous enough that eventually they no longer need the therapist

Signs of BPD

Symptoms often first appear in adolescence, with five or more symptoms indicating BPD. *For instance, he or she may…*

- **Make frantic efforts to avoid real or imagined abandonment.**
- **Have tumultuous, intense relationships.**
- **Have an unstable self-image**.
- **Act impulsively and self-destructively** (overspending, binge eating, excessive drinking, risky sex).
- **Experience intense mood swings** and excessive emotional reactions.
- **Have chronic feelings of emptiness.**
- **Feel intense rage** or have difficulty controlling anger.
- **Experience brief episodes of being out of touch with reality.**
- **Engage in self-injury** (such as cutting) or make repeated suicide attempts.

to meet these core needs—because they learn to do so themselves.

Do you think that you or someone you love might benefit from schema therapy for BPD? Dr. Farrell recommended working with a therapist certified by the International Society of Schema Therapy.

Referrals: *www.isstonline.com/find-a-therapist.*

Schema therapy usually is done in one-on-one sessions. However, research from Dr. Farrell and colleagues demonstrates a high level of effectiveness from a group-therapy version.

How to Break a Bad Habit for Good

Charles Duhigg, an investigative journalist for *The New York Times,* New York City. He is author of the recent best-seller *The Power of Habit: Why We Do What We Do* (Random House). *www.charlesduhigg.com*

Almost all of us have bad habits that we have tried to break but can't. That's because we have relied on willpower. Willpower can be effective, but it's like a muscle that grows fatigued after a while, and we tend to slip back into old patterns.

Charles Duhigg, an investigative journalist for *The New York Times,* spent the past few years uncovering new scientific research on the neurology and psychology of habits. *The findings indicate a much more effective way to break bad habits…*

THE HABIT LOOP

Habits are neurological shortcuts that we use to save mental effort and get through life more efficiently. But the dependence on automatic routines—MIT researchers say more than 40% of our daily actions are habits—has a downside. Our brains go on autopilot, and we reach for a cigarette, bite our nails or turn on the TV without thinking.

Habits like these may seem complicated, but they all can be broken down into three components…

•**Cue,** which triggers an urge or a craving that we need to satisfy and causes a habitual

behavior to unfold (for example, you feel sluggish and want to perk up).

•**Routine** or actual behavior you want to change (you reach for a can of cola).

•**Reward,** the deep-seated desire satisfied by your behavior (the soda's sugar, caffeine and fizziness energize you).

Over time, these three components become so intertwined and encoded in the structures of our brains that they form an intense loop of craving and anticipation of the associated reward.

STEP 1: ANALYZE THE LOOP

Awareness of the mechanisms of your own particular habit can make it easier to change…

Identify the routine. It's the most obvious and visible part of the loop.

Example: Every day, I would get up from my desk at The New York Times building, wander to the cafeteria and eat a cookie while I chatted with whomever was there. I am a disciplined person, so it was frustrating and embarrassing that this daily habit had caused me to gain several pounds over the course of a year despite my efforts to resist. I would even put notes on my computer that read "No More Cookies." But most days, I gave in.

•**Isolate the cue.** Scientists have determined that almost all habitual cues fit into one of five categories. Ask yourself the following questions when you feel an urge that sets off a behavior pattern—What time is it?...Where am I?...Who else is around?...What was I just doing?...What emotion am I feeling? One or more of the answers is your cue. It took me several days of self-observation to discover the trigger for my cookie binge. It would happen every day between 3 pm and 4 pm. I wasn't hungry or stressed out at the time, but I did feel isolated after working alone in my office for many hours.

•**Figure out the actual reward.** Because I wasn't eating cookies to stem my hunger, some other powerful craving was being satisfied. You can pinpoint the craving with some experimentation using alternate rewards.

Example: One day when I felt the urge to go to the cafeteria and get a cookie, I walked briskly around the block without eating anything. The next day, I brought a cookie from home and ate it at my desk. The day after, I had an apple and a cup of coffee with people at the cafeteria. After each experiment, I waited 15 minutes. If I still felt the urge to go to the cafeteria for a cookie, I assumed that the habit wasn't motivated by that particular reward. I soon realized what I was craving was the distraction and relief that came from socializing. Only after gossiping with colleagues in the cafeteria was I able to get back to work without further urges.

STEP 2: ADJUST THE ROUTINE

Trying to ignore my craving and suppress my behavior took what seemed like bottomless reserves of willpower. Studies suggested that I would have much more success if I tinkered with the routine, simply modifying it to be less destructive. That's the secret to gaining leverage—cues and rewards are primal needs that are difficult to deny, but routines are quite malleable and often can be replaced. Every afternoon when I felt the urge to have a cookie, I would visit the office of a friend and chat with him for at least 10 minutes.

STEP 3: GIVE IT TIME

My new behavior pattern, which I tracked on paper each day, still required effort and willpower. I often felt like slipping back into the old routine, and in fact, I did have setbacks, especially when I was under a lot of stress or out of my usual environment. But resisting the cookie was more manageable than applying blind dis-

cipline and writing notes to myself. Habits are an accretive process—each time you perform a modified loop, there is a thickening of neural pathways in the brain and the new behavior gets marginally easier. After about a month, I suddenly realized that I had a powerful craving to chat with a friend in the afternoon—but I no longer felt the urge to eat cookies.

Other helpful findings...

•**Begin with minor, easy-to-change habits.** A series of small wins makes you believe that you can cope with deeply entrenched cravings in a different way.

•**Get involved with others trying to break the same habit.** Becoming part of a like-minded social group provides more than just inspiration and a measure of accountability. Their experience is helpful in analyzing your cues and rewards and in suggesting alternative routines and behaviors.

CREATING GOOD HABITS

Trying to start a positive, new habit, such as exercising more or eating better, presents a different kind of challenge. Instead of analyzing and altering an existing loop, you have to establish one from scratch. *What works...*

•**Focus on "keystone" habits.** There are certain good habits that seem to echo through one's life and make it easier to change other habits. For instance, people who exercise regularly

Therapy to Fall Asleep

Fifty-one adults who had difficulty falling asleep (sleep-onset insomnia) were divided into two groups. Both groups were taught good sleep practices (maintaining a standard wake-up time, using the bed only for sleeping, etc.). One group, however, also received cognitive refocusing therapy (CRT)—which involves thinking about something interesting but unexciting, such as song lyrics or recipes, when preparing for sleep or upon wakening during the night. After one month, the CRT group fell asleep much faster than the group that didn't do CRT. If you try CRT but insomnia persists, see a sleep medicine specialist.

Les A. Gellis, PhD, assistant professor of psychology, Syracuse University, New York.

To Keep Anxiety in Check...

• **Avoid sugar and white flour**—they have been linked to an increase in brain chemicals that cause anxiety.

• **Get some sun daily**—anxiety sufferers often feel more relaxed after spending 20 to 40 minutes outdoors when the sun is shining.

• **Seek solitude**—find a quiet spot to read, write, listen to music or just think for 30 to 60 minutes each day.

• **Work out**—exercising for 30 to 40 minutes three to five times per week can help reduce stress.

• **Get enough sleep**—at least eight hours per night. Take a shower 15 minutes before you go to bed to help you relax, and set the thermostat no higher than 68° to sleep more soundly.

Rhonda Martin, licensed professional clinical counselor and anxiety therapist at the Akron Family Institute in Akron, Ohio.

Cure for Cell-Phone Addiction

Karen Larson, editor of *Bottom Line/Personal*.

A friend of mine seems to be addicted to her iPhone. She checks it every few minutes for messages and e-mails. And she's far from alone. About one in every five baby boomers—and one in every three teenagers—checks his/her cell phone at least once every 15 minutes.

Technically, my friend doesn't have an "addiction" to her phone. She has a "compulsion," says Larry Rosen, PhD, past chair of psychology at California State University, Dominguez Hills, and author of *iDisorder: Understanding Our Obsession with Technology and Overcoming Its Hold on Us* (Palgrave Macmillan). Addicts do things because it triggers the release of dopamine in their brains, which feels pleasurable. Compulsives do things because it relieves anxiety—and anxiety is precisely what people who endlessly recheck their phones are feeling. They're worried that someone might be trying to reach them, that there could be breaking news or that they might have lost their phones.

Cell-phone compulsion can be a serious problem. It makes us seem distant and detracts significantly from our focus, which can damage our relationships and job performance. It prevents our brains from truly relaxing. Just keeping a cell phone within arm's reach at night reduces the quality of our sleep—even if the phone doesn't ring.

Dr. Rosen suggests that my friend turn her phone's ringer to silent and place the phone upside down or out of sight so that she can't see

start eating better, stop using their credit cards quite so much, procrastinate less and have more patience with colleagues and family. Other keystone habits include a healthful, consistent sleep routine...maintaining good track of your finances...and keeping your living space organized.

• **Use a concrete and consistent cue.** Studies show that if you are hungry when you get home at the end of the day and there is nothing readily available to eat for dinner, you are much more likely to eat poorly. Just a simple cue like leaving vegetables out on the counter—even if you don't eat them—results in healthier eating.

• **Make sure that the reward you choose is something you really crave.** For instance, you want to get in better shape. When you first start jogging or going to the gym, the rewards (such as losing weight or gaining more energy) may not happen quickly enough to keep you motivated or to turn the behavior into an automatic habit. You may need to trick your brain the first few weeks by rewarding yourself with something more lavish and immediate after you exercise, such as a piece of chocolate or a soak in a hot tub.

incoming messages. Then she should set a timer or a wristwatch alarm to buzz every 15 minutes, when she can quickly check her phone. She should gradually push the 15-minute interval up to 20 or beyond. Knowing that she'll soon be able to check her phone should be enough to allow her to calmly focus on other matters between buzzes.

Is Someone You Know An "Almost Alcoholic"?

Robert L. Doyle, MD, assistant medical director in the Child and Adolescent Inpatient Unit at McLean Hospital in Belmont, Massachusetts. Dr. Doyle is coauthor, with Joseph Nowinski, PhD, of *Almost Alcoholic: Is My (or My Loved One's) Drinking a Problem?* (Hazelden/Harvard Health).

Everyone knows that alcoholism poses a real danger to health, relationships and work. On the other end of the spectrum, modest alcohol consumption can be pleasant and harmless for most people and may even bring some health benefits.

What many people aren't aware of: There's a large gray area between these two scenarios—drinking that doesn't fit the criteria of alcohol abuse or addiction, yet may be taking a subtle or substantial toll on a person's life. This area is known as almost alcoholism.

Chances are you know someone whose drinking falls into this gray area...or you might even suspect that you're an almost alcoholic.

TAKE THE QUIZ

Because the physical and mental reaction to alcohol varies from person to person (and even from one time of life to another), the number of drinks you have per day or week is not a reliable indicator of an alcohol problem.* *The type of alcohol you drink—hard liquor versus beer or wine—is not of utmost importance either. Instead, if you have concerns about your alcohol habits, take this quick quiz...*

*If you do drink, the recommended limit is up to one drink a day for women and up to two drinks a day for men.

•**Do you continue drinking despite experiencing negative consequences,** such as disrupted sleep or hangovers?

•**Do you look forward to drinking and arrange your schedule to be sure you can have a drink?**

•**Do you drink alone?**

•**Do you sometimes drink to control negative feelings such as boredom...**or to relieve anxiety or other unpleasant symptoms?

•**Is your drinking causing suffering to yourself or a loved one?**

Take Charge of Your Anger to Protect Your Health

In small doses, anger can be a helpful emotion. However, if not managed effectively, anger can blaze out of control and harm your health. Unchecked anger can contribute to heart and stroke risk, digestive disorders, muscle tension and breathing issues.

THREE SMART WAYS TO DEFUSE ANGER...

•**Sit down!** Your brain interprets a seated or reclining position as safe and relaxing, interrupting the flow of anger-enhancing adrenaline. The next time you're in an argument, get yourself (and the other person) to sit down. Say something like, "Let's sit and discuss this." If you're already sitting down when angered, try leaning back and relaxing your muscles.

•**Never go to bed angry.** Research proves that the old saying is right! A recent study found that hitting the sack after having negative emotions appears to reinforce them. Try to resolve disagreements before bedtime.

•**Become an observer.** The next time your blood boils, step back and view the situation from a distance. Evaluate how angry you are on a scale of 0 to 100. Then project what may happen if you don't lower that figure by using relaxation techniques. This will help you remain calm.

W. Robert Nay, PhD, clinical psychologist and clinical associate professor of psychiatry at Georgetown University School of Medicine in Washington, DC. He is author of *Taking Charge of Anger* (Guilford). *www.wrobertnay. com*

THE RESULTS

If you said yes to the first or last question, drinking definitely is a problem—even if amounts are modest and harm seems minor—and you need to make changes. But if you answered affirmatively to any question (especially more than one), you also should give serious thought to the role of alcohol in your life and whether you need to make changes. *What else may be behind some of the questions above...*

•**Looking forward to drinking may seem natural**—we anticipate what we enjoy—but this can be a sign that your relationship with alcohol is heading down a dangerous path. Maybe it's becoming too important to you, stressing significant relationships or affecting your daily responsibilities or schedule.

Ask yourself: Do you often stop by the local bar or hurry home to have a drink after work? If you refrain from drinking during the week, is alcohol a major reason you look forward to the weekend?

•**Drinking alone isn't always a problem either but can be a danger sign.** For most people, drinking is primarily a social activity—it's part of the fun of getting together. But drinking alone, or being the only one drinking in a group, suggests that a person may be drinking solely to get intoxicated, which is unhealthy physically and emotionally.

Drinking alone is of particular concern if boredom or loneliness is involved because, while drinking may be a distraction, it doesn't help solve these problems. Better solutions include finding fun activities to replace boredom or cultivating new friends to alleviate loneliness.

Important: Social drinking isn't necessarily benign. If watching sports on TV with friends is a favorite pastime, is it the friends, the game or the chance to drink more beers than usual that's the attraction? Would you spend so much time with those friends if alcohol weren't involved?

If a Loved One Has a Drinking Problem...

If you're concerned about a loved one's drinking, encourage him/her to think carefully about his alcohol use and consider the need to change. Be empathetic and avoid creating guilt or shame or name-calling.

You might say something like, "I notice when you drink you seem to be kind of flat. You've also said that you feel depressed lately. I wonder if alcohol is making it worse."

Suggest that your loved one have a discussion with his family doctor about mood problems and other issues associated with drinking.

Drinking to ease unpleasant emotions or stress isn't necessarily bad if it's occasional and part of a repertoire of coping strategies, such as exercising, talking to friends or pursuing a hobby. But relying on alcohol may keep you from using healthier solutions to resolve distress.

Ask yourself: During a stressful day, do you often find yourself thinking, "I really need a drink"? Is alcohol your usual remedy for feeling down, stressed or nervous?

IF YOU'RE STILL NOT SURE...

Sometimes almost alcoholism slips under the radar because the change from normal drinking has been gradual and the damage hidden. *If you are still concerned, ask yourself these additional questions...*

•**Has your alcohol use changed?** Are you drinking a little more than you used to? Or do you feel differently about drinking? Maybe you do set limits but grit your teeth to follow them.

•**Has your reaction to alcohol changed?** The body's ability to eliminate alcohol slows with age, and the same drink at age 60 commonly has more punch than it did at age 50. Also, the aftereffects of drinking tend to become worse with age.

•**Is drinking causing problems in your day-to-day life?** After an initial lift to your spirits, alcohol can bring you down. Mood can be negatively affected by even modest drinking. And just one drink in the evening may disrupt sleep. Performance at work also may suffer, increasing stress.

•**What do others think about your drinking?** The impact of drinking on relationships can be subtle—maybe you're a little less patient with your spouse or less attentive to his/her needs. Share your concerns about alcohol with a trusted friend or family member and ask him what he thinks. Perhaps a loved one has already approached you with concern about your drinking habits.

Helpful: To clarify alcohol's effects on your life, go without it for two weeks to a month. The time frame is up to you. How do you feel? Are you sleeping better, working better? Is it harder or easier to deal with stress? Due to differences in metabolism and previous drinking patterns, some people will notice a difference right away, while for others it can take longer.

If you find it very difficult—or impossible—to do without alcohol temporarily, you know you need to make some changes.

Important: People with significant to severe alcohol dependency may need to taper off alcohol or go through detoxification under the guidance of a clinician to prevent withdrawal side effects.

HOW TO CUT DOWN...

•**Change your routine.** If drinking is an integral part of your schedule, substitute other activities.

For example: Instead of stopping off for happy hour, treat yourself to a workout at the gym.

•**Make new friends.** If much of your social life includes drinking, cultivate new friends who don't drink as much.

•**Practice refusing drinks.** Health concerns are a socially acceptable reason to say no.

Examples: "No thanks. I'm watching my weight, and a glass of wine has about 100 calories." Or you could simply say, "I'm not crazy about the way alcohol makes me feel."

•**Find new ways to deal with stress.** Doing relaxation exercises, listening to calming music and practicing meditation are healthier ways to unwind than drinking alcohol. However, you may need to confront your stress at the source, whether it means working on a personal relationship or finding a new job.

•**Get help if you need it.** If you determine that you've been drinking to "self-medicate" depression or anxiety, speak to your family doctor about addressing these problems with lifestyle changes, psychotherapy and/or prescription medication.

Alcoholics Anonymous (AA) isn't just for people who identify themselves as alcoholics. Anyone interested is welcome to attend most AA meetings, and many people who are concerned about their drinking find the approach very helpful.

Men Know to Steer Clear of Friends' Wives

University of Missouri, news release.

M en appear to have a biologically based control to prevent them from committing adultery with their friends' wives, a recent study says.

RESEARCH ON TESTOSTERONE LEVELS

Researchers discovered that adult males' testosterone levels dropped when they interacted with the wife of a close friend, and said this may be an evolutionary adaptation that helped humans live in large groups.

"Although men have many chances to pursue a friend's mate, propositions for adultery are relatively rare on a per-opportunity basis," said Mark Flinn, PhD, a professor of anthropology at the University of Missouri.

"Men's testosterone levels generally increase when they are interacting with a potential sexual partner or an enemy's mate. However, our findings suggest that men's minds have evolved to foster a situation where the stable pair bonds of friends are respected," he explained.

The results from adult and adolescent males in a rural Dominican community, published in the journal *Human Nature,* may help explain how people manage to cooperate in neighborhoods, cities and even worldwide, the researchers say.

IMPLICATIONS

"Ultimately, our findings about testosterone levels illuminate how people have evolved to form alliances," Dr. Flinn said. "Using that biological understanding of human nature, we can look for ways to solve global problems. The same physiological mechanisms that allow villages of families to coexist and cooperate can also allow groups like NATO and the U.N. to coordinate efforts to solve common problems."

One example would be the threat of climate change, he said.

During evolution, men who constantly betrayed their friends' trust and endangered the stability of families may have caused a survival disadvantage for entire communities, Dr. Flinn suggested. The lack of trust in these communities would have made them fragile and vulnerable to attack and conquest.

info For more information on the causes and effects of infidelity, visit the Web site of the American Association for Marriage and Family Therapy, *http://www.aamft.org,* and search "infidelity."

Are You a Picky Eater? It Can Be a Serious Problem

Nancy Zucker, PhD, director of the Duke Center for Eating Disorders at Duke University Medical Center in Durham, North Carolina. She also is associate professor of psychiatry and behavioral sciences at Duke University.

We have all known little ones who are picky eaters—children who turn up their noses at vegetables…never try new foods…and often have just three favorite foods. But not adults, right? As it turns out, picky eating in adults is much more common than you might think.

Although most children eventually expand their palates and eat normally, many don't—and their finicky eating habits persist into adulthood. In recent years, researchers have begun to recognize that this type of picky eating, also known as selective eating disorder (SED) or food neophobia, adversely affects a significant number of adults, leading to nutritional deficiencies and even interfering with a normal social life.

AN EATING DISORDER?

Picky eating is not yet considered by health professionals to be a diagnosable disorder in adults, but that may soon change. Currently, this eating problem is officially recognized only as a diagnosis in children younger than age six and is characterized by selective eating that causes significant weight loss or a failure to grow normally.

However, an American Psychiatric Association task force is now investigating whether a new disorder should be proposed—one that is redefined to include children of all ages and adults whose food aversions and/or food avoidances lead to marked weight loss…nutritional deficiencies…dependence on tube feeding or supplements…and/or impaired social functioning. The proposed name of this newly defined disorder is avoidant/restrictive food intake disorder.

THE PROBLEM IN ADULTS

Researchers do not yet know exactly why this disorder occurs, although several factors may contribute. Some picky eaters may have a genetic predisposition to taste sensitivity…or they may have grown up with parents who were selective eaters. For some selective eaters, a prior illness, such as food poisoning or acid reflux, can make them fearful of eating and worried about getting sick again.

Because few studies have been done on picky eating in adults, the characteristics are still being discovered. Researchers do know, however, that picky eaters are highly sensitive and reactive to taste, food textures and odors.

For example, they often avoid foods that are chewy, stringy or slimy, such as cooked vegetables, and instead prefer crispy, crunchy foods, such as chips. They often dislike bitter foods, such as broccoli, but frequently have no problem with sweets. Sometimes, even the sight or smell of certain foods can bring on feelings of anxiety and/or disgust…and make them gag. Most people dislike some foods intensely—but it's different for adults who are picky eaters. They not only have extreme reactions to many foods, their reactions also cause them extreme emotional distress.

Adults with the disorder are often ashamed and embarrassed about their eating habits. Social occasions that revolve around food, such as family functions or business dinners, cause these adults severe anxiety. In fact, extreme anxiety about their eating habits may even hold them back professionally.

WHEN TO GET TREATMENT

•**If a person's limited range or quantity of food is threatening his/her functioning—for example, one's health, job or relationships—it's time to seek help.** Health professionals who are trained to help people with the disorder (not all doctors have even heard of it) do so through a combination of cognitive behavioral therapy, occupational therapy that focuses on the sensory aspects of eating and nutritional guidance. *Techniques found to help...*

•**Support groups.** Selective eating isn't a well-known problem, which can make people with the disorder feel isolated. Many might not even realize it is a problem that others share. Participating in an online support community, such as Picky Eating Adult Support (*www.picky eatingadults.com*), may be useful.

•**Behavioral therapy.** One key aspect of therapy for these patients is to help them acknowledge that they have an eating disorder—that is, in essence, a physical disorder like so many others. These people are not trying to be "difficult" when it comes to their food choices, they simply experience food differently from those who don't have the disorder. The goal of treatment will differ for each individual. However, in general it should help limit the restrictions that eating may be imposing on the person's daily life. This may involve improving the range of foods the person feels comfortable tasting or even liking. For others, treatment may focus on targeting the social isolation that has become associated with their dietary habits.

•**Dietary help.** Nutrition professionals who are trained in treating this disorder will try to help patients move toward consuming a more balanced diet. Although it is not known how much a picky eater's food repertoire can be expanded, there are some ways that nutrition experts might work with a patient to expand his diet. (See box.)

A Not-So-Picky Diet

Techniques that may allow a picky eater to expand his/her diet...

•**Experiment with different preparation methods.** If you don't like plain cooked vegetables, try adding them to a soup or stew. Some people who avoid broccoli, for example, have no trouble eating broccoli and cheese soup.

•**Try the same food, different texture.** Sometimes it's the consistency rather than the taste of a food that is offensive to a picky eater. A person who doesn't care for the texture of applesauce may enjoy apples, whole or cut up. People who dislike cheese may be able to eat a small amount melted on a piece of toast. Or put a tiny bit between two crackers. That way, in addition to tasting the cheese, you'll experience the crunch of the crackers.

•**Find a healthier alternative.** Many selective eaters favor crispy, crunchy foods like potato chips. Instead, try a crunchy raw vegetable such as celery with a little salt.

•**Take it slow.** Introduce one new food at a time, and allow yourself to get comfortable with it before attempting to add another one.

Franca Alphin, RD, MPH, CSSD, LDN, associate professor and director of nutrition services at Duke University, Durham, North Carolina. She regularly works with patients who have eating disorders.

Complementary Medicine A Boon to Soldiers With PTSD

Scripps Health, news release.

Complementary medicine techniques known as healing touch and guided imagery can help reduce symptoms of post-traumatic stress disorder in military personnel who have been in combat, a recent study says.

Healing touch is described as an energy-based treatment meant to restore and balance the human biofield in order to decrease pain and promote healing. It is sometimes used in surgery or other medical procedures to help patients relax and reduce pain and anxiety. Guided imagery uses imagination and visualization to help reduce stress and anxiety and enhance overall well-being.

STUDY DETAILS

The study included 123 active-duty US Marines who had at least one of the following post-traumatic stress disorder (PTSD) symptoms—flashbacks of their traumatic experience, nightmares, intrusive thoughts, emotional numbness, insomnia, irritability, exaggerated startle response, avoidance of people or places that remind them of the traumatic experience, or exaggerated emotional responses to trauma.

The participants were assigned to receive either standard treatment for PTSD or standard treatment plus healing touch and guided imagery. There were six complementary therapy sessions over three weeks.

The study found that patients who received standard treatment plus these complementary therapies had greater improvement in quality of life and lower levels of depression and cynicism than those who received standard treatment alone.

The study, published in the journal *Military Medicine,* was led by the Scripps Center for Integrative Medicine in San Diego. It also involved the Samueli Institute in Alexandria, Virginia.

"Service members are seeking out non-drug complementary and integrative medicine as part of their overall care and approach to wellness," said Wayne Jonas, MD, president and chief executive officer of Samueli Institute.

"This treatment pairs deep relaxation with a self-care approach that can be used at home," he said. "The results of this study underscore the need to make effective, non-stigmatizing treatments for PTSD available to all our service members."

info The US National Institute of Mental Health has more information about post-traumatic stress disorder at its Web site, *www.nimh.nih.gov* (search "PTSD").

Real Help From Hypnosis

Bruce N. Eimer, PhD, a clinical psychologist and hypnotherapist in private practice in Huntingdon Valley, Pennsylvania. He is author of *Hypnotize Yourself Out of Pain Now!* and coauthor, with C. Roy Hunter, of *The Art of Hypnotic Regression Therapy* (both from Crown House). *www.bruceeimer.com*

Hypnosis is best known for helping with weight loss and tobacco addiction. But research now shows that it also can be used for such conditions as anxiety, irritable bowel syndrome (IBS), gastroesophageal reflux disease (GERD), high blood pressure and diabetes to help relieve symptoms and reduce one's need for medication.

WHAT IS HYPNOSIS?

The main idea behind hypnosis is that the mind and body work together and cannot be separated. Unconscious negative thought patterns and unresolved emotions can cause physical and mental illness…and the subconscious mind can be used to help resolve these issues.

During hypnosis, the doorway to the subconscious mind is opened. In this state, suggestibility heightens, mental absorption increases, senses become more acute and the imagination communicates with the subconscious to create change.

Hypnosis is not meant to replace standard medical treatment, but it can enhance the effectiveness of traditional treatment methods, including medication and surgery, for many conditions. In addition, it's simple, safe, effective and has no side effects.

LATEST DEVELOPMENTS

Recent research confirms that hypnotherapy can help treat a wide variety of medical problems. For example, it significantly reduced pain in IBS patients—ultimately allowing these patients to take far less medications and have fewer doctor visits.

Similar research has demonstrated the effectiveness of hypnosis in reducing blood pressure in individuals with hypertension and blood sugar levels in people with diabetes. One recent study found that hypnosis reduced the frequency of hot flashes by 75% in menopausal women.

HOW HYPNOSIS WORKS

Unlike modern treatments, such as cognitive behavioral therapy, which require patients to consciously shift negative thought patterns, hypnosis bypasses the thinking mind and relies on the subconscious to relay messages.

The therapist induces a trance by having the patient focus on a single object such as a flickering candle...a sound such as a ticking clock...or a physical sensation such as breathing. The therapist then leads the patient into a peaceful, twilight state through relaxation and breathing exercises. This state awakens the imagination and produces heightened suggestibility. The therapist then can implant carefully selected suggestions in the patient's subconscious mind, which accepts these suggestions as already fact, and the new behavior becomes automatic.

Example: For a patient who suffers from panic attacks, a hypnotherapist would induce a trance state and suggest specific posthypnotic cues (actions, thoughts, words or images that will trigger a desired response after hypnosis). The patient can use these posthypnotic cues in his/her everyday, waking life to achieve a calm state on his own.

During the trance state, the hypnotherapist might say: "Whenever you feel anxious, you'll notice and feel the ring on your finger and take a slow, deep breath. This will make you feel grounded, safe and secure."

In general, people who can visualize, daydream or imagine can be hypnotized. The number of sessions needed depends on the person and his specific situation. Some people solve a problem after one session. For others, it takes longer. Patients typically have five sessions that last about 50 minutes to one hour each.

When To Try Hypnosis...

Research shows hypnosis helps the following conditions and more...

- Addictions
- Allergies and asthma
- Anxiety and stress
- Diabetes
- Gastrointestinal and other digestive disorders
- High blood pressure
- Hot flashes
- Insomnia
- Pain
- Phobias
- Skin conditions
- Weight gain

Each session with a licensed health professional trained in hypnotherapy related to the patient's specific problem costs about $150 to $300. Even though there is significant research-backed evidence supporting the use of hypnosis and hypnotherapy, they often are considered "alternative" or "complementary" therapies and are rarely covered by medical or mental health insurance. However, some hospital-based pain-management centers do provide insurance-covered hypnosis.

Caution: Anyone can call himself a "certified hypnotherapist" or "clinical hypnotist." Most states don't regulate the practice of hypnosis. Choose a licensed health professional—a psychologist, psychiatrist, medical doctor or clinical social worker—whom you trust and feel safe and comfortable with.

To find a qualified clinical hypnotherapist, contact the American Society of Clinical Hypnosis (ASCH) at 630-980-4740 or *www.asch.net.*

DO IT YOURSELF

After you have successfully entered a hypnotic state in a clinician's office, a qualified hypnotherapist can teach you self-hypnosis. Used regularly, self-hypnosis gives you the ability to relax at will, builds your capacity to control your mind and body and furthers the process of positive change.

How self-hypnosis works: First, choose one or two suggestions to repeat to yourself four or five times during self-hypnosis.

Examples: For high blood pressure, you might repeat, "I stay relaxed as I complete my daily responsibilities"...for pain you might say, "I can manage discomfort."

The next step is to put yourself into a trance, which allows you to enter a state of heightened suggestibility. This can be done by focusing your complete attention on something (as described

Better Treatment for Post-Traumatic Stress Disorder

In a recent study, 137 victims of trauma, such as car accidents or rape, began receiving cognitive behavioral therapy within 12 hours of the event. They had three weekly sessions that involved talking about what had happened and being exposed to safe stimuli related to the trauma.

Result: Victims were significantly less likely to develop PTSD symptoms, such as nightmares or depression, than those who had standard care, including assessment and therapy, more than 12 hours after the event.

Theory: Immediate therapy can change the memory of traumatic events so that PTSD is less likely to develop.

Barbara Olasov Rothbaum, PhD, director, Trauma and Anxiety Recovery Program, Emory University School of Medicine, Atlanta.

earlier). Then your focus can move to your breathing. Feel your belly expand on inhalation and contract on exhalation.

To relax more deeply, imagine slowly walking down a set of 20 stairs. Feel the soft carpet under your feet, the smooth, polished wood of the handrail. With each step, your relaxation deepens. At the bottom of the stairs, you find a door. You open it and enter a place where you feel happy, content, safe and comfortable. Maybe it's a balmy beach, cool meadow or favorite room. Notice the specific details of this "favorite place."

Once you master this deep relaxation, use positive suggestions and positive imagery to help change undesirable attitudes and behaviors and limiting beliefs. When you're ready to emerge from this hypnotic state, walk back up the stairs and into the present moment.

Family Matters

How to Make Caregiving Much Easier

No one has to tell the more than 65 million Americans who provide unpaid care to loved ones with chronic illness that their job is difficult, stressful and exhausting—physically and emotionally.

Nor do caregivers (full or part time) need to hear yet again that they must build a support system so they can take breaks to pamper themselves from time to time. What caregivers need most are methods for making the day-to-day act of caregiving a little less exhausting.

What often gets overlooked: With the grueling demands of caregiving—whether it's shopping, handling a loved one's finances or helping with bathing and dressing—it's easy to overlook the critical aspect of effective communication.

So often, it's the misunderstandings, hurt feelings and unspoken expectations that drain pre-cious energy from the caregiver at the very time he/she needs it most. *Here are eight secrets to help caregivers...**

SECRET #1: Set the ground rules. It's common for caregiving to begin with a general intention of "helping out." However, the needs of your loved one are bound to grow over time. That's why it is crucial for every caregiving arrangement (even with a spouse) to have a written agreement, initiated by the caregiver with input and consent from the loved one. What are you, as the caregiver, able and willing to do? How much time can you realistically commit to providing care? When creating the agreement, which can be reviewed and changed periodically, remind the ill person that it will

*These recommendations are not necessarily effective for people with dementia—seek the advice of a geriatric psychologist if you are caregiving for someone affected by this disorder, which may affect his/her ability to communicate effectively.

Walter St. John, EdD, a former professor of communications and an administrator at Keene State College in New Hampshire. He is author of *Solace: How Caregivers and Others Can Relate, Listen and Respond Effectively to a Chronically Ill Person* (Bull).

help protect the relationship and prevent misunderstandings.

SECRET #2: Don't give in. Whether it's eating a food that's not on his diet or stopping physical therapy, it's tempting to allow a chronically ill person to have his way just to keep the peace. Do not do it. Instead, try to figure out the reason for the request. Listen closely and then repeat the request, so the person knows you're paying attention. Take some time to consider the request, even when you know the answer is no.

When you do tell the person no, be firm but explain your reasons so you don't come across as arbitrary. Try to find another way to address the request in a safer and/or more appropriate way. If the person is, say, asking to eat spicy foods that you know upset his stomach, offer to contact a nutritionist for advice on what else he can eat.

SECRET #3: Pay attention to body language. In many cases, a person may say one thing but really be feeling something else. For example, your loved one may say that he likes the meal you've prepared, but his fidgeting at the table most likely indicates that he feels frustrated with the food choice or perhaps the table setup. Or your loved one may say that he feels comfortable taking a walk in the backyard, but if he's looking down when he makes the statement he may, in fact, feel unsafe. Be attuned to these signals, and you'll be better able to meet that person's real needs.

SECRET #4: Practice listening. Many chronically ill people are angry about what they're experiencing and need to vent. As the caregiver, one of your primary roles is to simply listen. (If you are a family member, it may be appropriate for you to help find a solution or look for someone who can.)

Let your loved one know that you're willing to listen, as long as he's not hurting or attacking you. If you get frustrated, say, "OK, I need to leave now. But I'll be back in a while." By saying you'll be back, you let the person know you're still in a relationship with him.

SECRET #5: Apologize if you're wrong. If you're spending a lot of time with a loved one, chances are you'll forget to follow through on

a request, act irritated when you should not or do something else at some point that will offend or hurt that person. If this occurs, give the person an opportunity to air his grievance. Never interrupt. After hearing out the person, repeat what he has said back to him. If it's obvious that you offended your loved one, apologize immediately and sincerely.

SECRET #6: Use the power of touch. Day-to-day caregiving can easily focus so much on the chores that need to be done that the relationship you have with the ill person gets somewhat neglected. In these cases, touch can be a powerful antidote. Simply holding someone's hand can ease sadness. A peck on the cheek shows you're happy to see your loved one. Touching shows acceptance, compassion and caring—and the result is a stronger bond between you and your loved one. Make sure the touch is appropriate to your relationship, and avoid touching anyone who dislikes physical contact.

SECRET #7: Let your loved one cry. Crying is a normal reaction to the sadness and suffering that often result from chronic illness.

Caregiving Safety

Posing as consumers, researchers recently surveyed 180 in-home adult-care agencies around the country to learn how their caregivers were hired, trained and supervised.

Surprising result: Only 55% of these agencies did a federal background check on employees, just one-third did drug testing or tested skill competence, and merely 30% sent supervisors into homes to check on caregivers.

If you are considering hiring someone to care for a loved one: Be sure the agency does background checks and provides proper training and supervision. Ask to see documentation of the background check, and consider dropping in unannounced at random times when the caregiver is working.

Lee Lindquist, MD, MPH, associate professor of medicine, Northwestern University Feinberg School of Medicine, Chicago.

Even men need to cry. When someone cries, don't interrupt him with, "Why are you crying?" or "Don't cry." Simply sit silently and look empathetic. Interrupt only if you're handing the person a tissue.

When the tears stop, wait awhile and then say, "I can see you're very disturbed, and this makes me feel for you." While leaning forward with an expectant look on your face, say, "Is there anything you'd like to talk about?" Don't force your loved one to explain the tears. Often, a good cry is all it takes to ease distressful feelings.

SECRET #8: Avoid confrontation. Do your best to avoid clashes, especially over minor issues. Use phrases such as, "As I see it…" or "In my opinion…" to suggest that you are giving your opinion, not hard facts. If you do have an argument, stay calm. Allow the other person to talk—or show anger as long as it isn't excessive or abusive—uninterrupted. When he finishes, calmly explain your position. If the conversation is still heated, suggest that you save the discussion for later when he calms down.

What to Do About a Loved-One's Hearing Loss

Richard E. Carmen, AuD, an audiologist and editor, co-author or author of several books, including editor of *The Consumer Handbook on Hearing Loss & Hearing Aids,* and author of *How Hearing Loss Impacts Relationships: Motivating Your Loved One* (both from Auricle Ink).

About 36 million Americans suffer from hearing loss—but only one in five people who would benefit from a hearing aid actually wears one.

How does untreated hearing loss affect the sufferer's loved ones? Over time, it can seriously strain—even destroy—a marriage or parent-child relationship due, for example, to misunderstandings and frayed nerves in the person who must constantly repeat himself/herself. *Fortunately, you can motivate your loved one to take action…*

MORE THAN JUST HEARING LOSS

Understanding the full extent to which hearing loss impacts your loved one will strengthen your resolve to motivate him to get treatment. The psychological effects are huge. People with untreated hearing loss tend to become withdrawn and are significantly more prone to depression and anxiety than those with adequate hearing. Anger, confusion, discouragement, loss of self-esteem and shame often occur as well.

Important recent discovery: Researchers at Johns Hopkins University and the National Institute on Aging found that even mild hearing loss was associated with twice the risk for dementia, while people with severe hearing loss were five times more likely to develop the condition—a link that gives sufferers yet another reason to consider getting hearing aids.

BREAKING THROUGH DENIAL

More than two-thirds of people who refuse hearing aids do so because they think "my hearing isn't bad enough," according to research conducted by the National Council on Aging. It is also easy for the person with hearing loss to blame other people ("you're just mumbling").

The most direct way to respond to this situation is to use "tough love." This means that you must stop being your loved one's ears. Take sensible steps to optimize communication—for example, speak clearly and face to face, not from another room. However, do not repeat yourself every time your loved one asks what you said and don't shout yourself hoarse just so he can hear. If you stop filling in the information that your loved one isn't hearing, he will be more likely to get treated.

Helpful: Tell your loved one that you're going to begin this practice out of love and concern and to make both your lives better. It is not a step that you're taking out of anger or vindictiveness.

If it feels too extreme to stop helping your loved one when he doesn't hear something, try this: Keep repeating yourself and/or conveying what others are saying, but preface it each time with the phrase "hearing help." This reminds your loved one of the hearing problem without cutting off communication.

Important: If you can't bear to try one of these approaches with your loved one, take an honest look at your own feelings about the situation. Is it possible that you find some degree of satisfaction in being your spouse's or parent's link to the world and having that person depend on you so much? Wanting to help is a wonderful human trait, but when you *need* to help your loved one, it locks you both into a pattern of codependence. If you suspect that you're caught in such a cycle, seeing a therapist can help—even in just a session or two.

KNOWLEDGE IS POWER

If your loved one recognizes his hearing problem but still won't get treated, here are some possible reasons why—and how to respond...

•**Vanity.** Research shows that 20% of those who refuse to have their hearing corrected said the following about using a hearing aid: "It makes me feel old"..."I'm too embarrassed to wear one"...or "I don't like what others will think of me."

What to do: Tell your loved one that the inability to hear is far more noticeable than a hearing aid and may well be interpreted as a cognitive problem or other illness. Then ask your loved one if he is familiar with modern hearing devices, which are much smaller and far less intrusive than those used years ago.

•**Expense.** Even many people who can well afford the cost of a hearing aid use price as an excuse to avoid treatment.

What to do: Ask if your loved one knows exactly how much hearing aids cost. Mention that many different devices are available and that costs vary widely.

Then remind your loved one how hearing loss impacts his life, yours and other family members'—and ask, "What's it worth for you to keep these relationships intact?"

•**Inferior equipment.** Many people say, "I've been told that hearing aids don't work so well."

What to do: Ask for the source of your loved one's information to determine how reliable it is. Then ask whether he's willing to take a 30-day trial to test the effectiveness of hearing aids. Most state laws mandate a trial period. Check

local laws by contacting your state's Department of Consumer Affairs. If your state does not require a 30-day trial, ask that it be written into any hearing-aid sales agreement—reputable sellers will agree to this.

If a loved one says, "I tried hearing aids and they didn't work," find out when and where the devices were purchased and suggest that he go to another audiologist. To find one near you, check with the American Academy of Audiology, *www.audiology.org*.

STRONG MEDICINE

If you try these approaches and your loved one still won't address his hearing loss, even stronger actions may be necessary. Be sure to consider your loved one's personality—can he deal with more direct confrontation, even if done in a gentle, loving way?

If so, you might try...

•**Videotape.** Make a videotape of your loved one in a situation where he struggles to hear, such as a family get-together. Then sit down and view the tape with him privately to prevent embarrassment.

•**Intervention.** Without prior warning to the loved one, family members meet with him for 10 to 15 minutes to talk about how the problem has affected them. The overall message of the meeting should be how much the family members care...and want a higher quality of life for the person with hearing loss (and for themselves).

Don't Let Your Bed Partner Ruin Your Sleep

Jeffry H. Larson, PhD, licensed marriage and family therapist and professor of marriage and family therapy at the School of Family Life at Brigham Young University in Provo, Utah. He is author of *The Great Marriage Tune-Up Book: A Proven Program for Evaluating and Renewing Your Relationship* (both from Jossey-Bass).

Sooner or later, one in every four American couples ends up sleeping in separate beds. Maybe it's your spouse's tossing and turning or TV watching in bed. Whatever the reason, it may seem easier just to turn that spare bedroom into a nighttime sanctuary of your own. But is that arrangement healthy?

Recent thinking: Even with the challenges that can come with sharing a bed, the net effect is usually positive for your health. While the exact mechanism is unknown, scientists believe that sleeping with a bed partner curbs levels of the stress hormone cortisol and inflammation-promoting proteins known as cytokines…while boosting levels of the so-called "love" hormone oxytocin.

Sleeping in the same bed also cultivates feelings of intimacy and security, which can strengthen a relationship and promote better sleep—factors linked to living a longer life. *Here, therapist Jeffry Larson, PhD, offers six common challenges and how to overcome them…*

•**You like to keep the room dark, while your partner prefers it light.** Sleep experts recommend keeping the room dark to help stimulate the production of the naturally occurring sleep hormone melatonin.

My advice: Room-darkening shades or light-blocking curtains help create the darkness we need for a good night's rest. But if your partner insists on having some light in the room, consider placing a dim night-light near his/her side of the bed. The person who prefers darkness may want to wear a sleep mask.

•**You're always cold, but your bed partner is too warm.** Sleep experts agree that a cooler room is generally more conducive to sleep and complements the natural temperature drop that occurs in the body when you go to sleep.

My advice: Optimal room temperature for the best sleep varies from person to person—most insomnia experts recommend a range of 60°F to 68°F. To help achieve your personal comfort level, use separate blankets so you can easily cover yourself or remove the blanket during the night without disturbing your bed partner. If you like to use an electric blanket during the winter, choose one with separate temperature controls.

•**You're a night owl, but your partner is a lark.** If the two bed partners prefer different bedtimes, this can cause both of them to

lose sleep and can be a major contributor to marital strife. In a study involving 150 couples, which I conducted with several colleagues at Brigham Young University, the University of Nebraska–Lincoln and Montana State University, those who had mismatched body clocks argued more, spent less time doing shared activities and had slightly less sex.

The first step in trying to resolve conflicting bedtimes is to understand that one's circadian rhythm, the internal body clock that regulates sleep and wakefulness as well as other biological processes, dictates whether you are a natural early riser or a night owl. One's particular circadian rhythm is determined by genetics but can be influenced by sunlight, time zone changes and work schedules. Bedtime tendencies also can be socially learned.

My advice: Have a conversation with your partner. Avoid blaming the other party for having a different sleep schedule—we can't control our circadian rhythms or such factors as work schedules. Then, like everything else in a partnership, you'll need to compromise.

For instance, say your partner likes to go to bed at 10 pm and get up at 6 am, while you're rarely in bed before 1 am and sleep until 10 am. As a compromise, you might agree to get in bed with your partner at 9:30 pm to talk, snuggle, relax, read together, etc. Then, when your partner is ready to go to sleep, you can get up and continue with your night. Alternatively, you and your partner could agree to go to bed at the same time two or three nights a week. A night owl could also lie in bed and listen to music or an audiobook with headphones while his partner sleeps.

•**Your bed partner wants to watch TV, but you want peace and quiet.** Watching TV—or looking at any illuminated screen, such as a laptop or smartphone—promotes wakefulness and can interfere with sleep. So it's not really something anyone should do just before lights out. However, if one partner wants to watch TV or use a laptop before bed, he should do it in another room.

•**Your partner thrashes all night long.** Some individuals are naturally restless sleepers, tossing and turning throughout the night.

Others may have restless legs syndrome (RLS) and/or periodic limb movement disorder (PLMD)—two related but distinct conditions.

RLS causes unpleasant sensations, such as tingling and burning, in the legs and an overwhelming urge to move them when the sufferer is sitting or attempting to sleep. PLMD causes involuntary movements and jerking of the limbs during sleep—the legs are most often affected but arm movements also can occur.

With RLS, the sufferer is aware of the problem. Individuals with PLMD, on the other hand, frequently are not aware that they move so much.

My advice: To help ease symptoms, you may want to try natural strategies such as taking warm baths, walking regularly and/or using magnesium supplements, which also promote sleep. But be sure to check with a doctor. If you have RLS or PLMD, it could signal an underlying health condition, such as iron deficiency.

If symptoms persist, you may want to talk to the doctor about medications such as *ropinirole* (Requip) and *pramipexole* (Mirapex), which can help relieve symptoms. Side effects may include nausea and drowsiness. (For more information on RLS see page 52.)

•**Your partner snores a lot**—and loudly. This is not only a nuisance, it also makes it hard for you to sleep.

ADHD May Be Sleep Apnea

Children diagnosed with ADHD may have a sleep disorder instead. Breathing problems from sleep apnea can cause chronic sleep deprivation, which may lead to behavioral problems associated with attention-deficit/hyperactivity disorder (ADHD).

Conditions that can produce sleep apnea in kids: Small jaws...large tongues... enlarged adenoids and/or tonsils. If a child breathes noisily during sleep, consult a pediatrician.

Chris Meletis, ND, executive director of Institute for Healthy Aging and author of *The Awakening of a Sleeping America* (Greenwood).

My advice: In some cases, running a fan, listening to music through earbuds or using a white-noise machine can help.

If the snoring occurs almost every night, however, your partner may need to see an otolaryngologist (ear, nose and throat doctor) to determine whether there's an underlying medical condition.

Loud snoring that is accompanied by periods in which the person's breathing stops for a few seconds and then resumes may indicate sleep apnea, a serious—but treatable—disorder usually caused by a blocked or narrowed airway.

Study Sees No Vaccine-Autism Link

Frank DeStefano, MD, MPH, director, Immunization Safety Office, US Centers for Disease Control and Prevention, Atlanta.

Paul Offit, MD, chief, infectious diseases, Children's Hospital of Philadelphia; Geraldine Dawson, PhD, chief science officer, Autism Speaks, New York City.

Geraldine Dawson, PhD, chief science officer for Autism Speaks.

Journal of Pediatrics, online

Although some parents worry about the sheer number of vaccines babies typically receive, a recent US government study finds no evidence that more vaccinations increase the risk of autism.

"This should give more reassurance to parents," said lead researcher Frank DeStefano, MD, MPH, director of the CDC's Immunization Safety Office.

The findings, which appear online in the *Journal of Pediatrics,* cast further doubt on a link between vaccines and autism spectrum disorders—a group of developmental brain disorders that impair a child's ability to communicate and socialize.

The first concerns that vaccines could lead to autism came from a small British study in 1998 that proposed a connection between the measles-mumps-rubella (MMR) vaccine and socializing disabilities in children. A spate of research since has found no link, and the original study was eventually retracted by the *Lancet,* the journal that published it.

Then came worries about thimerosal, a preservative once used in certain childhood vaccines (but never MMR) that contains small amounts of ethyl mercury. Again, international studies failed to show a link to autism.

More recently, concerns have shifted to the notion that children are getting "too many vaccinations, too soon." In the United States, children can be immunized against 14 different diseases by the time they are two.

STUDY DETAILS

Looking at about 1,000 US children with or without autism, researchers at the Centers for Disease Control and Prevention found no connection between early childhood vaccinations and autism risk.

The findings are based on 256 children with an autism spectrum disorder and 752 autism-free kids who were matched to them based on age, sex and health insurance plan.

The children with autism and those without had the same total exposure to vaccine antigens—the substances in vaccines that trigger the immune system to develop infection-fighting antibodies.

Dr. DeStefano said his team focused on antigen exposure, rather than just the number of vaccinations, because that gives a more precise idea of the "immune system stimulation" kids received through vaccines.

The CDC team found that kids' total antigen exposure in the first two years of life was unrelated to their risk of developing an autism disorder.

That was also true when they considered babies' antigen exposure in the first three months of life, and the first seven months. Nor was there any connection between autism risk and the amount of vaccine antigens children received on any single day.

"This provides evidence that concerns about immune system overstimulation are unfounded," Dr. DeStefano said.

Every day, babies' immune systems battle many more antigens than are present in vaccines, Dr. DeStefano explained. "Most infants can handle exposure to many antigens," he said.

Children and Too Much TV

Children who play in rooms where a TV is on and tuned to an adult show spend less time with individual toys and switch their attention more quickly from one activity to another—compared with their behavior when the television is off. And kids pay less attention to what a parent says when a TV is on in the background.

Troubling: Children younger than age eight spend nearly four hours a day near unattended televisions—and those from eight months to two years old have a TV on, in the background, for an average of nearly six hours a day.

Study of more than 1,500 households with at least one child between eight months and eight years old by researchers from the University of North Carolina Wilmington, University of Iowa, Iowa City, and University of Amsterdam, the Netherlands, published in *Pediatrics*.

EXPERT COMMENTARY: DON'T DELAY VACCINATION

A recent survey found that about one-third of parents thought children receive too many vaccinations in their first two years of life, and that the shots could contribute to autism.

But there's no scientific evidence of that, said Paul Offit, MD, chief of infectious diseases at the Children's Hospital of Philadelphia.

He said it's understandable that parents might worry. "You see your baby receiving all these vaccines. It looks like too much. It feels like too much," Dr. Offit said.

But, he said, there's no biological basis for the idea that vaccines "overstimulate" the immune system, and that somehow leads to autism.

Geraldine Dawson, PhD, chief science officer for the advocacy group Autism Speaks, said the study "adds to the existing literature showing no connection between vaccines and autism in large epidemiological studies."

She added, though, that further research is needed "to explore whether, in rare cases, a genetic vulnerability might increase susceptibility to vaccine-related side effects, including the triggering of autism symptoms in a genetically and medically susceptible child."

Both Drs. Offit and DeStefano stressed that there is no reason for parents to delay vaccinating their child.

"This is one more piece of evidence to help reassure parents," Dr. Offit said.

info The American Academy of Pediatrics has information on vaccine safety at its Web site, *www.aap.org/immunization/families/ safety.html.*

Most Kids With Autism Overcome Language Delays

Ericka Wodka, MD, neuropsychologist, assistant professor of psychiatry, Kennedy Krieger Institute Center for Autism and Related Disorders, Baltimore.

Andrew Adesman, MD, chief of developmental and behavioral pediatrics, Steven and Alexandra Cohen Children's Medical Center of New York, New Hyde Park.

Sarah Paterson, PhD, scientist, Developmental Neuroimaging Laboratory, Children's Hospital of Philadelphia.

Pediatrics

Severe language delays early in the life of a child with autism can be overcome, especially if a child exhibits nonverbal intelligence.

A recent study that looked at speech delays in children with autism spectrum disorders found that 70% of children who were not stringing words together into even the simplest of phrases by age four went on to do so by age eight, and in some cases, even achieved fluent speech.

"Autism spectrum disorders" is an umbrella term for neurodevelopmental conditions ranging from Asperger's syndrome to severe autism. Hallmarks of these conditions include problems with social interaction and repetitive behaviors.

The findings, published in the journal *Pediatrics,* offer hope, said lead author Ericka Wodka, MD, a neuropsychologist and assistant professor of psychiatry at the Kennedy Krieger Institute's Center for Autism and Related Disorders, in Baltimore.

"The study gives doctors and parents a sense that when these delays persist—when a child presents at age six or seven without phrase speech—they still have growth opportunity," Dr. Wodka said. "There's still a lot of hope that these children can go on to gain meaningful language."

The scientists evaluated data on more than 500 children with an autism spectrum disorder who were part of a national multisite study that involved complete evaluations on every child.

"Our data are based on actual measurements of current functioning and parent interviews, not chart review," Dr. Wodka said.

As toddlers, none of the children in the study had achieved "phrase speech," the ability to put together more than two or three words to communicate—to say basic sentences such as, "I want juice," for example.

Demographics—including parent income and education level, and child psychiatric characteristics—were not associated with whether a child with language delay attained phrase speech, Dr. Wodka said. Repetitive behaviors, such as hand-flapping, were not linked with delayed speech either.

Strong predictors of a child's ability to go on to develop phrase or fluent speech skills included his or her non-verbal IQ and being less impaired socially, Dr. Wodka said.

EXPERTS COMMENT

The size of the study lends the findings weight, said Sarah Paterson, PhD, a scientist in the Developmental Neuroimaging Laboratory at the Children's Hospital of Philadelphia. Dr. Paterson conducts brain imaging and cognitive studies of infants at risk for autism.

"There is a large number of children involved," Dr. Paterson said. "It's hard to get a sample that big in an autism study and I think it gives us some insight into what's happening with language."

Dr. Paterson said the results are not surprising. "I think the take-home message is that, as we've thought for a long time, social skills and nonverbal communication skills really are building blocks for language. Those who do have those skills generally have better language than those who don't."

Parents need to keep the results in perspective, though, said another autism expert.

"Parents should be cautious about applying statistics from studies like these to their individual child's outcome," said Andrew Adesman, MD, chief of developmental and behavioral pediatrics at Cohen Children's Medical Center of New York, in New Hyde Park.

Dr. Adesman said it's also important to note that although autism has to be considered whenever evaluating a child with language delay, the majority of children with language delay at age two or three don't have an autism spectrum disorder. "That's an important point," he said. "This study wasn't looking at severe language delay without diagnosis of autism."

Dr. Adesman said if children have good nonverbal communication skills—if they use gestures to communicate even though they don't use words, for example, and if they engage with people appropriately and are socially responsive—that would suggest something other than autism spectrum disorder is the likely cause of language delay.

WHAT PARENTS CAN DO

Parents with concerns about their toddler's lack of language development can ask their pediatrician about autism screening, or look for a community resource. "Every child can get a free evaluation when language delay is suspected," he said.

Dr. Wodka said she hopes the study findings will help guide parents and health professionals who work with children with autism to set both language and behavioral goals.

"What complicates issues for children with autism is that it's not purely a language disorder," she said. "It's a communication disorder, and it's important to consider the child's intellectual level as well as the social issues."

info Visit the US National Institute of Mental Health Web site at *www.nimh.nih.gov* (search "autism") to learn more about autism.

The "Kiss" That Unblocks Noses

Stephanie Cook, BM, BCh, a general practitioner in East Sussex, England, and lead author of a review on the safety and efficacy of the "mother's kiss." The study was conducted when Dr. Cook was at Buxted Medical Centre and was published in *Canadian Medical Association Journal*.

If you have children or grandkids, you might be called upon to perform this nifty trick to remove stuck objects out of tiny noses. After all, it's quite common for tots to stick raisins, seeds, pebbles, Legos or other stuff up their nostrils. *So here's what you need to know...*

The info comes from a recent review of case reports examining the safety and effectiveness of a technique called the "mother's kiss." Though first described in the medical literature back in 1965, the technique is not widely known. The researchers found that it was effective about 60% of the time...worked on both smooth objects and irregularly shaped ones... and had been used on children ranging in age from one to eight years old. No adverse effects were reported.

One main advantage of the technique is that it may prevent the need for a child to receive general anesthesia simply to remove a foreign body from the nose, researchers said. The technique generally is safe, with no minimum age limit on its use.

Be prepared: The researchers recommended that the "mother's kiss" be done under medical supervision unless a parent (or grandparent) is familiar with it, in which case it could be done at home. So familiarize yourself! Talk to your child's doctor now...ask if it would be OK to try the technique if ever the need should arise...and review the instructions together to make sure you understand how to do it properly. Keep the following instructions in a handy location.

When the moment comes: Start by telling the youngster that you are going to give her (or him) a "big kiss" so she has an idea of what to expect. Place your mouth over her open mouth to form a firm seal, as if you were about to give mouth-to-mouth resuscitation, and gently hold the unaffected nostril closed with a finger. Gently blow until you feel resistance caused by closure of the child's glottis (the opening between the vocal cords)...then exhale a short, sharp puff of air into her mouth, using about the same amount of pressure as would be generated by a sneeze. You may have to repeat the technique a number of times, but if the object isn't pushed too far inside, it should come out.

What if the darn thing stays stuck despite your best "kisses"? Do not try to pull it out with tweezers or suck it out with a rubber bulb syringe. Such implements could push the object farther in, with a risk of it winding up in the child's airway or lung. Instead, it's time to let a health-care professional take over the extraction. Don't delay—the longer an object is left inside the nose, the harder it may be to remove.

Keep Tots' Milk to Two Cups a Day

Jonathon Maguire, MD, pediatrician and scientist, St. Michael's Hospital, Toronto.
Emilia Baczek, RD, pediatric nutritionist, La Rabida Children's Hospital, Chicago.
Pediatrics

D rinking two cups of milk a day gives toddlers adequate amounts of vitamin D without lowering their iron levels, according to recent research.

Vitamin D and iron are crucial nutrients, especially for toddlers' growing brains and bodies. In this study, researchers confirmed that there's a tradeoff between the two when consumption of cow's milk exceeds two cups a day.

"We found that...around two cups a day is appropriate. For the average child, any more milk than that seems to reduce iron stores," explained study author Jonathon Maguire, MD, a pediatrician and scientist at St. Michael's Hospital in Toronto.

Before this study, which was published online in the journal *Pediatrics*, milk recommendations haven't always been clear, Dr. Maguire explained.

Vitamin D helps the body absorb calcium, which is necessary to develop strong bones. Vitamin D also may help prevent autoimmune, respiratory and cardiovascular diseases, according to background information in the study. Vitamin D is found mostly in fortified foods, such as milk. The body also produces vitamin D after sunlight exposure.

Iron is needed for brain development. A shortage of iron, even if it's not severe enough to be diagnosed as anemia, can impair development of physical and mental skills, according to the study.

STUDY DETAILS

To see if they could come up with a recommendation that would take into account both vitamin D and iron, Dr. Maguire and his colleagues recruited more than 1,300 toddlers between two and five years old. Parents reported how much milk the youngsters usually consumed. The children's vitamin D and iron levels were measured through a blood test.

The researchers found that as cow's milk consumption increased, vitamin D levels increased but iron levels decreased. Two cups of cow's milk daily provided sufficient vitamin D for most children, according to the study. For children with darker skin pigmentation during the winter months, however, two cups of milk wasn't enough to maintain adequate vitamin D levels. (Darker skin pigmentation makes it harder for the sun's rays to trigger vitamin D production.)

The study's authors suggested that for these children, wintertime supplementation with vitamin D might be necessary.

The researchers also found that drinking from a bottle didn't raise vitamin D levels, but it did result in lower iron levels. This supported some previous studies that suggested children using a bottle are at increased risk of iron deficiency.

In most cases, Dr. Maguire said it's likely that the low iron resulted from the kids drinking so much milk that they were too full to have other foods that contain sufficient iron.

"Milk is a very good source of nutrition, but only up to a point," he said. "Too much of a good thing may not be a good thing."

Emilia Baczek, a pediatric nutritionist at La Rabida Children's Hospital in Chicago, said that although vitamin D doesn't affect iron levels, calcium—which is also found in abundance in milk—can interfere with the body's absorption of iron.

"The calcium makes iron absorption a little bit harder," Baczek said. "Toddlers often aren't getting enough iron in their diet in the first place."

Baczek said she agrees with the recommendation to get two cups of milk daily. "It's enough to promote adequate vitamin D with minimal decreases in [iron]," she said.

Although it's important to drink milk, it's important to remember that it's only one part of a healthy diet, she added.

Baczek said for those who need vitamin D supplements, the daily recommended amount for kids older than one year is 600 international units a day.

More information: Learn more about toddler nutrition from the American Academy of Pediatrics Web site *www.healthychildren.org* (click on "Ages and Stages," then "Toddler," then "Nutrition").

Let Babies "Cry It Out," Study Suggests

Temple University, news release.

Most babies who wake up during the night should be allowed to self-soothe and fall back to sleep on their own, researchers say.

"By six months of age, most babies sleep through the night, awakening their mothers only about once per week. However, not all children follow this pattern of development," said Marsha Weinraub, PhD, Temple University psychology professor.

"If you measure them while they are sleeping, all babies—like all adults—move through a sleep cycle every one-and-a-half to two hours where they wake up and then return to sleep. Some of them do cry and call out when they awaken, and that is called 'not sleeping through the night,'" she added.

STUDY DETAILS

In conducting the study, researchers led by Dr. Weinraub examined patterns of awakenings during the night among more than 1,200 infants ranging in age from six months to 36 months. The researchers asked the babies' parents about their child's awakenings during the night at six, 15, 24 and 36 months of life. Based on their findings, the researchers divided the babies into two groups—sleepers and transitional sleepers.

By six months of age, 66% of babies considered "sleepers" did not wake up at night or woke up only once per week, the study revealed.

Meanwhile, at the same age, 33% of the children woke up seven nights per week. By the time these babies were 15 months old, they were only waking up two nights per week. At 24 months old, nighttime awakenings dropped to just one night per week, the investigators found.

Most of the babies that woke during the night were boys. These babies—considered transitional sleepers—were also assessed as being more irritable or difficult. They were also more likely to be breast-fed. The mothers of these transitional sleepers were more likely to be depressed and have greater maternal sensitivity, the study authors found.

The authors concluded that genetic factors could play a role in difficult temperaments. "Families who are seeing sleep problems persist past 18 months should seek advice," Dr. Weinraub advised.

BABIES NEED TO LEARN HOW TO FALL ASLEEP

Babies should learn how to fall asleep without help, the researchers added. "When mothers tune in to these nighttime awakenings and/or if a baby is in the habit of falling asleep during breast-feeding, then he or she may not be learning how to self-soothe, something that is critical for regular sleep," Dr. Weinraub said.

"Because the mothers in our study described infants with many awakenings per week as creating problems for themselves and other family members, parents might be encouraged to establish more nuanced and carefully targeted routines to help babies with self-soothing and to seek occasional respite," Dr. Weinraub noted. "The best advice is to put infants to bed at a regular time every night, allow them to fall asleep on their own and resist the urge to respond right away to awakenings."

The study was recently published in *Developmental Psychology*.

info The American Academy of Pediatrics provides tips on how to get your baby to sleep at its Web site, *www.healthychildren. org* (search "Getting Your Baby to Sleep").

Teething Baby? Avoid *Benzocaine,* FDA Says

Consumer update, US Food and Drug Administration.

Parents should not use products containing *benzocaine* to relieve teething pain in babies except under the advice and supervision of a health care professional, the US Food and Drug Administration (FDA) says.

Benzocaine is a local anesthetic found in over-the-counter products such as Anbesol, Orajel, Baby Orajel, Orabase and Hurricane.

The use of benzocaine gels and liquids to relieve gum and mouth pain can lead to a rare but potentially deadly condition called methemoglobinemia, in which the amount of oxygen carried through the bloodstream is greatly reduced. Children under two years old are at particular risk for the condition, according to the FDA.

The agency first warned about the potential dangers of benzocaine in 2006 and has since received 29 reports of benzocaine gel-related cases of methemoglobinemia. Nineteen of those cases occurred in children, 15 of them under two years of age.

The FDA also noted that parents may have difficulty recognizing the symptoms of methemoglobinemia, which include pale, gray or blue-colored skin, lips and nail beds…shortness of breath…fatigue…confusion…headache…light-headedness and rapid heart rate.

Symptoms can occur within minutes to hours after benzocaine is applied (for the first time or after several uses). Parents should immediately call 911 (or the local emergency number outside the United States) if a child has symptoms of methemoglobinemia, the FDA said.

WHAT TO USE INSTEAD

Instead of using benzocaine to ease teething pain, the American Academy of Pediatrics suggests that parents give a child a teething ring chilled in the refrigerator, or use a finger to gently rub or massage the child's gums.

info The MedlinePlus Medical Encyclopedia has more about teething at its Web site, *www.nlm.nih.gov/medlineplus/* (search "teething").

Drugs Hold Promise for Severe Juvenile Arthritis Patients

Nicolino Ruperto, MD, MPH, Istituto G. Gaslini, Di Ricovero e Cura a Carattere Scientifico (IRCCS) Istituto Gaslini, Genoa, Italy.

Patience White, MD, vice president for public health, Arthritis Foundation, and professor of pediatrics and medicine at George Washington University School of Medicine and Health Sciences, Washington, DC.

New England Journal of Medicine

Children who suffer from a rare and painful form of arthritis that's accompanied by fever and rashes may soon have more treatment options.

Two studies published in a recent issue of the *New England Journal of Medicine* suggest that two drugs—*canakinumab* and *tocilizumab*—reduce symptoms, including severe joint pain experienced by children with systemic juvenile idiopathic arthritis (JIA).

The disease is one of seven types of juvenile idiopathic arthritis that affect one in 1,000, or roughly 294,000, children in the United States, according to the US National Institutes of Health. It is characterized by inflammation of one or more joints, fever and rash, among other health problems. "Idiopathic" means the cause is unknown.

"Systemic juvenile idiopathic arthritis is a form of severe arthritis that until a few years ago was treated mainly with corticosteroids, which have known side effects, especially growth impairment," said Nicolino Ruperto, MD, a pediatric rheumatologist at G. Gaslini Children's Hospital in Genoa and coauthor of the studies.

TWO DRUGS MAY BRING NEEDED RELIEF

The research looked at the safety and effectiveness of the interleukin-1 inhibitor canakinumab and the interleukin-6 inhibitor tocilizumab.

In the canakinumab study, funded by drug maker Novartis Pharma, two trials took place. In one, patients received the drug subcutaneously (injected just below the skin) or a placebo. In the other, canakinumab was taken knowingly, or open-label.

"The study demonstrated that among 190 children with systemic JIA, about 60% of the children treated for several months had a complete disappearance of both arthritis, fever and rash," said Dr. Ruperto. One-third also discontinued corticosteroids, he said.

Dr. Ruperto said canakinumab works by reducing the level of a cytokine (a protein) called interleukin-1 that leads to the inflammation—the arthritis and fever—in children with systemic juvenile idiopathic arthritis.

In the study of tocilizumab, researchers from the Ospedale Pediatrico Bambino Gesu, a children's hospital in Rome, randomly assigned 112 children, aged two to 17, with systemic juvenile idiopathic arthritis to one of two doses given intravenously or a placebo every two weeks for three months. Patients who did not respond were offered the drug open label after that and followed for about a year. At 12 weeks, 71% who received tocilizumab had no fever and improved pain compared with 8% in the placebo group. The drug maker Hoffmann La Roche funded this study.

WHAT EXPERTS SAY

The research breaks new ground, according to Christy Sandborg, MD, and Elizabeth Mellins, MD, both from Stanford University, who wrote an accompanying journal editorial. "There is no doubt that the agents tested in these trials signal a new era in the treatment of systemic JIA and will shed light on the mechanisms driving this enigmatic disorder," they wrote.

But Drs. Sandborg and Mellins also said important questions remain about the drugs' side effects, and they noted that some children in the trials experienced macrophage activation syndrome, a serious, systemwide inflammation that is a complication of JIA and could also be related to the interleukin drugs.

Patience White, MD, vice president for public health at the Arthritis Foundation and a professor of pediatrics and medicine at George Washington University School of Medicine and Health Sciences, said, "These trials are very exciting because the response rates are much better than responses to other biologic drug trials to date."

Still, concerns exist. "While it is exciting work, from a parent point of view, it can be an anxiety-provoking decision to decide to start their child on a new drug for which the full side-effect profile is not known," she said.

Dr. White said that neither drug has a long track record in treating this condition, and unknown side effects don't always arise in early drug trials. Mass-market use sometimes reveals additional pros and cons of a medication.

She said families interested in trying the interleukin drugs should first see a physician who specializes in juvenile rheumatology. "See someone who knows about these drugs, and make sure your child is part of a registry so that everybody learns from the experience with it," she said.

WHAT'S AVAILABLE NOW AND WHAT'S TO COME

Currently, only tocilizumab is approved to treat systemic juvenile idiopathic arthritis, said Dr. Ruperto. For canakinumab, the evaluation process is ongoing in the United States and Europe. If it's approved, he said, "It is likely that insurance companies will have to pay for it."

"Before this," said Dr. White, "we really haven't had drugs that really made that much difference whereas these clearly do. The beauty of these trials is that they're opening up opportunity to see the results of targeting new steps in the inflammatory process."

info The US National Institutes of Health has more about juvenile arthritis at its Web site, *http://ghr.nlm.nih.gov/condition/juvenile-idiopathic-arthritis*.

Honey a Sweet Remedy For Kids' Coughs

Herman Avner Cohen, MD, professor and chairman, Pediatric Community Ambulatory Center, and Clalit Health Services, Petah-Tikva, Israel, and Sackler Faculty of Medicine, Tel-Aviv University.

Ian Paul, MD, professor, pediatrics, Penn State College of Medicine, Hershey, Pennsylvania, and member, American Academy of Pediatrics' committee on drugs.

Pediatrics

Instead of reaching for a commercial medicine when your child is coughing through the night because of a common cold, Israeli researchers suggest giving honey a try.

A teaspoon or two of honey before bedtime can safely relieve the symptoms of an upper respiratory tract infection, they report.

"The cough due to a viral [upper respiratory infection] is generally a self-limited disease," said study author Herman Avner Cohen, MD, chairman of the Pediatric Community Ambulatory Care Clinic with Clalit Health Services in Petah-Tikva, Israel.

"However, parents often [want] some active intervention," Dr. Cohen said. This often leads to the use of over-the-counter cough medications, which are potentially dangerous because of the possibility of accidental overdose, he said.

For this reason, "honey may be a preferable treatment for the cough and sleep difficulty associated with childhood [upper respiratory infection]," said Dr. Cohen, who also hails from Sackler Faculty of Medicine at Israel's Tel-Aviv University.

"In light of our study, honey can be considered an effective and safe alternative, at least for those children over one year of age," he said.

HOW HONEY MIGHT HELP TO HEAL COUGHS

The authors pointed out that honey has long been appreciated for its antioxidant properties, derived from vitamin C and flavonoids among other sources. It is also known for its antimicrobial potential.

Some researchers have suggested that the proximity of the nerve fibers that control coughing with the nerve fibers that control sweetness may empower sweet substances with a natural ability to suppress coughing.

Still others believe the syrupy thickness of honey, alongside its ability to cause salivation (and thereby throat lubrication), are key characteristics that might explain its potential as an anti-coughing intervention.

STUDY DETAILS

To test honey's therapeutic potential, Cohen and his colleagues focused on 300 children between the ages of one and five, all of whom had been diagnosed with upper respiratory infections.

The children, who were brought in to one of six pediatric clinics in Israel, had been ill for seven days or less and all suffered from nighttime coughing and runny noses. None had signs of asthma or pneumonia.

The children were randomly given one of four possible treatments a half hour before bed—roughly two teaspoons of eucalyptus honey, citrus honey or libiatae honey, or an extract that tasted and looked like honey but contained none.

Based on parents' responses to a survey completed the day before treatment and the day after, the research team found that while all the children showed improvement in terms of sleep quality and coughing severity, those who received honey fared significantly better than those who consumed the non-honey extract.

The authors thereby concluded that honey might be a "preferable treatment" to relieve the kinds of symptoms that typify childhood upper respiratory infection.

Cohen's investigation, funded by the Israel Ambulatory Pediatric Association, the Materna Infant Nutrition Research Institute and the Honey Board of Israel, was published in the journal *Pediatrics*.

EXPERT CONFIRMATION

As an expert on the subject of honey as a potential treatment for respiratory infection, Ian Paul, MD, a professor of pediatrics at Penn State College of Medicine, was not surprised by the findings.

"Honey is an effective alternative to over-the-counter cold and cough medicines," he noted.

"In fact, we found that honey was the best treatment and provided the most relief."

The bottom line for parents is that the common medicines that many families use are "not very effective, if at all, and there's potential for side effects," said Dr. Paul, who is also a member of the American Academy of Pediatrics' committee on drugs. "Whereas honey for children over the age of one is both safe and highly effective."

info For more information on upper respiratory infections, visit the US National Institutes of Health Web site at *www.nlm.nih.gov* (search "Common Cold").

Easier Ways to Give Children Medicine

Ask your doctor for more concentrated medication—if the medicine is twice as strong, the child has to swallow only half as much. Try chilling liquid medicine to improve the taste. Taste medication yourself—and tell the child if it tastes bad so that he/she can get ready. Rub an ice cube over a child's taste buds to numb them and reduce a bad taste.

Vicki Lansky has written more than 30 books, including *Practical Parenting Tips: New Edition* (Book Peddlers). She is based in Deephaven, Minnesota.

Doctors to Parents: No Trampolines

Robert Glatter, MD, emergency physician, Lenox Hill Hospital, New York City.
Pediatrics

Trampolines may be hazardous to your child's health, pediatricians warn. The American Academy of Pediatrics reaffirms its earlier cautions about home trampoline use in a recent report, published in the journal *Pediatrics*.

"The very forces that make trampoline use fun for many children also lead to unique injury mechanisms and patterns of injury," according to the study authors. "Pediatricians should only endorse use of trampolines as part of a structured training program with appropriate coaching supervision and safety measures in place."

TRAMPOLINE-RELATED INJURIES

Rates of trampoline-related injuries have decreased since 2004, but accidents still happen and many have serious consequences, they added.

Nearly 98,000 trampoline-related injuries occurred in the United States in 2009, which resulted in 3,100 hospitalizations, according to the National Electronic Injury Surveillance System. Children appear to be injured more often than older jumpers.

Fractures and dislocation accounted for nearly half the injuries treated in kids ages five and younger, according to the academy, a professional association of pediatricians.

Common injuries in all age groups include sprains, strains and bruises. Falling off the trampoline—which accounts for up to 39% of all injuries—often has serious consequences. Likewise, doing somersaults and flips can lead to permanent head and spinal injury, the authors warned.

According to the new article, three-quarters of trampoline-related injuries take place when more than one person is on the mat, and many accidents occur when an adult is watching.

The same cautions recommended for home trampoline use apply to trampolines in jump parks, the authors added.

NEW SAFETY FEATURES DO NOT DECREASE INJURIES

Trade groups and manufacturers have made efforts to improve the safety of trampolines in recent years, adding heavier padding and stricter warnings about appropriate use, for example.

But the report says research on netting and other safety features hasn't shown a lowering of injury rates, and experts say home trampolines are still unsafe.

"Although injury rates in children associated with trampoline use have been declining since 2004, the chance of sustaining a severe injury still remains exceedingly high, even with adult supervision," said Robert Glatter, MD, an emergency medicine physician at Lenox Hill Hospital in New York City. "The use of padding with trampolines does not, in reality, safeguard against the high number of injuries on the mat, and may lead to a false sense of protection."

EXPERT RECOMMENDATIONS

Dr. Glatter said pediatricians should continue to discourage recreational trampoline use among children and teenagers. "But for those families of children who continue to engage in trampoline use, it is recommended that only a single jumper be present on the mat at any particular time," he said. He also advised against allowing flips and somersaults in a recreational environment.

info The US National Institutes of Heath Web site has more information about preventing head injuries in children, *http://www.nlm. nih.gov/medlineplus/ency/patientinstructions/ 000130.htm.*

Strict Moms Influence Kids' Friends: Study

Holly B. Shakya, PhD, postdoctoral research fellow, Gates Foundation Social Networks Project, University of California, San Diego School of Medicine.
Bruce Goldman, LCSW, director, Substance Abuse Services, Zucker Hillside Hospital, Glen Oaks, New York.
Simon Rego, PsyD, director, psychology training, Montefiore Medical Center/Albert Einstein College of Medicine, New York City.
Archives of Pediatric and Adolescent Medicine, online

Mothers who are strict with their teen children also influence the behavior of their teens' friends, a recent study suggests.

In fact, the researchers found, the friends were 40% less likely to get drunk, 38% less likely to binge drink, 39% less likely to smoke and 43% less likely to smoke marijuana, compared with friends of teens whose mothers were less strict.

"Authoritative parenting—using a style that balances warmth and communication with appropriate control and supervision—is not only associated with reduced substance abuse in our own children, but it is also associated with reduced substance abuse in our own children's friends," said lead researcher Holly Shakya, PhD, a postdoctoral research fellow with the Gates Foundation Social Networks Project at the University of California, San Diego School of Medicine.

"We also find that some of the effect may be spreading through the adolescent social network—parents' behaviors affect their children, and that effect spreads to their friends," she added.

"So, good parents may be helping both their own children and the friends of their children. Thus, the benefits of parenting interventions may be multiplied throughout the community beyond parent to child," Dr. Shakya said.

STUDY DETAILS

To reach their conclusions, Dr. Shakya's team analyzed data from several years of the National Longitudinal Study of Adolescent Health study, which is an ongoing study of teen behavior across the United States.

An authoritative parenting style "appears to create the most optimal long-term benefits for adolescents, including: academic success, positive peer relationships, minimal delinquent behavior and reduced likelihood of having delinquent peer networks, risk avoidance and positive psychosocial adjustment, including higher levels of well-being," said Simon Rego, PsyD, director of psychology training at Montefiore Medical Center/Albert Einstein College of Medicine in New York City.

The report was published in the online edition of the *Archives of Pediatric and Adolescent Medicine.*

EXPERT COMMENTARY

Bruce Goldman, LCSW, director of Substance Abuse Services at Zucker Hillside Hospital in Glen Oaks, New York, said the results of this study should be encouraging to parents "who sometimes feel out of control and that they have no influence at all—in fact, that's not true."

In addition, Dr. Rego said, adolescents appear to be influenced by more than just their peers and family members when it comes to substance abuse. The parenting practices of their friends' parents play a role in their substance abuse outcomes as well, he added.

"We may need to change the concept of parenting to include the indirect effects of the adolescent's friends' parents," he said.

Goldman also pointed out that troubled teens often seek out other teens who come from stable homes. "That can help these youths avoid negative outcomes," he said.

info For more on parenting teens, visit the Nemours Foundation Web site, *http:// kidshealth.org/parent/growth/growing/adolescence.html*.

Parents: Revealing Your Past Substance Abuse May Not Help Your Kids

Human Communication Research, news release.

It's time for that heart to heart with your kids about the dangers of smoking, drinking or illicit drugs. *One thing that's best not to bring up:* Your own dabbling in such substances in your youth, a recent study suggests.

The study found that kids are more likely to have negative views of smoking, drinking and drugs if their parents don't reveal that they used these substances.

RESEARCH DETAILS

The researchers asked 253 Hispanic and 308 white children in grades six to eight about conversations they had with their parents about alcohol, cigarettes and marijuana.

Previous research found that teens said they were less likely to use drugs if their parents told them about their own past drug use. But this recent study found that children whose parents talked to them about the negative effects of or regret over their use of alcohol, cigarettes or marijuana were less likely to oppose the use of these substances.

The researchers said their findings suggest that there may be unintended consequences for children when their parents share their history of past substance use, even if it is meant as a warning.

The study, published online recently in the journal *Human Communication Research*, did identify specific ways that parents can talk to children to discourage them from using alcohol, cigarettes or drugs.

This includes telling children about the harm caused by these substances, how to avoid them and stories about others who have gotten into trouble from using them. Parents can also tell children that they disapprove of substance use and outline family rules against substance use.

"Parents may want to reconsider whether they should talk to their kids about times when they used substances in the past and not volunteer such information," said study coauthor Jennifer Kam, of the University of Illinois at Urbana-Champaign.

"Of course, it is important to remember this study is one of the first to examine the associations between parents' references to their own past substance use and their adolescent children's subsequent perceptions and behaviors," she added.

info The American Academy of Pediatrics offers parents tips on preventing child and teen substance abuse at its Web site, *www. healthychildren.org* (search "Drug Abuse Prevention").

"Synthetic Pot" Sending Thousands of Young People to ER

Peter J. Delany, rear admiral, director, Center for Behavioral Health Statistics and Quality, US Substance Abuse and Mental Health Services Administration, Rockville, Maryland.
Adam Bisaga, MD, professor of psychiatry, Columbia University, and addiction psychiatrist, New York State Psychiatric Institute, New York City.
SAMHSA Drug Abuse Warning Network, The DAWN Report.

US emergency rooms tended to more than 11,400 cases of drug-related health complications specifically linked to the use of synthetic marijuana in 2010 (latest statistics), a recent government report reveals.

The DAWN Report from the US Substance Abuse and Mental Health Services Administration (SAMHSA) attaches a hard figure to the potential health risks associated with the growing

Inflatable Bounce Houses and Moonwalks Are Dangerous

In 2010 (most recent data available), an average 30 children a day were treated in hospital emergency rooms throughout the US for fractures, strains, and head and neck injuries from playing on inflatable bouncers.

Study of emergency departments records of children injured in inflatable bouncers by researchers at Center for Injury Research and Policy, Nationwide Children's Hospital, Columbus, Ohio, published in *Pediatrics*.

use of synthetic marijuana. The report also puts such use in context, observing, for example, that actual marijuana use accounted for far more ER visits (exceeding 461,000) in the same time frame.

"It's not an epidemic," acknowledged Rear Admiral Peter Delany, director of SAMHSA's Center for Behavioral Health Statistics and Quality. "But it's a growing problem. And people need to be thinking about it, and how we're going to deal with it."

Since it first came on the scene in the United States in 2008, synthetic marijuana has commonly been sold under the guise of being an innocuous "herbal incense," according to the White House Office of National Drug Control Policy.

Until recently, however, customers have sought it out—under names like "Spice" and "K2"—as a legal alternative to real marijuana, based on its reputation as being able to prompt a similar high.

But though it's varying ingredients are typically sprayed in liquid form on top of plant materials, such so-called "fake" marijuana is exactly that: an entirely synthesized and unlabeled chemical concoction, rather than a naturally grown plant.

In the last few years, synthetic marijuana has seen a rapid increase in popularity, particularly among American teens who initially could turn to local convenience stores and the Internet for legal access. The authors of the report point to a 2011 drug-use study that found that more than 11% of high school seniors admitted having tried the drug in the prior year.

In light of such numbers, health risk concerns led to sales restrictions in 38 states, and in the summer of 2012 the US Food and Drug Administration imposed a wholesale ban on all sales of synthetic cannabinoids.

The current SAMHSA report uses public health surveillance data on all 2.3 million drug abuse or misuse-related visits to US emergency departments in 2010 involving both male and female patients between the ages of 12 and 29 (who account for the bulk of users).

Male patients made up 78% of synthetic pot emergencies, the report team noted, compared with 66% among authentic marijuana emergencies.

Most (59%) of those seeking emergency care following synthetic marijuana use were not using any other drug at the time, while 36% had used it in conjunction with one other drug such as actual marijuana, alcohol or prescription drugs.

Most of the synthetic pot patients were ultimately discharged directly from the ER, with less than one-quarter requiring follow-up care after their initial visit, the report noted.

Nevertheless, Delany pointed out that the host of complications that can land a synthetic pot user in the emergency department in the first place are not to be taken lightly.

"I think parents and communities need to become more informed about this drug," Delany said. "They should be aware that you don't know what you're buying when you buy it. You don't know the potency and the chemical compound. And they should also know that young people who use it are ending up in the ER, due to high blood pressure, nausea, vomiting, anxiety, agitation and sometimes seizures. So you can't say this is a safe drug. Especially if you decide to mix it with other chemicals."

EXPERT RESPONSE

The thought is seconded by Adam Bisaga, MD, a professor of psychiatry at Columbia University and an addiction psychiatrist with the New York State Psychiatric Institute.

"Certainly in the context of other forms of drug abuse, the numbers they show here related to synthetic marijuana are nowhere near the numbers associated with, say, painkillers," Dr. Bisaga said.

"But with something sold as part of a 'spice package' you might think you're smoking herbs. And they're not herbs. You're not smoking tea or oregano. These are chemicals that are synthesized from scratch to act on the same receptors in the brain as real marijuana. But they are just pure chemicals, with no quality control and with the real potential to be toxic," he explained.

"So there was a time when selling them, and probably the use of them, was perceived as non-harmful," Dr. Bisaga noted. "But hopefully now, with the bans that have been put in place and the release of this kind of data, we are catching up to reality."

info For more information, visit the White House Office of National Drug Control Policy at its Web site, *www.whitehouse.gov/ ondcp* (search "synthetic marijuana").

Dangerous Rage May Be Common Among US Teens

Ronald Kessler, PhD, McNeil Family Professor of Health Care Policy, Harvard Medical School, Boston.
Simon Rego, PsyD, director, psychology training, Montefiore Medical Center, New York City.
Archives of General Psychiatry

Almost two-thirds of US teens have had an anger attack so severe they have destroyed property, or threatened or attacked another person, a recent study finds.

When these attacks persist, the syndrome is known as intermittent explosive disorder. One in 12 US teens may have the condition, which usually surfaces in late childhood, the researchers said.

"This is one of the most common adolescent disorders in America, and the most important ignored disorder among youth in America," said lead researcher Ronald Kessler, PhD, professor of Health Care Policy at Harvard Medical School in Boston.

"For reasons that are unclear to me, [this] has not been on the radar screen of the psychiatric profession," he added.

Whether the anger problem has increased or was just under-recognized is unclear, Dr. Kessler said. "But we know it's a big problem."

The condition can continue into adulthood and lead to depression and drug and alcohol abuse, he said.

While it is common for a child to have an explosion of anger, it is not normal for uncontrolled anger to be a steady pattern, Dr. Kessler said. "And if we are talking about a teen, it is definitely not normal and it really gets in the way of your life."

INHERITED TENDENCIES

Many teens with intermittent explosive disorder have parents with violent tendencies or mothers with panic disorder, Dr. Kessler noted. Children in these situations may learn that anger is an acceptable reaction to problems, he said.

Although the problem is widespread, "there is not a great deal of scientific evidence on how to treat [intermittent explosive disorder]," Dr. Kessler said.

STUDY DETAILS

For the study, Dr. Kessler's team collected data from the US National Comorbidity Survey Replication Adolescent Supplement, a survey of teens 13 to 17 years old. Information provided by nearly 6,500 teen-parent pairs was included in the study.

These data revealed that one in 12 US teens—about 8%—met the criteria for intermittent explosive disorder, meaning they've had three episodes of impulsive aggressiveness "grossly out of proportion to any precipitating psychosocial stressor," at any time during their life, according to the *Diagnostic and Statistical Manual of Mental Disorders.*

The researchers excluded anyone diagnosed with other mental health problems, such as bipolar disorder, attention-deficit/hyperactivity disorder, oppositional defiant disorder or conduct disorder, all of which are associated with aggressive behavior.

The condition was more common among teenagers not living with two biological parents and those with the most siblings.

More than one-third of those teens identified with chronic rage had received some treatment for emotional problems, but only 6.5% were treated specifically for anger, the researchers found.

The report was published in the *Archives of General Psychiatry*.

EXPERT COMMENT

Simon Rego, PsyD, director of psychology training at Montefiore Medical Center in New York City, said the findings indicate that the condition warrants more attention.

"Although it is not surprising that the researchers found [intermittent explosive disorder] to be a commonly occurring disorder among US adolescents, what is surprising is the fact that the data also show that [intermittent explosive disorder] is being undertreated," Dr. Rego said.

This conclusion, plus the condition's potential for serious consequences, suggests more research is needed on this disorder, he said.

"Research should focus on the factors that put adolescents at risk, as well as any identifiable protective factors," Dr. Rego said. The goal, he added, is to help researchers and clinicians develop effective treatments that can be applied at an early age in those at risk.

Dr. Kessler's team believes school-based violence prevention programs might help with early detection.

Pediatricians Say No to Expulsions, Suspensions At Schools

Jeffrey Lamont, MD, clinical assistant professor, University of Wisconsin, Madison, and pediatrician, Marshfield Clinic, Weston, Wisconsin.

Katherine Cowan, director, communications, National Association of School Psychologists, Bethesda, Maryland.

Pediatrics

Suspending or expelling a child from school should be a rare last resort and not a routine punishment for bullying, drug use or other infractions, according to a recent policy statement from the American Academy of Pediatrics (AAP).

The AAP, a leading group of pediatricians, said school "zero-tolerance" policies toward kids' behavior problems do no good.

If the parents are at work when a child is out of school, more inappropriate behavior often occurs, the authors said in the statement, which was published online in the journal *Pediatrics*. Students who are suspended or expelled are more likely to never get a high school diploma, end up in the juvenile justice system or eventually land a low-paying job or no job at all.

"There's a tremendous price to pay not just for the kid involved, but for society," said Jeffrey Lamont, MD, a pediatrician at Marshfield Clinic in Weston, Wisconsin, who wrote the new AAP statement.

But if zero-tolerance policies keep troublemakers out of school, don't the "good" kids benefit? That's not what the research shows, Dr. Lamont said.

What's more, Dr. Lamont said, the policies are not only targeting kids who are a danger to their peers but also students with a wide range of behavior issues.

BACKGROUND

US schools started turning to the zero-tolerance approach in the 1980s, as a way to curb drug use and violence. The idea got a boost in the 1990s with the passage of the Gun-Free School Zone Act, which required schools to expel students caught with firearms on school grounds.

"The problem was that schools adopted zero-tolerance policies that extended to lesser offenses, like disrespecting a teacher," Dr. Lamont said.

In 2006, a task force set up by the American Psychological Association found after a decade of research that there was no evidence that zero-tolerance policies had made schools any safer or helped kids' school performances. But there was evidence, the task force found, that the policies were disproportionately targeting black and Hispanic kids.

The AAP had no estimate for how many US school districts had zero-tolerance policies. But they are "very common," said Katherine Cowan, director of communications for the National Association of School Psychologists.

Cowan said the new AAP policy is in line with her group's thinking on the issue. "It's great to have pediatricians weighing in on this now," she said, noting that pediatricians play a big role in spotting kids' behavioral and health issues early on.

Cowan said there are "obvious, silly examples" of zero-tolerance being too rigidly applied, such as suspending elementary school kids because their parents packed a butter knife with their lunch. Recently, a Pennsylvania kindergartener was suspended for threatening classmates with her Hello Kitty "bubble gun."

ALTERNATIVES TO EXPULSIONS

Most often, however, suspensions and expulsions are doled out when kids do misbehave. The issue, Dr. Lamont and Cowan said, is that the punishment doesn't fit the crime.

"And we have alternatives that are proven to work," Cowan said.

One example the AAP points to is a program called Positive Behavioral Interventions & Supports, already used in more than 16,000 US schools. Many state education departments have "technical assistance" centers that help schools implement the plan.

The program's goal is to prevent behavior problems or keep them from escalating. The first step is for schools to come up with expectations for all students' behavior—such as keeping your hands to yourself when you're in the hallway or speaking up when you see a student being bullied—and making those expectations clear.

The response to rule-breaking is also made clear. If it's minor, a teacher might handle it with a simple reminder of the school's expectations. If it's serious, parents might be called in or the child might get counseling from a school psychologist or other professional.

The other key is that kids are also recognized for good behavior, Dr. Lamont said. "Put yourself in the kids' place," he said. "Not many adults would stay with a job where all they hear is criticism. Why do we expect something from children that we wouldn't expect of adults?"

Dr. Lamont said there is evidence that the program does improve behavior problems in schools. "From the federal government on down, people support this," he said.

info Learn more about getting Positive Behavioral Interventions & Supports into schools at *www.pbis.org*.

Heart & Stroke

Are You Doing Everything You Can to Prevent a Heart Attack?

You already know the best ways to prevent a heart attack—give up cigarettes if you smoke…get regular exercise…lose weight if you're overweight…and prevent (or control) high blood pressure (hypertension), elevated cholesterol and diabetes.

Yet millions of Americans continue to jeopardize their cardiovascular health by not fully understanding how to address these key risk factors.

Example: One common misconception is that you must do hard aerobic exercise to protect the heart. While it's true that people who increase the intensity and duration of their exercise may have greater reductions in cardiovascular disease, that doesn't mean you have to run on a treadmill or work up a sweat on a

stair-climber to help your heart. A daily brisk walk (ideally, 30 minutes or more) will provide significant improvements in blood vessel function and heart-muscle efficiency.

Other misconceptions…

Misconception #1: Reducing dietary fat is the best way to control cholesterol. In the 1960s, the average American consumed about 45% of calories from fats and oils. After decades of warnings that a high-fat diet increased cholesterol, that percentage has dropped to about 33%.

That sounds like good news, but it's not. Research clearly shows that the best diet for improving cholesterol is not a low-fat diet.

Reason: People who cut back on fat tend to reduce all fats in the diet, including healthful monounsaturated fats such as olive and canola oils. These fats improve the ratio of LDL "bad"

Steven Nissen, MD, chairman of the Robert and Suzanne Tomsich Department of Cardiovascular Medicine at the Cleveland Clinic main campus. He is coauthor, with Marc Gillinov, MD, of *Heart 411: The Only Guide to Heart Health You'll Ever Need* (Three Rivers).

cholesterol and HDL "good" cholesterol—a critical factor in reducing heart disease.

What to do: Cut back on saturated fat (ideally, less than 7% of total calories)—this fat does increase cholesterol.

But make sure that your diet includes healthful monounsaturated and polyunsaturated fats. In addition to olive and canola oils, foods that are high in monounsaturated fats include avocados, almonds, pecans, and pumpkin and sesame seeds. We get most of our polyunsaturated fats from sunflower, corn, soybean and other oils. Foods containing polyunsaturated fats include walnuts, fish and flaxseed.

Important: Of course you should avoid trans fats—engineered fats that are commonly used in commercially made cookies, crackers and other baked goods, as well as in deep-fried fast food. It's been estimated that for every 2% of calories that are consumed daily in the form of trans fats, the risk for heart disease rises by as much as 23%!

Misconception #2: Blood pressure medication should be stopped if it causes side effects. Everyone knows that hypertension is a very strong risk factor for heart disease and a subsequent heart attack. Yet studies show that many patients who have been diagnosed with hypertension don't achieve adequate control.

Blood pressure drugs are usually effective—but only if taken as directed. The problem is that these medications often cause uncomfortable side effects, including fatigue, dizziness or even fainting.

As a result, many patients—consciously or not—find excuses to skip doses or stop the medications altogether. It's been estimated that only about 60% of patients follow all of the instructions for taking these medications.

But reducing or stopping blood pressure medications abruptly can cause a rebound, in which blood pressure suddenly spikes to dangerous levels.

What to do: Don't suddenly stop medications because of side effects. And do your best not to forget doses or neglect to fill a prescription on time. Even if you do experience side effects when you first start a blood pressure medication, try to be patient and speak to your doctor, if necessary. Side effects typically go away on their own within a few weeks as your body adjusts to the lower blood pressure.

Important: If a side effect is severe (fainting, for example), seek immediate medical attention.

With good control, people with high blood pressure can dramatically reduce their risk for heart attack and stroke. Studies have shown, for instance, that people who lower their systolic (top number) pressure by just five points can reduce heart attacks by 15% to 20% and strokes by 25% to 30%.

Misconception #3: There's nothing you can do about your family history. We all know that heart disease "runs in the family." If a close sibling or either of your parents developed heart disease before age 55, your risk of developing it is approximately one and a half to two times as high as someone without the family link. And if you have a first-degree relative (a parent or sibling) who developed atrial fibrillation (an irregular and often rapid heartbeat) at any age, your chance of developing heart disease is increased two to three times.

What to do: Even though family history is considered a nonmodifiable risk factor, you still can take precautions that will reduce your risk. If you have a family history of atrial fibrillation, for example, ask your doctor if you should have a yearly EKG. It can be included as part of an annual exam.

You should also be particularly vigilant about managing other risk factors for heart disease. Multiple risk factors—say, family history plus high cholesterol or hypertension—increase your risk far more than any one factor alone.

Misconception #4: Stress isn't a danger once you've calmed down. It's widely known that acute emotional stress caused by a near accident or some other frightening event causes a momentary spike in blood pressure and heart rate that can have harmful consequences. Anger, one of the most common stressful emotions, has been found to precede 2% of all heart attacks.

However, ongoing stress (due to financial or health worries, for example), which triggers chronically high levels of the stress hormone cortisol, is an often underrecognized threat to one's heart and blood vessels.

What's more, even though obesity is a factor in about 90% of patients with diabetes, some research suggests that chronic stress also may increase risk for diabetes—a known risk factor for heart attack and stroke.

What to do: Do whatever it takes to avoid chronic stress. Exercise, including yoga, is among the best ways to reduce stress while also protecting the heart. But find whatever works for you to defuse stress—for example, listening to music and reading are also helpful.

Uncommon Causes of Heart Disease

Stephen Sinatra, MD, board-certified cardiologist and assistant clinical professor of medicine at University of Connecticut School of Medicine in Farmington. Dr. Sinatra is author or coauthor of numerous books, including The Healing Kitchen *(Bottom Line Books). www.bottomlinepub lications.com/healingkitchen*

There are well-known risk factors for heart disease, such as high blood pressure, diabetes, being overweight and a family history of early heart attacks. But some little-known risk factors are as threatening to your heart as those you're familiar with—in some cases, doubling your risk for disease.

Here Stephen Sinatra, MD, shares six of these "secret" risk factors, revealed by recent scientific studies—and how to reduce your risk...

BISPHENOL-A (BPA)

BPA is a chemical frequently found in food and beverage containers, such as plastic bottles and the lining of metal cans. It can harm your arteries.

Recent research: In a study of 591 people published in *PLoS One,* those with the highest urinary levels of BPA were the most likely to have advanced coronary artery disease—severely narrowed arteries ripe for the blockage that triggers a heart attack.

What happens: BPA sparks the chronic inflammation that drives arterial damage and heart disease.

My recommendation: Reduce your exposure to BPA. Avoid canned foods as much as possible because cans may have an epoxy liner that leaches BPA into food. Or look for cans labeled BPA-free. Drink water out of glass or stainless steel bottles that don't have a plastic liner. Don't microwave food in plastic or use plastic containers for hot foods or liquids—the heat can cause BPA to leach out.

Exception: Soft or cloudy-colored plastics typically do not contain BPA—they usually are marked on the bottom with the recycling labels #1, #2 or #4.

SHIFT WORK

Dozens of studies have linked shift work—an ongoing pattern of work that is not roughly 9 am to 5 pm—to higher heart disease risk, but the link has always been speculative. The latest study—a so-called "meta-analysis" of previous research—changes the shift work/heart disease hypothesis into scientific fact.

Recent research: The study, published in *BMJ,* analyzed data from 34 studies involving more than two million people and found that shift work was linked to a 23% increased risk for heart attack. The researchers concluded that

---

Tasty Way to Lower Heart Attack Risk

In a recent study of 93,600 women, those who ate more than three servings of strawberries or blueberries each week had a 34% lower risk for heart attack compared with those who rarely ate these berries.

Theory: Berries are rich in antioxidant anthocyanins, which have been shown to help regulate blood pressure and improve blood vessel function.

For heart health: Eat a handful of fresh or frozen berries a few times a week.

Eric Rimm, ScD, associate professor of epidemiology and nutrition, Harvard School of Public Health, Boston.

7% of all heart attacks—about one out of every 14—are directly attributable to shift work.

What happens: Shift work disrupts the normal sleep-wake cycle, throwing every system in your body out of balance, including the autonomic nervous system, which regulates heartbeat. An irregular heartbeat (arrhythmia) can cause a type of heart attack.

My recommendation: A key way to balance your autonomic nervous system is to increase your intake of foods rich in omega-3 fatty acids, such as wild-caught fatty fish (salmon, sardines, mackerel, tuna), grass-fed red meats, free-range poultry, walnuts and flaxseed oil. Also, take a daily fish oil supplement that delivers one to two grams of the essential fatty acids EPA and DHA.

If your work schedule includes shift work, pay attention to other heart disease risk factors and go for regular screenings.

DIABETES DRUGS

A generic, low-cost class of antidiabetes drugs called sulfonylureas (*glipizide, glyburide* and *glimepiride*) help control type 2 diabetes by stimulating the pancreas to produce insulin, a hormone that regulates blood sugar levels, but these drugs can be dangerous to your heart.

Recent research: Researchers at the Cleveland Clinic analyzed data from nearly 24,000 patients who had taken either a sulfonylurea drug or *metformin*, another generic, low-cost drug used to control diabetes. Compared with metformin, the sulfonylureas were linked to a 50% greater risk for death.

What happens: It's likely that sulfonylurea drugs are toxic to the body's mitochondria, the energy-generating structures in every cell that are crucial to health and longevity.

My recommendation: If you're taking a sulfonylurea drug, ask your doctor to switch you to metformin.

Even better: In a major, multiyear study, losing weight and exercising outperformed metformin in regulating blood sugar.

FATTY DEPOSITS AROUND THE EYES

Recent research: In a 35-year study involving nearly 11,000 people, researchers found that those with three out of four signs of visible aging had a 39% increased risk for heart disease and a 57% increased risk for heart attack. The four signs (in both men and women) are receding hairline at the temples…crown top baldness…earlobe creases…and fatty deposits around the eyes.

Important: Of these four signs, fatty deposits around the eyes were the strongest predictor of heart attack and heart disease.

My recommendation: If your doctor finds at least three of these risk factors—or just fatty deposits around your eyes—he/she should schedule you for regular screenings for heart disease.

EARLY MENOPAUSE

Menopause, and its accompanying drop in heart-protecting estrogen, increases the risk for heart disease. So it's no surprise that early menopause (starting at age 46 or younger) is a risk factor.

Recent research: In an eight-year study published in *Menopause,* researchers found that women who enter menopause early are twice as likely to suffer from heart disease and stroke.

My recommendation: There are several ways menopausal women can lower their risk for heart disease…

•**Eat more noninflammatory foods,** such as fresh, organic vegetables and fruits and wild-caught fatty fish.

•**Minimize your intake of inflammatory simple sugars** (white bread, pastries, cookies, pastas, candies, etc.).

•**Exercise regularly,** such as a daily 30-to-60-minute walk.

•**In addition to a multivitamin,** take daily supplements that strengthen the heart and circulatory system, including CoQ10 (60 mg to 100 mg)…fish oil (one to two grams)…vitamin C (1,000 mg)…and magnesium (400 mg to 800 mg).

•**Reduce stress with meditation,** yoga and/or tai chi. Other ways to reduce stress include socializing with friends and doing hobbies you enjoy.

PSORIASIS

The chronic inflammatory disease of psoriasis causes patches of dry, itchy skin. A recent study shows that it also damages arteries.

Recent research: In a study in *Journal of Investigative Dermatology,* researchers found that chronic inflammation of the skin is accompanied by chronic inflammation in blood vessels. And in a study published in *Circulation: Cardiovascular Imaging,* researchers found that treating psoriasis patients with the anti-inflammatory drug *adalimumab* decreased inflammation in the arteries (carotid and ascending aorta) often involved in heart attack and stroke.

My recommendation: All psoriasis patients should go on a gluten-free diet, eliminating inflammation-sparking grains such as wheat, rye and barley. They also should take inflammation-reducing omega-3 fatty acids (three to four grams daily). In addition, people with psoriasis should be screened regularly for heart disease.

When a Brother or Sister Dies…

When a brother or sister dies, heart attack risk rises. In an 18-year study of more than 1.6 million middle-aged people, those whose adult siblings had died of any cause were 20% more likely to have a fatal heart attack a few years after the event than peers who had not lost a sibling.

Interesting: Heart attack risk was not highest immediately after the sibling's death—but two to six years later.

Theory: Chronic stress and grieving, as well as family risk factors, could lead to heart attack.

If your adult sibling has died: Talk with your doctor about your heart attack risk, which also has been shown to increase after the death of a spouse or child.

Mikael Rostila, PhD, associate professor of sociology, Centre for Health Equity Studies, Stockholm, Sweden.

Don't Miss These Risk Factors For Heart Attack

When determining one's odds of having a heart attack, two factors often are overlooked…

• **Periodontal disease.** Many doctors have been slow to recognize how poor dental hygiene can increase a person's heart attack risk.

Here's what happens: If you don't brush and floss regularly, small particles of food get trapped between your teeth and gums, which promotes the buildup of plaque as well as inflammation and infection. Periodontal disease, in turn, causes a generalized inflammatory response that can increase heart attack risk.

In fact, a recent seven-year study of more than 100,000 people with no history of heart attack or stroke showed that those who had their teeth cleaned by a dentist or hygienist at least twice a year over a two-year period had a 24% lower risk for heart attack compared with people who did not go to the dentist or went only once in a two-year period.

My approach: Brush and floss regularly… and see your dentist at least every six months.

• **Sleep apnea.** Recent research shows that this nighttime breathing disorder increases a person's risk for heart attack and stroke.

What's the connection? With sleep apnea, the upper airway narrows or collapses during sleep, often disrupting sleep hundreds of times each night. This sleep disturbance decreases oxygen saturation in the bloodstream. Sleep apnea also raises adrenaline and inflammation—both of which increase risk for heart attack.

My approach: Patients who have signs or symptoms of sleep apnea—such as snoring, periods of breathing cessation during sleep, daytime fatigue and/or morning headaches—should see a doctor. There is some evidence that treating sleep apnea can lower heart attack risk.

Michael Ozner, MD, medical director of the Center for Wellness & Prevention at Baptist Health South Florida in Miami and author of *Heart Attack Proof: A Six-Week Cardiac Makeover for a Lifetime of Optimal Health* (BenBella). *www.drozner.com*

The Red Flags for Heart Attack That Often Get Overlooked

Antonio M. Gotto, Jr., MD, DPhil, dean emeritus, Lewis Thomas University Professor and cochairman of the board of overseers for Weill Cornell Medical College in New York City. He is also coauthor of *The Living Heart in the 21st Century* (Prometheus).

Former talk-show host Rosie O'Donnell recently became one of the 195,000 Americans each year who experiences a heart attack and does not know it. O'Donnell, age 50 at the time of her attack, reportedly did not realize what was happening to her when she became nauseated and started to feel clammy, two of the subtle, often-missed heart attack symptoms that are frequently experienced by women. (Other "atypical" heart attack symptoms in women include back or jaw pain, extreme fatigue, dizziness and light-headedness.)

An even more insidious risk: It's common for women and men to fail to tell their doctors about elusive heart disease symptoms that often precede a heart attack. If recognized, these symptoms often can be effectively treated to stop a heart attack before it occurs.

WHAT GETS MISSED

Most people do not realize just how important it is to report new symptoms during a doctor visit. With heart disease, in particular, there can be such a wide range of mild and/or fleeting changes in the heart, that the way you describe any possible abnormality to your doctor can mean the difference between an accurate diagnosis and a missed one. That's why you always should be sure to include details whenever you tell your physician about a symptom.

Examples: Don't just say that you're short of breath—do you feel this way all the time or just when you're climbing stairs? And don't just say that you've noticed changes in your heartbeat—is it too fast, too slow, fluttery, irregular, etc.?

Other important symptoms that should be discussed...

•**Intermittent chest pain.** The majority of heart attacks are preceded by the development of atherosclerosis, accumulations of fatty deposits in the arteries that inhibit the normal flow of blood and oxygen. When these deposits restrict blood flow to the heart, the result can be myocardial ischemia, a condition that typically causes chest pain due to a lack of oxygen.

Main symptom: Sharp chest pains or pressure that can last anywhere from a few seconds to about five minutes. This type of chest pain, known as angina, usually occurs during physical exertion, such as climbing stairs or working in the yard. It also can occur during cold weather, which causes blood vessels to constrict, or during stressful situations, which can increase demands on the heart and cause it to beat faster.

Exceptions: Angina isn't always painful, and you won't necessarily feel it in your chest. Patients with myocardial ischemia affecting the base of the heart might have abdominal discomfort instead of chest pain. (Some people mistake it for heartburn.) People with diabetes who have nerve damage, or those with a high pain threshold, might have no pain at all.

My advice: Suspect angina when you have chest and/or abdominal pain that occurs only during physical exertion. Rest if you experience pain in these areas. The pain should go away within five minutes if angina is the cause. In this case, call your doctor promptly to make an appointment. Call 911 if the pain isn't gone after five minutes.

•**Shortness of breath (dyspnea).** It is one of the main symptoms of heart disease, yet patients don't always mention it because they attribute it to other factors, such as smoking, advancing age and/or a lack of exercise.

Important: Shortness of breath can be caused by atypical angina. These angina patients do not experience pain as the main symptom. They are more likely to have episodes of breathlessness, weakness, fatigue and/or sweating. This is particularly common in older adults and those with diabetes.

My advice: To distinguish "normal" shortness of breath from a heart-related condition, ask yourself whether the dyspnea is out of proportion to what you're doing.

Don't Let Unemployment Hurt Your Heart

People who were jobless because they had been fired, laid off or quit a job earlier in life had a 35% higher risk for heart attack after age 50 than people who remained employed. Multiple job losses posed as much of a threat to heart health as smoking, high blood pressure and diabetes. Talk to your doctor about heart-health strategies, such as reducing stress.

Matthew Dupre, PhD, assistant professor of community and family medicine, Duke University, Durham, North Carolina, and leader of a study of 13,451 people, ages 51 to 75, published online in *Archives of Internal Medicine*.

For example, people do not normally get winded from unloading the dishwasher or walking to the mailbox. If you do—and you haven't been diagnosed with a condition to explain it, such as lung disease—see your doctor. Also, any change in your tolerance for exercise could indicate a heart problem. If you experience unexplained shortness of breath or a significant change in your tolerance for exercise, see your doctor as soon as possible.

Call 911 if you have severe shortness of breath that comes on suddenly, especially if it's accompanied by chest pain, fainting or nausea—these could be signs of heart attack or pulmonary embolism.

•**Palpitations.** Everyone has occasional changes in the heart's pumping rhythm. You might notice that your heartbeat is rapid, pounding or fluttering, particularly during exercise or when you're stressed. The heart is probably still pumping blood effectively, but you'll want to talk to your doctor anyway.

The risk: Heart palpitations can indicate that you have arrhythmias, problems with the heart's electrical systems. A heartbeat that's too rapid (tachycardia), too slow (bradycardia) or irregular (atrial fibrillation, among others) can be life-threatening.

Example: Atrial fibrillation is common in older adults. The heart usually regains its normal rhythm within a few seconds, but not always. There's an increased risk for stroke if the irregular heartbeat continues for more than 24 hours.

My advice: Call 911 immediately if palpitations are accompanied by other symptoms, such as fainting, heavy sweating or extreme anxiety—all of which can signal a heart attack or an impending one. If you have palpitations without other symptoms, make an appointment to see your doctor as soon as possible.

•**Leg pain.** It's normal to experience occasional "charley horses," cramps in the muscles in your legs. It's not normal to have frequent pain in a foot, calf, thigh or buttock when you're walking or doing other activities. Leg pain that develops during exertion is often a sign of peripheral artery disease, a form of atherosclerosis that occurs in arteries in the leg. Patients with peripheral artery disease have a high risk of having (or developing) cardiovascular disease.

My advice: If you notice aching, cramping or pain in one or both legs during physical activity, see your doctor. Peripheral artery disease also can cause a sensation of "burning," tingling or numbness in the legs and/or feet. These symptoms indicate that the leg isn't getting enough oxygen-rich blood—and there's a good chance that your heart arteries are also at risk. With advanced peripheral artery disease, the symptoms occur even at rest.

•**Hair loss on the legs/feet.** Sedentary patients with peripheral artery disease might not notice leg pain or cramps. However, they might have other "silent" symptoms that indicate impaired circulation, including hair loss on the legs and/or feet.

My advice: See your physician as soon as possible if you notice hair loss on the legs or feet or one of the other possible signs of peripheral artery disease—one leg/foot that is colder than the other…sores that are slow to heal…a "shine" to the skin…or thick, slow-growing toenails. The symptoms may occur in both legs, but patients often report that only one leg is affected.

WHEN TO CALL 911...

Severe chest pain (often described as "crushing" pain) is the heart attack symptom that everyone knows about—and fears. You most likely are having a heart attack if you have severe, unexplained chest pain that lasts longer than 20 minutes. But do not wait that long before getting help.

Call 911 even if your chest pain has lasted just a few minutes—or if you do not have chest pain but are experiencing other symptoms that could indicate a heart attack, such as unexplained nausea, breaking out in a cold sweat, dizziness, shortness of breath or extreme anxiety accompanied by a feeling of impending doom.

Emergency personnel may advise you to chew aspirin while you wait for help to arrive, so always keep a bottle of aspirin handy.

Clean Out Your Arteries

Catherine Ulbricht, PharmD, cofounder of Natural Standard Research Collaboration, which collects data on natural therapies, and senior attending pharmacist at Massachusetts General Hospital in Boston. She is also author of *Natural Standard Herbal Pharmacotherapy* and *Natural Standard Medical Conditions Reference* (both from Mosby).

You are walking or climbing up a set of stairs, and suddenly you notice a dull, cramping pain in your leg. Before you write off the pain as simply a sign of overexertion or just a normal part of growing older, consider this: You may have intermittent claudication, the most common symptom of peripheral artery disease (PAD).

PAD, also known as peripheral vascular disease, is a condition in which arteries and veins in your limbs, usually in the legs and feet, are blocked or narrowed by fatty deposits that reduce blood flow.

Intermittent claudication, leg discomfort (typically in the calf) that occurs during exertion or exercise and is relieved by rest, usually is the first symptom of PAD. But other possible symptoms may include leg sores that won't heal (chronic venous ulcers)…varicose veins (chronic venous insufficiency)…paleness (pallor) or discoloration (a blue tint) of the legs…or cold legs.

Why is "a little leg trouble" so significant?

If it's due to PAD, you have got a red flag that other arteries, including those in the heart and

Mediterranean Diet Tops for Heart Health

The American Heart Association diet doesn't work, says Jonny Bowden, PhD, CNS. A recent study found that about 30% of heart attacks, strokes and deaths from heart disease can be prevented in people at high risk if they switch to a Mediterranean diet rich in olive oil, nuts, beans, fish, fruits and vegetables. The low-fat, high-carb diet recommended by the AHA did not reduce heart attack risk. The study ended early because the results were so clear.

Jonny Bowden, PhD, CNS, a nutritionist based in Los Angeles and author, with Stephen Sinatra, MD, of *The Great Cholesterol Myth* (Fair Winds). *www.jonnybowden.com*

brain, may also be blocked. In fact, people with PAD have a two- to sixfold increased risk for heart attack or stroke.

An estimated eight million to 12 million Americans—including up to one in five people age 60 or older—are believed to have PAD. While many individuals who have PAD experience the symptoms described earlier, some have no symptoms at all.

Those at greatest risk: Anyone who smokes or has elevated cholesterol, high blood pressure or diabetes is at increased risk for PAD.

What you need to know…

BETTER TREATMENT RESULTS

The standard treatment for PAD typically includes lifestyle changes (such as quitting smoking, getting regular exercise and eating a healthful diet). Medical treatment may include medication, such as one of the two drugs approved by the FDA for PAD—*pentoxifylline* (Trental) and *cilostazol* (Pletal)—and, in severe cases, surgery.

For even better results: Strong scientific evidence now indicates that several natural therapies—used in conjunction with these treatments—may help slow the progression of PAD and improve a variety of symptoms more effectively than standard treatment alone can.

Important: Before trying any of the following therapies, talk to your doctor to determine which might work best for you, what the most effective dose is for you and what side effects and drug interactions may occur.

Do not take more than one of the following therapies at the same time—this will increase bleeding risk.

Among the most effective natural therapies for PAD…

•**Ginkgo biloba.** A standardized extract from the leaf of the ginkgo biloba tree, which is commonly taken to improve memory, is one of the top-selling herbs in the US. But the strongest scientific evidence for ginkgo biloba may well be in the treatment of PAD.

Scientific evidence: Numerous studies currently show that ginkgo biloba extract can decrease leg pain that occurs with exercise or at rest. The daily doses used in the studies ranged from 80 mg to 320 mg.

Warning: Because it thins the blood and may increase risk for bleeding, ginkgo biloba should be used with caution if you also take a blood thinner, such as *warfarin* (Coumadin) or aspirin. In addition, ginkgo biloba should not be taken within two weeks of undergoing surgery.

•**Grape seed extract.** Grapes, including the fruit, leaves and seeds, have been used medicinally since the time of the ancient Greeks. Grape seed extract is rich in oligomeric proanthocyanidins, antioxidants that integrative practitioners in Europe use to treat varicose veins, chronic leg ulcers and other symptoms of PAD.

Scientific evidence: In several recent studies, grape seed extract was found to reduce the symptoms of poor circulation in leg veins, which can include nighttime cramps, swelling, heaviness, itching, tingling, burning, numbness and nerve pain.

Caution: Don't use this supplement if you're allergic to grapes. It should be used with caution if you take a blood thinner.

•**Hesperidin.** This flavonoid is found in unripe citrus fruits, such as oranges, grapefruits, lemons and tangerines.

Scientific evidence: Research now shows that hesperidin may strengthen veins and tiny blood vessels called capillaries, easing the symptoms of venous insufficiency. Hesperidin also has been shown to reduce leg symptoms such as pain, cramps, heaviness and neuropathy (burning, tingling and numbness).

Some hesperidin products also contain *diosmin* (Daflon), a prescription medication that is used to treat venous disease, vitamin C or the herb butcher's broom—all of which strengthen the effects of hesperidin.

Caution: Many drugs can react with hesperidin. If you take a diabetes medication, antihypertensive, blood thinner, muscle relaxant, antacid or antinausea medication, be sure to use this supplement cautiously and promptly alert your doctor if you experience any new symptoms after starting to use hesperidin.

•**Horse chestnut seed extract.** The seeds, leaves, bark and flowers of this tree, which is native to Europe, have been used for centuries in herbal medicine.

Scientific evidence: Several studies now indicate that horse chestnut seed extract may be helpful for venous insufficiency, decreasing leg pain, fatigue, itchiness and swelling.

Caution: Horse chestnut may lower blood sugar and interfere with diabetes medication.

•**L-carnitine.** Also known as acetyl-L-carnitine, this amino acid may improve circulation and help with PAD symptoms.

Recent finding: Taking L-carnitine in addition to the PAD medication cilostazol increased walking distance in people with intermittent

---

Extreme Exercise Hurts the Heart

Recent finding: Marathon runners who were followed over three decades had a 19% lower rate of death than nonrunners—but those who ran more than 20 to 25 miles each week ended up with the same risk as the couch potatoes in the study.

Self-defense: Exercise vigorously for no more than one hour a day.

James O'Keefe, MD, head of preventive cardiology at Mid America Heart Institute at Saint Luke's Health System, Kansas City, Missouri, quoted at Today.com.

Get Happy—It's Good for Your Heart

It's long been known that negative feelings can be bad for the heart. Now a recent review of more than 200 studies has found that a positive psychological state has significant health benefits, including up to a 50% lower risk for a first cardiac event, such as heart attack.

Interesting: Optimism, happiness and satisfaction with life were related to reduced cardiovascular disease rates regardless of a person's age, weight and socioeconomic status.

To increase your well-being: Foster positive relationships with others...express gratitude and kindness...and think optimistically about the future.

Julia K. Boehm, PhD, research fellow, department of society, human development, and health, Harvard School of Public Health, Boston.

---

claudication up to 46% more than taking cilostazol alone, reported researchers from the University of Colorado School of Medicine in a recent issue of *Vascular Medicine.*

• **Inositol nicotinate.** This is a form of niacin (vitamin B-3) that is less likely to create the typical "flushing" (redness and heat) that is produced by high doses of niacin.

Several studies show that it is helpful in treating PAD. It is commonly used in the UK to treat intermittent claudication.

• **Policosanol.** This is a natural cholesterol-lowering compound made primarily from the wax of cane sugar.

Comparative studies show that policosanol treats intermittent claudication as effectively as the prescription blood thinner *ticlopidine* (Ticlid) and more effectively than the cholesterol-lowering statin *lovastatin* (Mevacor).

OTHER THERAPIES

You may read or hear that acupuncture, biofeedback, chelation therapy, garlic, omega-3 fatty acids and vitamin E can help with PAD.

However: The effectiveness of these particular therapies is uncertain at this time. For this reason, it is best to forgo these approaches until more scientific evidence becomes available.

Fainting in Healthy People May Signal Heart Trouble

Satish R. Raj, MD, assistant professor of medicine and pharmacology in the division of clinical pharmacology at Vanderbilt University School of Medicine in Nashville.

Martin Ruwald, MD, postdoctoral research fellow, heart research follow-up program, University of Rochester Medical Center, Rochester, New York.

Suzanne Steinbaum, MD, preventive cardiologist, Lenox Hill Hospital, New York City.

Journal of the American College of Cardiology

Fainting isn't fun. The cause is often relatively harmless, such as standing up too quickly, getting overheated, becoming dehydrated, receiving bad news or experiencing intense fear. Unfortunately, it's often tough for physicians to determine just what caused a first fainting episode.

A large recent Danish study provides a nationwide picture of how one-time fainters fare over several years. The researchers found these people were 74% more likely to eventually be admitted to the hospital for heart attack or stroke and five times more likely to need a pacemaker or implantable cardioverter-defibrillator, devices implanted under the skin to treat an irregular heartbeat, at some point in the future.

If you've fainted for the first time (and have no idea what could have caused it), play it safe and contact your doctor to find out whether you need to be examined. People who suddenly experience more than one fainting episode in a short period of time—especially those who have been diagnosed with another health problem—should definitely see their doctors. A long history of fainting spells makes it less likely that the cause is serious.

IT COULD BE YOUR HEART

Structural heart problems, such as cardiomyopathy (a weakened heart) or heart-valve conditions, can cause fainting spells. An abnormal heart rhythm, which may increase risk for cardiac arrest or a heart attack, can lead to fainting, too.

If your doctor suspects that your fainting is due to a cardiovascular problem, he/she might advise that you wear a heart monitor to detect problems with heart rates or rhythms.

Important: If you faint and have a first-degree relative (parent, sibling or child) who has suffered an unexplained sudden cardiac death, you may need to be examined by a heart-rhythm specialist (cardiac electrophysiologist).

The Dutch study suggests that even low-risk people who faint need to be carefully evaluated.

"Patients, relatives and clinicians should be aware that syncope [fainting] in seemingly healthy people is associated with higher risks of death and that syncope may be a first symptom of cardiovascular disease," said Martin Ruwald, MD, lead author of the study and postdoctoral research fellow at the University of Rochester Medical Center in Rochester, New York.

Suzanne Steinbaum, DO, a preventive cardiologist at Lenox Hill Hospital in New York City, explained that while fainting is common, it's challenging to identify who is in danger and who is not. "Some people do well, some people don't do well, and some people die," she said. "This study suggests that although fainting could mean nothing if you're 44 or older, it could be a sign of cardiovascular disease. See your doctor if you faint."

The study was published in the *Journal of the American College of Cardiology,* and while it found an association between fainting in otherwise healthy people and future heart complications, it did not establish cause-and-effect.

Fainting First Aid

When you see someone lose consciousness and collapse, you won't know at first if the person is injured, still breathing or even alive.

Someone who faints will recover spontaneously (typically in less than a minute). This is usually not an emergency.

However: Unless you're a health professional, you won't know what's going on. The person could have fainted or experienced something far worse, such as a heart attack. Don't take any chances.

If someone loses consciousness…

• **Place the person on his/her back.** Check the ABCs—airway, breathing and circulation. If the person isn't breathing, call 911 and begin chest compressions.

• **Allow the person to lie on the ground.** This increases circulation to the brain. Loosen his collar, belt or other restrictive clothing. When it's time to help him stand up, do it slowly.

• **Call 911 if the person does not regain consciousness within a minute.**

The Spice That Could Save Your Heart

Wanwarang Wongcharoen, MD, department of internal medicine, faculty of medicine, Chiang Mai University, Chiang Mai, Thailand.

People tend to think that bypass surgery is pretty safe. But the reality is, patients who undergo coronary artery bypass graft surgery—its official name—are vulnerable to an in-hospital heart attack in the first few days after the operation.

Now here's good news: Curcuminoids, chemicals in the spice turmeric (the spice that gives curry its yellow color), may help prevent many of these post-op heart attacks, according to recent research from Thailand.

HEART OF THE MATTER

In the study, beginning three days prior to their bypass surgery, participants were given either a placebo or 4,000 milligrams (mg) of a curcuminoid supplement daily. They remained on that dose for five days after surgery, along with any necessary medications that they were given before, during and after surgery. The results were striking—30% of the patients who took the placebo had heart attacks in the 72 hours following the surgery...while only 13% of those who took the supplement had heart attacks.

"We believe that the anti-inflammatory and antioxidative effects of curcuminoids are mainly what helped prevent heart attacks," the study's lead author, Wanwarang Wongcharoen, MD, told me.

It's possible that curcuminoids might also help patients who aren't undergoing bypass surgery but are at high risk for heart attack, said

What Exercises Are Best for You?*

If you have cardiovascular disease...

A key benefit of exercise is reduced heart attack risk. But if you have already had a heart attack or undergone bypass surgery...or have symptoms, such as chest pain (angina), that signal established heart disease, you may worry that physical exertion is too risky.

For the vast majority of people with heart disease, it's not—if it's supervised. This usually involves initial and periodic testing to establish safe levels of exercise and monitoring of heart rate and blood pressure for some sessions. Once you're cleared, you can do most sessions on your own.

When performed at the proper intensity, standard aerobic activities are usually suitable. This means you can most likely walk, jog, use a stationary bike or treadmill (or even participate in aerobic dance) as long as you do it at a moderate level that doesn't raise your heart rate too high. Talk to your doctor about the heart rate you should strive for. Once you have that number, you may want to wear a heart rate monitor—several models are widely available for under $100.

Another option: Use the "Talk Test." If you can talk while exercising, this will indicate with 95% accuracy that your heart rate is in a safe range.

If you have hypertension: Higher-intensity exercise may trigger potentially dangerous spikes in your blood pressure—talk to your doctor about appropriate heart rate goals, and remember to breathe (do not hold your breath) and stay away from heavier weights when doing strength training.

Important: Be sure to ask your doctor to reevaluate your target heart rate if you change blood pressure medication—some drugs, such as beta-blockers, will affect your heart rate.

*Always talk to your doctor before starting a new exercise program. If you have a chronic illness, it may be useful to consult a physical therapist for advice on exercise dos and don'ts for your particular situation.

John P. Porcari, PhD, program director of the Clinical Exercise Physiology (CEP) program at the University of Wisconsin–La Crosse.

Dr. Wongcharoen, but further research is needed to confirm.

SHOULD YOU EAT MORE CURRY?

Before you head to the nearest Indian or Malaysian restaurant thinking that a great-tasting, curry-flavored meal will help protect your heart, keep in mind that the amount of curcuminoids that you get in such a meal is typically less than 10 mg—which is very, very little compared with the massive amount that patients in the study received (4,000 mg). So it's unlikely that consuming curcuminoids through foods would have anywhere near the dramatic effect seen by the bypass patients in the study. Curcuminoid supplements, however, would be more likely to help because they contain much higher amounts, said Dr. Wongcharoen—usually about 250 mg to 500 mg per capsule.

If you're about to undergo bypass surgery, ask your doctor whether taking 4,000 mg of a curcuminoid supplement daily (available at health-food stores or Web sites)—for three days before the operation and for five days after it—is a good idea, said Dr. Wongcharoen. Just be sure not to abandon your surgery meds. "I do not recommend replacing any drugs with a curcuminoid supplement," Dr. Wongcharoen said. "But it might be a helpful addition." Just make sure that the word "curcumin" is on the label, said Dr. Wongcharoen.

It's generally considered to be a very safe supplement, said Dr. Wongcharoen. Potential side effects include nausea, dizziness and/or diarrhea, and it can slow blood clotting, so if it's taken with other drugs or supplements that may also slow blood clotting (including *clopidogrel, ibuprofen, naproxen, warfarin,* garlic, ginger, ginkgo and/or ginseng), that could be dangerous. (Dr. Wongcharoen found in his study that the supplement group did not bleed any more than the placebo group, which suggests that the anticlotting effect of these curcuminoids may not be very strong—therefore, in his opinion, the reduction in heart attack risk outweighs an additional risk of bleeding.) Keep in mind that taking any supplement in an extreme amount does raise the risk for side effects and adverse interactions—so definitely check with your doctor first.

And if you had bypass surgery more than 72 hours ago, the danger of having an operation-related heart attack has passed, so Dr. Wongcharoen does not recommend that you take a curcumin supplement to prevent heart attacks until future research shows whether it's helpful.

Infection Protection for Cardiac Implant Patients

Bruce Wilkoff, MD, director of Cardiac Pacing and Tachyarrhythmia Devices at the Cleveland Clinic and a professor of medicine at Cleveland Clinic Lerner College of Medicine at Case Western Reserve University in Ohio. He is also the president of the Heart Rhythm Society. *www.hrsonline.org*

If you or someone you love has a cardiac implantable electronic device (CIED), such as a pacemaker or cardio defibrillator, you should know about a potentially deadly problem that is becoming increasingly common— CIED-related infection.

Between 1993 and 2008, the number of CIEDs in use doubled while the number of infections associated with the devices more than tripled, reaching 2.41%, according to a recent study in the *Journal of the American College of Cardiology.* Sadly, 18% of patients with CIED infections do not survive for a year. For those who live, treatment can be economically devastating, with an average cost of more than $146,000.

Bruce Wilkoff, MD, director of Cardiac Pacing and Tachyarrhythmia Devices at the Cleveland Clinic, explained that most CIED-related infections are caused by *staphylococcus aureus* or *staphylococcus epidermidis* bacteria. Infection can get started if, at the time of surgery, bacteria contaminate the surface of the device, the patient's skin or the area in the chest beneath the skin where the surgeon creates a "pocket" to hold the CIED. The surgeon's scrupulous attention to proper sterile techniques can greatly reduce but not completely eliminate this risk. Sometimes an infection develops soon after surgery, but in other cases it becomes apparent only after a year or more has passed.

Could staph also can get into the pocket long after the surgery—for instance, by migrating from some other infected site in the body? Dr. Wilkoff said, "It is possible but very uncommon, particularly for these staph bacteria. But about 10% of the time, other bacteria are involved… and 1% to 2% of patients could have the infection occur through another mechanism."

Compared with the infection risk after an initial implantation, the risk is four to six times greater when a patient has another surgery to replace a device (for instance, because its battery is depleted, a component has stopped working or the patient requires a device with additional features). *Reason:* Reopening the pocket where the device was placed may allow a colony of bacteria that the body had previously "walled off" to overwhelm the immune system's defenses, Dr. Wilkoff explained. Since a CIED typically lasts about four to eight years, a patient is quite likely to need such repeat surgery.

Warning signs: There is no one symptom that appears in all cases of infection, Dr. Wilkoff said. *But see your doctor quickly if any of the following occur…*

•**You run a fever of 101° or higher.**

•**There is swelling, redness or pain at the site where the device was implanted.**

•**The skin covering the device becomes dimpled or oozes.**

•**The device appears to be shifting position.**

Be especially vigilant about watching for such signs if you have diabetes or compromised kidney function. Either of these conditions can increase your susceptibility to CIED-related infection.

If you do get a CIED infection: Both the device and all of its leads (wires that deliver energy from the CIED to the heart muscle) need to be removed and replaced. *Reason:* Staph bacteria can bind to a sticky substance called fibronectin that circulates in the blood and clings to the surface of implanted devices. Once this biofilm of persistent bacterial bugs takes hold, it is very antibiotic-resistant and almost impossible to get rid of without removing the device.

Before and after the surgery, for a period that can range from several days to several weeks, you receive antibiotics through an IV. You may be given a temporary pacemaker or an external defibrillator during this time. When the infection is gone, your doctor will schedule another surgery to implant a new CIED, often before you go home.

To reduce your risk for a subsequent infection: It is best to use an experienced cardiologist who does a high volume of device implantation and device change procedures. Dr. Wilkoff suggested asking the doctor and/or hospital whether they report the number of CIED procedures they do on a Web site or in a booklet—the larger the number, the better the outcomes tend to be. Also, he noted that women sometimes ask to have the CIED implanted underneath a muscle so that it's less visible. But since this makes it more difficult to remove if an infection does develop, it's important to discuss the pros and cons with your doctor before opting for such placement. And, of course, follow your doctor's advice on minimizing CIED infection risk after surgery.

Risky Blood Thinners May Be Unnecessary After Stent Surgery

Christopher Cove, MD, associate professor, medicine, and assistant director, cardiac catheterization lab, University of Rochester Medical Center, Rochester, New York.

Kirk Garratt, MD, director, clinical research, Lenox Hill Heart and Vascular Institute of New York, New York City.

Journal of the American College of Cardiology

A full year of aggressive anti-clotting therapy—which can lead to heavy bleeding—may not be needed after surgery to implant a drug-coated cardiac stent, two recent studies suggest.

BACKGROUND

Standard treatment for patients receiving so-called drug-eluting cardiac stents, which prop open clogged arteries after angioplasty, typically entails 12 months of double anti-platelet therapy consisting of aspirin and prescription blood thinners. Korean and Spanish research indicates, however, that patients who discontinue such risky therapy after several months suffer no more ill effects than those treated for a year.

ABOUT CARDIAC STENTS AND ANTI-PLATELET THERAPY

Cardiac stents—metal mesh tubes that prevent heart arteries from re-closing—are implanted in more than 500,000 Americans each year, according to the US Centers for Disease Control and Prevention. Some stents are coated with medication that is released slowly (eluted) to prevent the growth of scar tissue in the artery lining.

Prescription blood thinners used in double anti-platelet therapy, such as *clopidogrel* (Plavix) and *warfarin* (Coumadin), are tricky to dose properly and can lead to life-threatening bleeding complications.

THE STUDIES

The Korean study split more than 2,100 patients, all of whom underwent stent surgery after angina (chest pain) or a heart attack, into groups treated with either three months of double anti-platelet therapy or the standard 12-month course. After a year, just less than 5% of both groups had suffered complications such as death, bleeding, heart attack or clotting near the stent.

The Spanish study addressed interruptions in double anti-platelet therapy due to noncompliance, surgery or other medical decisions in a group of 1,600 patients. Most of the 10.6% of patients who discontinued the therapy did so temporarily, but this practice didn't translate into more serious consequences compared with those whose therapy was not interrupted.

The studies were published in the *Journal of the American College of Cardiology.*

EXPERT REACTION

"The interesting thing is, we went through a period of time so panicked about anti-platelet therapy interruptions and the effect they might have," said Kirk Garratt, MD, director of clinical research at Lenox Hill Heart and Vascular Institute of New York City, who was not involved in the studies. "But over the last few years, a series of reports and clinical trials say the same thing—that we probably don't need to be as worked up about it as we used to be."

But Christopher Cove, MD, associate professor of medicine and assistant director of the cardiac catheterization lab at the University of Rochester Medical Center in New York, cautioned it would be a mistake to think it's safe to stop double anti-platelet therapy based on the recent research. Larger studies are needed, he added.

"We know that [double anti-platelet therapy] is beneficial as compared to aspirin alone in large groups of patients, and that there's a high risk of bleeding with it," Dr. Cove said. "What we really need to know is, if we have to stop double anti-platelet therapy, when is the safe time to do that."

info The American Heart Association has more information about treating heart disease at its Web site, *www.heart.org*. Search "treatments for heart disease."

Common Painkillers Might Boost Odds for Second Heart Attack

Anne-Marie Schjerning Olsen, MD, department of cardiology, University of Copenhagen, Denmark.
Gregg Fonarow, MD, spokesman, American Heart Association, and professor, cardiology, University of California, Los Angeles.
Circulation

People who've already suffered a heart attack may face higher odds of death or subsequent heart attack if they regularly take a common form of painkiller, Danish researchers report.

The painkillers are known as nonsteroidal anti-inflammatory drugs (NSAIDs), and include over-the-counter drugs such as *ibuprofen* (Advil, Motrin) and *naproxen* (Aleve), as well as prescription drugs such as *celecoxib* (Celebrex), the researchers noted.

The report was published in *Circulation*.

STUDY FINDINGS

For the study, researchers collected data on nearly 100,000 people who had experienced a heart attack between 1997 and 2009. They found that 44% of these patients had filled at least one prescription for an NSAID.

Compared with non-users, people who took the painkillers had a 59% higher risk of dying from any cause within a year after their heart attack, and a 63% higher risk within five years, the researchers found.

In addition, the risk of having another heart attack or dying from heart disease increased 30% within one year, and 41% after five years, the Danish team said.

These findings were the same for men and women regardless of age and income, the researchers found, and the study also accounted for factors such as other illnesses or medications.

Still, the data comes from what's known as an observational study, so it cannot prove that NSAIDs helped cause the deaths and heart attacks—only that there was an association.

Nevertheless, the use of these drugs should be limited and the ability to buy them over-the-counter should be reconsidered, the researchers concluded.

RECOMMENDATIONS

"These results support previous findings that NSAIDs have no apparent safe treatment window among patients with a [prior] heart attack," said lead researcher Anne-Marie Schjerning Olsen, MD, from the department of cardiology at the University of Copenhagen. "Long-term caution with use of NSAIDs is advised in all patients after a heart attack," she said.

Dr. Olsen added that "it is important to get the message out to clinicians taking care of patients with cardiovascular disease that NSAIDs are harmful, even several years after a heart attack."

EXPERT COMMENTARY

"It has been shown in multiple prior studies that regular use of NSAIDs, including those that are available over the counter, is associated with increased risk of cardiovascular events," noted Gregg Fonarow, MD, a spokesman for the American Heart Association and a professor of cardiology at the University of California, Los Angeles, who was not involved with the study.

"Even short-term use in patients after a heart attack or with heart failure has been associated with excess risk," he said.

Since 2007, American Heart Association guidelines have warned of the potential cardiovascular risk of NSAIDs in patients with established cardiovascular disease and after a heart attack and discouraged their use in these patients, Dr. Fonarow noted.

"This study highlights that substantial caution is necessary when considering NSAIDs in patients after a heart attack no matter how long ago the heart attack occurred," he said.

"Patients with a history [of heart attack] should consult with their physicians before taking NSAIDs, including those that are available over the counter," Dr. Fonarow added.

ASPIRIN SAFE IN HEART ATTACK PATIENTS

After a heart attack, patients are usually prescribed aspirin, which is also an NSAID. However, "these findings do not apply to aspirin, which is a protective therapy after a heart attack," Dr. Fonarow stressed.

info For more information on assessing your risk for heart attack, visit the American Heart Association Web site, *www.heart.org*, and search "heart attack risk assessment."

Breakthroughs in Stroke Recovery

Murray Flaster, MD, PhD, an associate professor of neurology and neurological surgery and director of Loyola Outpatient Clinics at Loyola University Chicago Stritch School of Medicine, where he specializes in vascular neurology and neurological intensive care.

Physician scientists have now discovered that a series of surprisingly simple treatments—performed in the first 24 to 48 hours after a stroke—can prevent additional brain damage and help reduce the risk for disability and complications, including cognitive impairments.

Important: The recommendations described in this article apply only to patients who have had an ischemic stroke (caused by a blood clot). Almost 90% of all strokes are ischemic. Unless it's otherwise noted, these recommendations do not apply to patients who have suffered a hemorrhagic (bleeding) stroke.

Most important treatments following stroke…

•**Maintain or raise blood pressure.** It sounds counterintuitive because high blood pressure is one of the main risk factors for stroke—and because most stroke patients have a spike in blood pressure of about 20 points. But studies have shown that higher-than-normal blood pressure can help patients recover faster, with less brain damage.

Giving blood pressure–lowering drugs in the hospital can cause a decrease in cerebral perfusion pressure (a measurement of blood flow to the brain) that can increase damage.

Recommended: As a general rule, your blood pressure should not be lowered immediately after a stroke, even if you have existing hypertension. As long as your blood pressure reading is below 220/120 (normal is about 120/80), it should be left alone.

In some patients, particularly those with a blockage in a major blood vessel, it might be advisable to actively raise blood pressure with a vasopressive medication, such as *phenylephrine* (Neo-Synephrine).

Exceptions: Blood pressure may still need to be lowered in patients who have had a hemorrhagic stroke (caused by bleeding in the brain) or in those who are taking clot-dissolving drugs. Raising blood pressure in patients who are actively bleeding or at risk for bleeding can potentially cause more bleeding.

•**Reduce body temperature.** Fever is common in stroke patients due to infection or the stroke itself, with up to 25% having a temperature of 100.4°F or higher within 48 hours after being admitted to the hospital. A fever is dangerous because it increases the metabolic demands of damaged brain tissue—energy that should go toward healing. It also triggers the release of inflammatory substances that can cause additional damage.

Recommended: *Acetaminophen* (Tylenol) and hydration. Cooling blankets may be used for fever above 101°F. An experimental treatment called therapeutic hypothermia involves rapidly lowering body temperature with a cooled saline solution given intravenously.

•**Rehydrate.** Dehydration is common in stroke patients because fever and other complications can reduce the body's fluids. If you've had a stroke and are dehydrated, your risk of forming additional blood clots is increased by fivefold.

Reason: Dehydration reduces the volume of blood in the body. This, in turn, reduces blood pressure and increases the tendency of blood to clot.

Recommended: Intravenous (IV) saline solution for at least 24 to 48 hours.

•**Lower the bed.** When the head of the bed is raised, the increased elevation can decrease cerebral blood flow, particularly when the stroke affects the middle cerebral artery, which is common in ischemic stroke.

Important finding: Studies suggest that lowering the head of the bed from 30 degrees to 15 degrees increases blood flow through the middle cerebral artery by 12%. There's an additional 8% increase when the bed is flat.

The trade-off: Many patients aren't comfortable when the bed is completely flat. They also have more trouble swallowing, which increases the risk that they'll get pneumonia after inhaling (aspirating) foreign material from the mouth. Therefore, the head of the bed should initially be elevated to about 15 degrees. If the patient doesn't improve, the bed can be lowered.

•**Use an insulin drip.** It's common for stroke patients to have high blood sugar because of preexisting diabetes or prediabetes. In addition, the stroke itself can temporarily raise blood sugar (in fact, any major stressor in the body can raise blood glucose levels). High blood sugar, or hyperglycemia, is associated with a 2.7-fold increase in poor outcomes following stroke. Poor outcomes could include language difficulties, paralysis, cognitive impairments, etc.

Recommended: Stroke patients should be tested for hyperglycemia immediately after arriving in the hospital emergency department and then as frequently as needed. If blood sugar is higher than 155 mg/dL, insulin should be administered intravenously.

Important: To help prevent stroke-related complications that are worsened by elevated blood sugar, these patients should not be given saline that contains glucose—even if they could benefit nutritionally from the additional sugar.

•**Give a statin quickly.** Stroke patients routinely have their cholesterol tested in the hospital.

Recommended: There's no need to wait for the results before giving patients a cholesterol-lowering statin drug, such as *atorvastatin* (Lipitor) or *pravastatin* (Pravachol).

Reason: Even if your cholesterol is normal, statins reduce the inflammatory brain damage that's caused by stroke. Giving these medications quickly can help patients recover more promptly. Continuing statin therapy (if you have high cholesterol and are already taking a statin) can help prevent a subsequent stroke.

•**Start activity early.** Hospitalized patients who are physically active to any degree—even if it is just sitting up in bed—improve more quickly and have fewer complications than those who are initially immobile.

Other benefits: Physical activity also reduces the risk for pneumonia, deep-vein thrombosis, pulmonary embolism and bedsores.

Recommended: Some form of activity within hours after having a stroke if the patient is neurologically stable. We encourage patients to spend as little time in bed as possible even if

Anemia and Stroke Danger

A review of the medical records of 3,750 men who had suffered an ischemic stroke found that those with severe anemia were 3.5 times more likely to die while in the hospital and 2.5 times more likely to die within one year than those without anemia. In study participants with moderate anemia, one-year risk for death was increased twofold...for those with mild anemia, it was 1.5 times higher.

Possible explanation: Anemia may reduce oxygen delivery to the brain, which inhibits recovery from stroke.

If you are a stroke survivor: Ask your doctor whether you should get tested for anemia.

Jason Sico, MD, assistant professor of neurology and internal medicine, Yale University School of Medicine, New Haven, Connecticut.

their mobility is impaired and to do as much as they can tolerate.

Important: Activity should always be carefully guided by nurses, therapists or other members of the hospital team to avoid injury.

Catching a Stroke Before It Starts

Fiona Webster, PhD, an education scientist and assistant professor in the department of family and community medicine at the University of Toronto in Ontario and lead author of a study on stroke prevention clinics published in *Stroke*.

When you think of saving lives that would otherwise be lost to stroke, you probably imagine frightened but clear-thinking family members calling 911 or efficient ER doctors administering crucial medication just in the nick of time. Those things matter, of course—but a lifesaving approach that often is overlooked is the stroke prevention clinic.

Researchers recently compared the medical records of 16,468 patients who had experienced either an ischemic stroke (caused when a clot blocks blood flow to the brain) or a transient ischemic attack (TIA), often called a "mini-stroke." TIAs produce symptoms that are similar to stroke—sudden weakness or numbness on one side of the body, slurred speech, dizziness, vision problems—but usually last a much shorter time and often cause no permanent damage. However, the risk of having a full-blown and potentially fatal stroke within three months after a TIA is as high as 20%.

Study findings: TIA and ischemic stroke patients who were referred to stroke prevention clinics that aimed to identify and address risk factors were 26% less likely to die of stroke in the following 12 months than patients who did not attend such programs. These findings underscore the importance of secondary prevention for at-risk patients, researchers said.

Why it works: Many factors that place a person at increased risk for stroke are modifiable. When a patient learns which particular risk factors are putting her in danger and takes steps to

control those, her risk is significantly reduced. A stroke prevention clinic is an outpatient program staffed by medical professionals trained to assess, diagnose and treat stroke risk factors. *The treatment duration and exact services provided vary, but typically patients...*

• **Have their blood monitored** to measure how well any medications they take are working to control clotting, modulate blood pressure and/or regulate cholesterol.

• **Receive support to exercise more,** lose weight, reduce stress and/or quit smoking, as needed.

• **Are assessed and treated as necessary for heart conditions,** sleep apnea and other chronic conditions that contribute to stroke risk.

Not all hospitals have stroke prevention clinics—and not all doctors refer their TIA or stroke patients to such programs. If you have had a TIA or stroke, talk to your doctor about whether a stroke prevention clinic could benefit you... and ask your insurer whether your policy covers the cost.

Stroke: It's on the Rise Among Younger People

Brett M. Kissela, MD, professor and vice-chair of the department of neurology at the University of Cincinnati College of Medicine. He was the lead researcher of the National Institutes of Health–funded study, published in *Neurology*, that documented increasing strokes in younger adults.

Few people in their 40s or 50s can imagine having a stroke, particularly if they are generally healthy. But the risk is higher than you might think—dispelling the common belief that stroke is a risk for only the elderly.

An unexpected trend: Over the last several years, there has been an increase in strokes among adults in their 40s, 50s and 60s. What's most alarming about this development is that doctors don't expect to see strokes in these relatively young patients, so the diagnosis sometimes gets overlooked.

Important finding: One in seven young stroke patients was initially misdiagnosed as

Surprising Red Flags For Stroke

Stroke symptoms aren't always dramatic. If you've had a minor stroke or a transient ischemic attack (a brief interruption of blood flow known as a "ministroke"), the symptoms might be fleeting and easy to miss.

What's more, in rare cases, symptoms may occur that you may not think of in relation to a stroke. For example, you may initially feel disoriented or experience nausea, general weakness, face or limb pain, chest pain or palpitations—all of which typically come on suddenly. Depending on the part of the brain that's affected, you may not be aware of your symptoms and must rely on someone else to call for help.

•**Don't take chances.** Get to an emergency room if you have these and/or the classic symptoms below—FAST (Face, Arm, Speech and Time) is a helpful guide.

•**Face.** The most common stroke symptom is weakness on one side of the body, including on one side of the face. You may have difficulty smiling normally.

•**Arm.** One-sided weakness often affects one of the arms. Hold both arms out to your sides. You could be having a stroke if one of your arms drops down.

•**Speech.** Your words could sound slurred, or you might be unable to say a simple sentence correctly.

•**Time.** In the past, the "window" to receive clot-dissolving medication was considered to be three hours. Recent research indicates that stroke patients can benefit if they get treated within 4.5 hours after having the first symptom.

having another problem, such as a seizure or alcohol intoxication, researchers at Wayne State University–Detroit Medical Center found in a recent study.

What to do: First and foremost, be alert. Stroke can occur at any age, so it's important for all adults to pay close attention to symptoms (see box). If you are diagnosed and treated within about four hours of having a stroke, you are far more likely to recover than someone whose diagnosis and treatment are delayed. Unfortunately, only about 20% to 30% of young patients with stroke symptoms go to the emergency room, according to research. The others are likely to shrug off the symptoms (especially if they were relatively minor and/or short-lived) and do not learn that they have suffered a stroke until a subsequent problem is detected later on.

WHAT'S CAUSING EARLIER STROKES?

Many of the so-called "age-related" diseases that greatly increase stroke risk, such as high blood pressure (hypertension), diabetes and high cholesterol, are now appearing in patients who are middle-aged or younger—primarily because so many Americans are eating more junk food, gaining too much weight and not getting enough exercise. Family history is also a risk factor for stroke.

But even if you don't have any of these conditions (or a family history of stroke), you are in good physical shape and generally eat a well-balanced diet, do not be lulled into a false sense of security. Anyone can suffer a stroke. That's why it's very important for all adults to be on the lookout for red flags that could signal a stroke.

PREVENTION WORKS

Stroke is the fourth-leading cause of death in the US. Those who survive a stroke often face a lifetime of disability, including paralysis and speech and emotional difficulties.

Fortunately, younger patients, in general, are more likely to recover than older ones because their brains have greater plasticity, the ability to regain functions after stroke-related trauma. Even so, many young stroke patients will have permanent damage.

Important: Regardless of your age, fast treatment is critical if you experience stroke symptoms. The majority of strokes are ischemic, caused by blood clots that impair circulation to the brain. Patients who are given clot-dissolving drugs, such as tissue plasminogen activator (tPA), within the first few hours after a stroke are far more likely to make a full recovery than those who are treated later.

Tomatoes May Lower Stroke Risk

Recent finding: Researchers measured antioxidant levels in the blood of more than 1,000 men (ages 46 to 65) and tracked their health for 12 years. Those with the highest levels of the powerful antioxidant lycopene, found mainly in tomatoes and foods containing tomatoes, were 59% less likely to suffer ischemic stroke than those with low levels.

Theory: Lycopene reduces inflammation and blood clotting.

Other good sources of lycopene: Watermelon, papaya, guava, apricots and pink grapefruit.

Jouni Karppi, PhD, researcher, University of Eastern Finland, Kuopio.

Up to 80% of strokes can be avoided by preventing or treating the main risk factors, according to the National Stroke Association. For example, not smoking is crucial—people who smoke are twice as likely to have an ischemic stroke as nonsmokers.

Also important…

•**Do not ignore hypertension.** Like stroke, hypertension is often viewed as a problem only for the elderly. But there's been an increase in hypertension in younger patients, who often go undiagnosed.

Warning: Uncontrolled high blood pressure damages the brain—even in patients who haven't had a stroke, according to a recent study published in *The Lancet Neurology.*

If your blood pressure is high (normal is below 120/80), you are two to four times more likely to have a stroke than someone with normal blood pressure.

What to do: All adults should always have their blood pressure taken during routine doctor visits (at least once every two years if your blood pressure is normal…and at least annually if you've been diagnosed with hypertension or prehypertension). You can reduce both blood pressure and the risk for stroke by maintaining a healthy body weight…eating a healthful diet… getting regular exercise…and taking medication

if your blood pressure remains elevated despite lifestyle changes.

•**Manage diabetes.** It's second only to hypertension as a risk factor for stroke. Diabetes increases the risk for all cardiovascular diseases, including hypertension. People who have diabetes are up to four times more likely to have a stroke than those without the condition.

What to do: Get tested. The American Diabetes Association recommends that all adults age 45 and older get screened for diabetes every three years.

If you already have diabetes, do everything you can to keep your blood sugar stable—for example, eat properly, get exercise and lose weight, if necessary.

•**Keep an eye on your cholesterol.** It's the third most important stroke risk factor because LDL ("bad") cholesterol can accumulate in the arteries, impede circulation to the brain and increase the risk for blood clots.

What to do: Beginning at age 20, get your cholesterol tested at least every five years. If your LDL is high (less than 100 mg/dL is optimal), you'll want to get the number down by eating less saturated fat…getting more vegetables and other high-fiber foods…and possibly taking a statin medication, such as *simvastatin* (Zocor). Depending on the drug and dose, statins typically lower cholesterol by about 25% to 50%.

•**Pay attention to your alcohol consumption.** People who drink heavily (three or more alcoholic beverages daily for men and two or more for women) are more likely to have a stroke earlier in life than moderate drinkers or nondrinkers.

In fact, in a study of 540 stroke patients, French researchers found that heavy drinkers suffered their strokes at age 60, on average—14 years earlier than patients who drank less or not at all.

Warning: Heavy use of alcohol is also associated with increased risk for hemorrhagic stroke, which is caused by bleeding in the brain (rather than a blood clot). This type of stroke can occur even in patients without a history of serious health problems.

What to do: If you drink, be sure to follow the standard advice for alcohol consumption—

no more than two drinks daily for men…or one for women.

Do You Get Enough of the Anti-Stroke Mineral?

Susanna Larsson, PhD, an associate professor at the Institute of Environmental Medicine at the Karolinska Institutet in Stockholm, Sweden, and lead author of a study on dietary magnesium and stroke risk published in *The American Journal of Clinical Nutrition.*

Our moms always told us to eat our greens and beans…and now a recent study reveals yet another important reason why these wise women were right. People who consume plenty of foods rich in magnesium—such as leafy green veggies and legumes—appear to have fewer strokes.

Researchers analyzed data from seven studies involving a total of 241,378 people from the US, Europe and Asia who were followed for an average of nearly 12 years.

What they found: For every additional 100 mg of magnesium consumed daily, a person's risk for ischemic stroke (the most common type, which is caused by a blood clot) was reduced by 9%.

Concern: Study participants from the US fell far short of the ideal, consuming foods that provided, on average, just 242 mg of magnesium per day—though the RDA is 320 mg for most adult women and 420 mg for most adult men.

Because this study focused specifically on food, researchers did not make a recommendation regarding the use of magnesium supplementation. However, it is easy to boost your intake of the brain-protecting mineral with food. *For instance, you can get about 100 mg of magnesium each from…*

- **Beans** (black, lima, navy, white), 1 cup.
- **Beet greens,** 1 cup cooked.
- **Bran cereal,** ½ cup.
- **Brazil nuts,** 1 ounce.
- **Cashews,** 1¼ ounce.
- **Halibut,** 3 ounces.
- **Lentils,** 1¼ cup.
- **Okra,** 1 cup cooked.
- **Spinach,** ⅔ cup cooked.

Loud Traffic Noise Increases Stroke Risk

Previous studies have linked traffic noise with heart attack risk and increased blood pressure, and a recent study shows that persistent exposure to loud traffic can significantly increase the risk for stroke in people older than 64½. Every 10-decibel increase in traffic noise increases the risk for stroke by 27%. Researchers theorize that persistent road noise disrupts older people's sleep patterns (which already tend to be more fragmented), which in turn increases stress hormones, blood pressure and heart rate.

Mette Sørensen, PhD, senior researcher, Institute of Cancer Epidemiology, Danish Cancer Society, Copenhagen, Denmark, and lead author of a study of 57,053 people, published in *European Heart Journal.*

Fish, But Not Fish Oil Supplements, May Shield Against Stroke

BMJ news release

Eating fish, particularly oily fish, a couple of times a week may help protect you against stroke, but fish oil supplements don't have the same effect, a recent study finds.

STUDY DETAILS

Researchers analyzed the results of 38 previous studies to examine the association between fish consumption and the risk of stroke or mini-stroke (known to doctors as transient ischemic attack). The studies included nearly 800,000 people in 15 countries.

After adjusting for several risk factors, the researchers concluded that people who ate two to four servings of oily fish per week had a 6%

lower risk of stroke or mini-stroke than those who ate one or less servings per week. People who ate five or more servings per week had a 12% lower risk.

Two servings per week of any fish was associated with a 4% reduced risk. However, fish oil supplements did not reduce the risk of stroke or mini-stroke, according to a team led by Rajiv Chowdhury, PhD, of the University of Cambridge, in England.

The study was published online in the *BMJ*.

HOW FISH MIGHT HELP VASCULAR HEALTH

Prior research has linked regular consumption of fish with a reduced risk of coronary heart disease and current guidelines recommend eating at least two portions of fish a week, preferably an oily fish such as mackerel or sardines.

This study shows that eating fish can also reduce the risk of stroke, according to a *BMJ* journal news release.

There are a number of possible reasons why eating fish can benefit vascular health, the study authors said. It may be due to interactions between a wide range of nutrients, such as vitamins and essential amino acids, commonly found in fish.

Or it may be that eating more fish leads people to eat less red meat and other foods that harm vascular health, or that higher fish consumption may be an indicator of a generally healthier diet or greater wealth, both of which are associated with better vascular health.

info For more information on how to prevent stroke, visit the Web site of the US Centers for Disease Control and Prevention at *http://www.cdc.gov/stroke/healthy_living.htm*

Infectious Diseases

This Common Cause of Death Can Be Cured— If Detected Quickly

Sepsis is the tenth-leading cause of death in the US. It doesn't have to be. *The challenge:* There isn't a single test that can diagnose sepsis. Because its symptoms can be very similar to those caused by the original infection, the diagnosis sometimes is overlooked—and even a brief delay in treatment can be deadly.

Every year, at least 750,000 Americans develop severe sepsis and about 40% of patients with severe sepsis will die from it. The death rate approaches 50% in patients who develop septic shock (a dangerous drop in blood pressure that can lead to organ failure), which can't be reversed by the administration of intravenous (IV) fluids.

WHO'S AT RISK

Sepsis often is triggered by a bacterial infection. It also can be caused by viral or fungal infections. Pneumonia is the infection most likely to lead to sepsis.

The risk for sepsis is highest among adults age 65 and older, particularly those in the hospital who get IV lines, urinary catheters or other invasive devices. But you don't have to be elderly or seriously ill or be in a hospital to develop sepsis. About half of all cases occur in nonhospital settings. If you have any type of infection—an infected cut, a urinary tract infection, the flu—it can progress to sepsis.

Examples: Many of the 18,000 deaths that were linked to the swine flu outbreak in 2009 actually were caused by sepsis. In 2012, a New York sixth-grader cut his arm during a basketball

Derek C. Angus, MD, MPH, the Mitchell P. Fink Endowed Chair in Critical Care Medicine and professor of critical care medicine, medicine, health policy and management, and clinical and translational science at University of Pittsburgh School of Medicine.

game and got an infection. He died from sepsis three days later.

WARNING SIGNS

For reasons that still aren't clear, some infections are accompanied by an exaggerated immune response. It's normal for the body to respond to an infection with local inflammation. In patients with sepsis, the inflammation is systemic—it spreads throughout the body and often causes a loss of fluids that leads to plummeting blood pressure and shock. It also triggers microscopic blood clots that can block circulation to the heart, kidneys and other organs.

WARNING SIGNS...

• **You're sicker than expected.** Suppose that you have a bladder infection or an infected cut. If the severity of your symptoms seems to be out of proportion to the illness, call your doctor.

Go to the emergency room if you or a loved one also has two or more of the following symptoms...

• **Rapid heartbeat.** Patients who are developing sepsis usually will have tachycardia, a rapid heartbeat that exceeds 90 beats/minute.

• **High or low temperature.** Both hypothermia (a body temperature below 96.8°F) and fever (above 100.4°F) can indicate sepsis.

• **Rapid breathing, or tachypnea.** Patients with sepsis may have a respiration rate of 20 breaths/minute or higher.

• **Mucus.** The common cold is unlikely to cause sepsis, but it's not impossible. Call your doctor if a cold or other respiratory infection is accompanied by foul-smelling, discolored (rather than clear) mucus. This could indicate that you have developed a more serious infection.

• **Mental confusion.** When sepsis has reached the stage that it's interfering with circulation, it often will cause mental confusion.

• **Mottled skin.** There may be blue patches on the skin. Or if you press on the skin, there might be a delay before it returns to its normal color. Both of these changes indicate that circulation is impaired—a sign of severe sepsis.

Important: When patients begin to develop signs and symptoms suggesting that vital organ function is compromised, sepsis already is an emergency. For example, altered mental status, falling blood pressure, difficulty breathing or mottled skin all suggest that the inflammatory response intended to help is now, in fact, causing life-threatening harm.

WHAT COMES NEXT

• **Sepsis always is treated in the hospital.** To confirm that you have it, your doctor will do a variety of tests, including a blood pressure check and a white blood cell count. You also will need blood cultures to identify the organism that is causing the infection so that your doctor can choose the most effective treatment.

• **Treat first, diagnose later.** A study in *Critical Care Medicine* reported that the risk of dying from sepsis increases by 7.6% for every hour that passes without treatment. If your doctor suspects that you have sepsis, he/she will immediately start treatment with an antibiotic— usually a broad-spectrum antibiotic that's effective against a wide variety of organisms. Later the drug may be changed, depending on what the blood cultures show.

• **Intravenous fluids.** They often are needed to counteract the capillary leakage that causes blood pressure to drop.

• **Vasopressor treatment.** Depending on the severity of sepsis, you might be given *dopamine* or *norepinephrine*—medications that increase blood pressure and improve circulation to the heart, kidneys and other organs.

Other treatments may include supplemental oxygen, anti-inflammatory steroids and sometimes kidney dialysis.

PREVENTING SEPSIS

There's no way to predict who will get sepsis or the type of infection that's most likely to cause it in a particular person. So don't watch and wait. If you suspect sepsis, call your doctor. *And to build up your defense against sepsis in the future...*

• **Get a pneumococcal pneumonia vaccination** if you're 65 years old or older...have chronic health problems...take medications that lower immunity...or you're a smoker. Most people should get a pneumonia vaccination every five years.

•**Get an annual flu shot.** The rate of sepsis increases by about 16% during flu season. Getting an annual flu shot—along with washing your hands several times a day—reduces your risk for sepsis.

•**Clean wounds thoroughly.** If you have a cut, scrape or burn and are taking care of it yourself, wash it several times a day with soap and water, and apply an antibacterial ointment. Call your doctor immediately if there is pus, increased or streaking redness, or if the wound feels warm.

Millions of Americans Have Hepatitis C—Why You Need a Test Now

Bryce D. Smith, PhD, lead health scientist in the division of viral hepatitis at the Centers for Disease Control and Prevention in Atlanta, where he is the project officer for the program to improve hepatitis C–screening practices and testing for primary-care patients.

S hocking fact: One of every 30 baby boomers has been infected with a virus—most of them unknowingly—that greatly increases the risk for liver cancer, liver cirrhosis and liver transplants.

Latest development: The Centers for Disease Control and Prevention now recommends that every boomer get tested for the hepatitis C virus (HCV), which often causes no symptoms until the liver is severely damaged. Certain other people of any age, including those who received a blood transfusion or an organ transplant before blood-screening tests were widely available, also should be tested for the stealthy virus.

Because testing and treatment frequently can cure the HCV infection, these new guidelines are projected to prevent more than 120,000 unnecessary deaths in the US.

A GENERATION AT RISK

An estimated 3.2 million Americans, largely baby boomers, have a chronic HCV infection.

This generation accounts for more than 75% of all adult cases.

Most of these infections occurred in the 1970s and 1980s, before there were tests to detect them and before the nation's blood supply was routinely screened for the virus. The risk of transmitting the virus in bodily fluids was not widely known at the time.

HCV is transmitted only through blood. Anyone who received either a blood transfusion or an organ transplant prior to 1992, when blood screening and other HCV precautions came into widespread use, is also at increased risk. So are health-care workers exposed to blood (such as from accidental needle sticks)...and people who inject drugs (including those with diabetes, who might have shared a needle when injecting diabetes medications).

Even though baby boomers are the age group most likely to be infected with HCV, no one can assume that he/she is safe. You can get HCV from microscopic amounts of infected blood. This could occur during sex, from sharing a razor or toothbrush, or when getting a tattoo at an unsterile shop. About 45% of infected patients report no risk factors.

SILENT AND DEADLY

Most viral infections, including those caused by other forms of hepatitis, are "cleared" by the immune system—that is, the virus is eliminated from the body after the initial infection.

HCV is different. While the virus is cleared from the body in about 25% of cases, the HCV infection becomes chronic in 75% of infected patients. In these people, the virus (for unknown reasons) eludes the immune system and stays active in the body, where it causes on-going liver damage. The majority of those exposed to the virus have no initial symptoms. The infection can persist for decades before it is recognized and treated.

Even in the 20% to 30% of patients who do have symptoms (such as fatigue, fever and joint pain), the illness is so mild that it's often mistaken for a cold or the flu. Most people don't get tested because they never even bother to see a doctor for such mild symptoms.

GETTING DIAGNOSED

Blood tests to diagnose HCV…

An initial antibody test will determine whether you've ever been infected with HCV. If the test is negative, no further tests are needed—unless you have ongoing risk factors, such as the continued use of injected drugs, which requires more frequent testing.

Cost: $30 to $35. If the test is positive, you'll need the following test to determine whether the infection is chronic.

A nucleic acid test will show whether the virus is still active.

Cost: $100 to $250. If you test positive, you have chronic HCV and will need to talk to your doctor about treatment options. If you are infected, but have no liver damage, your doctor should monitor your liver at your annual physical.

BEST TREATMENT OPTIONS

Deaths from HCV are on the rise because many chronic HCV patients aren't diagnosed or treated until the liver is severely damaged. If the condition is detected and treated, many of these deaths could be prevented. There is no vaccine currently available to prevent HCV infection, though studies are under way.

The main treatments for chronic HCV…

•*Pegylated interferon* **and** *ribavirin.* This two-medication treatment is standard for certain types of chronic HCV, although a new approach (described below) may be faster-acting. The interferon, given by injection twice a month, helps the immune system fight the virus. *Ribavirin* (Copegus, Rebetol and others), taken orally twice a day, fights the virus directly.

•**Triple therapy.** With this approach, patients take *boceprevir* (Victrelis) or *telaprevir* (Incivek), in addition to the interferon and ribavirin. This three-drug therapy can shorten the treatment time to as little as 24 weeks, compared with 48 weeks with the older treatment.

The side effects of both treatments can be grueling and may include extreme fatigue and/or muscle aches. But the virus is completely eliminated in 70% to 75% of cases. The rest will remain chronically infected.

This Vitamin Fights the Deadly Virus You Don't Know You Have

According to a recent study, adding vitamin B-12 to the standard healing regimen for hepatits C virus (HCV) significantly improves the success rate for the treatment of this life-threatening disease.

How the study was done: HCV patients were randomly assigned to receive either the standard treatment of a twice-daily antiviral pill called *ribavirin* and a weekly injection of *interferon*…or these same medications plus monthly injections of 5,000 micrograms of vitamin B-12. Treatment continued for 24 to 48 weeks, and researchers checked periodically to see whether the virus was eliminated from the body.

Results: Twelve weeks into the study, the response rate was already 21% higher among patients receiving vitamin B-12, compared with the standard treatment group…and six months after treatment ended, patients in the B-12 group were 34% more likely to be free of the virus. Interestingly, the beneficial effects of B-12 were especially pronounced among patients with a particularly difficult-to-treat type of HCV called genotype 1. Vitamin B-12 injections were not associated with any increased risk for side effects.

Update: The recent introduction of two new antiviral drugs, *boceprevir* and *telaprevir*, now provides additional options for HCV patients. However, these medications can have serious side effects…they are very expensive…they raise concerns about the development of drug-resistant HCV strains…and, as with any new drug, their long-term risks are unknown. So until more is revealed about the new drugs, the study researchers say that the addition of vitamin B-12 represents a safe and inexpensive option for improving the effectiveness of the standard HCV treatment. In addition, it is possible that B-12 may even boost patients' response to these new drugs.

Gerardo Nardone, MD, professor in the department of clinical and experimental medicine of the gastroenterology unit at the University of Naples "Federico II" in Italy and coauthor of an article on hepatitis C published in *Gut*.

Doctor's Exam Is Not Enough To Diagnose Pneumonia

Recent study: Physicians were asked, based only on medical history and a physical exam, whether 2,810 patients with an acute cough had pneumonia or bronchitis. Each patient then received a chest X-ray to confirm the diagnosis.

Result: The physicians had correctly identified only 29% of pneumonia cases.

Self-defense: If you have such symptoms as a cough, fever, shortness of breath, chills and chest pain, and your doctor has said that you don't have pneumonia, contact him/her again—especially if your symptoms do not improve in a few days or get worse.

Saskia van Vugt, MD, researcher, Julius Center for Health Sciences and Primary Care, Utrecht, the Netherlands.

TWO OTHER HEPATITIS VIRUSES

Hepatitis A virus (HAV) infections have dropped by 92% since 1995, when a vaccine first came into widespread use. In 2009, fewer than 2,000 cases were reported in the US.

Cause: Poor sanitation. It's spread through the fecal-oral route. For example, someone who's infected and doesn't wash his/her hands after using the bathroom could transmit it to someone else.

Other causes: Contaminated water (usually in less-developed countries) and eating food that has been contaminated, often by an infected food-service worker. Certain sexual practices (specifically oral contact with an infected partner's anus) also increase risk for HAV.

Some patients infected with HAV have no symptoms. In others, it may cause jaundice (yellowing of the skin and/or eyes), fatigue and flulike symptoms. Most patients recover in one to two months. Get vaccinated for HAV if you travel to areas where the virus is common. You'll need two injections over a six-month period.

Hepatitis B virus (HBV) has also declined in the US in recent years. In 2009, 3,374 new

Pneumococcal Vaccine Recommended for People Ages 50 and Over

The vaccine Prevnar was recently approved by the FDA to protect people 50 and older against infection by Streptococcus pneumoniae bacteria, which can cause pneumonia, meningitis, and blood and middle-ear infections. Prevnar lasts longer than the older vaccine, Pneumovax, and has been given to children for several years. Now it is approved for older adults as well.

UC Berkeley Wellness Letter. *www.wellnessletter.com*

cases were reported. Since many patients have no or only mild symptoms and don't get tested, the actual number of cases is probably 10 times higher.

Cause: Contact with blood or other body fluids, such as semen and saliva. Most people are infected during sex with an infected partner... from injecting drugs with an unsterile needle... or from sharing personal items such as razors or toothbrushes. It is not spread by sharing eating utensils, sneezing, etc. The virus is unlikely to be spread by kissing unless the noninfected partner has an open wound in his/her mouth.

Between 30% and 50% of HBV patients will experience fatigue, nausea, jaundice or other symptoms. The symptoms can persist for a few weeks to up to six months.

HBV can become chronic, but this occurs in only about 5% of adults. Between 15% and 25% of those with a chronic infection will eventually develop liver cirrhosis and/or liver cancer.

No treatment is needed for an acute HBV infection. Patients with chronic HBV may be treated with antiviral drugs and need regular checkups to monitor liver changes that could lead to cirrhosis or cancer.

Important: Patients with risk factors for HBV—including health-care workers...people who travel to parts of the world with a high rate of HBV...or men who have sex with men—should get vaccinated. Three shots are given over six months.

Tap Water Used in Neti Pots Tied to Rare, Fatal Brain Infection

Jonathan Yoder, MPH, coordinator, waterborne diseases and outbreak surveillance, US Centers for Disease Control and Prevention.

Ann Falsey, MD, professor of medicine, University of Rochester Medical Center, Rochester, New York.

Clinical Infectious Diseases, online

Two people in Louisiana died in 2011 from a rare brain infection contracted after using neti pots containing tap water to flush their sinuses.

The infection, known as primary amebic *meningoencephalitis*, occurs after water containing the amoeba *Naegleria fowleri* enters the nose and travels through the olfactory nerve into the brain.

This is the first time tap water and neti pots have been connected to infection with N. fowleri, according to a report appearing online in *Clinical Infectious Diseases*.

Neti pots are small vessels that are filled with water and saline solution and used to flush the sinuses.

Although the infection is extremely rare, it is almost uniformly fatal, said Ann Falsey, MD, a professor of medicine at the University of Rochester Medical Center, who was not involved with the study.

According to Jonathan Yoder, MPH, lead author of the paper, 123 cases have been reported since 1962, the year it was discovered. Yoder is coordinator of waterborne diseases and outbreak surveillance at the US Centers for Disease Control and Prevention.

N. fowleri is generally found in warmish freshwater ponds, lakes and rivers and can be contracted by swimming, fishing, boating, diving or tubing in such bodies of water.

RECENT CASES

The first patient to succumb to the infection via a neti pot was a 28-year-old man from southern Louisiana who developed a severe headache along with neck stiffness, back pain and vomiting in June 2011. The next day he arrived

DID YOU KNOW?

Infections Cause One in Six Cancer Cases Worldwide

Many infections are preventable or treatable. Human papillomavirus can lead to cervical cancer and is preventable through vaccine. Hepatitis affects the liver, leading to inflammation and scarring, which can cause cancer. Hepatitis treatments are available. Helicobacter pylori bacteria can lead to gastric cancer, but the infection can be treated with an antibiotic cocktail.

Study of two million new cancer cases in 2008 by researchers from International Agency for Research on Cancer, Lyon, France, published in *The Lancet Oncology*.

at a New Orleans hospital disoriented, confused and combative.

He received a tentative diagnosis of amebic meningoencephalitis, was treated immediately with a combination of drugs but unfortunately died in the neurologic critical care unit.

The man lived with his mother, who reported that he had not been near any freshwater recently but that he did irrigate his sinuses daily with a neti pot. She said he added a commercially sold salt packet to tap water.

A similar case occurred three months later involving a 51-year-old woman in northern Louisiana,

The woman was admitted to a hospital in September 2011 with nausea, vomiting, neck stiffness and "altered mental status."

She died in October 2011 and an autopsy revealed amebic meningoencephalitis.

Again, the woman's parents reported that their daughter had had no freshwater exposure in the past two weeks but also regularly used a neti pot.

In both cases, N. fowleri was found in the tap water of the individuals' homes.

Although N. fowleri cannot survive in salt water, the saline solutions used in these neti pots were unable to kill the organisms.

255

Infectious Diseases

New Test Quickly Identifies Bacterial Infections

The FDA recently approved a blood test that can identify 12 different types of bacterial infection, such as Staphylococcus, Streptococcus and Listeria, in a few hours after a positive blood culture (instead of the standard two to four days). Results from the new test, called the Verigene Gram-Positive Blood Culture (BC-GP) nucleic acid test, were compared with those from traditional tests in 1,642 blood culture samples. Results from the BC-GP test were as accurate as those from the traditional tests. Faster identification of the type of bacteria causing an infection may allow for more effective treatment.

Alberto Gutierrez, PhD, director, Office of In Vitro Diagnostic Device Evaluation and Safety, FDA, Silver Spring, Maryland.

Officials don't know why these two cases occurred in Louisiana, but there is some evidence that N. fowleri may be expanding its reach, particularly into northern areas, which are experiencing warmer weather. A case of primary amebic meningoencephalitis was reported for the first time in Minnesota in 2010 and also in Kansas in 2011.

WHAT NETI-POT USERS CAN DO

Despite the severity of the infection, "very simple measures could prevent it," Dr. Falsey said.

Yoder recommended using boiled or filtered water when preparing to use a neti pot.

"Even though tap water is safe...for drinking, showering and bathing, it's certainly not sterile water and we don't think it's appropriate for something like nasal irrigation," he said.

And there are other reasons not to use tap water for nasal irrigation, including the presence of E. coli and the bacteria legionella, Dr. Falsey said.

info The US Centers for Disease Control and Prevention has more on N. fowleri and primary amebic *meningoencephalitis* at its Web site, *www.cdc.gov/parasites/naegleria/*.

Scientists Explore How Zinc Fights Infection

Ohio State University, news release.

Many Americans take zinc supplements to zap colds, and a recent study seeks to explain how the mineral works.

Zinc helps fight infections by balancing the immune system's response, according to the study led by Daren Knoell, PharmD, a professor of pharmacy and internal medicine at Ohio State University.

"We believe that our findings help to narrow an important gap that has existed in our understanding of how this relatively simple metal helps us defend ourselves from infection," said Dr. Knoell.

Zinc deficiency affects about two billion people worldwide, including roughly 40% of the elderly in the United States. It can have severe consequences among vulnerable people, the researchers noted.

Red meat and poultry are rich in zinc, according to the US National Institutes of Health. Other foods that contain zinc are beans, nuts, some shellfish, whole grains, fortified cereals and dairy products.

The essential mineral works by stopping the action of a protein known to play an important role in the immune response to infection. As a result, it prevents out-of-control inflammation, the researchers said.

A zinc deficiency at the time of an infection, particularly sepsis—a devastating systemic response to infection common among patients in a hospital's intensive care unit, or ICU—could be damaging or even deadly, according to the researchers.

256

Fecal Transplant Cures Gastrointestinal Illness

The bacteria C. difficile claims thousands of lives a year. If two attempts using the first-line treatment—the antibiotic *metronidazole* (Flagyl)—don't work, transplanting the feces of a healthy person into someone who is sick is effective more than 90% of the time. Feces contain the right mix of bacteria to fight C. difficile. Fecal transplants are done at the Mayo Clinic in Arizona and Minnesota and at several other health-care institutions.

Robert Orenstein, DO, associate professor of medicine and chair, division of infectious diseases, Mayo Clinic, Phoenix.

RESEARCHERS REVIEWED HUMAN AND ANIMAL STUDIES

After analyzing human cell culture and animal studies, the researchers found that a specific protein draws zinc into infection-fighting cells where it balances the immune response. In a previous animal study, Dr. Knoell's team found that unlike mice on a normal diet, those deficient in zinc developed significant inflammation in response to sepsis.

"We believe that to some extent, these findings are going to be applicable to other important areas of disease beyond sepsis," Dr. Knoell said. "Without zinc on board to begin with, it could increase vulnerability to infection. But our work is focused on what happens once you get an infection—if you are deficient in zinc you are at a disadvantage because your defense system is amplified, and inappropriately so."

The study appeared in the journal *Cell Reports*.

WHAT THIS MEANS FOR THE VERY SICK

However, it's uncertain for now if very sick ICU patients would benefit from zinc supplements.

"I think the question is whom to give zinc to, if anybody at all. We predict that not everybody in the ICU with sepsis needs zinc, but I anticipate that a proportion of them would," added Dr. Knoell, who is also an investigator in Ohio State's Davis Heart and Lung Research Institute.

"Zinc is a critical element that we get from our diet, but we do not think we can give zinc and fix everything. Usually, if there is a zinc deficiency, we would expect to see other nutrient deficiencies, too."

Theses findings could help explain why taking zinc supplements at the start of a cold seems to ease the effects of the illness, the researchers suggest.

"There might be therapeutic implications about giving supplemental zinc in a strategic manner to help improve some people with certain conditions. But also, could we learn from this so someday we can be more diagnostic about who it is that needs zinc? And if so, what dose and for how long?" Dr. Knoell said.

DAILY MINIMUM REQUIREMENT OF ZINC FOR ADULTS

Most adults should get eight to 11 milligrams of zinc daily. With supplements, the researchers noted it is possible but relatively uncommon to consume toxic levels of zinc.

info The US Office of Dietary Supplements has more about zinc.

Dishwashing Doesn't Kill Tummy-Troubling Norovirus

Ohio State University Center for Clinical and Translational Science, news release.

Commercial dishwashers can kill everyday bacteria but not norovirus, the cause of stomach flu and many foodborne illnesses around the world, according to a recent study.

The researchers noted that norovirus is responsible for 90% of nonbacterial cases of gastroenteritis outbreaks.

Norovirus, which can easily contaminate food or water, spreads rapidly through confined populations, such as cruise ships, dormitories and prisons. According to the US Centers

Common Hepatitis Treatment Increases Risk for Depression

Hepatitis is the most common chronic blood-borne infection in the US, affecting at least 3.2 million people. It's mainly treated by the antiviral agent Interferon.

Self-defense: Certain antidepressants, such as *citalopram* (Celexa), have been effective in treating depression in hepatitis patients treated with interferon.

Study of hepatitis C patients by Loyola University Medical Center, Maywood, Illinois, published in International Journal of Interferon, Cytokine and Mediator Research.

for Disease Control and Prevention, norovirus each year causes an estimated 91,000 emergency room visits and 23,000 hospitalizations for severe diarrhea among children younger than five years.

Although restaurant-industry guidelines for cleaning dishes and silverware eliminate bacteria, they are not effective against norovirus, said researchers from Ohio State University. The virus can withstand both manual and mechanical washing, according to the recent study.

"We know that when public food establishments follow the cleaning protocols, they do a very good job at getting rid of bacteria," said study leader Melvin Pascall, PhD, associate professor in the department of food science and technology. "Now we can see that the protocols are less effective at removing and killing viruses, and this may help explain why there are still so many illnesses caused by cross-contaminated food."

STUDY DETAILS

For the study, published recently in the journal *PLoS One,* researchers contaminated cream cheese and reduced-fat milk with a norovirus, E. coli or Listeria, three common causes of foodborne illness. These dairy products were then applied to stainless-steel utensils, ceramic plates and drinking glasses. The utensils were washed by hand or in a dishwasher following sanitizing protocols that used chlorine and quaternary ammonium compound (germicidal detergent).

Both hand-washing and dishwashers reduced E. coli and Listeria to safe levels. Although dishwashers were more effective at eliminating potentially harmful bacteria and viruses, the researchers found neither cleaning method could reduce the presence of norovirus.

"Even though the protocols were able to kill some of the virus, norovirus is highly contagious and it takes only a few viral particles to infect humans," noted Jianrong Li, PhD, assistant professor of food virology. "These results would indicate that neither the detergents nor sanitizers used in current cleaning protocols are effective against the norovirus at the currently used concentrations."

"Proper sanitation and handling remain the single biggest factor that can prevent cross-contamination of food and dishware at food-service establishments," Dr. Pascall said. "However, it appears that we need to identify better agents or methods to significantly reduce the presence of norovirus and work to update the protocols."

The researchers said they plan to test the effectiveness of cleaning methods against hepatitis A and influenza viruses

info For more information on norovirus, visit the Web site of the US Centers for Disease Control and Prevention at *www.cdc.gov/norovirus/.*

New Antibiotic May Treat Skin Infections in Shorter Time

Michele Green, MD, dermatologist, Lenox Hill Hospital, New York City.

Scott Gorenstein, MD, clinical director, Hyperbaric Medicine Program, Winthrop-University Hospital, Mineola, New York.

Journal of the American Medical Association, news release

A short course of treatment with a newer antibiotic called *tedizolid* works as well against bacterial skin infections as longer

FDA Approves New Test to Identify Cause of Gastroenteritis

Many viruses, bacteria and parasites can cause infectious gastroenteritis, inflammation of the stomach and intestines that causes vomiting and watery diarrhea. A new test, the xTAG Gastrointestinal Pathogen Panel (GPP), screens for 11 possible causes of infectious gastroenteritis from a single stool sample and provides results much more rapidly than traditional tests. This allows diagnosis and any necessary treatment to begin much sooner.

Alberto Gutierrez, PhD, director, Office of In Vitro Diagnostics and Radiological Health, FDA, Silver Spring, Maryland.

treatment with the antibiotic *linezolid*, a recent study finds.

"These infections, which include cellulitis and other wound infections, can be life threatening," noted one expert not connected to the study, Michele Green, MD, a dermatologist at Lenox Hill Hospital, in New York City. "Because so many of these infections have become antibiotic-resistant, the development of a novel antibiotic which is effective is very important," she added.

STUDY DETAILS

The recent phase 3 clinical trial included 667 adult patients in North America, Latin America and Europe who received either 200 milligram pills once a day of tedizolid phosphate for six days, or 600 mg of linezolid every 12 hours for 10 days.

The drugs showed similar levels of effectiveness after two to three days and after 11 days, according to the study in the *Journal of the American Medical Association*.

Side effects, mostly mild or moderate, occurred in nearly 41% of patients taking tedizolid and about 43% of those taking linezolid. Rates of serious side effects were low and similar in both groups, according to a journal news release.

The study was led by Philippe Prokocimer, MD, of Trius Therapeutics Inc., San Diego, which makes tedizolid and funded the study.

EXPERTS EVALUATE RESULTS

According to Dr. Green, the study suggests tedizolid is "a reasonable alternative" to the older drug, especially for infections with MRSA (methicillin-resistant Staphylococcus aureus), "which is a growing problem, due to antibiotic resistance and the continued use of prolonged antibiotics."

Another physician agreed. Scott Gorenstein, MD, is an expert in wound healing therapies at Winthrop-University Hospital in Mineola, New York. He said it is important to find shorter-course antibiotic therapies to help reduce antibiotic resistance and the risk for complications.

Dr. Gorenstein, who is also clinical director of the hospital's Hyperbaric Medicine Program, called the study "a great starting point" for further research to confirm these findings.

info For more information about skin infections, visit MedlinePlus, *www.nlm.nih.gov/medlineplus/skininfections.html.*

Emerging SARS-Like Virus Well-Suited to Attack Humans

American Society for Microbiology, news release.

The new SARS-like "coronavirus" that first emerged in the Middle East can invade the lungs and immune system as easily as the common cold, according to a recent study.

But in the event of a large-scale outbreak, researchers in Switzerland found the virus—known as HCoV-EMC—may be treatable with components of the immune system, known as interferons. This immunotherapy has shown promise in the treatment of the respiratory disease SARS and hepatitis C, the study authors said.

"Surprisingly, this coronavirus grows very efficiently on human epithelial cells," said study coauthor Volker Thiel, PhD, of the Institute of Immunobiology at Kantonal Hospital in St. Gallen, in a news release from the American Society for Microbiology. Epithelial cells line hollow organs and glands.

"The other thing we found is that the viruses [HCoV-EMC, SARS, and the common cold virus] are all similar in terms of host responses: they don't provoke a huge innate immune response," he said.

The study was published online in *mBio*.

HCoV-EMC, which may have jumped from animal to human very recently, was first isolated in Spring 2012 after a man in Saudi Arabia died from a severe respiratory infection and kidney failure. Following his death, health officials identified 11 more people infected with the virus, the latest in Great Britain. As of early 2013, seven people with known infections have died. Nearly all patients have lived or traveled in the Middle East.

Concerns have been raised that the new strain could trigger a pandemic similar to the SARS outbreak of 2002–2003, which infected more than 8,000 people and killed 774.

"We don't know whether the cases we observed are the tip of the iceberg, or whether many more people are infected without showing severe symptoms," noted Dr. Thiel.

The World Health Organization said that doctors should test patients for the new coronavirus if they have unexplained pneumonia or unexplained complicated respiratory illness not responding to treatment.

As of February 2013, no cases of the coronavirus have been reported in the United States, according to the US Centers for Disease Control and Prevention.

To test the new virus, the researchers used cultured bronchial cells to mimic the lining of the human airway. The study authors found that pre-treating the airway with proteins that play a critical role in immune response to infections—known as lambda-type interferons—significantly reduced the number of infected cells.

Although their findings suggest there is promise for an effective treatment against HCoV-EMC, the researchers added ongoing cooperation between scientists and health agencies around the world is needed to prevent outbreaks of this virus and other diseases.

info For more information about the coronavirus infection, visit The World Health Organization Web site at *www.who.int/csr/disease/coronavirus_infections/en/*.

Is That a Germy Toothbrush?

Is it true that you should replace your toothbrush after a cold or the flu?

A toothbrush does not typically carry enough germs to make you sick. Even if a virus from a recent illness is lingering on your toothbrush, you've developed antibodies to it, so the chance of reinfection is very small. But it's best to always follow good hygiene practices, especially after an illness. Choose a soft or ultrasoft toothbrush…rinse it thoroughly…and let it air dry after brushing. Store your toothbrush standing up in a container that does not cover the bristles. Replace your toothbrush every three to four months or when it starts to look frayed.

Kavita P. Ahluwalia, DDS, MPH, public health dentist, associate professor of clinical dentistry, Columbia University College of Dental Medicine, New York City.

Whooping Cough Strains Outsmart Vaccine

Paul Cieslak, MD, medical director, Oregon Immunization Program, Portland, Oregon.
Kenneth Bromberg, MD, chairman of pediatrics and director of the Vaccine Research Center, Brooklyn Hospital Center, New York City.
New England Journal of Medicine

The bacteria responsible for whooping cough may be evolving into different strains, and the current vaccine can't offer complete protection against these new strains, researchers report.

In recent years, cases of whooping cough have risen dramatically. Tens of thousands have been sickened, and multiple deaths have been reported, mostly in infants, according to the US Centers for Disease Control and Prevention (CDC).

Several recent studies have focused on the potential of waning immunity from the whooping cough vaccine over time. In a letter printed in the *New England Journal of Medicine,* researchers pointed out that there may be another culprit: an evolution in the bug itself.

The vaccine contains a number of components that help give the body immunity against the whooping cough bacteria (Bordetella pertussis). One of these components is called pertactin. Strains of the whooping cough bacteria that are pertactin-negative have been found in Japan, France, Finland and, now, the United States, the researchers reported. That means that at least one component of the current vaccine is ineffective against these newly found strains.

"There are several theories as to why we're seeing more pertussis," said Kenneth Bromberg, MD, chairman of pediatrics and director of the Vaccine Research Center at the Brooklyn Hospital Center, in New York City. "One theory is better diagnosis. A second [theory] is that the vaccines are not as good in terms of longevity as the whole-cell vaccine was. The third theory is that there have been genetic changes in the strains of pertussis, such that it makes new strains immune or relatively immune to the current vaccines."

"The thought is that the bacteria have gotten smart and are eliminating the pertactin in themselves," said Dr. Bromberg, who was not involved in the current research.

EFFECTIVENESS OF CURRENT VACCINE IS QUESTIONED

A second letter in the same journal issue addressed another of the theories that Dr. Bromberg outlined—the effectiveness of the current vaccine.

In the late 1990s, the vaccine was switched from a whole-cell vaccine to what's known as an acellular vaccine.

"The whole-cell vaccine contains the whole cell of killed bacteria, so every protein that the bacteria makes is in it, forcing the person to mount an immune response to every part of the bacteria," said the letter's coauthor, Paul Cieslak, MD, medical director of the Oregon Immunization Program, in Portland. "With the

New Lupus Trigger?

Recent finding: Lupus and other autoimmune diseases could be triggered by Staphylococcus, a common bacterium. It's possible that treating the infection could reduce flare-ups—or even prevent the disease.

Mayo Clinic.

new, acellular vaccine, they picked the proteins they thought were most important. Without the whole cell, there are fewer side effects, but it may be a little less effective."

Oregon experienced a significant increase in the number of whooping cough cases last year. Oregon maintains statewide records on immunizations, as well as records of who has had a confirmed case of whooping cough. This information allowed Dr. Cieslak and his colleagues to go back and review what type of vaccine had been given to those who later were infected with whooping cough.

They found that the reported cases of whooping cough were significantly lower in youngsters who had their first immunization with the whole-cell vaccine rather than the acellular vaccine.

PUTTING CURRENT VACCINE TO BETTER USE

Does that mean that whole-cell vaccine should make a comeback? "No one is making the argument for whole-cell vaccine," Dr. Cieslak said. "Without the whole cell in the vaccine, there are fewer side effects. It may be a little less effective, but it's got to be safe."

Dr. Bromberg agreed. "The whole-cell vaccine isn't coming back. The acellular vaccine is significantly better in terms of not causing reactions, but it doesn't work for as long as we thought," he said.

Dr. Cieslak said that even though the current vaccine isn't perfect, "we certainly recommend getting the vaccine. You are still far better off with the vaccine."

Dr. Bromberg added that experts are trying to figure out ways to better use the current vaccine. For example, the CDC recently added a recommendation that all pregnant women

261

should receive the whooping cough vaccine late in pregnancy to offer protection to their newborns.

info For more information about preventing whooping cough, visit US Centers for Disease Control and Prevention Web site at *www.cdc.gov/pertussis/about/prevention.html.*

"Nightmare" Bacteria Spreading in US

Marc Siegel, MD, clinical associate professor, medicine, NYU Langone Medical Center, New York City.

Ghinwa Dumyati, MD, associate professor, medicine, University of Rochester, Rochester, New York.

Thomas Frieden, MD, MPH, director, US Centers for Disease Control and Prevention.

Michael Bell, MD, director of the CDC's Division of Healthcare Quality Promotion.

US Centers for Disease Control and Prevention report, *Vital Signs.*

A "nightmare" bacteria that is resistant to powerful antibiotics and kills half of those it infects has surfaced in nearly 200 US hospitals and nursing homes, according to the US Centers for Disease Control and Prevention (CDC).

The CDC said 4% of US hospitals and 18% of nursing homes had treated at least one patient with the bacteria, called Carbapenem-Resistant Enterobacteriaceae (CRE), within the first six months of 2012 and that number increased in 2013.

CRE are in a family of more than 70 bacteria called enterobacteriaceae, including Klebsiella pneumoniae and E. coli, that normally live in the digestive system.

In recent years, some of these bacteria have become resistant to last-resort antibiotics known as carbapenems.

"CRE are nightmare bacteria. Our strongest antibiotics don't work and patients are left with potentially untreatable infections," CDC Director Thomas Frieden MD, MPH, said. "Doctors, hospital leaders and public health [officials] must work together now to implement the

Better Cure for C. Diff Infection

Clostridium difficile (C. diff), a dangerous bacterial infection that causes severe diarrhea, sometimes is difficult to treat with antibiotics and/or probiotics.

Recent study: When researchers implanted donated human stool from healthy family members into the intestines of 49 patients (average age 66) with C. diff, all of the patients recovered dramatically within four days, with no recurrence within the 100 days following treatment.

Theory: Healthy stool contains good bacteria that reestablish normal intestinal flora.

If you have C. diff that has not responded to antibiotics or probiotics: Ask your doctor about a fecal transplant.

Mayur Ramesh, MD, infectious diseases physician, Henry Ford Hospital, Detroit.

CDC's 'detect and protect' strategy and stop these infections from spreading."

"The good news," Dr. Frieden added, "is we now have an opportunity to prevent its further spread." But, he continued, "We only have a limited window of opportunity to stop this infection from spreading to the community and spreading to more organisms."

Although CRE bacteria are not yet found nationwide, they have increased fourfold within the United States in the past decade, with most cases reported in the Northeast.

Health officials said they're concerned about the rapid spread of the bacteria, which can endanger the lives of patients and healthy people. For example, in the last 10 years, the CDC tracked one CRE from one health-care facility to similar facilities in 42 states.

One type of CRE, a resistant form of Klebsiella pneumoniae, has increased sevenfold in the past decade, according to the CDC's *5 Vital Signs* report.

"To see bacteria that are resistant is worrisome, because this group of bacteria are very common," said Marc Siegel, MD, clinical associate professor of medicine at NYU Langone Medical Center in New York City.

WHO GETS CRE AND HOW IT SPREADS

Most CRE infections to date have been in patients who had prolonged stays in hospitals, long-term facilities and nursing homes, the report said.

The bacteria kill up to half the patients whose bloodstreams get infected and are easily spread from patient to patient on the hands of health-care workers, the CDC said.

Moreover, CRE bacteria can transfer their antibiotic resistance to other bacteria of the same type.

This problem is the result of the overuse of antibiotics, Dr. Siegel said. "The more you use an antibiotic, the more resistance is going to emerge," he said. "This is an indictment of the overuse of this class of antibiotic."

What's needed are new antibiotics, Dr. Siegel said, adding that pharmaceutical companies lack the financial motivation to develop them right now. "Eventually, there will be enough resistance so drug companies will have a financial incentive. In the meantime, lives can be lost," he said.

EXPERT COMMENTARY

"At this time, our best prevention is detection and infection control. The incidence [of CRE] is low and we are looking to prevent it before it gets much higher and we cannot control it," commented Ghinwa Dumyati, MD, associate professor of medicine at the University of Rochester in New York.

Wipe Off the Top

Wipe off the top of a soda can, or rinse it with water, before drinking from it. Cans of soda bought at stores and from machines carried a variety of bacteria on the tops. Cans bought from stores and gas stations had the most germs...those from vending machines had fewer...those bought in 12-packs had the fewest.

Laboratory study arranged by CBS 11, Fort Worth, Texas, reported online at *www.consumerist.com*.

To beat back the spread of these bacteria, the CDC wants hospitals and other health-care facilities to take the following steps...

- **Enforce infection-control precautions.**
- **Group together patients with CRE.**
- **Segregate staff, rooms and equipment to patients with CRE.**
- **Tell facilities when patients with CRE are transferred.**
- **Use antibiotics carefully.**

Additional funding of research and technology is critical to prevent and quickly identify CRE, the CDC said.

HOSPITALS CAN CONTROL CRE

Countries where CRE is more common have had some success controlling it.

Israel, for example, worked to reduce CRE in its 27 hospitals, and CRE rates dropped by more than 70%. Some US facilities and states have also seen similar reductions, the agency said.

"We have seen in outbreak after outbreak that when facilities and regions follow the CDC's prevention guidelines, CRE can be controlled and even stopped," said Michael Bell, MD, acting director of the CDC's Division of Healthcare Quality Promotion. "As trusted health-care providers, it is our responsibility to prevent further spread of these deadly bacteria."

WHAT PATIENTS CAN DO

Dr. Siegel said there are measures patients can take to reduce their risk of infection.

"Number one on the list is to not push for a longer hospital stay. Patients think they are safer at the hospital, but that may not be true," he said. "And try to go into a clean hospital."

Patients should also make sure doctors and staff wear gloves and wash their hands when treating them, he said.

info For more information on CRE bacteria, visit the US Centers for Disease Control and Prevention Web site at *www.cdc.gov/hai/organisms/cre/cre-patients.html*.

Know the Facts About Lyme Disease

Henry Feder, MD, professor of family medicine at University of Connecticut Health Center, Farmington, Connecticut.

Every summer, there are more than 30,000 new cases of Lyme disease in the US, with 93% occurring in 10 states—Connecticut (where the disease was originally identified, in the towns of Lyme, Old Lyme and East Haddam), Delaware, Maryland, Massachusetts, Minnesota, New Jersey, New York, Pennsylvania, Rhode Island and Wisconsin. The Pacific deer tick—a close relative of the species found east of the Rockies—causes Lyme disease in California.

Most recent development: University researchers, in cooperation with the federal Centers for Disease Control and Prevention, conducted the largest-ever field study of Lyme disease, publishing their results in the February 2012 issue of *The American Journal of Tropical Medicine.* They found Lyme-infected ticks in the 10 states listed above—and also in northern Virginia… along the Illinois/Indiana border…along the New York/Vermont border…in southwestern Michigan…and in east North Dakota.

That's a fact. But a lot of frightening misinformation has shadowed scientific findings about Lyme disease. *What you need to know now…*

THE FACTS

Lyme disease is an infection by the bacteria *Borrelia burgdorferi,* caused by a bite from an infected deer tick. The tick regurgitates the bacteria while sucking a "blood meal" from its host. Most humans are infected through the bites of immature ticks called nymphs, which are the size of a poppy seed. Adult deer ticks also can transmit Lyme disease, but because they are so much larger—the size of an apple seed—they are more likely to be discovered before having time to transmit the disease.

From the first, inaccurate stories have emerged about Lyme disease.

Example: In 1977, the tabloid headline "Mystery Disease in Connecticut Cripples Children" introduced Lyme disease to the public. Yes,

Poison Ivy Is Growing More Dangerous

Increased carbon dioxide in the atmosphere is causing the plants to grow bigger and produce more *urushiol,* the oil that causes an immune reaction in human skin.

Self-defense: When in areas where poison ivy grows, use a barrier cream such as Ivy Block to prevent urushiol from getting on your skin. Wear heavy protective gloves and clothing. Also use gloves to bathe your pet if you think that the animal has been exposed to poison ivy.

If you think you have been exposed: Wear clean gloves when removing clothing and shoes that have come in contact with the plant. Thoroughly scrub exposed skin with lots of soap and lukewarm water within five to 10 minutes of touching the plant.

Caution: Never burn poison ivy plants. Doing so releases urushiol, which can cause severe lung damage if inhaled.

University of Berkeley Wellness Letter. www.well nessletter.com

Lyme arthritis—inflammation and swelling of the joints, particularly the knee joint—is a possible symptom of Lyme disease when it's not treated with antibiotics in its earliest stage. But of the thousands of children who have developed Lyme arthritis, not a single child, to my knowledge, has ever been crippled.

My perspective: I have been diagnosing and treating Lyme disease since it was first identified in the 1970s, and I have helped conduct more than a dozen scientific studies on the condition—including an investigation of information about Lyme disease on the Internet.

I found that of the eight Web sites with the word "Lyme" in their domain name, seven gave inaccurate information. (The accurate Web site is *www. aldf.com,* maintained by the American Lyme Disease Foundation.) An accurate Web site without Lyme in its domain name is *www.cdc.gov.*

DO YOU HAVE IT?

If you remove a deer tick within 24 to 48 hours after it has taken up residence on your body, the tick is unlikely to have infected you with Lyme disease. And chances are, even if you don't remove it and you are bitten, you won't get Lyme anyway. Of all people bitten by an infected tick, only about one in 20 develops Lyme disease. Also, not every deer tick is infected with *Borrelia burgdorferi*—in some areas, the rate is as high as one in five ticks…in other areas, the rate is less than one in 100.

If you have been bitten by a tick, the guidelines of the Infectious Diseases Society of America (IDSA) do not routinely recommend that you receive antibiotics unless you develop the obvious rash of Lyme disease—a red, circular "bull's-eye" (targetlike) rash. Lyme disease's nonrash symptoms don't warrant immediate treatment with antibiotics because they're shared by many conditions and because antibiotics have their own health risks. However, if you are very nervous about developing Lyme disease after a tick bite, talk to your doctor about taking a single, 200-milligram (mg) dose of *doxycycline*.

The bull's-eye rash begins three to 30 days after the bite, starting out the size of a quarter and widening to the size of a football as bacteria spread out.

ANTIBIOTIC REGIMEN

Treatment for "early Lyme disease" (the first month or so after a tick bite with an identifiable rash) is one of the following—doxycycline (100 mg twice a day for 10 to 21 days)…*amoxicillin* (500 mg three times a day for 14 to 21 days)…or *cefuroxime axetil* (500 mg twice a day for 14 to 21 days). It typically is not necessary to treat Lyme disease for more than four weeks, and intravenous therapy rarely is needed except for those patients hospitalized with Lyme meningitis (inflammation surrounding the brain and spinal cord).

To Prevent Tick Bites…

If you live in an area with Lyme-infected ticks, take the following precautions when ticks are feeding, usually from early April through September…

- **Spray exposed skin with the insect repellent DEET** before going outdoors into a grassy or wooded area. Research shows that DEET effectively repels deer ticks and that a product with 30% DEET lasts all day.

- **Check your clothes and body for ticks** after coming indoors from a grassy or wooded area. Then take a shower, which is a good way to prevent bites.

- **If you find a feeding tick, remove it**—and don't worry about your technique. Grab the tick with a tissue or handkerchief, and pull it out slowly. You don't need to remove it in any other "special" way. Don't worry if the tick's head breaks off and remains in the skin. Treat it like a splinter, removing it with a needle, or let it work its way out on its own.

If the disease isn't treated with antibiotics, at least one out of 10 people will develop Lyme arthritis, which requires a specific antibiotic regimen.

Infection with Lyme disease can be diagnosed with antibody-detecting blood tests (ELISA and immunoblots), but the tests are inaccurate in the first two weeks after infection—clinical signs are the best way to diagnose early Lyme. The two tests are helpful in confirming Lyme arthritis or other rarer manifestations of Lyme disease, such as meningitis, Bell's (facial) palsy (if bacteria affect nerves in the face) or Lyme carditis (if bacteria infect the heart).

POST-LYME DISEASE

About 10% to 20% of people with Lyme disease develop what infectious disease specialists call post-Lyme disease—they continue to feel bad for months afterward, with symptoms such as joint pain and fatigue, even though blood tests show no active infection. This is a poorly understood phenomenon, but it is not due to persistent infection.

Several double-blind, randomized, placebo-controlled trials show that long-term antibiotic treatment for the symptoms of post-Lyme disease offers little or no benefits, and it frequently is dangerous and occasionally deadly. I recommend emotional support and medical management of the pain, fatigue and other symptoms.

SYMPTOMS OF LYME DISEASE

- **Bull's-eye rash**
- **Fever**
- **Fatigue**
- **Headache**
- **Neck pain**
- **Muscle and joint pain**

When Doctors Get It Wrong... Lyme Disease

If a person has Lyme disease and it's missed, he/she may go on to develop joint inflammation, heart-rhythm disturbances and even problems with concentration and memory.

Lyme disease, the most common tick-borne disease, now has been reported in most US states, but doctors often do not look for it outside the Northeast, where the disease originated. The initial symptoms, such as muscle aches and fatigue, are often confused with the flu, particularly when patients don't even know that they were bitten.

What to do: Look for a rash. About three-quarters of patients will develop a "bull's eye" rash along with the flulike symptoms that last for weeks. Lyme disease can be diagnosed with a blood test (see previous article). Patients who are treated with oral antibiotics at the onset of symptoms almost always make a full recovery. The longer someone goes untreated for Lyme, however, the more challenging the course of recovery.

Joe Graedon, MS, and Teresa Graedon, PhD, consumer advocates. *www.peoplespharmacy.com*

Taking Anti-HIV Meds Prior to Exposure Wards Off Infection

CMAJ (Canadian Medical Association Journal), news release

Preventive antiretroviral treatment appears to be an effective way to help protect high-risk people against HIV infection, a recent study suggests.

HIV, the virus that causes AIDS, can be transmitted through unprotected sex and contaminated needles.

Immediate treatment after HIV exposure can be successful in preventing HIV infection, previous research has found. More recently, several large randomized, controlled trials—the gold standard of medical research, in which people are randomly assigned to treatment or no treatment—have shown that giving antiretroviral drugs before people are exposed may also prevent infection.

RESEARCH DETAILS

In a recent report, published in the *CMAJ* (Canadian Medical Association Journal), researchers reviewed studies published between January 1990 and April 2012 and found that preventive antiretroviral treatment could reduce the risk of HIV infection in high-risk groups such as gay men, intravenous drug users and women in areas with high rates of HIV.

For example, one recent study that included 900 women from a region with a high rate of HIV found that applying a topical vaginal microbicide 12 hours before and after sex led to a 39% reduction in HIV infection rates.

"All pre-exposure prophylaxis [prevention] interventions should be considered one part of a more comprehensive plan for preventing the spread of HIV infection, including standard counseling on safer sexual practices and condom use, testing for and treating other sexually transmitted infections and, in select circumstances, male circumcision and needle exchange programs," Isaac Bogoch, MD, of Harvard Medical School and Massachusetts General Hospital in Boston and colleagues wrote.

While pre-exposure treatment is promising, there are a number of unanswered questions, such as which groups would benefit most, and the possibility of the development of drug resistance, the researchers noted.

info The US Centers for Disease Control and Prevention has more information on HIV transmission at its Web site, *www.cdc. gov/hiv/resources/qa/transmission.htm*.

How to Get Over a Stomach Virus

To get over a stomach virus quickly, combine repletion with palliation.

Repletion means restoring crucial nutrients that your body loses in gastrointestinal distress. One way to do that is with egg drop soup from any Chinese restaurant—it combines water-based chicken stock with whole egg. It also contains salt, which a depleted body needs. In addition, take Larix, the trade name for the inner bark of the Western larch—this sweet-tasting white powder, very soluble in water, calms mucous membranes.

Palliation means making the stomach and large intestine feel better. For the stomach, sip a tea made with gentian and slippery elm bark. The herbs are available at *www. teahaven.com.* Use a mixture of two-thirds gentian and one-third slippery elm with a teaspoon of the combination in each cup. Steep for eight minutes. For the intestine, try Thorne Research's Formula SF734, which includes deglycyrrhizinated licorice root and berberine in a base that is mainly bismuth citrate—it effectively calms the large intestine.

Andrew L. Rubman, ND, founder and director, Southbury Clinic for Traditional Medicine, Southbury, Connecticut. www.southburyclinic.com

How to Bounce Back from Food Poisoning

Jamison Starbuck, ND, naturopathic physician in family practice and a guest lecturer at the University of Montana, both in Missoula. She is past president of the American Association of Naturopathic Physicians and a contributing editor to *The Alternative Advisor: The Complete Guide to Natural Therapies and Alternative Treatments* (Time Life).

As the infecting organisms of food poisoning invade your intestines, the symptoms can be debilitating—nausea, stomach pain, loose bowel movements and slight fever. It often gets worse before it gets better. You're likely to start vomiting and have ongoing abdominal cramps—and just feel lousy.

The good news is that natural medicine can shorten an episode of food poisoning dramatically. *Here are my favorite methods...**

•**Take activated charcoal.** At the first sign of food poisoning, take two capsules of activated charcoal (available from natural-food stores) and repeat every four waking hours until your symptoms are gone. Toxins attach to the surface of the activated charcoal and are drawn out of the stomach and intestines.

•**Use antiseptic herbs.** Oregon grape root, uva ursi and gingerroot will help kill the organism causing your food poisoning. You can use any of these herbs individually or buy a tincture that contains all three of them for the greatest benefit.

Typical adult dose: Sixty drops (about one-quarter teaspoon) in one ounce of water every four waking hours for up to three days.

•**Try carob powder.** Unsweetened carob powder, available in bulk at most natural-food grocers, will ease diarrhea. Add two teaspoons of carob powder and two teaspoons of slippery elm powder to one-quarter cup of unsweetened applesauce. Eat the mixture slowly throughout the day. Repeat daily until symptoms are gone.

•**Drink clear liquids.** If you limit your diet to mostly clear liquids, you can reduce diarrhea by slowing down the activity of your gut.

Good choices: Vegetable broth...peppermint, chamomile and/or raspberry leaf herbal teas... and plain water.

Also helpful: Try rice water—cook one cup of brown or white rice in four cups of water, strain off the liquid and drink six ounces several times a day. This gives you starch, which slows diarrhea, without taxing your gut to digest the rice.

Caution: Seek prompt medical attention if you experience diarrhea for more than three days. Also see a doctor if you have a fever above 101.5°F...blood in the stool or in vomit...severe abdominal pain...lack of urination...or more than one episode of difficulty swallowing, vision changes, fainting or dizziness. These can be signs that infection has spread throughout your body.

*Check with your doctor before using herbal therapies.

Longevity & Optimum Aging

5 Surprising Foods to Help You Live Longer

Whether your blood sugar (glucose) levels are normal and you want to keep them that way…or you have diabetes and glucose control is your mantra…it is smart to eat a well-balanced diet to help keep your glucose readings healthy. In fact, maintaining healthy glucose levels may even help you live longer by avoiding diabetes—one of the leading causes of death in the US.

Most people already know that cinnamon is an excellent choice for blood sugar control. Consuming just one-half teaspoon to three teaspoons a day can reduce glucose levels by up to 24%. Cinnamon is great on cereals, vegetables, cottage cheese and snacks (think fresh apple slices sprinkled with cinnamon).

Other smart food choices…*

GLUCOSE-CONTROLLING FOOD #1: BLACK BEANS

Beans, in general, are the most underrated food in the supermarket.

Beans are high in protein as well as soluble and insoluble fiber. Soluble fiber helps you feel fuller longer, and insoluble fiber helps prevent constipation. Beans also break down slowly during digestion, which means more stable blood sugar levels.

Black beans, however, are particularly healthful because of their especially high fiber content. For example, one cup of cooked black beans contains 15 g of fiber, while a cup of pink beans has just 9 g.

*If you take diabetes medication, consult your doctor before making significant changes to your diet—drug dosages may need to be adjusted.

Bonnie Taub-Dix, RD, a registered dietitian and owner of BTD Nutrition Consultants located in New York City. A nationally recognized nutrition expert and author of *Read It Before You Eat It* (Plume), she has advised patients on the best ways to control diabetes for more than three decades. *www.bonnietaubdix.com*

Bonus: Beans protect the heart by lowering cholesterol and reducing damage from free radicals. For example, one study showed that you can lower your total and LDL ("bad") cholesterol by about 8% simply by eating one-half cup of cooked pinto beans every day.

Helpful: To shorten cooking times, use canned beans instead of dried beans. They are equally nutritious, and you can reduce the sodium in salted canned beans by about 40% by rinsing them.

Another healthful way to use beans: Hummus. In the Middle East, people eat this chickpea (garbanzo bean) spread as often as Americans eat bread. It is much healthier than bread because it contains both protein and olive oil—important for slowing the absorption of carbohydrate sugars and preventing blood sugar "spikes."

Hummus is a good weight-loss dish because it is high in fiber (about 15 g per cup) as well as protein (about 19 g). Ample amounts of protein and fiber allow you to satisfy your appetite with smaller portions of food.

Hummus is made with mashed chickpeas, tahini (a sesame seed paste), lemon juice, garlic, salt and a little olive oil. Stick to the serving size on the label, which is typically two to four tablespoons.

GLUCOSE-CONTROLLING FOOD #2: COCOA

The flavanols in cocoa are potent antioxidants that not only fight heart disease but also help guard against diabetes. In recent studies, cocoa improved insulin sensitivity, the body's ability to transport sugar out of the bloodstream. It's wise for people with diabetes or high blood sugar to choose unsweetened cocoa and add a small amount of sugar or sugar substitute.

A Simple Blood Sugar Buster

Taking two tablespoons of apple-cider vinegar in eight ounces of water with meals or before bedtime can slow the absorption of sugar into the blood—vinegar helps to block the digestive enzymes that change carbs to sugar.

Cinnamon hot cocoa combines two glucose-controlling ingredients in one delicious recipe.

To prepare: Mix one-quarter cup of baking cocoa, one tablespoon of sugar (or Truvia to taste) and a pinch of salt. Gradually add one-quarter cup of boiling water and blend well. Add one cup of skim or 1% low-fat milk and a cinnamon stick. While stirring occasionally, heat on low for 10 minutes. Remove the cinnamon stick and enjoy!

GLUCOSE-CONTROLLING FOOD #3: DATES

These little fruits are sweet enough to qualify as dessert but have more antioxidants per serving than oranges, grapes and even broccoli. The antioxidants can help prevent heart disease as well as neuropathy—nerve damage that frequently occurs in people who have diabetes.

A single serving (for example, seven deglet noor dates) has 4 g of fiber for better blood sugar management.

Be careful: Seven dates also have 140 calories and 32 g of sugar, so this must be added to your total daily carbohydrate intake, especially if you have diabetes. Dates, in general, have a low glycemic index, so they don't spike glucose levels. Medjool dates, however, are not an ideal choice. They have significantly more sugar and calories per serving than deglet noor dates.

GLUCOSE-CONTROLLING FOOD #4: SARDINES

Many people know about the heart-healthy benefits of cold-water fish, such as salmon and mackerel. An analysis of studies involving hundreds of thousands of adults found that just one to two fish servings a week reduced the risk of dying from heart disease by more than one-third.

What's less well-known is that the high concentration of omega-3 fatty acids in cold-water fish also helps prevent a too-rapid rise in blood sugar. Besides being low on the glycemic index, fish contains protein, which blunts blood sugar levels.

Best for helping to prevent high blood sugar: In addition to salmon and mackerel, sardines are an excellent choice (when canned with bones, they also are a good source of calcium).

Sugar Makes You Look Older

People were asked to guess the age of volunteers. The study found that every 0.18-gram increase in the volunteers' blood sugar level was associated with a five-month increase in perceived age.

Possible reason: Glucose can damage skin's collagen and elastin, causing wrinkles and sagging.

Study by researchers from Unilever Discover, Colworth House, Sharnbrook, Bedfordshire, UK, and Leiden University Medical Center, the Netherlands, published in *AGE: Journal of the American Aging Association.*

Tuna, to a somewhat lesser extent, offers omega-3s (choose canned light—albacore white has higher levels of mercury). Also avoid large fish, such as king mackerel and swordfish, which have more mercury than smaller fish. Aim for a 3.5-ounce serving two or three times a week.

GLUCOSE-CONTROLLING FOOD #5: ALMONDS

High in fiber, protein and beneficial fats, nuts can significantly lower glucose levels. In fact, women who ate a one-ounce serving of nuts at least five times a week were nearly 30% less likely to develop diabetes than women who rarely or never ate nuts, according to one study.

The poly- and monounsaturated fats in nuts improve the body's ability to use insulin. Nuts also help with cholesterol control—important because diabetes increases risk for heart disease.

All nuts are beneficial, but almonds contain more fiber, calcium and protein than most nuts (and are best for blood sugar control). Walnuts are highest in antioxidants and omega-3 fatty acids. Avoid salted nuts—they have too much sodium.

Excellent way to add nuts to your diet: Nut butters. Almost everyone likes peanut butter, and it is healthier than you might think. Like butters made from almonds, cashews or other nuts, the fats it contains are mostly monounsaturated, which are good for the heart. The fiber in nut butters (about 1 g to 2 g per tablespoon, depending on the nut) can help lower blood sugar.

Good choice for blood sugar control: One serving (one to two tablespoons) of almond butter (rich in potassium, vitamin E and calcium) several times a week. Look for nut butters that have a short list of ingredients—they are the most nutritious.

Become an Optimist for Better Health and Longer Life...It's Easier Than You Think

Elaine Fox, PhD, director of the Affective Neuroscience Laboratory in the department of psychology at the University of Essex, Colchester, UK. She is also author of *Rainy Brain, Sunny Brain: How to Retrain Your Brain to Overcome Pessimism and Achieve a More Positive Outlook* (Basic). *www.rainybrainsunnybrain.com*

Optimists generally are more successful at most things in life—from business to personal relationships—than pessimists. And they probably have more fun, too. But even more importantly, there's now scientific evidence that optimists are healthier and live longer.

Recent study: A 2012 Harvard School of Public Health study found that optimistic individuals had up to 50% less risk of having a first heart attack, stroke or other cardiovascular event than their less optimistic peers.

BORN THAT WAY?

Many people believe that outlook or disposition, be it gloomy or sunny, is something you're just born with. To some extent, that's true—a person's brain tends to be wired either toward optimism or pessimism. But these tendencies are reinforced by mental habits.

Latest research: By changing how you think, live and act, it's actually possible to change your disposition.

RETRAIN YOUR BRAIN

Here's how you can train yourself to be more optimistic using positive emotions and experiences...

•**What makes you feel good?** Research shows that people exhibit flourishing mental health when positive emotions, such as hope, joy and wonder, exceed negative emotions, such as anger, disgust, fear, sadness and shame, by a ratio of three to one. While you can't eliminate all problems and negativity in life, you can offset them with an ample supply of things that make you feel good.

Think about simple things that make you feel positive. Maybe it's petting a dog, listening to music, working out or meeting a friend for coffee. Make an effort to include some of these things in your daily routine—and jot down your positive experiences in a notebook to reinforce them.

•**Live in the present.** Increasing evidence shows that mindfulness meditation—a practice in which you become more aware of your own sensations, thoughts and emotions without judgment—not only relaxes and calms your mind, but also boosts your ability to curb negativity.

What to do: Take a 10- to 15-minute break for mindfulness meditation several times a day. Turn off the phone and close your door, or take a walk in the park. Devote this time to tune in to the thoughts and feelings that pass through your mind and body. If upsetting thoughts enter your mind, don't dwell on them—let them simply drift away.

After adding mindfulness meditation to their routines, most people find they're able to deal more effectively with problems and worries.

•**Act like an optimist.** Research has shown that activating the muscles used for smiling—by holding a pencil between your front teeth, for example—can boost your mood. In the same way, adopting the behavior patterns of optimism, even if they are not natural to you, will go a long way toward cultivating a sunnier nature. *Try the following…*

•**Give it a go.** Optimists are not afraid to take risks or try things out. Unsuccessful results tend to be viewed as learning experiences rather than failures. And optimists are game to try again.

Example: Go ahead and apply for your dream job. If you don't get it, you will be disappointed but will learn from the process so you can try again.

•**Be more flexible.** Do something new—even if it's as minor as taking a different route on your morning run or chatting with a neighbor you usually pass by with a nod. Each positive alteration in your routine, no matter how small, helps to retrain your brain and builds the flexibility and creativity that characterize optimism.

•**Take command.** Optimists tend to feel a sense of control over their lives, which has been shown to reduce stress and provide other health benefits. *Best:* Increase your sense of control in small steps. For example, if you'd like to have fewer interruptions at work, you might start by curbing the number of times you check your e-mail—set aside specific times to review it, and don't look at it any other time.

Important: Recognize each small advance so you'll gain confidence to make other changes that will help you feel more in control.

> ## Optimism 101
>
> Optimists tend to be…
>
> •**Proactive.** They take action and get things done.
>
> •**Persistent.** They pursue goals and try again after failure.
>
> •**Creative.** If one approach fails, they find another one.
>
> •**Confident.** They expect things to work out in the long run.
>
> *Crucial:* Optimists tend to notice and focus on the positive things in their lives, such as rewarding experiences and possibilities, rather than the negative.

Could an Aging Face Reflect an Unhealthy Heart?

Anne Tybjaerg-Hansen, MD, professor of clinical biochemistry, University of Copenhagen, Denmark.

David A. Friedman, MD, chief, Heart Failure Services, North Shore-LIJ's Plainview Hospital, Plainview, New York.

Kenneth Ong, MD, acting chief, cardiology, Brooklyn Hospital Center, New York City.

Annual meeting, American Heart Association, Los Angeles.

Anxious about those telltale signs of aging? A recent study gives you one more reason to worry: Facial aging might point to worsening cardiovascular health.

The Danish study found that people who had three or four signs of aging—fatty deposits around the eyelids, receding hairlines, baldness, and creased earlobes—were 39% more likely to develop heart disease and 57% more likely to have a heart attack over 35 years of follow-up, compared with people of similar age who looked younger.

"Looking old for your age is a good marker for poor cardiovascular health," said study lead author Anne Tybjaerg-Hansen, MD, a professor of clinical biochemistry at the University of Copenhagen. She presented the findings in Los Angeles at the annual meeting of the American Heart Association (AHA).

According to Dr. Tybjaerg-Hansen, many doctors explicitly or unconsciously take into account how old patients look for their age when assessing their health. The idea behind this is that a prematurely aged person must be less healthy than someone who has retained the bloom of youth into middle or old age.

"But, really, it's not really well-examined whether this is correct," she said.

STUDY DETAILS

To find out, her team looked at aging signs in nearly 11,000 people aged 40 or older who were taking part in the Copenhagen City Heart Study, which began in the late 1970s. The researchers looked at common signs of aging such as wrinkles, graying hair, receding hairline at the temples, baldness at the top of the head (typically for men), earlobe creasing and yellow deposits of cholesterol around the eyelids (called xanthelasmata).

Tracked over 35 years, about 3,400 participants developed heart disease and more than 1,700 had a heart attack.

Certain aging signs seemed related to normal chronological aging, but not heart disease. "Adjusted for chronological age and for sex, wrinkles were no longer associated with increased risk for disease," Dr. Tybjaerg-Hansen noted, and the same held true for graying hair.

But four other outward signs were closely linked with poorer heart health: Receding hairlines at the temples, balding at the crown of

the head, fatty deposits around the eyelids and creasing of the earlobes.

For example, Dr. Tybjaerg-Hansen said, "if you are a 70- to 79-year-old male and you have three to four [of these] aging signs, then you have a 10-year, 40% risk of [developing] ischemic heart disease," significantly higher than men of similar age with fewer aging signs.

Based on the study's results, Dr. Tybjaerg-Hansen said that a routine doctor's office exam should include a quick check of these indicators of aging.

EXPERT COMMENTARY

Physicians tended to agree with the study findings.

"These subtle skin findings are a helpful part of every clinician's routine physical exam screening," said David Friedman, MD, chief of heart failure services at North Shore-LIJ's Plainview Hospital in Plainview, New York. "I specifically look for signs around the nasal crease and upper eyelid area as a marker for potentially elevated blood cholesterol; and it's interesting that the earlobe crease once again might suggest elevated cardiac risk, which has been mentioned in old physical exam textbooks."

Kenneth Ong, MD, is acting chief of cardiology at the Brooklyn Hospital Center in New York City. He agreed that "these physical findings may assist in earlier identification and management of heart problems."

But he stressed that signs of aging only reflect—not cause—heart disease. "People should realize that it is important to distinguish the difference between an association and a risk factor; there may not be much you can do about a receding hairline, but risk factors such as high blood pressure can be treated," Dr. Ong said.

And Dr. Friedman cautioned about reading too much into the findings. "One shouldn't jump to conclusions if slight fatty skin bumps around the eyes or certain patterns of baldness are seen," he said.

info Find out more about the risk factors for heart disease at the Web site of the US Centers for Disease Control and Prevention, *www.cdc.gov/heartdisease/risk_factors.htm.*

How Testosterone Can Help You Live Longer

Chris D. Meletis, ND, executive director of the Institute for Healthy Aging and coauthor of *His Change of Life: Male Menopause and Healthy Aging with Testosterone* (Praeger). *www.drmeletis.com*

Bill Gottlieb, CHC, health coach certified by the American Association of Drugless Practitioners and author of *Maximum Manhood: Sexual Healing Secrets and Anti-Aging Breakthroughs* (OPM). *www.billgottliebhealth.com*

The sex hormone testosterone gives a man his beard, deep voice and sex drive. It also may give all of us—men and women—better health and a longer life.

Research shows that low levels of testosterone may increase the risk for heart disease, stroke, type 2 diabetes, osteoporosis, depression and Alzheimer's disease. Low testosterone also can trigger fatigue, low libido, erectile dysfunction, enlarged prostate (benign prostatic hyperplasia), muscular weakness, poor endurance, irritability, poor concentration and poor memory. *What you need to know now…*

LIVE LONGER

An estimated 40% of men age 45 and older have testosterone deficiency—total testosterone below 300 ng/dL. (This phenomenon is called by various names, including andropause, male menopause and hypogonadism.) *This deficiency is linked to…*

•**Cardiovascular disease (CVD).** In a four-year study, men with one risk factor for heart disease (such as high blood pressure) were four times more likely to develop CVD if they had low testosterone. Other studies link low testosterone to an increased risk for stroke, blood clots, high total cholesterol, high LDL "bad" cholesterol and arrhythmias (irregular heartbeats that can trigger a heart attack or stroke). One such study concluded that "testosterone levels may be a stronger predictor of coronary artery disease than high cholesterol, blood pressure, diabetes, smoking and body mass index."

•**Metabolic syndrome and type 2 diabetes.** Metabolic syndrome—a risk factor for type 2 diabetes—is a constellation of health problems that can include insulin resistance, abdominal obesity, high blood pressure, high triglycerides and low HDL "good" cholesterol. In a recent two-year study, metabolic syndrome was completely reversed in 65% of men on testosterone replacement therapy (TRT).

•**Osteoporosis.** A study found that men with low testosterone had an 88% higher risk for hip fracture.

•**Midlife male depression.** A study from Columbia University showed that TRT completely reversed depression in more than 50% of depressed men.

•**Alzheimer's disease.** Research links higher levels of testosterone with better blood flow to the brain, better memory and less risk for Alzheimer's disease.

•**Death from any cause.** In a study of 900 men, those with low testosterone had a 43% higher risk for all-cause mortality (dying from any cause). In another, seven-year study, every 173 ng/dL increase in total testosterone levels was linked to a 21% lower risk for all-cause mortality.

TESTOSTERONE TESTING

The Androgen Deficiency in the Aging Male (ADAM) Questionnaire (see page 320 in the Men's Health chapter) can determine if you have symptoms of low testosterone. If you do, you should be tested for a low blood level. However, you can have so-called "normal" test results for total testosterone and still have a deficiency. That's because testosterone may be bound to a compound called sex hormone binding globulin, so only a small percentage reaches your cells.

Best: Ask your doctor to test you for total testosterone and free (unbound) testosterone. You may need a doctor trained in the use of bio-identical hormones or a naturopathic physician.

Another problem with testosterone tests is that "normal" values vary widely from laboratory to laboratory. One study from Harvard Medical School found 17 different sets of "normal" values for total testosterone among 25 labs.

What to do: If you have the symptoms of low testosterone…and your level of either total or free testosterone is below normal or borderline normal at whatever lab your doctor chooses… you should consider TRT.

Standing Could Save Your Life

Among more than 200,000 adults age 45 and older, those who sat for 11 or more hours a day—at home, at work or in their cars—were 40% more likely to die of any cause over the next three years than those who sat for fewer than four hours daily.

Explanation: Physical activity of any kind —even standing—is crucial for longevity.

Hidde van der Ploeg, PhD, senior research fellow, The University of Sydney, Australia.

MAKE LIFESTYLE CHANGES

If you have low testosterone, you can first try to boost it by…

- **Losing weight**
- **Managing stress**
- **Weight-training**
- **Getting eight hours of sleep**
- **Eating healthy,** monounsaturated fats and limiting processed carbohydrates, such as sugar and white flour
- **Eating organic food** (estrogen-like pesticides can stymie testosterone).

TREATMENT

If you still have low testosterone after making lifestyle changes, you may need TRT. There are four forms of TRT for men. All are effective and safe. *You and your doctor can determine the best treatment for you…*

- **Prescription 1% or 1.62% testosterone gel,** such as Testim and AndroGel, which is applied once a day.
- **Testosterone injections,** which typically are given once every two weeks, though some doctors prefer to give them once a week.
- **Testosterone pellets,** which are surgically inserted.
- **Compounded 1% to 10% testosterone cream** is custom-formulated by a compounding pharmacy and applied once a day.

Whatever the form of testosterone, the following is advisable…

- **Aim for a total testosterone blood level of 600 ng/dL** or just a little higher (up to 900 ng/dL).

- **Recheck blood levels.** Many primary care doctors prescribe testosterone gel—and never recheck their patients. Your doctor should check your levels after one month…then every three months for one year…every four months for the second year…and every six months for the third year and thereafter.

WOMEN AND TRT

A deficiency of testosterone in perimenopausal or menopausal women can cause symptoms similar to testosterone deficiency in middle-aged and older men, such as fatigue, depression, weight gain, low libido and osteoporosis.

What to do: Ask your doctor to test your free testosterone. If your level is low, consider treatment with testosterone cream from a compounding pharmacy at a dose of 0.5 milligrams (mg) to 2 mg daily. (This is an off-label use of testosterone, not approved by the FDA.) Most women notice more energy, younger-looking skin, thicker hair and increased libido.

Some women worry that testosterone will give them "manly" characteristics, but this does not happen with female-appropriate doses.

Simple Test May Reveal Longevity

According to a recent study, more than 2,000 healthy adults (average age 62) were scored on the number of hand, knee or other supports required to sit on the floor and then stand unaided.

Result: Those who needed the most support had up to six times greater risk for death than those who needed the least support.

Theory: These movements indicate musculoskeletal fitness, a key component of longevity.

Self-defense: If you require more than one support to sit on or rise from the floor, talk to your doctor about ways to improve your muscle strength and flexibility.

Claudio Gil Soares de Araujo, MD, PhD, professor of exercise science and sports, Universidade Gama Filho, Rio de Janerio, Brazil.

"SuperAgers" Have Thicker Cortexes Than Their Peers

Emily Rogalski, PhD, assistant research professor, Cognitive Neurology and Alzheimer's Disease Center, Northwestern University, Chicago.

Russell Swerdlow, MD, professor, neurology, and director, Alzheimer's Disease Center, University of Kansas, Kansas City.

Journal of the International Neuropsychological Society

Elderly people who experience no decline in memory have certain brain characteristics that differ from their peers who show more typical age-related memory loss, recent research reveals.

Scientists from Northwestern University's Cognitive Neurology and Alzheimer's Disease Center identified 12 people aged 80 and older who did as well or better on memory tests as people who were 20 to 30 years younger. Researchers dubbed them "SuperAgers."

MRI scans showed that the cortex of Super-Agers was thicker than a comparison group of people aged 80 and older. The cortex is the outer layer of the brain involved in memory, attention and other thinking abilities.

A thinning cortex suggests a loss of brain cells, or gray matter, explained senior study author Emily Rogalski, PhD, assistant research professor at Northwestern.

Brain scans also showed that people in their 80s and 90s who exhibited more typical memory declines (though not the marked decline associated with Alzheimer's disease or other thinking impairments, researchers said) had a thinner cortex.

"The SuperAgers looked more like the middle-aged controls, despite being 20 to 30 years older," Dr. Rogalski said. "We didn't see any significant atrophy or brain cell loss."

The SuperAgers also had a larger cingulate cortex than the middle-aged participants. This is another brain region involved in attention and memory. What's unknown is if SuperAgers were born with a more prominent cingulate cortex or if that region resisted atrophy in later life, according to the study.

Some degree of forgetfulness is a common complaint among the elderly, Dr. Rogalski said. "These complaints are so widespread that it's come to be thought of as a normal part of aging," she noted.

The study was published in the *Journal of the International Neuropsychological Society.*

HOW THIS BRAIN STUDY DIFFERS

Many prior studies have shown that brain atrophy and loss of thinking abilities go hand in hand, said Russell Swerdlow, MD, director of the Alzheimer's Disease Center at the University of Kansas.

This study is unique in that it starts with people with exceptionally good memories for their age, and then looks at what makes their brains different, he said.

He noted, however, that the study shows a correlation between good memories in later life and a thicker cortex and larger brain volume, but it doesn't show cause-and-effect. What is unknown is if retaining brain volume protects thinking abilities, or if maintaining thinking abilities protects brain volume.

"It could be that those whose brains are better 'built to last' structurally are probably those brains that are better built to last from a functional perspective, or that those who are exercising their brains may have less atrophy," he said.

MORE THAN ONE ROUTE TO SUPERAGING

With studies like this, one thing people want to know is what it takes to be among the Super-Agers. Unfortunately, there aren't yet any clear answers, Dr. Rogalski said.

"Genetics are likely to play a role. And, in general, a healthy lifestyle is supportive of good memory," Dr. Rogalski said. "But in our experience, some of our SuperAgers smoke cigarettes. Others have never touched them. Some go to the gym three to five days a week. Others don't exercise. Some are still working and others have never worked. It seems there might be more than one route to being a SuperAger."

info The US National Institutes of Health has more information on the brain at its Web site, *www.ninds.nih.gov/disorders/brain_basics/know_your_brain.htm.*

More Aches and Less Sleep...What's Normal and What's Not as We Age

John Whyte, MD, MPH, an internist and chief medical expert and vice president, health and medical education, at the Discovery Channel. He is author of *Is This Normal?: The Essential Guide to Middle Age and Beyond* (Rodale). *www.discoverychannel.com*

With all the physical changes that occur as we grow older, it's tempting to chalk up all our infirmities to the effects of aging.

But that's a mistake. In some cases, physical changes that appear to be a normal part of aging signal the onset of a treatable condition. To protect yourself—and feel as good as possible!—it's crucial to know what's normal and what's not as we grow older. *For example...*

STOOPED POSTURE

The vertebrae in the spine are separated by intervertebral discs, which act like shock absorbers. It's normal for the discs to dehydrate and flatten with age. This is why the average person loses about half an inch in height every decade after about age 40. The same changes can alter the curve of the spine and cause a slight stoop.

What isn't normal: Extreme curvature of the upper spine. In general, aging should cause no more than a 20-degree curvature of the spine. An extreme curvature is typically due to a condition known as "dowager's hump" (kyphosis), which is usually caused by osteoporosis. Weak bones in the spine eventually crumble, changing the alignment of the spine and causing a stooped posture. Osteoporosis that has advanced this far can't be reversed.

That's why prevention is critical. Perform weight-bearing exercises, preferably before the bones have weakened. Walking and even dancing promote the development of new bone and protect your posture later in life. Weight-bearing exercise also can help even after bones are weakened—just be sure not to overdo it since you don't want to cause more damage. Depending on the condition of your bones, you may need to switch to non–weight-bearing exercise, such as swimming.

Important: Make sure you're getting enough vitamin D. Depending on where you live, it's possible to get more than 90% of the vitamin D that you need just from sun exposure—the rest can come from D-fortified foods and/or supplements. Vitamin D enables the movement of calcium from the bloodstream into the bones. Ask a doctor for a blood test to check your vitamin D level. If it's low, he/she can suggest the best ways for you to get more of this crucial vitamin.

PAIN

We all notice more aches and pains as we get older, often due to back problems, arthritis or other common conditions. These aches are normal if they are occasional.

What isn't normal: Pain that's severe or chronic.

Good rule of thumb: See a doctor if you have severe pain and don't know why—or if chronic pain interferes with your ability to live a normal life.

Important: Consider your mental health as well as your physical health. Pain and depression frequently go together—they actually share some of the same biochemical pathways.

That's why drugs called tricyclic antidepressants, such as *imipramine* (Tofranil), are sometimes used to relieve chronic pain—even in patients who aren't depressed. When pain is due to a physical problem, such as arthritis, depression also is common.

Get help right away, either from a doctor or a mental health professional (or both). Otherwise, you could be setting yourself up for a difficult cycle—ongoing pain increases depression, and the more depressed you are, the more pain you'll experience.

Helpful: I strongly advise pain patients to do some kind of exercise, even if it's just gentle stretches. Exercise increases endorphins, the body's natural painkillers.

LESS SLEEP

After about age 50, most people tend to sleep less soundly, and they may sleep fewer total hours than younger people. The reasons for these differences in sleep habits are varied but

Best Multivitamins for Seniors

Centrum Silver, Costco's Kirkland brand, Dollar General's DG Health, Sam's Club/Member's Mark and Wal-Mart's Equate. These were found to help seniors meet nutrient needs without exceeding safe intake levels. Centrum Silver costs about 11 cents a day... the other brands, three to four cents a day.

Editor's note: Save $29.20 a year with the cheapest brands versus the most expensive brands.

Tod Cooperman, MD, president, ConsumerLab.com, White Plains, New York.

may include more pain, medication use and nighttime urination in older adults.

What isn't normal: Taking more than 10 to 15 minutes to fall asleep. See your doctor if you have trouble falling asleep more than, say, two nights a week. This delay in sleep onset might be due to stress. Or you could be having side effects from medications. Offenders include decongestants, beta-blockers and some asthma drugs. Don't ignore sleep problems—over time, they can increase one's risk for heart disease, diabetes and other serious conditions.

SLEEPWALKING

We still don't know why people sleepwalk, but it's been shown that sleepwalkers can engage in surprisingly complex activities, such as going to the refrigerator, then preparing—and consuming—a complete meal.

Sleepwalking is more common in children but also occurs in older adults. It's usually not cause for concern unless you are putting yourself in dangerous situations, such as leaving the house or walking outside onto an unprotected balcony.

What isn't normal: A condition known as sun-downing, which can mimic sleepwalking. With sun-downing, older adults sometimes are awake late at night and wander around the house. They're partly conscious but confused and often combative. You can distinguish sun-downing from sleepwalking by the person's degree of engagement. Sun-downers can in-

teract with other people—sleepwalkers usually don't.

If you suspect that you or a loved one may be suffering from sun-downing, see a doctor. It could be a sign of early-stage dementia. Sun-downing can also be a side effect (or wearing off) of medications, such as antidepressants, sleeping pills or antipsychotic drugs. In addition, it can be caused by narcotic painkillers, such as *meperidine* (Demerol). Once a physician changes the person's medications—or adjusts the dosages—the nighttime wandering may stop.

BLURRED VISION

Do you have trouble reading small letters? Welcome to the over-50 club. The lenses of the eyes get less elastic with age, which impairs close vision, such as that required for reading. You can solve it with reading glasses or bifocals.

What isn't normal: Consistently blurry vision. You could be developing "dry" macular degeneration, a leading cause of impaired vision. It occurs when cells in the macula (a structure in the center of the retina) start to deteriorate.

You might notice that words on a page are getting increasingly blurry. You also might have trouble adjusting to dim light. In addition, you'll probably notice a general haziness and perhaps a blurred spot in the center of your vision.

Important: See a doctor immediately if you notice any of the above vision changes. Dry macular degeneration sometimes leads to the "wet" form, a leading cause of blindness. (To read more about macular degeneration, see page 278.)

Interesting: Although color blindness is usually present at birth in those who suffer from the condition, some people lose the ability to see certain colors later in life. For example, many adults age 50 and older have trouble distinguishing greens from blues. The lenses of the eyes, like tooth enamel, yellow with age. The yellow filters out these other colors. This problem is usually minor and requires no treatment.

LOSS OF LIBIDO

It's common for men and women to experience gradual changes in their ability/desire to have sex. In men, there is a decrease in the frequency/strength of erections, often due to reduced blood flow. Women may have reduced lubrication after menopause because of declines in estrogen.

What isn't normal: Significant changes in your desire for sex might be a problem. In general, physical factors, such as pain and/or lower levels of hormones, can cause a loss of libido. But you should consider your history when assessing desire for sex—a 50% or more reduction in frequency is worth discussing with your doctor. It is usually due to excessive stress—from money worries, relationship conflicts, etc.

Helpful: Stress-reducing practices, which can include regular exercise, making time for hobbies and/or practicing relaxation techniques, such as meditation.

Save Your Eyesight— New Ways to Stop Macular Degeneration

Stephen Rose, PhD, chief research officer of the Foundation Fighting Blindness. Dr. Rose is former director of the Division of Clinical Recombinant DNA Research at the Office of Biotechnology Activities of the National Institutes of Health (NIH). *www.blindness.org*

Age-related macular degeneration (AMD), the most common cause of vision loss in people over age 55, has always been considered a difficult—if not impossible—condition to treat.

Now: There is more reason than ever before to be hopeful that this dreaded eye disease, which affects about 10 million Americans, can be slowed, stopped or even reversed.

Exciting scientific findings…

BREAKTHROUGHS FOR DRY AMD

Dry AMD, which affects about 90% of people with AMD, occurs when the light-sensitive cells in the macula slowly break down, gradually blurring central vision—which is necessary for reading and driving.

There is no treatment for dry AMD, though many drugs are in clinical trials. In the mean-time, we now have evidence that certain nutrients can help control the disease, and exciting advances are taking place in stem cell therapy.

•**Nutrients that can help.** The Age-Related Eye Disease Study (AREDS), landmark research conducted by the National Eye Institute, found that a supplement containing high levels of antioxidants and zinc reduced the risk for advanced dry and wet AMD (the latest stages of AMD) in people with vision loss in one or both eyes.

The daily regimen: 500 mg of vitamin C…400 international units (IU) of vitamin E…15 mg of beta-carotene…80 mg of zinc…and 2 mg of copper. People with all stages of AMD were studied. With early-stage AMD, there may be no symptoms or vision loss. The condition is detected when an eye-care professional can see *drusen* (yellow deposits under the retina) during a dilated eye exam.

Scientists also are studying other nutrients for dry AMD, and there have been several positive reports. *For example…*

•**Zeaxanthin and lutein.** When 60 people with mild-to-moderate dry AMD took 8 mg a day of zeaxanthin for one year, they reported a marked improvement in vision (more "visual acuity" and a "sharpening of detailed high-contrast discrimination") along with visual restoration of some blind spots, researchers reported in the November 2011 issue of *Optometry*. A group receiving 9 mg of lutein daily along with zeaxanthin also had improvements in vision.

Many supplements that contain all of the nutrients mentioned earlier are available over-the-counter (OTC). But these should not be taken without a diagnosis of large drusen and monitoring by a doctor—some of these nutrients could be harmful for certain individuals, such as current and former smokers.

•**Stem cell therapy.** Perhaps one of the most remarkable findings ever reported in the literature of AMD treatment occurred earlier this year when new retinal cells grown from stem cells were used to restore some of the eyesight of a 78-year-old woman who was nearly blind due to a very advanced form of dry AMD.

The breakthrough therapy involved the use of human embryonic stem cells, which are capable of producing any of the more than 200 types of specialized cells in the body. New retinal cells grown from stem cells were injected into the patient's retina. Four months later, the patient had not lost any additional vision and, in fact, her vision seemed to improve slightly.

info ***For more information:*** Go to *www.clini caltrials.gov* and search "advanced dry age-related macular degeneration and stem cells."

BREAKTHROUGHS FOR WET AMD

Wet AMD, which affects about 10% of people with AMD, is more severe than the early and intermediate stages of the dry form. It occurs when abnormal blood vessels behind the retina start to grow. This causes blood and fluid to leak from the vessels, and the macula to swell. Because the condition progresses quickly, it requires prompt treatment for the best chance of saving your vision. You are at an increased risk for wet AMD if you have dry AMD in one or both eyes…or you have wet AMD in one eye (the other eye is at risk).

The two standard treatments for wet AMD are the injection of a medication directly into the eye to block the growth of the abnormal blood vessels…and photodynamic therapy, in which a drug that's injected into the arm flows to the abnormal blood vessels in the eye and is activated there by a laser beam that destroys the vessels.

What's new…

•**More affordable drug choice.** The drugs *ranibizumab* (Lucentis) and *bevacizumab* (Avastin), which are injected into the eye, halt or reverse vision loss. However, these drugs have a huge price disparity. Lucentis, which is FDA-approved as a treatment for wet AMD, costs $2,000 per injection, while Avastin, a cancer drug that is used "off-label" to treat AMD, costs $50.

Recent finding: In a two-year study, both drugs worked equally well, with two-thirds of patients having "driving vision" (20/40 or better).

Another option: *Aflibercept* (Eylea), also injected into the eye, was approved by the FDA for wet AMD in November 2011. Research shows that every-other-month injections of Eylea (about $1,800 per injection) can be as effective as monthly injections of Lucentis.

What Is Macular Degeneration?

Age-related macular degeneration (AMD) causes progressive damage to the macula, the part of the eye that allows us to see objects clearly. With "dry" AMD, there is a thinning of the macula, which gradually blurs central vision but generally does not cause a total loss of sight. With "wet" AMD, a more severe form of the disease, abnormal blood vessels grow beneath the macula, leaking fluid and blood. Wet AMD often progresses rapidly, leading to significant vision loss or even blindness.

Bottom line: You now have three safe and effective AMD treatment options to discuss with your doctor.

•**At-home monitoring.** Monthly monitoring by an ophthalmologist or optometrist for the subtle visual changes that herald wet AMD (or indicate a diagnosed case is worsening) is impractical for many.

New: An at-home system, the ForeseeHome AMD Monitoring Program, was recently approved by the FDA. You look into this lightweight and portable monitor for a few minutes daily. If results indicate a problem, you and your doctor are alerted to schedule an eye appointment.

Don't Let Glaucoma Steal Your Sight

Lucy Q. Shen, MD, an instructor in ophthalmology at Harvard Medical School and a glaucoma specialist at Massachusetts Eye and Ear Infirmary, both in Boston. She has been awarded a Harvard Medical School Catalyst grant in support of her research.

Glaucoma, the number-two cause of blindness in the US, often causes no early symptoms…yet unless the condition is detected early, permanent vision loss is likely.

The good news is that a five-minute, in-office laser procedure can successfully treat glaucoma in many cases, according to Lucy Shen, MD, a Harvard Medical School instructor and glaucoma specialist at Massachusetts Eye and Ear Infirmary. But of course, to take advantage of that option, you first have to have given your eye doctor a chance to discover the problem! Glaucoma risk increases with age, which is one reason why the American Academy of Ophthalmology recommends getting a baseline comprehensive eye exam at age 40, plus regular follow-up exams.

Glaucoma basics: In most cases, glaucoma develops when an imbalance in the production and drainage of fluid in the eye allows pressure to build up within the eye. The abnormally high intraocular pressure (IOP) damages the optic nerve that carries visual information from the eye to the brain, resulting in progressive and irreversible vision loss.

Though there are various types of glaucoma, by far the most common is open-angle glaucoma. Open-angle glaucoma occurs when the trabecular meshwork, a system of microscopic drainage channels encircling the iris, slowly become clogged with debris and dysfunctional, and thus cannot drain eye fluid effectively.

Note: We're talking about fluid inside of the eye. "Many patients think this is related to tearing—but tearing is because the fluid made on the surface of the eye does not drain well through a channel outside of the eye, on the eyelid," Dr. Shen explained.

With open-angle glaucoma, optic nerve damage is slow and painless and peripheral (side) vision is affected first. That is why people often don't notice a problem until a significant portion of their vision is irretrievably lost.

Once the condition is detected, the first line of treatment usually consists of medicated eyedrops that reduce production of eye fluids and/or help increase drainage. Oral medications, such as certain diuretics, also may be used. If those treatments don't halt the disease—or if the patient develops an allergy to the eyedrops, as happens with about 5% to 10% of patients in her practice Dr. Shen said—the ophthalmologist may recommend a procedure called laser trabeculoplasty to improve the drainage function of the trabecular network.

Sight-saving laser treatment: The procedure generally is done in the ophthalmologist's office. After administering eye-numbing drops, the doctor positions a special contact lens on the eye to control blinking, reduce small eye movements and facilitate focusing of the laser. Then the laser is aimed at the trabecular meshwork, the internal drainage area of the eye, in a procedure that takes about five minutes. Though it is not painful, some patients report feeling a little sore afterward, Dr. Shen said.

There are two laser options. With argon laser trabeculoplasty (ALT), a high-energy laser typically is applied in evenly spaced spots over the trabecular meshwork, causing shrinkage that creates openings to improve drainage. However, because tiny scars can eventually form, ALT cannot be repeated in the same area even if IOP eventually rises again.

Recent advance: The newer selective laser trabeculoplasty (SLT) uses a lower-energy laser to selectively target the trabecular meshwork. It stimulates the cells in the drainage channels to clean up the debris that is compromising drainage. Because scarring is unlikely, SLT can be repeated to keep pressure under control— which is one reason why Dr. Shen uses SLT instead of ALT.

Possible complications after ALT or SLT, though rare, include inflammation, pain, temporary cloudy vision and a potential rise in IOP.

To minimize risks: Ask the ophthalmologist you are considering how many patients he or she has treated and the treatment success rate, defined as achieving a 30% reduction in IOP. You want a doctor whose success rate is around 80% or better. Also ask how many of the doctor's patients have needed to be treated a second time. Ideally, the majority of patients are treated only once—but do understand that it is not uncommon to require additional laser treatment.

Important: Even after successful ALT or SLT, most patients still need medication to keep open-angle glaucoma from progressing. And of course, follow-up eye exams are essential to protect vision.

Easy-to-Do Exercises That Keep You Young

Barbara Bushman, PhD, a professor in the department of kinesiology at Missouri State University in Springfield, a fellow of the American College of Sports Medicine (ACSM) and editor of *ACSM's Complete Guide to Fitness & Health* (Human Kinetics).

N eed to sit down to put on socks? That's a common sign of what happens as we age—balance, coordination and agility fade. Fortunately, we can boost those skills with simple moves that fit into the fancy-sounding category of neuromotor exercise training. The point is to reduce the risk for falls and injury and enhance "functional fitness," or the ability to go about our daily business.

Update: Newest guidelines from the American College of Sports Medicine (ACSM) recommend doing 20 to 30 minutes of neuromotor exercise training two or three days per week, for a total of about 60 minutes weekly.

Tai chi and yoga are good examples—but you don't need to take a class to become more functionally fit. "Lots of neuromotor exercises can be done at home. All it takes is a bit of creativity and some time," said Barbara Bushman, PhD, a professor in the department of kinesiology at Missouri State University and editor of ACSM's *Complete Guide to Fitness & Health.* Ideally, you'll add neuromotor activities to your existing workout regimen without sacrificing cardio, resistance training or stretching time.

As with any new exercise routine, get your doctor's OK first. Then try the activities below, starting with a minute or two per exercise and gradually increasing your time, Dr. Bushman recommended. Activities can be done in any order and spread throughout the day, if desired. If balance is a challenge, do the exercises while standing near a countertop or other sturdy object that you can grasp for support if necessary.

• **Box Step.** On the floor, line up half a dozen empty boxes of varying sizes, positioning them about 12 to 15 inches apart, then practice stepping up and over them.

Red Flags That You May Need to Give Up Driving

You are having trouble with...
- **Seeing cars or pedestrians at night**
- **Braking quickly when needed**
- **Reacting to sirens or flashing emergency lights**
- **Traffic violations and are receiving frequent traffic tickets**
- **Other drivers and are getting honked at**
- **"Close calls" in traffic accidents,** or you have been involved in a crash or near-miss in the last two years.

Also: If you have conditions such as angina, severe arthritis, cataracts or cognitive problems, ask your doctor to assess whether or not your condition is affecting your ability to drive.

University of California, *Berkeley Wellness Letter.* www.wellnessletter.com

As you improve: Increase the height and width of the boxes...step over the boxes sideways...or design your own more complex stepping pattern.

If you're a beginner: Skip the boxes and simply practice walking backward and shuffling from side to side.

• **Sock Stand.** Barefoot, stand on your right foot. Bending your left knee, lift your left foot and put on a sock without sitting or using any other support...then, left foot still lifted, remove the sock. Repeat several times, trying not to touch your left foot to the ground, then switch legs.

As you improve: Try putting on, tying and then removing a shoe as you stand on one leg.

If you're a beginner: Just practice standing on one leg for 20 to 30 seconds, then rest and repeat several times...then switch legs.

• **Chair Squat.** Stand in front of a sturdy chair, facing outward, and hold your arms straight out in front of you. Slowly bend your knees and stick your rear end out, lowering

DID YOU KNOW?

Age Is Just a Number for Kidney Transplants

You may not be too old for a kidney transplant. Nine-thousand adults over age 65 who should have been considered "excellent" candidates for a kidney transplant and another 40,000 "good" candidates were not referred by their doctors for the procedure, according to a review of medical data from 1999 to 2006.

Theory: Not all physicians or patients are aware of the advantages of kidney transplants in older adults—and that friends or relatives may be able to serve as living donors.

If you're an older adult with advanced renal disease: Ask your doctor about being evaluated for a kidney transplant.

Dorry L. Segev, MD, PhD, associate professor of surgery and epidemiology, Johns Hopkins University School of Medicine, Baltimore.

yourself toward the chair as if about to sit. Allow your rear end to touch the chair seat only very lightly—without resting—then slowly rise to standing again. Repeat. This activity builds strength as well as balance.

•**Paper Towel Tube Pickup.** Place the empty cardboard tube from a roll of paper towels on the floor about 12 inches in front of you. Stand on your right foot, lifting your left foot out behind you. Carefully lean forward, bending your right knee…reach down to pick up the roll…then stand up straight. Repeat several times without touching your left foot to the ground, then switch legs.

As you improve: Use a smaller object, such as a pencil, instead of the paper towel tube.

If you're a beginner: Standing on your right foot, lift your left foot slightly. With the toes of the left foot, touch the floor in front of you…then touch the floor to your left side… then touch the floor behind you. Repeat several times, then switch legs.

•**Ball Toss.** Sit or stand and toss a tennis ball repeatedly back and forth from one hand to the other.

As you improve: Toss the ball higher…hold your hands farther apart…use a larger, heavier ball (such as a softball)…and/or stand on one leg while you toss. Try not to drop the ball!

Biggest Road Risk for Seniors Isn't Driving

Jonathan J. Rolison, PhD, a psychology lecturer at Queen's University, Belfast, Ireland. His study was published in *Journal of the American Geriatrics Society.*

Are senior citizens at greatest risk of dying from a car-related injury while walking, riding in the passenger seat of a car or driving?

Most people would probably guess driving. It's just part of being human—as we age, our eyesight and reflexes (and maybe even our mental focus) all diminish…and those are all vital for something as risky and difficult as driving.

Well, a recent British study found that seniors are actually in most danger while *walking.*

How is that possible? *We spoke with the researcher to find out…*

PEDESTRIAN PERILS

A research team lead by Jonathan J. Rolison, PhD, analyzed all fatal injuries reported by police in Britain between 1989 and 2009 that were classified as "road traffic fatalities." Meanwhile, the UK National Travel Survey had estimated the number of excursions—whether as a driver, passenger or pedestrian—made each year by individuals age 21 and up. When the researchers combined these two sets of data, they were able to calculate the risk that an individual would be fatally injured for each excursion. *Here's what they found…*

When it came to both driver and passenger fatality rates, people age 70 and older had a higher rate than people who were considered "middle-aged" (between 30 and 69). But the rate of the older set was about equal to that of the youngest set—people between ages 21 and 29.

When it came to the pedestrian fatality rate, however, seniors were far more likely to die than people in any other age group—and they were far more likely to die as pedestrians than while driving or sitting in a passenger seat.

SAFEGUARDING SENIORS

Anyone who is elderly should be extra careful while walking on or near roads. Seniors typically walk more slowly than younger individuals, and they more often misjudge the speed of approaching vehicles—often due to declining hearing and/or sight. And because they are usually more frail and susceptible to injury than younger people, they should cross streets only at designated crossing areas, ideally when no cars are in sight.

Keep Your Hands Young and Strong in Just Minutes a Day

Anjum Lone, OTR/L, CHT, an occupational and certified hand therapist and chief of the department of occupational therapy at Phelps Memorial Hospital Center in Sleepy Hollow, New York.

I f you have been diagnosed with arthritis, it's wise to protect your hands right away. Approximately 40% of arthritis patients must eventually restrict their daily activities because of joint pain or stiffness—and the hands often get the worst of it.

Both osteoarthritis (known as "wear-and-tear" arthritis) and rheumatoid arthritis (an autoimmune disease) can damage cartilage and sometimes the bones themselves. (For natural remedies to help ease arthritis, see page 330.)

What's missing from the typical arthritis prescription: Unfortunately, most patients with either type of arthritis do not recognize the importance of simple daily hand exercises, which can improve joint lubrication…increase your range of motion and hand strength…and maintain or restore function. These exercises also are helpful for people who have a hand injury or who heavily use their hands.

SAVE YOUR HANDS WITH EXERCISE

Most hand and wrist exercises can be done at home without equipment. But don't exercise during flare-ups, particularly if you have rheumatoid arthritis. Patients who ignore the pain and overuse their hands and wrists are more likely to suffer long-term damage, including joint deformity.

Important: Warm the joints before doing these exercises—this helps prevent microtears that can occur when stretching cold tissue. Simply run warm water over your hands in the sink for a few minutes right before the exercises. Or you can warm them with a heating pad.

Before doing the hand exercises here, it also helps to use the fingers of the other hand to rub and knead the area you'll be exercising. This self-massage improves circulation to the area and reduces swelling.

If you have osteoarthritis or rheumatoid arthritis, do the following exercises five times on each hand—and work up to 10 times, if possible. The entire sequence should take no more than five minutes. Perform the sequence two to three times a day.*

#1: TENDON GLIDES

Purpose: Keeps the tendons functioning well to help move all the finger joints through their full range of motion.

What to do: Rest your elbow on a table with your forearm and hand raised (fingertips pointed to the ceiling). Bend the fingers at the middle joint (form a hook with your fingers), and hold this position for a moment. Then bend the fingers into a fist, hiding your nails. Don't clench—just fold your fingers gently while keeping the wrist in a "neutral" position. Now make a modified fist with your nails showing. Next, raise your fingers so that they are bent at a 90-degree angle and your thumb is

---

*For more exercises, see an occupational therapist. To find one, consult the American Occupational Therapy Association, *www.aota.org.*

resting against your index finger (your hand will look similar to a bird's beak). Hold each position for three seconds.

#2: THUMB ACTIVE RANGE OF MOTION

Purpose: Improves your ability to move your thumb in all directions. Do the movements gently so that you don't feel any pain.

What to do: Rest your elbow on a table with your forearm and hand in the air.  Touch the tip of the thumb to the tip of each finger (or get as close as you can). Then, flex the tip of your thumb toward the palm. Hold each of these positions for three seconds.

#3: WEB-SPACE MASSAGE

Purpose: Using one hand to massage the other hand strengthens muscles in the "active" hand while increasing circulation in the "passive" hand.

What to do: Clasp your left hand with your right hand as if you are shaking hands. With firm but gentle pressure, use the length of your left thumb to massage the web (space between the thumb and the index finger) next to your right thumb. Then, reverse the position and massage the web next to your left thumb. Massage each web for 30 seconds.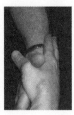

#4: WRIST ACTIVE RANGE OF MOTION

Purpose: To maintain proper positioning of the wrist, which helps keep the fingers in correct alignment.

What to do: Rest your right forearm on a table with your wrist hanging off the edge and your palm pointing downward—you'll only be moving your wrist. Then place your left hand on top of your right forearm to keep it stable. With the fingers 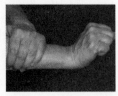 on your right hand held together gently, raise the wrist as high as it will comfortably go. Hold for three seconds.

Next, make a fist and raise it so the knuckles point upward. Now, lower the fist toward the floor. Hold each position for three seconds.

#5: DIGIT EXTENSION

Purpose: Strengthens the muscles that pull the fingers straight—the movement prevents chronic contractions that can lead to joint deformity.

What to do: Warm up by placing the palms and fingers of both hands together and pressing the hands gently for five seconds. Then place your palms flat on a table. One at a time, raise each finger. Then lift all the fingers on one hand simultaneously while keeping your palm flat on the table. Hold each movement for five seconds.

#6: WRIST FLEXION/ EXTENSION

Purpose: Stretches and promotes muscle length in the forearm. Forearm muscles move the wrist and fingers. Flexion (bending your wrist so that your palm approaches the forearm) and extension (bending your wrist in the opposite direction) help maintain wrist strength and range of motion.

What to do: Hold your right hand in the air, palm down. Bend the wrist upward so that the tips of your fingers are pointed toward the ceiling. Place your left hand against the fingers (on the palm side) and gently push so that the back of your right hand moves toward the top of your right forearm. Hold for 15 seconds. Switch hands and repeat.

Now, bend your right wrist downward so that the fingers are pointed at the floor. Place your left hand against the back of your right hand and gen- 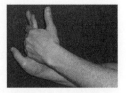 tly push so your palm moves toward the bottom of the forearm. Hold 15 seconds. Switch and repeat.

#7: FINGER-WALKING EXERCISE

Purpose: Strengthens fingers in the opposite direction of a deformity. This exercise is particularly helpful for rheumatoid arthritis patients.

What to do: Put one hand on a flat surface. Lift the index finger up and move it toward the thumb, then place the finger down. Next, lift the middle finger and move it toward the index finger. Lift the ring finger and move it toward the middle finger. Finally, lift the little finger and move it toward the ring finger. Repeat on your other hand.

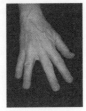

Photos of hand exercises: Courtesy of Anjum Lone

You Can Have a Much Younger Body and Mind

Mike Moreno, MD, who practices family medicine in San Diego, where he is on the board of the San Diego Chapter of the American Academy of Family Physicians. He is also author of The *17 Day Plan to Stop Aging* (Free Press). *www.the17daydiet.com*

What is it that allows some people to remain robust and healthy well into their 80s and 90s while others become frail or virtually incapacitated? It's not just luck. Recent studies indicate that aging is largely determined by *controllable* factors.

Case in point: Millions of people have chronic inflammation, which has been linked to practically every "age-related" disease, including arthritis, heart disease and dementia.

Inflammation can usually be controlled with stress management, a healthful diet, weight loss (if needed) and other lifestyle changes, but there are other, even simpler, steps that can strengthen your body and brain so that they perform at the levels of a much younger person.

To turn back your biological clock…

CHALLENGE YOUR LUNGS

You shouldn't be short of breath when you climb a flight of stairs or have sex, but many adults find that they have more trouble breathing as they age—even if they don't have asthma or other lung diseases.

Why: The lungs tend to lose elasticity over time, particularly if you smoke or live in an area with high air pollution. "Stiff" lungs cannot move air efficiently and cause breathing difficulty.

Simple thing you can do: Breathe slowly in and out through a drinking straw for two to three minutes, once or twice daily. Breathe only through your mouth, not your nose. This stretches the lungs, increases lung capacity and improves lung function.

Helpful: Start with an extra-wide straw, and go to a regular straw as you get used to breathing this way.

DRINK THYME TEA

When the lungs do not expand and contract normally (see above), or when the tissues are unusually dry, you're more likely to get colds or other infections, including pneumonia. The herb thyme contains *thymol,* an antioxidant that may help prevent colds, bronchitis and pneumonia and soothe chronic respiratory problems such as asthma, allergies and emphysema.

Simple thing you can do: Add a cup of thyme tea to your daily routine. If you have a chronic or acute respiratory illness, drink two cups of thyme tea daily—one in the morning and one at night.

To make thyme tea: Steep one tablespoon of dried thyme (or two tablespoons of fresh thyme) in two cups of hot water for five minutes, or use thyme tea bags (available at most health-food stores).

If you take a blood thinner: Talk to your doctor before using thyme—it can increase risk for bleeding. Also, if you're allergic to oregano, you're probably allergic to thyme.

Another simple step: Drink at least six to eight eight-ounce glasses of water every day. This helps loosen lung mucus and flushes out irritants, such as bacteria and viruses.

LOWER YOUR HEART RATE

Heart disease is the leading cause of death in the US. The average American would live at least a decade longer if his/her heart pumped blood more efficiently.

Elite athletes typically have a resting heart rate of about 40 beats a minute, which is about half as fast as the average adult's resting heart rate. This reduced heart rate translates into lower blood pressure, healthier arteries and a *much* lower rate of heart disease. But you don't have to be an athlete to lower your heart rate—you just have to get a reasonable amount of aerobic exercise.

Simple thing you can do: Aim for a resting heart rate of 50 to 70 beats a minute—a good range for most adults. To do this, get 30 minutes of aerobic exercise, five days a week. Good aerobic workouts include fast walking, bicycling and swimming. Even if you're not in great shape, regular workouts will lower your resting heart rate.

To check your pulse: Put your index and middle fingers on the carotid artery in your neck, and count the beats for 15 seconds, then multiply by four. Check your pulse before, during and after exercise.

WALK JUST A LITTLE FASTER

A study published in *The Journal of the American Medical Association* found that people who walked faster (at least 2.25 miles per hour) lived longer than those who walked more slowly.

Why: Faster walking not only lowers your heart rate and blood pressure but also improves cholesterol and inhibits blood clots, the cause of most heart attacks.

Simple thing you can do: You don't have to be a speed-walker, but every time you go for a walk, or even when you're walking during the normal course of your day, increase your speed and distance *slightly.*

Time yourself and measure your distance to monitor your progress, and create new goals every two weeks. Walk as fast as you can but at a speed that still allows you to talk without gasping, or if you're alone, you should be able to whistle. You'll notice improvements in stamina and overall energy within about two to three weeks.

TRY THIS FOR BETTER MEMORY

A study found that people who got even moderate amounts of exercise—either leisurely 30-minute workouts, five days a week, or more intense 20-minute workouts, three times

---

That Music's Too Loud!

Can very loud music blasted in restaurants and other public spaces cause hearing loss? What can be done about it?

Repeated exposure to high levels of noise (such as loud music in restaurants and other public places) can damage the sensitive cells in the inner ear that convert sounds into signals that travel to the brain. Once these cells are damaged, they cannot be restored.

How can you tell if the restaurant music is so loud it is potentially damaging? Download a free sound meter app on your smartphone to measure sound levels—try Too Loud? for your iPhone or deciBel for an Android.

The National Institute for Occupational Safety and Health advises a limit of 85 decibels (dB). If the music is louder than that, be sure to tell the manager that the restaurant is violating national safety recommendations.

Murray Grossan, MD, a Los Angeles–based otolaryngologist in private practice and author of *Stressed? Anxiety? Your Cure Is in the Mirror* (CreateSpace). *www. grossaninstitute.com*

---

a week—had better memories than those who exercised less.

Why: Physical activity increases oxygen to the brain and boosts levels of *neurotransmitters* that improve mood as well as memory.

Simple thing you can do: Try an aerobic dance class, such as Zumba or salsa, or power yoga. These activities provide the physical activity needed to boost memory…and learning and remembering complicated routines will activate brain circuits and promote the growth of new brain cells for further brain benefit. *Bottom line:* Just keep moving—even housecleaning and yard work count. *More on boosting brain function below…*

SHAKE UP
YOUR MENTAL ROUTINES

In a study of about 3,000 older adults, those who performed mentally challenging tasks, such as memorizing a shopping list or surfing the Internet to research a complex topic, were found to have cognitive skills that were the typical equivalent of someone *10 years younger.* You'll get the same benefit from other activities that promote thinking and concentration.

Why: These tasks trigger the development of new neurons in the brain, which boost cognitive function.

Simple thing you can do: Try to change your mental routines daily.

Fun ideas: If you're right-handed, use your left hand to write a note. Study the license number of the car in front of you, and see if you can remember it five minutes later. Listen to a type of music that's new to you. Rearrange your kitchen cabinets so that you have to think about where to find things. Overall, don't let your brain get into the rut of performing the same tasks over and over.

FIGHT BRAIN
INFLAMMATION

You've probably heard that good oral hygiene can reduce the risk for heart disease. A recent study suggests that it also can promote brain health. Researchers found that men and women over age 60 who had the lowest levels of oral bacteria did better on cognitive tests involving memory and calculations than those who had more bacteria.

Why: Bacteria associated with gum disease also cause inflammation in the brain. This low-level inflammation can damage brain cells and affect cognitive function.

Simple thing you can do: Brush your teeth after every meal—and floss twice a day. I also recommend using an antiseptic mouthwash, which helps eliminate bacteria. Visit your dentist at least twice a year for thorough cleanings. Eat a diet low in sugar and high in vitamin C.

Safer Senior Living at Home with New High-Tech Services

Jim Miller, an advocate for older Americans, writes "Savvy Senior," a weekly information column syndicated in more than 400 newspapers nationwide. Based in Norman, Oklahoma, he also offers a free senior news service at *www.savvysenior.org.*

Helping an aging parent or other loved one to remain independent and living in his/her own home has become much easier in recent years, thanks to a host of new or improved products and services.

Some of the best…

IN-HOME ALERT DEVICES

One of the most common concerns is that an elderly loved one may fall and need help when no one is around. For this danger, a medical-alert device—also known as a personal emergency response system (PERS)—has long been the tool of choice. New versions of these devices overcome past shortcomings.

At the press of a button, your loved one could call and talk to a trained operator through the system's base station receiver, which works like a powerful speakerphone. (Two base stations often are used in large or two-story homes.) The operator will find out what's wrong and notify a contact person, a neighbor, friend or emergency services, as needed.

Concerns about the old versions of these devices include seniors falling and becoming disoriented and forgetting to activate the device. Older devices also have range limitations and will work only if the senior is in the house.

To overcome some of these challenges, Philips, maker of the Lifeline, the most widely used home medical-alert service in the US, offers an Auto Alert option that has sensors built into the SOS button to detect falls. When triggered by these sensors, the device automatically can summon help without your loved one having to press a button. The Lifeline with Auto Alert costs $48 a month, and the standard medical alert service without Auto Alert runs $35 per month. (800-380-3111, *www.lifelinesys.com*)

HOME MONITORS

A more sophisticated technology for keeping tabs on an elderly loved one at home is a monitoring system. These systems will let you know whether your loved one is waking up and going to bed on time, eating properly, showering and taking his/her medicine.

They work through small wireless sensors (not cameras) placed in key locations throughout the home. The sensors track movements and learn the person's daily activity patterns and routines. The system will notify you or other family members via text message, e-mail or phone if something out of the ordinary is happening.

For instance, if your loved one doesn't open the medicine cabinet at the usual time, it could mean that he/she forgot to take his medication… or if he went to the bathroom and didn't leave it, that could indicate a fall or other emergency.

You also can check up on your loved one's patterns anytime you want through the system's password-protected Web site. And for additional protection, most services offer SOS call buttons that can be worn or placed around the house.

One reliable company that offers these services is BeClose (866-574-1784, *www.beclose. com*), whose system costs from $400 for three sensors to $500 for six, plus a service fee that ranges from $70 to $100 per month.

GrandCare Systems (262-338-6147, *www.grand care.com*) adds a social connectivity component to go along with the activity monitoring. It does this through a touch-screen computer that provides your loved one with easy access to Skype for video calls and to e-mail, photos, caller ID, games and brain exercises, as well as a calendar to keep up with appointments and events.

If your loved one doesn't want to use a computer, GrandCare can set up a dedicated channel on his television set so that he can see pictures, e-mails, calendar events, news, weather and more. The contents of the channel can be changed remotely by a caregiver through a Web site.

GrandCare Systems typically run between $950 and $1,500 for a one-bedroom apartment, with a monthly subscription fee of $30 to $50. Leasing options also are available.

OUTSIDE THE HOME

To deal with falls or health emergencies outside the home, there are a number of new mobile-alert products available that work anywhere. These pendant-style devices, which fit in the palm of your hand, work like cell phones with GPS tracking capabilities and can be carried in a purse, worn on a belt or attached to a key chain.

To call for help, your loved one pushes one button and an operator from the device's emergency-monitoring service is on the line to assist him. The devices allow your loved one to speak and listen to the operator through the pendant, and because of the GPS technology, the operator knows the exact location, which is critical in emergency situations. These alerts, however, do not have fall-detection sensors.

Top products in this category include the 5Star Urgent Response from GreatCall (800-733-6632, *www.greatcall.com*) for $50 plus a $35 activation fee and a $15 monthly service fee…and Mobile-Help (800-800-1710, *www.mobilehelpnow.com*), which offers a duo system that includes a mobile device, an indoor base station and pendant buttons for home use—$37 per month if paid a year in advance with no activation fee to $42 per month with a $100 activation fee.

MEDICATION MANAGEMENT

To help loved ones keep up with medication regimens, there's a wide variety of pillboxes, medication organizers, vibrating watches and beeping dispensers that can help them stay organized and be reminded. To find these types of products, visit *www.epill.com* (800-549-0095), where there are dozens to choose from.

One popular option is the Cadex 12 Alarm Medication Reminder Watch for $100. It provides up to 12 daily alarms and displays a message of what medication to take at scheduled times throughout the day.

And there is the monthly MedCenter System ($80), which comes with 31 color-coded pillboxes, each with four compartments for different times of the day and a four-alarm clock for reminders.

There also are a number of Web-based services that can notify your loved one when it's time to take a medication.

Examples: MyMedSchedule (908-234-1701, *www.mymedschedule.com*) and RememberItNow (925-388-6030, *www.rememberitnow.com*) offer free text-message and e-mail reminders. OnTimeRX (866-944-8966, *www.ontimerx.com*) provides phone call reminders in addition to text messages and e-mails for all types of scheduled activities, including daily medications, monthly refills, doctor appointments, wake-up calls and other events. These charge between $10 and $30 per month depending on how many reminders you need.

Another option is CARE Call Reassurance (602-265-5968, extension 7, *www.call-reassurance.com*), which provides automated call reminders to your loved one's phone. If he fails to answer or acknowledge a call, the service will contact a family member or a designated caregiver via phone, e-mail or text message. The cost is $15 per month if paid in advance for a year.

If your loved one needs a more comprehensive medication-management system, consider the MedMinder Automated Pill Dispenser (888-633-6463, *www.medminder.com*). This is a computerized pillbox that flashes when it's time for your loved one to take his medication and beeps or calls his phone with an automated reminder if he forgets. It will even alert him if he takes the wrong pill.

This device also can be set up to call, e-mail or text a family member and caregiver if the loved one misses a dose, takes the wrong medication or doesn't refill the dispenser. The MedMinder rents for $40 per month.

Another good medication dispensing system is the Philips Medication Dispensing Service (888-632-3261, *www.managemypills.com*), a countertop appliance that dispenses medicine on schedule, provides verbal reminders and notifies caregivers if the pills aren't taken. Monthly rental and monitoring fees for the Philips service run $75 (plus $99 installation fee).

After Hospital Discharge, Other Ills May Land Seniors Back in Again

Harlan Krumholz, MD, professor, Yale University School of Medicine, New Haven, Connecticut.

Amy E. Boutwell, MD, president, Collaborative Healthcare Strategies, internist, Newton-Wellesley Hospital, Newton, Massachusetts.

New England Journal of Medicine

The days and weeks after hospital discharge are a vulnerable time for people, with one in five older Americans readmitted within a month—often for symptoms unrelated to the original illness.

Now, one expert suggests it's time to recognize what he's dubbed "post-hospital syndrome" as a health condition unto itself.

A hospital stay gives patients vital or even life-saving treatment. But it also involves physical and mental stresses—from poor sleep to drug side effects to a drop in fitness from a prolonged time in bed, explained Harlan Krumholz, MD, a cardiologist and professor of medicine at Yale University School of Medicine in New Haven, Connecticut.

"It's as if we've thrown people off their equilibrium," Dr. Krumholz said. "No matter how successful we've been in treating the acute condition, there is still this vulnerable period after discharge."

POOR SLEEP IN HOSPITALS REQUIRES RECOVERY

Disrupted sleep-wake cycles during a hospital stay, for instance, can have broad and lingering effects, Dr. Krumholz writes in the *New England Journal of Medicine*.

Sleep deprivation is tied to physical effects, such as poor digestion and lowered immunity, as well as dulled mental abilities.

"The post-discharge period can be like the worst case of jet lag you've ever had," Dr. Krumholz said. "You feel like you're in a fog."

WHAT HOSPITAL STAFF CAN DO

There's no way to eliminate what Dr. Krumholz called the "toxic environment" of the hospital stay. Patients are obviously ill, often in pain, and away from home. But Dr. Krumholz said hospital staff can do more to "create a softer landing" for patients before they head home.

Staff might check on how patients have been sleeping, how clearly they are thinking and how their muscle strength and balance are holding up, Dr. Krumholz said.

Involving family members in discussions about after-hospital care is key, too. "Patients themselves rarely remember the things you tell them," Dr. Krumholz noted—whether it's from sleep deprivation, medication side effects or other reasons.

Previous research has shown that about 20% of older Americans on Medicare are readmitted to the hospital within 30 days. And more often than not, that return trip is not for the illness that originally landed them in the hospital. Instead, infections, accidents and gastrointestinal disorders are among the common reasons.

Take heart failure, for example. It is a common cause of hospitalization for older Americans, but when those patients are readmitted within 30 days, heart failure is the cause only 37% of the time, according to a study previously published in the *New England Journal of Medicine*.

EXPERT COMMENTARY

One expert, Amy Boutwell, MD, said the editorial underscores a "very important" point.

"We have to think about discharge from the hospital in a whole new way," said Dr. Boutwell, president of Collaborative Healthcare Strategies Inc., which works on projects to improve care and prevent hospital readmissions.

"The good news is most hospitals across the country are now paying attention to this," said Dr. Boutwell, who is also an internist at Newton-Wellesley Hospital in Newton, Massachusetts.

For several years, programs have aimed to cut avoidable hospital readmissions. Dr. Boutwell cofounded one, called STAAR (State Action on Avoidable Rehospitalizations), which involves hospitals in Massachusetts, Michigan, Ohio and Washington state.

And hospitals now have a financial motivation to cut readmissions, Dr. Boutwell added. In 2012, Medicare began penalizing hospitals with higher-than-expected rates of readmission within 30 days of patients' original stay.

Hospitals vary in the specific steps they take to reduce readmissions, Dr. Boutwell said. But one example is that centers are trying to ensure that families understand what has to happen when the patient goes home, and helping them with "logistics"—such as making appointments for follow-up care and sending patients home with an adequate supply of prescription medications.

"Those are the types of things we've traditionally left up to families," Dr. Boutwell said.

Whether it's necessary to officially recognize a "post-hospital syndrome" is not clear, said Dr. Boutwell. But she praised Dr. Krumholz's article for helping to bring the issue to the attention of more doctors.

AWARENESS AND PRECAUTIONS

For now, Dr. Krumholz said hospital patients and their families should be aware that the few weeks after discharge are a "period of risk and vulnerability."

So it would be wise to take some precautions, he said. These include making sure that the recently released patient does not drive a car for at least a week or so, and stays away from people with flu-like infections, since his or her immune function may be compromised.

info To learn more about taking care of yourself after hospitalization, visit the Web site of the US Agency for Healthcare Research and Quality at *www.ahrq.gov* (search "Taking Care of Myself").

Medical Newsmakers

Steroid Meningitis Outbreak Spreads to 20 States

The first reports of serious fungal infections from tainted steroid injections for back pain came in September 2012 from Tennessee and quickly became a national health crisis.

As of August 2013, 63 people have died and 749 have been sickened in 20 states during the outbreak of fungal meningitis, with Tennessee and Michigan hit the hardest, according to US health officials and the Centers for Disease Control and Prevention (CDC).

"Tennessee really got inundated with this," said Marc Siegel, MD, an associate professor of medicine at NYU Langone Medical Center in New York City.

A report published online in the *New England Journal of Medicine* explains how the outbreak began and gives details on 66 cases in Tennessee. The state eventually reported 153 cases of infection and 15 deaths.

This is rare fungal infection, Dr. Siegel said. "What's important about this report is that it documents an unusual way of transmitting this fungus," he explained.

The crisis started when a Tennessee doctor reported a single case of fungal meningitis to the state Department of Health on September 18, 2012, and the agency began an investigation. Two days later two more cases were identified in Tennessee and authorities notified the CDC.

By September 25, 2012, there were eight cases of meningitis, which is inflammation of the lining surrounding the brain and spinal cord. All of the patients had been injected with a steroid compound in hopes of relieving neck or back pain.

Investigators quickly linked the outbreak to contaminated products made by a single company, the New England Compounding Center in Framingham, Massachusetts. The company has

Marc Siegel, MD, associate professor of medicine, NYU Langone Medical Center, New York City.
New England Journal of Medicine, online

recalled all of its products and was eventually shut down.

When the Tennessee Department of Health compiled data on the cases, it found that the age of patients ranged from 23 to 91, and it generally took about 18 days from the steroid injection until symptoms appeared.

Symptoms included headache, new or worsening back pain, nausea, stiff neck and neurological symptoms, such as sleep problems and sensitivity to light, the report said.

The investigators were able to trace the tainted products to specific lots of a steroid, preservative-free methylprednisolone acetate. Patients particularly at risk were those whose injections came from older vials or those who were given high doses or multiple injections, the investigators found.

Among these 66 patients, eight died—seven from strokes, the report said.

Effective collaboration between public health officials and physicians were essential to this investigation, the authors said. "An aggressive public health response to a single report of an unusual infection resulted in the identification of a multistate outbreak of fungal infections and the rapid recall of the implicated product involved," they concluded.

According to the CDC, as many as 14,000 people were exposed to the contaminated steroids.

MORE OVERSIGHT NEEDED

While praising the Tennessee Department of Health and the CDC for their swift action, Dr. Siegel said the lesson from this outbreak is the need for more oversight of compounding pharmacies like the New England Compounding Center.

These pharmacies combine, mix or alter ingredients to create drugs to meet the specific needs of individual patients, according to the US Food and Drug Administration (FDA). Such customized drugs are frequently required to fill special needs, such as a smaller dose or removal of an ingredient that might trigger an allergy in a patient.

Currently, these pharmacies are regulated by each state's Board of Pharmacy. The FDA has limited regulatory power over these companies,

Dr. Siegel noted. Several members of Congress have called for greater FDA oversight of compounding pharmacies in the wake of the outbreak.

"This is a situation where something is made in one state but administered in another state. This is a federal problem," Dr. Siegel said. "This is not supposed to happen. This loophole needs to be closed."

"From the point of manufacture to the point of injecting a person's body, the amount of surveillance should not diminish," he added.

info To learn more about fungal meningitis, visit the US Centers for Disease Control and Prevention Web site at *www.cdc.gov/men ingitis/fungal.html.*

Sugary Drinks Tied to 25,000 US Deaths a Year

Gitanjali Singh, PhD, research fellow, Harvard School of Public Health, Boston.
Lona Sandon, RD, MEd, assistant professor, clinical nutrition, University of Texas Southwestern Medical Center at Dallas.
Suzanne Steinbaum, DO, director, Women and Heart Disease, Lenox Hill Hospital, New York City.
American Beverage Association, news release.
American Heart Association, news release.

More than 180,000 deaths worldwide in 2010 were linked to a high intake of sugar-laden drinks, a recent study estimates, including 25,000 deaths in the United States.

Most deaths occurred in middle- to low-income countries, the Harvard researchers noted.

The findings are surprising because "we often think of this as a problem only in high-income countries, like the US," said lead researcher Gitanjali Singh, PhD, a research fellow at Harvard School of Public Health, in Boston.

She said her findings, presented at an American Heart Association meeting in New Orleans, point to a need for policies that curb people's sugary drink intake.

One such effort, in New York City, is Mayor Michael Bloomberg's controversial limit on large sweetened sodas and other sugary beverages, which was struck down a day before the rule was to go into effect. Bloomberg said he would appeal the decision and defended his plan, which would have limited the size of sugary drinks sold at restaurants, food carts and theaters to 16 ounces.

Dr. Singh said that's not the only type of measure officials could take. Others could include taxing sugar-added drinks, or limiting advertising of the beverages to children.

But "anti-soda" moves are a tough sell—not only because the beverage industry and many consumers resist. It's also hard to pin ill health effects on one component of people's diets, even if it's a nutritionally dubious one.

These latest findings do not prove that sugary drinks kill people. They only show a correlation between high consumption and deaths from heart disease, diabetes and certain cancers.

"This type of study cannot prove cause-and-effect," said Lona Sandon, RD, MEd, an assistant professor of clinical nutrition at the University of Texas Southwestern Medical Center at Dallas.

"Sugary beverage consumption is often paired with other unhealthy food choices or behaviors," said Sandon, who was not involved in the study. "Chronic diseases, such as heart disease and diabetes, are the result of many factors, not just excess sugar intake."

That said, everyone should be limiting added sugar—from drinks and food—Sandon stressed. "We just do not need added sugar that is empty calories," she said.

AMERICAN BEVERAGE ASSOCIATION COMMENTARY

The beverage industry also weighed in on the findings.

"This [study], which is neither peer-reviewed nor published, is more about sensationalism than science," said the American Beverage Association (ABA).

"In no way does it show that consuming sugar-sweetened beverages causes chronic diseases such as diabetes, cardiovascular disease or cancer—the real causes of death among the studied subjects," the ABA added. "The researchers make a huge leap when they illogically and wrongly take beverage intake calculations from around the globe and allege that those beverages are the cause of deaths which the authors themselves acknowledge are due to chronic disease."

STUDY DETAILS

Study author Dr. Singh agreed that for any one person, many factors go into the risk of developing heart disease, cancer or other chronic conditions. But she said that on the "population level," it is still possible to estimate the number of deaths attributable to sugary drink consumption.

To do that, she and her colleagues used national nutrition surveys from around the world to gauge how high people's sugary drink intake was in each country. Then they estimated how sugar-added drinks affected obesity levels in those countries. Finally, Dr. Singh said, they turned to data on how obesity sways people's risk of heart disease, type 2 diabetes and certain cancers—such as breast, colon and pancreatic cancers.

Overall, they estimate that upwards of 180,000 deaths were "attributable to" sugary drink consumption in 2010. That included more than 130,000 from diabetes, about 45,000 from heart disease and stroke, and 4,600 from various cancers.

As for sugary drink intake, young Cuban men beat the rest of the world—men younger than 45 typically downed more than five servings per day. And in general, Latin America and the Caribbean had the most deaths linked to sugar-sweetened drinks.

EXPERT COMMENTARY

"This sheds light on the linear connection between sugary drink consumption and deaths," said Suzanne Steinbaum, DO, a cardiologist and director of Women and Heart Disease at Lenox Hill Hospital in New York City. She was not involved in the study.

She agreed that it's difficult to blame deaths on high-sugar drinks alone. But she also said the findings highlight one important, and simple, move that people can make to improve their diets.

"Make this one change, to stay away from sugar-sweetened beverages," Dr. Steinbaum said. "Is it the only fix? Certainly not." But, she added, replacing even one sugary drink a day with water can cut a significant amount of calories.

Dr. Steinbaum also noted that sodas are not the only culprits. "Often, these fruit juices that people think are healthy are loaded with sugar," she said.

One of the big concerns in the sugary-drink "war" is that many children and teenagers are downing huge amounts of liquid calories. Because this study focused on deaths from chronic diseases, Dr. Singh said it says nothing about the potential health effects on kids across the globe.

"We need research to figure out how high their consumption of sugary drinks really is," Dr. Singh said, "and to see how it affects their health."

The ABA countered that it is daily caloric intake, not high-calorie beverages, that really matters. "When it comes to risk for heart disease, there is nothing unique about the calories from added sugars, or sugar-sweetened beverages for that matter," the group said.

info For more information on cutting back on sugar, visit the American Heart Association Web site, *www.heart.org*, and search "sugars 101."

Breakthrough Cure for Chronic Insomnia

Michael Terman, PhD, head of the Center for Light Treatment and Biological Rhythms at Columbia University Medical Center in New York City. Dr. Terman is coauthor, with Ian McMahan, PhD, of *Chronotherapy: Resetting Your Inner Clock to Boost Mood, Alertness and Quality Sleep* (Avery).

If you can't fall asleep at a reasonable hour, you might tell yourself that you are a "night owl" or just suffer from insomnia. But turning to sleeping pills, as many insomnia sufferers do, can be a big mistake. These medications may not improve your situation and could even make it worse if you have a type of sleep disorder known as delayed sleep phase disorder (DSPD)—a condition that affects about 10% of people who complain of chronic insomnia.

Even worse: Your situation can be exacerbated by the shorter days and later sunrises of winter.

Could you have DSPD? How to find out—and what to do about it…

WHY CAN'T YOU GET TO SLEEP?

People who have DSPD find it hard to fall asleep before 2 am or sometimes even later. With this disorder, the sufferer's circadian rhythm, or internal sleep clock, is shifted later at night and, as a result, he/she awakens later in the morning. If you have DSPD, you might, for example, naturally fall asleep at 2 am and feel ready to get up about 10 am.

The problem is, most people need to get up at around 7 am or so to get to work or start their daily activities. If you drag yourself out of bed in order to meet a typical daily schedule, you will then have to deal with the fatigue, grogginess and irritability that can occur when you do not get enough sleep.

While most cases of DSPD are due to a circadian rhythm disorder, symptoms of insomnia also could be due to other causes, such as depression, anxiety disorders, neurological impairments (including dementia) or even certain drugs such as the beta-blockers commonly used for high blood pressure.

Important: Talk to your doctor about your sleep symptoms so that he/she can confirm that they are due to problems with your circadian rhythm. You may be advised to consult a sleep specialist.* If you are diagnosed with DSPD, chronotherapy, which aims to reset your body's biological rhythms, usually improves symptoms within a week.

A SECRET THAT REALLY WORKS

Your body's inner clock expects sleep to begin at a certain time, which varies from person to person. About two hours before that time, the clock signals the pineal gland, a small, pinecone-shaped gland located near the center of the brain, to begin releasing small amounts of the "sleep hormone" melatonin. For the average sleeper, melatonin levels start to rise about

*To find a sleep specialist, consult the American Academy of Sleep Medicine, *www.aasmnet.org*.

9 pm to prepare the body to fall asleep around 11 pm. The melatonin itself is not putting you to sleep the way sleeping pills do—rather it is signaling the sleep centers in the brain, via the inner clock, that nighttime is beginning.

While using a melatonin supplement, sold over-the-counter in drugstores, might seem like an obvious aid to help you fall asleep earlier, most people take it right before sleep, which overwhelms the body with excessive levels of the hormone. This can lead to side effects such as difficulty awakening, fatigue and even a feeling of sadness the next day.

However, melatonin can be used very successfully to synchronize one's circadian rhythms and shift the body clock earlier so that the urge to sleep occurs earlier. The secret is to take tiny amounts of the hormone—no more than what the pineal gland releases naturally. The other crucial point is to take the melatonin well before the inner clock typically signals the pineal gland to release melatonin.

Important study: At the Center for Light Treatment and Biological Rhythms at Columbia University Medical Center in New York City, researchers developed and tested a controlled-release melatonin tablet that allows a fine stream of melatonin to be absorbed over hours. In research volunteers, the microdose tablet (0.2 mg) produced blood levels of melatonin that were in the same range as those produced naturally by the pineal gland.

What's more, the melatonin from the tablet was washed out of the blood by the morning, mimicking the body's normal removal of pineal melatonin. In contrast, when the volunteers took a higher-dose tablet, melatonin was still lingering in the blood the next day, which can counteract the desired effect and actually shift the inner clock even later.

What to do: Until the microdose tablet is commercially available, DSPD sufferers can try using a 1-mg tablet cut into quarters with a pill cutter—one-quarter of the tablet should be taken six hours before your "natural bedtime" (driven by your natural circadian sleep–wake cycle).

Caution: A 1-mg tablet cut into quarters is not a precise dose, and some people may experience grogginess in the early evening.

To determine your natural bedtime: Take the quiz at *www.cet.org*, the Web site of the Center for Environmental Therapeutics (CET), a nonprofit organization that educates the public and professionals on sleep disorders. Click on "Therapeutic Resources & Tools"…"Self-Assessment Tools"…"Your Circadian Rhythm Type." Once you determine your natural bedtime, count back six hours and take the melatonin tablet at that time.

DON'T FORGET TO DIM THE LIGHTS

Exposure to bright indoor or outdoor lights suppresses melatonin levels. *What to do…*

•**Use low-level "soft white" bulbs**—they are easy on the eyes and produce minimal glare.

•**Dim computer and TV screens to the lowest comfortable level at least two hours before bedtime.**

•**Wear "blue-blocking" protective glasses if you must be in bright light after taking your evening melatonin.** The filter on the lenses screens out the blue rays from computer and TV screens and bright lights. Unlike sunglasses, blue-blocking glasses enhance night vision. These glasses (on the CET Web site for about $80) can fit over prescription glasses.

Once you start taking melatonin and dimming the lights in the evening, DSPD should improve within one week (some people improve the first night). Be sure not to get into bed until you start feeling sleepy, which will likely be earlier than usual. If you get into bed before the urge to sleep kicks in, you can worsen insomnia. As your sleep-onset time becomes earlier, be sure to gradually move up the time you take the melatonin so that it continues to be six hours before you are ready for sleep.

If you stop chronotherapy and return to a later sleep pattern, the problem should subside when you resume the melatonin regimen. Some people will need to take melatonin indefinitely—this is fine.

Solving the Medical Mystery of Cold Feet

Maqsood Chotani, PhD, Center for Cardiovascular & Pulmonary Research: The Research Institute at Nationwide Children's Hospital, and assistant professor, department of pediatrics, Ohio State University Wexner College of Medicine, Columbus, Ohio.

Martin Michel, MD, professor, department of pharmacology, Johannes Gutenberg University, Mainz, Germany.

American Journal of Physiology—Cell Physiology, online.

I f you've ever been booted out of bed because of your icy feet, recent research may help explain your plight.

Scientists have pinpointed specific proteins within the skin's blood vessels that play a part in the body's reaction to cold stimuli, whether it's exposure to chilly weather or touching a frigid surface with your bare hand.

The body's response to cold is to cut off circulation to the extremities to preserve blood flow to warm the internal organs. But for some people, this response is too strong, or it occurs mistakenly.

In Raynaud's disease, for instance, as the body responds to cold or stress, blood vessels narrow in the fingers and toes, which may feel numb and turn from white to blue to red during an attack.

A recent study explores the physiological mechanisms at work that makes the extremities numb with cold. The findings of this study and an accompanying editorial appear in a recent issue of the *American Journal of Physiology—Cell Physiology*.

STUDY DETAILS

The researchers used muscle cells from tiny blood vessels in skin-punch biopsies from healthy volunteers as well as muscle cells from an artery found in mouse tails with circulation similar to human skin.

"Our bodies are engineered by evolution to conserve heat and energy," explained Martin Michel, MD, a professor at Johannes Gutenberg University in Germany, and the coauthor of the editorial. "One way of doing this is limiting blood flow to the skin by making blood vessels constrict, and *norepinephrine* (a hormone and neurotransmitter) does this via alpha-adrenergic receptors on muscle cells in the blood vessel wall. But we only want this to happen when it is cold."

For some people, he said, it appears that the healthy reaction goes awry.

"The mechanisms get active at 'normal' outer temperature," Dr. Michel said. "This could involve too many alpha-adrenergic receptors or that the [temperature] set-point or something in the regulation mechanism goes wrong. Now we know for certain that two molecules called Epac and Rap1 play an important role in the process."

The study identified new players that influence adrenergic receptor function in small blood vessels, said senior study author Maqsood Chotani, PhD, a principal investigator at the Research Institute at Nationwide Children's Hospital in Columbus, Ohio.

"The alpha-2C receptors had been identified many years ago, but the exact function of this alpha-2C subtype in blood vessels was very intriguing to me," Dr. Chotani said. "Early observations showed the alpha2C to be inside the cell and not on the cell surface like other receptors in the same family. The general belief [had been] that the receptor doesn't do anything in blood vessels—it was like a vestigial, or like a silent receptor."

Not so, the study found.

"The alpha-2C receptor has a specialized role; in fact, we believe it is a stress-responsive receptor and in this case it's actually conserving body heat," he said. "So we know how the receptor is regulated in health. In disease—like Raynaud's—there could be a dysfunction, there could be overactivity of the new players we have identified in this study."

RAYNAUD'S DISEASE DEFINED

The US National Institute of Arthritis and Musculoskeletal and Skin Diseases (NIAMS) describes two levels of Raynaud's.

Primary Raynaud's, which usually starts between the ages of 15 and 25, is seen most often in women and people living in cold places. Preventive measures include keeping hands and feet warm and dry, avoiding air conditioning and wearing gloves to touch frozen or cold food.

Secondary Raynaud's starts later in life and is seen with connective tissue diseases like scleroderma, Sjögren's syndrome and lupus, according to the NIAMS. Severe cases can lead to tissue death in the fingers and toes.

In secondary Raynaud's, Dr. Chotani said, "the underlying cause could be an immune response, and it could be a complicated mixture of responses. Whereas in primary Raynaud's, its underlying cause is really not known."

IMPLICATIONS

Now, Dr. Michel said, "we can look specifically at whether the newly discovered mediators of blood flow control in the extremities are malfunctioning in such people. If they do, we may find a way to handle this."

And, Dr. Chotani said, "in the disease process, the implications for the findings that we have, these new players potentially could be targets for pharmaceutical drugs."

What about people at the other extreme, whose hands and feet always feel hot?

"That's another physiological response of the body trying to open up the blood vessels and just remove the heat from the body, so it doesn't overheat," Dr. Chotani said. "The receptor, I would think, is not working. It's just the opposite scenario."

info For more information, visit the Web site of the US National Institute of Arthritis and Musculoskeletal and Skin Diseases (*www. niams.nih.gov/health_info/raynauds_phenomenon/raynauds_ff.asp*) to learn more about Raynaud's phenomenon.

Cell-Based 'Tracking Devices' Might Help Monitor Treatments

David Newby, PhD, professor and chair of cardiology, Centre for Cardiovascular Science, University of Edinburgh, Scotland.

Matthew Tirrell, PhD, professor and Pritzker director of the Institute for Molecular Engineering, University of Chicago.

Circulation: Cardiovascular Imaging

C all it a fantastic voyage. Scientists have successfully found a way to inject tiny iron filings into the human body to potentially monitor medical therapies. The particles work as tracking devices that may help physicians determine if certain treatments are working.

The development of methods to track cells is critical to stem-cell and other therapies that rely on the delivery of particular cells to a target site, such as the heart or other organ, according to the authors of a small recent study.

"Eventually we'll be able to prove stem cells are going where they are supposed to be and track cells going into other tissues," said David Newby, PhD, study coauthor and professor and chair of cardiology at the Centre for Cardiovascular Science at the University of Edinburgh, in Scotland.

The study, published recently in *Circulation: Cardiovascular Imaging*, showed that immune cells tagged with nano-sized iron filings and injected into the bloodstream can be tracked by magnetic resonance imaging (MRI) as they move through the human body. The researchers also demonstrated that the process was safe and did not interfere with normal cell function.

A type of normal white blood cell known as macrophages ingest pathogens and cellular debris—including the filings—and take them along wherever they go. The iron filings are only about 20 nanometers across. In comparison, the average red blood cell is 8,000 nanometers wide.

Dr. Newby said the critical question the researchers wanted to answer was whether the tracking cells, once injected into the body, would migrate where the researchers wanted them to go. "We needed to be able to know if they wander off," he said.

The research showed it is possible to track tagged, injected cells for seven days. Because MRI technology is nonradioactive, the tracking system would not subject patients to radiation exposure, Dr. Newby noted.

STUDY DETAILS

The study involved two phases. First, the researchers determined that blood cells with attached iron filings moved normally, and were indeed able to survive. Twenty study volunteers participated. Some people were given injections into their thigh muscles of either unlabeled cells, iron-filing labeled cells or just the filings. Others received intravenous injections of the labeled blood cells.

To show that the tracking method could be used to facilitate the development of cell-based therapies in the future, the researchers injected one person with labeled immune blood cells, and they tracked the cells as they migrated to an inflamed area of skin on the thigh. The inflammation was caused by a Mantoux tuberculosis test, an injection just under the skin that typically becomes slightly inflamed.

"This is a pretty convincing demonstration that there's real merit to this idea of using cells as carriers," said Matthew Tirrell, PhD, a professor and Pritzker director of the Institute for Molecular Engineering at the University of Chicago.

Dr. Tirrell said the research opens up new territory for other kinds of visualization experiments. "There are few examples of any kind of targeting particles in humans," he said. "To have the confidence and guts to do it is impressive, and I think other people will be building on this work," he said.

Dr. Newby said that the research team hopes to investigate the use of these techniques to diagnose inflammatory conditions of the heart, such as transplant rejection, myocarditis or inflammation of the heart, and sarcoidosis, where there is inflammation in multiple organs. The work may also be useful in five to 10 years in stem-cell research, he added.

info Visit PEW's Project on Emerging Nanotechnologies to learn more about nanotechnology at the Web site *www.nanotechproject. org/topics/nano101/*.

Brain May Treat Wheelchair as Part of the Body

PLoS One

Mariella Pazzaglia, PhD, assistant professor, Sapienza University of Rome, Italy.

Alexander Dromerick, MD, vice president for research, National Rehabilitation Hospital, and chief of rehabilitation medicine, Georgetown University Medical Center, Washington, DC.

The brains of disabled people adjust to a wheelchair and treat it as an extension of their body, essentially replacing limbs that don't function properly anymore, recent research suggests.

The findings provide more insight into how the brain compensates when it uses tools like a wheelchair, or even something as simple as a hammer or toothbrush, said study lead author Mariella Pazzaglia, PhD, an assistant professor at the Sapienza University of Rome, in Italy.

In the future, Dr. Pazzaglia said, this kind of research could lead to ways to enhance the body in people who are physically impaired. "Bodily representations can be extended to include exoskeletons, prostheses, robots and virtual avatars," she said.

At issue is what scientists call "brain plasticity," which describes the brain's ability to learn and adjust, something people do regularly when young and continue to do as they get older.

Human brains also can compensate for bodily changes such as the loss of a limb by adjusting what's known as the internal body map. The recent study sought to understand how the brains of disabled people change their body maps to include wheelchairs.

STUDY DETAILS AND FINDINGS

The researchers surveyed 55 people in wheelchairs with spinal cord injuries about their lives, and then analyzed their responses. The study authors determined that the participants treated wheelchairs as part of their bodies, not simply as extensions of their limbs.

The study also found that people who had more movement in their upper limbs could interact more with wheelchairs, and this improved their ability to incorporate them into their body images.

Essentially, the participants' brains go into an automatic mode when it comes to using the wheelchairs. This leads to "more efficient and safer use, with lower costs, risks and dangers to the body," Dr. Pazzaglia said.

"To elude dangerous objects in the environment and the collisions that may occur during wheelchair use, the brain needs to encode an internal representation of the body that includes the wheelchair," she said.

"Moreover, the simple action of picking objects up from the floor without tipping out of the

Prosthetic for the Eye

A new device implanted directly on a blind patient's retina allowed him to read words. The experimental therapy uses a small camera mounted on a pair of glasses to send signals directly to the retina via electrical stimulation.

Frontiers in Neuroprosthetics

wheelchair implies a change in the representation of the body to enable this to happen successfully and without the risk of possible damage to the individual due to a fall," she added. "All daily activities become an automatic way of thinking, not merely a mechanical or practical process."

The study appeared in the journal *PLoS One*.

BRAIN PLASTICITY IN EVERYDAY LIFE

Automatic thinking—based on body maps that encompass inanimate objects—plays plenty of other roles in people's lives, Dr. Dromerick said. For example, people who can wield a hammer effectively or parallel park with ease have learned to treat hammers and cars as extensions of themselves, he said.

"If we learn how to play a piano or drive somewhere, that's plasticity in action," said Alexander Dromerick, MD, chief of rehabilitation medicine at Georgetown University Medical Center in Washington, DC.

info For comprehensive information on disability programs and services in communities nationwide, visit the Web site *disability.gov*.

Experimental Chemical Helps Blind Mice See

University of California, Berkeley, news release.

A novel chemical temporarily restored some vision to blind mice, and this success may eventually lead to a treatment to help people with degenerative blindness see again, according to a recent study.

Those who could benefit include people with retinitis pigmentosa and age-related macular degeneration (AMD). Retinitis pigmentosa is a genetic disease that is the most common inherited form of blindness, while AMD is the most common cause of acquired blindness in the developed world.

In both diseases, light sensitive cells in the retina called rods and cones die and leave the eye without functioning photoreceptors.

The mice used in this study had genetic mutations that made their rods and cones die within months of birth. Injections of the chemical AAQ into the eyes of the blind mice temporarily restored their light sensitivity, according to the study published in the journal *Neuron*.

AAQ makes the remaining, normally "blind" cells in the retina sensitive to light, explained lead researcher Richard Kramer, PhD, a professor of molecular and cell biology at the University of California, Berkeley.

This approach "offers real hope to patients with retinal degeneration," study coauthor Russell Van Gelder, MD, PhD, chair of the ophthalmology department at the University of Washington in Seattle, said in the news release.

"We still need to show that these compounds are safe and will work in people the way they work in mice, but these results demonstrate that this class of compound restores light sensitivity to retinas blind from genetic disease," he added.

The researchers noted that the chemical eventually wears off, which may make it a safer alternative to other experimental methods for restoring sight, such as gene or stem cell therapies, which permanently change the retina. Chemical treatment is also less invasive than implanting light-sensitive chips in the eye, the researchers said.

"The advantage of this approach is that it is a simple chemical, which means that you can change the dosage, you can use it in combination with other therapies, or you can discontinue the therapy if you don't like the results. As improved chemicals become available, you could offer them to patients. You can't do that when you surgically implant a chip or after you genetically modify somebody," Dr. Kramer explained.

However, experts note that while studies involving animals can be useful, they frequently fail to produce similar results in humans.

The research was supported by the US National Institutes of Health's National Eye Institute and Research to Prevent Blindness.

info For more information about age-related macular degeneration, visit the Web site of the US National Eye Institute at *www.nei. nih.gov/health/maculardegen/armd_facts.asp.*

Possible Vaccine to Cure Nicotine Addiction

Weill Cornell Medical College, news release.

A vaccine could someday help smokers kick the habit once and for all, according to a study that found the shot successfully treated nicotine addiction in mice in just one dose.

Although the findings hold promise, experts note that research involving animals frequently fails to lead to benefits for humans. In addition, the vaccine must be tested in rats and then primates before it can be tested in humans.

The researchers who developed the vaccine, however, say it could be the strategy that finally helps millions of smokers quit.

"While we have only tested mice to date, we are very hopeful that this kind of vaccine strategy can finally help the millions of smokers who have tried to stop, exhausting all the methods on the market today but finding their nicotine addiction to be strong enough to overcome these current approaches," the study's lead investigator, Ronald Crystal, MD, chairman and professor of genetic medicine at Weill Cornell Medical College in New York City, said in a news release.

"Smoking affects a huge number of people worldwide, and there are many people who would like to quit but need effective help," he added. "This novel vaccine may offer a much-needed solution."

Blind Man "Drives"

A man who is 95% blind recently "drove" one of Google's self-driving cars to a restaurant near his home. The car made the trip, without the driver using the steering wheel or pedals, thanks to a variety of video, radar and laser sensors.

New Scientist

The vaccine works by preventing nicotine from reaching the brain and heart. It uses the liver to continuously produce antibodies, which eat up the nicotine before it enters the bloodstream, depriving smokers of their "fix."

"As far as we can see, the best way to treat chronic nicotine addiction from smoking is to have these Pac-Man-like antibodies on patrol, clearing the blood as needed before nicotine can have any biological effect," Dr. Crystal said. "[People] will know if they start smoking again, they will receive no pleasure from it due to the nicotine vaccine, and that can help them kick the habit."

Previously tested vaccines that delivered nicotine antibodies directly failed in clinical trials because they lasted only a few weeks and had inconsistent results.

In conducting the recent study, researchers engineered a nicotine antibody and inserted it into a harmless virus. The vaccine was made to target liver cells, which, in turn, produce a steady stream of the nicotine antibodies.

When used on mice, the researchers found their vaccine produced high levels of the nicotine antibody, preventing the chemical from ever reaching the brain.

The researchers said the vaccine is completely safe and may someday even be used to prevent addiction to nicotine in people who never smoked.

"Just as parents decide to give their children a [human papillomavirus] vaccine, they might decide to use a nicotine vaccine," Dr. Crystal said. "We would, of course, have to weigh benefit versus risk, and it would take years of studies to establish such a threshold."

The study is scheduled for publication in the journal *Science Translational Medicine.*

info The American Cancer Society has more about how to quit smoking at its Web site, *www.cancer.org/healthy/stayawayfromtobacco/guidetoquittingsmoking/index.*

Condoms Don't Diminish Sexual Pleasure

Debby Herbenick, PhD, MPH, associate research scientist, codirector for the Center for Sexual Health Promotion, Indiana University, Bloomington.

Jill Rabin, MD, chief, ambulatory care, obstetrics and gynecology, Long Island Jewish Medical Center, New Hyde Park, New York.

Journal of Sexual Medicine

Try it, you'll like it—probably more than you think. With or without a condom, Americans find sex very satisfying, according to a recent study that took a peek into the bedrooms of men and women, straight and gay.

"There's this commonly held belief that condom use makes sex feel less natural or pleasurable," said study lead author Debby Herbenick, PhD, MPH, associate research scientist and codirector for the Center for Sexual Health Promotion at Indiana University in Bloomington. "But when people use them, sex happens to be great."

The study, published in the *Journal of Sexual Medicine*, found that in a nationally representative sample of men and women aged 18 to 59, ratings of sex were high, with few differences based on condom or lubricant use. No significant differences were found in men's ability to have erections with or without condoms or lubricants.

WHY DO CONDOMS GET A BAD RAP?

Jill Rabin, MD, chief of ambulatory care, obstetrics and gynecology, at the Long Island Jewish Medical Center in New Hyde Park, New York, who was not involved with the study, said she thinks it's a myth that men hate to use condoms. "Lots and lots of men like them. The women who don't like them feel they might decrease sensation and sensitivity," she said.

Lubricants also are underestimated for their ability to improve sex, said Dr. Herbenick. And women of any age may misinterpret the need to use a lubricant as an indication of non-arousal. "I knew a 26-year-old woman who said she dreaded using lubricant," said Dr. Herbenick. "She said there needs to be a Web site that says, 'Younger women need lubricant, too.'"

Women who experience vaginal dryness after menopause can also feel frustrated, seeing the need for a lubricant as a sad sign of aging.

"But one-third of American women experience the need for lubricants," said Dr. Herbenick. "Now, in the last five to seven years on TV, lubes are talked about as related to pleasure and excitement."

MORE SEX ED NEEDED

The study tapped data from the National Survey of Sexual Health and Behavior, which includes the sexual experiences and condom-use behaviors of 5,865 Americans.

While other studies have looked at attitudes toward condoms, this is the first to focus on Americans, said Dr. Herbenick.

In addition to the findings about sexual pleasure from condoms and lubricants, the study found that women were less able to identify what material the condom was made of than men— about 24% of women were unsure versus 9% of men. This was probably because men typically purchase condoms, said the study authors.

Not knowing the type of condom used has health implications for both partners. Water-based lubricants are safer to use with condoms, while oil and petroleum-based products can cause latex to deteriorate, explained Dr. Rabin.

Knowing what people do and do not know about condoms and lubricants shows health educators what they need to teach, said Dr. Herbenick.

"We continue to have high rates of sexually transmitted infections, unintended pregnancies and HIV, and people's attitudes are part of the problem," she said.

The key to helping people understand the benefits of condoms and lubricants is education, Dr. Herbenick said.

info Learn how condoms help prevent sexually transmitted diseases at the US Centers for Disease Control and Prevention Web site, *www.cdc.gov/condomeffectiveness/brief.html.*

Scientists ID Gene That Shows Progression in ALS Patients

Methodist Hospital, news release.

Agene that's an indicator of disease progression in most patients with amyotrophic lateral sclerosis (ALS) has been identified by researchers.

ALS, also known as Lou Gehrig's disease, is a neurodegenerative disease that slowly causes paralysis and death. It affects about five in 100,000 people and there is no known cure.

WHAT RESEARCHERS DISCOVERED

The researchers at the Methodist Hospital in Houston found that the debilitating symptoms of ALS appear to be increased by a lack of inflammation-reducing T cells. Specifically, they discovered that expression of the gene FoxP3—which helps control the production of anti-inflammatory T cells—was an indicator of disease progression in 80% of the ALS patients they studied.

Low FoxP3 levels were likely in patients whose ALS progressed rapidly, while higher FoxP3 levels were associated with slower disease progression, according to the study published online recently in the *EMBO Molecular Medicine Journal*.

"This is the first demonstration that regulatory T cells may be slowing disease progression, since low FoxP3 indicates a rapidly progressing disease," said lead author Jenny Henkel, PhD, an assistant professor of neurology. "Levels of FoxP3 may now be used as a prognostic indicator of future disease progression and survival."

INFLAMMATION AND ALS

The link between inflammation and ALS progression is well established, and many genes associated with the disease have been identified, according to the Methodist Hospital news release on the study.

"While inflammation exacerbates [worsens] disease in ALS patients, this inflammation is suppressed in some patients," Dr. Henkel said.

"The data in our article suggest that regulatory T cells can suppress this inflammation."

She said researchers are closing in on specific targets for modifying the inflammation that drives ALS progression, and that they are also getting closer to developing new treatments for the disease.

info For more information about amyotrophic lateral sclerosis, visit the US National Institute of Neurological Disorders and Stroke Web site at *www.ninds.nih.gov/disorders/amy otrophiclateralsclerosis/als.htm*.

Salty Diet Might Trigger MS and Arthritis

David Hafler, MD, professor, neurology and immunobiology, and chair, department of neurology, Yale School of Medicine, New Haven, Connecticut.
John O'Shea, MD, director, intramural research program, US National Institute of Arthritis and Musculoskeletal and Skin Diseases, Bethesda, Maryland.
Nature

Eating lots of foods loaded with salt may do more than raise your blood pressure. Researchers report that it could also contribute to the development of autoimmune diseases, where the body's immune system mistakenly mounts an attack upon some part of the body.

Three recent studies suggest salt may be a prime suspect in a wide range of autoimmune diseases, including multiple sclerosis (MS), psoriasis, rheumatoid arthritis and *ankylosing spondylitis* (arthritis of the spine).

A significant increase in the incidence of autoimmune diseases, especially multiple sclerosis and type 1 diabetes, suggests that environmental factors, and not genetics, may explain the trend, the researchers noted.

"The diet does affect the autoimmune system in ways that have not been previously recognized," said senior study author David Hafler, MD, a professor of neurology and immunobiology at the Yale School of Medicine, in New Haven, Connecticut.

It was an accidental discovery that triggered the researchers' interest in salt; they stumbled

Top Doctor's Natural Strategies for...

Lou Gehrig's Disease

Amyotrophic lateral sclerosis (ALS), also known as Lou Gehrig's disease, is a rare neurodegenerative disorder that affects nerve cells in the brain and spinal cord. It's a progressive disease and results in total paralysis. No two ALS patients will progress at the same rate.

ALS patients should take a daily multivitamin and mineral supplement without iron that includes B-complex, C, D and E vitamins…and calcium and magnesium to help strengthen the immune system as well as muscle and nerve function.

The progression of muscle weakness, cramping and spasms can be eased with the homeopathic remedies Magnesium phosphoricum, Cuprum metallicum, Plumbum metallicum or nux vomica (follow label instructions for dosage). Alternating hot and cold compresses to areas with muscle cramps will help increase blood flow and reduce pain. Acupuncture can also help relieve symptoms.

Thomas Kruzel, ND, naturopathic physician, Rockwood Natural Medicine Clinic, Scottsdale, Arizona.

upon the fact that people who ate at fast food restaurants seemed to have higher levels of inflammatory cells than others, Dr. Hafler explained.

RESEARCH DETAILS

In the study, Dr. Hafler and his team found that giving mice a high-salt diet caused the rodents to produce a type of infection-fighting cell that is closely associated with autoimmune diseases. The mice on salt diets developed a severe form of multiple sclerosis, called autoimmune encephalomyelitis. Findings from animal studies are not always mirrored in human trials, however.

Inflammatory cells are normally used by the immune system to protect people from bacterial, viral, fungal and parasitic infections. But, in the case of autoimmune diseases, they attack healthy tissue.

Dr. Hafler's study is one of three papers, published in the journal *Nature*, that show how salt may overstimulate the immune system. In addi-

tion to Dr. Hafler's research, scientists from the Broad Institute in Boston explored how genes regulate the immune response, and researchers from Harvard Medical School and Brigham and Women's Hospital in Boston zeroed in on how autoimmunity is controlled by a network of genes.

All three studies help explain, each from a different angle, how "helper" T-cells can drive autoimmune diseases by creating inflammation. Salt seems to cause enzymes to stimulate the creation of the helper T-cells, escalating the immune response.

"We think of helper T-cells as sort of the orchestra leaders, helping the immune system know what the cells should be doing in response to different microbial pathogens," explained John O'Shea, MD, director of intramural research at the US National Institute of Arthritis and Musculoskeletal and Skin Diseases, in Bethesda, Maryland. "The strength of these papers is that they have found another factor that drives [helper T-cell] differentiation—salt."

While salt may play a role in autoimmune diseases, the researchers said the picture is most likely complicated. "We don't think salt is the whole story. It's a new, unexplored part of it, but there are hundreds of genetic variants involved in autoimmune disease and environmental factors, too," said Dr. Hafler.

It's also unclear just how much salt is required to stimulate the autoimmune response, Dr. Hafler added.

IMPLICATIONS

Should consumers who are concerned about autoimmune disease switch to a low-salt diet, even before tests in humans have been done?

"If I had an autoimmune disease, I would put myself on a low-salt diet now," Dr. Hafler said. "It's not a bad thing to do. But we have to do more studies to prove it."

Dr. O'Shea agreed. "But the extent to which salt is important, I think we don't know. These papers show it experimentally, but we still can't be sure," he said.

info To learn more about low-salt diets, visit the MedlinePlus Web site at *www.nlm. nih.gov/medlineplus* (search "Low-Salt Diet").

No More Running to the Bathroom!

Tomas L. Griebling, MD, MPH, professor and vice-chair in the department of urology and faculty associate in The Landon Center on Aging, University of Kansas School of Medicine, Kansas City.

For millions of American women and men who suffer from overactive bladder (OAB), going to the bathroom is a stressful part of daily life. They urinate much more frequently than they should and suffer from a "got to go now" feeling multiple times a day.

Latest development: There are now newly approved FDA drugs and high-tech treatment options that help sufferers overcome their troubling symptoms.

Important: Behavioral approaches (see box on next page) can effectively treat OAB in some people and should typically be tried first for six to eight weeks. If these approaches don't adequately improve symptoms, then one or more of the following treatments can be added to the regimen.

Even if you're already taking an OAB drug, there are new options that may be more effective or convenient than your current treatment. *What you need to know…*

HOW THE BLADDER SHOULD WORK

Normally, when the bladder is relaxed, it fills up like a balloon, stretching but not leaking. Then when you urinate, it gets squeezed empty. But in people who have OAB, the bladder starts squeezing even when it's not full. If it squeezes hard enough, you leak urine.

OAB causes one or more of the following symptoms…

•**Urgency**—Sudden episodes of having to get to the toilet very fast. This may involve leakage.

•**Frequency**—On average, adults without OAB urinate roughly every three or four waking hours—about six times a day. But individuals with OAB need to urinate more than that and consider their frequent urination bothersome.

•**Nocturia**—Having to get up from sleep to urinate. More than once a night is not normal.

IS THERE A PROBLEM?

If you suspect that you have OAB, see your primary care doctor. He/she will take your medical history…perform a physical exam—to check for a prolapsed (dropped) uterus in women, for example, or an enlarged prostate gland in men—and test for a urinary tract infection.

Make sure your doctor also: Rules out other medical conditions that can lead to frequent and/or urgent urination—including diabetes, a history of stroke or a neurological condition such as Parkinson's disease, multiple sclerosis or Alzheimer's disease. Once you're sure you have OAB, treatment can begin.

NEW TREATMENT OPTIONS

A number of prescription medications, including *darifenacin* (Enablex), *fesoterodine* (Toviaz), *oxybutynin* (Ditropan, Oxytrol) and *tolterodine* (Detrol), are commonly used in pill form to help improve bladder control in OAB patients. Now, there are new options that may cause fewer side effects and/or be more convenient to use.

Recent development I: The FDA has just approved for women with OAB an over-the-counter version of Oxytrol in a patch that is placed on the skin every four days. A patch is more convenient than pills for some people. (The drug is available only by prescription for men.)

The patch's possible side effects, including dry mouth and constipation, are believed to be milder than those that can occur with the pills, since the dose is lower. The patch may cause minor skin irritation where it is placed.

Recent development II: The FDA approved Botox injections for patients with OAB who do not respond to medication. Small amounts of botulinum toxin are injected at various sites in the bladder. The treatment may need to be repeated in nine to 12 months if symptoms persist. Side effects could include urinary tract infection and incomplete emptying of the bladder.

Other OAB treatments now covered by some insurance companies (check with your insurer)…

•**Peripheral tibial nerve stimulation** involves inserting a small needle electrode near the ankle to stimulate the tibial nerve, which helps control urination. The electrode is then charged with electrical current (it is not painful). Thirty-minute sessions are typically scheduled

Overactive Bladder: Natural Care

The following behavioral approaches, used alone or in conjunction with the treatments described in the main article, can help relieve overactive bladder (OAB)…

•**Keep tabs on yourself.** Write down how often you go to the toilet to urinate…how often you experience urgency (this may not precede each urination)…what you eat and drink (dietary factors can play a role in OAB) and when. Doing this for at least three days can help pinpoint some lifestyle factors that might be making your OAB worse—for example, drinking fluids right before bedtime.

For a printable bladder diary or information on bladder diary applications for smartphones, go to the American Urological Association Web site (*www.urologyhealth.org/oab/patients.cfm*) and click on "Assess Your OAB Symptoms."

•**Do pelvic-floor exercises the right way.** With these exercises, also known as Kegels, you train the muscles that stop and start the flow of urine. This can reduce the urgent sensations and give you more time to get to the toilet.

What to do: Squeeze your muscles as if you are trying to stop yourself from urinating. Hold the muscle for five seconds, then relax for five seconds. Repeat this 10 times, three to five times a day. Work up to holding each contraction for 10 seconds, then relaxing for 10 seconds between contractions.

Common mistakes to avoid: Contracting the wrong muscles, such as abdominal, thigh or buttock muscles…bearing down as if you're going to have a bowel movement and straining the ab-dominal muscles (this may actually worsen symptoms)…and doing too many repetitions, which can fatigue the muscles and cause discomfort.

Important: Some people learn to do the exercises, feel improvement and then quit. Unfortunately, the symptoms often come back when patients stop the exercises.

•**Watch your diet.** Avoid foods and beverages that trigger symptoms. For example, caffeine, carbonated beverages, alcohol and, in some people, acidic foods, such as citrus and tomatoes, bother the bladder. *Also…*

•**Drink more water, not less.** Many patients think that if they cut way back on the amount they drink, their bladder symptoms will improve because they'll need to urinate less. But it can make things worse—urine becomes concentrated, which has an irritating effect and increases urgency.

•**Prevent constipation—it can make bladder problems worse.** Eat a high-fiber diet. If you take a fiber supplement, drink plenty of water with it. A stool softener also may help.

Important: People who smoke tend to have more OAB problems and urinary urgency. There's also a strong link between cigarette smoking and bladder cancer.

•**Bladder training.** The goal is to increase the time between urinations to minimize urgency incontinence.

What to do: When you get a sensation of needing to urinate, the natural reaction is to rush to the toilet, but the bladder is often contracting while you do that so you may leak on the way.

Better: Stop everything—don't head for the bathroom—and do a series of rapid Kegels until the sense of urgency passes. It may take several weeks for urgency to improve.

once weekly for 12 weeks. Thereafter, maintenance sessions are usually required every two to three weeks.

•**Sacral neuromodulation (SNM).** This treatment, also known as sacral nerve stimulation (SNS), and sometimes referred to as a "pacemaker for the bladder," involves implanting a device near the tailbone where it can send electrical signals to the sacral nerve, which helps control the bladder and muscles that are related to urination. A handheld remote control device is used to change the settings, allowing patients to adjust it to their symptoms.

New clinical trial: Researchers are now recruiting women for a clinical trial that compares the effectiveness of SNM/SNS versus Botox for OAB that is not caused by a chronic health condition. If you are interested in participating in this trial or any other, ask your doctor or go to *www.clinicaltrials.gov* and search "Overactive Bladder."

Men's Health

How to Prevent Erectile Dysfunction

Erectile dysfunction (ED) drugs have become so popular in the US— about 20% of American men over age 45 have used them—that the most obvious and safest solution to the problem is now being largely overlooked.

What works best for ED: Instead of taking a medication that can bring on side effects ranging from vision problems to headaches, it's much smarter to prevent the condition from developing.

Good news: Recent research shows that there are simple yet effective techniques to prevent ED. Men who already suffer from ED can improve their symptoms, too, by addressing these health issues.

THE NEW THINKING

While doctors have long known that ED can sometimes be caused by emotional factors, such as depression, there's now a growing body of evidence that shows how closely this problem is related to the same physical problems that can lead to heart disease, high blood pressure (hypertension) and stroke.

Example: The main artery in the penis is only about 0.02 inches in diameter. A man with atherosclerosis (plaques in the arteries) will often develop impotence years or even decades before he's diagnosed with cardiovascular disease.

What men need to know about the underlying causes of ED...

BELLY FAT

Men who are overweight or obese have a high risk of developing ED, particularly if they also have diabetes, hypertension or heart disease— all of which can damage the blood vessels and/ or nerves that are needed for erections.

The risk is even higher in men who have excessive belly fat. That's because fat that accumulates in the abdomen, known as vis-

Sheldon Marks, MD, associate clinical professor of urology, University of Arizona College of Medicine, Tucson, and author of *Prostate & Cancer* (Da Capo).

ceral fat, converts testosterone to estrogen. Men with a low testosterone-to-estrogen ratio frequently suffer from ED. Low energy is another warning sign.

What to do: Men who have excessive belly fat should lose weight. If weight loss does not eliminate the ED, it then makes sense to get a hormone test. Your doctor can check your testosterone-estrogen ratio with blood and/or saliva tests. Men with this hormone imbalance often improve when taking an aromatase inhibitor (such as Arimidex). This class of medications blocks the conversion of testosterone to estrogen.

Important: I don't recommend testosterone supplements because they could disrupt the balance between testosterone and estrogen, creating more visceral fat.

GUM DISEASE

Scientists have known for years that men with periodontal (gum) disease tend to have more cardiovascular disease, but gum problems also have recently been linked to an increased risk for ED.

It's possible that bacteria from infected gums can get into the bloodstream and cause inflammation in the arteries in the penis. Inflammation can, in turn, accelerate arterial obstructions that can lead to ED as well as heart disease.

What to do: Take better care of your gums with daily brushing and flossing.

Important: Dentists recommend brushing for at least two minutes twice daily—most people do not brush for nearly that long.

HEART DISEASE

There's now strong evidence showing that ED is often a marker for undiagnosed heart disease.

Here's what happens: When the narrow arteries in the penis become blocked by plaque (leading to ED), this is a good indicator that arteries in the heart also could be obstructed. It's crucial to recognize that arterial blockage in the heart can occur long before a man develops chest pain, shortness of breath or other cardiovascular symptoms.

MRI Is a Smart Choice for Prostate Patients

When 388 men who were newly diagnosed with low-risk prostate cancer had an MRI, those whose tumors were barely visible on the scan were later found through prostate biopsy to be good candidates for so-called "watchful waiting." Patients with highly visible tumors were more likely to have disease severity upgraded and require more aggressive treatment such as surgery.

Implication: MRI is a valuable tool in helping prostate cancer patients weigh treatment options.

Hebert Alberto Vargas, MD, assistant attending physician, department of radiology, Memorial Sloan-Kettering Cancer Center, New York City.

What to do: I advise men with ED to see a cardiologist first. They should assume, until testing proves otherwise, that ED is an early sign of heart disease. You'll probably be given an echo stress test. With this test, you'll use a treadmill or bicycle while a technician monitors your heartbeat and uses ultrasound to show the heart's movements.

If you have early-stage heart disease, you can save your life—and your sex life—with a combination of lifestyle changes (such as regular exercise) and, if necessary, medication to lower cholesterol.

HIGH BLOOD PRESSURE

Both high blood pressure and the drugs used to treat it are among the most common causes of ED.

If you have high blood pressure, damage to the arteries from excessive blood pressure can interfere with erections. Unfortunately, the problem can get worse if you take blood pressure medication.

What to do: In addition to reducing high blood pressure—by lifestyle changes (such as getting more exercise, dropping some pounds if you're overweight and eating less salt) and taking medications, if needed—tell your doctor right away if you're suffering from ED. He/she might be able to switch you to a different antihypertensive medication that doesn't itself cause you to have ED. Every man responds to blood pressure drugs differently.

Also important: Prescription antidepressants are notorious for causing ED in some men. As with blood pressure drugs, switching to a different antidepressant is sometimes enough to solve the problem. Drugs for male pattern baldness, such as *finasteride* (Propecia), also may cause ED.

SLEEP APNEA

Sleep apnea is a condition in which breathing intermittently stops and starts during sleep. It causes a decrease in oxygen in the blood and an increase in carbon dioxide that can lead to hypertension, heart disease—and ED.

Obesity is among the main causes of sleep apnea. Apnea also can be caused, or increased, by excessive alcohol consumption, medications (such as sedatives) and smoking.

What to do: If you are a loud snorer or your partner reports that you frequently gasp or snort during sleep, you might have sleep apnea. Other symptoms include morning headaches and extreme daytime fatigue.

Ask your doctor if you should have a sleep test. If you're diagnosed with sleep apnea, you'll probably be advised to lose weight if you're overweight and perhaps be prescribed treatment such as a CPAP (continuous positive airway pressure) device. It delivers pressurized air to the nose and/or mouth while you sleep and can sometimes eliminate both apnea and ED.

Real Relief for Prostate Pain

H. Ballentine Carter, MD, professor of urology and oncology and director of adult urology at Johns Hopkins University School of Medicine, Baltimore. He is coauthor, with Gerald Secor Couzens, of *The Whole Life Prostate Book: Everything That Every Man—at Every Age—Needs to Know About Maintaining Optimal Prostate Health* (Free Press).

A man who goes to his doctor with prostate-related pain will probably be told that he has prostatitis and that he needs an antibiotic for the infection that is assumed to be causing his discomfort.

In most cases, that diagnosis would be wrong. He probably doesn't have an infection, and antibiotics won't make a bit of difference.

Only 5% to 10% of men with prostate-related symptoms have a bacterial infection. Most have what's known as chronic nonbacterial prostatitis/chronic pelvic pain syndrome (CP/CPPS). It's a complicated condition that typically causes pain in the perineum (the area between the testicles and the anus) and/or in the penis, testicles and pelvic area.

The pain can be so great—and/or long lasting—that it can significantly interfere with a man's quality of life. *Here's how to ease the pain…*

A COMMON PROBLEM

More than one-third of men 50 years old and older suffer from CP/CPPS, according to the National Institutes of Health. In this age group, it's the third-most-common urological diagnosis, after prostate cancer and lower urinary tract conditions.

CP/CPPS isn't a single disease with one specific treatment. The discomfort has different causes and can originate in different areas, including in the prostate gland, the ejaculatory ducts, the bladder or the muscles in the pelvic floor. It can affect one or all of these areas simultaneously.

If you have pelvic pain that has lasted three months or more, you could have CP/CPPS. The pain typically gets worse after ejaculation and tends to come and go. Some men will be pain-free for weeks or months, but the discomfort invariably comes back.

THE UPOINT EXAM

A man with CP/CPPS might not get an accurate diagnosis for a year or more. Many family doctors, internists and even urologists look only for a prostate infection. They don't realize that CP/CPPS can be caused by a constellation of different problems.

You may need to see a urologist who is affiliated with an academic medical center. He/she will be up-to-date on the latest diagnostic procedures and treatments for ongoing pelvic pain.

Recent approach: Researchers recently introduced the UPOINT (urinary, psychosocial, organ specific, infection, neurologic/systemic and tenderness of skeletal muscles) exam. It categorizes the different causes of CP/CPPS and helps doctors choose the best treatments.

Your doctor will perform a physical exam and take a detailed history. He will ask where the pain is, how often you have it and how severe it is. He also will ask if you've had recurrent urinary tract infections, sexually transmitted diseases, persistent muscle pain, etc.

Important: Arrive for your appointment with a full bladder. You might be asked to perform a two-glass urine test. You will urinate

It's OK to Trim—Not Pluck—Nose Hairs

Is it safe for men to pluck their nose hairs?

Most men love a good head of hair, but not necessarily flowing from their nose. It's fine to trim (not remove) nose hairs that visibly protrude beyond the nostrils, using an electric trimmer or scissors designed for this purpose. Aggressive removal or "plucking" can cause painful ingrown hairs or a skin infection that may require antibiotics.

If redness or tenderness appears after trimming, apply an antibiotic ointment twice daily to the inner skin of the nasal passage for a few days to reduce the chance of infection.

Nose hairs are necessary to filter airborne particles, so be sure to leave enough to avoid compromising this important function.

Richard M. Rosenfeld, MD, MPH, professor and chairman of otolaryngology, SUNY Downstate Medical Center, Brooklyn, New York.

once into a container to test for bacteria/cells in the bladder. Then you will urinate a second time (following a prostate "massage") to test for bacteria/cells from the prostate gland.

NEXT STEPS

What your doctor looks for and what he may recommend…

•**Infection.** Even though it affects only a minority of men with pelvic pain, it's the first thing your doctor will check.

Consider yourself lucky if you have an infection: About 75% of men with bacterial prostatitis will improve when they take an antibiotic such as *ciprofloxacin* (Cipro).

The discomfort from an acute infection—pain, fever, chills—usually will disappear within two or three days. You will keep taking antibiotics for several weeks to ensure that all of the bacteria are gone.

In rare cases, an infection will persist and become chronic. Men who experience symptoms after the initial antibiotic therapy will need to be retested. If the infection still is there, they will be retreated with antibiotics.

•**Urinary symptoms.** These include frequent urination, urinary urgency and residual urine that's due to an inability to completely empty the bladder. Your doctor might prescribe an alpha-blocker medication, such as *tamsulosin* (Flomax), to relax muscles in the prostate and make it easier to urinate.

Also helpful: Lifestyle changes such as avoiding caffeine and limiting alcohol…not drinking anything before bedtime…and avoiding decongestants/antihistamines, which can interfere with urination.

•**Pelvic pain.** It is the most common symptom in men with CP/CPPS. It's usually caused by inflammation and/or tightness in the pelvic floor, a group of muscles that separates the pelvic area from the area near the anus and genitals. The pain can be limited to the pelvic area, or it can radiate to the lower back, thighs, hips, rectum or bladder.

Helpful treatments…

•**Kegel exercises to ease muscle tension and pain.** The next time you urinate, try to stop the flow in mid-stream—if you can do it,

PSA Testing Can Be Skewed

Can a cold or dehydration elevate a man's PSA level?

Yes, they could have an effect. Prostate-specific antigen (PSA) is a protein produced by cells of the prostate gland. An elevated level may indicate prostate cancer, but it also could result from an enlarged prostate gland or prostate inflammation.

Urinary tract infections or recent manipulation of the prostate, which may occur with the use of a catheter, also can cause the PSA level to rise. Health conditions such as a cold or dehydration, as well as ejaculation within the past 24 hours, have been reported to cause some minor elevations.

If your PSA is elevated or increasing, you should get another test in six to eight weeks. If it remains elevated, see a urologist to get further testing such as an ultrasound.

Sheldon H.F. Marks, MD, associate clinical professor of urology, University of Arizona College of Medicine, Tucson, and author of Prostate & Cancer: A Family Guide to Diagnosis, Treatment and Survival (DeCapo).

you're contracting the right muscles. To do a Kegel, squeeze those muscles hard for about five seconds…relax for five seconds…then squeeze again. Repeat the sequence five or 10 times—more often as the muscles get stronger. Do this five times a day.

•**Mind-body approaches,** including yoga and progressive relaxation exercises, can help reduce muscle spasms and pelvic pain.

•**Anti-inflammatory drugs,** such as *ibuprofen* or aspirin, as directed by your doctor. If you can't take these medications because of stomach upset or other side effects, ask your doctor about trying quercetin or bee pollen supplements. They appear to reduce inflammation in the prostate gland. Follow the dosing instructions on the label.

•**Sitz bath** (sitting in a few inches of warm water) can relieve perianal/genital pain during flare-ups. Soak for 15 to 30 minutes.

•**Depression, anxiety or stress.** Therapy and/or stress reduction are an important part of

treatment because both approaches can reduce muscle tension. Also, patients who are emotionally healthy tend to experience less pain than those who are highly stressed.

Helpful: Cognitive behavioral therapy, which helps patients identify negative thought patterns and behaviors that increase pain.

I also strongly advise patients to get regular exercise. It's a natural mood-booster that helps reduce stress, anxiety and pain.

PSA Testing Linked To Improved Prostate Cancer Survival

The Journal of Urology, news release

Prostate cancer survival rates in the United States have improved since the introduction of prostate-specific antigen (PSA) testing, researchers report.

PSA is a protein released into the body by the prostate gland. PSA screening involves measuring the amount of PSA in a man's blood. The higher the PSA level, the more likely it is that a man has prostate cancer.

The recent study, published in *The Journal of Urology,* found that routine use of PSA testing for prostate cancer screening and monitoring has resulted in earlier and more sensitive detection of the disease. This has led to improved survival for patients with newly diagnosed prostate cancer that has spread to the bones or other parts of the body ("metastatic prostate cancer").

In addition, the survival rate for black patients has improved and is now about the same as for whites, the investigators found.

STUDY DETAILS

For the study, researchers analyzed data from three clinical trials conducted over the last three decades that evaluated patient survival after androgen (hormone)-deprivation treatment for prostate cancer. Two of the clinical trials were conducted before the introduction of PSA screening, and one took place after.

Tea Time May Be Dangerous For Men

In a new study of 6,016 men who were tracked for up to 37 years, those who drank seven cups or more of black tea a day were 50% more likely to develop prostate cancer than those who drank three cups or less. Researchers do not yet have an explanation for the link.

Men who enjoy black tea: Drink it moderately—three cups or less a day. Herbal teas were not studied.

Kashif Shafique, MD, MPH, doctorate fellow, Institute of Health and Wellbeing, University of Glasgow, Scotland, UK.

Median survival was 30 months in the first trial (conducted from 1985 to 1986), 33 months in the second trial (conducted from 1989 to 1994), and 49 months in the third trial (conducted from 1995 to 2009). Patients in the most recent trial also had a 30% decreased risk of death, the study found.

While not all of the improvements in prostate cancer survival "can be attributed strictly to PSA testing, without a doubt it has played a role in extending many lives," Dr. Thompson concluded.

IMPROVEMENT IN HIGHER-RISK CATEGORIES

Among black patients, median survival was 27 months in the first trial and 48 months in the third trial, which is close to that of white patients, the study authors noted in a journal news release.

This improvement in black patients' survival may be due to greater awareness of prostate cancer and increased likelihood that they will seek health care, suggested lead investigator Ian Thompson, MD, director of the Cancer Therapy and Research Center, a US National Cancer Institute-designated cancer center, and a professor in the urology department at the University of Texas Health Science Center at San Antonio.

However, Dr. Thompson noted that black men have a twofold to threefold greater incidence of newly diagnosed metastatic prostate cancer than white men, which contributes to

a similarly higher death rate. This shows the need for a greater effort to eliminate disparities in prostate cancer, he pointed out in the news release.

RECENT FINDINGS VERSUS RECOMMENDATIONS

PSA testing has been controversial.

In May 2012, the US Preventive Services Task Force recommended against routine PSA screening, saying too many non-dangerous cancers were being treated aggressively and resulting in unnecessary harm.

But a July 2012 study in the journal *Cancer* found that not screening American men would triple the number developing advanced cancer, and the American Society of Clinical Oncology recommended that men with a life expectancy of more than 10 years talk with their doctors about getting the test.

While the recent study uncovered an association between routine PSA testing and improved rates of prostate cancer survival, it did not prove a cause-and-effect relationship.

info The US National Cancer Institute has more about PSA testing at its Web site *www.cancer.gov/cancertopics/factsheet/detection/psa*.

Does Green Tea Really Help Fight Prostate Cancer?

Susanne Henning, PhD, RD, adjunct professor, David Geffen School of Medicine, University of California, Los Angeles.

Mark Soloway, MD, professor and chairman emeritus, urology, University of Miami Miller School of Medicine.

Presentation, American Association of Cancer Research annual prevention conference, Anaheim, California.

Six cups of green tea a day may slow the progression of prostate cancer, a recent study suggests.

The finding stems from research that showed prostate patients scheduled for a type of surgery known as a prostatectomy, where the prostate is removed, reduced their levels of some disease-associated inflammation by drinking lots of brewed green tea in the weeks preceding the operation. And that reduction in inflammation may inhibit tumor growth, the researchers suggested.

Their results were presented at the American Association for Cancer Research's annual prevention conference in Anaheim, California.

The notion that the polyphenol compounds found in green tea might have a protective effect against prostate cancer has yet to be confirmed outside a laboratory setting. However, this latest report builds on previous Italian research that suggested that consuming green tea extract may help lower the risk that a precancerous condition will develop into full-blown prostate cancer.

And related research that was also presented at the cancer research conference suggested that the flavonoids found in fruits and vegetables may be associated with a lower risk of developing aggressive prostate cancer.

RECENT STUDY

In this green tea study, men who drank the beverage for three to eight weeks prior to surgery experienced a noticeable drop in both serum prostate-specific antigen (PSA) concentrations and PSA protein expression by the time they went under the knife. The fall-off in such telltale signs of disease was accompanied by reductions in both disease-linked inflammation and oxidative DNA damage, the study authors said.

"To see this effect, you would need to drink a lot of green tea," stressed study author Susanne Henning, PhD, RD, adjunct professor with the University of California, Los Angeles David Geffen School of Medicine. "Two cups a day is not going to help. In fact, we had our men drink six cups spread out all throughout the day, which I think was beneficial because green tea polyphenols are excreted very rapidly, so if you drink it that way you keep your levels up. And that seems to be the important factor in keeping the protection going."

To explore the anticancer potential of green tea, the authors focused on 67 prostate cancer patients, all of whom were weeks away from surgery. About half the men were randomly assigned to a six-cup-a-day regimen of green tea leading up to surgery, while the others consumed water instead.

The result: Blood and urine samples analyzed alongside tissue samples taken during surgery revealed that the green tea group fared significantly better on key signs of inflammation, PSA levels and expression and DNA damage.

However, no notable difference was found between the two groups in terms of tumor cell growth.

IMPLICATIONS

Dr. Henning stressed the need for more research on the potential green-tea/prostate cancer connection, and her team is currently planning new animal investigations involving combinations of green tea and other natural foods.

While this research showed an association between green tea and prostate cancer, it did not prove a cause-and-effect link.

"Actually, several food agents have been under investigation for their protective impact," she noted. "Lycopene and omega-3 fatty acids, for example. So, I would say that if you have cancer and you want to make a decision about all of this, then think of incorporating all of those as a part of a lifestyle change. I know that if I were diagnosed with prostate cancer, I would try to change my lifestyle. And that would mean, in addition to eating lots of fruits and vegetables and trying to lose weight and exercising, that I would definitely drink green tea."

EXPERT COMMENTARY

Mark Soloway, MD, professor and chairman emeritus of urology at the University of Miami Miller School of Medicine said that while drink-

More Milk May Mean Increased Risk for Prostate Cancer

According to a recent finding, men who said that they drank milk daily during adolescence were three times more likely to be diagnosed with advanced prostate cancer than men who said they drank more moderate amounts.

Jóhanna Torfadóttir, MSc, PhD, student and nutrition scientist, University of Iceland, Reykjavik, and leader of a study of 2,268 men, published in *American Journal of Epidemiology*.

ing green tea probably does not have a downside, this "limited study" does not confirm its impact as a prostate cancer intervention.

"[There's] not much solid data to prove it," he said. "This is a small study, and it would take a longer study with hundreds of patients to 'prove' its benefit."

Dr. Soloway also noted that the jury is still out on whether inflammation even plays a significant role in cancer development. "It is very much a question," he said. "Not proven at all."

But, he agreed that until larger studies come along to explore green tea's potential, "it might be worth giving it a shot."

info For more on prostate cancer risk, visit the Web site of the American Cancer Society, *www.cancer.org*, and search "prostate cancer risk factors."

Baldness May Predict Prostate Cancer

In a recent study of 214 men (median age 64) who had a prostate biopsy for suspected cancer, those who had male-pattern baldness (in which the hairline gradually recedes) were 2.4 to 2.5 times more likely to have cancer than men who had not lost hair.

Possible explanation: Prostate cancer, like baldness, is driven by the hormone androgen.

Men who have male-pattern baldness: Ask your doctor about more frequent prostate-specific antigen (PSA) testing.

Neil Fleshner, MD, MPH, professor of surgery, University of Toronto, Canada.

The Danger of "Toughing It Out"—How To Recognize Depression In Men and Get the Best Treatment

Thomas Joiner, PhD, the Robert O. Lawton Distinguished Professor of Psychology at The Florida State University in Tallahassee. Dr. Joiner has written or edited 17 books, including *Myths About Suicide* (Harvard University) and *Lonely at the Top: The High Cost of Men's Success* (Palgrave Macmillan).

Many people think of depression as a woman's problem—and for the most part that's true. Depression tends to affect twice as many women as men.

What often gets overlooked: Depression takes a huge toll on men as well, and an increasing body of research shows that it can have a wide variety of devastating consequences for them.

That's why it's vital to know how and why depression affects men…

DANGEROUS COMPLICATIONS

Depression often goes undiagnosed and untreated in men. That's because men, in general, are less likely than women to admit that they feel depressed and will often downplay their emotions.

They also are less apt to seek help, thinking they can "tough it out." Many men dislike sharing their feelings and may view seeking treatment for depression as being unmanly or weak.

Men also are less likely than women to replace the friendships that they lose throughout the years, which contributes to loneliness—a key risk factor for depression and suicide. Research shows that older men are more likely than any other demographic group to commit suicide. The rate of male suicides for those age 65 and older was 5.4 times greater than that of female suicides in the same age group.

Research has shown that depression is an independent risk factor for coronary artery disease. A study published in the journal *Psychophysiology* found that people who had depression had slower heart rate recovery after exercise, a finding that may explain the link.

In addition, depression can cause men to suppress their feelings and become more aggressive and irritable, which can wreak havoc on relationships with a spouse, children and colleagues. And it can make it difficult to function at work.

Recently Approved Prostate Cancer Medicine Extends Lives

Men given the hormone pill *enzalutamide* (formerly known as MDV3100) lived an average of 18 months after starting treatment, compared with less than 14 months for men given a placebo. The survival edge was substantial enough that the study was halted early so that men taking a placebo could be offered enzalutamide. The pill attacks testosterone and its related hormones called androgens that fuel prostate cancer growth. In August 2012 the Food and Drug Administration approved enzalutamide for use.

Study of nearly 1,200 prostate cancer patients by researchers at Memorial Sloan-Kettering Cancer Center, New York City, presented at the 2012 American Society of Clinical Oncology Genitourinary Centers Symposium.

SPOTTING DEPRESSION IN A MAN

Some sadness in life is normal. After all, life is filled with ups and downs. But pinpointing a depression diagnosis based solely on mood can be difficult. Diagnosing depression involves a variety of symptoms.

What isn't normal: When you no longer take pleasure in activities you once enjoyed. It is especially problematic if the loss of enjoyment is accompanied by persistent feelings of sadness, hopelessness and helplessness.

Changes in sleep habits—such as difficulties falling asleep or staying asleep or oversleeping—are another major sign of depression, as are a sharp drop in energy levels and difficulty focusing and concentrating.

Unlike women, who tend to express their feelings of hopelessness and helplessness, men often try to hide their depression with short-term "fixes" and risky behavior such as extramarital sex and drug and alcohol abuse. Additionally, depressed men may become obsessed with hobbies such as golf or work very long hours.

TREATING MALE DEPRESSION

Even though it can be hard for men to ask for help, getting treated for depression is critical.

The first step toward treatment is acknowledging the problem. The next step is to have an honest conversation with your primary care physician, who may treat you or refer you to a mental health professional. *Possible treatments for depression include…*

•**Physical activity.** Regular exercise has been found to have a profound effect on mood. For example, doing just 45 minutes of brisk walking three times a week can make a difference.

•**Cognitive behavioral therapy (CBT).** This type of psychotherapy involves changing negative thought patterns that are contributing to depressive thoughts. When combined with medication, CBT is especially effective.

•**Medication.** Some individuals achieve relief with medication. Drugs to treat depression include selective serotonin reuptake inhibitors such as *fluoxetine* (Prozac) and *sertraline* (Zoloft)…norepinephrine reuptake inhibitors such as *duloxetine* (Cymbalta) and *venlafaxine* (Effexor)…tricyclics such as *amitriptyline* (Elavil) and *nortriptyline* (Aventyl)…and monoamine oxidase inhibitors such as *phenelzine* (Nardil) and *isocarboxazid* (Marplan). Some antidepressants cause sexual side effects such as erectile dysfunction.

If you have sexual side effects: Try scheduling sexual activity before taking your antidepressant. Or try switching to one of the drugs less likely to cause sexual side effects such as *bupropion* (Wellbutrin). You could also ask your doctor about adding a medication to improve sexual function such as *sildenafil* (Viagra) or *tadalafil* (Cialis).

Tell your doctor if you take any medications or supplements other than the antidepressant, since antidepressants can interact with both. Be aware that depression may worsen in the first weeks after starting or changing the dose of an antidepressant. Report any severe symptoms, including thoughts of suicide, to your doctor. If you or someone you know is contemplating suicide, immediately call the American Association of Suicidology hotline at 800-273-TALK (8255).

•**Behavior activation therapy.** This treatment works by altering your behaviors to change your mood. Working with a mental health professional, you create a hierarchy of activity goals

Bald Men Appear More Powerful

Men with shaved heads are seen as being more masculine, dominant and better able to lead others than men with thinning hair or longer locks.

Results of three studies that tested people's perceptions of men with shaved heads by researchers at The Wharton School, University of Pennsylvania, Philadelphia, published online in *Social Psychological and Personality Science.*

for the week, starting with the easiest (or most necessary) and advancing to the most difficult. A depressed person who has been housebound, for instance, may start by stepping outside the house, then advance to walking to the mailbox before going to a neighbor's house to visit.

•**Socializing.** It's crucial for depressed men to find people (or even one person) they feel comfortable sharing their feelings with—someone who listens without judging and who will not tell them how to think or feel.

Participating in social activities, such as a weekly golf game, alumni groups, church committees and other forms of socializing, also can play a critical role in alleviating depression. Even weekly phone calls to friends and connecting with others on social-networking sites such as Facebook can be beneficial.

Helping a depressed man: A concerned wife, partner or loved one should first urge the individual to seek professional help if he has not done so already. Once the diagnosis has been made, a partner can help by stressing that depression is nothing to be ashamed of, listening to concerns and being patient.

Turn Off the Game If You're Trying to Conceive

According to a recent study, men who watched more than 20 hours of TV a week had sperm counts that were 44% lower than those who watched less.

British Journal of Sports Medicine

Male Sexual Abuse Survivors—Many Are Not Truly "Over It"

Howard Fradkin, PhD, a psychologist and male sexual abuse advocate based in Columbus, Ohio. He is cofounder of *Male Survivor and author of Joining Forces: Empowering Male Survivors to Thrive* (Hay House).

The recently publicized accusations of sexual abuse that were filed against 1,247 Boy Scout leaders and the crimes committed by Jerry Sandusky at Penn State University are troubling reminders that boys and young men very often are the victims of sexual abuse.

In fact, various studies show that approximately one in six boys are victimized before age 18 in the US. Think about that. It means that there are more male sexual abuse victims than there are males with diabetes or heart disease.

Yet despite these startling statistics, it's a problem that is rarely talked about. Our society tells male victims that they should be strong and stoic—so they often fear that asking for help may be an acknowledgement of weakness and may lead to judgment.

But one man has been crusading for a different approach. A victim of sexual abuse himself, a psychologist and author of *Joining Forces: Empowering Male Survivors to Thrive*, Howard Fradkin, PhD, is a psychotherapist to and advocate for thousands of other male survivors. And he shared why it's so important for male victims to face their memories of abuse—whether they feel like they're "over it" or not.

YOU CAN THRIVE

If you're a man in your 30s or older who suffered sexual abuse, the abuse likely happened at least a decade ago—and maybe many decades ago. So you might think, *Life has gone on—I'm fine. Why dig up painful memories from the past?*

Just because you're not still having nightmares about the abuse doesn't mean that it isn't affecting you, said Dr. Fradkin. Negative feelings can manifest themselves in different ways, so it's important to take a close look at your whole life. For example, many male abuse survivors suffer from depression, anxiety and/or relationship problems—in particular, they may have trouble getting close to a partner. Or they might work excessively, or they might struggle with alcoholism, drug addiction or sex addiction. "People who bury the truth for years tend to use coping mechanisms to numb the pain," he said.

In other words, there's a difference between surviving and thriving. Ask yourself which best describes you. "Many men survive but don't thrive when they keep their abuse a secret," he said. "A dark cloud still travels with them."

If you're surviving but not thriving, Dr. Fradkin has advice that may help.

ACKNOWLEDGING ABUSE

The first challenge is recognizing abuse for what it was. Men who were abused by a woman, for instance, might frame the incident as a favor—an early sexual introduction by an affectionate teacher or a friend's mom. And even adolescents who were abused by a Sandusky-type predator can feel some ambivalence because sexual abusers tend to give their young victims special privileges, such as money, gifts, trips and even nonsexual attention. "Many survivors say, 'But he or she loved me,'" said Dr. Fradkin. "Now, to thrive, they must learn how to accept the truth."

Men Can Get Genital Yeast Infections Too

While they are rare, it is possible for a man to develop a yeast infection after having unprotected intercourse with a partner who has one. Symptoms include a reddish rash and itching or burning at the tip of the penis.

To treat the infection: Use an over-the-counter antifungal treatment such as Monistat—which works for men, too—and apply the medication twice daily. See a doctor if symptoms don't go away or yeast infections happen frequently.

mayoclinic.com

IF YOU WERE ABUSED

Beyond acknowledging the abuse, Dr. Fradkin suggested more strategies that may help men thrive…

•**Chat with other survivors.** Go to malesurvivor.org, the site for the nonprofit organization that Dr. Fradkin cofounded. It offers articles on the topic…discussion boards where people can post questions and get answers…and a chat room where men can talk (instantly, in real time) with other male survivors.

•**Meet with a mental health counselor.** Find one through *Psychology Today*'s therapy directory on the American Mental Health Counselors Association site.

•**Learn more about sexual abuse and how to overcome it.** The American Psychological Association offers a variety of articles and other resources.

•**Meet other survivors.** Male Survivor sponsors recovery weekends that take place in cities nationwide and bring together a few dozen survivors at a time to share their stories. The organization also holds an annual conference. For more details about the weekends and the conference, visit *www.malesurvivor.org.*

How Men Can Shed Belly Fat, Get a Healthier Heart And Have Better Sex

Timothy McCall, MD, a board-certified internist, medical editor of *Yoga Journal* and author of *Yoga as Medicine* (Bantam). He teaches workshops on yoga as medicine that are open to health-care professionals, yoga teachers and anyone seeking help with a specific medical condition. *www.DrMcCall.com*

About 16 million Americans regularly practice yoga for health and healing—but four out of five of them are women.

What few people realize: Despite its reputation as a "soft" exercise that's more suited to women, yoga can provide special health benefits for men—even helping to slow the growth of prostate cancer.

What all men need to know…

Marijuana Increases Risk for Testicular Cancer

According to a recent finding, men who answered "yes" to the question "Have you ever smoked marijuana?" are 2.42 times more likely to develop an aggressive type of testicular tumor later in life than men who have never used the drug.

Possible reason: Marijuana may interfere with hormone signals between the brain and the testes.

Victoria Cortesis, MSPH, PhD, assistant professor of preventive medicine, Keck School of Medicine, University of Southern California, Los Angeles, and coauthor of a study of 455 men, published in Cancer.

BENEFITS FOR MEN

Hundreds of scientific studies on yoga have shown that it can improve health conditions ranging from sleep problems and sinusitis to high blood pressure and schizophrenia. *Many of these benefits are particularly relevant for men. For example, yoga has been shown to…**

•**Slow prostate cancer.** In a study published in *The Journal of Urology,* some men with prostate cancer did 60 minutes daily of gentle yoga (stretching, breathing, meditation, guided imagery and relaxation) for one year while others did not. Those who didn't do yoga had eight times more growth of cancer cells than those who performed yoga daily.

•**Reduce abdominal fat.** Stress is behind many "spare tires," because it triggers high levels of the hormone cortisol, which stimulates appetite and overeating and then plays a key role in turning extra calories into extra belly fat. For unknown reasons, visceral fat, which releases disease-causing inflammatory chemicals, is more prevalent in men than in women.

*Before starting yoga, check with your doctor if you have severe osteoporosis, problems with your spine or artificial joints—you may be at greater risk for injury. Also consult your doctor if you have any chronic health conditions or recent injuries. If you develop pain, dizziness or other symptoms while doing yoga, stop the pose and tell your teacher immediately.

Good news: Yoga reduces cortisol, which helps control abdominal fat.

•**Help prevent a heart attack.** Each year more than 900,000 Americans have heart attacks, and the majority of them are men.

Recent research: Yoga can reduce many of the heart attack risk factors in people who have heart disease, including high blood pressure, elevated total and LDL "bad" cholesterol and high triglycerides.

•**Improve sexual performance and satisfaction.** In a study of 65 men reported in *The Journal of Sexual Medicine,* practicing yoga an hour a day for three months improved every dimension of sexual functioning—libido…erections…ejaculatory control…satisfaction with performance, intercourse and orgasm…and sexual confidence.

HOW TO START

Many middle-aged men make the mistake of thinking that because yoga looks easy, it is easy. While there are some easy versions that anyone can do, faster, more vigorous yoga styles require a fair degree of fitness and strength to even start. Even though yoga is generally safe for most people of all ages, if you're middle-aged or older and have never practiced yoga, it's best to start with a slower, less vigorous style. *My advice…*

•**Start with a yoga class, not with a book or DVD.** Taking a class led by a skilled yoga teacher is invaluable because the teacher can look at you, review what you're doing and guide you to the best injury-free experience. Expert instruction, mindfulness and not pushing too hard during practice can prevent most injuries, such as muscle spasms and ligament strains.

Helpful: If you do use a book or DVD to learn yoga, have a skilled yoga teacher look over your routine now and then to help you correct any mistakes.

•**Find a good class for men.** Ask a male family member, friend or colleague who practices yoga for his recommendation. If you don't know any men who practice yoga, ask a woman, or visit the Web site of the International Association of Yoga Therapists, *www.iayt.org.*

•**Don't rush results.** Men are often achievement-oriented and want fast results. That's a mistake. Yoga is not about performance or competition—it's about how the poses help you.

•**Just do it!** This is the secret to success with yoga—simply doing a yoga routine, 15 to 20 minutes a day, every day.

For overall fitness, yoga is a good complement to cardio exercise and strength training. But remember, yoga also provides stress reduction, flexibility and mental focus.

WHAT YOGA ISN'T...

Misconceptions about yoga can keep some men from trying it. *Yoga is not...*

•**A religion.** It is practiced by Christians, Jews, Muslims and atheists.

•**Just stretching.** Yoga includes stretching poses (asanas), as well as many other techniques, such as breathing exercises and meditation.

•**A single style of exercise.** There are many styles of yoga, from slow and gentle (such as Ananda or Kripalu) to fast and vigorous (such as Power Yoga or Vinyasa Flow).

Vitamins, Minerals May Help Older Men's Sperm Stay Healthy

Andrew Wyrobek, PhD, senior staff scientist, Lawrence Berkeley National Library, Berkeley, California.
US Department of Energy/Lawrence Berkeley National Laboratory, news release.

A diet that contains high amounts of certain vitamins and minerals is associated with improved sperm DNA quality in older men, researchers say.

STUDY DETAILS

In a study of 80 healthy men, ages 22 to 80, investigators found that those older than 44 who consumed the most vitamin C, vitamin E, zinc and folate had 20% less sperm DNA damage than those who consumed the lowest amounts of these so-called "micronutrients."

However, a higher intake of these vitamins and minerals was not associated with improved sperm DNA quality in younger men.

The study, published in the journal *Fertility and Sterility*, was led by scientists at the US Department of Energy's Lawrence Berkeley National Laboratory.

"It appears that consuming more micronutrients such as vitamin C, E, folate and zinc helps turn back the clock for older men. We found that men 44 and older who consumed at least the recommended dietary allowance of certain micronutrients had sperm with a similar amount of DNA damage as the sperm of younger men," said Andrew Wyrobek, PhD, senior staff scientist of the Life Sciences Division at the Lawrence Berkeley National Laboratory.

IMPLICATIONS

"This means that men who are at increased risk of sperm DNA damage because of advancing age can do something about it. They can make sure they get enough vitamins and micronutrients in their diets or through supplements," Dr. Wyrobek added.

The findings are important because an increasing number of men over 35 years of age are having children, which raises public health concerns, the researchers pointed out.

Previous research has shown that as men age, they are more likely to have sperm DNA damage. This explains why older men are less fertile and at increased risk for having children with genetic defects.

Until now, scientists haven't known whether a diet high in antioxidants and micronutrients might help protect against age-related damage in sperm DNA. Further research is needed to determine if higher vitamin intake and improved sperm DNA quality in older men will help improve their fertility and the health of their children.

info For more information about older men and fertility, visit the Web site of the American Society for Reproductive Medicine, *www.asrm.org*, and search "aging male fertility."

Father's Age Linked To Autism and Mental Illness

Nature

"Can you believe it? She's expecting—at her age!" When a woman who's pushing or past 40 announces a pregnancy, loved ones' hearty congratulations often are accompanied by concerns about her age. That's because certain genetic problems, such as Down syndrome, are more common among babies born to older moms.

But nobody blinks when it's the dad who is of a more advanced age.

That may be about to change.

Reason: Recent research from Iceland shows that fathers pass on nearly four times as many genetic mutations as mothers do...and that the risk rises significantly as men get older.

This is no small concern, because some such mutations have been linked to various developmental and mental health problems—including autism and schizophrenia.

Dietary Fat Reduces Men's Fertility

Recent finding: Men whose diets included 37% or more calories from fat or 13% or more calories from saturated fat had 40% lower sperm production and concentration than men who consumed less fat. Further research is needed, but in light of other known dangers of high fat intake, such as cardiovascular disease, men concerned about fertility should moderate their dietary-fat intake.

Jill A. Attaman, MD, a reproductive endocrinologist at Dartmouth-Hitchcock Medical Center, Lebanon, New Hampshire, and leader of a study published online in *Human Reproduction*.

It makes sense when you stop to think about it. Females are born with all the eggs they'll ever have. But sperm are continually produced throughout a man's life—and that nonstop production provides constant opportunities for genetic mutations to occur.

What does this mean for couples hoping to have kids later in life?

WHEN DAD'S DNA LETS HIM DOWN

Participants in the study from Iceland included 78 family groupings (each consisting of a mother, father and one child). Researchers looked for new mutations in each child that were not present in either parent...then determined whether that genetic material had come from the mother's egg or from the father's sperm.

What they found: Fathers passed on nearly four times as many genetic mutations as mothers—on average, 55 versus 14. And the number of new mutations in children increased by two for every additional year of the father's age, with the total number doubling every 16.5 years.

This means, for instance, that compared with a 20-year-old man, a 36-year-old man passes along twice as many mutations to his children... a 53-year-old man passes on four times as many mutations...and a 70-year-old man passes on eight times as many mutations.

Now, we can't say for sure whether these results would apply across the board, because the study participants included a disproportionate number of families in which the children had autism or schizophrenia. But the research nonetheless raises important questions about a father's age—questions that often go unasked.

MUTATION RISK REDUCTION

There are steps a man can take to reduce the odds of passing genetic mutations to offspring. *For instance, you can consider...*

•**Having children sooner rather than later.**

•**Working with a geneticist or a genetics counselor** before you and your partner try to conceive to gauge your risk of having a child with a genetic disorder. Your doctor can refer you to a counselor in your area.

•**Freezing some of your sperm now for use later** if you think you are likely to want to father a child years down the road. Sperm-freezing costs about $300 for the initial processing plus $400 per year for storage—which isn't cheap but may end up being a small price to pay for peace of mind. If you do consider going this route, ask your doctor for a referral to a well-regarded sperm cryobank—improper storage reduces the viability of sperm and lowers the odds of conception.

Do You Have Low Testosterone?

John E. Morley, MB, B.Ch, St. Louis University.

The ADAM Questionnaire is a standard test used by doctors to determine whether a man has symptoms of low testosterone and therefore might have a testosterone deficiency. *Answer yes or no to each of the following questions...*

1. Do you have a decrease in libido (sex drive)?

2. Do you have a lack of energy?

3. Do you have a decrease in strength and/or endurance?

4. Have you lost height?

5. Have you noticed a decreased "enjoyment of life"?

6. Are you sad and/or grumpy?

7. Are your erections less strong?

8. Have you noticed a recent deterioration in your ability to play sports?

9. Are you falling asleep after dinner?

10. Has there been a recent deterioration in your work performance?

What to do: If you answered "yes" to questions 1 or 7, or to any other three questions, you might have low testosterone—and you should be tested for total and free testosterone. (See article on page 273 for more information.)

Pain Relief

Foods That Fight Pain— Some Work Better Than Drugs

Many of us turn to medications to relieve pain. But research has shown that you can help reduce specific types of pain—and avoid the side effects of drugs—just by choosing the right foods. Here, the common causes of pain and the foods that can help. *Unless otherwise noted, aim to eat the recommended foods daily...*

OSTEOARTHRITIS

Osteoarthritis causes pain and inflammation in the joints.

Best foods: Bing cherries, ginger, avocado oil and soybean oil.

A study in *The Journal of Nutrition* found that men and women who supplemented their diets with Bing cherries (about two cups of cherries throughout the day) had an 18% to 25% drop in C-reactive protein, a sign of inflammation. Bing cherries contain flavonoids, plant-based compounds with antioxidant properties that lower inflammation.

Ginger also contains potent anti-inflammatory agents that can reduce joint pain. A double-blind, placebo-controlled study found that 63% of people who consumed ginger daily had less knee pain when walking or standing. I recommend one to two teaspoons of ground fresh ginger every day.

Avocado oil and soybean oil contain avocado soybean *unsaponifiables* (ASUs), which reduce inflammation and cartilage damage in arthritis patients.

David Grotto, RD, founder and president of Nutrition Housecall, LLC, a consulting firm based in Chicago that provides nutrition communications, lecturing and consulting services as well as personalized, at-home dietary services. He is author of *The Best Things You Can Eat: For Everything from Aches to Zzzz* (Da Capo). *www.david grotto.com*

RHEUMATOID ARTHRITIS

This autoimmune disease causes systemic inflammation—your joints, your heart and even your lungs may be affected.

Best foods: Fish and vitamin C–rich foods.

The omega-3 fatty acids in fish increase the body's production of inhibitory prostaglandins, substances with anti-inflammatory effects. A recent study found that some patients who consumed fish oil supplements improved so much that they were able to discontinue their use of aspirin, *ibuprofen* and similar medications.

Ideally, it's best to eat two to three servings of fish a week. Or take a daily fish oil supplement. The usual dose is 1,000 milligrams (mg) to 3,000 mg. Be sure to work with a qualified health professional to determine what supplement regimen is right for you.

Foods rich in vitamin C (citrus fruits, berries, red bell peppers) are effective analgesics because they help decrease joint inflammation. These foods also help protect and repair joint cartilage. A study in *American Journal of Nutrition* found that patients who ate the most vitamin C–rich fruits had 25% lower risk for inflammation.

GOUT

Gout is a form of arthritis that causes severe joint pain that can last for days—and that "flares" at unpredictable intervals.

Weight loss—and avoiding refined carbohydrates, such as white bread, commercially prepared baked goods and other processed foods—can help minimize flare-ups. You also should eat foods that reduce uric acid, a metabolic by-product that causes gout.

Best foods: Celery and cherries.

Celery contains the chemical compound 3-n-butylphalide, which reduces the body's production of uric acid. Celery also reduces inflammation.

Both sweet (Bing) and tart (Montmorency) pie cherries contain flavonoids, although the bulk of science supporting the anti-inflammatory and pain-relieving properties of cherries has been done using tart cherries. (An exception is the study that found that Bing cherries relieve osteoarthritis.) It is hard to find fresh tart cherries, so I recommend dried tart cherries or tart cherry juice.

MIGRAINES

These debilitating headaches are believed to be caused by the contraction and dilation of blood vessels in the brain.

Best foods: Oats, coffee and tea.

Oats are high in magnesium, a mineral that helps reduce painful muscle spasms—including those in the muscles that line the arteries. In one study, researchers found that people who took 600 mg of magnesium daily had a 41.6% reduction in the number of migraines over a 12-week period, compared with only a 15.8% reduction in those who took a placebo.

You can get plenty of magnesium by eating high-magnesium foods. A small bowl of cooked oat bran (about one cup), for example, provides more than 20% of the daily value. Other high-magnesium foods include oatmeal, almonds, broccoli and pumpkin seeds.

The caffeine in coffee and tea helps relieve migraine pain. The antioxidants in both beverages also are helpful.

Caution: Consuming too much caffeine—or abruptly giving it up if you are a regular coffee or tea drinker—can increase the frequency and severity of headaches. Limit yourself to a few cups daily.

MUSCLE PAIN

It usually is caused by tension, overuse or an actual injury, such as a strain or sprain. Because tendons and ligaments (the tissues that attach your muscles to your bones) have little circulation, muscle-related pain can be very slow to heal.

Best foods: Tart cherries and rose hip tea.

Eating as few as 20 dried tart cherries can help reduce pain. So can tart cherry juice.

Example: At the Sports and Exercise Science Research Centre at London South Bank University, researchers gave one-ounce servings of tart cherry juice twice daily to athletes who did intense workouts. These athletes regained more of their muscle function more quickly than those who didn't drink the juice. Studies also have shown that the juice can reduce muscle pain after exercise.

Office Buildings Are Linked to Headaches

When exposed to an uncomfortable indoor environment, 38% of workers reported having a headache one to three days a month…18% had a headache one to three days a week…and 8% had headaches daily. An uncomfortable indoor environment was defined as one with abnormal levels of carbon monoxide, carbon dioxide, volatile organic compounds, light, humidity and/or temperature. Headaches ranged from mild to migraine, and women were more likely to report headaches than men.

Study of 4,326 office workers in 100 large office buildings led by researchers in the department of physiology and health science, Ball State University, Muncie, Indiana, published in *Annals of Indian Academy of Neurology*.

Rose hip tea is high in vitamin C, as well as anthcyanins and a substance called galactolipid—all of which have been shown to combat inflammation and may help ease muscle and joint pain. Have several cups daily.

NERVE PAIN

Inflammation or injury to a nerve can cause a burning, stabbing pain that is difficult to control with medications. Examples of conditions that cause nerve pain include sciatica (pain along the sciatic nerve from the lower spine down the back of the leg) and neuropathy (nerve damage), a painful complication of diabetes.

Best foods: Turmeric, figs and beans.

Turmeric, a yellow-orange spice that commonly is used in Indian and Asian cooking, is a very effective analgesic. Like ginger, it is an anti-inflammatory that has been shown to reduce pain about as well as ibuprofen—and with none of the side effects.

Both figs and beans—along with whole grains and green leafy vegetables—are rich in B-complex vitamins, which are essential for nerve health. One study, which looked at a form of vitamin B-1, found that patients who took as little as 25 mg four times daily had an improvement in neuropathy. Other B vitamins may have similar effects.

What to Take for a Tension Headache— No Drugs Needed

Trupti Gokani, MD, a board-certified neurologist and director of the Zira Mind & Body Center in Glenview, Illinois. Her special interests include alternative approaches to headache management and women's issues. *www.ziramindandbody.com*

Its trivial-sounding name seems to imply that the problem is "just stress"…but the viselike pain of a tension headache can make you truly miserable and significantly disrupt your day. Popping a painkiller is not a great solution because such drugs can have nasty side effects, including increased risk for gastrointestinal bleeding, blood pressure problems and liver or kidney damage.

So what can you take when a tension headache grabs hold? Integrative neurologist Trupti Gokani, MD, director of the North Shore Headache Clinic in Highland Park, Illinois, suggested trying any or all of the following options. Products are available at health-food stores and/or online. *Consider taking…*

•**A few bites of food or a big drink of water.** If hunger or dehydration is triggering your headache, the pain may disappear once you assuage your body's basic needs. Just about any healthful food will do…but stay away from known headache triggers such as processed meats, aged cheeses, red wine and anything with monosodium glutamate, Dr. Gokani said.

•**Butterbur supplements.** Though various supplements may prevent headaches when taken regularly, Dr. Gokani said that butterbur works best to help halt a headache you already have. This anti-inflammatory herb should be taken as soon as you feel the pain coming on. Try the brand Petadolex (*www.petadolex.com*), which contains a purified form of butterbur free from liver-damaging pyrrolizidine alkaloids. Or consider HAessentials by Pure Balance, a product Dr. Gokani helped develop, which contains Petadolex and other headache-relievers (available at *www.ziramindandbody.com/store*).

Caution: Do not use butterbur if you are pregnant or have liver disease.

•**Some whiffs of an aromatherapy remedy.** Finding the right scent may require some experimentation, Dr. Gokani said, because an aroma that soothes pain for one person can irritate another.

Options to try: Essential oil of lavender… basil…or clary sage.

To use: Sprinkle three drops of the desired essential oil onto a tissue or handkerchief and take a sniff every few minutes…or sprinkle three drops onto a hot or cold compress and apply to your forehead until the pain lets up.

•**A moment to ask yourself why you have this headache.** A tension headache usually has an underlying trigger, Dr. Gokani noted.

Consider: Do you need a break from your computer screen? Are you working in a poorly lit room? Might a short walk or a chat with a friend help relieve whatever stress you're under? Once you identify the root problem and take action to rectify it, your pain should ease up.

Migraine Drugs Can Actually Worsen the Pain

Jay S. Cohen, MD, author of MedicationSense.com, an online newsletter that provides information about medications and natural therapies, and an adjunct associate professor of psychiatry and family and preventive medicine at the University of California, San Diego. Dr. Cohen is also author of the book *15 Natural Remedies for Migraine Headaches* (Square One).

Anyone who has ever had a migraine knows that the excruciating pain will drive you to do almost anything to get relief.

Case in point: Powerful migraine medications, including triptans, are rife with side effects, such as dizziness, drowsiness and nausea, but these drugs are among the most widely prescribed for migraine sufferers.

Latest development: Important recent research completed in Great Britain has found that painkillers, including nonsteroidal anti-in-

flammatory drugs (NSAIDs) and triptans, often worsen headaches due to overuse (defined as 15 or more days of NSAID use per month or 10 or more days of a triptan or opiate-based painkiller). So what's the solution?

POWERFUL NONDRUG THERAPIES

Increasing scientific evidence now supports the use of natural therapies that, in many instances, are just as effective—and sometimes even more effective—in preventing migraines than the standard medications.

Important: Unlike prescription drugs, which usually reach high concentrations in the body almost immediately, natural remedies work more slowly and, as a result, rarely cause side effects. It may take about three months before a particular remedy is fully effective.

My advice: Start with riboflavin (see below) and take it for about one month. This may be all that you need. If migraine frequency and severity don't seem to be subsiding, keep taking riboflavin and add one (and then another) of the other supplements below every month or so until symptoms improve. If you require more than one supplement, take them individually rather than in a manufactured combination product for optimal therapeutic effect. *Three of the following supplements are the most anyone should require…**

•**Riboflavin.** This B vitamin is believed to improve oxygen metabolism within the energy-producing mitochondria of nerve cells. Researchers speculate that a dysfunction in oxygen metabolism is an underlying cause of migraines.

Scientific evidence: When researchers studied patients who averaged four migraine attacks a month, the number dropped to two per month after three months of taking riboflavin. It also reduced the duration of the attacks by an average of 44%.

Typical dose: 400 mg daily.

*Consult your doctor before trying these supplements if you have a chronic medical condition and/or take prescription medication—some remedies may interact with commonly used medications. If you use migraine medication, you'll need advice on tapering off that drug while adding these therapies.

Side effects: Very rarely, patients who take high-dose riboflavin will experience nausea or other gastrointestinal side effects. These can be avoided by splitting the dose—take 200 mg at breakfast and another 200 mg with dinner.

Note: In some people, riboflavin turns the urine an iridescent yellow color. Don't worry—it's harmless.

•**Magnesium.** Estimates show that 70% to 80% of the US population is deficient in magnesium. In some people, low magnesium triggers spasms in the cerebral arteries that lead to migraines.

Scientific evidence: A study that looked at 81 migraine patients found that supplemental magnesium, taken for three months, decreased the frequency of migraines by 42%. It also reduced the duration and severity of the attacks.

Typical dose: Start with 100 mg in the morning and 100 mg at night. Every few weeks, increase the dose until you're taking 400 mg daily, in divided doses.

Side effects: About 40% of patients who take magnesium experience loose bowel movements. Experiment with different forms of this supplement until you find one that doesn't cause this.

For example, the magnesium hydroxide form used in Milk of Magnesia is more likely than most to cause diarrhea at high doses. This is less likely to occur with magnesium citrate, magnesium lactate or magnesium malate.

Important: Drink plenty of water—about eight glasses daily—when taking magnesium. This prevents excessive levels from accumulating in the body, which can lead to diarrhea.

•**Co-enzyme Q10 (CoQ10).** This supplement is a strong antioxidant that reduces the release of inflammatory substances that have been linked to migraines.

Scientific evidence: One study reported that 94% of patients who took CoQ10 had at least a 25% reduction in the frequency of their migraines.

Typical dose: Start with 150 mg once daily. If needed, you can increase the dose to 300 mg, divided into three daily doses.

Side effects: Less than 1% of people who take CoQ10 will experience stomach upset or other side effects. Dividing the dose usually prevents this.

•**5-HTP (5-hydroxytryptophan).** This is a naturally occurring substance that's produced from an amino acid (tryptophan) in foods. The body uses 5-HTP to produce serotonin, a neurotransmitter with paradoxical effects—that is, in some patients, elevated serotonin dilates the blood vessels, while in others it causes constriction. This is why 5-HTP prevents migraines in some patients, but not in everyone.

Scientific evidence: In one study, more than half of migraine patients taking 5-HTP reported less pain and frequency of headaches after two months.

Typical dose: 50 mg to 100 mg daily. Take the lower dose for several weeks, then gradually increase it if your migraines aren't improving. Don't take more than 400 mg daily.

Side effects: In rare cases, sedation and/or strange dreams will occur. 5-HTP should not be taken with an antidepressant and may interact with other medications.

•**Butterbur.** This powerful herbal medicine is considered a natural product in the US but requires a doctor's prescription in Germany. Butterbur has compounds that are thought to reduce arterial spasms. It also inhibits the body's production of leukotrienes, inflammatory substances that can trigger migraines.

Scientific evidence: A double-blind study of 202 migraine patients found that a twice-daily dose of 75 mg of butterbur decreased the frequency of migraines by an average of 48%.

Typical dose: 50 mg to 75 mg twice daily.

Side effects: In rare instances, patients may experience burping or stomach upset when taking butterbur.

Important: Use a butterbur extract labeled PA-free (free of the harmful chemicals pyrrolizidine alkaloids). Butterbur may cause allergic reactions in people who are sensitive to plants in the ragweed family.

FDA Approves First Skin Patch to Treat Migraines

Fawad Khan, MD, neurologist, Ochsner Neuroscience Institute, New Orleans.

Nancy Waltman, PhD, nurse practitioner, University of Nebraska Medical Center College of Nursing, Lincoln Division.

NuPathe Inc., news release.

Bloomberg News

A skin patch for the treatment of migraines, and the intense waves of nausea that often accompany these debilitating headaches, has been approved by the US Food and Drug Administration.

Called Zecuity, the patch contains *sumatriptan*, one of the most widely prescribed medications for migraines.

ABOUT MIGRAINE TREATMENTS

According to Fawad Khan, MD, a neurologist with Ochsner Neuroscience Institute in New Orleans, few drugs are approved for the treatment of acute, symptomatic migraine. To complicate matters, many migraine sufferers can also experience severe bouts of nausea and vomiting.

Another expert described the problem this way.

"I've had some patients where the nausea and vomiting was so bad they couldn't even swallow a pill," said Nancy Waltman, PhD, a nurse practitioner with the University of Nebraska Medical Center College of Nursing, Lincoln Division.

Treat a Migraine ASAP

Start treating a migraine as soon as symptoms appear. Migraine sufferers often wait for the pain to become severe, even unbearable, before taking any medication—because they believe they should not take it until they absolutely must.

But: Migraine treatment is much more effective when started as soon as possible—preferably within the first 20 minutes.

Study by researchers at Beth Israel Deaconess Medical Center, Boston, presented at the American Neurological Association annual conference, held in Boston.

A nasal spray is available, as is an injection, but many patients aren't comfortable with these options, Dr. Khan and Dr. Waltman noted.

ABOUT THE MIGRAINE PATCH

Dr. Khan said the Zecuity patch is "simple, efficient and can deliver the exact amount of dosage with minimal variability."

The patch is attached to the upper arm or thigh, and when the patient pushes a button the drug is delivered through the skin. Zecuity, which is battery-operated, delivers 6.5 milligrams of sumatriptan over the course of about five hours and can relieve nausea, as well as reduce sensitivity to light and sound.

NuPathe Inc., which makes Zecuity, hopes to have the patch on the market by 2014.

STUDY FINDINGS

Research involving 800 patients ultimately led to the approval of Zecuity. One study found that 18% of patients using the patch were headache-free after two hours, compared with 9% of those using an inactive placebo. About half achieved a reduction in their headache after two hours, compared with 29% of those using the placebo.

And 84% of patients using the patch were relieved of their nausea, compared with 63% of those in the placebo group, according to NuPathe Inc.

The most frequent side effects were pain at the site of application along with tingling, itching, warmth and discomfort.

CAUTIONS AND COST

Patients with heart disease or who are using antidepressants known as selective serotonin reuptake inhibitors should also be careful when taking sumatriptans, said Dr. Waltman, who added that she thought the patches "are wonderful."

One concern, though, is cost, Dr. Waltman cautioned.

It's not clear how much the patches will cost, but the class of medications known as triptans can be expensive, as much as $300 a month (although sumatriptan now has a generic version), Dr. Waltman said.

In general, though, "the more options that are available to migraine headache patients, the better," Dr. Waltman said. "Migraine patients tend to be underdiagnosed and undertreated and inappropriately treated."

info The US National Library of Medicine has more information about migraine at *http://www.ncbi.nlm.nih.gov/pubmedhealth/PMH0001728.*

Change Your Sleep Position to Heal Your Pain

Mary Ann Wilmarth, PT, DPT, chief of physical therapy at Harvard University. She is also the founder and CEO of Back2Back Physical Therapy, a private practice based in Andover, Massachusetts. *www.back2backpt.com*

When you slip into bed at night, you probably go straight to your favorite sleep position—perhaps on your side or on your back. But sleep positions can sometimes be tricky. Certain positions can help—or worsen—frequent body pain.

The best—and worst—sleep positions for common body aches...

SHOULDER PAIN

Sleeping on your back is often a good option if you have shoulder pain. To avoid compressing shoulder nerves, tendons and/or joints, make sure that your head, neck and shoulders are in a neutral position. Put a small pillow under your head (with a rolled-up towel under your neck, if needed). You may even want to put a small towel roll or pillow under your shoulder to give it more support, if needed.

Should you sleep on your side when your shoulder hurts?

Is It Time to Replace Your Mattress?

If you can't remember when you bought your mattress, you're probably due for a new one. Mattresses start to sag and lose their support after about eight or 10 years.

Choose a mattress that's on the firm side or firm, but with some cushioning on top, such as a plush-top mattress. About every three months, rotate the mattress. Flip it over if it has two sleep sides.

Also: Invest in more pillows. You can use them in different ways when you need more support or padding—for example, between your legs, for hugging and under your knees. Depending on the size of the pillows, two to four will generally be enough to provide added support for your body.

And if so, which side? It depends on the cause of your shoulder pain.

For sprains and rotator-cuff injuries: When opting for side-sleeping, most people with this type of shoulder pain are most comfortable hugging a pillow with the painful shoulder up.

Some people, however, are more comfortable—and hurt less in the morning—if they sleep with the painful side down. The joint will be supported by the mattress, and your weight will keep the affected shoulder from moving. Just be sure to place a pillow in front of your chest and under the painful shoulder for support.

For arthritis: The irritation and inflammation can worsen if you sleep on the painful shoulder. Keep pressure off the affected joint by lying on your back or on the other side with the arm supported by hugging a pillow.

KNEE PAIN

Do not lie on your stomach if you have knee pain—whether it's from arthritis, an injury or a surgical procedure. The pressure on the kneecap can be painful. Also, people who sleep on their stomachs often stretch out the back of the knee joint. This can cause an overextension of the hamstring and the knee joint, leading to pain in the knee or hamstring.

Better: Sleep on your side with a pillow between your knees. The pillow should be thick enough so that the top leg remains in alignment with the hip. This prevents the top hip from dropping down, which can stress the leg and the spine. The pillow reduces friction and pressure on the knees and keeps the legs in proper alignment.

Another choice: Sleep on your back. You may want to sometimes use a small pillow or towel roll under your knees.

Caution: If you have arthritis or any acute injury and use a pillow in this way often, it can increase swelling in your knees and limit the knees' range of motion. For this reason, you might need to alternate between side-lying and sleeping on your back throughout the night or on different nights.

BACK PAIN

Back-sleeping is a good position for people with back pain. However, if you're lying flat on your back, you may feel more comfortable with a pillow under your knees. This will keep your back in a more natural position and eliminate an excessive arch between your lower back and the mattress.

Self-test: If you can easily slip your hand into an open space between your lower back and the mattress, raise your knees a little more. Your lower back should be flat against your hand.

For back pain, you may also find it comfortable to sleep on your side with a pillow between your legs.

NECK PAIN

If your neck is tight and/or painful, do not sleep on your stomach.

Reason: Unless you sleep with your face pressed into the mattress, you'll need to turn your head to the side. This puts a lot of stress on the neck joints as well as the muscles and soft tissues in the neck and upper back.

Better: Sleep on your side with a pillow under your neck. The pillow should fill the distance between your neck and shoulder. You can use a special pillow for side-sleeping with more support for your neck and a cutout for your head (available online or from home-goods stores). Alternately, you can use a rolled-up towel to give your neck more support. You also can sleep on your back as long as you don't prop up your head too high, which will strain your neck. (Usually one pillow is enough.)

FOOT PAIN

If you have extreme pain on the sole of your foot, you may have plantar fasciitis. This condition causes painful inflammation of the tissues on the bottom of the foot. If you have plantar fasciitis, it will likely worsen if you sleep on your stomach.

Reason: You generally point your feet when you're on your stomach. This shortens the muscles of the calf and soles of the feet and can cause painful cramps.

You will do better if you sleep on your back or side using a pillow between the legs. If you must sleep on your stomach, at least hang your feet over the end of the bed so that your feet and ankles are in a more neutral position.

HOW TO CHANGE HOW YOU SLEEP

Suppose that you are a side-sleeper, but you know that you should be sleeping on your back. Before you go to sleep, think about the position that you want to maintain and start in that position. Remind yourself of this whenever you happen to wake up and return to the desired position.

It may take a few weeks (or even months), but the mental reminders and time in the desired position will eventually change the way that you sleep most of the time.

Do You Have Mysterious Pain or Numbness in Your Arms or Legs?

Michael Costigan, PhD, an assistant professor of neurology at Boston Children's Hospital and Harvard Medical School and a specialist in neuropathic pain medicine. His research on the peripheral nervous system led to the discovery of GCH1, a gene that activates enzymes involved in neuropathic pain and that could be a target for more effective treatments.

Have you ever felt pain or numbness in your hands, legs or feet? This can be caused by a condition called peripheral neuropathy (PN), a form of nerve damage.

PN is relatively common—about 20 million Americans have it—and most people associate it with diabetes. But there are literally hundreds of forms of PN.

The condition can be caused by athletic injuries, repetitive motions and autoimmune diseases. Continual pressure on one part of the body (from using crutches, for example) or a ligament compression (such as carpal tunnel syndrome) also can cause PN, as can exposure to toxic chemicals. Even hormonal changes in women could be the cause.

What you need to know…

HUNDREDS OF CAUSES

About one-third of neuropathy patients also have diabetes. And up to 70% of people with diabetes will eventually develop PN. Elevated blood sugar damages vessels carrying blood to the extremities, causing PN. The highest risk for PN is in people who have had diabetes for at least 25 years.

Other causes of PN…

•**Nerve entrapment injuries.** Activities involving repetitive motions—for example, typing, working a cash register or riding a bike—are a common cause of nerve inflammation and damage. You should suspect a local injury if you have symptoms in just one area (mononeuropathy). Patients who have diabetes or other systemic diseases are more likely to have damage to multiple nerves (polyneuropathy).

•**Vitamin B-12 deficiency** damages the coating that surrounds and protects nerves (the myelin sheath), which can lead to PN. Between 10% and 25% of older adults are deficient in B-12 because of an age-related decline in intrinsic factor, a protein that's needed for absorption of the vitamin.

•**Autoimmune diseases** (such as lupus and rheumatoid arthritis) can cause the immune system to attack and damage the myelin sheath. Nerve damage also can be caused by conditions such as kidney disease, hypothyroidism, hepatitis C and Lyme disease.

•**Toxic neuropathy,** usually caused by chemotherapy during cancer treatments, can result in severe nerve damage. Additionally, exposure to environmental chemicals, such as heavy metals or agricultural pesticides, can cause PN.

LITTLE-KNOWN SYMPTOMS

Although pain is often a symptom of PN, many patients with the condition experience uncomfortable but painless sensations, including tingling, itching and/or numbness. For example, most patients who have diabetic neuropathy experience foot numbness rather than pain—in fact, some cannot feel their feet at all.

Warning: Pain, tingling, numbness or burning sensations in the feet may be the first sign of diabetes.

DIFFICULT TO DETECT ROOT CAUSE

Most cases of PN can be diagnosed in a doctor's office with simple tests, including reflex and manual muscle testing, along with "touch tests" that can identify a loss of sensation in a particular location.

You also might need nerve conduction studies, which determine how fast the nerves can carry the signal and how well the muscles can respond to it, or electromyography, which helps distinguish nerve damage from muscle-related disease. In addition, your doctor might order blood tests to check for infection, hormone deficiencies or nutritional status.

The catch: Even though it's usually easy to identify PN, it can be a challenge to find the underlying cause. In nearly one-third of cases, the cause is never determined. In these patients, treatments can only relieve symptoms, and damage to the nerve or nerves will probably continue because the mechanism can't be identified. Research is under way to try to find solutions.

RECOVERY IS POSSIBLE

The good news is that the majority of patients with PN will gradually heal once the underlying cause is identified and treated—although it could take years before the nerves fully recover.

Example: Patients with diabetes who improve their glucose control will frequently experience a reduction in neuropathy symptoms over a period of months, but it might take a year or longer before their symptoms are mainly or completely gone.

The odds for making a complete recovery improve when the nerve damage is recent and treatment is started quickly.

Example: The nerve will completely regenerate in most patients with carpal tunnel syndrome if they're diagnosed and surgically treated within six months.

Important: Go to a doctor right away if you suspect that you have PN. The longer you wait, the higher the risk that you'll have permanent nerve damage—and a lifetime of pain and/or other undesirable symptoms.

BEST TREATMENTS NOW

The current treatments available for PN only relieve discomfort—they do not affect the ability of nerves to regenerate. Scientists are developing medications that specifically target nerve pain and improve the ability of nerves to heal, but these drugs are still in the experimental stage. *For now…**

•**Don't depend on aspirin, *ibuprofen* or related medications.** They are not very effective for PN—and the potential side effects (such as gastrointestinal bleeding and kidney or liver damage) make them a poor choice for most patients.

•**Tricyclic antidepressants,** such as *nortriptyline* (Aventyl, Pamelor) or *desipramine* (Norpramin, Pertofrane), are an effective treatment for PN, particularly when the nerve discomfort is caused by diabetes. Taken at low doses, they reduce pain even in patients who don't suffer from depression. Side effects, which may include a dry mouth and constipation, are somewhat rare.

Also helpful: Selective serotonin and norepinephrine reuptake inhibitors (SSNRIs), such as *duloxetine* (Cymbalta). Side effects may include nausea.

•***Gabapentin* (Neurontin) and *pregabalin* (Lyrica).** First developed for seizures, they change electrical activity in the brain and reduce pain caused by many types of PN, including the pain caused by cancer and cancer treatments.

Bonus: Pregabalin reduces anxiety in some patients—helpful because stress and anxiety often increase due to chronic pain. Possible side effects include dizziness, sedation and sometimes cognitive impairment in older adults. Side effects can be reduced, however, by starting patients on a low dose that's increased over a period of weeks.

•**Topical *lidocaine*** (such as Lidoderm and Topicaine) used in patch or gel form is a good choice for patients whose painful neuropathy is limited to specific, localized areas. Even at high doses (three patches daily, applied for a

*Tell your doctor if you take other medications to avoid possible interactions.

total of 12 hours), little of the drug enters the bloodstream, which reduces risk for side effects. A local rash where the gel/patch is applied may occur in some patients.

•**Opioid painkillers,** such as *oxycodone* (OxyContin) and *levorphanol* (Levo-Dromoran), can be effective for reducing neuropathic pain. However, many doctors avoid them because they cause sedation and could lead to addiction. These drugs are mainly used for patients with severe pain who do not respond to other treatments. In addition to sedation and dependency, side effects may include nausea and constipation.

info For more information, including clinical trials and the latest research, contact the Foundation for Peripheral Neuropathy at 877-883-9942 or *www.foundationforpn.org*.

Natural Cures for Arthritis

Steven Ehrlich, NMD, a naturopathic physician and founder of Solutions Acupuncture & Naturopathic Medicine in Phoenix. He has spent the last decade using natural medicine to treat chronic pain and illness. Dr. Ehrlich has also taught naturopathic techniques to both conventional and alternative medicine practitioners.

If you have arthritis, you may have shied away from natural medicine in the past because you didn't think that it would relieve your pain.

After all, there is no rigorous scientific evidence to back up these remedies, right?

Wrong.

Now: While it's true that many nondrug approaches for pain relief have been based primarily on their thousands of years of use by Asian, Indian and other traditional cultures, there is now an impressive body of scientific evidence that makes natural medicine a smarter choice than ever before for many arthritis sufferers. (These therapies have been studied most often for osteoarthritis but may also relieve pain due to rheumatoid arthritis. Check with your doctor.)

PAIN RELIEF WITH LESS RISK

Millions of Americans depend on high-dose pain relievers that cause side effects, including gastrointestinal upset or bleeding, in up to 60% of patients.

What you may not realize is that some natural therapies, which are far less likely to cause side effects, work just as well as the powerful pain-relieving drugs that are so commonly used for arthritis.

Many Americans take glucosamine (a dietary supplement that stimulates production of key components in cartilage) to help fight arthritis. However, arthritis pain symptoms improve only slightly or moderately in some patients—even when they take glucosamine sulfate, the most widely studied form of this supplement. (Research currently indicates that adding chondroitin, a supplement derived from shark or bovine cartilage or produced synthetically, isn't necessarily helpful for arthritis.)

In my practice, I often recommend the following regimen (with or without glucosamine) to relieve arthritis pain—the typical arthritis patient might start with curcumin and fish oil (pain relief should begin within one week to a month). Ginger can be added if more pain relief is needed...*

•**Curcumin.** A chemical compound in the spice turmeric, it helps inhibit inflammatory enzymes and reduces joint pain without the gastrointestinal side effects that often occur with aspirin and related drugs.

Scientific evidence: A study published in *The Journal of Alternative and Complementary Medicine* found that curcumin reduced arthritis pain and improved knee function about as well as *ibuprofen* (Motrin).

How to use curcumin: To obtain a concentrated dose of the active ingredient, try curcumin supplement capsules with a standardized curcuminoid complex (rather than kitchen turmeric, which would be difficult to consume in therapeutic amounts). Follow the label instructions—typically taking it three times daily during flare-ups. Between arthritis episodes, you can take half this amount to prevent inflammation.

Caution: Curcumin can inhibit the ability of blood to clot. Use this supplement only under a doctor's supervision, particularly if you're also taking a blood-thinning medication such as *warfarin* (Coumadin) or aspirin.

•**Fish oil.** The omega-3 fatty acids in fish oil supplements increase the body's production of inhibitory prostaglandins, substances that prevent inflammation.

Scientific evidence: A study published in *Arthritis & Rheumatism* discovered that some arthritis patients who took fish oil improved so much that they were able to discontinue their use of conventional painkillers.

How to use fish oil: The amount of omega-3s found in dietary sources is insufficient for pain relief. Use a fish oil supplement—doses range from about 2,000 mg to 6,000 mg daily. Start with the lower dose, then gradually increase it until you notice improvement in pain and stiffness (the rate at which the dose is increased depends on the patient). If you take more than 2,000 mg of fish oil daily, you should be monitored by a physician—this supplement has a blood-thinning effect.

•**Ginger.** This spice has compounds that inhibit the effects of cyclooxygenase, an inflammatory enzyme.

Scientific evidence: A study that looked at 261 patients with knee arthritis discovered that those who took ginger supplements had less pain—and required fewer painkillers—than those taking placebos.

How to use ginger: Ginger spice will not provide enough of the active ingredient, so use a ginger supplement. The standard dose is 250 mg taken four times daily. Talk to your doctor before trying ginger—especially if it's used with a blood-thinning drug, curcumin and/or fish oil. Ginger can increase the risk for bleeding in some patients.

OTHER THERAPIES THAT HELP

The following approaches can accelerate and increase the pain-relieving effects offered by the supplements described earlier...

*Consult a doctor before trying these supplements—especially if you have a chronic condition or take medication. To find a physician near you with experience prescribing botanical medicines, consult the American Association of Naturopathic Physicians at *www.naturopathic.org*.

331

•**Balance Method acupuncture.** Acupuncture can be extremely effective because it increases the flow of blood and oxygen into painful areas while accelerating the removal of inflammatory chemicals.

Scientific evidence: A study involving more than 3,500 patients with chronic hip and/or knee arthritis found that those given acupuncture (in addition to conventional care, including doctor visits and use of painkillers) had fewer symptoms and a better quality of life than those given only conventional treatments.

My advice: Consider trying Balance Method acupuncture. Rather than inserting needles above or near the painful areas (as occurs with standard acupuncture), the practitioner will use points on your arms or legs that "remotely" affect the joints. It seems to be more effective than standard acupuncture.

How acupuncture is used: Virtually all arthritis patients improve by the end of the third session—some after the first session. Most practitioners advise an initial series of 12 to 15 sessions, given once or twice a week, followed by monthly "tune-ups."

•**Meditation.** Meditation works in part by lowering levels of stress hormones. This decreases inflammation as well as the perception of pain. Patients who do meditation may still have pain, but it won't bother them as much as it did before.

Scientific evidence: In a study reported at an American College of Rheumatology meeting, arthritis patients who did meditation for 45 minutes a day, six days a week for six months had an 11% decrease in symptoms, a 46% decrease in erythrocyte sedimentation rate (a measure of inflammation) and a 33% reduction in psychological stress.

How meditation is used: Practice meditation for five to 10 minutes, once or twice a day—even during symptom-free periods.

Helpful: "Tapping meditation," which incorporates elements of acupressure as the patient taps different areas of his/her body. It has been especially helpful for arthritis patients in my practice. Most health practitioners who recommend meditation can teach you how to perform tapping meditation.

•**Yoga.** Any form of exercise is helpful for arthritis as long as it doesn't put excessive pressure on the joints. Yoga is particularly beneficial because it gently stretches and strengthens the muscles. It also increases the movement of synovial (lubricating) fluid across bone surfaces.

Scientific evidence: Researchers recently found that patients with knee osteoarthritis who took a weekly yoga class had improvements in pain and mobility after just eight weeks.

How yoga is used: The yoga that's practiced in many health clubs and yoga studios may be too aggressive for patients who have arthritis. Start with a beginner's class, preferably one that's taught by an instructor who specializes in therapeutic yoga, which is designed to treat specific medical conditions. To find a yoga instructor who specializes in therapeutic yoga, consult the International Association of Yoga Therapists at *www.iayt.org*.

Arthritis? No…Bursitis— Here's Why It Matters

James V. Luck, Jr., MD, an orthopedic surgeon, professor and residency program director of the UCLA/Orthopaedic Hospital Department of Orthopaedic Surgery. He is chairman of the national Medical Advisory Board for the Shriners Hospital for Children.

D on't assume that an aching joint means that you have arthritis. If the pain came on suddenly, hurts more at night and gets better when you're active, you might have bursitis.

Many of the body's joints have one or more *bursae* (bur-SEE), fluid-filled sacs that rest between bones and tendons. Irritation of a bursa (the singular form) can cause intense pain that makes it difficult to move.

Bursitis usually occurs in the shoulder, hip, elbow or knee, but it also can occur in the heel and base of your big toe. Depending on the location and the degree of irritation, the pain can range from merely irritating to excruciating.

WHAT GOES WRONG

Bursae provide a lubricating surface between joint bones and the tendons and muscles that lie above. When you move, the tendons/muscles glide, with almost no friction, across the bursae.

Bursitis is caused when pressure and/or repetitive movements irritate a bursa and cause inflammation. Inflammation not only is painful, but it also increases the friction of moving tendons/muscles, which exacerbates the problem.

Bursitis can be triggered by trauma, such as a hard knock to the elbow or knee. However, most cases are due to repetitive movements (such as frequently lifting your arms over your head) or pressure (from kneeling or leaning on your elbows). People with hobbies or professions—electrician, carpet installer, musician, factory worker—that involve repetitive movements and/or pressure have the highest risk.

If the discomfort from the bursitis severely inhibits your range of motion and you quit moving normally, you can develop scar tissue that can lead to chronic inflammation and stiffness.

Example: One common disorder, adhesive capsulitis, often occurs in patients who first had shoulder bursitis and then put up with limited joint motion. This condition, also known as "frozen shoulder," can cause severe pain and take many months to resolve.

Arthritis in One Joint Can Affect Entire Body

Untreated arthritis in one joint can cause pain throughout the body. Osteoarthritis reprograms the central nervous system and should be treated early with medicines that target the central nervous system to prevent the disease from becoming crippling. Weight loss if you are overweight, exercise and a healthy diet with an emphasis on omega-3 fatty acids also may help.

Joanne Jordan, MD, MPH, director of the Thurston Arthritis Research Center and chief of the division of rheumatology, allergy and immunology at University of North Carolina, Chapel Hill.

Another risk: An infected bursa, known as septic bursitis.

BURSITIS OR SOMETHING ELSE?

Your doctor will press on different points around your painful joint to see if there's tenderness above one or more bursae. It's difficult to distinguish bursitis from tendonitis, inflammation of a tendon. Patients with bursitis often have tendonitis as well, because the increased friction from an inflamed bursa can irritate the tendon. Also, tendonitis can spread to the adjacent bursa. The distinction usually isn't important because the treatments for each condition typically are the same.

Your doctor usually can distinguish bursitis from arthritis by your symptoms. In general, the pain caused by osteoarthritis (the most common form of arthritis) is more persistent...gets worse rather than better with continued movements... and usually is worse during the day, when patients are most active.

If your doctor isn't sure what's causing your pain, you probably will need an X-ray. It's the only way to definitively distinguish arthritis from bursitis.

If your doctor suspects that a bursa might be infected, he/she will remove fluid with a needle and test it for infection.

Bonus: Although the procedure is mildly uncomfortable, it usually will reduce bursitis pain almost immediately.

SELF-HELP FOR BURSITIS

Apply ice or a cold pack as soon as you feel pain. Chill the area for 10 to 15 minutes at a time, and repeat it once or twice an hour—or as often as you can—for at least 48 hours. Applying cold will help reduce swelling as well as pain. After 48 hours, intermittent heat is appropriate to increase circulation and promote healing.

You also can take an over-the-counter anti-inflammatory, such as *ibuprofen* (i.e., Advil, Motrin), following the directions on the label.

MEDICAL HELP

If you have severe pain, your doctor can inject the bursa with a mixture of cortisone and an anesthetic. The anesthetic will stop the pain instantly. The cortisone gradually will reduce swelling as well as pain. Most patients with bursitis who get an injection need only one treatment.

If you have septic bursitis, you'll need antibiotics—the type will depend on the bacterium that's causing the infection. Most patients will take antibiotics orally. Severe infections might need to be treated with intravenous antibiotic therapy.

When bursitis is severe and doesn't improve after treatment, surgery may be needed to remove the bursa—but this is rarely necessary.

PREVENTION

To avoid bursitis…

Protect your joints as much as possible. For example, someone who spends a lot of time kneeling can wear knee pads. Or rest your weight on your forearms rather than on your elbows.

•**Take frequent breaks.** If you're laying tile, for example, stand up and walk around every 15 or 20 minutes.

Routinely move your joints through their full range of motion.

Examples: Periodically move your arm in a complete circle—from front to back and from side to side. You can work the knee joint by lying on your back, with your knees bent, and slowly bringing the heel of your foot close to the buttocks.

Walking also is helpful, and using a bicycle is an excellent exercise for knees and hips. Doing shoulder exercises in a warm shower often is beneficial.

Four Surprising Cures For Joint Pain

Jamison Starbuck, ND, naturopathic physician in family practice and a guest lecturer at the University of Montana, both in Missoula. She is columnist for *Bottom Line/Health.*

Exercise has so many health benefits that it's hard to understand why everyone isn't doing it on a regular basis. But what if it hurts to exercise? If you have joint pain, you may wonder whether exercise is good for you or even possible to do. In conventional medicine, joint pain is treated with synthetic medication, typically nonsteroidal anti-inflammatory drugs (NSAIDs), such as *naproxen* (Aleve) or *ibuprofen* (Motrin). These medicines usually are effective for short-term use, but they do not cure the problem, and they can harm your stomach. For these reasons, I prefer to start with natural methods, which usually do a terrific job at reducing—and sometimes even eliminating—joint pain. *My favorite remedies for joint pain—roughly in order of importance…*

REMEDY #1: Get serious about stress reduction. An increasing body of evidence now shows that stress reduction really does reduce pain. You may have noticed this through your own experiences—for example, your pain lessens while you're on vacation or during a relaxed weekend. Three stress-reducing methods that I highly recommend are yoga, meditation and massage. I advise patients to engage in one or more of these practices on a regular basis. An ideal stress-reducing regimen might include daily meditation, yoga three times a week and/or massage once a week.

REMEDY #2: Investigate food allergies. Eating food to which you are allergic can significantly increase pain. Wheat, soy and peanuts are common food allergens. To start, eliminate suspected foods to see if your symptoms improve and then reappear when the foods are reintroduced. Or ask a naturopathic physician to test you for food allergies using a blood test for IGG immunoglobulins (antibodies reach high levels with food allergies). If food allergies don't seem to be contributing to your pain, you may want to consider giving up animal-based foods, including meat. Animal-based foods are generally inflammatory, which means that they contain a high percentage of arachidonic acids that can promote and aggravate pain. Keep in mind that you can often get more inflammation-fighting omega-3s from plant sources, such as flaxseed and walnuts, than from fish.

REMEDY #3: Try Boswellia serrata. This herbal remedy contains nutrients that reduce inflammation and improve both acute and chronic joint pain.

Typical dose: 300 mg three times a day for four weeks, then 300 mg one to three times a day if needed for pain. It's generally safe, but check with your doctor before trying this remedy.

REMEDY #4: Get some mild exercise. Many people mistakenly assume that exercise will damage joints and increase pain, but studies show that regular mild exercise, such as swimming, yoga or pilates, promotes circulation within joints and will reduce inflammation and pain. Work out up to the point of pain, then stop and repeat the exercise the next day—ideally, until you can do the activity for an hour a day, six days a week. If you have joint degeneration or severe pain, check with your doctor first.

Need a New Joint?— Check Out "Pre-Hab"

Karen Pechman, MD, medical director of the department of physical medicine and rehabilitation at Burke Rehabilitation Hospital in White Plains, New York. She is an assistant professor of rehabilitation medicine at Weill Cornell Medical College in New York City.

Joint-replacement surgery may be a good solution if your joint pain interferes with everyday activities.

Secret to getting better results: A targeted form of physical conditioning known as "pre-hab" can dramatically reduce the often-painful recuperation period that follows joint-replacement surgery.

Even though surgeons have encouraged pre-hab for as long as they've been doing joint replacements, not enough patients take advantage of it.

When performed for six weeks before your surgery, pre-hab can reduce your recovery time by up to 73% for common joint-replacement surgeries such as those for the knee and hip—and even less common replacement procedures, including those for the ankle and elbow.

What you need to know…

WHY PRE-HAB?

With pre-hab, a physical therapist coordinates an exercise program that helps build the physical "reserves" you'll need to recover from surgery.

To accomplish this, pre-hab focuses on specific exercises that strengthen multiple muscle groups without stressing the affected joint…improves balance and flexibility…and increases stamina and coordination.

BUT IS PRE-HAB REALLY WORTH THE EFFORT?

Consider these facts: Pre-hab not only results in shorter hospital stays, but also shorter stints in inpatient and outpatient rehab…and a quicker return to the activities and lifestyle that had to be put on hold due to unbearable joint pain.

What's more, there's significant scientific evidence that supports the use of pre-hab for people undergoing joint replacement.

For example, participation in pre-hab has been found to greatly increase your chances of having a successful surgical outcome—that is, having little or no pain and regaining full joint mobility and functional capacity—according to research published in *Physiotherapy Theory and Practice, Clinical Orthopaedics and Related Research* and *The Journal of Strength and Conditioning Research*.

Although pre-hab is not a substitute for rehab that's done after joint replacement, there are several advantages to strengthening one's body before surgery. A faster recovery is perhaps the most important benefit.

Someone who undergoes a few weeks of pre-hab prior to a hip replacement, for example, might complete a postsurgery rehabilitation program in only five to seven days, while another person who hasn't undergone pre-hab and isn't in the best of health could require several weeks in rehab.

With pre-hab, you will exercise to strengthen the muscles around the joint that is going to be replaced. While this is done in several ways to avoid straining the joint, you may experience some discomfort.

If you're planning to undergo a knee replacement, for example, you might do exercises that strengthen muscles around the knee, rather than flexing the knee itself. In rare cases, patients are in so much pain that pre-hab isn't possible.

Helpful: Doing pre-hab at the same facility handling your rehab creates a seamless pre- and postsurgical "program."*

WHAT TO EXPECT IN PRE-HAB

In general, the therapist will choose exercises that strengthen—but don't overly stress—the affected joint. Pre-hab is usually done two or three times a week for 45 minutes to an hour. Patients are also given a program to do at home for 30 to 45 minutes on the days they are not in pre-hab.

Some examples…

•**Straight-leg raises** are often used for patients who are about to undergo a knee replacement.

What to do: While lying down (with the pain-free knee slightly bent), the patient raises and lowers his/her painful leg. This strengthens muscles around the knee, such as the quadriceps in the thigh. Those who are preparing for joint-replacement surgery in both knees perform the exercise on each of their legs.

•**Side leg raises are exercises commonly used for a hip replacement.**

What to do: While standing upright (and holding on to the back of a chair for balance), the patient slowly raises his leg out to the side, then slowly brings it back to the starting position. This strengthens side hip muscles.

•**Isometric shoulder extensions help prepare patients for shoulder surgery.**

What to do: The patient stands with his back against a wall and arms straight at his sides. Keeping arms straight, he

*To find a physical therapist or pre-hab program near you: Ask your surgeon…or check with the director of the rehabilitation clinic at the hospital where your surgery and/or rehab will take place.

pushes his arms into the wall, holds for five seconds, relaxes and repeats.

Also useful: Pre-hab optimally includes exercises performed in a swimming pool, where there's virtually no direct impact on joints and minimum pain during muscle strengthening and flexibility workouts. Since the body is buoyed, there's better balance, too.

Important: Because some pre-hab exercises increase heart rate, anyone with high blood pressure, heart disease or other significant health issues should consult his physician before beginning this type of program.

WHO PAYS FOR PRE-HAB?

Pre-hab is usually covered by insurance, but you may be responsible for some out-of-pocket expenses. Your insurer may cover a specific number of sessions, which include both pre-hab and rehab.

Pre-hab can cost as little as $10 for a group class or up to $200 for an initial consultation with a physical therapist. Check with your insurer.

Check List to Fix Back Pain

Julie Silver, MD, physiatrist and assistant professor in the department of physical medicine and rehabilitation at Harvard Medical School. She is author of *Say Goodbye to Back Pain! How to Handle Flare-Ups, Injuries and Everyday Back Health* (Chicken Soup for the Soul).

More than 80% of Americans will experience at least one episode of low-back pain during their lives. *Here's how to relieve the pain and prevent it from coming back…*

•**Act quickly.** Most back pain is caused by damage to muscle fibers. Frequent causes include overuse, repetitive motions or anxiety, tension or stress. The damage is accompanied by the release of substances that constrict blood vessels and reduce the oxygenation of tissues. Treating the pain can interrupt this chemical cascade. Take an over-the-counter anti-inflammatory medication such as *ibuprofen*. For mild pain, take 400 milligrams (mg)—you can treat more severe pain with 800 mg, but always talk to your doctor first.

Also helpful: Moist heat from a hot shower or bath. Or you can apply a cold pack to the area for about 20 minutes several times a day. Heat and cold both can be helpful. Use the one that seems to work best for you.

•**Keep moving even when it hurts.** Relaxing and contracting muscles with normal movements—walking, turning, climbing stairs, etc.—will increase blood flow and help the muscles relax.

Caution: Don't exercise if you have severe pain…a flare-up of sciatica (nerve pain that typically travels down the leg)…or pain from a traumatic injury such as a sprained back. See your doctor if the pain persists or gets worse over multiple days.

•**Treat depression.** Studies have shown that patients who manage their emotions in a healthy way tend to experience less pain. Your doctor can refer you to a mental health professional.

•**Change position every 15 minutes.** People who spend hours in the same position are more likely to have back pain than those who move around.

•**Lighten your load.** Pain in the middle or lower back is often caused by carrying a heavy bag on one side of the body. You can lighten your load or increase your core strength (see below). Preferably, do both.

•**Strengthen your core.** Strong abdominal muscles are essential for treating and preventing back pain.

Self-test: Lie on your back with your arms folded across your chest. Try to sit up without using your arms. If you can't do it, you don't have enough core strength and should do curl-ups or other core-strengthening exercises.

To do a curl-up: Lie on your back with your knees bent and your hands under the small of your back. Slowly curl your head and shoulders a few inches off the floor. Pause for a moment, then lower back down. Repeat eight to 12 times.

•**Check your shoes.** If you wear the same pair of shoes often and they are more than six months old, the heels and soles are probably showing signs of wear. The uneven surfaces force your body to compensate, which puts unnecessary stress on your back. Get new shoes or have the bottoms replaced every six months or so.

The Correct Way to Use Steroids for Back Pain

David Borenstein, MD, clinical professor of medicine at The George Washington University Medical Center in Washington, DC, in private practice. The author of *Heal Your Back* (M. Evans & Company), Dr. Borenstein is also the host of Speaking of Health with Dr. B, a weekly radio program on WomensRadio.com. *www.arapc.com*

S teroid injections have long been considered a much needed pain-relieving treatment for people with sciatica and other back conditions.

Now: Many patients are thinking twice about having the injections after contaminated doses of the drug created a nationwide outbreak of meningitis that began in late 2012 and has now claimed more than 60 lives and sickened 749 people (see page 291 for more information).

Important fact: Although it was not widely reported at the time, the tragedy of the meningitis deaths and illnesses is magnified by the fact that many of the victims probably didn't

Wool Underwear Relieves Lower Back Pain

In a recent finding, men with lower back pain who wore merino wool underwear for two months reported 89% less pain and needed fewer pain medications than men who wore cotton underwear. Wool's heat-retaining properties help keep back muscles flexible, reducing pain. Merino wool is comfortable to wear.

Study by researchers at Atatürk University, Erzurum, Turkey, published in *Collegium Antropologicum*.

even need the injections. While spinal injections are clearly beneficial for some patients, experts now agree that they're used too often for conditions for which they're not effective. *What you need to know...*

WHO CAN BENEFIT

When given by injection, steroids such as *cortisone* or *methylprednisolone* can reduce inflammation and pain within hours. The injections are also less likely to cause side effects than oral steroids, which may suppress the naturally occurring hormone cortisol and increase risk for bone loss and eye problems when used long term.

Back pain is one of the conditions for which steroid injections are commonly recommended. But these injections are not for everyone with back pain.

The injections, which typically cost $600 to $2,500 each, are not helpful for simple back pain caused by muscle spasms. In fact, professional guidelines discourage the use of steroid injections if you've had symptoms for six weeks or less.

Reason: The majority of patients with back pain have temporary muscle spasms and will recover without treatment in less than six weeks.

When steroid injections may be used appropriately for back pain...

•**Sciatica.** Typically caused by a herniated disc, this nerve pain (or numbness) originates in the lower back and radiates through the buttock into the right or left leg. A steroid injection can reduce pain and disability significantly in 50% or more of patients. But do not expect more than temporary relief.

This type of injection, known as an epidural, is administered into the outer part of the spinal canal. The steroid reduces swelling and inflammation of the spinal nerve compressed by the herniated disc. Sometimes one injection is all that is needed for pain relief, which typically lasts up to six months.

Scientific evidence: An analysis of 23 scientific studies involving sciatica patients confirmed that the nerve pain relief provided by the injections was only temporary. Those who received the injections had no significant differences in leg or back pain one year later than those who were given placebos.

•**Spinal stenosis.** This is an abnormal narrowing (stenosis) of the spinal canal. The narrowed opening, often due to arthritis or osteoporosis, can press against spinal nerves and cause leg or neck pain. In severe cases, it can cause nerve damage that leads to bowel or bladder incontinence.

An injection into the epidural space just outside the spinal column can reduce swelling and remove pressure from the affected nerve(s). Injections usually relieve pain within 24 hours, but it can take as long as seven days to get full relief. Typically, pain relief lasts for a few months.

WHAT TO EXPECT

Before a doctor recommends a steroid injection in or near the spine, he/she will probably suggest an oral anti-inflammatory medication such as *ibuprofen* (Motrin) or aspirin. If this doesn't help, a one-week course of an oral steroid such as *prednisone* (Deltasone) might be prescribed. If you're still in pain, or if the pain is accompanied by leg weakness (a sign of nerve damage), you might need one or more steroid injections.

Injections typically are given by an anesthesiologist or an interventional radiologist in a clinic, hospital or doctor's office. The procedure takes 15 to 30 minutes.

What happens: You'll lie flat on your stomach on an X-ray table. Using fluoroscopy (a real-time imaging technique), your doctor will insert a needle into the spinal canal. This shouldn't be painful because the area is usually numbed with a topical anesthetic, but you might experience uncomfortable pressure when the solution is injected.

If you have nerve pain from a herniated disc, you'll probably be given three separate injections over a six- to eight-week period. If the pain doesn't improve significantly, additional injections are unlikely to help.

For spinal stenosis, you'll probably be given three injections, one every two months. In some patients, the initial series relieves pain for six months or more...in others, the benefits last only a few weeks. You can get additional injections with your doctor's approval. Some patients get the injections for years as an alternative to surgery but must be monitored closely for side effects, such as cataracts, osteoporosis and elevated blood pressure.

POSSIBLE RISKS

Injected steroids are much less likely to cause side effects than oral steroids, but there are some risks…

•**Severe infection.** This occurs in only about 0.01% to 0.1% of injections. Even so, steroid injections usually are not recommended for people with compromised immunity due to diabetes or cancer treatments, for example, or those with an active infection.

Important: To reduce contamination risk, your doctor should use a brand-name drug rather than a drug from a compounding pharmacy (as was the case in the meningitis outbreak).

•**Bleeding.** This can occur in patients taking blood thinners or in those with underlying health problems (such as cirrhosis of the liver) that interfere with blood clotting.

•**Nerve damage.** This occurs in only about one in every 10,000 cases but could happen if the doctor accidentally jabs a nerve during the procedure. Nerve damage could result in incontinence, chronic back pain and, in rare instances, paralysis.

How to Cure Chronic Pelvic Pain— For Women and Men

Geo Espinosa, ND, LAc, a naturopathic doctor and acupuncturist who specializes in prostate disorders, male sexual health and chronic pelvic pain. He founded the Integrative Urology Center at New York University (NYU) Langone Medical Center in New York City. *www.drgeo.com*

It is one of the most common but least talked about medical conditions. Chronic pelvic pain (CPP)—dull aching, cramping and/or sharp pains in the area between the navel and the hips—is mostly thought of as a woman's disorder. But men account for approximately 20% of the 11 million Americans who suffer from CPP.

It's a tricky condition to diagnose because the symptoms—which in women and men may include painful intercourse, difficulty sleeping, low energy and/or alternating constipation and diarrhea—can be caused by many different conditions, such as endometriosis in women… or prostate enlargement in men. In both women and men, infection of the urethra or bladder and food sensitivities can trigger CPP.

And even though the condition is chronic—that is, lasting for six months or longer—it might wax and wane daily…or you might have a weeklong flare-up after a pain-free month.

WHERE TO START?

Every woman with CPP symptoms should see a gynecologist, who will perform a thorough pelvic exam to look for such problems as abnormal growths and tension in the pelvic muscles. Men affected by CPP symptoms should be seen by a urologist. Specific testing will depend on what your physician finds—or suspects—during the initial exam as the underlying cause of CPP.

Examples: Ultrasound to examine the organs for abnormalities such as ovarian cysts in women and prostate enlargement in men…and laboratory tests to look for infections. In some cases, a woman may also undergo laparoscopy, the insertion of a thin tube into the abdomen to look for endometriosis.

Some patients get relief once the underlying problem is identified and treated, but many patients don't.

Reason: Within just months, CPP can trigger sometimes permanent changes in the spinal cord that allow the persistent passage of pain signals to the brain—even when the underlying cause of the pain has been corrected.

THE NEXT STEP

Patients with CPP can improve with conventional treatments (such as the use of painkillers or surgery to remove growths), but these approaches won't necessarily give them the greatest odds of adequately relieving their pain.

Better: Taking a complementary approach that combines conventional and alternative treatments.

Best therapies to try—in addition to mainstream treatments...

•**Relax trigger points.** Most women and men with CPP have one or more trigger points (areas of knotted muscle) somewhere in the pelvic area—for example, on the lower abdomen or on the upper thighs. Trigger points themselves can be excruciatingly painful and can transmit pain throughout the pelvic region.

Example: Vaginal pain could be caused by a trigger point elsewhere on the pelvis.

Massage therapists are typically trained to identify and treat trigger points. Simply pressing on one of these points for 20 to 30 seconds—and repeating the pressure several times during an hour-long massage—can relax the tension and help ease the pain. Having a weekly massage for several months sometimes can eliminate symptoms of CPP.

To find a massage therapist who specializes in trigger point treatment, go to *www.massage therapy.com*, click on "Find a Massage Therapist" and select "Trigger Point Therapy."

Drawback: Pressure on a trigger point can be painful. You can get the same relief, with less discomfort, with electroacupuncture. Two or more hair-width acupuncture needles are inserted into the skin above the trigger point. Then, a mild electrical current is administered, which causes the muscle to relax.

Treatment for CPP will typically require about six to 20 sessions of electroacupuncture. Many acupuncturists are trained in electroacupuncture. However, because the technique is less well-studied than standard acupuncture, it may not be covered by your health insurer. Electroacupuncture typically costs about $70 to $100 per session.

Electroacupuncture should not be used on patients who have a history of seizures, epilepsy, heart disease, stroke or a pacemaker.

•**Try standard acupuncture.** Even if you don't have trigger points, acupuncture is among the most effective treatments for CPP. A study of 67 women who had bacterial cystitis (infection of the bladder wall that commonly causes CPP)

found that 85% of them were virtually pain-free after receiving 20-minute acupuncture sessions, twice weekly for four weeks. Reinfection rates were also reduced.

Acupuncture is believed to help block the transmission of pain signals. It's also an effective way to reduce muscular as well as emotional stress, both of which increase all types of chronic pain. Most CPP patients will need 10 to 20 treatments. Acupuncture is often covered by insurance.

•**Identify food sensitivities.** Many women and men with CPP are sensitive to one or more foods, particularly wheat and dairy. *What happens:* When these patients eat "problem" foods, they have increased intestinal permeability, also known as "leaky gut" syndrome. Large, undigested food molecules that are normally contained within the intestine pass into the bloodstream, where they trigger the release of inflammatory chemicals that can cause pain throughout the body and in the pelvic region, in particular.

A blood test known as ALCAT (antigen leukocyte cellular antibody test) can identify specific food sensitivities. Although it is reasonably reliable, the test usually isn't covered by insurance because it is considered an "alternative" diagnostic tool. It costs about $400.

Another option: An elimination-challenge diagnostic diet.

What to do: Quit eating wheat, dairy and other likely food triggers, such as soy, wine and sugar, for 21 days. If your symptoms improve, at least one of the foods was a problem. Then, reintroduce the foods, one at a time over a period of weeks, to see which food (or foods) causes symptoms to return.

Patients may get frustrated, initially, because they feel like there are few foods left to eat, but many of the foods that they give up during the test will turn out to be harmless. Foods found to cause problems should be given up indefinitely.

•**Take probiotics.** Because infections, such as those described earlier, are a common cause of pelvic pain, patients often receive multiple courses of antibiotics. Antibiotics eliminate infection, but they also kill beneficial bacteria in

Topical Pain Relievers May Cause Burns

Topical pain relievers may cause burns even after just one application. Over-the-counter creams, lotions, ointments and patches for joint and muscle pain often contain menthol, methyl salicylate and/or capsaicin, all of which can irritate skin. Some users reported a burning sensation, swelling, pain and skin blistering within 24 hours of use. Tightly bandaging or applying heat to areas treated with these products may increase risk.

US Food and Drug Administration, Silver Spring, Maryland.

the intestine. This can lead to digestive problems such as irritable bowel syndrome and leaky gut syndrome—both of which are linked to CPP.

Helpful: A daily probiotic supplement with a mix of at least 10 billion live, beneficial organisms, such as Acidophilus and Lactobacillus. A probiotic supplement should be taken indefinitely.

Also helpful: Glutamine—100 mg to 200 mg, taken twice daily until symptoms improve. It nourishes the cells that line the intestine and can help prevent leaky gut syndrome. People with liver or kidney disease should not take glutamine.

Caution: Do not take a B-complex nutrient if you're suffering from CPP. In my practice, patients who take B vitamins have more CPP symptoms for reasons that aren't clear.

•**Learn to relax.** Emotional stress doesn't cause CPP, but people who are stressed and anxious tend to be more aware of their pain. Women and men who practice stress-reduction techniques—such as deep breathing and meditation—report about a 50% reduction in CPP symptoms, on average.

Very helpful: Yoga. It is probably the best workout if you have CPP. That's because it relaxes muscle tension as well as trigger points... increases levels of painkilling endorphins...and promotes overall relaxation.

Medical Marijuana Works Better Than Pills For Certain Kinds of Pain

Gregory T. Carter, MD, physiatrist, clinical professor at the University of Washington, Seattle, and medical director of the Muscular Dystrophy Association Regional Neuromuscular Center in Olympia, Washington. He is coauthor of *Medical Marijuana 101* (Quick American Archives).

The US government classifies marijuana as a Schedule 1 controlled substance—a dangerous drug with no medical value. Yet the Institute of Medicine, an elite group of scientists and physicians, has concluded that the chemical compounds in marijuana do have therapeutic properties.

According to Gregory T. Carter, MD, the wrangling between scientists and policy makers won't stop anytime soon. Neither will the wrangling between the federal government and the states, 18 of which, along with the District of Columbia, allow the use of medical marijuana and two of which (Colorado and Washington) recently legalized marijuana for recreational use for people over age 21. But he sees marijuana as a viable medicine for some patients and a very effective painkiller.

Caution: Always use medical marijuana under a doctor's supervision.

•**Neuropathic pain.** Researchers at the University of California, Davis, reported in *The Journal of Pain* that patients with neuropathy (nerve pain) who used cannabis (the word scientists prefer to the slang "marijuana") were more likely to have significant relief than those taking a placebo. The chemical compounds in cannabis affect cell receptors in the brain, reducing pain and making it an alternative for patients who are unresponsive to standard drug therapies.

Neuropathy is common in diabetics, HIV patients and other neuropathic disorders. The prescription medications that currently are used aren't very effective. In my practice, about 90% of neuropathy patients who use cannabis have good results—often with fewer side effects than those who take drugs such as *gabapentin* (Neurontin).

•**Crohn's disease.** This is a potentially life-threatening inflammatory gastrointestinal (GI) disease that often causes severe abdominal pain, nausea and malnutrition, along with unpredictable bouts of diarrhea and/or constipation. Researchers at Tel Aviv University recently reported that 21 of 30 Crohn's patients who used cannabis had less pain and were able to reduce their use of other medications. They also were less likely to require surgery.

The chemical compounds in cannabis reduce not only pain but also inflammation that causes ongoing tissue damage in the intestinal tract. Currently, some Crohn's patients depend on narcotic medications for pain relief. Constipation is a common side effect of these drugs, which is dangerous for Crohn's patients. Cannabis is safer because it doesn't interfere with bowel movements.

•**Arthritis.** The anti-inflammatory and pain-relieving substances in cannabis appear to make it a good choice for different forms of arthritis, including rheumatoid arthritis and osteoarthritis.

•**Weight loss from cancer treatment.** Cancer patients who undergo chemotherapy and/or radiation treatments often suffer from severe weight loss and malnutrition. Cannabis stimulates appetite and can help patients get the calories they need to maintain a normal weight. Also, it's easier for patients with nausea to inhale a medication than to take—and keep down—a pill.

HOW TO USE IT

Dr. Carter doesn't recommend that patients who use cannabis smoke it. Smoking can increase the risk for bronchitis or other respiratory problems.

Better methods…

•**Vaporization.** When patients use a vaporizer, the active compounds in cannabis "boil" and turn into vapor—the plant material doesn't get hot enough to burn. This eliminates the harsh compounds in the smoke. It also causes less intoxication because the lower temperatures don't activate tetrahydrocannabinol (THC), the compound that causes most of the "high" associated with smoking marijuana.

•**Sublingual tincture.** With a prescription, you can buy this form of cannabis at some dispensaries. You also can make it at home by steeping about one ounce of cannabis flowers (available at dispensaries) in six ounces of glycerin for about a week. You put three or four drops under your tongue when you need a dose. It works almost as quickly as vaporized cannabis.

•**Juicing.** You can put a small amount of cannabis in a blender, add your choice of liquids such as milk or juice and drink it as a beverage. The intoxicating effects are reduced because the THC isn't heated.

Some people eat cannabis by adding it to brownies or other prepared foods. Don't do it. The intoxicating effects can be very strong. And because it can take an hour or longer to work, patients may think that they're not getting enough. They consume even more—and wind up getting too much.

HOW MUCH TO TAKE

Some cannabis dispensaries (and growers) use devices called gas chromatographs to measure the amounts of THC and other compounds in their products. This makes it easier to achieve batch-to-batch consistency. Typically, the cannabis sold by dispensaries has a THC concentration of about 15% to 20%.

Doctors who recommend cannabis usually rely on patient-titrated dosing. This simply means taking a small amount when you need a dose…waiting for about 20 to 30 minutes to see how you feel…and then increasing or decreasing subsequent doses, as needed. Effects typically last one to two hours.

WHAT AND WHERE TO BUY

Different types of cannabis have markedly different effects. Cannabis that is rich in cannabidiol (CBD) has fewer psychoactive effects than cannabis with a lot of THC. Patients who want to minimize the intoxicating effects can choose a strain with a higher percentage of CBD.

You can buy marijuana at dispensaries in the states where it is legal. Describe your symptoms to the clerk so that he/she can help you choose the right type of cannabis. If, for example, you have pain that mainly bothers you at night, you probably will want a cannabis that's high in CBD—it will help you fall asleep. Patients with certain conditions where fatigue is a symptom and who need a "lift" might do better with a higher-THC product.

SIDE EFFECTS

Recreational users of marijuana want to get high. For medical patients, this often is the main drawback.

Dr. Carter recommends to his patients that they "start low, go slow." Take the lowest possible dose at first. Later, you can increase the dose if you need more relief. If you find that you're getting intoxicated, use less.

Obviously, you shouldn't drive, operate tools or machinery, or perform tasks that require a lot of concentration up to three hours after using cannabis, though residual effects have been reported up to 24 hours after using any medication that impairs mental functions.

Caution: If you have a serious psychiatric illness, such as bipolar disorder or schizophrenia, don't use cannabis without the supervision of a psychiatrist.

Reducing Uric Acid

Michael A. Becker, MD, professor emeritus of medicine, The University of Chicago. He has published dozens of studies on hyperuricemia.

Should you be concerned about high levels of uric acid? It's not uncommon to have a high uric acid level—up to 40 million Americans do. Most people with chronic high uric acid levels (called hyperuricemia) never develop gout, an arthritic condition marked by high uric acid levels and resulting in painful joint inflammation, often in the big toe. Medication to lower uric acid is often prescribed for people with gout.

Hyperuricemia (even without gout) is also associated with other conditions, such as high blood pressure, obesity, diabetes, cardiovascular disease and reduced kidney function. However, because hyperuricemia seems unlikely to cause these diseases, drug treatment is not advised unless gout is also present.

Other things you can do to help lower uric acid levels: Reduce your intake of purine-rich foods, including seafood and meat (especially organ meats, such as liver). Reduce or avoid alcohol (especially beer), soda and juice with high fructose content. Reach and maintain a normal body weight. Take about 500 mg of vitamin C each day.

Natural Ways to Feel Much Better After a Fall...

Jamison Starbuck, ND, naturopathic physician in family practice and a guest lecturer at the University of Montana, both in Missoula. She is a columnist for *Bottom Line/Health*.

We tend to think of falls as affecting only older adults and causing primarily physical injuries. But neither is true. People of all ages fall, and the aftereffects can be harmful in a variety of ways.

Unexpected falls destabilize the nervous system. Even if you aren't badly hurt, these falls are scary. Our inner protective mechanisms become hypervigilant—our muscles become tense and we hold ourselves more rigidly. We also struggle with a lingering sense of unease and begin to mistrust our ability to safely do everyday activities.

After ruling out a concussion and fractures with a doctor's exam, patients should use ice to treat an injury for the first 48 hours, followed by heat and painkillers, if needed. Natural medicine can also help people avoid lasting problems from falls. *Favorite approaches...**

•**Use natural remedies.** Arnica is a well-known homeopathic remedy that is used topically for physical trauma. Arnica lotion, for example, can be applied to bruises or sprains several times a day until they are healed. Along with arnica, I recommend using homeopathic Aconite, a remedy that is excellent in treating the fright that follows sudden, violent accidents.

*Check with your doctor first if you have a chronic condition or take medication.

What Exercises Are Best for You?*

If you have arthritis...

If you have arthritis, certain exercises may be painful. That's why swimming and/or aerobic exercise such as "water walking" in a warm-water pool are good options. If you don't have access to a pool, choose non–weight-bearing exercise, such as a stationary bike, to minimize stress on your joints.

With arthritis, it's especially helpful to consult your doctor or physical therapist before starting a new exercise program—so your workout can be tailored to your specific type of arthritis.

Good rule of thumb: If an exercise hurts, don't do it.

If you have bone disease...

If you have bone disease, including osteoporosis or decreased bone density due to osteopenia: Weight-bearing exercise strengthens bone by exerting force against it. For this reason, walking is better than biking, for example, and swimming is usually the least likely to help.

Warning: Avoid exercises involving quick changes in direction, such as aerobic dance, which may increase fracture risk.

*Always talk to your doctor before starting a new exercise program. If you have a chronic illness, it may be useful to consult a physical therapist for advice on exercise dos and don'ts for your particular situation.

John P. Porcari, PhD, program director of the Clinical Excercise Physiology (CEP) program at the University of Wisconsin-La Crosse.

Aconite is best taken within 48 hours of a fall. I typically recommend one dose (two pellets of Aconite 30C) taken under the tongue. If 24 hours after taking Aconite you remain anxious or scared about your fall, repeat the same dose once a day for up to a week.

• **Try nervine herbs.** Chamomile, valerian and hops are plant medicines that calm the nervous system and help the body recover from a fall by promoting rest and muscle relaxation. Take these herbs alone or in combination in tea or tincture form. *Typical dose for a single herb or mixture:* Drink 10 ounces of tea three times a day or take 60 drops of tincture in one ounce of water three times a day for up to two weeks.

• **Get plenty of rest.** Soaking in a warm bath with Epsom salts relaxes muscles and helps you get a good night's sleep. Until you have fully recovered from the fall, it also helps to take 150 mg of magnesium citrate (the form most easily absorbed) twice daily. This mineral promotes relaxation.

• **Consider bodywork.** Soon after a fall, consider getting full-body massage or acupressure treatment several times. These therapies not only promote circulation and healing, but also help people regain trust in their bodies after a scary event.

Caution: If you hit your head, are bleeding significantly or suspect a fracture from a fall, get to a hospital emergency department. If you experience headache, vision changes, dizziness, confusion, nausea, vomiting or a balance problem (even days after the fall), you may have a head injury and must seek immediate medical help.

Women's Health

Women's Fatal Mistake In Seeking Help For Stroke

Imagine this scene: Your husband suddenly feels dizzy, goes numb in one arm or starts slurring his words. Odds are that you would urge him to call 911 or you'd do it yourself without delay, right? Now suppose you were the one with the symptoms. Would you carry on with your tasks, stoically ignoring the problem and hoping it would just go away? Many wives would. In fact, when it comes to seeking help for possible symptoms of stroke, there's an alarming discrepancy between husbands and wives, a recent study reveals.

Researchers analyzed data on 192 patients with acute stroke symptoms who were brought by emergency medical services (EMS) to the Mayo Clinic in Phoenix. Specifically, they looked at the number of minutes that elapsed between the time a patient first became aware of having

symptoms and the time at which 911 was called. They found that, on average, married patients summoned EMS 44 minutes after symptoms were noticed, while single patients called 911 after 46 minutes—so there was no real difference there. And while single men summoned help quicker than single women did, the difference was not statistically significant.

But: Breaking down the data a different way, researchers discovered that when the patient was a married man, EMS was summoned in an average of just 28 minutes. Yet when the patient was a married woman, the delay between symptom awareness and the 911 call averaged 67 minutes!

Researchers speculate that women are so used to being the caregivers in the family that their needs are always at the bottom of the list.

Why women's delay in summoning help is so worrisome: With stroke, every minute

Joyce K. Lee-Iannotti, MD, is a fellow in the department of neurology at the Mayo Clinic in Scottsdale, Arizona, and lead author of a study on acute stroke symptoms and activation of emergency medical services presented at the recent American Stroke Conference.

counts—the earlier patients get help, the more treatment options there are and the less devastating the consequences are likely to be. Also, women have a higher lifetime risk for stroke than men do…and more women than men die of stroke each year, according to the American Heart Association.

Self-defense: Memorize the symptoms of stroke and call 911 immediately if you experience any of the following…

•**Numbness or paralysis on one side of your face or body.** Try smiling into a mirror or raising both arms over your head at the same time—a one-sided smile or an arm that won't stay up could indicate a stroke.

•**Speech problems, such as slurring words or being unable to find the right words.** Try repeating a simple sentence—if you can't, that suggests a stroke.

•**Unexplained dizziness, loss of balance or difficulty walking.**

•**Vision problems, such as blurred, double or blackened vision.**

•**A sudden, severe "bolt out of the blue" headache.**

info To see a video about the study and stroke symptoms, go to *http://bit.ly/SLTtUU.*

What Your Age at Menopause Means For Your Heart

Dhananjay Vaidya, PhD, MPH, assistant professor in the division of general internal medicine at the Johns Hopkins University School of Medicine in Baltimore and coauthor of a study on heart risk published in *Menopause.*

What's the connection between menopause and heart health? When periods stop, production of heart-protecting estrogen decreases dramatically.

Now a recent study adds to that concern by highlighting the fact that women who reach menopause at a relatively young age are particularly likely to develop heart problems. Given that cardiovascular disease is the number-one killer of US women, we can't afford to ignore these findings. *Here's the scoop…*

Previous research linked early menopause to heart disease in Caucasian women, but there has been little such info about risk among other ethnicities. So for the recent study, researchers analyzed data on 2,509 women (ages 45 to 84) who were either non-Hispanic white…black… Chinese…or Hispanic. All were free of cardiovascular disease at the start of the study and were followed for an average of nearly five years.

Findings: 28% of the women reached menopause before age 46, either naturally or due to oophorectomy (surgical removal of the ovaries, often done in conjunction with hysterectomy). These women were more than twice as likely to suffer a fatal or nonfatal heart attack or stroke during the study as women who entered menopause later. This held true across all ethnicities and regardless of any other heart-related risk factors the women may have had.

If you're premenopausal: To help guard against early menopause, don't smoke—research shows that smokers reach menopause two years earlier, on average, than nonsmokers. Also, if your doctor suggests a hysterectomy, get a second opinion…and if surgical removal of your uterus truly is necessary, discuss whether you can keep your ovaries. This is particularly important for Hispanic and black women, who tend to hit menopause somewhat earlier than women of other ethnicities.

If you did reach menopause early: Though it's wise for everyone to follow a heart-healthy lifestyle, you should be especially careful about eating right, exercising regularly, maintaining an appropriate weight and not smoking. What about using hormone therapy (HT) to replace some of the estrogen lost at menopause? Whether HT helps or harms heart health is a subject of intense debate, though in this study, HT users did not have any cardiovascular advantage—and HT does increase the risk for breast cancer.

Better bet: Be sure that your current doctor is aware of the age at which you reached menopause…and work with your physician to keep any other cardiovascular risk factors, such as blood pressure and cholesterol levels, well under control.

Hypnosis May Ease Hot Flashes in Postmenopausal Women

Gary Elkins, PhD, director, Mind-Body Medicine Research Laboratory, Baylor University, Waco, Texas.

Margery Gass, MD, executive director, North American Menopause Society and consultant, Cleveland Clinic.

Menopause, online

Hypnosis may help reduce hot flashes in postmenopausal women, cutting down their frequency as much as 74%, researchers say.

Hot flashes affect about 80% of women as they go through menopause. The sudden rush of heat can be followed by chills and can reduce quality of life.

STUDY DETAILS

Researcher Gary Elkins, PhD, director of the Mind-Body Medicine Research Laboratory at Baylor University in Waco, Texas, assigned 187 women who had at least seven hot flashes daily to either five weekly sessions of clinical hypnosis with at-home practice or a comparison treatment called structured attention.

Those in the hypnosis group received five weekly sessions with a clinician versed in hypnosis. They were given suggestions for mental images of coolness, a safe place or relaxation, and picked the one they wanted to use. In addition, they were given an audio recording of a hypnotic induction to practice daily.

Women in the comparison group also met once a week for five weeks with a clinician. They discussed symptoms, avoided negative suggestions and were given a recording with information about hot flashes that they were told to listen to daily.

Women self-reported their hot flashes for 12 weeks, and the researchers also measured hot flash frequency by a skin conductance monitor.

After 12 weeks, the hypnosis group reported 74% fewer hot flashes, while the comparison group reported 17% fewer.

"Our results indicated both a reduction in perceived hot flashes and physiologically verified reduction in hot flashes over three months," Dr. Elkins said.

No adverse effects were reported, Dr. Elkins noted, except for temporary irritation from the skin conductance monitors used to verify hot flashes.

The study was published online in the journal *Menopause*.

IMPLICATIONS

In the wake of the Women's Health Initiative study results, released in 2003, which found increased health risks such as heart disease with long-term hormone therapy use, many women are seeking non-hormonal alternatives for hot flash relief. In a previous study, Dr. Elkins had found that hypnosis helped breast cancer survivors reduce hot flashes by nearly 70%.

One drawback, Dr. Elkins said, is the lack of people with training in hypnosis for hot flashes. He hopes to develop a CD or DVD program.

Meanwhile, women can get referrals from the American Society of Clinical Hypnosis and the Society for Clinical and Experimental Hypnosis, he said. Costs vary per session. Dr. Elkins estimates an initial visit to be about $170, and follow-ups run about $135.

EXPERTS COMMENT

The nearly 75% reduction "is a very good result," said Margery Gass, MD, executive director of the North American Menopause Society and a consultant at the Cleveland Clinic. She reviewed the findings.

According to Dr. Gass, the most likely drawback when using hypnosis for hot flashes is the effort required. Initial training must be given by a health care professional versed in hypnosis, she said, "and then you have to practice at home."

Experts don't know exactly how hypnosis may work to cool the hot flashes. Dr. Gass said it probably affects the body's thermostat regulation in the brain.

The study was funded by the National Center for Complementary and Alternative Medicine of the US National Institutes of Health.

info To learn more about hypnosis, visit the American Society of Clinical Hypnosis Web site at *www.asch.net* (click on the "Public" tab).

New Map for the Menopause Maze

William F. Young, Jr., MD, MSc, is president of The Endocrine Society, an international organization devoted to research on hormones and the clinical practice of endocrinology, based in Chevy Chase, Maryland.

Among women currently experiencing menopausal symptoms, more than 60% have not talked to their doctors about hormone therapy or nonhormone options, and 72% have not received any treatment for their symptoms, according to a survey from The Endocrine Society.

If you are in the middle of the menopause maze, there's an online resource that can help you sort out your treatment options and provide talking points to discuss with your doctor. The free interactive Web tool, called the Menopause Map, can be accessed at *www.hormone. org/menopausemap.*

Relief Rx: Recently launched by The Endocrine Society and its Hormone Health Network, the map consists of a series of questions about your menopausal symptoms (hot flashes, vaginal dryness, interrupted sleep)...personal health (high blood pressure, diabetes, excess weight, unexpected spotting, etc.)...family medical history (cancer, blood clots)...and other factors. Based on your answers, it offers information on the various treatment options—lifestyle changes, botanical and vitamin supplements, topical and oral hormones—that may be appropriate for you. And it provides an individualized list of questions to ask your own physician...giving you an easy way to jump-start this important conversation.

What Causes Hot Flashes? Study Gives New Clues

Naomi Rance, MD, PhD, neuropathologist, and professor and associate head of pathology, University of Arizona College of Medicine, Tucson.

Jill Rabin, MD, chief, ambulatory care, obstetrics and gynecology, and head of urogynecology, Long Island Jewish Medical Center, New Hyde Park, New York.

Proceedings of the National Academy of Sciences

Scientists are getting warmer in their attempts to zero in on what causes hot flashes, intense surges of heat and sweating that affect millions of middle-aged women in the years leading to menopause.

Studying rats, researchers at the University of Arizona College of Medicine have pinpointed a small region of the brain that may go awry during typical hot flashes, finding that a certain set of neurons acts as a virtual control switch for the problem when estrogen levels drop.

"I think the idea is to develop some alternate treatments for hot flashes, but how could we possibly develop appropriate treatments if we don't know what causes them?" said study author Naomi Rance, MD, PhD, a neuropathologist, professor and associate head of pathology at the university. "This is the first evidence these neurons have anything to do with [heat] regulation."

Scientists note, however, that research with animals often fails to provide similar results in humans.

An estimated 70% of women—along with some men—experience hot flashes, and previous research indicated the flashes originated in the *hypothalamus*, a section of the brain serving as the "switchboard" between hormone signals and the central nervous system.

University of Pittsburgh scientists published a study earlier this year showing that the parasympathetic nervous system—part of the autonomic nervous system, which regulates unconscious bodily functions such as heart rate and breathing—isn't working as efficiently as normal during a hot flash.

STUDY DETAILS

In the more recent research, Dr. Rance and her colleagues created an animal model of menopause by using a toxin to deactivate a group of brain cells known as KNDy (pronounced "candy") neurons in rats. After these neurons were deactivated, the rats' tail skin temperature consistently lowered, suggesting that the neurons control the widening of the blood vessels known as vasodilation that lead to hot flashes by increasing blood flow to the skin. The rats' tail skin temperature rose after removal of their ovaries, which produce estrogen.

"Hot flashes are really episodic vasodilation," Dr. Rance explained. "You can see it—that's why people get red, because blood rises to the surface of the skin. Flushing is the body trying to get rid of that heat. Their core temperature is normal, so it doesn't make sense at all."

Current treatment for hot flashes includes estrogen replacement therapy, which is controversial because of potential health risks, including higher odds of certain cancers. Another option is selective serotonin reuptake inhibitors (SSRIs), which are best known as a treatment for depression.

Although the current research helps identify the basic biologic mechanism behind hot flashes, it may be years before scientists are able to develop new choices for treating them, Dr. Rance said.

The study appeared in the journal *Proceedings of the National Academy of Sciences*.

EXPERT COMMENTS

Jill Rabin, MD, chief of ambulatory care and obstetrics and gynecology at Long Island Jewish Medical Center in New Hyde Park, New York, praised Dr. Rance's study as "groundbreaking and very well done."

"The study is done in rats, so it's really hard to [translate the results] into people, but it's very, very interesting," said Dr. Rabin, who also is head of urogynecology. "This issue has been looked at for a long time and this may open the way, possibly, for a study in humans."

info The National Women's Health Network offers more information about hot flashes at its Web site *http://nwhn.org/hot-flashes.*

Postmenopausal? What Your Doctor Should Know About Your Pregnancies

George Saade, MD, professor and chief of obstetrics and maternal-fetal medicine at the University of Texas Medical Branch in Galveston. He also is the president of the Society for Maternal-Fetal Medicine.

Unless you have been with the same primary care physician since before all of your babies were born, your current doctor may not know about any pregnancy complications you experienced.

What you need to know: Problems during pregnancy, even if they occurred long ago, provide important clues about your current and future risk for potentially serious disorders—clues your doctor must be aware of in order to offer you optimal care.

According to George Saade, MD, chief of obstetrics and maternal-fetal medicine at the University of Texas Medical Branch in Galveston, "Pregnancy complications are equally as important risk factors as whether you smoke or have a family history of chronic health conditions like heart disease or diabetes—so it strikes me as odd that many doctors neglect to ask patients about their pregnancy history."

Pregnancy complications of concern include…

• **Gestational hypertension** (high blood pressure that develops during pregnancy) or preeclampsia (high blood pressure and excess protein in the urine after the twentieth week of pregnancy).

• **Gestational diabetes** (diabetes that develops during pregnancy).

• **Delivering a baby with a low birth weight** (below five pounds, eight ounces).

• **Delivering a premature baby** (before 37 weeks' gestation).

• **Stillbirth.**

A history of such complications may increase your risk for…

• **Cardiovascular problems.** A recent study in Obstetrics & Gynecology looked at 15,065

Norwegian women who gave birth to their first child between 1967 and 1995, examining various aspects of their health an average of 16.5 years after their pregnancies. Compared with participants who had normal blood pressure during pregnancy, those who had had hypertension while pregnant had higher blood pressure and unfavorable levels of total cholesterol, LDL "bad" cholesterol and triglycerides (a type of blood fat). These factors increase a person's risk for heart attack and stroke.

•**That's not all.** Other studies found that women with a history of preeclampsia had approximately double the risk for coronary heart disease, stroke and blood clots…that women who had delivered a preterm infant had nearly triple the risk for cardiovascular disease…and that women who delivered a low-birth-weight baby had seven to 11 times the usual risk of dying from cardiovascular causes.

•**Diabetes.** Even if their blood glucose levels return to normal in the postpartum period, women who had gestational diabetes are at significantly increased risk for developing type 2 diabetes later in life. Women with a history of preterm delivery also are more likely to develop diabetes later on. And according to a Danish study, women who had had blood pressure problems during pregnancy had a more than threefold increased risk for subsequent diabetes.

•**Kidney disease.** Studies link preeclampsia, preterm delivery and/or having a low-birth-weight baby with later development of kidney problems. Also, Israeli researchers found that women who had delivered stillborn babies had a 4.7-fold increased risk of dying from kidney-related causes.

Though researchers don't yet fully understand why pregnancy complications increase certain health risks later in life, Dr. Saade said that it is likely that pregnancy unmasks a predisposition to these chronic diseases or conditions. "If you are already predisposed to hypertension, for example, it may first show up when you're pregnant because of the additional demands that pregnancy puts on your body," he explained.

To protect yourself…

•**Describe any pregnancy complications to your primary care doctor** in as much de-

---

Hormone Replacement Therapy May Reduce Alzheimer's Risk

According to a recent study, women who take hormones within five years of menopause have a 30% lower risk for Alzheimer's, compared with women who never take them. The issue of HRT remains complex and controversial—discuss your personal situation with your doctor.

Study of 1,768 women by researchers at Johns Hopkins Bloomberg School of Public Health, Baltimore, published in *Neurology*.

---

tail as you can recall…if possible, get a copy of your medical records from your obstetrician. If you experienced problems during more than one pregnancy, emphasize that fact—studies show that repeated pregnancy complications put you at even greater risk.

•**With your doctor, discuss getting extra screening tests** for cardiovascular, metabolic and kidney disorders, as appropriate.

•**Prevention is the best medicine**—so it is especially important that you commit to a healthy lifestyle. Eating nutritious foods, exercising regularly, controlling your weight and not smoking can go a long way toward offsetting the future health risks that accompanied the pregnancy complications of your past.

Chiropractic Cure for Achy Breasts

Mikell Suzanne Parsons, DC, CCN, founder of the Natural Path Health Center in Fresno, California. *www.naturalpathfresno.com*

You head for the chiropractor when your back is out of whack or your neck needs a good crack. But when the problem is breast pain, a chiropractor may be the last person you'd think to consult.

Yet that oversight could lead to continued and unnecessary suffering, according to Mikell Suzanne Parsons, DC, founder of the Natural

Path Health Center in Fresno, California. She said that she helps several patients each day who have breast pain—though that's rarely the reason why they've come to see her.

How are chiropractors equipped to treat this problem? "Chiropractors are detectives. We're trained to look at the body as a whole, to identify why a person has a particular symptom or disease, then dig deeper to correct the problem by restoring balance to the body," she explained.

Of course it's wise to alert your primary-care doctor to any breast symptoms you might have. But once serious problems are ruled out, call your chiropractor if discomfort persists. With just a few questions about symptoms and lifestyle, Dr. Parsons said, she usually can pinpoint the root cause of a woman's breast pain. *Here are three common problems she sees and the treatments that bring relief…*

BREAST PROBLEM #1

Telltale symptoms: Pain is sharp and worsens when you take a deep breath or prod the area…with symptoms arising suddenly (rather than occurring chronically).

Likely cause: Your body is out of alignment in the area where one of the ribs attaches to the sternum, which prevents the lungs from fully expanding as you breathe. What feels like breast pain is actually inflammation of deeper tissues. The misalignment may have occurred when you lifted something heavy, slept in an awkward position or twisted in an unnatural way (for example, by reaching into the back seat while driving).

Solution: Dr. Parsons treats this problem by identifying the specific rib involved and cor-

recting the alignment, either manually or with a handheld, spring-loaded device called an activator that delivers a rapid pulse. In addition, if muscle tissue in the area is affected, she also may do a manual press-and-release treatment called trigger point therapy. Most patients get relief almost immediately.

BREAST PROBLEM #2

Telltale symptoms: Pain is localized primarily on the sides of both breasts…with discomfort that is fairly consistent, occurring more often than not…and often is accompanied by constipation.

Likely cause: The real problem arises some inches south of your breasts, in your intestines—because your body is not detoxifying correctly. When toxins are not eliminated through the digestive system, they get reabsorbed and stored in fatty tissue, Dr. Parsons explained. Breasts consist primarily of fatty tissue, so toxins can accumulate there and create inflammation.

Solution: Cut caffeine, food additives and processed foods from your diet. Also, consider talking with a nutritionist to determine whether your diet is lacking in any particular detoxifying nutrients, such as the B vitamins. As you reduce your toxic load and resume daily bowel movements, your breast pain should diminish within a matter of days, Dr. Parsons said.

BREAST PROBLEM #3

Telltale symptoms: All-over breast achiness occurs nearly all the time…and often is accompanied by dry skin, especially on the hands and shins.

Likely cause: Your diet is too low in healthful fats, perhaps because you try to avoid fats altogether or because the fats you do consume are the unhealthful ones (such as those found in fried foods and baked goods). Dr. Parsons explained that healthful fats are needed to build healthy, pliable cell walls. When such good dietary fats are lacking, fatty tissue (including in the breasts) can generate inflammation.

Solution: Boost your intake of foods that provide healthful fats, such as olive oil, coconut oil, avocado and fatty fish…and ask your healthcare provider about taking a high-quality fish oil supplement. Breast pain should ease within a few weeks—and as a bonus, your skin will look and feel better, too.

Never Stick This In Your Bra!

Devra Davis, PhD, MPH, an epidemiologist and president and founder of the Environmental Health Trust. She is also author of *Disconnect: The Truth About Cell Phone Radiation, What the Industry Is Doing to Hide It, and How to Protect Your Family* (Plume). *www.ehtrust.org*

Jay K. Harness, MD, a clinical professor of surgery at the University of California, Irvine, a practicing breast surgeon at the St. Joseph Hospital Center for Cancer Prevention and Treatment in Orange, California. *www.drJayharness.com*

When you don't have a purse or pocket but still want to stay connected to the world, nestling your cell phone into your cleavage for safekeeping may seem like a great solution. In fact, so many women now do this that there's even a new type of bra with a pocket to hold a phone.

But beware: Stashing your cell in your bra is a dangerous habit—because the radiation it emits might increase your risk for breast cancer. After hearing about this concern at a recent medical conference in New York City, we contacted the conference speaker, Devra Davis, PhD, MPH, president and founder of Environmental Health Trust (EHT), an organization that provides research and education on cell phones and other environmental health hazards.

Dr. Davis has teamed with medical doctors from a breast imaging center and a cancer-testing laboratory. They are preparing a case study report on four young women with no known family history or risks for the disease who developed clusters of breast cancer in highly unusual areas after carrying cell phones in their bras for years. She explained, "Breast cancer typically develops as a single tumor in the upper outer quadrant of the breast, not in the center of the chest. But these cases all had multiple primary tumors in the outlines of where the cell phones lodged. And none of the patients had the known breast cancer mutations. So the tumor location, the young age, the multiplicity

of tumors and the lack of genetic markers are all very concerning."

Substandard standards: Cell phones have never been tested for radiation safety, only for their impact on temperature. Dr. Davis said that phones are tested to see how much heat they emit in two positions—held 10 millimeters (about three-eighths of an inch) from the ear…or carried in a holster on the hip and held nearly an inch off the body. However, both the skull and hip have thick bones, which don't absorb radiation well. In contrast, fat does absorb radiation—and breast tissue is mostly fat. Furthermore, Dr. Davis added, recent studies find that cell-phone radiation that does not change heat can have biological impacts.

Dr. Davis is certainly not alone in her concern. In August 2012, the US Government Accountability Office released a statement saying that federal cell-phone radiation standards are outdated and may not protect public health… and recommending that the Federal Communications Commission review its current radiofrequency energy exposure limits.

Children at risk: Using cleavage to carry a phone seems to be particularly popular among teens and young women—and that raises additional worries. For instance, Jay K. Harness, MD, a past president of the American Society of Breast Surgeons, said that he was especially concerned about cell phones' potentially damaging effects on young girls whose breasts are still developing.

In addition, researchers from the University of California, Los Angeles, found a link between

---

Aspirin vs. Skin Cancer

Preliminary research shows that risk for melanoma was reduced by nearly 30% in postmenopausal women who reported taking aspirin—perhaps because of the drug's anti-inflammatory properties. However, other nonsteroidal anti-inflammatory drugs were not associated with this beneficial effect (see page 92 for details).

Society for Investigative Dermatology

Better Bone Therapy

Among 160 postmenopausal women, those who had adequate vitamin D levels were seven times more likely to respond to osteoporosis therapy with bisphosphonate medication, such as *alendronate* (Fosamax) or *ibandronate* (Boniva), than those with lower levels of vitamin D. It's estimated that 43% of women taking the drug derive a lower benefit—perhaps because they don't get enough vitamin D.

If you take a bisphosphonate drug for osteoporosis: Get plenty of vitamin D—from sun exposure and foods, including salmon, tuna and milk. Vitamin D supplements also may be needed.

Richard Bockman, MD, PhD, chief of the endocrine service, Hospital for Special Surgery, New York City.

---

prenatal exposure to cell-phone radiation and behavior problems, such as hyperactivity.

For safer cell phoning...

• **Keep your phone off or in airplane mode** (so it's not sending or receiving signals) as much as possible. When your phone is simply on, even if not in use, it is emitting radiation.

• **Limit cell-phone use in areas with weak signals.** Cell phones are programmed to work harder—which means they're emitting more radiation—when signal strength is low.

• **Use a headset or speaker function** as much as possible.

• **Check out EHT's brand-by-brand warning lists here.** Cell-phone manufacturers are required to provide guidelines on the safest ways to use and carry their phones, but they don't always make these warnings easy to find.

• **Carry your cell phone in a purse or wear a hip holster**—preferably in a pouch with radiation-blocking or diffusing material (for instance, such as those from *www.lessemf.com, www.pong research.com* or *www.radirid.com*).

• **Whatever you do, keep that phone out of your bra!**

Bra or Braless in Bed?

Jill R. Dietz, MD, a breast surgeon, director of the Breast Cancer Program and program director of the Surgical Breast Fellowship at the Cleveland Clinic in Ohio. She also is a fellow of the American College of Surgeons and a contributing editor for *Women's Oncology Review*.

The main purpose of a bra is to prevent ligaments in the breast from stretching, as this can lead to soreness and sagging. The larger your breasts are, the more important it is to have the support of a well-fitting bra during the day when you are sitting, standing and moving.

But: Since there is not much pull on the breast ligaments when you are quietly lying down, there is no health-related reason to wear a bra at night.

However, if you feel more comfortable sleeping in a bra, there is no health-related reason not to do so. Despite the dire warnings you may have read on the Internet, wearing a bra to bed will not increase your risk for breast cancer, according to breast expert Jill R. Dietz, MD, of the Cleveland Clinic. It is best, though, to avoid sleeping in a bra that has an underwire or is so tight that it leaves marks on your skin—otherwise, delicate nerves and tissues could be compressed, leading to breast pain, vein blockage or inflammation and/or blocked lymph flow. Instead, Dr. Dietz recommended opting for a style labeled as a "sleep bra," a type that generally has no wires or tight bands. Also, unlike nylon bras, which can trap moisture and allow an overgrowth of yeast, sleep bras typically are made of a soft, breathable, comfortable material such as cotton.

Women Have a Happiness Gene

Women, here's something to smile about. Monoamine oxidase A (MAOA), a gene that is linked to happiness in women, has recently been identified by scientists. The gene was not associated with improved mood in men.

Progress in Neuro-Psychopharmacology & Biological Psychiatry

Job Stress Hurts Hearts

Over 10 years, researchers studied the link between work stress and cardiovascular health in 22,000 women (average age 57).

Result: Women with the most stressful jobs, including those with high demands and little opportunity to make decisions or use creativity, were 38% more likely to suffer heart-related events such as stroke or death than those with less stressful jobs.

Risk for heart attack was 70% higher. If you have a stressful job: Talk to your doctor about ways to protect your heart health, including effective strategies to cope with stress.

Michelle Albert, MD, MPH, associate professor of medicine, Harvard Medical School, Boston.

Pleasure-Enhancing Feminine Parts You Never Knew You Had

Laurie Steelsmith, ND, LAc, is coauthor, with her husband, Alex Steelsmith, of *Great Sex, Naturally: Every Woman's Guide to Enhancing Her Sexuality Through the Secrets of Natural Medicine* (Hay House) and author of *Natural Choices for Women's Health: How the Secrets of Natural and Chinese Medicine Can Create a Lifetime of Wellness* (Three Rivers). Dr. Steelsmith maintains a private practice in naturopathic and Chinese medicine in Honolulu. *www.drsteelsmith.com*

Countless women have pored over the book *Our Bodies, Ourselves,* starting when it first came out in the 1970s and continuing right up through the most recent edition published last year. It's probably safe to say that most women today are better acquainted with their sex organs than their mothers or grandmothers were.

Even so, you may be surprised by how much more there is to learn, particularly about the hidden parts—and how much pleasure that new knowledge can bring.

Bonus: Better sex often leads to a better relationship.

Laurie Steelsmith, ND, LAc, a Honolulu-based naturopathic physician and coauthor of *Great Sex, Naturally: Every Woman's Guide to Enhancing Her Sexuality Through the Secrets of Natural*

Medicine, encourages today's sensual women to explore the following three anatomical wonders, alone and/or with a partner, experimenting to discover new sources of joy.

Secret #1. There's more to the clitoris than meets the eye. In addition to the visible "nub" (the clitoral glans), its protective hood and the clitoral shaft directly under the glans, the clitoris includes two wing-shaped "legs" or crura (the singular form of the word is crus). These reach downward and to the sides, along the pubic arch, for about four inches.

The clitoris also includes two vestibular bulbs, typically about three to five inches long, extending from the clitoral shaft and continuing along the sides of the inner labia and vaginal opening. The crura and bulbs are made of erectile tissue—which means that stimulation of those areas causes the tissues to swell with blood, leading to very enjoyable sensations.

Pleasure maximizer: "With gentle pressure and massage to the vulva, including the labia and clitoris, these underlying structures will be stimulated. Some women choose to use vibrators or other devices to increase sensation," Dr. Steelsmith said.

Secret #2. The perineum (the area between the vagina and anus) provides another potential surprise because its midpoint is especially sensitive to touch. Called the perineal sponge, it too swells up when you're aroused and feels wonderful when gently massaged or stroked.

What's more, Dr. Steelsmith said, according to traditional Chinese medicine, the center of the perineum is the site of an important acupressure point called Hui Yin. Pressing on this point can enhance sexual energy.

Dr. Steelsmith's suggestion: "This area can be directly massaged during foreplay or intercourse. Some women report very pleasurable sensations when firm, rhythmic pressure is used."

Secret #3. Many women are unaware of the role that the urethral sponge—or G-sponge, to use the term coined by Dr. Steelsmith's coauthor and husband, Alex Steelsmith—can play in sexual fulfillment. Located directly behind the G-spot, the G-sponge consists of erectile tissue and specialized glands that produce a fluid that some women ejaculate from their bodies when sufficiently aroused. "The G-spot earned its reputation for triggering orgasmic ecstasy only because pressing on it during arousal means stimulating the G-sponge," Dr. Steelsmith said.

To find the G-sponge, use your index or middle finger to reach one to two inches inside your vagina…curl your finger upward to feel along the center of the front vaginal wall…then press directly on the swollen, spongy area. Ejaculation happens, typically after some minutes of consistent stimulation, when intense muscular contractions squeeze the built-up fluid in the sponge into the urethra. Dr. Steelsmith explained that the fluid, though it does emerge from the urethral opening, is not urine. Rather, it is a clear and watery fluid with a pleasant musky aroma.

Enjoyment enhancement: "It is easiest to stimulate this special area with a finger or a vibrator. And it is often stimulated by a man's penis during intercourse, especially if he is entering the woman's vagina from behind," Dr. Steelsmith said. It's well worth giving this a try—because when G-sponge stimulation leads to female ejaculation, the release may be accompanied by an orgasm that is deeply intense and immensely satisfying.

Good News for Fibromyalgia Sufferers!

In a recent study, 27 women with fibromyalgia received a low daily dose (4.5 mg) of *naltrexone* (Depade)—a drug normally used to treat narcotic addiction—for 12 weeks. They then took a placebo for four weeks. The drug reduced pain by an average of 48.5%, compared with 27.4% for the placebo.

Theory: Naltrexone may suppress functioning of hypersensitive immune cells, which can trigger fibromyalgia pain.

If you have fibromyalgia pain: Ask your doctor about an "off-label" prescription for naltrexone from a compounding pharmacy—the low dose used in the study isn't available at a regular pharmacy.

Jarred Younger, PhD, assistant professor, Stanford University School of Medicine, Palo Alto, California.

The Contraceptive You've Been Too Scared to Try

Anita L. Nelson, MD, a professor in department of obstetrics and gynecology at the David Geffen School of Medicine at the University of California, Los Angeles. She also is coeditor of *Sexually Transmitted Diseases: A Practical Guide for Primary Care* (Humana).

Memories of the notorious Dalkon Shield—a contraceptive intrauterine device (IUD) linked to pelvic inflammatory disease and infertility—have caused many women to remain leery of IUDs. If you share their concerns, you're hardly alone. Fewer than 6% of US women who use contraception choose IUDs.

But: Many experts are urging women to take a fresh look, because today's IUDs are among the safest, most effective and most economical forms of reversible birth control.

An IUD is a plastic, T-shaped device that a physician places in a woman's uterus. *Two brands are on the market…*

•**Mirena.** This device releases the hormone progestin, which thickens the cervical mucus and blocks the sperm from getting into the uterus. *Major bonuses for women with heavy periods:* Mirena reduces menstrual bleeding (and may even halt it) and lowers the risk for anemia and endometriosis. Mirena can be left in place for five years and costs about $800 to $1,000.

•**ParaGard.** This IUD releases a tiny amount of copper that interferes with the sperm's movement and ability to fertilize an egg. ParaGard does not lighten heavy periods—it may even increase flow and cramping at first (so women with heavy periods may prefer Mirena).

Advantage: It can be left in for 10 years. ParaGard costs about $600.

Anita L. Nelson, MD, a professor of obstetrics and gynecology at the David Geffen School of Medicine at the University of California, Los Angeles, discussed these devices and their benefits. *Today's IUDs…*

•**Have very low failure rates.** "IUDs are in the top tier of contraceptive protection and are as effective as sterilization," Dr. Nelson said, adding that in the first year of use, less than 1% of IUD users will wind up pregnant.

Comparison: About 6% of users of the Depo-Provera injection, 9% of users of the Pill and 17% of condom users wind up pregnant each year, given that these methods are not always used correctly.

•**Are reversible.** An IUD can be removed by a physician at any time. After that, Dr. Nelson said, a woman's fertility level immediately goes back to what it would have been had she not used the IUD.

•**Are hassle-free.** Once the device is inserted, all the woman has to do is reach a finger into her vagina once a month to feel for the little tail string that signals that the IUD is still in place. Unlike with certain other birth control methods, there is no need to interrupt the action prior to lovemaking.

•**Are economical**—particularly considering how many years an IUD lasts. Many health insurance policies cover the cost.

•**Protect against cancer.** IUDs reduce the risk for endometrial cancer...and a recent study from Spain suggests that they may cut cervical cancer risk in half.

Is it safe? Dr. Nelson said that there is a critical difference between the old-style IUD and those used today. The Dalkon Shield's tail string had a design that may have allowed it to convey bacteria from the vagina into the uterus...whereas today's IUDs have "monofilament" tail strings that do not facilitate movement of bacteria. About one in 1,000 women experience problems during the placement procedure (such as puncture of the uterus). Some IUD users develop ovarian cysts, which generally are harmless but sometimes can cause pain. In some cases, a woman loses her IUD early if her uterus pushes it out. Such expulsions most often occur within the first months after insertion.

In the past, the IUD was often considered most appropriate for women who had previously given birth because they are less likely to expel the device. But The American College of Obstetricians and Gynecologists (ACOG) recently declared IUDs safe for most women of childbearing age, including those who have never given birth...those with a history of ectopic (tubal) pregnancy...and teens. In addition,

ACOG now says that an IUD can be placed right after childbirth, miscarriage or a D&C, rather than delaying four to six weeks as traditionally has been advised. The device does have to fit correctly, however, so women with large fibroids, uterine cancer or infections are not candidates for the IUD, Dr. Nelson said.

If you decide to get an IUD: Placement of the device takes just a few minutes and is done in a doctor's office. You may be advised to take an over-the-counter nonsteroidal anti-inflammatory (not aspirin) beforehand to minimize discomfort during and after the insertion. Expect mild cramping and perhaps spotting or bleeding that persists for several weeks. After about five to 10 weeks, you return for a checkup.

Thereafter, you don't need any extra monitoring outside of your normal gynecological checkups. There are no limitations on your activities. *But do contact your physician if, at any time during your IUD use, you are concerned that...*

•**You might have a pelvic infection.** Possible warning signs include vaginal discharge, abnormal pelvic pain and/or fever.

•**You are losing your IUD (possible symptoms include heavy bleeding and cramping).**

•**You could be pregnant.**

Sex question you may be afraid to ask: Can the woman or her partner feel the IUD during sex? She told me that neither partner can feel

---

Help for Overactive Bladder

Over-the-counter treatment for overactive bladder is available for women, reports Leslie M. Rickey, MD, MPH. Oxytrol is a thin, flexible transdermal patch that releases oxybutynin, which is effective at controlling overactive bladder and decreasing urinary leakage. Side effects such as constipation, dry mouth and skin irritation usually are mild. But check with your doctor before using.

Leslie M. Rickey, MD, MPH, assistant professor in the departments of surgery and obstetrics and gynecology, division of female pelvic medicine and reconstructive surgery, University of Maryland School of Medicine, Baltimore.

the device itself because it is inside the woman's uterus...and the tail string tucks away and should not be bothersome.

Should You Be Screened For Uterine Cancer?

Debbie Saslow, PhD, director, Breast and Gynecologic Cancer, American Cancer Society, Atlanta.

A test for an insidious, lethal cancer isn't used very much even though it has been around for years and has a very high success rate of detecting risk. Why is that?

The cancer is uterine cancer, which sometimes can progress quickly and dangerously. But this test is not being recommended as a screening for all postmenopausal women, who are the most likely to get uterine cancer.

Then who should get the test? For answers, we turned to Debbie Saslow, PhD, director of breast and gynecologic cancer at the American Cancer Society in Atlanta.

THICK AND THIN

Also known as endometrial cancer, since it begins in the endometrium (the lining of the uterus), uterine cancer is the most common gynecological cancer, affecting more than 43,000 women and causing nearly 8,000 deaths in this country each year.

You may not realize that one physiological characteristic that a gynecologist is attuned to is the thickness of your uterine lining. It's normal for the lining of a woman's uterus to atrophy and grow thin with menopause, Dr. Saslow explained. There are several reasons why a woman might have a thickened uterine lining, but cancer is one of them, so the condition should be monitored. A test called transvaginal ultrasound (TVS) is one way this can be done.

How it works: A technician inserts a specially designed ultrasound probe into a woman's vagina and captures an image, which is sent to a display, enabling the technician to measure the thickness of the uterine lining. Though it can be somewhat uncomfortable, this test is not painful.

Researchers in the UK administered TVS to nearly 37,000 postmenopausal women, measuring the thickness of their uterine linings and then following them for a year to see how many developed cancer. The study, which was published in *The Lancet,* found that women with a uterine lining that was 5 mm or thicker were indeed at about 80% higher risk for uterine cancer within a year.

Even so, the study authors oppose using TVS for mass screening and, said Dr. Saslow, so does the American Cancer Society. One reason, she said, is that the risk of a false-positive result is high. Nearly 15% of women who undergo TVS and are found to have abnormally thick uterine linings will then end up having to endure an uncomfortable (and expensive) biopsy, with all the accompanying mental turmoil that brings—but they will not have cancer. Meanwhile, she said, the vast majority (90%) of women who do have endometrial cancer also will have abnormal bleeding as an early warning sign. These factors have led the researchers and other experts to conclude that it is unlikely there will be much benefit to screening asymptomatic women. "We found that there is no proof that detection through screening improves outcome over detection from symptoms (vaginal bleeding)," Dr. Saslow explained.

ARE YOU A CANDIDATE?

While TVS is not a routine test, it is widely available. Risk factors for uterine cancer include obesity...never having been pregnant...and exposure to synthetic estrogens, such as hormone replacement therapy, or *tamoxifen* (for breast cancer). Dr. Saslow said that at present the American Cancer Society is focused on limiting the number of false-positives and therefore recommends screening only for women with a rare hereditary disease called Lynch syndrome that increases the risk for both uterine and colorectal cancers.

Cancer screening tests remain a controversial topic, and this story sheds light on the complexities that make it so difficult—the risk-versus-benefits equation does not always present a clear case for making a recommendation. The one thing that every woman absolutely should know is that the most important warning sign of

uterine cancer is vaginal bleeding after menopause—if you experience this symptom, call
your doctor immediately.

Chemicals in Cookware, Carpets May Raise Arthritis Risk in Women

Sarah A. Uhl, MS, (former) researcher, Yale School of
Forestry and Environmental Studies, New Haven, Con-
necticut.
Environmental Health Perspectives, online

In what researchers are calling a first, a recent
analysis suggests that the greater a woman's
exposure to a type of common chemical
compound called PFCs, the greater her risk for
developing osteoarthritis.

Researchers did not find a similar risk among
men regarding these chemicals, which are now
found in everything from nonstick cookware to
take-out containers and carpeting.

Osteoarthritis, the most common type of arthritis, causes pain and stiffness and involves
degeneration of the cartilage in the joints.

And the study authors stressed that while their
investigation identified a robust link between
osteoarthritis and exposure to two specific PFC
chemicals—known as PFOA and PFOS—for
now the finding can only be described as an
association, rather than a cause-and-effect relationship.

"But we did find a clear and strong association between exposure to [these] compounds
and osteoarthritis, which is a very painful
chronic disease," said study lead author Sarah
Uhl, who conducted the study while working
as a researcher at the Yale School of Forestry
and Environmental Studies in New Haven, Connecticut.

"This adds to the body of information that we
have suggesting that these highly persistent synthetic chemicals are of concern when it comes
to the public health," she said.

Uhl noted that exposure to PFCs is nearly
universal, given their inclusion in a vast array
of products to enable (among other things) the

Know the Symptoms of Ovarian Cancer

Bloating…increased abdominal size…pelvic
or abdominal pain…difficulty eating…and/or
feeling full quickly. Consult your physician if
you begin to experience one or more symptoms every day or two—or more than 12 times
in a month. Though most likely the symptoms
are caused by a noncancerous condition,
they should not be ignored.

M. Robyn Andersen, MPH, PhD, member, public health
sciences division, Fred Hutchinson Cancer Research Center, Seattle, and coauthor of a study of an ovarian cancer
symptoms index, published in *Open Journal of Obstetrics
and Gynecology.*

grease-proofing of food packaging, waterproof-
ing of rain gear, and textile stain protection.

Previous research has linked PFC exposure to
a higher risk for the premature onset of menopause in women, higher levels of "bad" LDL
cholesterol in men and women, and reduced
effectiveness of routine vaccinations among
children.

RESEARCH FINDINGS

To explore a potential PFC-osteoarthritis connection, the authors looked at PFOA and PFOS
exposure data collected between 2003 and
2008 by the US National Health and Nutrition
Examination Survey.

The analysis covered more than 4,000 men
and women between the ages of 20 and 84
for whom osteoarthritis status information was
available.

The team found "significant associations" between osteoarthritis incidence and exposure to
PFOA or PFOS among women but not men.

Women exposed to the highest levels of either
chemical seemed to face up to nearly double
the risk for developing osteoarthritis, compared
with women exposed to the lowest levels.

The osteoarthritis-PFC connection also appeared to be stronger among younger women
(between 20 and 49) than among older women
(between 50 and 84). But the team said more
follow-up research is needed to confirm the
observation.

While the biological reason behind the potential connection remains unclear, the team suggested that the chemicals may have a particularly profound impact on hormonal balances for women.

"Our hormone systems are incredibly delicate and can be thrown off by tiny doses of hormone-disrupting chemicals," Uhl said. "And processes like inflammation and cartilage repair are associated with our hormones, and are also associated with osteoarthritis."

Whatever the culprit, Uhl cautioned that the problem is likely to persist for years to come despite a safety-driven downward trend in global PFOA/PFOS use.

"Once they get into the environment they just don't go away," she noted. "In people, they last years. So even if we were to reduce the use of these chemicals right away, they're still going to be around and in our bodies for a long time," she explained.

"Not being exposed is not an option, which is frustrating," Uhl added. "But as consumers, I would say that one of the best things to do is to lead a healthy lifestyle, and get exercise and eat well. Because we're finding that those steps can reduce susceptibility to factors that are outside our control."

The new study appears in the online issue of *Environmental Health Perspectives*.

info For more on PFCs, visit the US Environmental Protection Agency Web site at *www.epa.gov/opptintr/existingchemicals/pubs/actionplans/pfcs.html*.

New Pap Smear Guidelines

Women ages 21 to 65 should have Pap smears to test for cervical cancer no more than once every three years, according to recent guidelines from the US Preventive Services Task Force and the American Cancer Society. Testing every three years will protect against cervical cancer just as effectively as annual Paps, according to research, while also cutting down on the number of false-positives, which result in unnecessary biopsies. Pap smears are not recommended for women over age 65 who are not at increased risk for cervical cancer and who have had at least three consecutive negative Paps within the past decade.

Self-defense: Unless you have an unusual Pap result, a compromised immune system or a known cervical cancer risk, schedule your Pap smear for once every three years.

Wanda Nicholson, MD, MPH, associate professor of obstetrics and gynecology, University of North Carolina at Chapel Hill.

Thyroid Treatment Guidelines for Pregnant Women Revised

The Endocrine Society, news release.

Thyroid hormone is critical for normal fetal brain development, and hormonal problems among pregnant women must be properly managed, according to the Endocrine Society, which has recently revised its guidelines on treating thyroid-related medical issues before, during and after pregnancy.

Too much or not enough thyroid hormone can harm both women and their unborn babies, the experts said. The recent treatment guidelines update the 2007 version.

"Pregnancy may affect the course of thyroid diseases and, conversely, thyroid diseases may affect the course of pregnancy," said lead study author Leslie de Groot, MD, a research professor at the University of Rhode Island, in a society news release. "Pregnant women may be under the care of multiple health care professionals, including obstetricians, nurse midwives, family practitioners and endocrinologists, making the development of guidelines all the more critical."

Women who are hypothyroid (underactive thyroid function) are at greater risk for infertility and are more likely to have anemia, gestational hypertension and postpartum hemorrhage, the news release noted. If not treated, hypothyroidism during pregnancy can lead to premature birth, low birth weight and respiratory distress among newborns. Overactive thyroid function, or hyperthyroidism, also can lead to miscarriage.

The Endocrine Society made the following revisions to its clinical practice guidelines:

•**Doctors should interpret serum-free thyroxine levels cautiously during pregnancy.** The experts advised that using trimester-specific reference ranges would improve the interpretation of pregnant women's thyroid-function tests.

•**The drug *propylthiouracil*** (PTU) should be the primary treatment for hyperthyroidism during the first trimester of pregnancy. The experts cautioned the alternate treatment—*methimazole*—may increase the risk for birth defects. Methimazole, however, can be used if PTU is unavailable or if women have a negative reaction to the drug. Because PTU may be harmful to the liver in rare cases, once women complete their first trimester, they should switch from PTU to methimazole.

•**Women who are breast-feeding** should take 250 micrograms of iodine daily to ensure their infants are getting 100 micrograms of iodine each day.

•**Daily prenatal vitamins** should contain 150 to 200 micrograms of iodine to protect women from iodine deficiency.

•**Women with Graves' disease,** a history of Graves' disease, a previous newborn with Graves' disease or previously elevated thyroid stimulating hormone antibodies should have these antibodies measured before they are 22 weeks pregnant. These antibodies cross the placenta and can stimulate or restrict the fetal thyroid, the experts explained.

•**The fetuses of women who have thyroid stimulating hormone receptor antibodies** at least two to three times higher than normal or who are treated with anti-thyroid drugs should be screened for thyroid problems. This can be done during the fetal ultrasound women routinely undergo when they are between 18 and 22 weeks pregnant. An enlarged thyroid, growth restriction, severe swelling, presence of goiter, advanced bone age or heart failure could be signs of thyroid problems in a fetus.

•**Fine-needle aspiration** should be considered for women with nodules 5 millimeters to 1 centimeter in size who have a high-risk history or suspicious findings on an ultrasound. Women with complex nodules 1.5 centimeters to 2 centimeters also should undergo this procedure. The guidelines note that this can be delayed until after delivery for women who are at least 34 weeks pregnant.

The news release noted that consensus was not reached on whether all newly pregnant women should be screened for thyroid problems, but added that some experts support universal screening for thyroid problems by the time women are nine weeks pregnant.

The revised guidelines appear in the *Journal of Clinical Endocrinology and Metabolism.*

info The US Department of Health and Human Services has more about pregnancy and thyroid disease at the Web site, *www.endocrine.niddk.nih.gov/pubs/pregnancy/.*

Surprising Connection Between Autoimmune Disease and Endometriosis

Tine Jess, MD, a researcher in the department of epidemiology research at the Statens Serum Institut in Copenhagen, Denmark, and lead author of a study on endometriosis and IBD risk published in *Gut.*

With endometriosis, tissue from the uterine lining migrates outside the uterus and implants on other pelvic structures. During menstruation, this displaced tissue bleeds…and the trapped blood inflames surrounding tissues, causing intense pain and internal scarring. Previous studies suggested an association between this inflammatory disorder and various autoimmune diseases. So Danish researchers decided to investigate a possible link between endometriosis and inflammatory bowel disease (IBD), an umbrella term for a group of immune disorders that affect the gut and cause abdominal pain, diarrhea and bloody stools.

The study analyzed data on 37,661 women who were hospitalized for endometriosis between 1977 and 2007. During that 30-year period, 228 of the endometriosis patients also developed ulcerative colitis, a form of IBD that affects the inner lining of the colon…and 92 endometriosis patients also developed Crohn's disease, a type of IBD that affects all layers of both the small and large intestine.

Crunching those numbers: Compared with women in the general population, endometriosis patients were 50% more likely to develop some form of IBD…while those whose endometriosis was verified through surgery had an 80% higher risk for IBD. What's more, the increased IBD risk persisted even 20 years or more after the endometriosis diagnosis.

Why this matters so much: Certain symptoms, notably chronic abdominal pain and diarrhea, are common to both endometriosis and IBD. If a doctor assumes that a patient's ongoing symptoms are solely the result of her endometriosis, he or she may fail to diagnose and treat the woman's IBD—and thus the patient will continue to suffer.

Though it is unclear why endometriosis raises the risk for IBD, researchers suggested that the two conditions might share some underlying immunological features. Or, in some cases, the IBD might be a consequence of treating endometriosis with oral contraceptives (as is commonly done), given that oral contraceptive users are at significantly increased risk for IBD.

Vaginal Surgery Can Do More Harm Than Good

Synthetic vaginal mesh, used to treat pelvic organ prolapse, may cause bleeding, scarring and/or other complications. Possible alternatives include vaginal repairs with no mesh…synthetic mesh placed abdominally…vaginal repair using biologic grafts/animal tissue. For menopausal women with synthetic mesh in place, local/vaginal estrogen may be useful in preventing complications.

Cheryl B. Iglesia, MD, section director of female pelvic medicine and reconstructive surgery, Washington Hospital Center, and associate professor, Georgetown University, both in Washington, DC.

Endometriosis patients: If you have persistent abdominal pain or other symptoms, talk with your doctor about this possible link with IBD. Bring this article to your appointment if you think it will help!

The Injury-Prone Time Of the Month

Andrew L. Rubman, ND, founder and medical director of the Southbury Clinic for Traditional Medicines in Southbury, Connecticut. *www.southburyclinic.com*

There is a point in the menstrual cycle (aside from annoying periods) that draws a caution—ovulation. This warning note has nothing to do with getting pregnant (though fertility generally does peak at this time as the ovary releases a mature egg). The caution here concerns increased risk for injury, particularly during exercise.

Reason: Around the time of ovulation, the increases in levels of hormones such as *estrogen* and *relaxin* that allow the egg to pop through the ovarian capsule also cause a loosening and stretching of ligaments and tendons. These are the same hormones that, late in pregnancy, help loosen a woman's pelvic ligaments in preparation for childbirth. "Women who participate in intense exercise in the days around ovulation are at heightened risk for tearing any area where connective tissue may be aggressively stretched by a movement or an impact during sports," explained Andrew L. Rubman, ND, medical director of the Southbury Clinic for Traditional Medicines in Southbury, Connecticut. Vulnerable areas include the shoulders, knees, ankles and back.

A woman typically ovulates mid-cycle. The first day of your period is considered day one, so if your cycle lasts 28 days, ovulation is likely to occur around day 14—though it could happen earlier or later. Dr. Rubman noted that the peak injury-prone time lasts from a day before until a day after ovulation.

Self-defense: There's no need to avoid exercise entirely during this time, Dr. Rubman said, but you should take added precautions against injury. *Here's how...*

•**Be extra-sure to warm up before working out...**and to cool down and stretch afterward.

•**For weight lifting, use somewhat lighter weights than usual.** You can make up for this by increasing the number of repetitions.

•**Avoid sports that involve sudden angular movements** that would challenge tendons and ligaments, such as tennis and basketball—or at least try not to play full-out.

•**Focus on gentle stretching and low-impact activities such as bicycling, swimming and walking.**

Not sure when you're ovulating?

Watch for these signs: Lower abdominal discomfort or an ache in the general area of your ovaries (a sensation called mittelschmerz)...and/or vaginal secretions that increase in amount and that change from just wet to tacky and slippery (similar in look and feel to uncooked egg whites). If you still can't tell, take your temperature with a basal thermometer first thing every morning before getting out of bed—temperature rises slightly during ovulation. Charting your daily temperature for a few months will familiarize you with the rhythms of your cycle.

Natural Help for Painful Periods

Mark A. Stengler, NMD, a naturopathic medical doctor and leading authority on the practice of alternative and integrated medicine. Dr. Stengler is author of *The Natural Physician's Healing Therapies* (Bottom Line Books), founder and medical director of the Stengler Center for Integrative Medicine in Encinitas, California, and adjunct associate clinical professor at the National College of Natural Medicine in Portland, Oregon. *http://markstengler.com*

I'm frequently asked by patients—either for themselves or on behalf of family members—about natural treatments for menstrual cramps. Cramping, which is characterized by inflammation, is caused by high levels of certain prostaglandins that trigger uterine contractions. Often high prostaglandin levels are accompanied by estrogen dominance, where estrogen levels are too high relative to progesterone. Using specific nutrients, I am able to balance the ratio between these hormones in patients and greatly relieve cramping.

You can use just one of the remedies below or all of them, depending on what helps you. You need to take most of these remedies all month (as indicated), even though symptoms occur on only a few days, because these remedies don't just treat symptoms. Instead, they work to enhance the release of progesterone...improve circulation...or relax muscles.

•**Vitex.** This herb (also known as chasteberry) improves the production of progesterone and offsets estrogen dominance.

Dose: 160 mg to 240 mg, or 40 drops of tincture daily. Try it for at least three months. If it helps you, you can keep taking it. Don't use vitex if you are taking birth control pills.

•**Pycnogenol.** This pine bark extract contains potent anti-inflammatories and antioxidants. It boosts production of endothelial nitric oxide, which improves circulation and helps to reduce the pain of cramps. A Japanese study found that pycnogenol significantly decreased the amount of time women had menstrual cramps.

Dose: 100 mg to 150 mg daily.

•**Calcium and magnesium.** These minerals reduce premenstrual syndrome symptoms. Magnesium acts as a muscle relaxant, relieving cramps.

Dose: A daily calcium supplement of 500 mg to 1,000 mg that contains at least half as much magnesium. It may take one to two menstrual cycles to reduce symptoms.

•**Natural progesterone.** For severe menstrual cramps, I recommend bioidentical progesterone cream to reduce estrogen dominance. A typical dose is 20 mg twice daily starting two weeks before menses. Work with a holistic physician who can monitor your hormone levels while you use it.

Index